Love is an Illusion!

The Queen

1

Story & Art by
Fargo

LOVE IS AN ILLUSION! - THE QUEEN VOL. 1
STORY AND ART BY FARGO

© 2022. Fargo. All Rights Reserved.
Writer/Artist: Fargo
First published in the Republic of Korea by LEZHIN Entertainment, Inc.
English Print Edition is published by Seven Seas Entertainment, Inc. under the exclusive license granted by LEZHIN Entertainment, Inc.

English Translation: LEZHIN US

Translation: **Lezhin Entertainment, America Localization Team**
Lettering: **Karis Page**
Editor: **Lark Smith**
Managing Editor: **Bambi Eloriaga-Amago**

Published by Seven Seas Entertainment, Inc.

No portion of this book may be reproduced or transmitted in any form without written permission from the copyright holders. This is a work of fiction. Names, characters, places, and incidents are the products of the author's imagination or are used fictitiously. Any resemblance to actual events, locales, or persons, living or dead, is entirely coincidental. Any information or opinions expressed by the creators of this book belong to those individual creators and do not necessarily reflect the views of Seven Seas Entertainment or its employees.

Seven Seas Entertainment, Inc. | President: **Jason DeAngelis** | Vice President: **Adam Arnold** | Publisher: **Lianne Sentar** | Licensing Manager: **Y. Takahashi & Lena LeRay** | Editor-In-Chief: **Julie Davis** | Managing Editors: **Jack Sullivan & Shanti Whitesides** | Production Manager: **John Ramirez** | Assistant Production Manager: **Jinky Besa** | Prepress Technicians: **Salvador Chan Jr., Melanie Ujimori, & Jules Valera** | Digital Manager: **CK Russell** | Sales & Marketing Manager: **Lauren Hill** | Marketing Associate: **Leanna Cruz** | Administrative Associate: **Danya Adair** | Inventory & Logistics Manager: **Marsha Reid**

Seven Seas and the Seven Seas logo are trademarks of Seven Seas Entertainment.
All rights reserved.
sevenseasentertainment.com
sevenseaswebtoons.com

Love is an Illusion! - The Queen is rated Mature for language and sexual content. Reader discretion is advised.

ISBN: 979-8-89160-610-4
Printed in Canada
First Printing: October 2024
10 9 8 7 6 5 4 3 2 1

The Queen
CONTENTS

Chapter 1 7
Chapter 2 33
Chapter 3 55
Chapter 4 77
Chapter 5 99
Chapter 6 119
Chapter 7 147
Chapter 8 169
Chapter 9 195
Chapter 10 217
Chapter 11 241
Chapter 12 269
Chapter 13 297
Chapter 14 325
Chapter 15 353

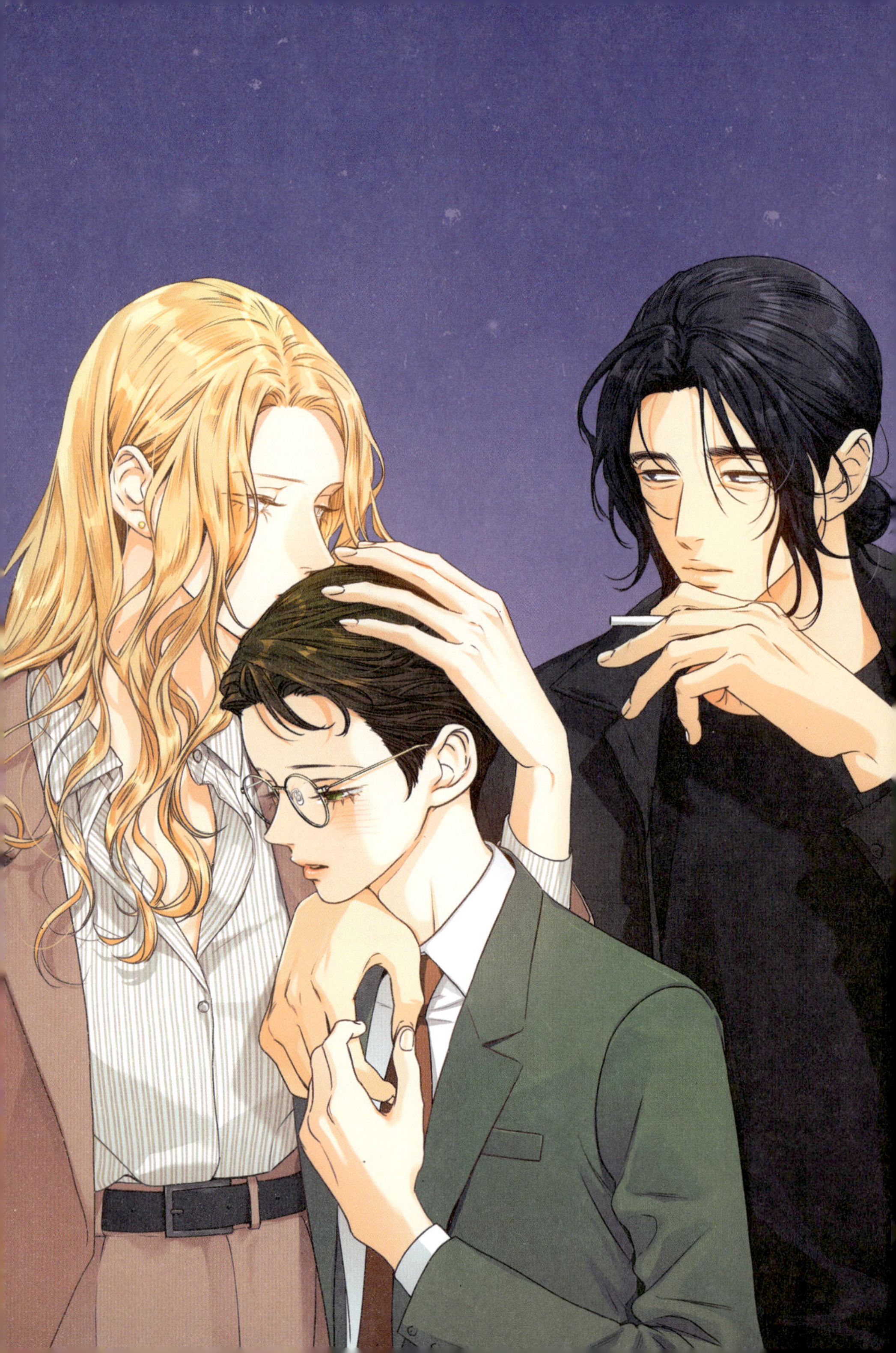

OMEGAVERSE

A world where everyone has a secondary biological gender and males can become pregnant.

Omega
Can be impregnated by an alpha, regardless of base gender.

Alpha
Responds to omegas' pheromones and can impregnate an omega.

Beta
Neither an alpha nor an omega, but a regular human.

Pheromone: The unique odor emitted by alphas and omegas.

Heat Cycle: A period of a few days where an omega secretes pheromones stronger than usual to seduce an alpha. Omegas often take medications to control this.

Love is an Illusion!
The Queen

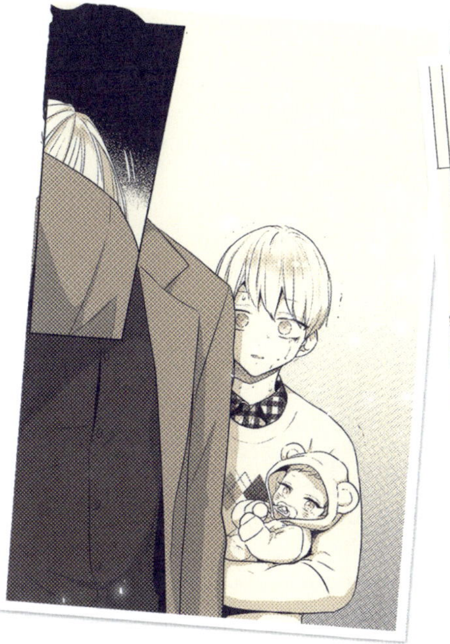

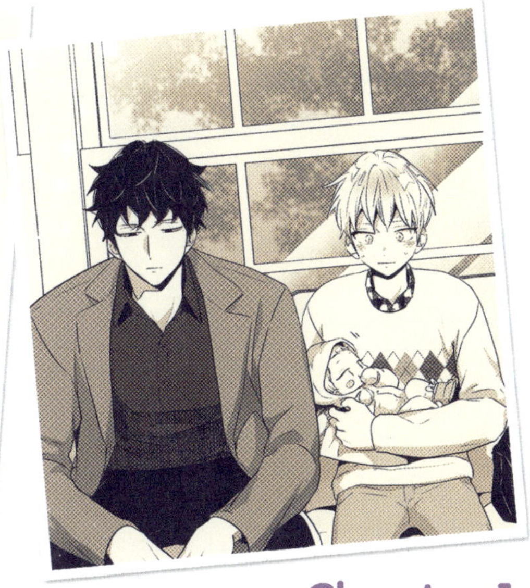

Chapter 1

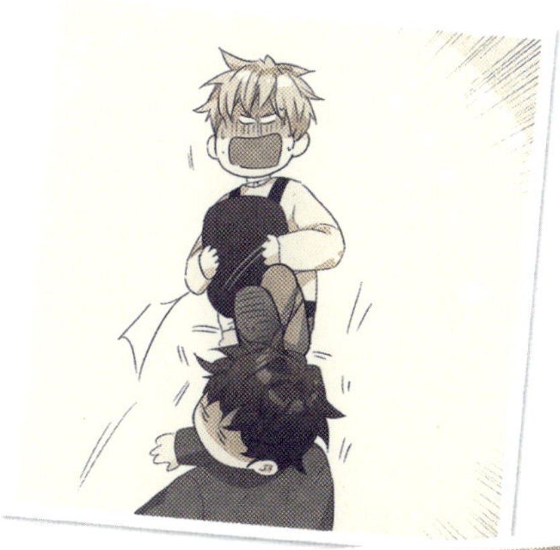

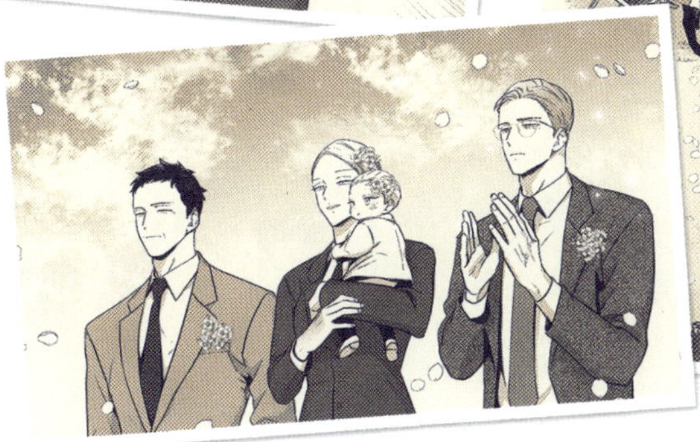

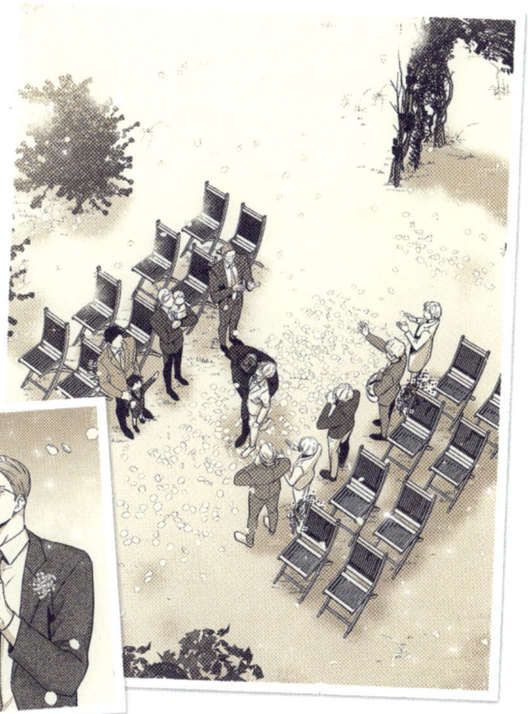

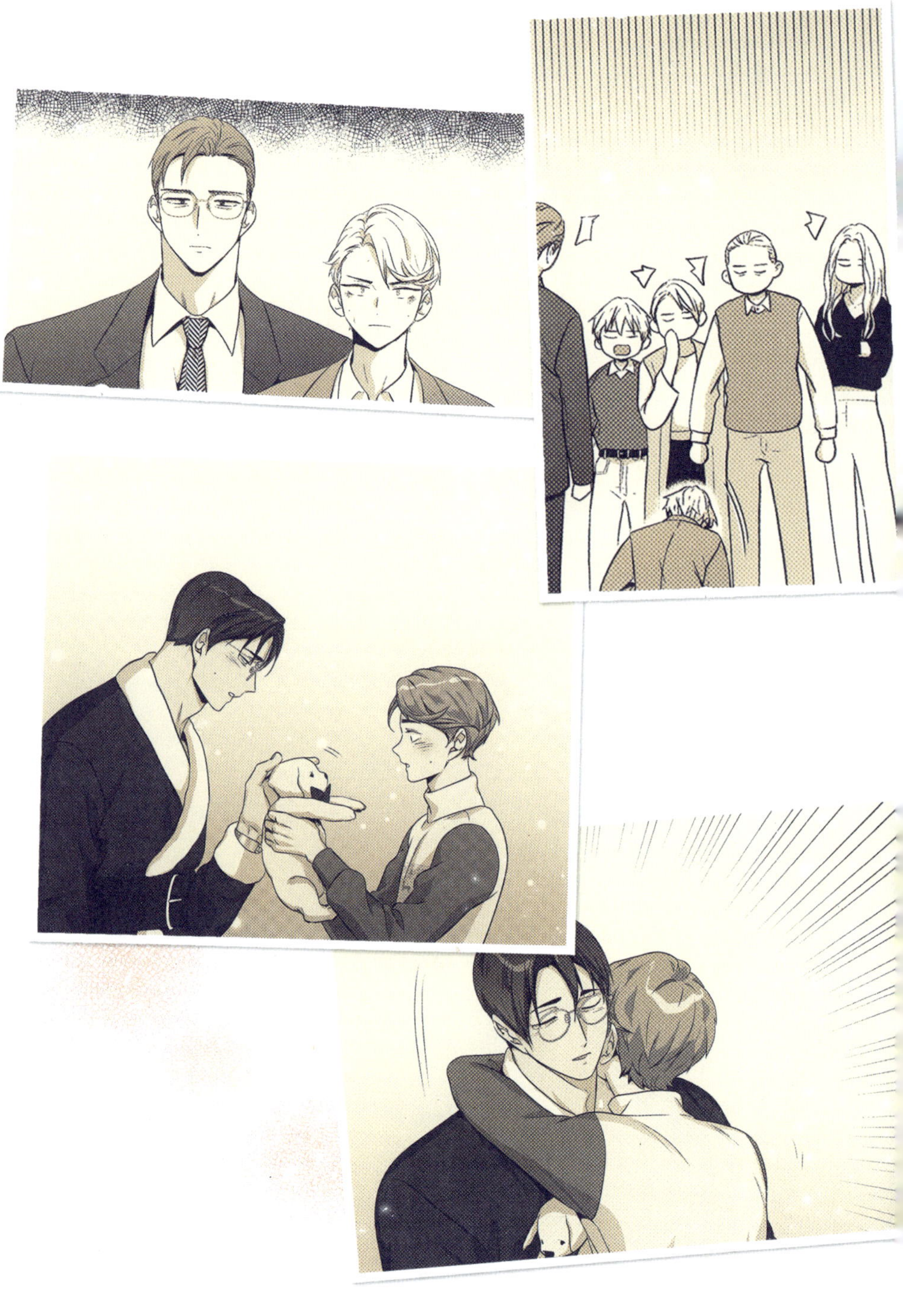

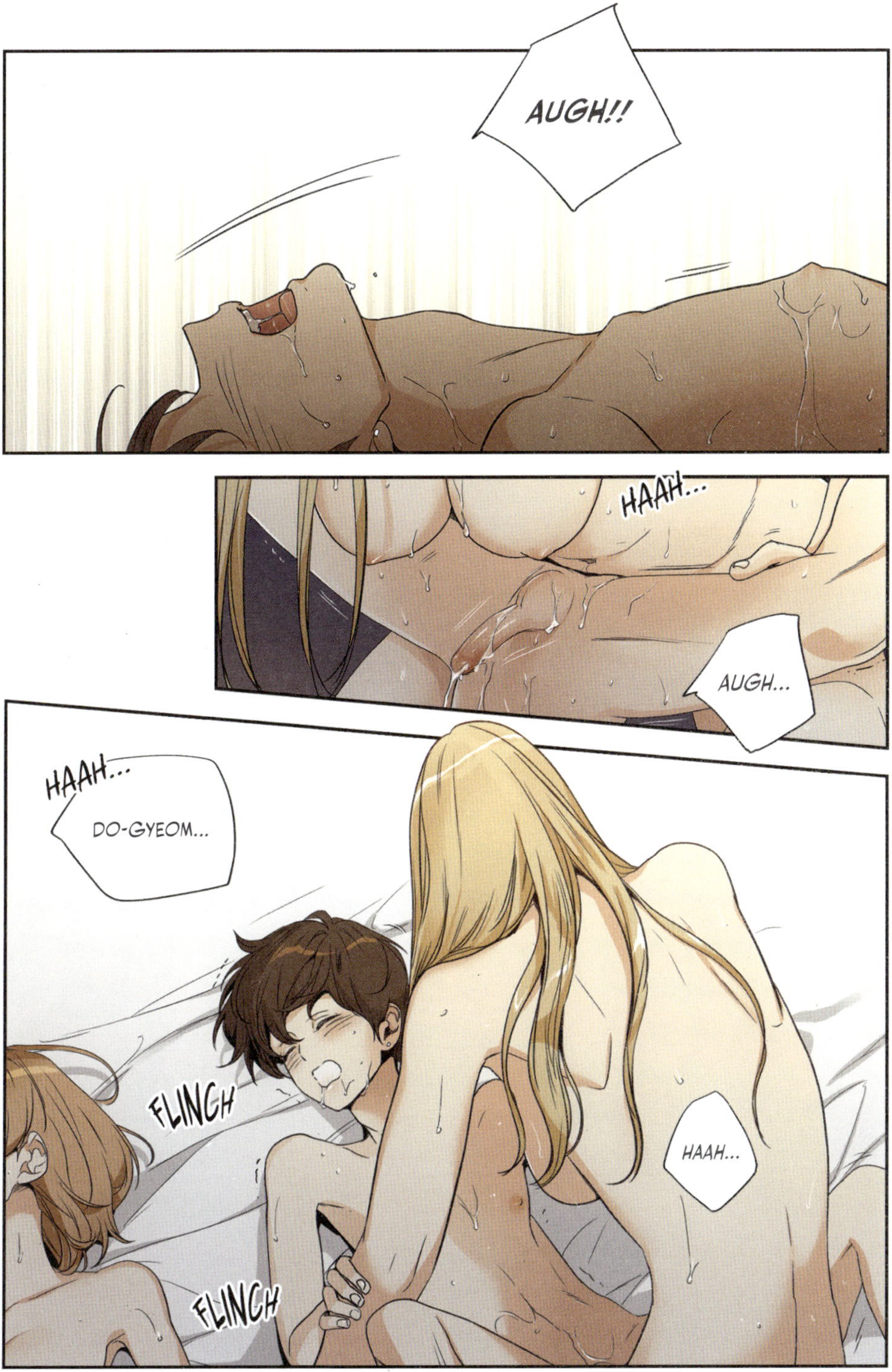
AUGH!!
HAAH...
AUGH...
HAAH...
DO-GYEOM...
FLINCH
FLINCH
HAAH...

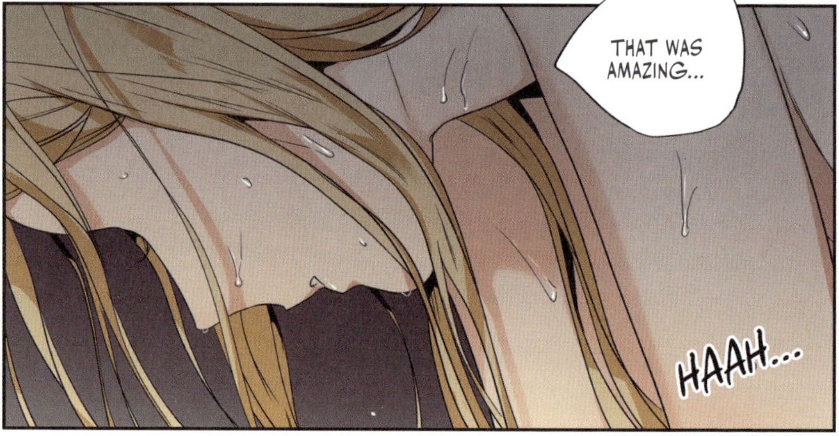
THAT WAS AMAZING...
HAAH...

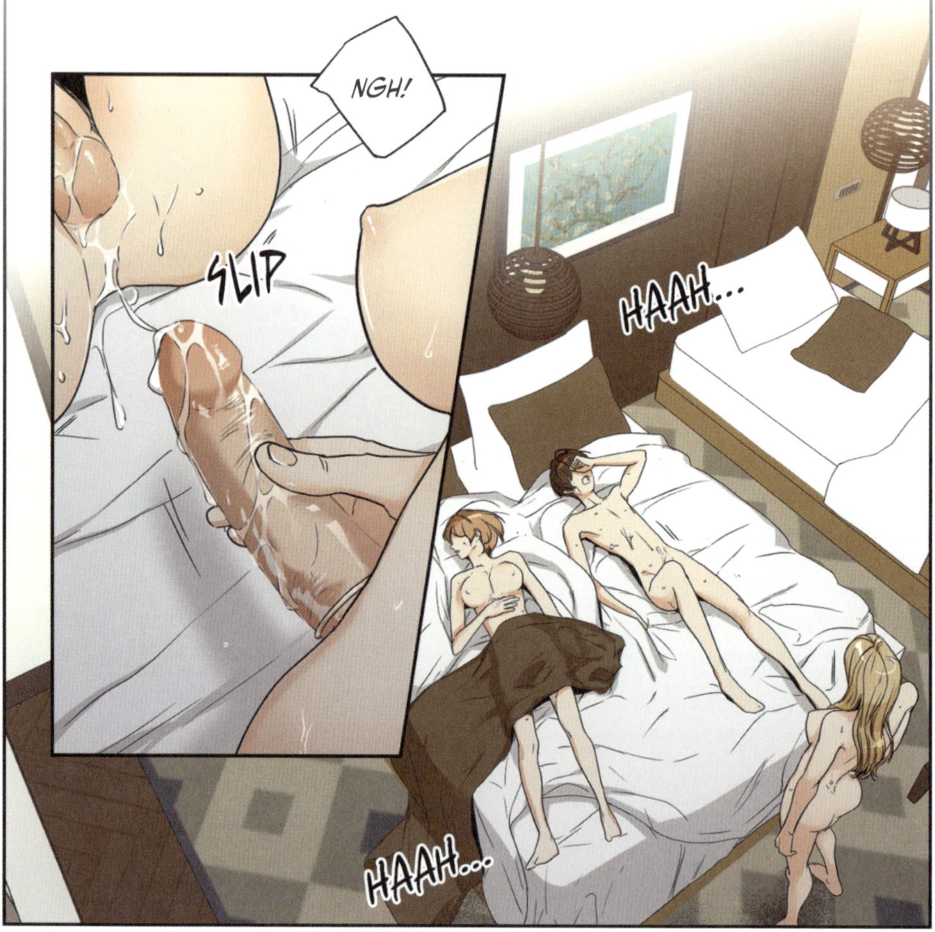
NGH!
SLIP
HAAH...
HAAH...

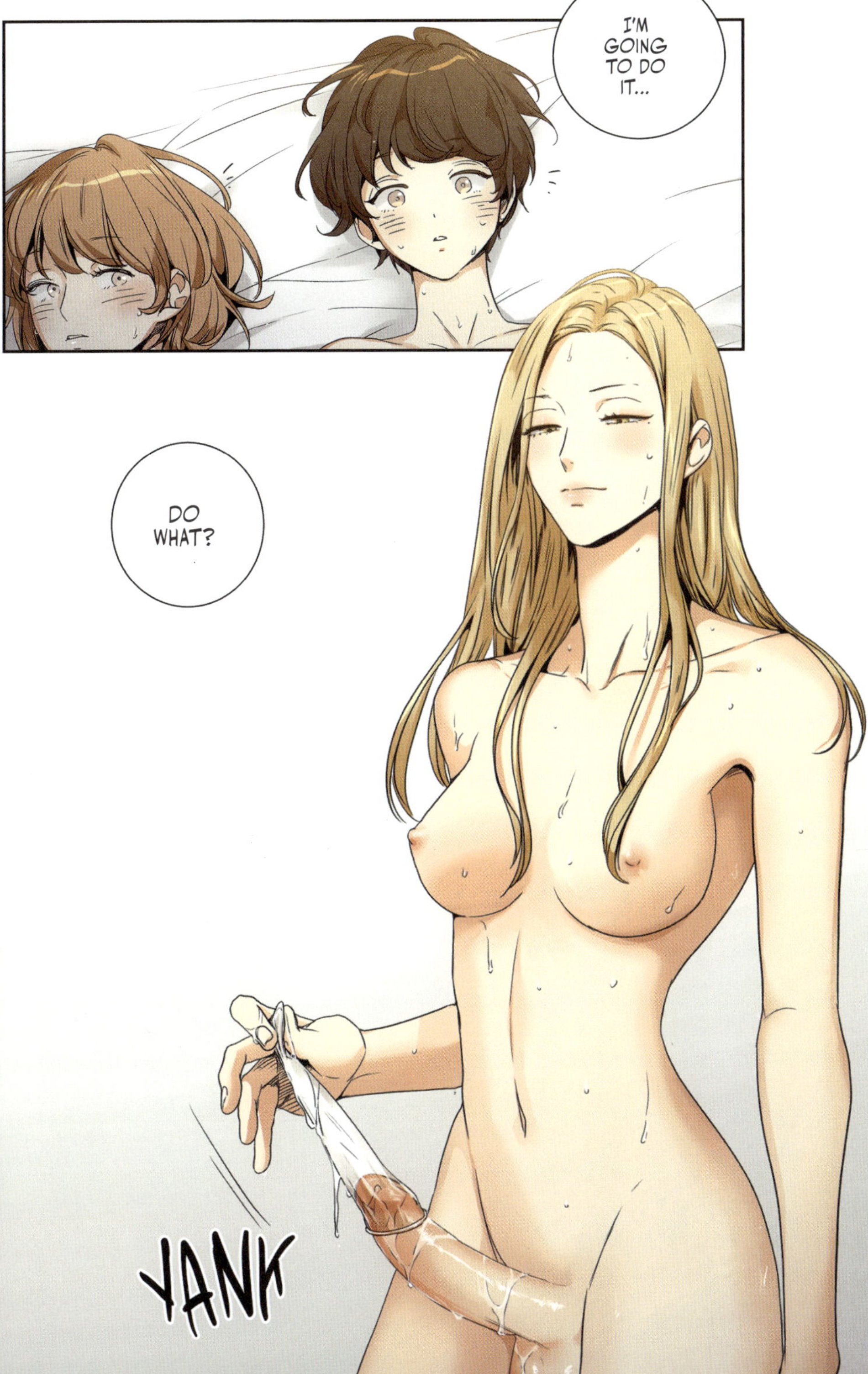
I'M GOING TO DO IT...
DO WHAT?
YANK

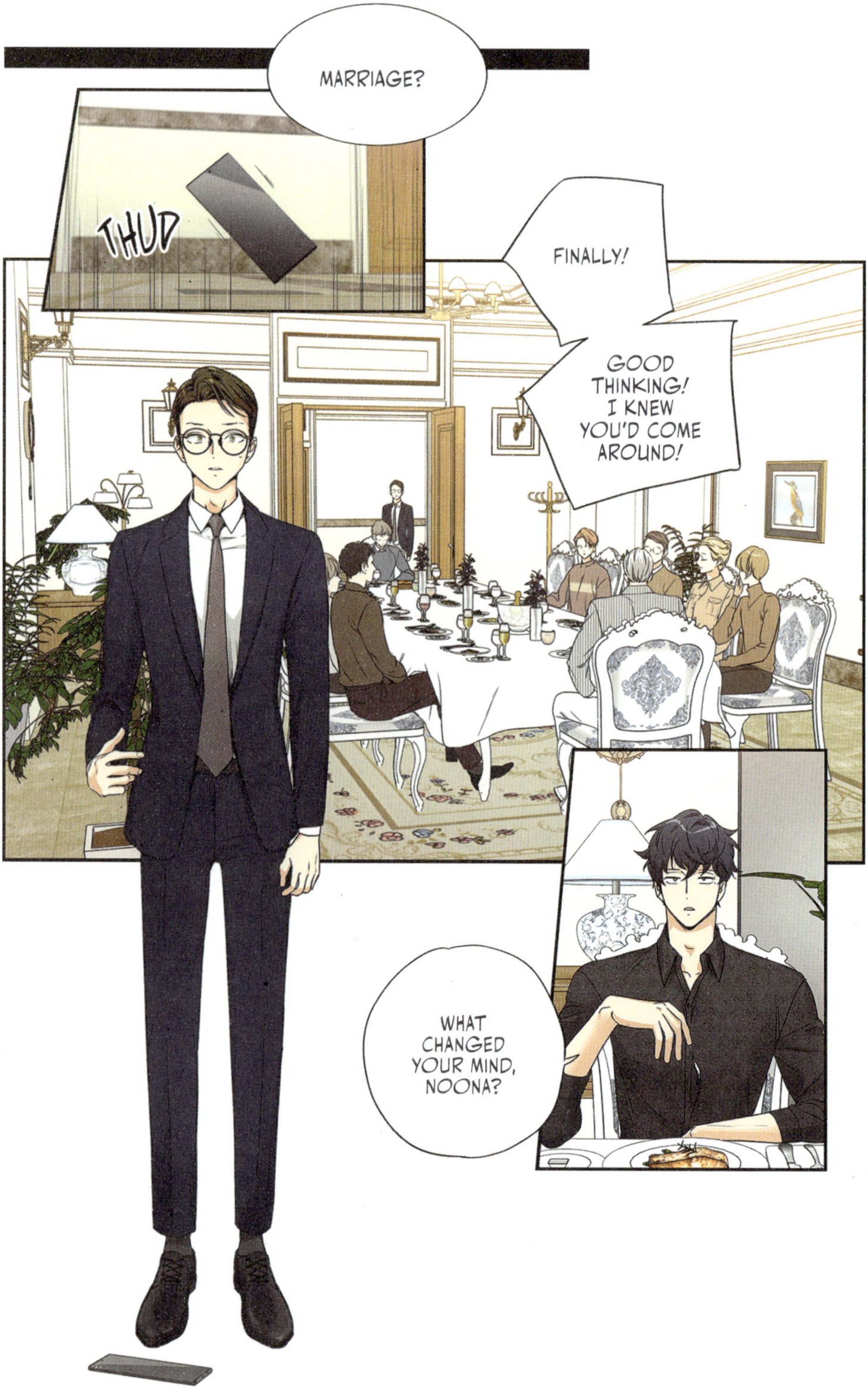
MARRIAGE?
THUD
FINALLY!
GOOD THINKING! I KNEW YOU'D COME AROUND!
WHAT CHANGED YOUR MIND, NOONA?

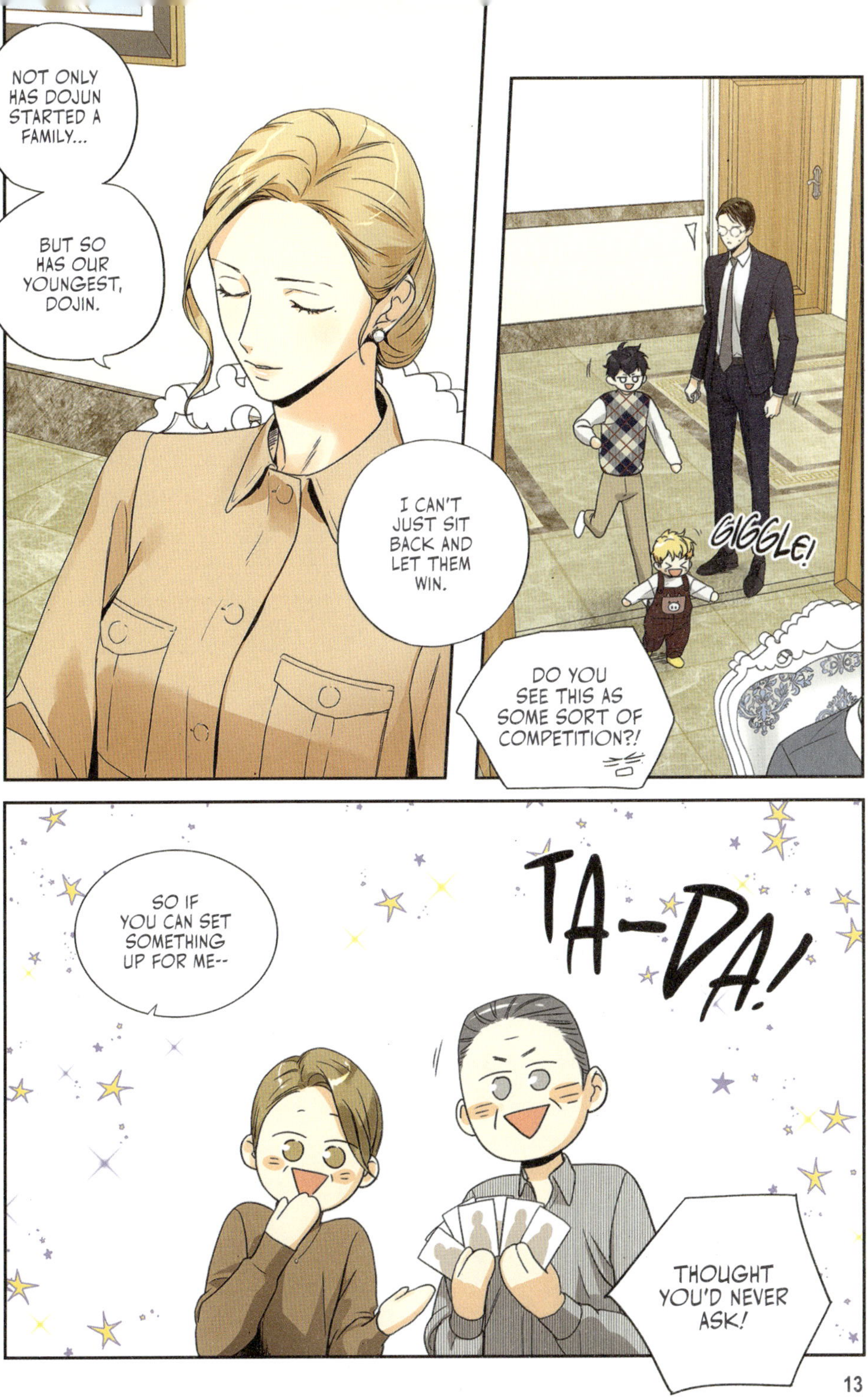
NOT ONLY HAS DOJUN STARTED A FAMILY...
BUT SO HAS OUR YOUNGEST, DOJIN.
I CAN'T JUST SIT BACK AND LET THEM WIN.
GIGGLE!
DO YOU SEE THIS AS SOME SORT OF COMPETITION?!
SO IF YOU CAN SET SOMETHING UP FOR ME--
TA-DA!
THOUGHT YOU'D NEVER ASK!

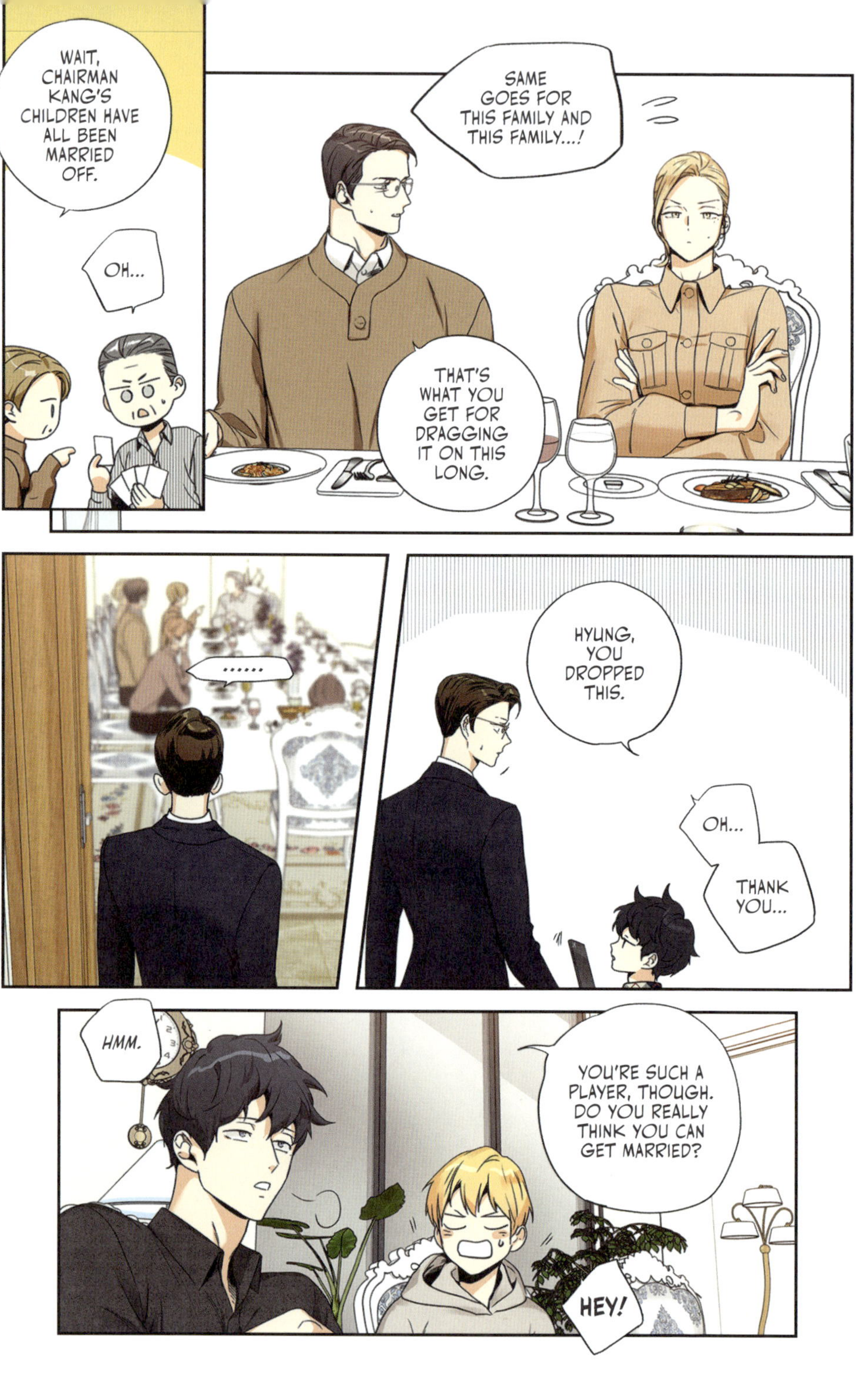
WAIT, CHAIRMAN KANG'S CHILDREN HAVE ALL BEEN MARRIED OFF.
OH...
SAME GOES FOR THIS FAMILY AND THIS FAMILY...!
THAT'S WHAT YOU GET FOR DRAGGING IT ON THIS LONG.
......
HYUNG, YOU DROPPED THIS.
OH...
THANK YOU...
HMM.
YOU'RE SUCH A PLAYER, THOUGH. DO YOU REALLY THINK YOU CAN GET MARRIED?
HEY!

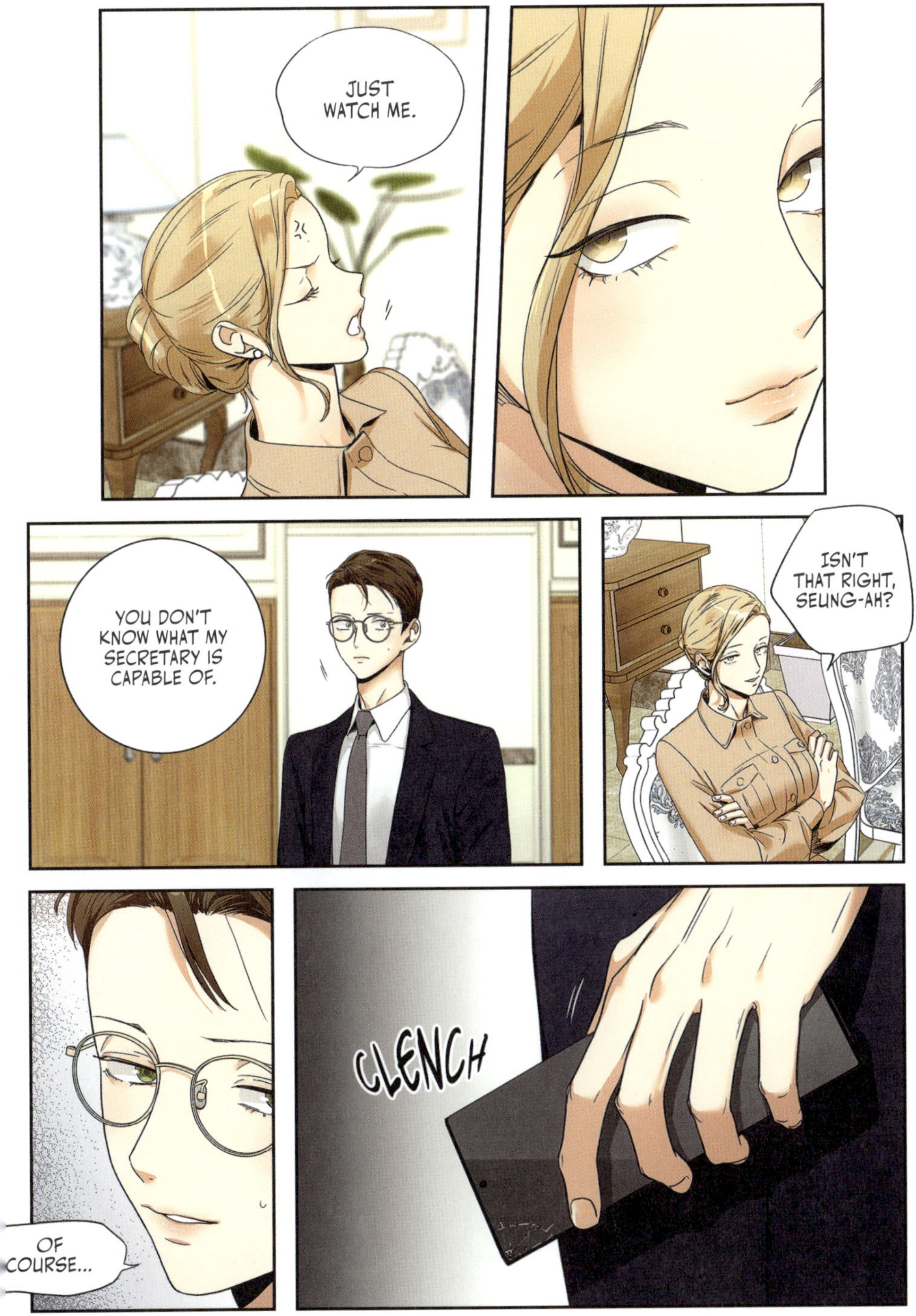
JUST WATCH ME.
YOU DON'T KNOW WHAT MY SECRETARY IS CAPABLE OF.
ISN'T THAT RIGHT, SEUNG-AH?
OF COURSE...
CLENCH

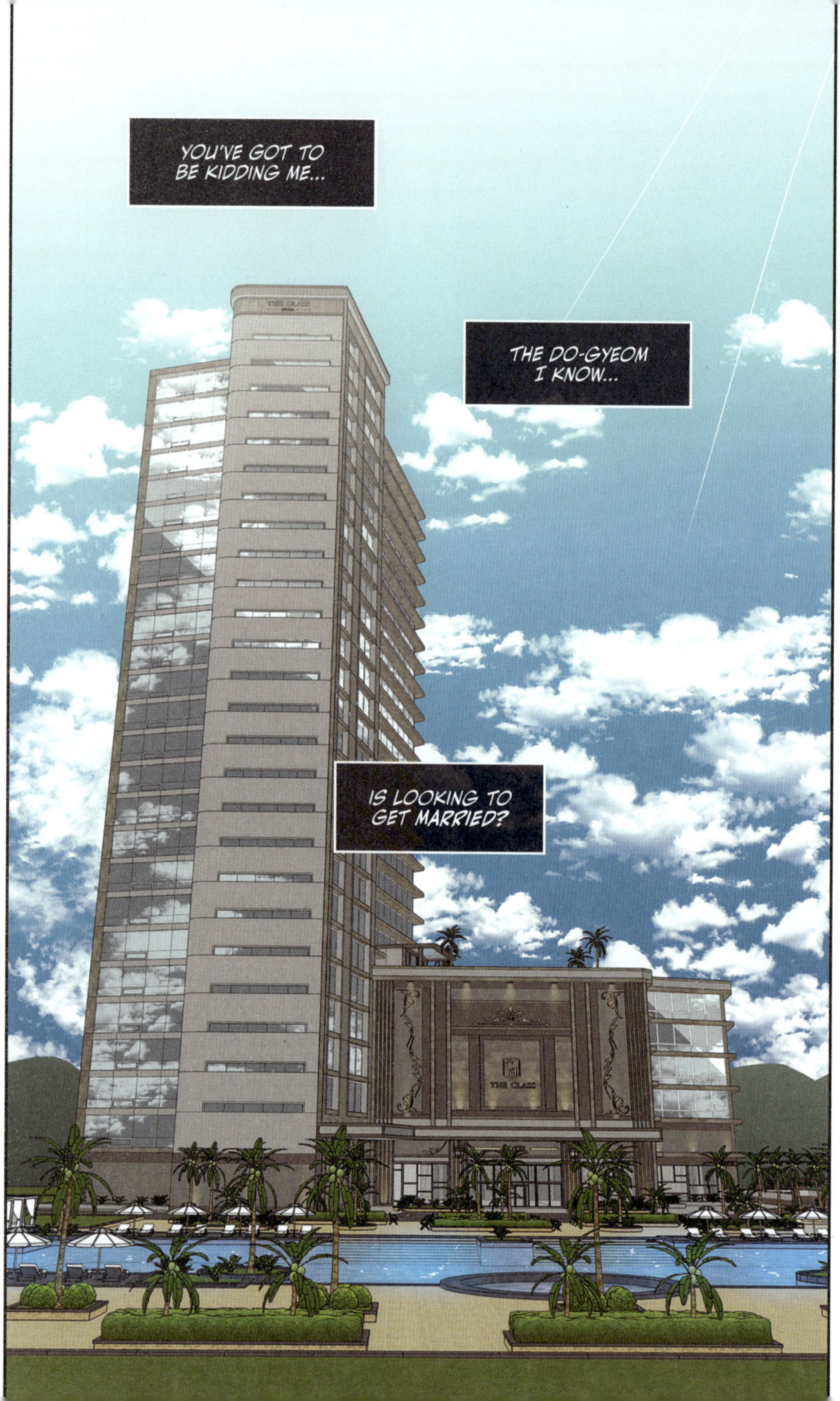
YOU'VE GOT TO BE KIDDING ME...
THE DO-GYEOM I KNOW...
IS LOOKING TO GET MARRIED?
THE CLASS

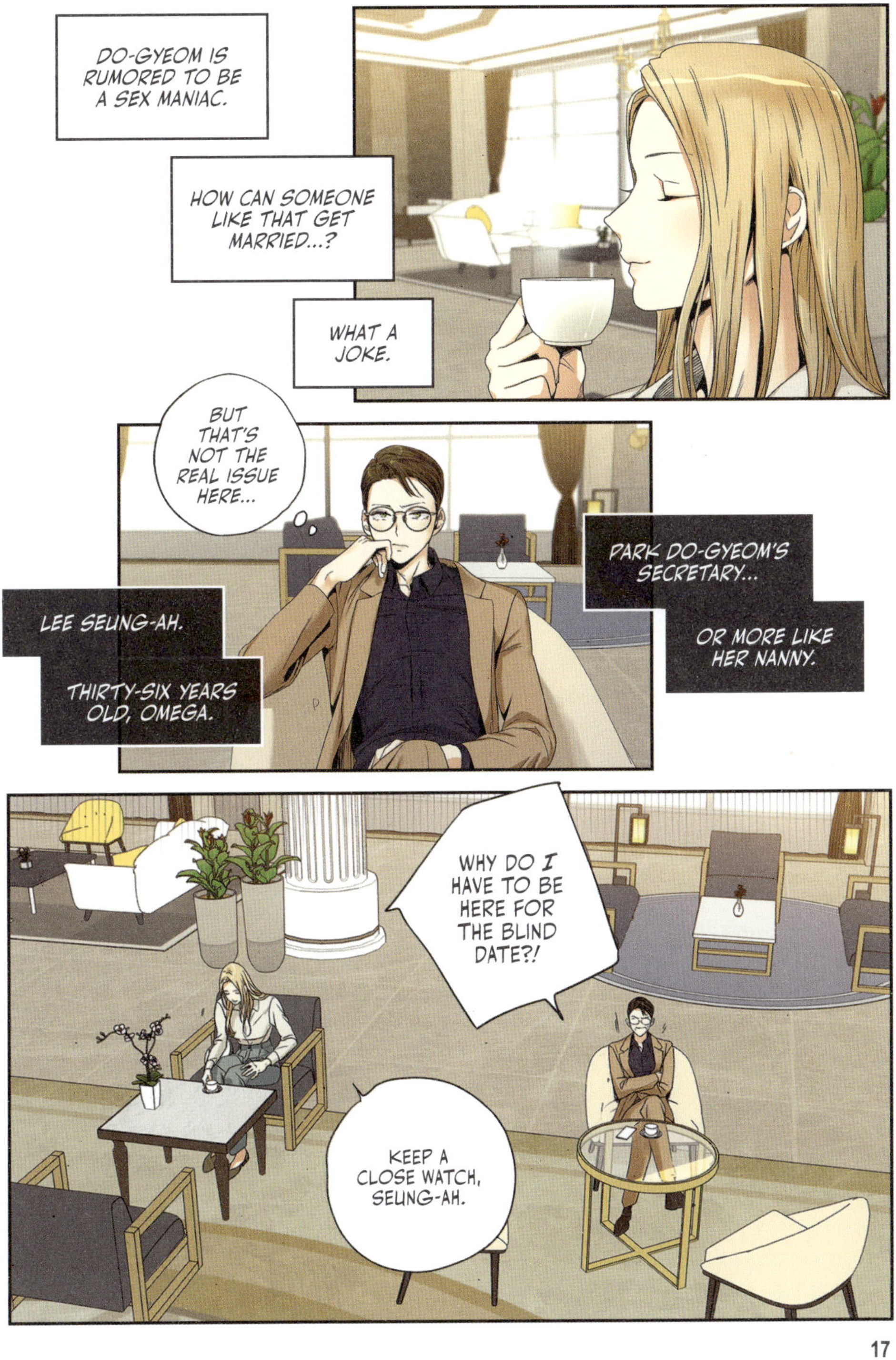
DO-GYEOM IS RUMORED TO BE A SEX MANIAC.
HOW CAN SOMEONE LIKE THAT GET MARRIED...?
WHAT A JOKE.
BUT THAT'S NOT THE REAL ISSUE HERE...
LEE SEUNG-AH.
THIRTY-SIX YEARS OLD, OMEGA.
PARK DO-GYEOM'S SECRETARY...
OR MORE LIKE HER NANNY.
WHY DO I HAVE TO BE HERE FOR THE BLIND DATE?!
KEEP A CLOSE WATCH, SEUNG-AH.

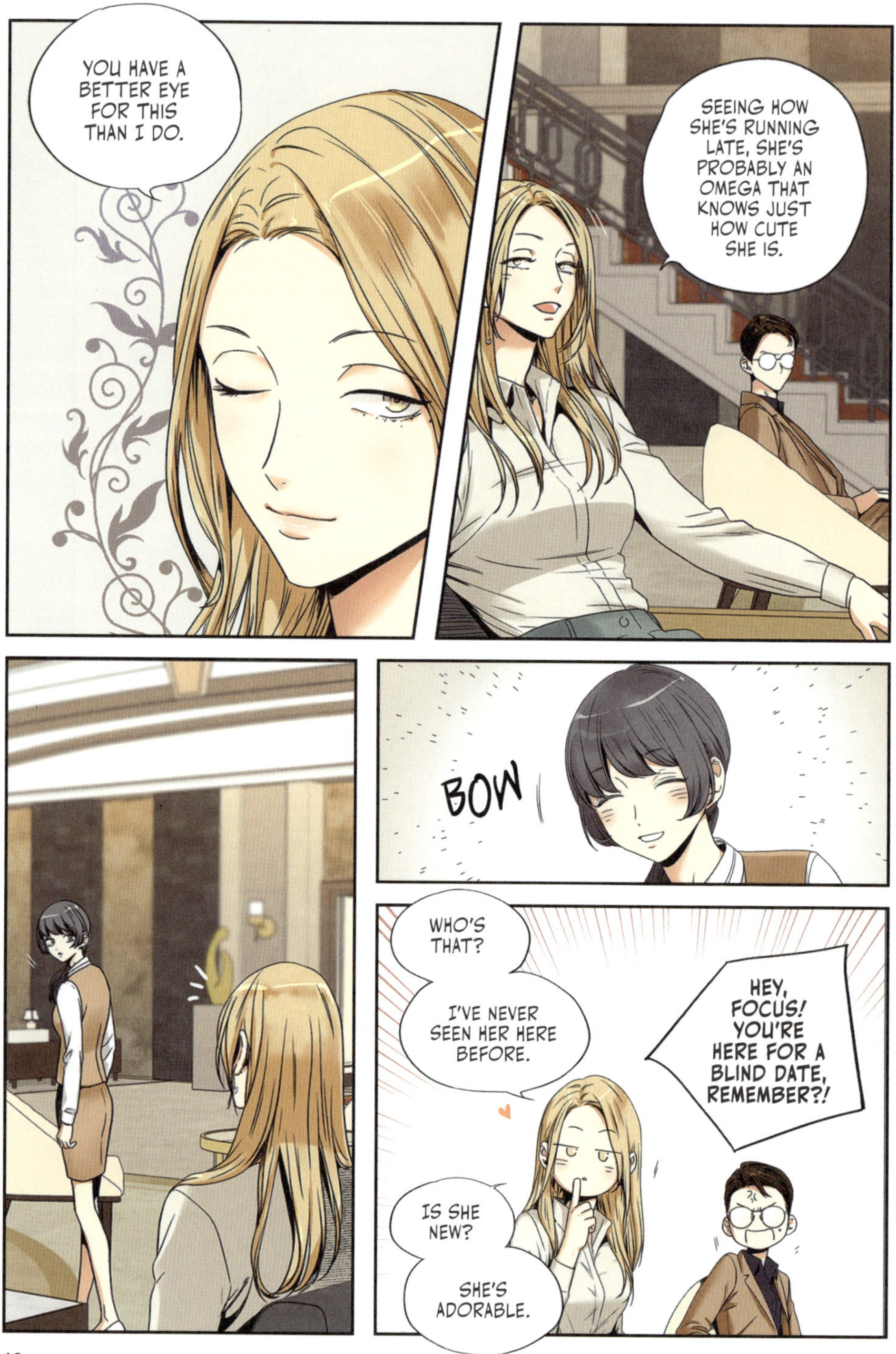
YOU HAVE A BETTER EYE FOR THIS THAN I DO.
SEEING HOW SHE'S RUNNING LATE, SHE'S PROBABLY AN OMEGA THAT KNOWS JUST HOW CUTE SHE IS.
BOW
WHO'S THAT?
I'VE NEVER SEEN HER HERE BEFORE.
HEY, FOCUS! YOU'RE HERE FOR A BLIND DATE, REMEMBER?!
IS SHE NEW?
SHE'S ADORABLE.

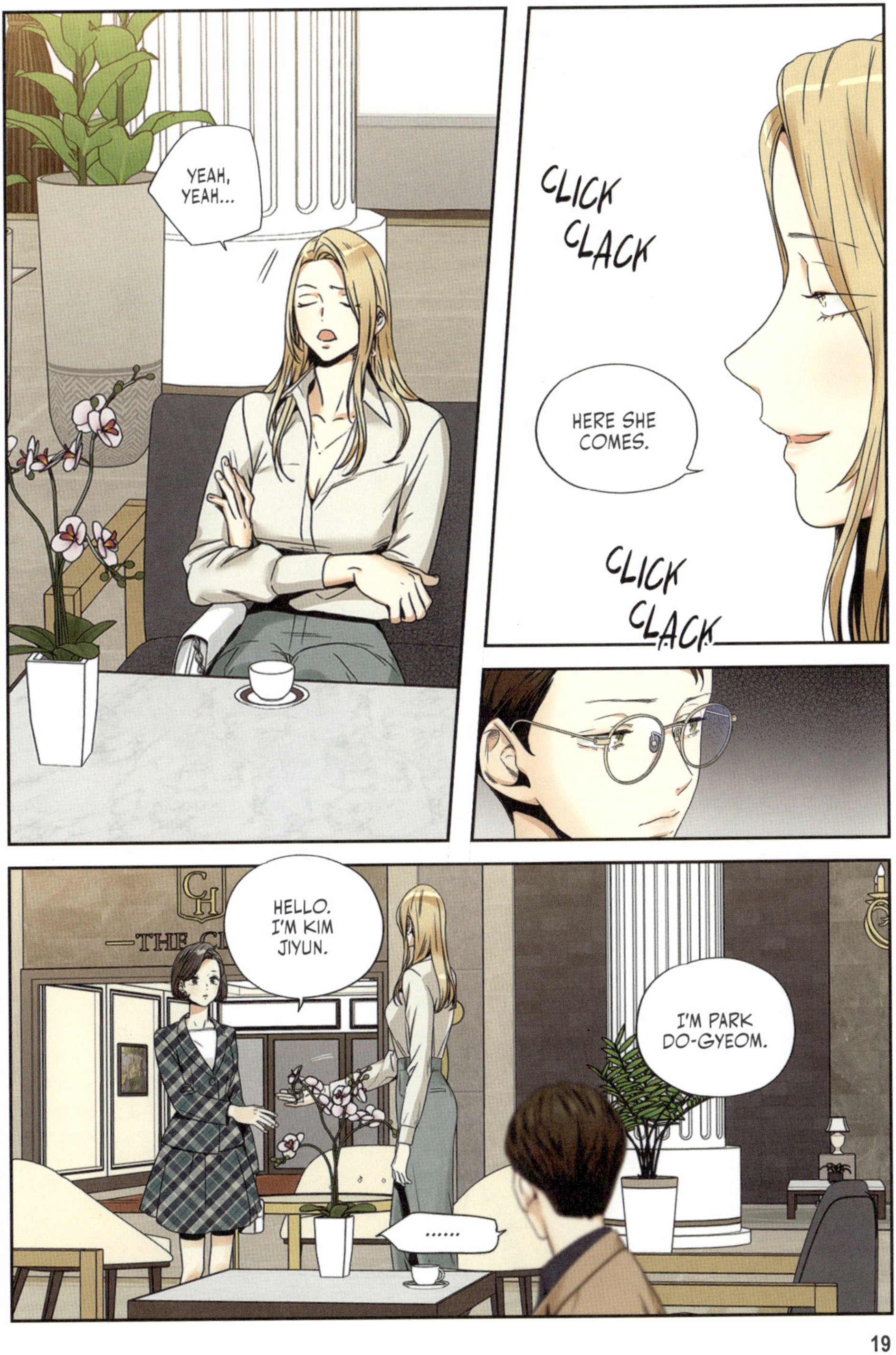
YEAH, YEAH...
CLICK CLACK
HERE SHE COMES.
CLICK CLACK
HELLO. I'M KIM JIYUN.
I'M PARK DO-GYEOM.
....

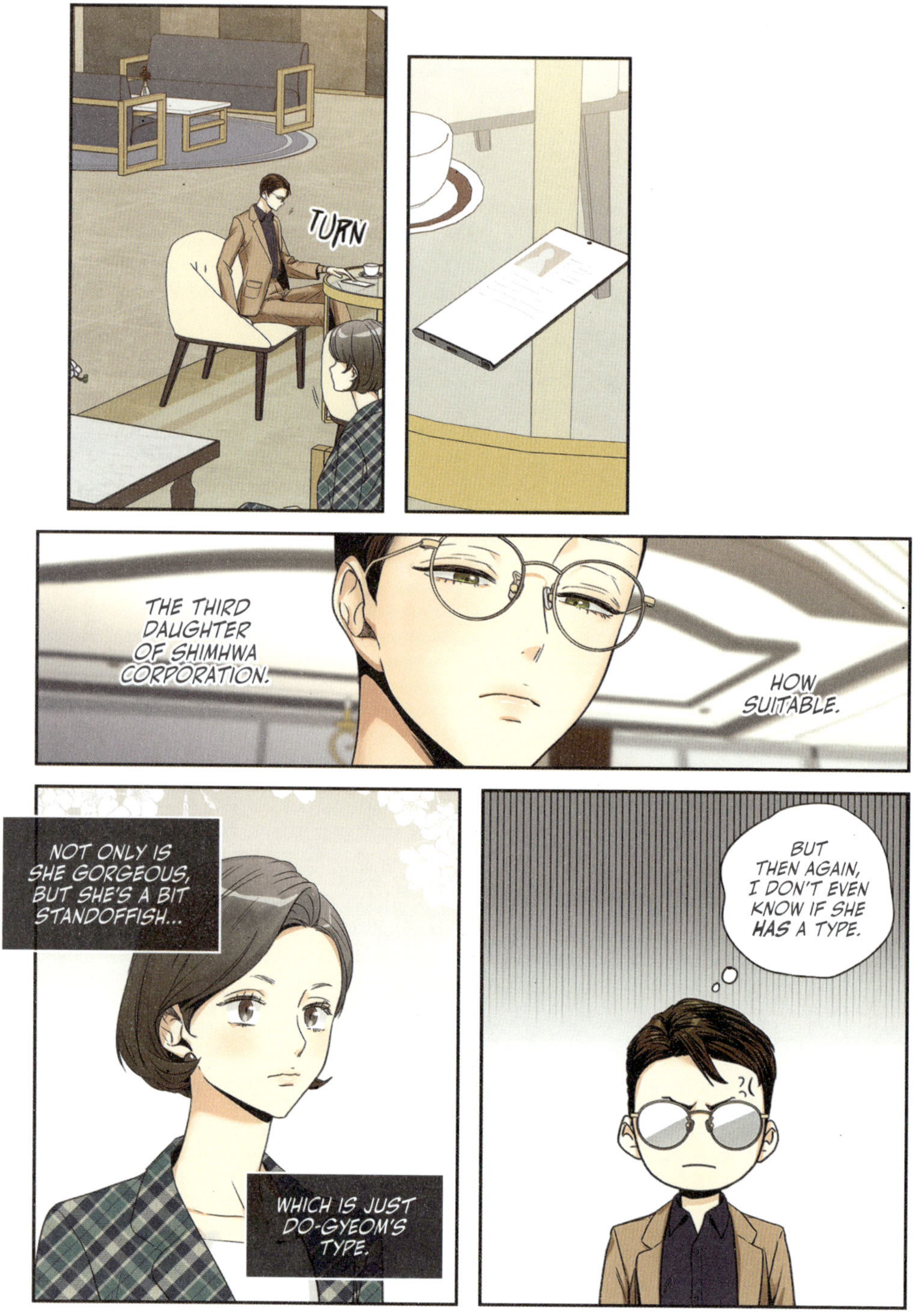
TURN
THE THIRD DAUGHTER OF SHIMHWA CORPORATION.
HOW SUITABLE.
NOT ONLY IS SHE GORGEOUS, BUT SHE'S A BIT STANDOFFISH...
WHICH IS JUST DO-GYEOM'S TYPE.
BUT THEN AGAIN, I DON'T EVEN KNOW IF SHE HAS A TYPE.

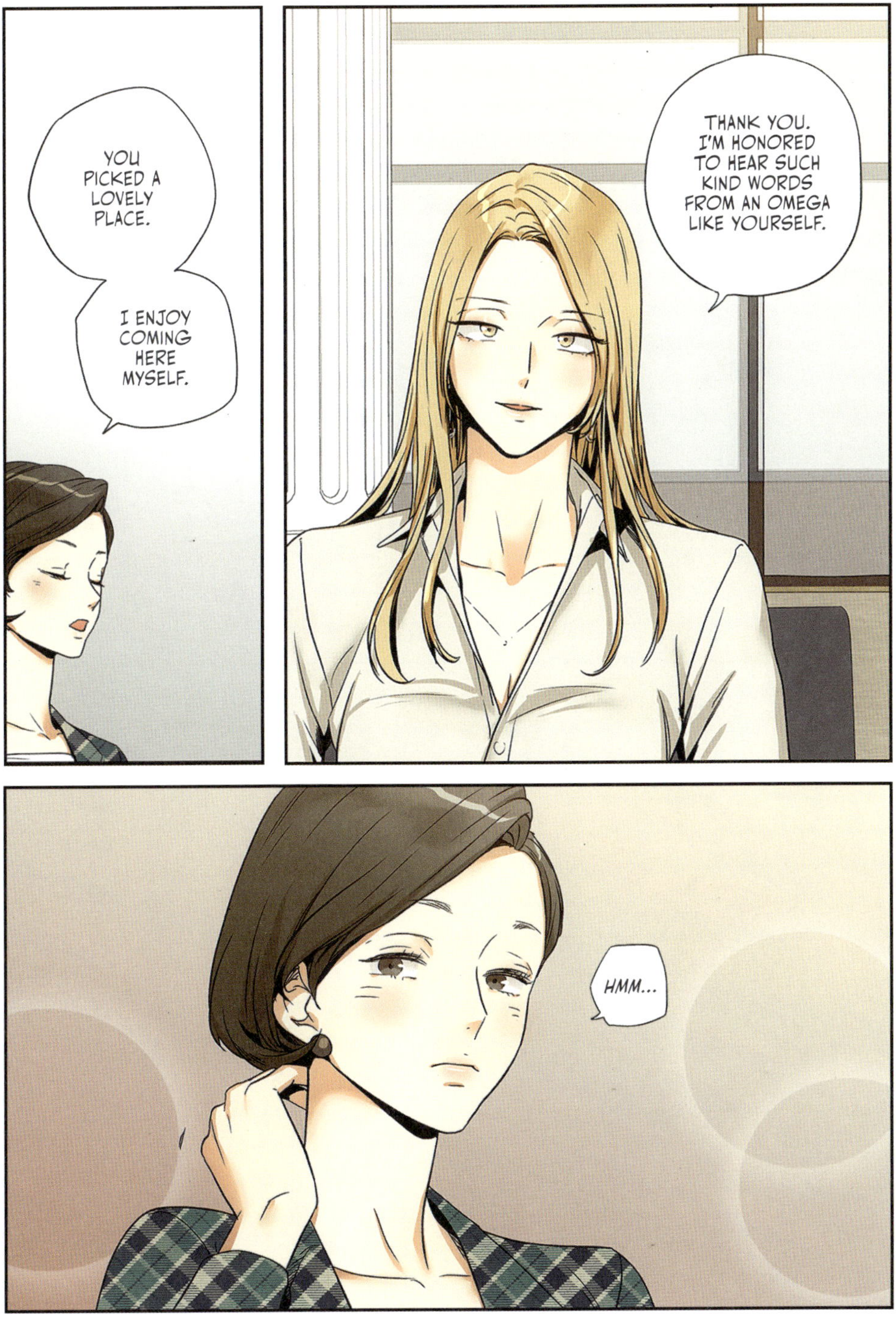
YOU PICKED A LOVELY PLACE.
I ENJOY COMING HERE MYSELF.
THANK YOU. I'M HONORED TO HEAR SUCH KIND WORDS FROM AN OMEGA LIKE YOURSELF.
HMM...

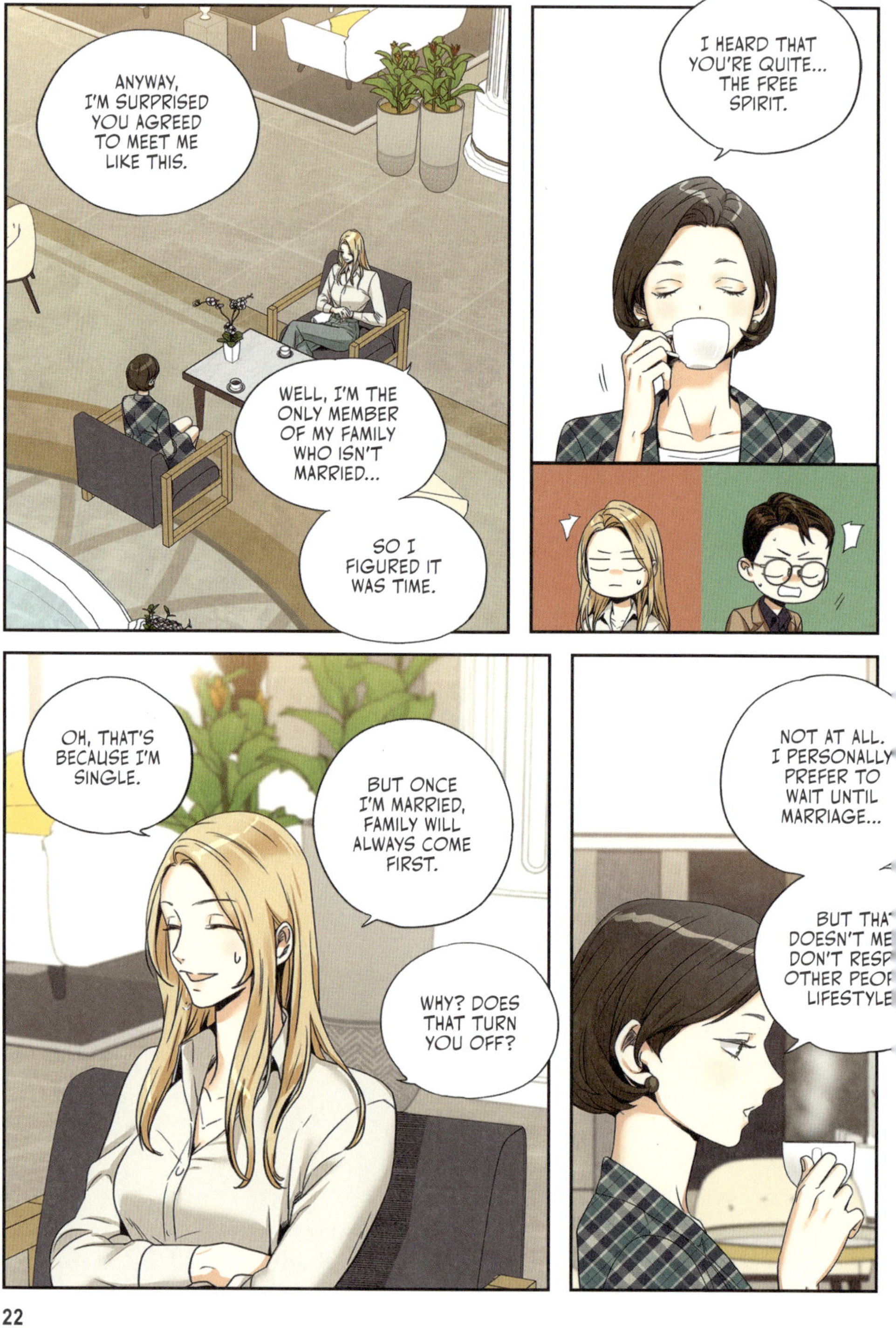
ANYWAY, I'M SURPRISED YOU AGREED TO MEET ME LIKE THIS.
WELL, I'M THE ONLY MEMBER OF MY FAMILY WHO ISN'T MARRIED...
SO I FIGURED IT WAS TIME.
I HEARD THAT YOU'RE QUITE... THE FREE SPIRIT.
OH, THAT'S BECAUSE I'M SINGLE.
BUT ONCE I'M MARRIED, FAMILY WILL ALWAYS COME FIRST.
WHY? DOES THAT TURN YOU OFF?
NOT AT ALL. I PERSONALLY PREFER TO WAIT UNTIL MARRIAGE...

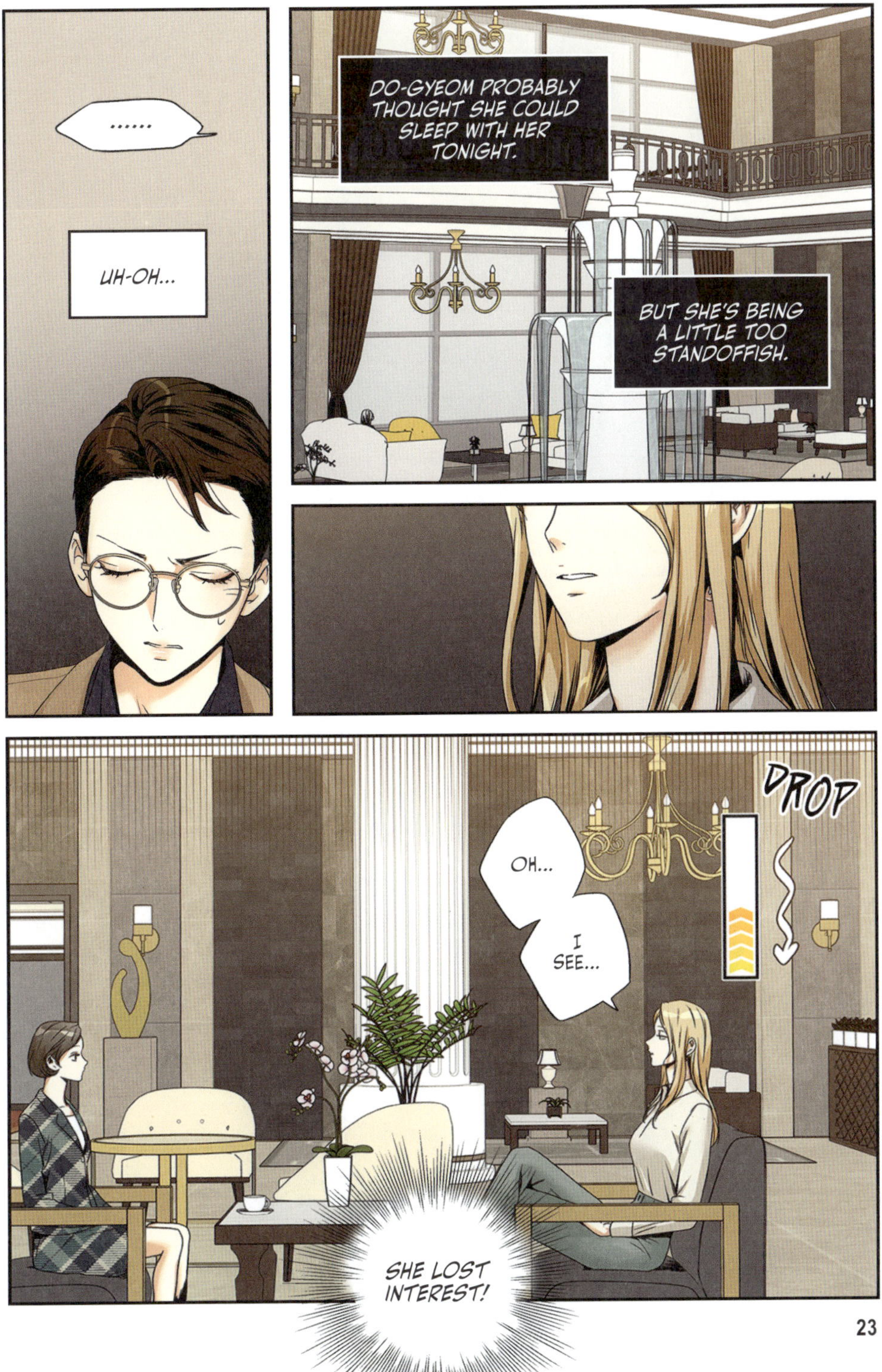
......
UH-OH...
DO-GYEOM PROBABLY THOUGHT SHE COULD SLEEP WITH HER TONIGHT.
BUT SHE'S BEING A LITTLE TOO STANDOFFISH.
OH...
I SEE...
DROP
SHE LOST INTEREST!

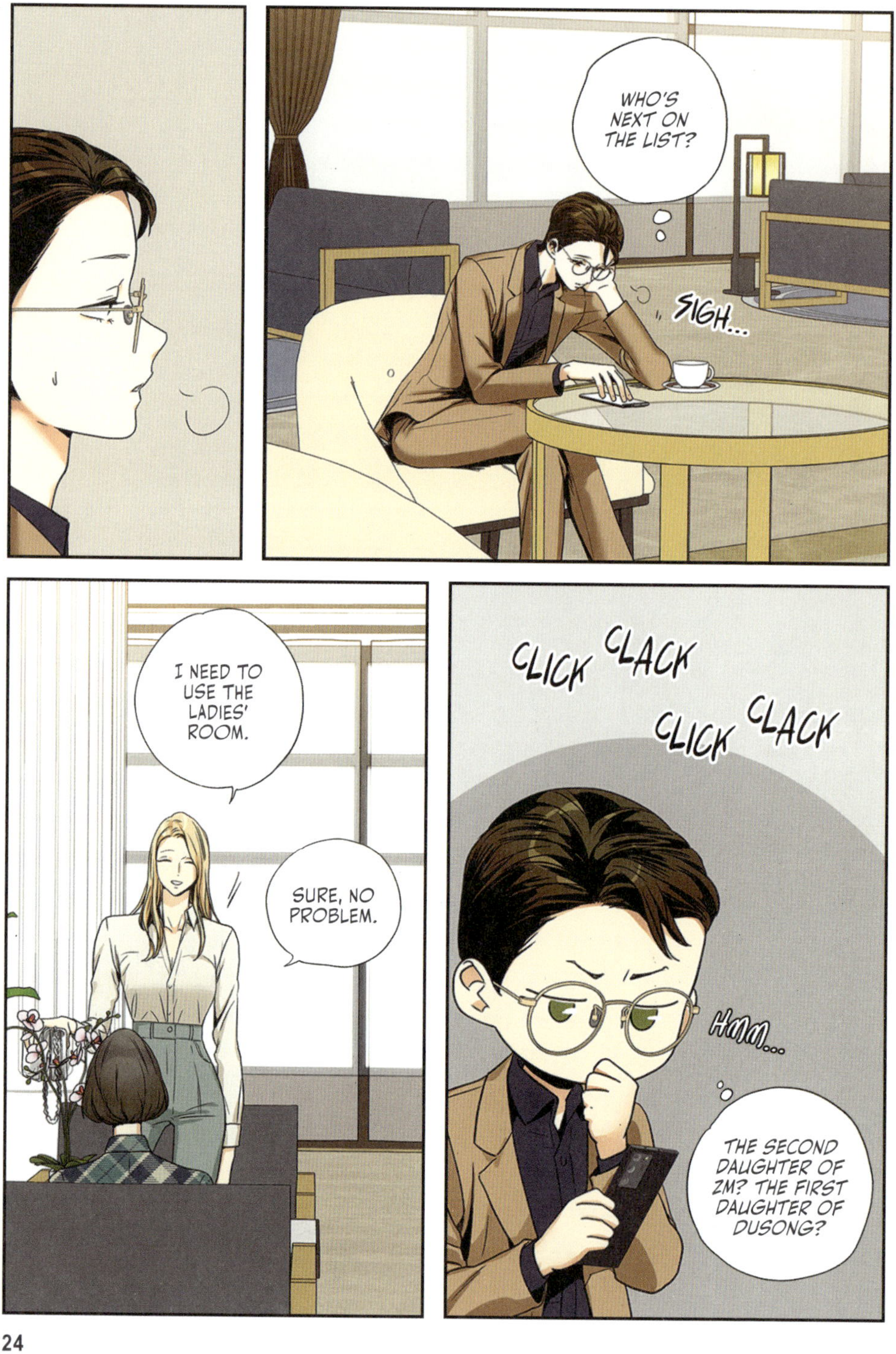
WHO'S NEXT ON THE LIST?
SIGH...
I NEED TO USE THE LADIES' ROOM.
SURE, NO PROBLEM.
CLICK CLACK
CLICK CLACK
HMM...
THE SECOND DAUGHTER OF ZM? THE FIRST DAUGHTER OF DUSONG?

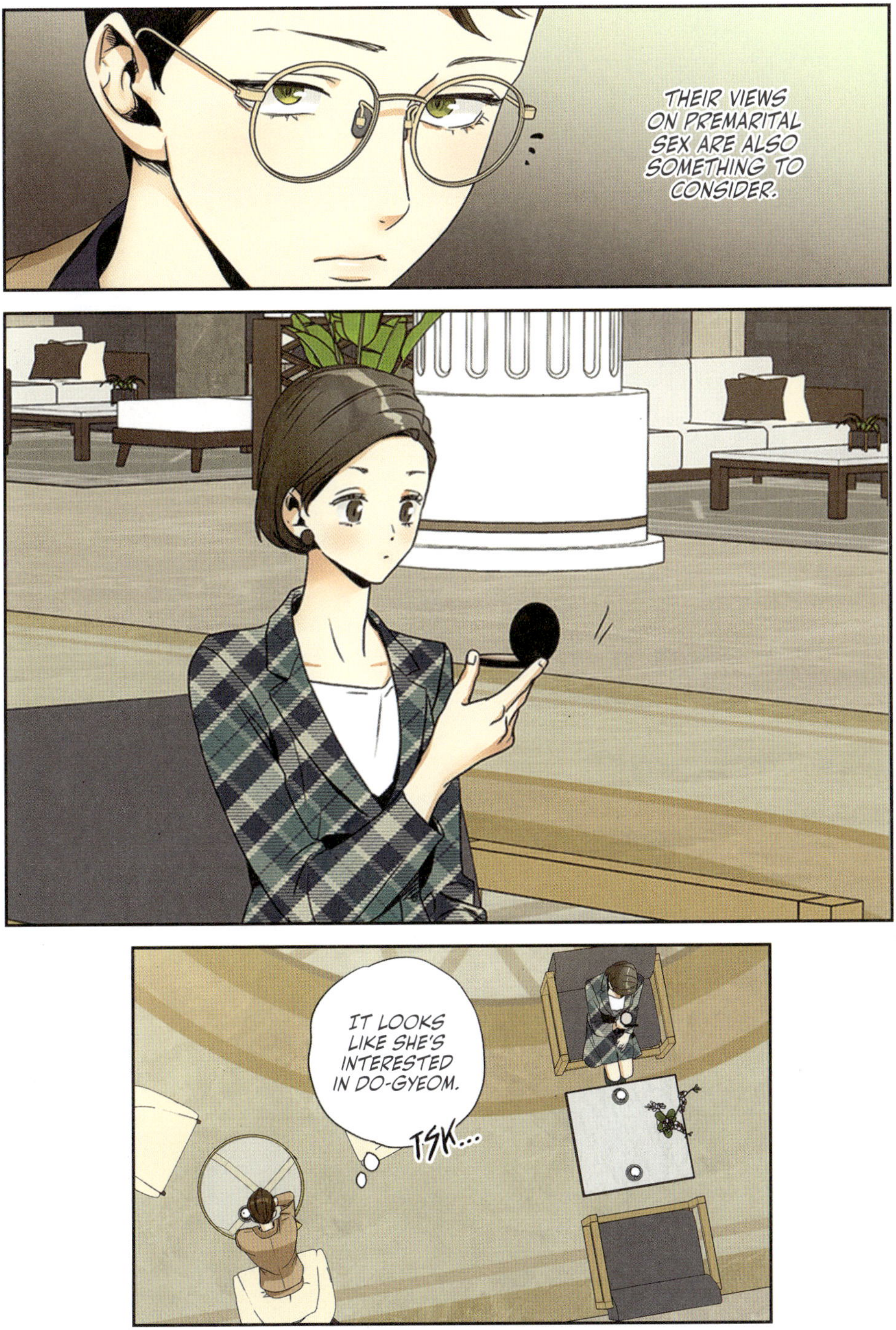
THEIR VIEWS ON PREMARITAL SEX ARE ALSO SOMETHING TO CONSIDER.
IT LOOKS LIKE SHE'S INTERESTED IN DO-GYEOM.
TSK...

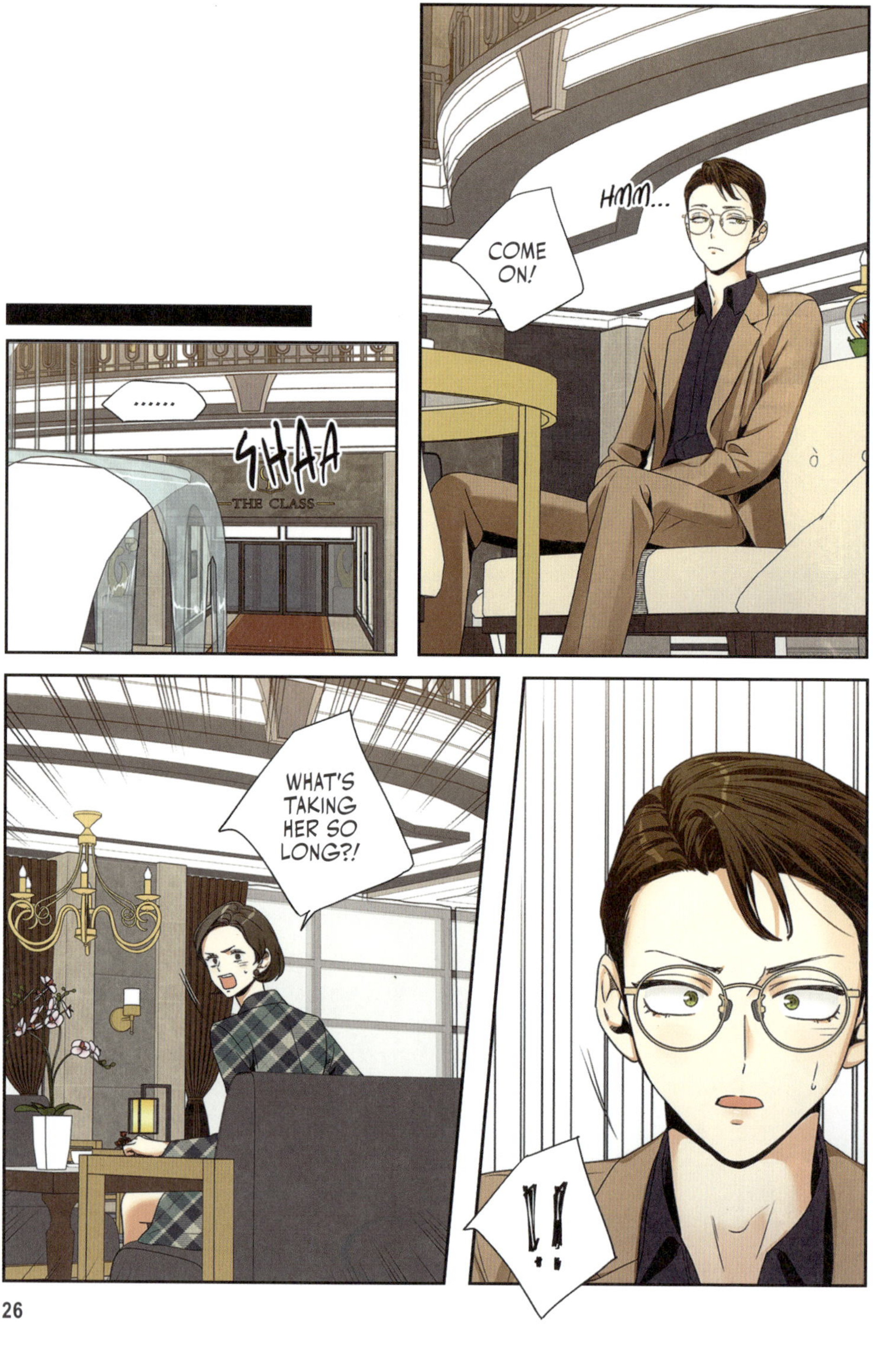
......
SHAA
THE CLASS
COME ON!
HMM...
WHAT'S TAKING HER SO LONG?!
!!

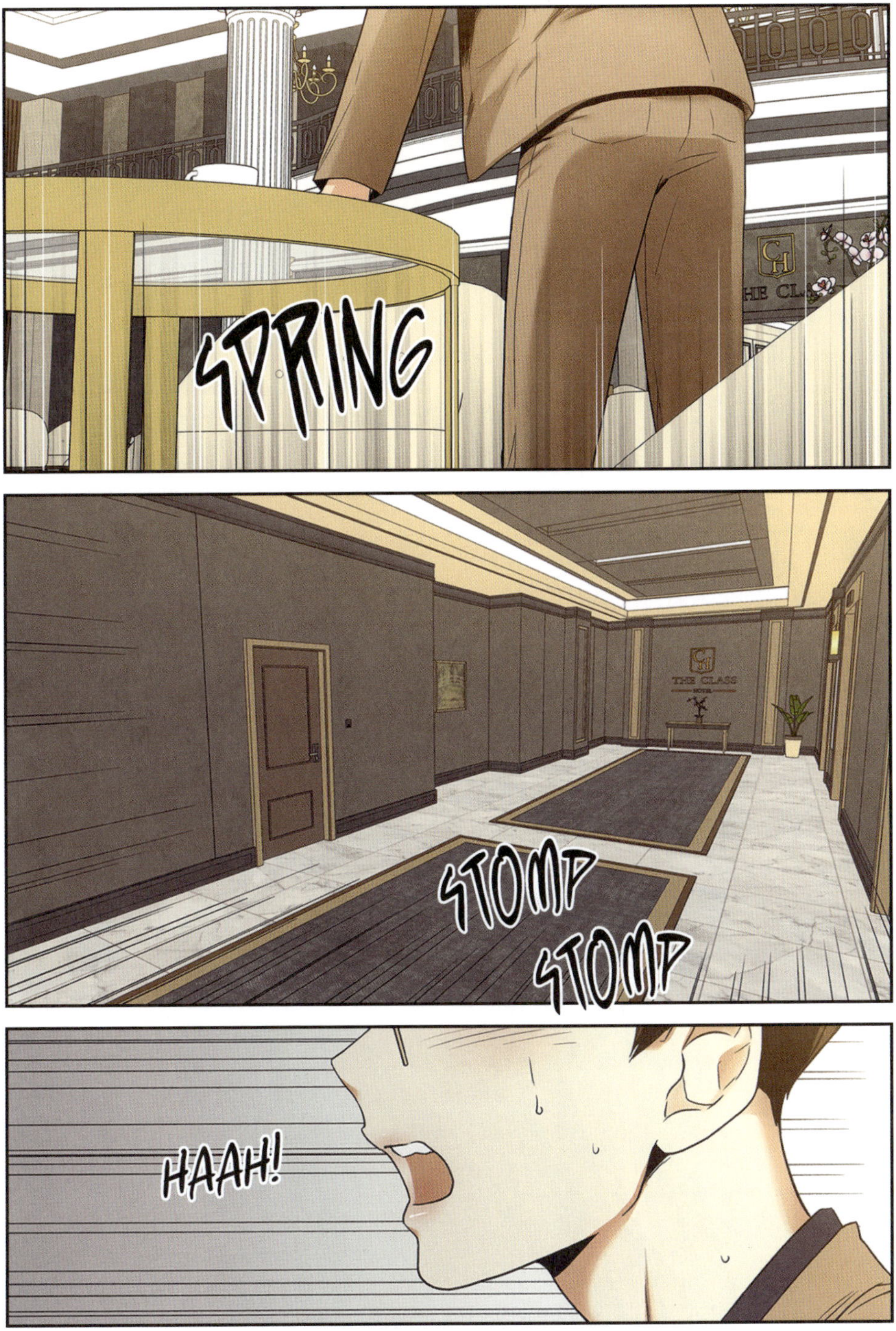
SPRING
STOMP
STOMP
HAAH!

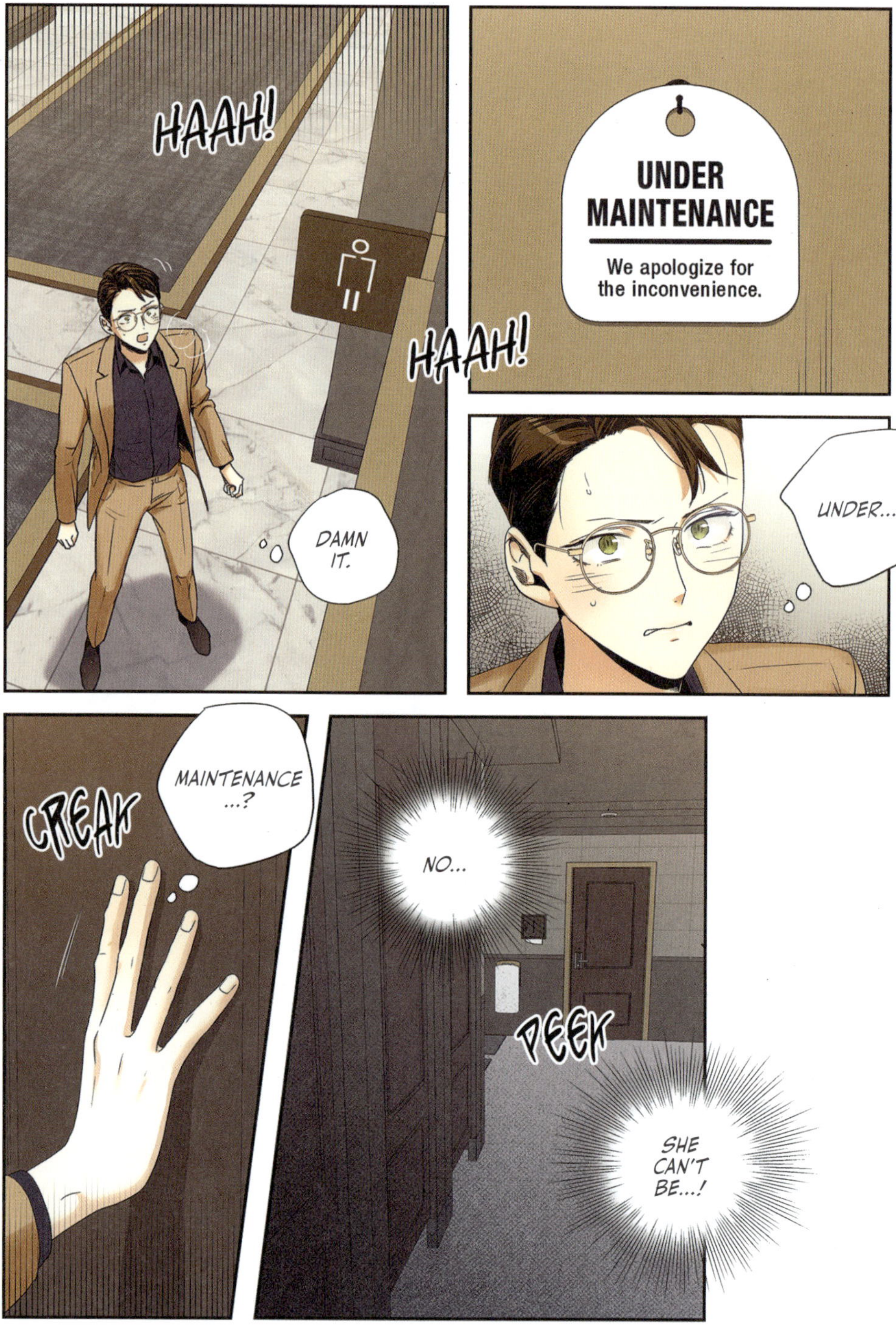
HAAH!
DAMN IT.
UNDER MAINTENANCE
We apologize for the inconvenience.
HAAH!
UNDER...
CREAK
MAINTENANCE ...?
NO...
PEEK
SHE CAN'T BE...!

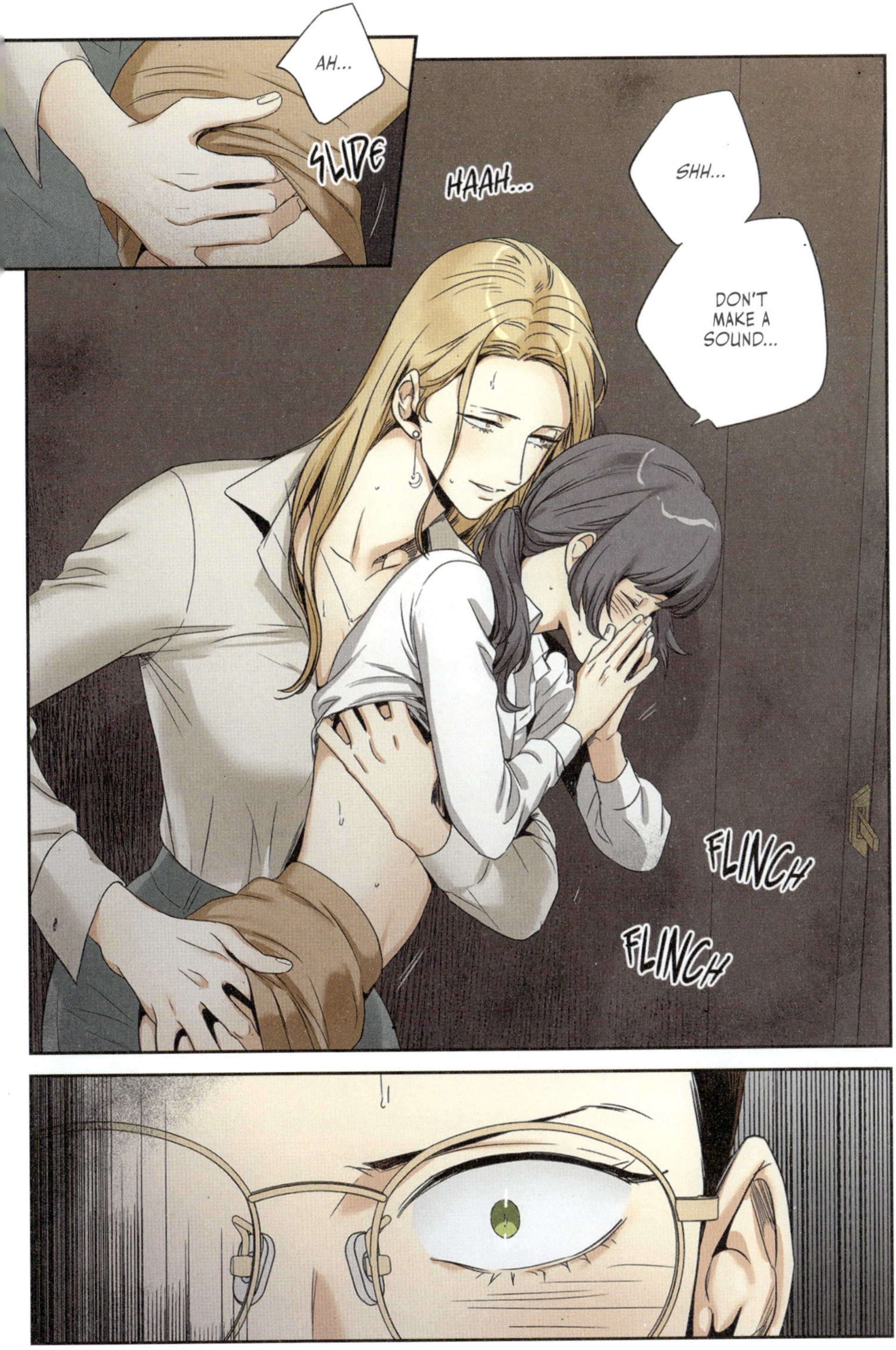
AH...
SLIDE
HAAH...
SHH...
DON'T MAKE A SOUND...
FLINCH
FLINCH

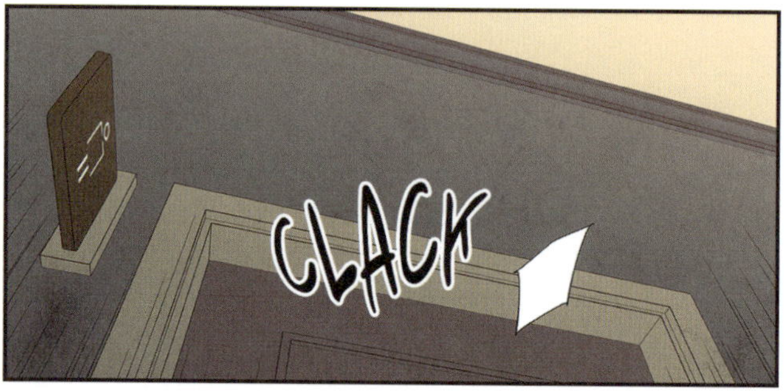
CLACK

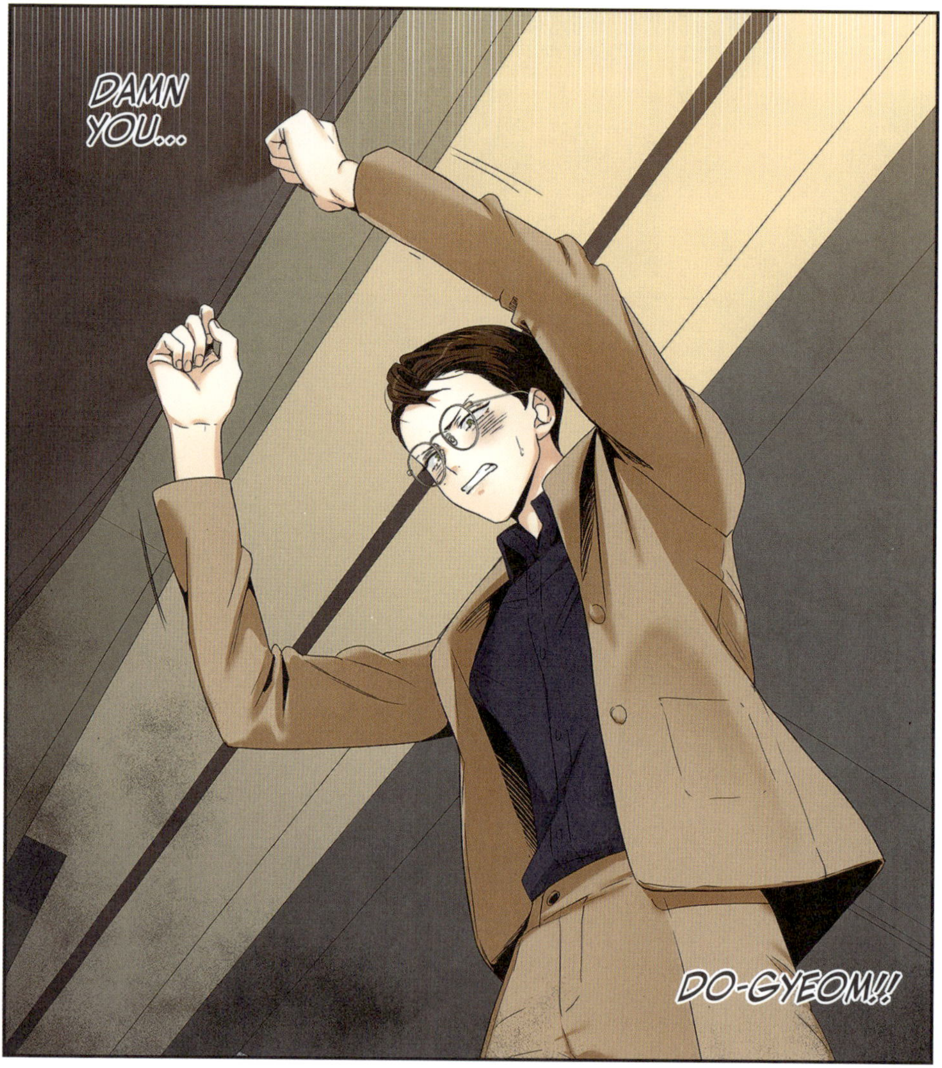
DAMN YOU...
DO-GYEOM!!

Love is an Illusion!
·•·—·◆·— The Queen —·◆·—·•·

Love is an Illusion!
The Queen

Chapter 2

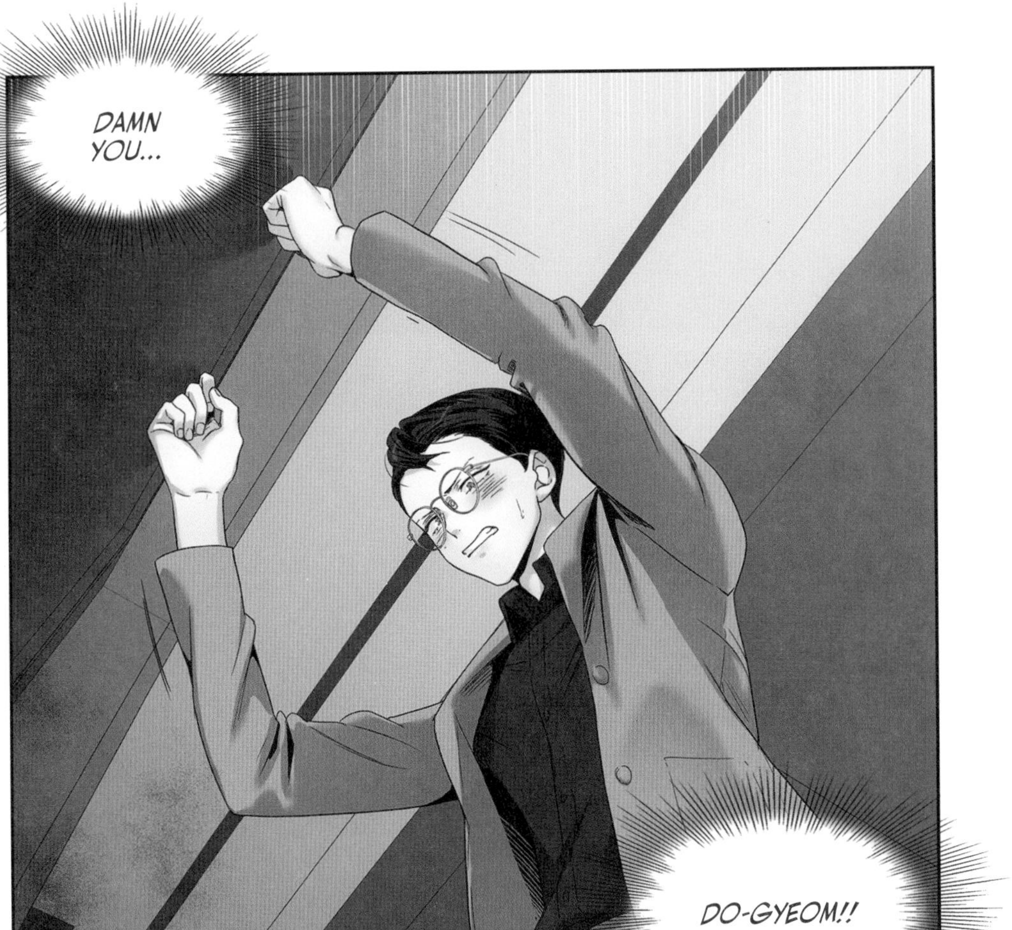
DAMN YOU...
DO-GYEOM!!

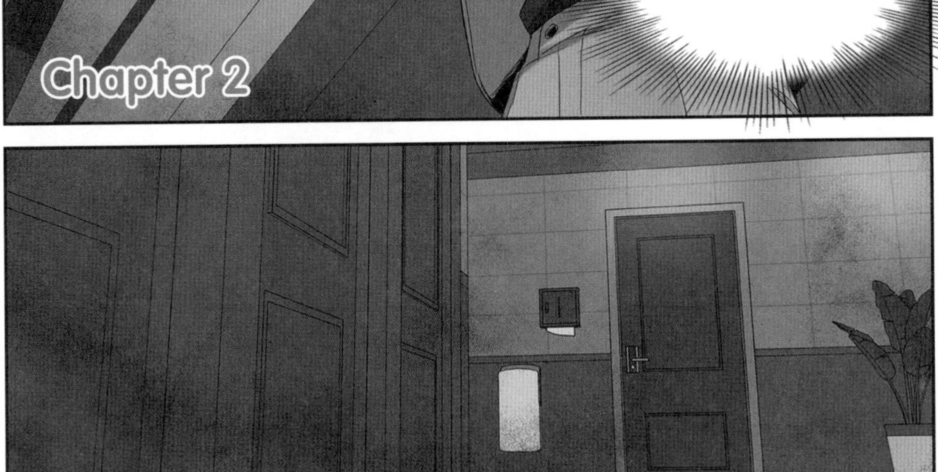

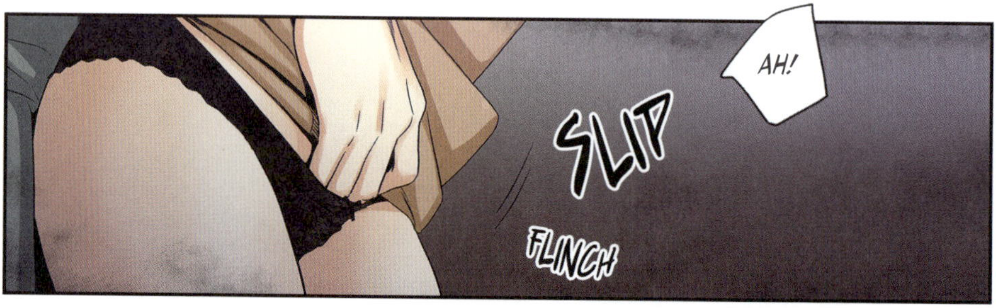
AH!
SLIP
FLINCH

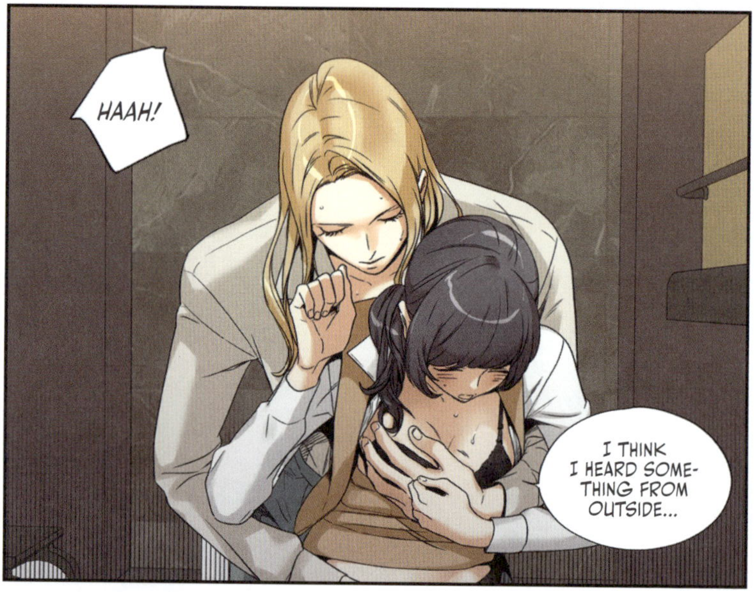
HAAH!
I THINK I HEARD SOMETHING FROM OUTSIDE...

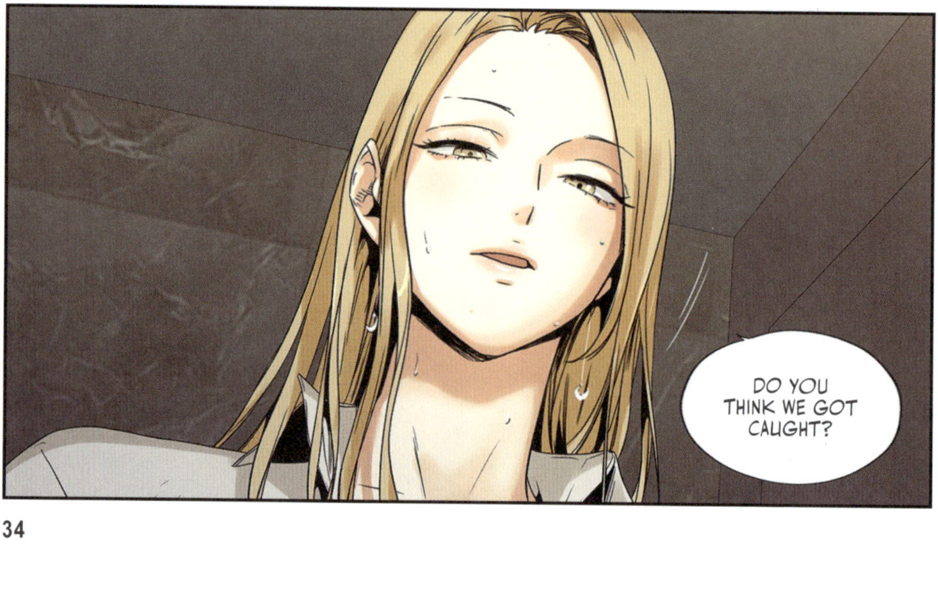
DO YOU THINK WE GOT CAUGHT?

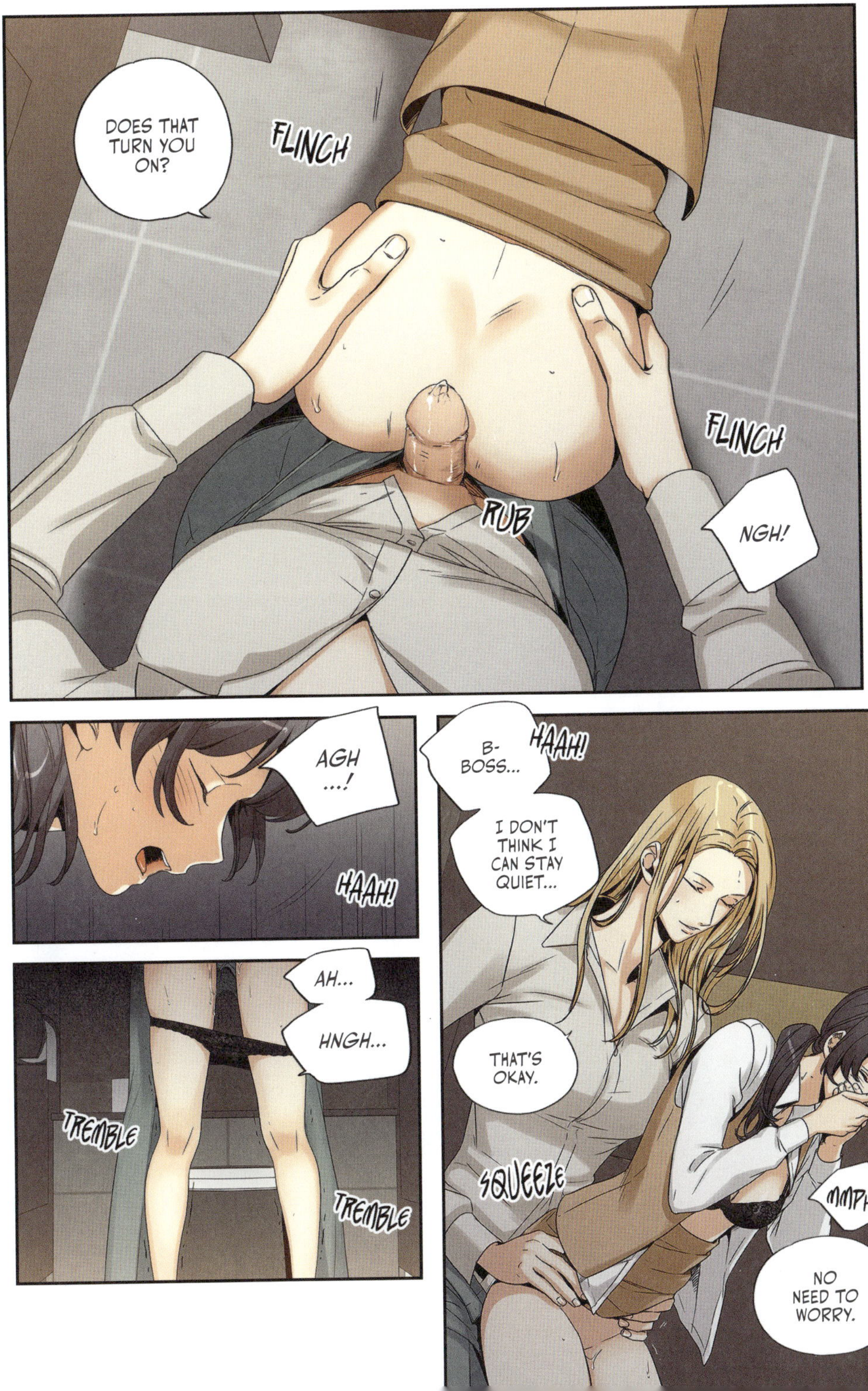
DOES THAT TURN YOU ON?
FLINCH
FLINCH
RUB
NGH!
AGH ...!
HAAH!
AH...
HNGH...
TREMBLE
TREMBLE
B- BOSS...
HAAH!
I DON'T THINK I CAN STAY QUIET...
THAT'S OKAY.
SQUEEZE
MMPH!
NO NEED TO WORRY.

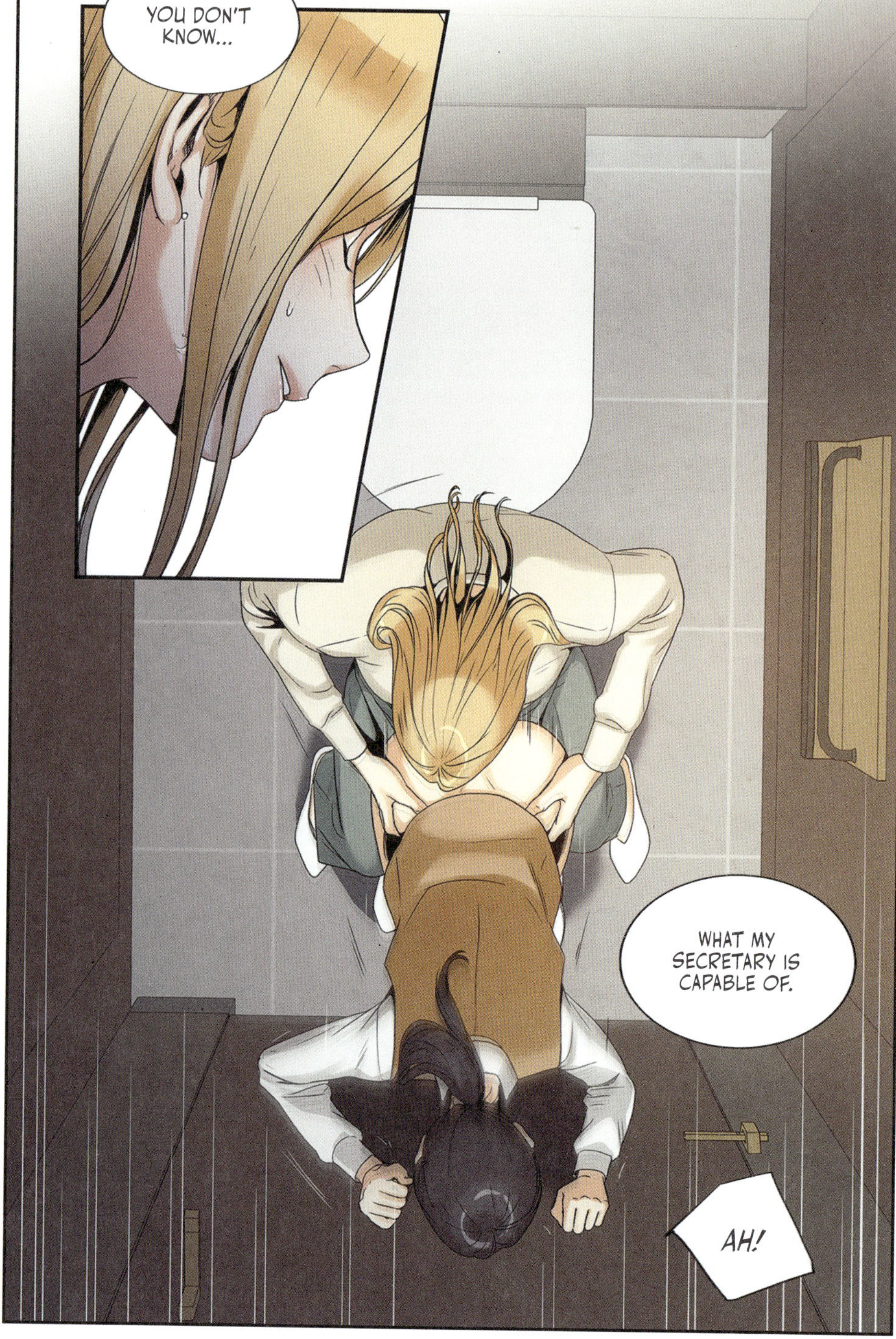
YOU DON'T KNOW...
WHAT MY SECRETARY IS CAPABLE OF.
AH!

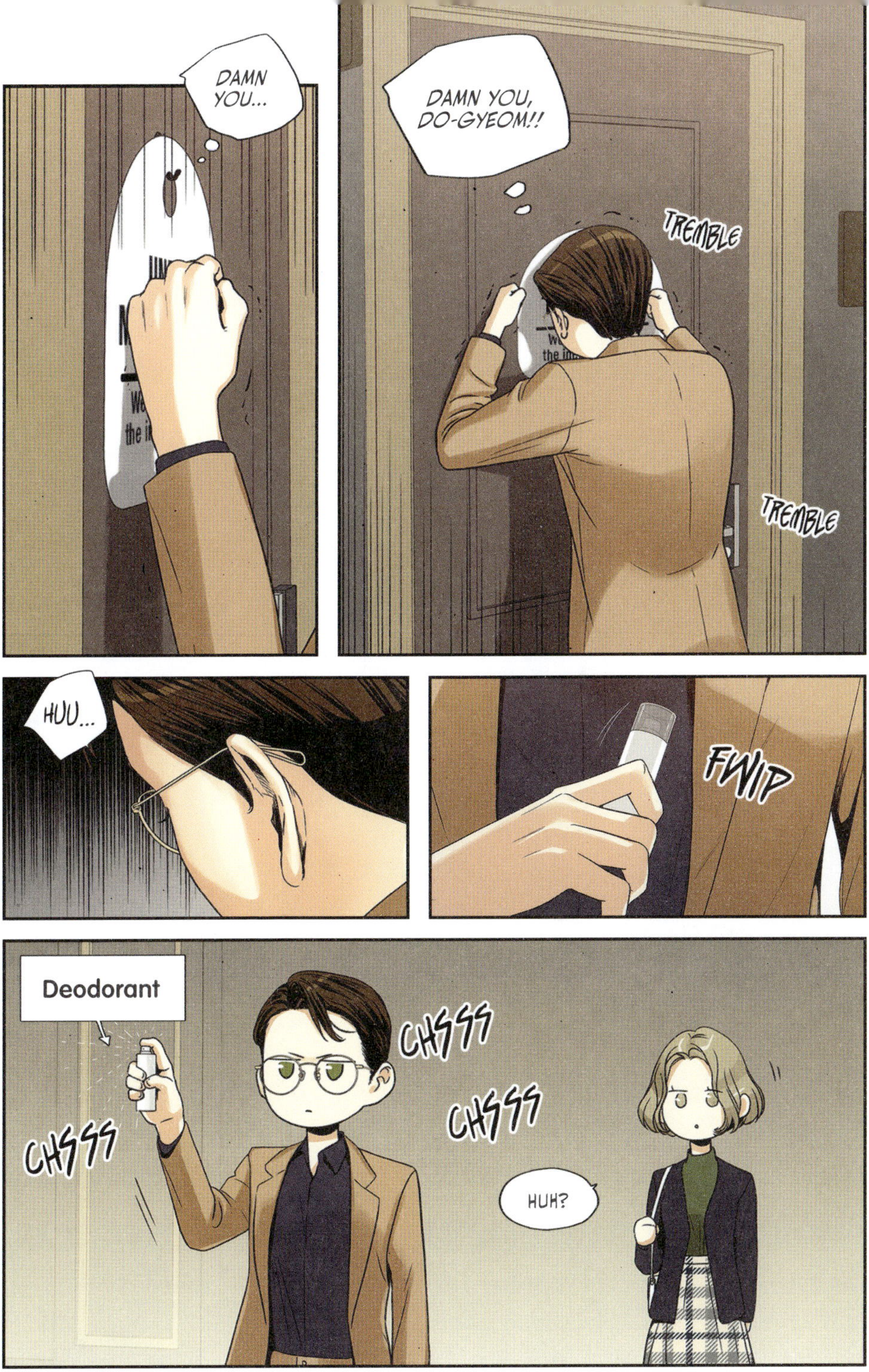
DAMN YOU...
DAMN YOU, DO-GYEOM!!
TREMBLE
TREMBLE
HUU...
FWIP
Deodorant
CHSSS
CHSSS
CHSSS
HUH?

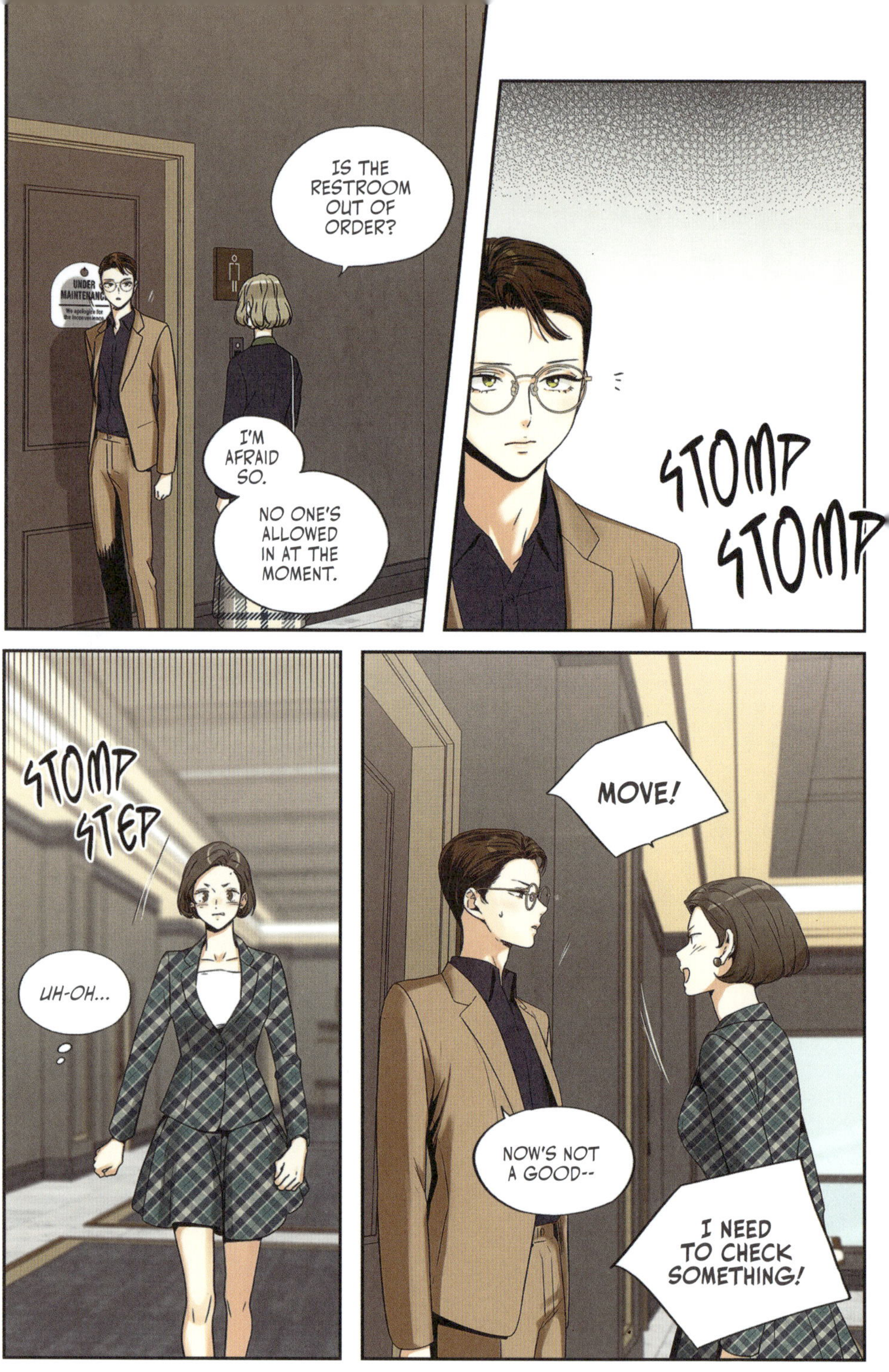
IS THE RESTROOM OUT OF ORDER?
I'M AFRAID SO.
NO ONE'S ALLOWED IN AT THE MOMENT.
STOMP STOMP
STOMP STEP
UH-OH...
MOVE!
NOW'S NOT A GOOD--
I NEED TO CHECK SOMETHING!

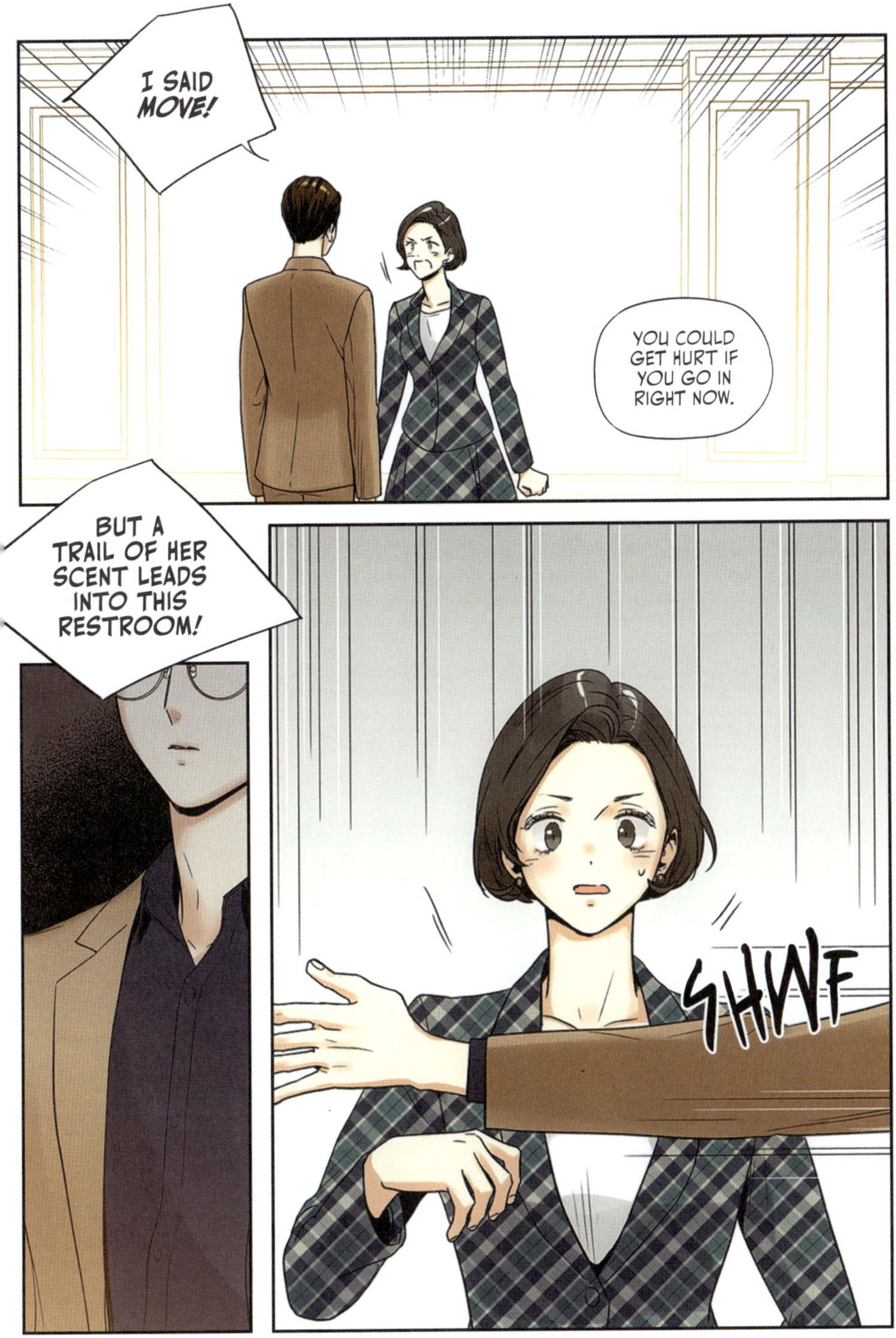
I SAID MOVE!
YOU COULD GET HURT IF YOU GO IN RIGHT NOW.
BUT A TRAIL OF HER SCENT LEADS INTO THIS RESTROOM!
SHWF

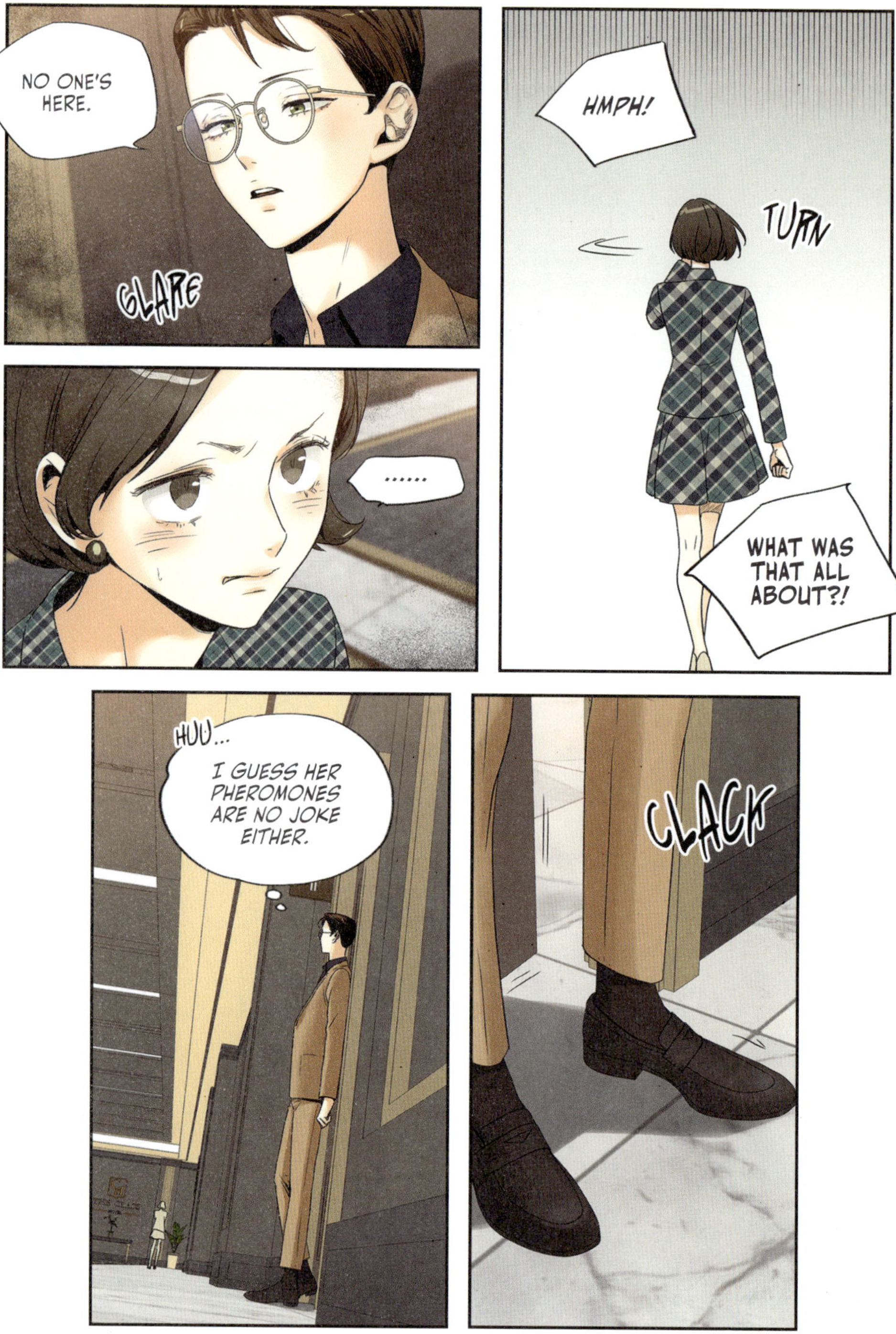
NO ONE'S HERE.
GLARE
HMPH!
TURN
WHAT WAS THAT ALL ABOUT?!
......
HUU...
I GUESS HER PHEROMONES ARE NO JOKE EITHER.
CLACK

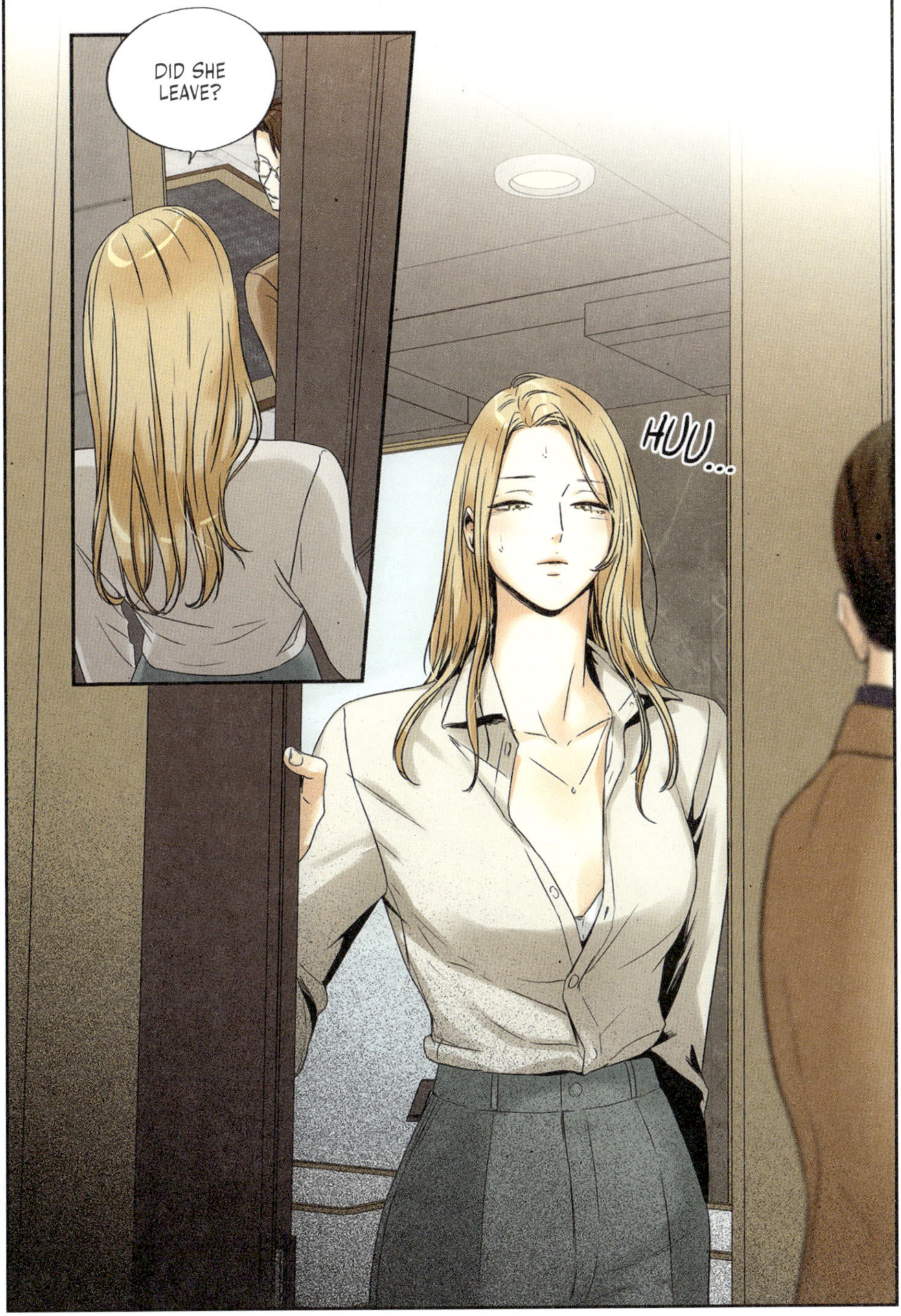
DID SHE LEAVE?
HUU...

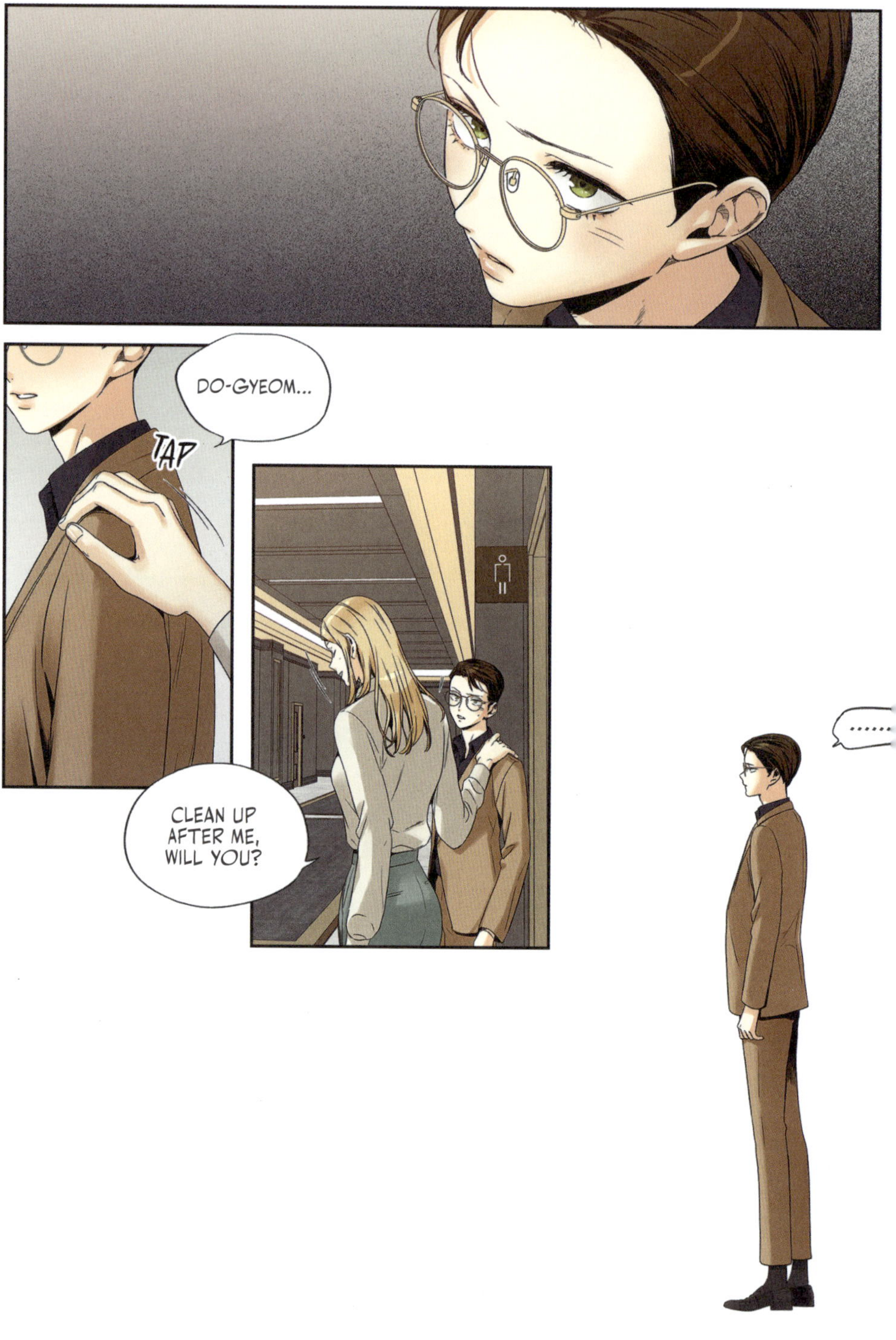
DO-GYEOM...
TAP
CLEAN UP AFTER ME, WILL YOU?
......

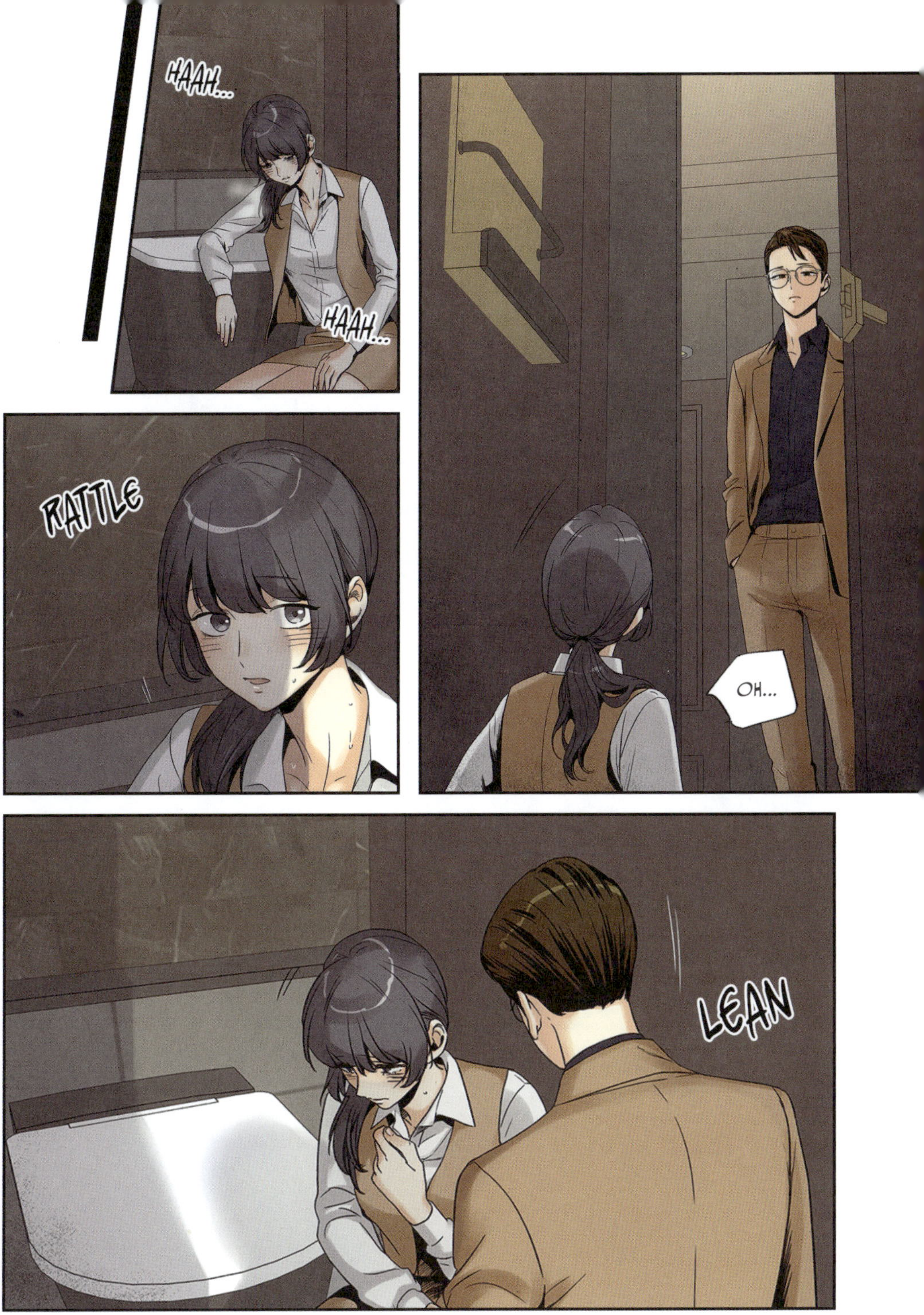
HAAH...
HAAH...
RATTLE
OH...
LEAN

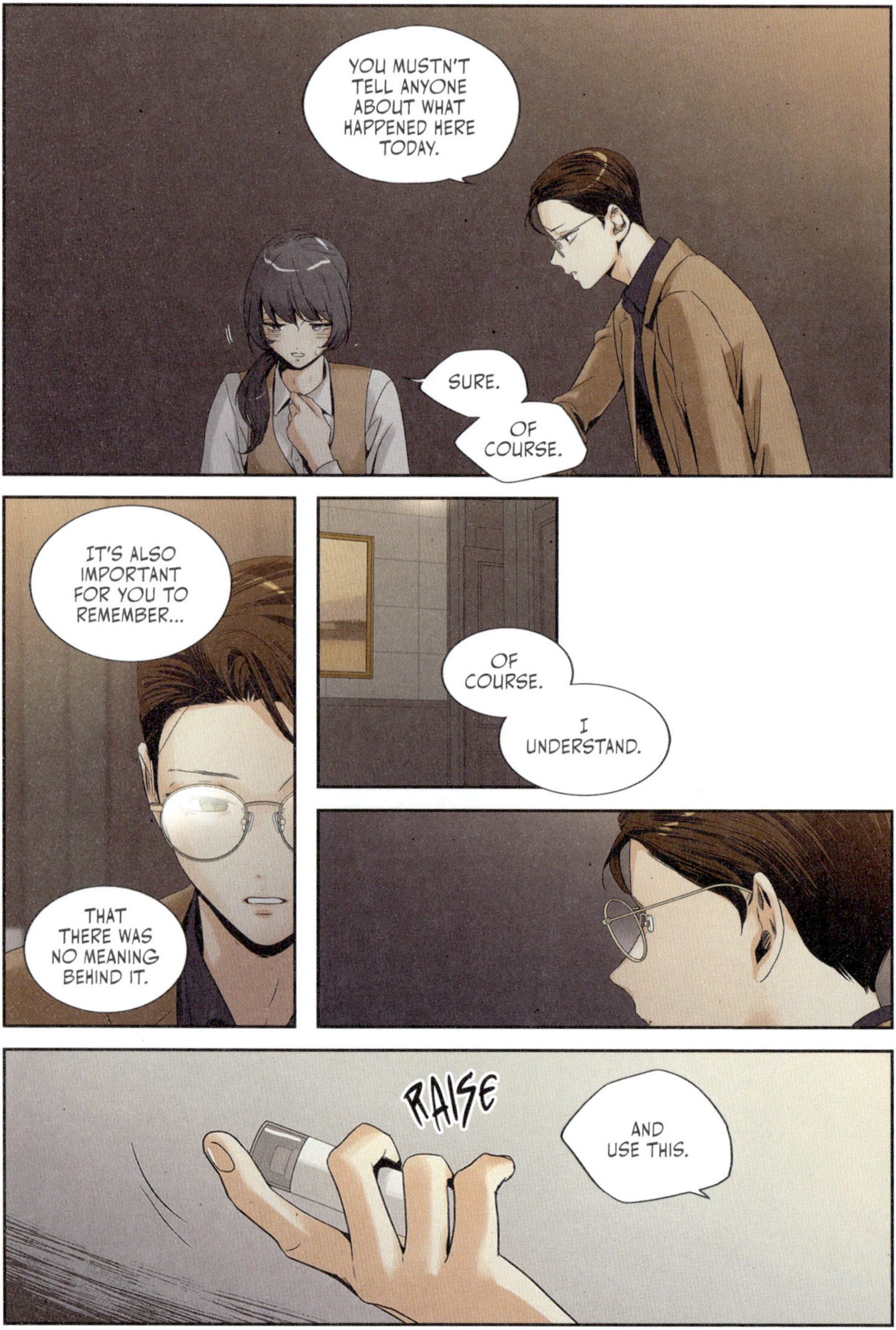

YOU MUSTN'T TELL ANYONE ABOUT WHAT HAPPENED HERE TODAY.
SURE.
OF COURSE.
IT'S ALSO IMPORTANT FOR YOU TO REMEMBER...
THAT THERE WAS NO MEANING BEHIND IT.
OF COURSE.
I UNDERSTAND.
RAISE
AND USE THIS.

YOU CAN GO NOW.

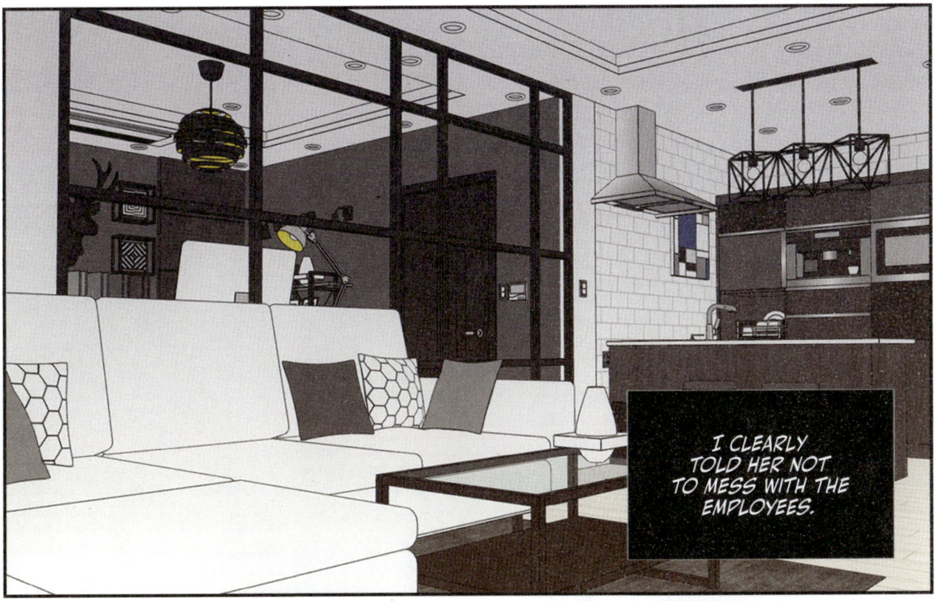
I CLEARLY TOLD HER NOT TO MESS WITH THE EMPLOYEES.

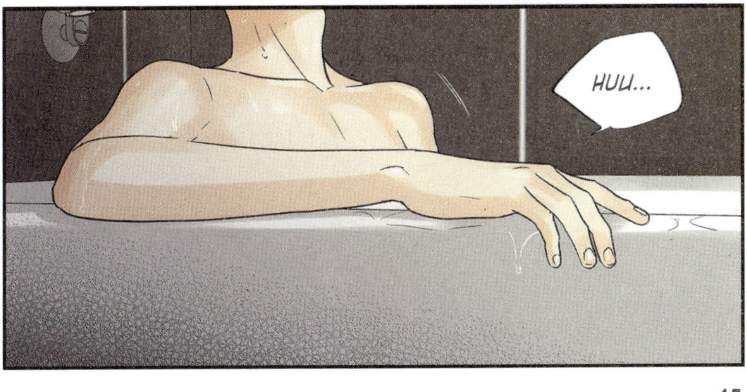
HUU...

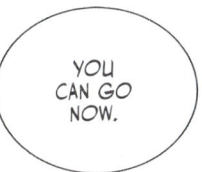

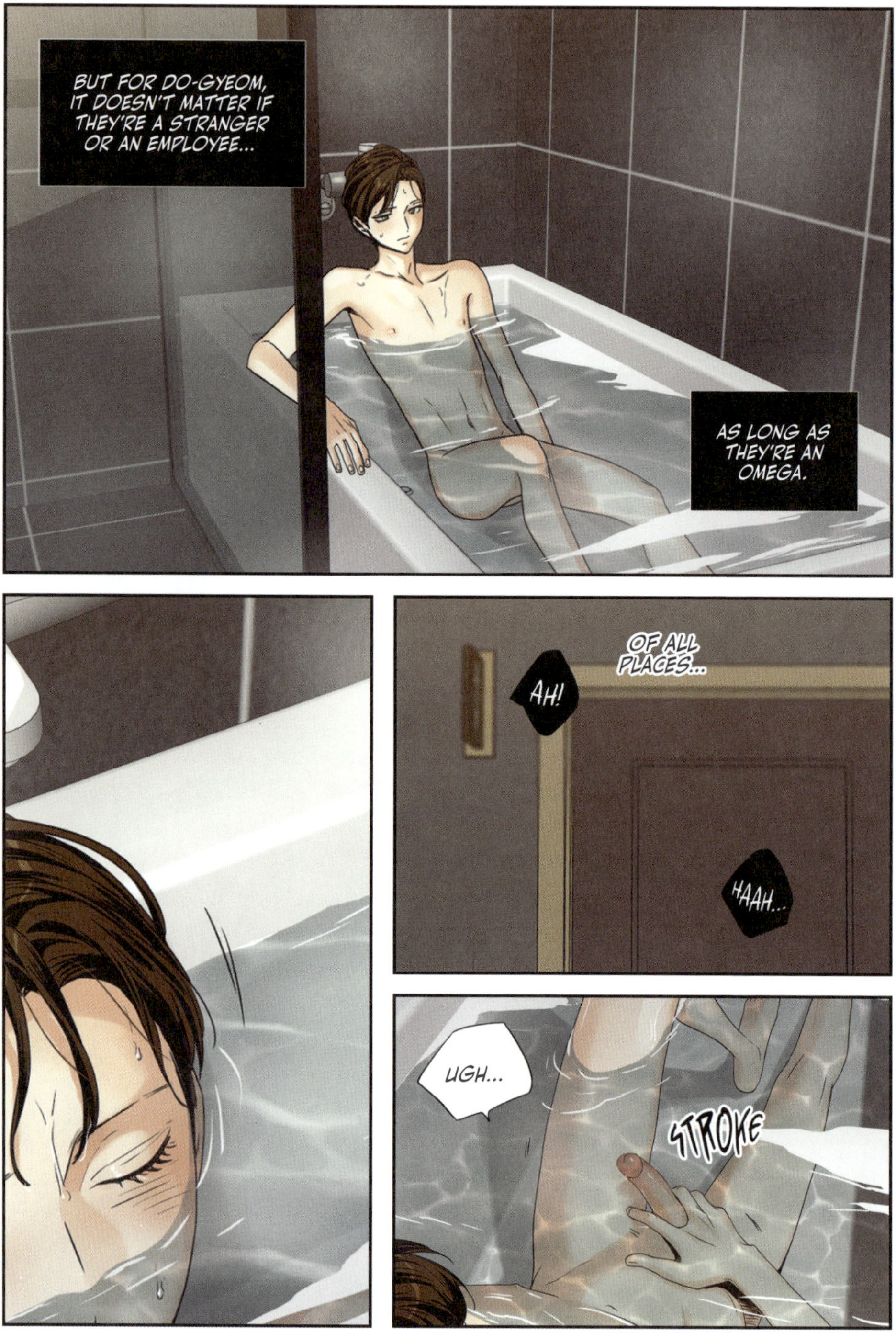
BUT FOR DO-GYEOM, IT DOESN'T MATTER IF THEY'RE A STRANGER OR AN EMPLOYEE...
AS LONG AS THEY'RE AN OMEGA.
OF ALL PLACES...
AH!
HAAH...
UGH...
STROKE

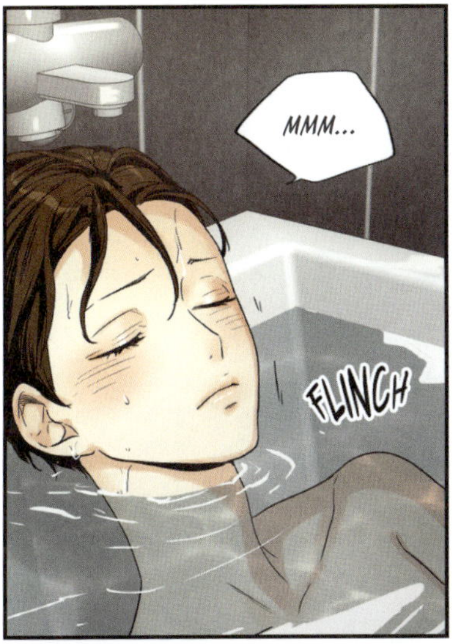
MMM...
FLINCH

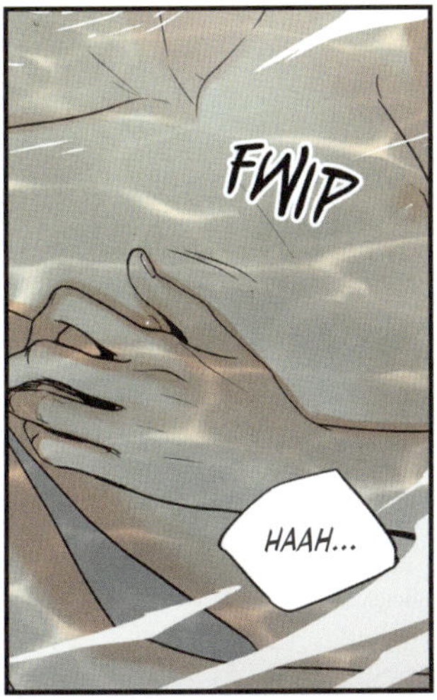
FWIP
HAAH...

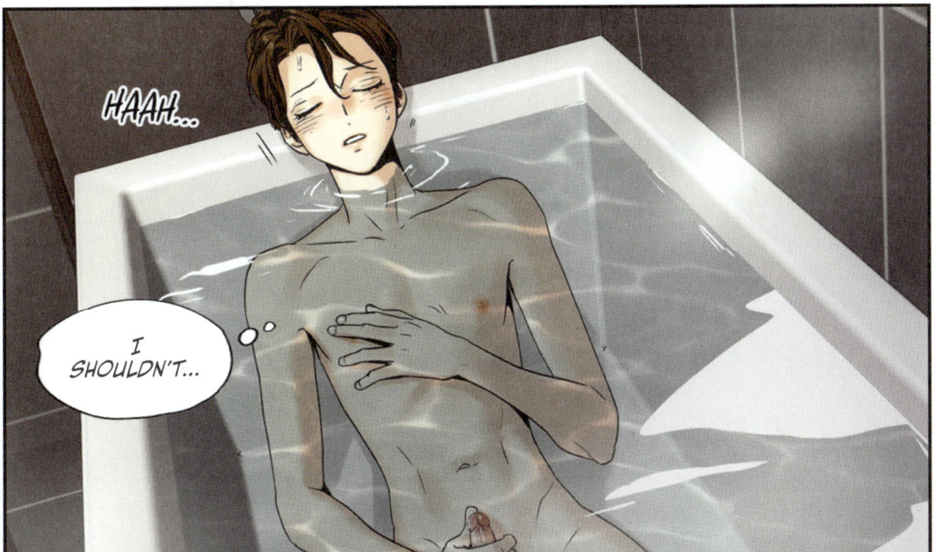
HAAH...
I SHOULDN'T...

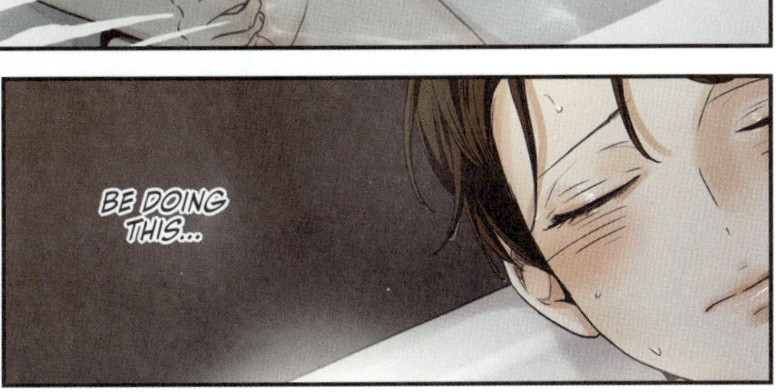
BE DOING THIS...

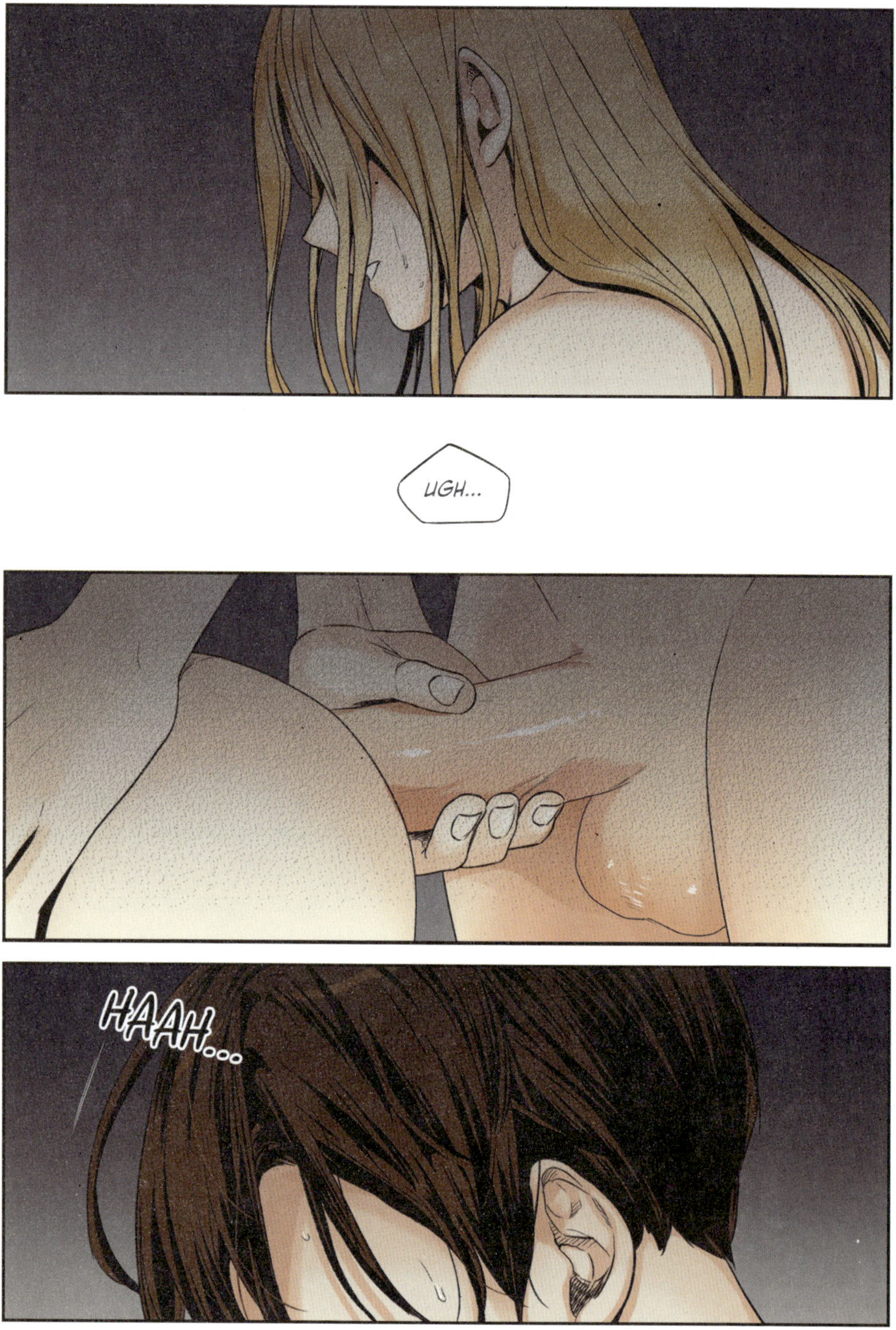
UGH...
HAAH...

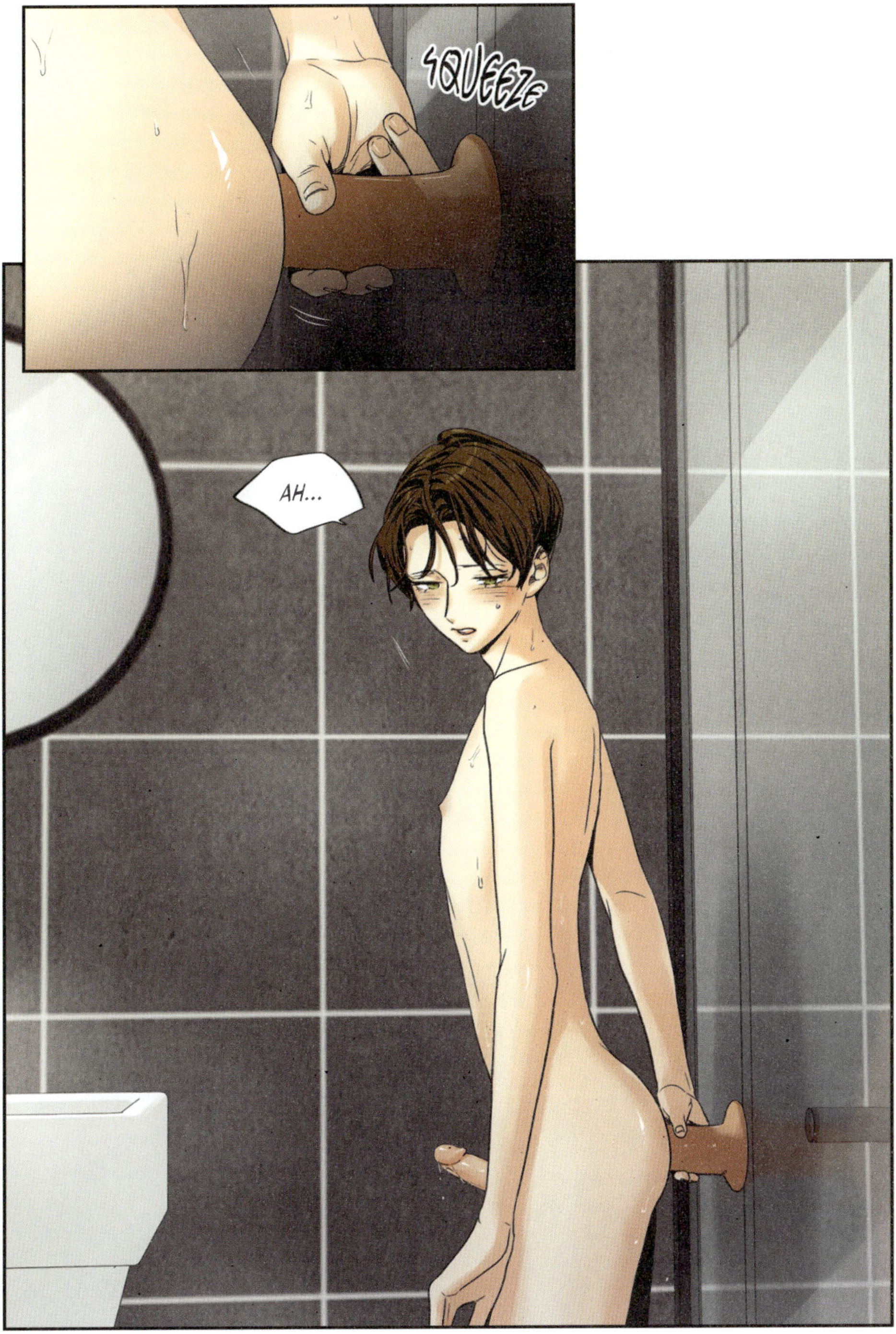
SQUEEZE
AH...

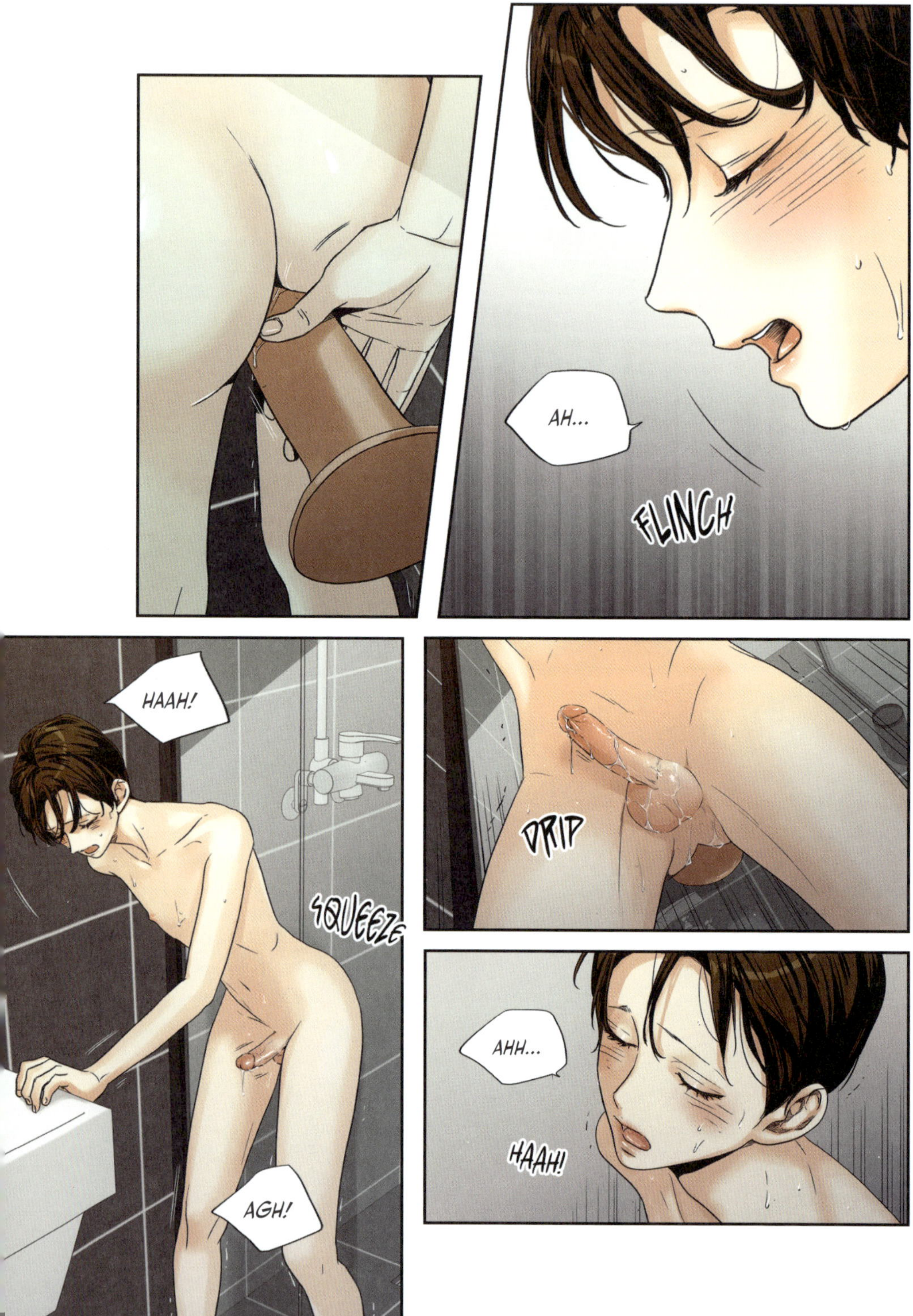
AH...
FLINCH
HAAH!
SQUEEZE
AGH!
DRIP
AHH...
HAAH!

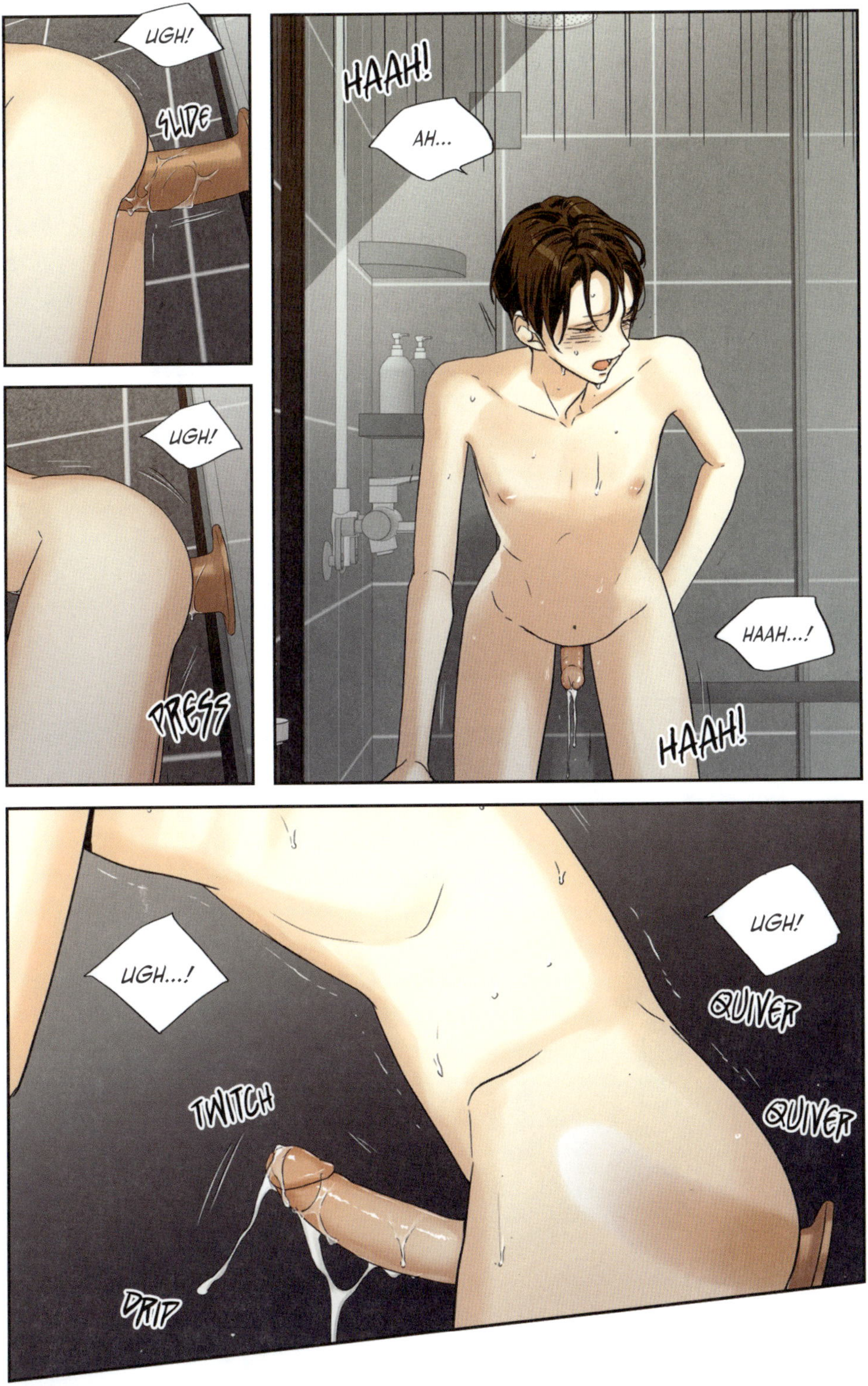
UGH!
SLIDE
UGH!
PRESS
HAAH!
AH...
HAAH...!
HAAH!
UGH!
UGH...!
QUIVER
TWITCH
QUIVER
DRIP

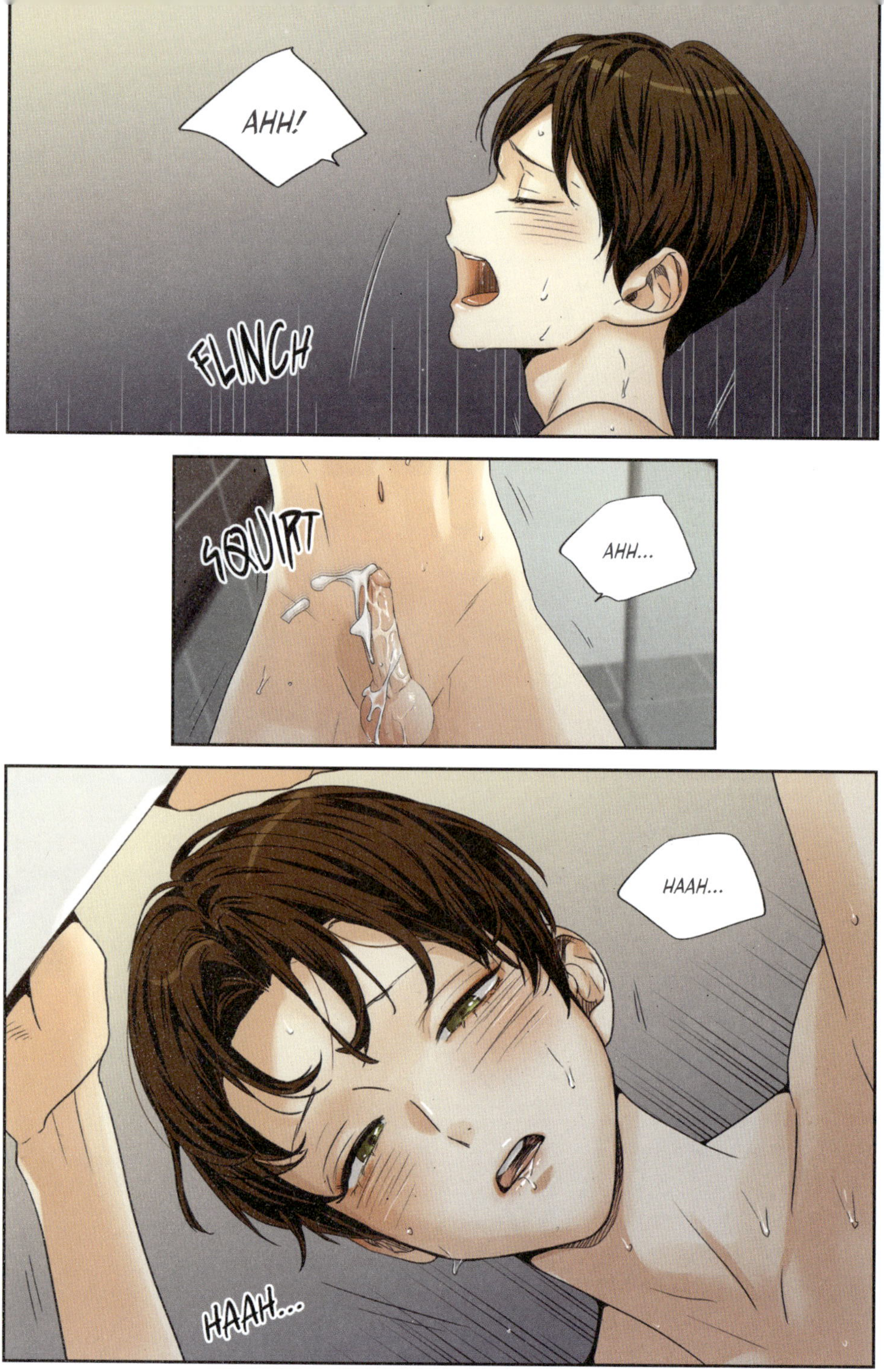
AHH!
FLINCH
SQUIRT
AHH...
HAAH...
HAAH...

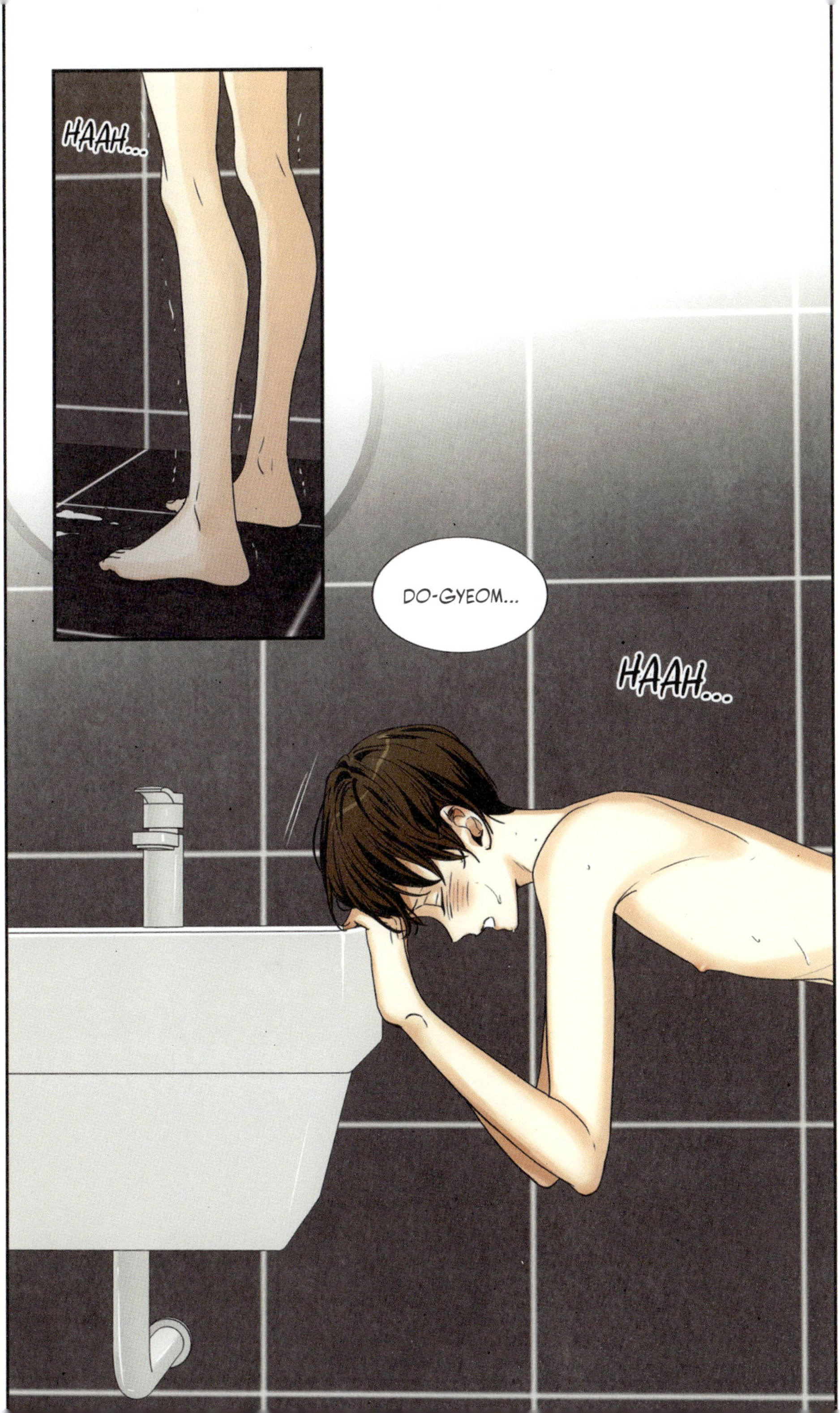
HAAH...
DO-GYEOM...
HAAH...

Love is an Illusion!
— The Queen —

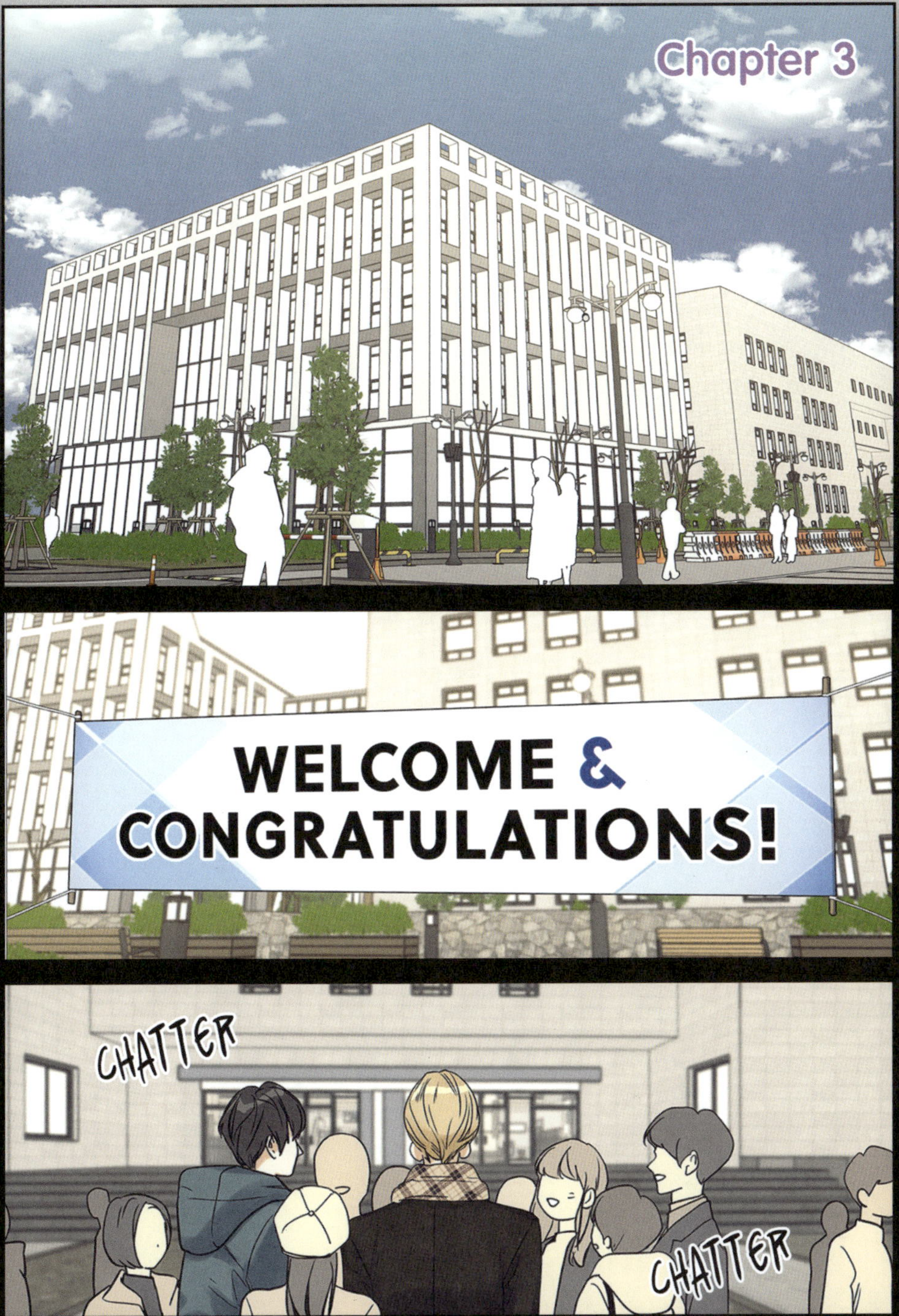
Chapter 3
WELCOME & CONGRATULATIONS!
CHATTER
CHATTER

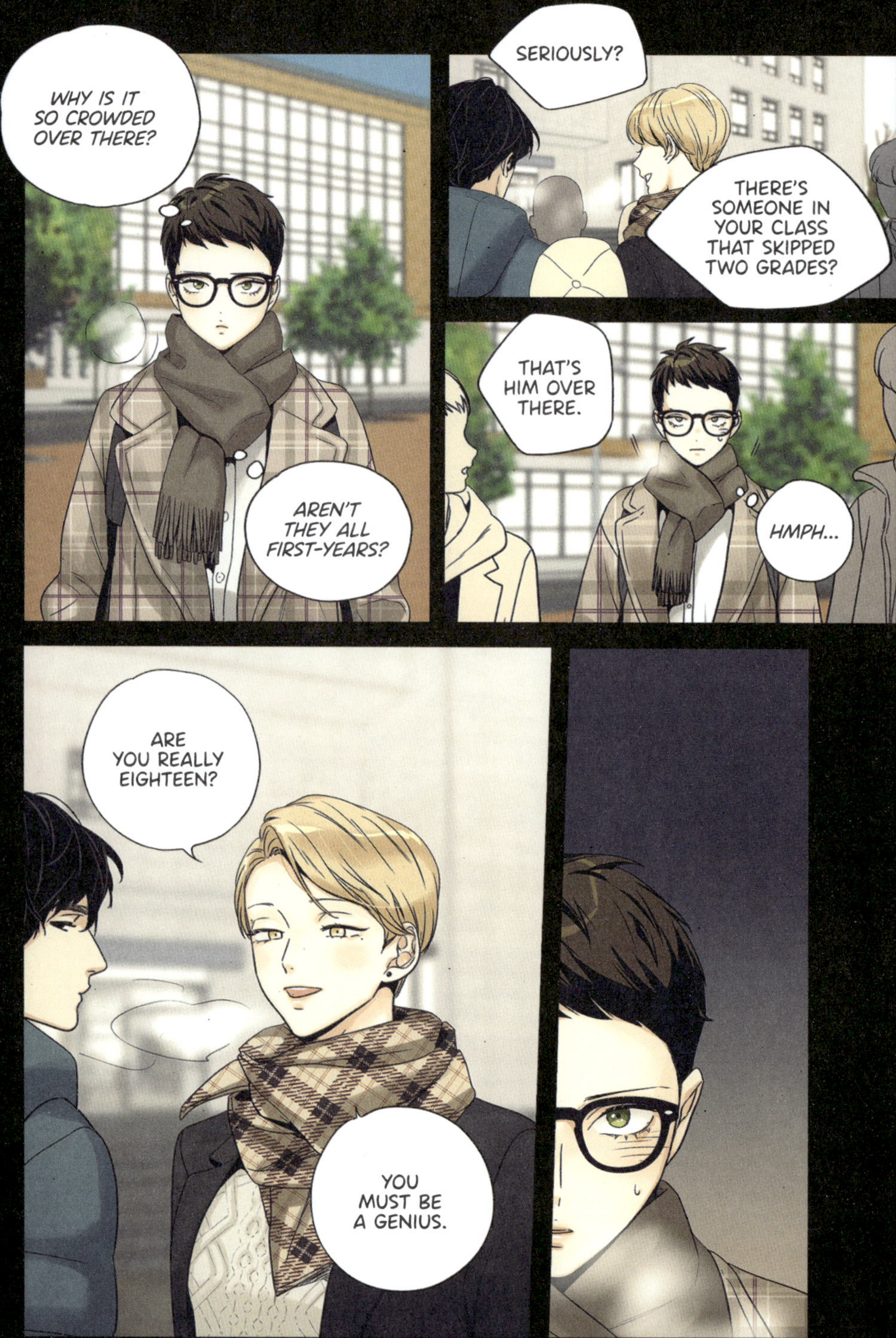
WHY IS IT SO CROWDED OVER THERE?
AREN'T THEY ALL FIRST-YEARS?
SERIOUSLY?
THERE'S SOMEONE IN YOUR CLASS THAT SKIPPED TWO GRADES?
THAT'S HIM OVER THERE.
HMPH...
ARE YOU REALLY EIGHTEEN?
YOU MUST BE A GENIUS.

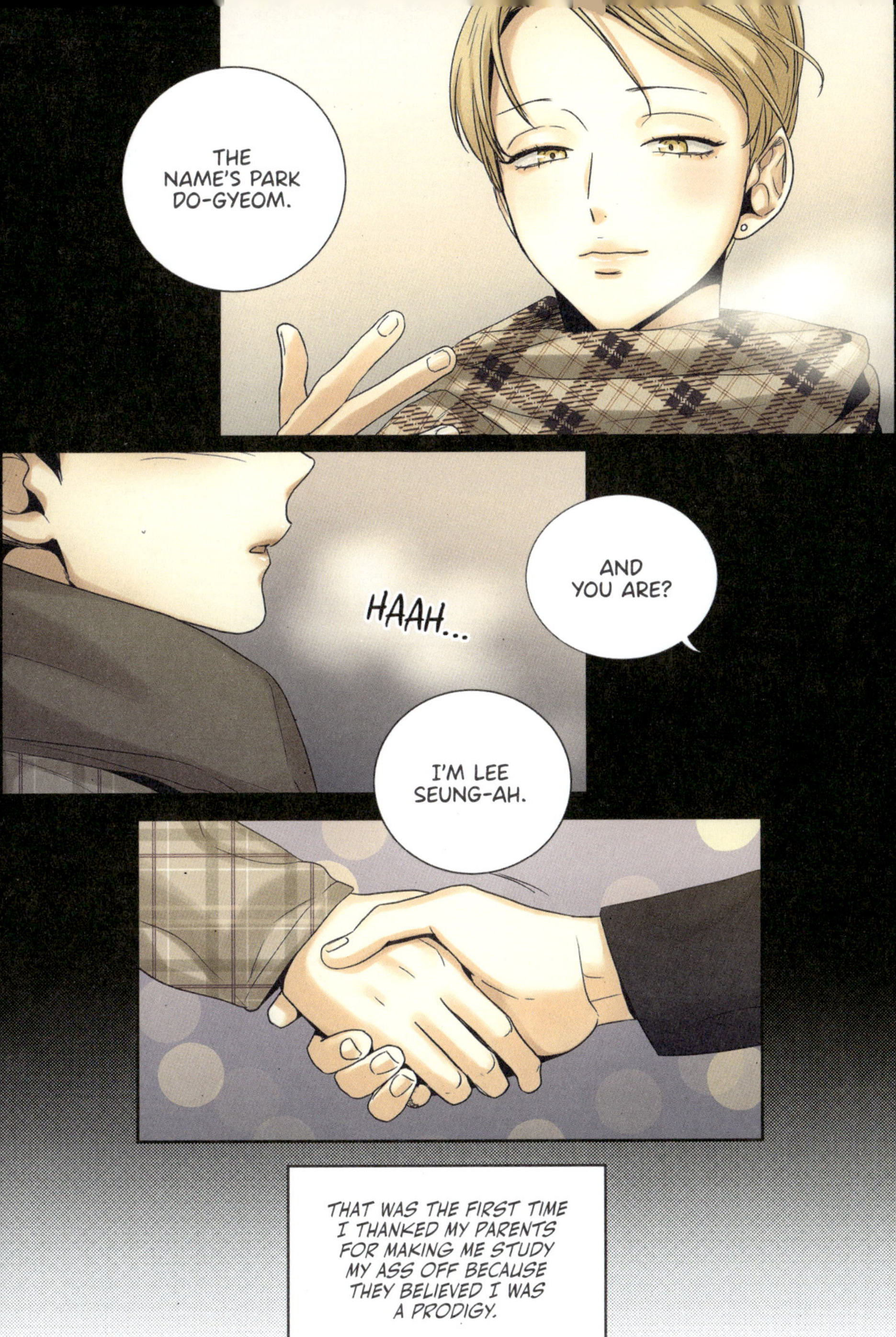
THE NAME'S PARK DO-GYEOM.
HAAH...
AND YOU ARE?
I'M LEE SEUNG-AH.
THAT WAS THE FIRST TIME I THANKED MY PARENTS FOR MAKING ME STUDY MY ASS OFF BECAUSE THEY BELIEVED I WAS A PRODIGY.

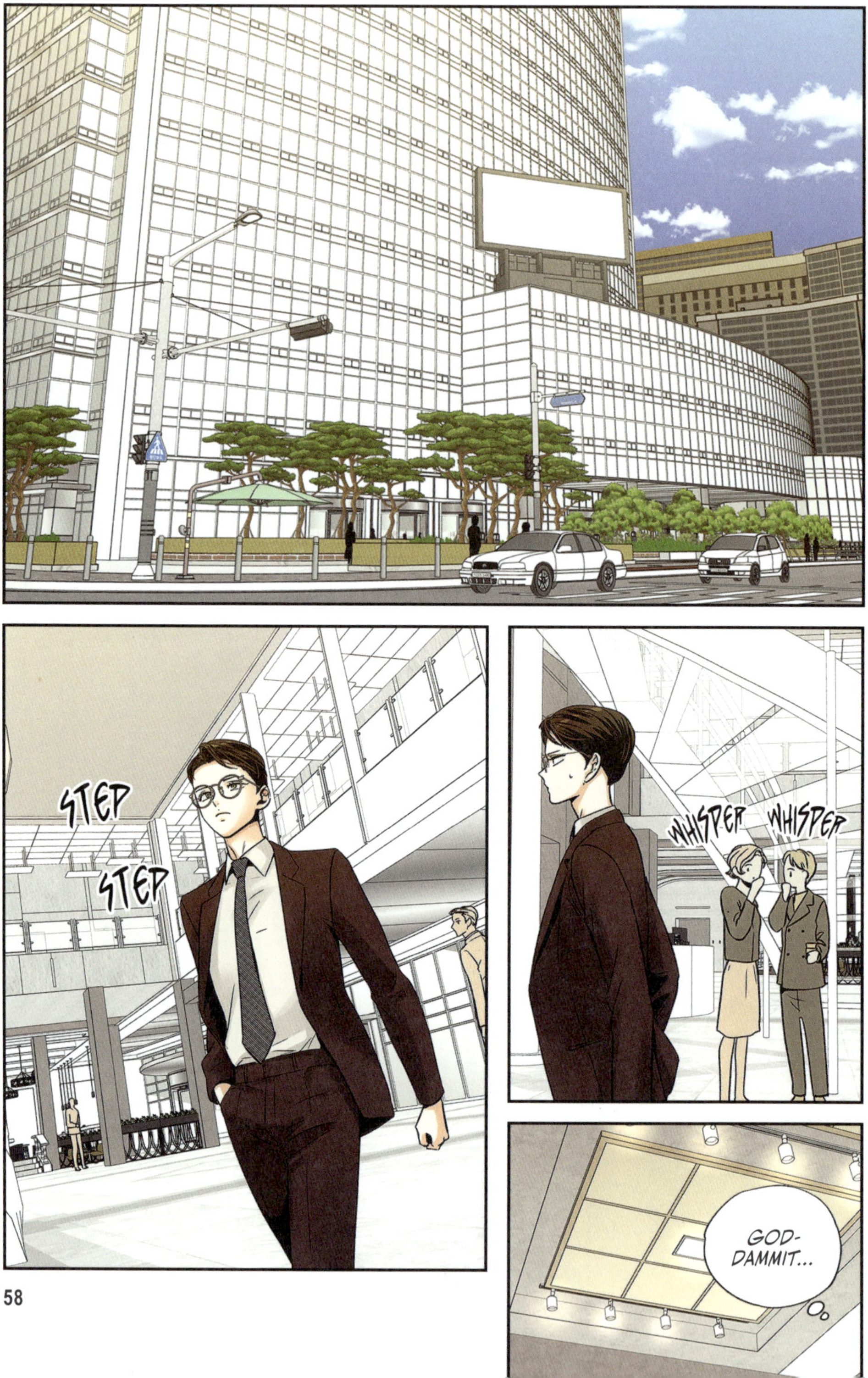
STEP
STEP
WHISPER
WHISPER
GOD-
DAMMIT...

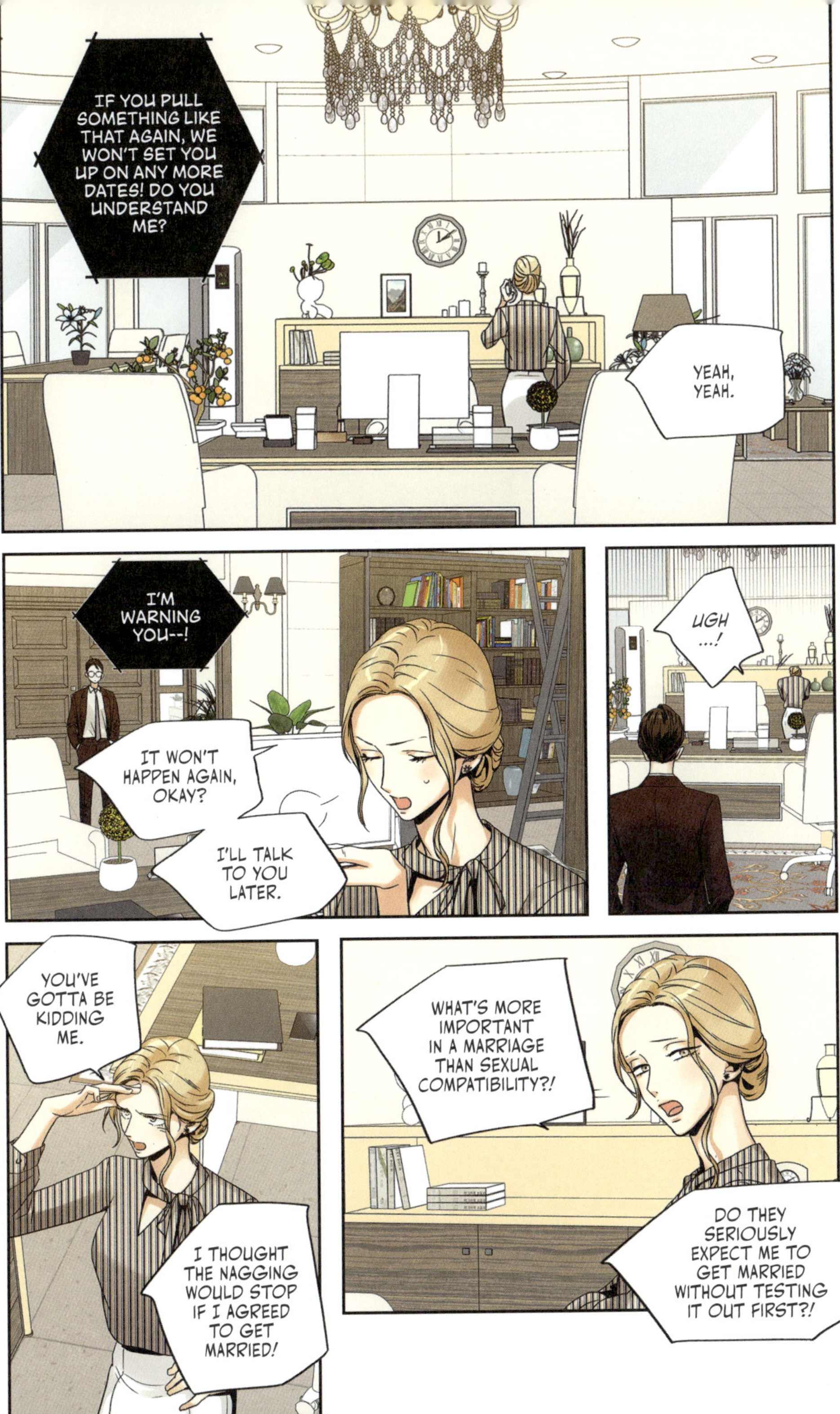
IF YOU PULL SOMETHING LIKE THAT AGAIN, WE WON'T SET YOU UP ON ANY MORE DATES! DO YOU UNDERSTAND ME?
YEAH, YEAH.
I'M WARNING YOU--!
IT WON'T HAPPEN AGAIN, OKAY?
I'LL TALK TO YOU LATER.
UGH ...!
YOU'VE GOTTA BE KIDDING ME.
I THOUGHT THE NAGGING WOULD STOP IF I AGREED TO GET MARRIED!
WHAT'S MORE IMPORTANT IN A MARRIAGE THAN SEXUAL COMPATIBILITY?!
DO THEY SERIOUSLY EXPECT ME TO GET MARRIED WITHOUT TESTING IT OUT FIRST?!

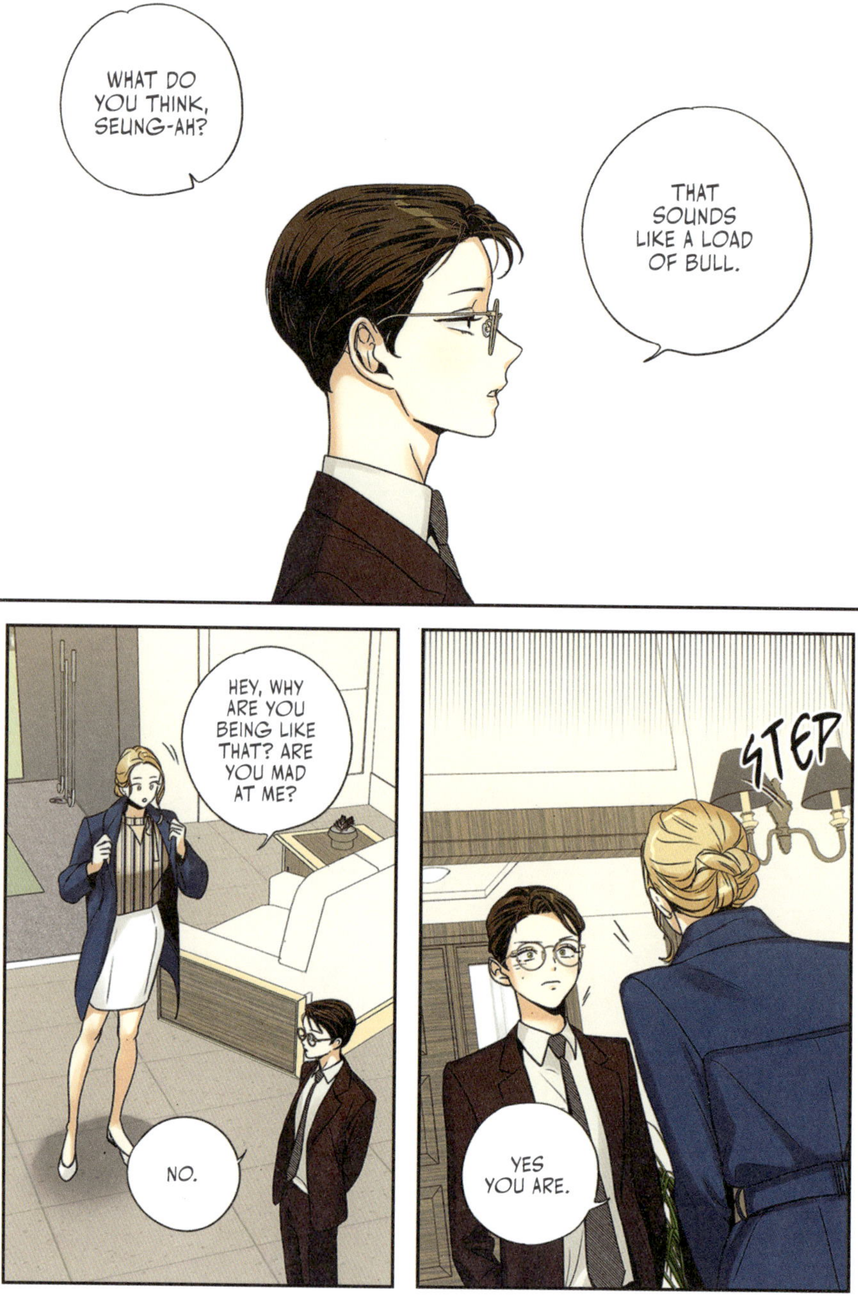
WHAT DO YOU THINK, SEUNG-AH?
THAT SOUNDS LIKE A LOAD OF BULL.
HEY, WHY ARE YOU BEING LIKE THAT? ARE YOU MAD AT ME?
NO.
STEP
YES YOU ARE.

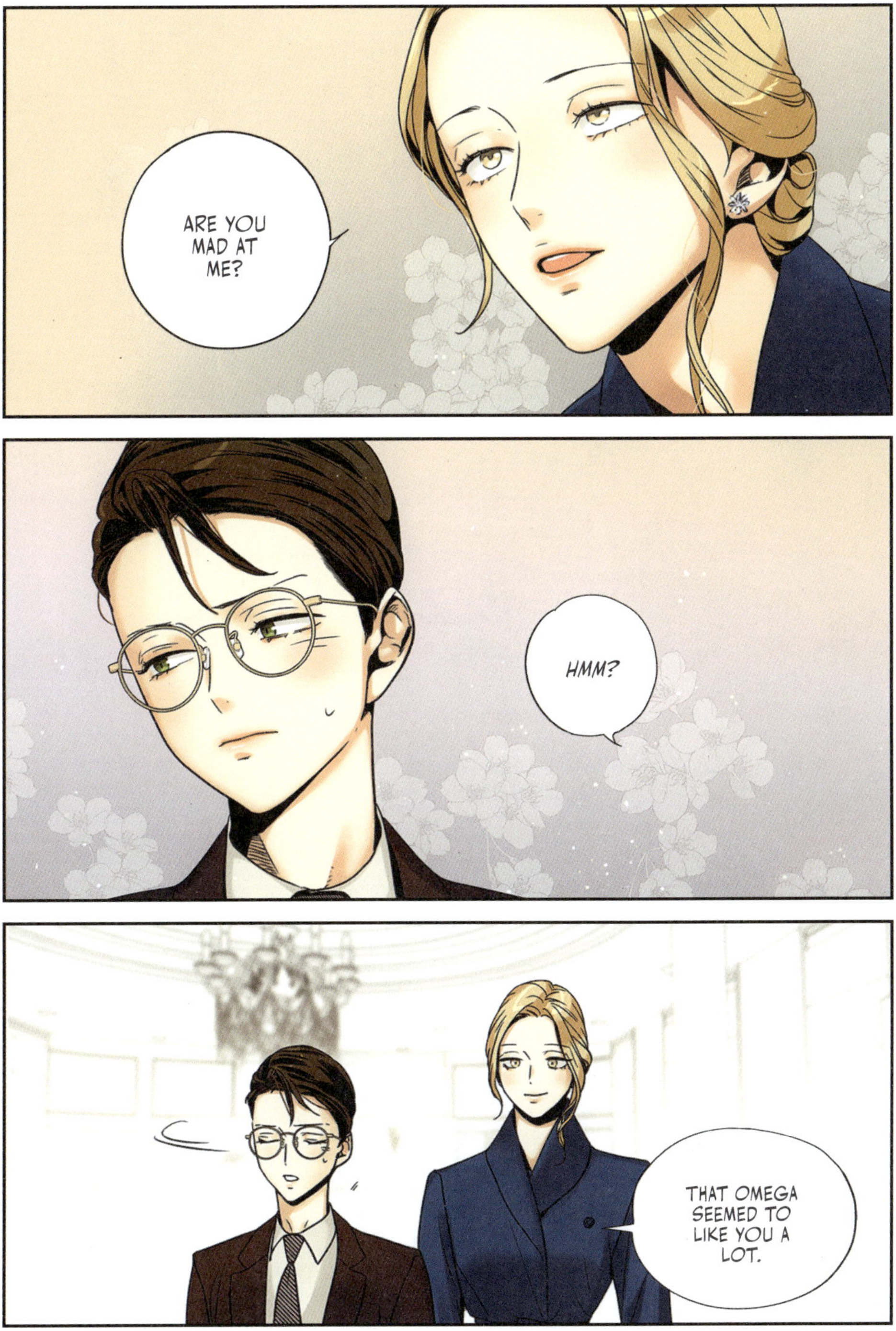
ARE YOU MAD AT ME?
HMM?
THAT OMEGA SEEMED TO LIKE YOU A LOT.

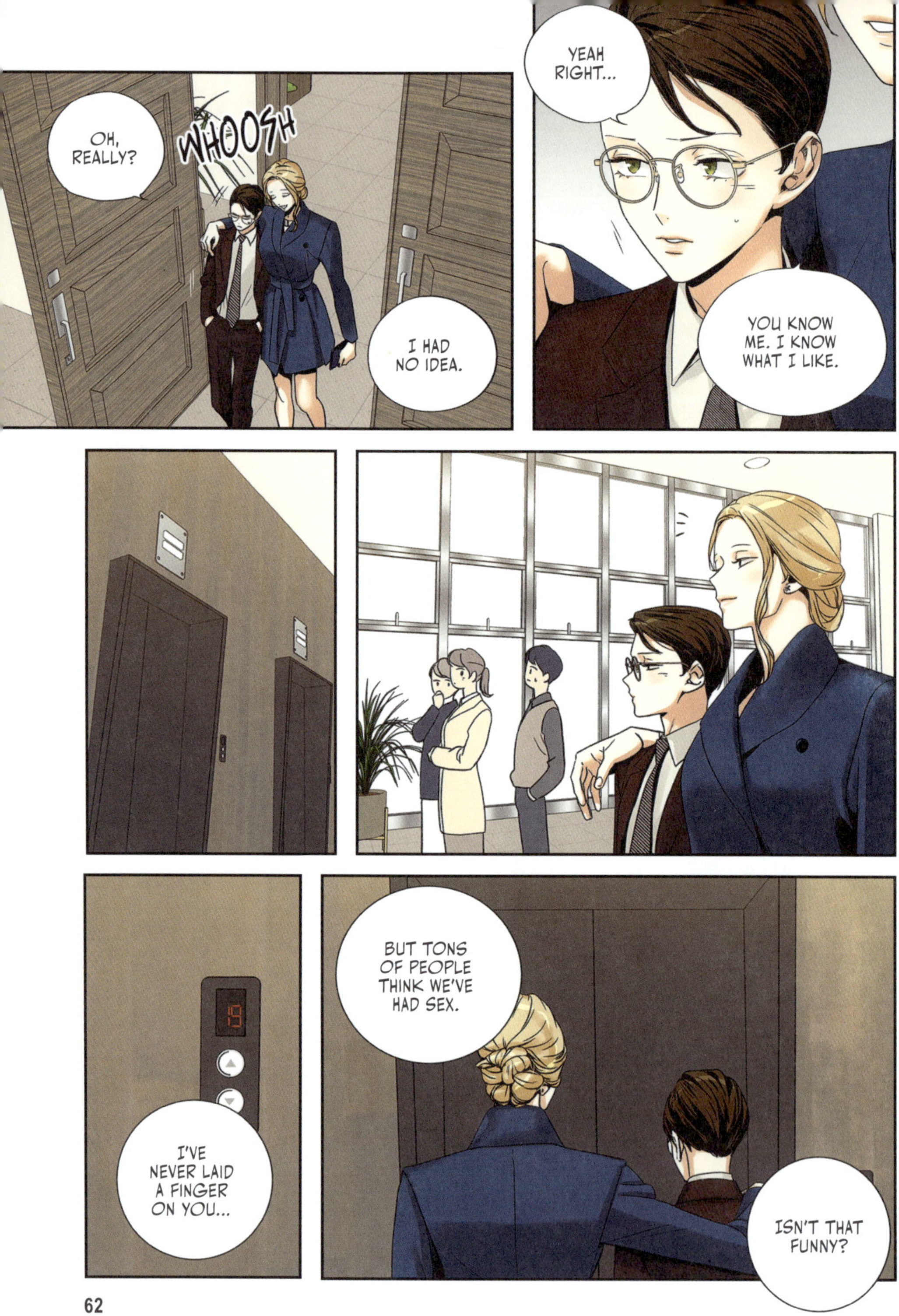
OH, REALLY?
WHOOSH
I HAD NO IDEA.
YEAH RIGHT...
YOU KNOW ME. I KNOW WHAT I LIKE.
I'VE NEVER LAID A FINGER ON YOU...
BUT TONS OF PEOPLE THINK WE'VE HAD SEX.
ISN'T THAT FUNNY?

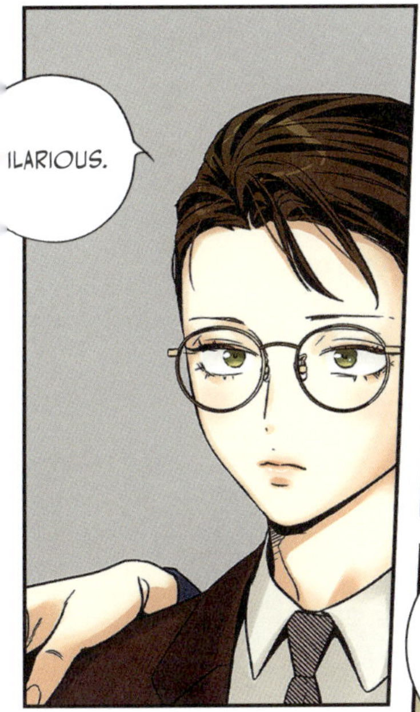
ILARIOUS.
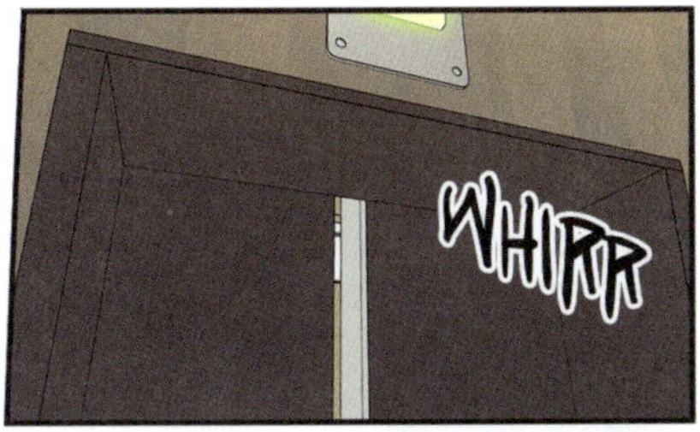
WHIRR
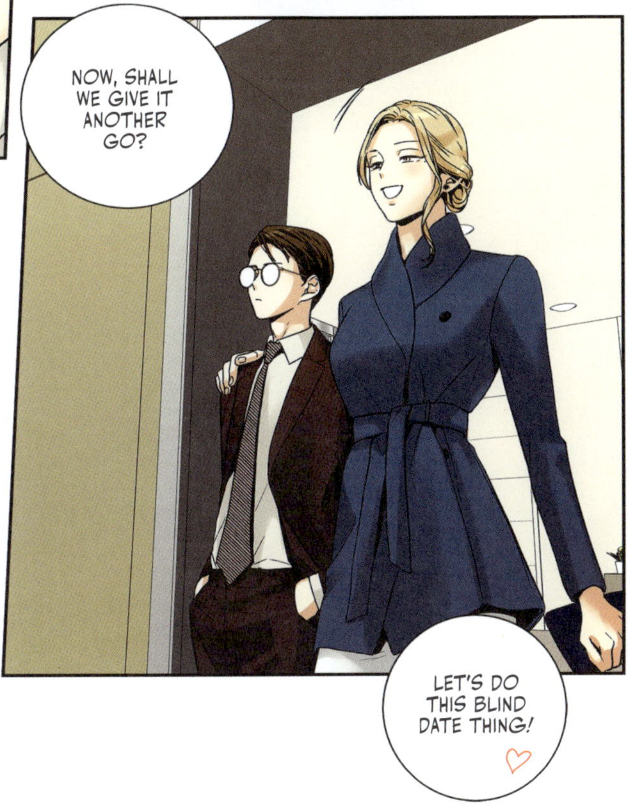
NOW, SHALL WE GIVE IT ANOTHER GO?
LET'S DO THIS BLIND DATE THING!

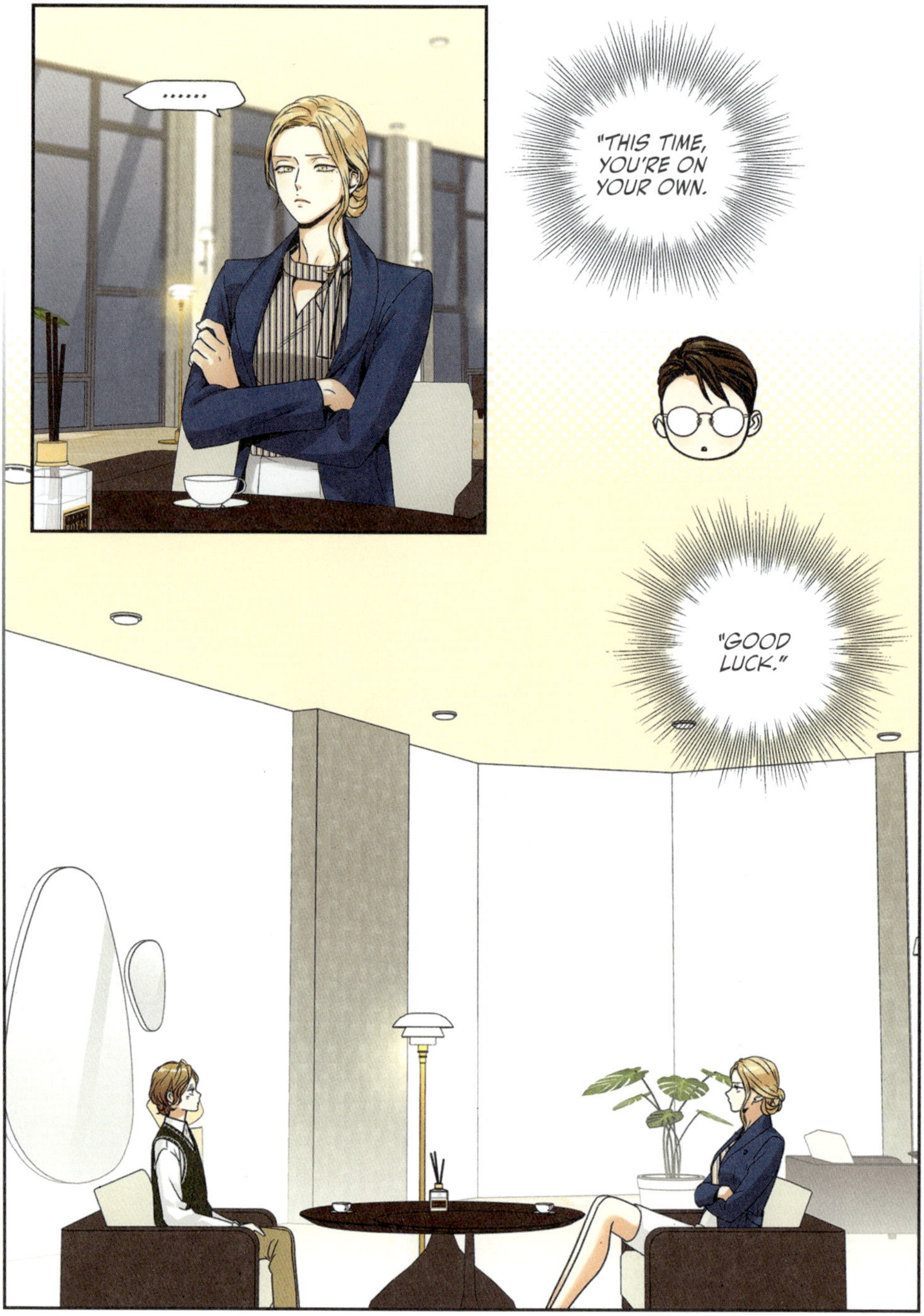
......
"THIS TIME, YOU'RE ON YOUR OWN.
"GOOD LUCK."

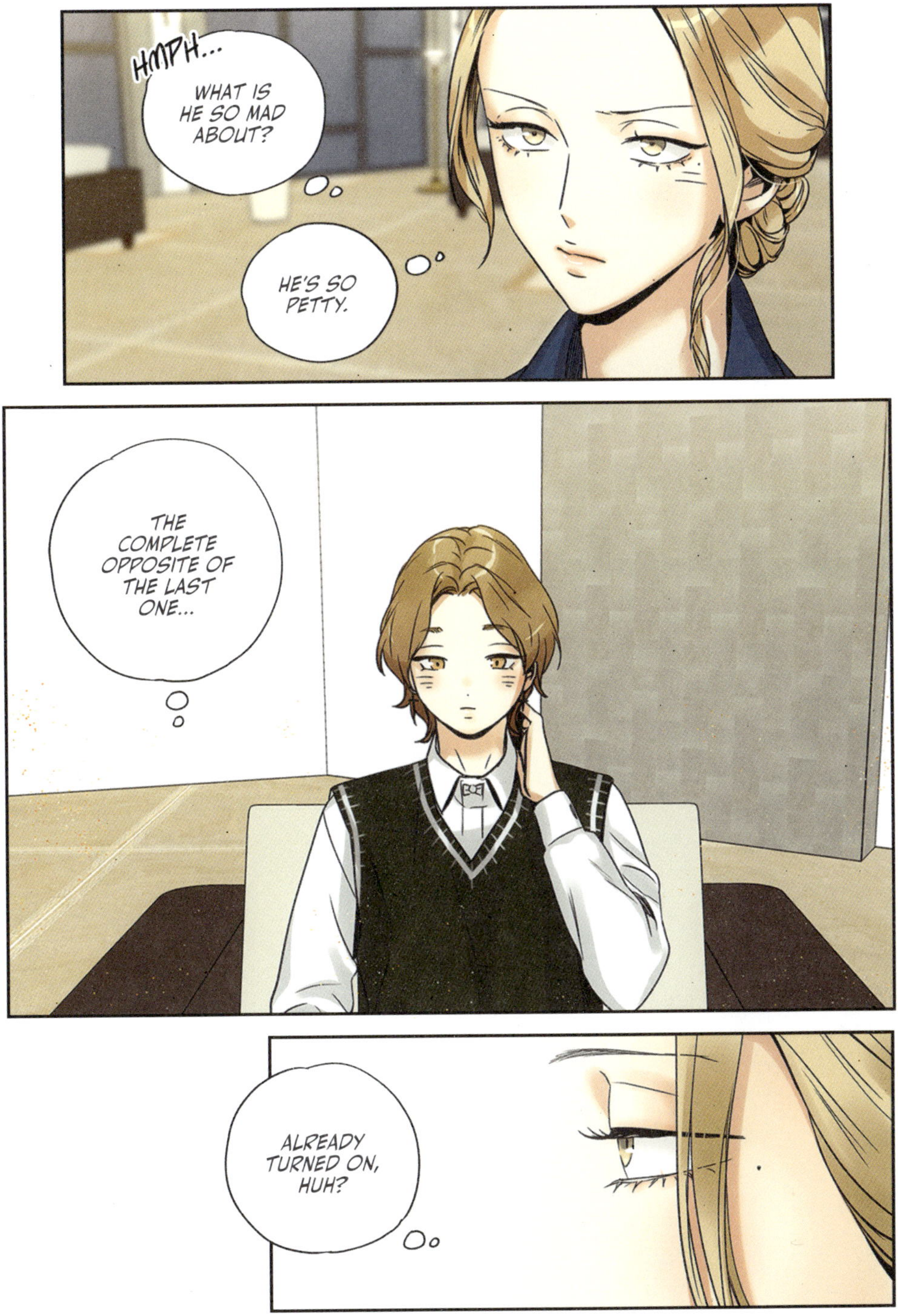
HMPH...
WHAT IS HE SO MAD ABOUT?
HE'S SO PETTY.
THE COMPLETE OPPOSITE OF THE LAST ONE...
ALREADY TURNED ON, HUH?

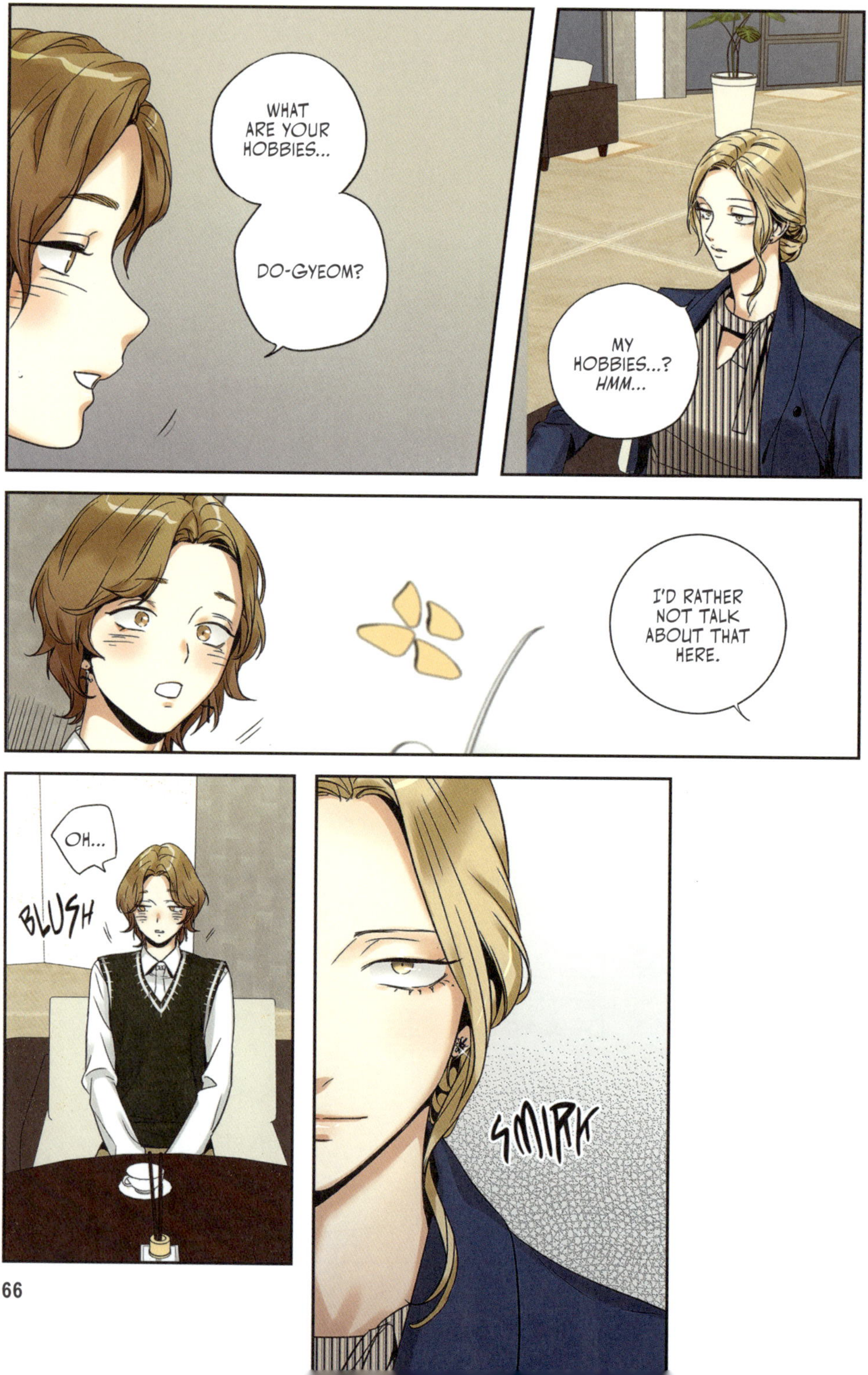
WHAT ARE YOUR HOBBIES...
DO-GYEOM?
MY HOBBIES...? HMM...
I'D RATHER NOT TALK ABOUT THAT HERE.
OH...
BLUSH
SMIRK

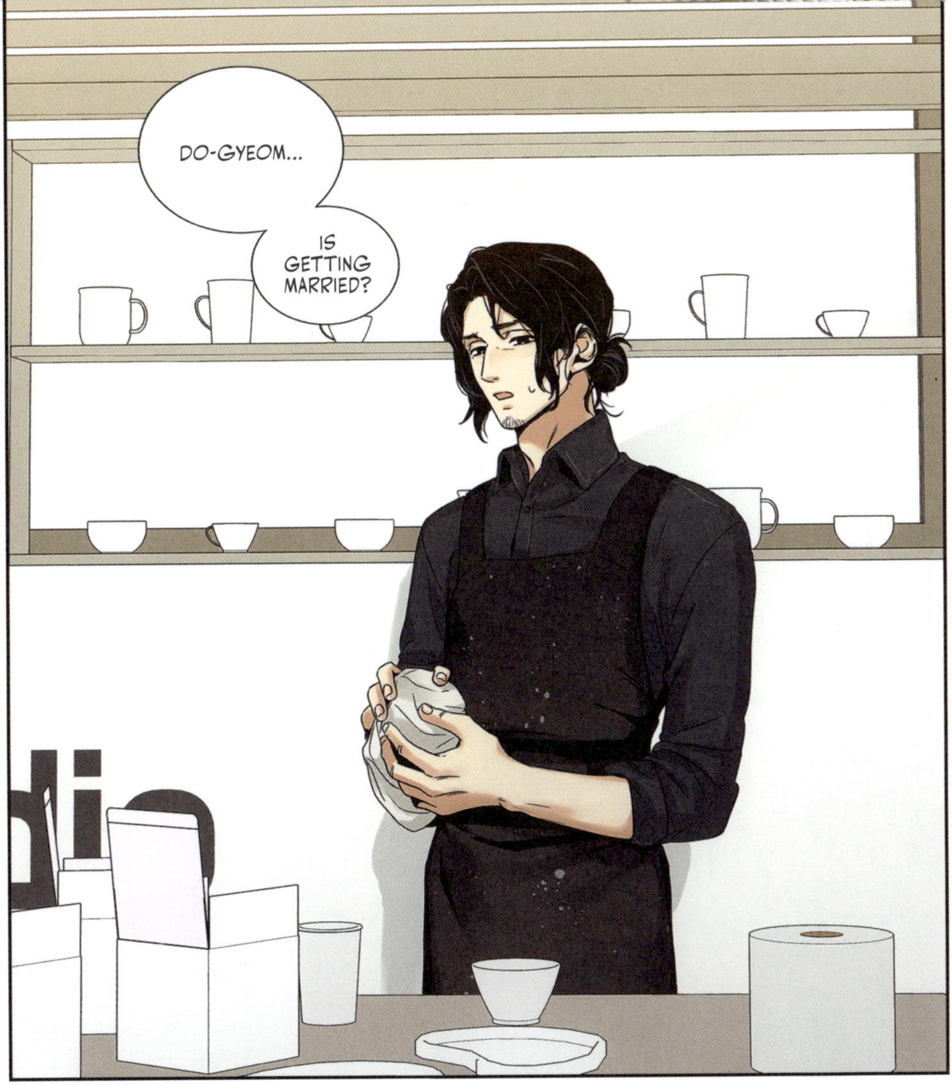
DO-GYEOM...
IS GETTING MARRIED?
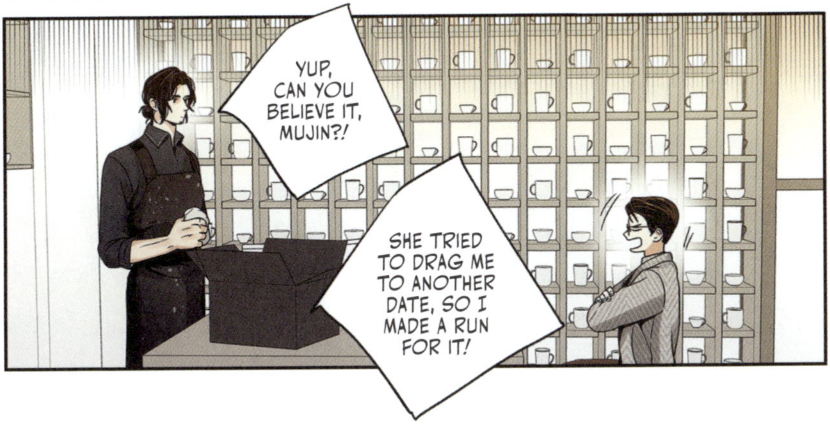
YUP, CAN YOU BELIEVE IT, MUJIN?!
SHE TRIED TO DRAG ME TO ANOTHER DATE, SO I MADE A RUN FOR IT!

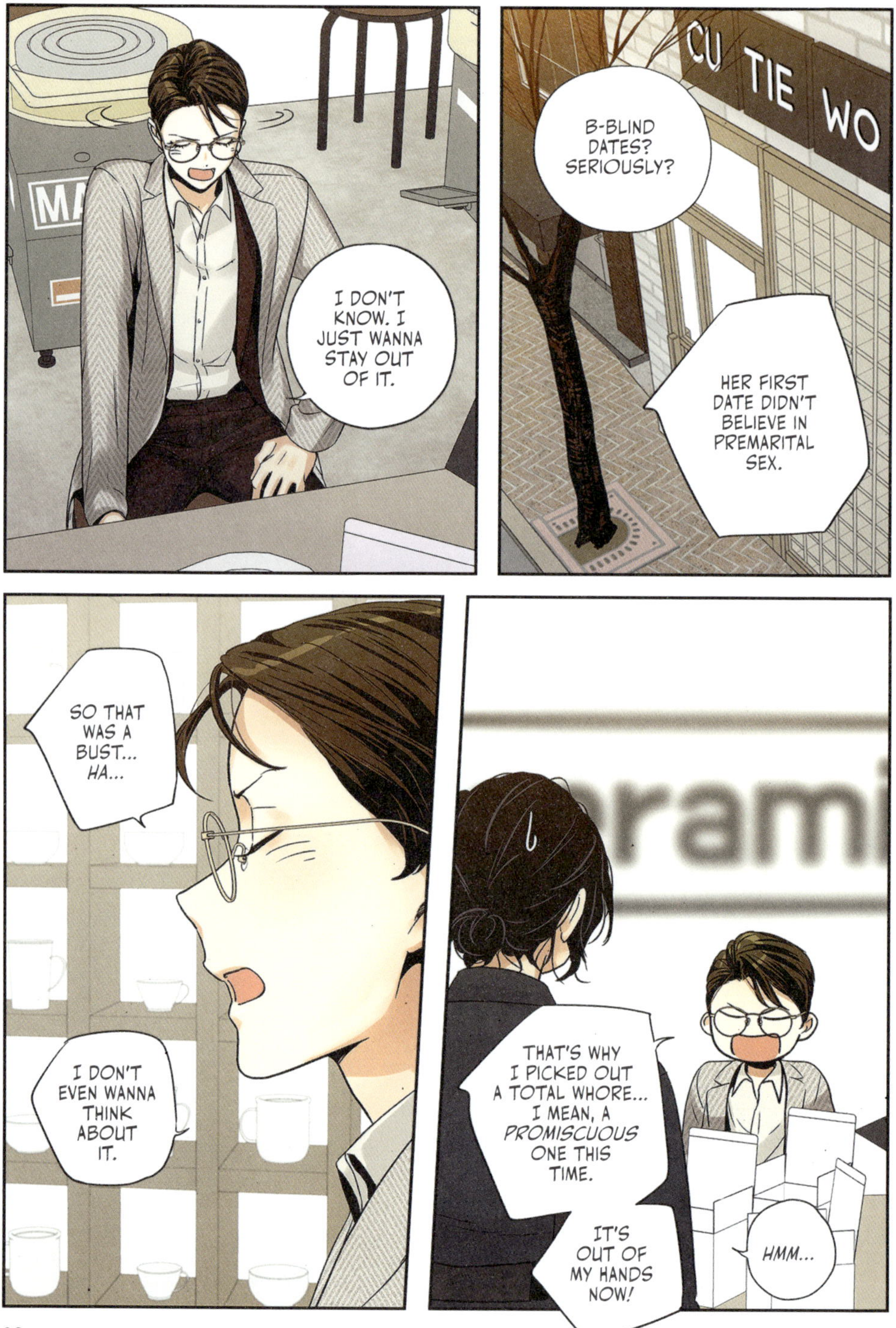
I DON'T KNOW. I JUST WANNA STAY OUT OF IT.
CU TIE WO
B-BLIND DATES? SERIOUSLY?
HER FIRST DATE DIDN'T BELIEVE IN PREMARITAL SEX.
SO THAT WAS A BUST... *HA...*
I DON'T EVEN WANNA THINK ABOUT IT.
rami
THAT'S WHY I PICKED OUT A TOTAL WHORE... I MEAN, A *PROMISCUOUS* ONE THIS TIME.
IT'S OUT OF MY HANDS NOW!
HMM...

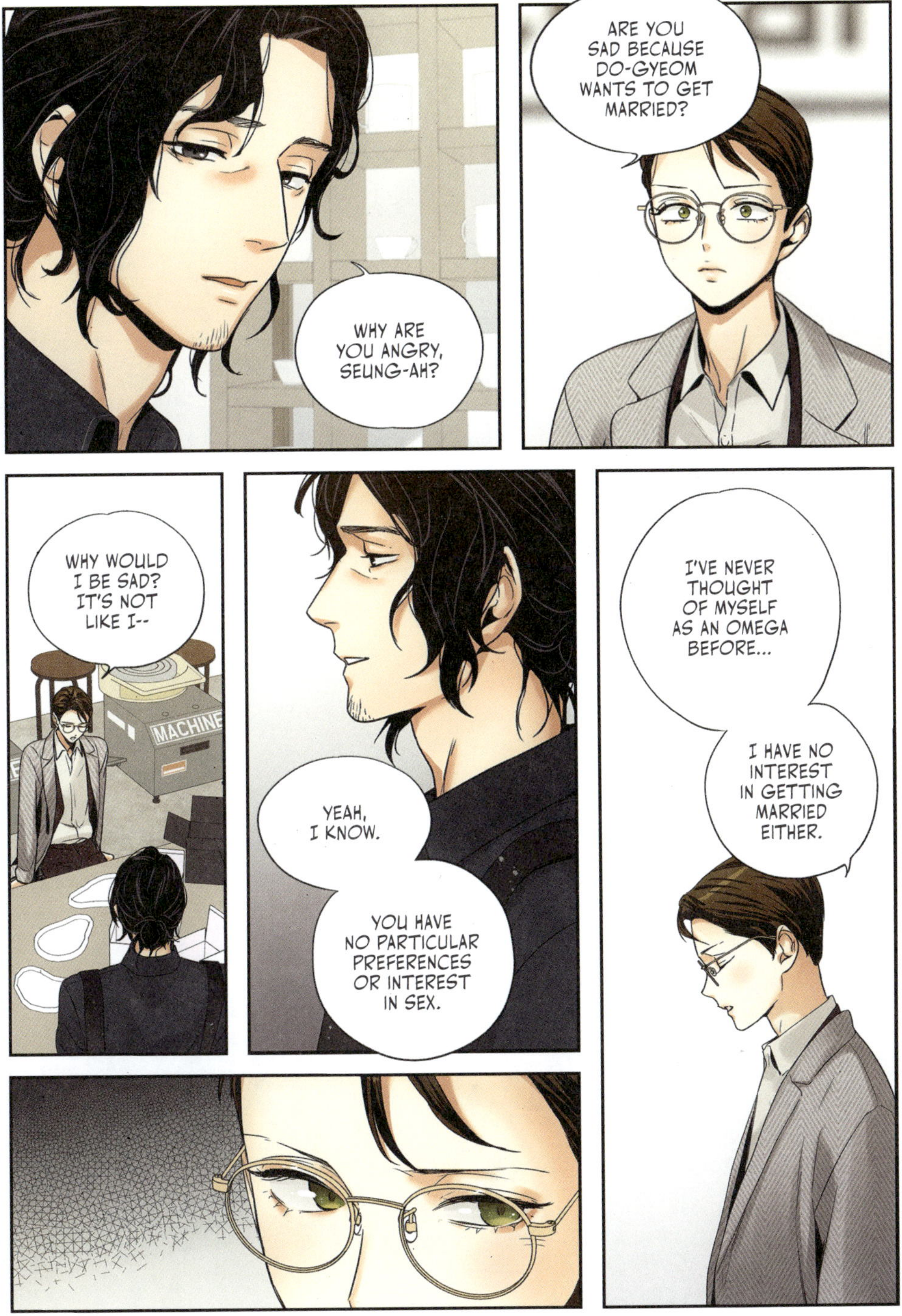
WHY ARE YOU ANGRY, SEUNG-AH?
ARE YOU SAD BECAUSE DO-GYEOM WANTS TO GET MARRIED?
WHY WOULD I BE SAD? IT'S NOT LIKE I--
MACHINE
YEAH, I KNOW.
YOU HAVE NO PARTICULAR PREFERENCES OR INTEREST IN SEX.
I'VE NEVER THOUGHT OF MYSELF AS AN OMEGA BEFORE...
I HAVE NO INTEREST IN GETTING MARRIED EITHER.

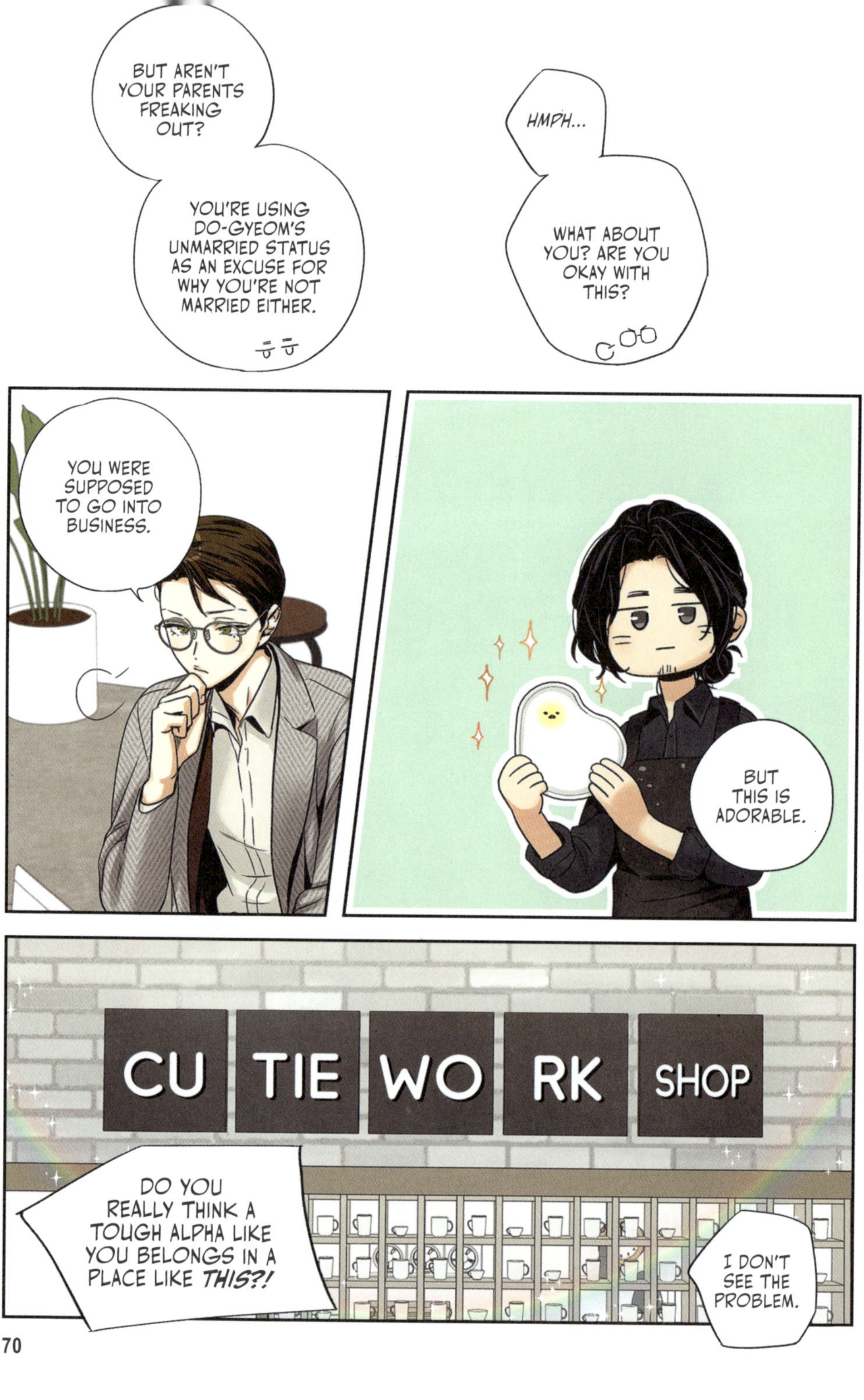
BUT AREN'T YOUR PARENTS FREAKING OUT?
YOU'RE USING DO-GYEOM'S UNMARRIED STATUS AS AN EXCUSE FOR WHY YOU'RE NOT MARRIED EITHER.
HMPH...
WHAT ABOUT YOU? ARE YOU OKAY WITH THIS?
YOU WERE SUPPOSED TO GO INTO BUSINESS.
BUT THIS IS ADORABLE.
CU TIE WO RK SHOP
DO YOU REALLY THINK A TOUGH ALPHA LIKE YOU BELONGS IN A PLACE LIKE *THIS?!*
I DON'T SEE THE PROBLEM.

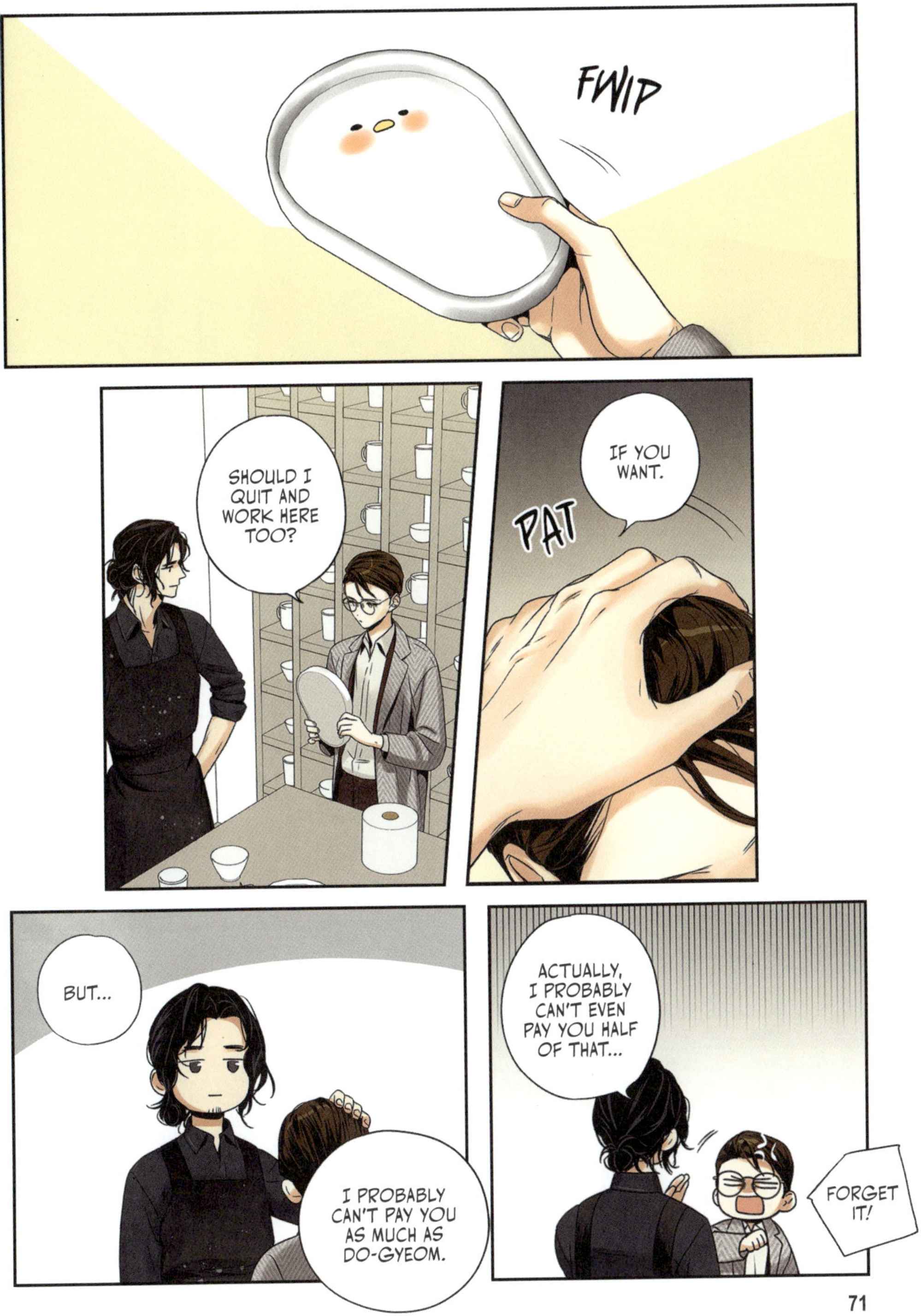
FWIP
SHOULD I QUIT AND WORK HERE TOO?
IF YOU WANT.
PAT
BUT...
I PROBABLY CAN'T PAY YOU AS MUCH AS DO-GYEOM.
ACTUALLY, I PROBABLY CAN'T EVEN PAY YOU HALF OF THAT...
FORGET IT!

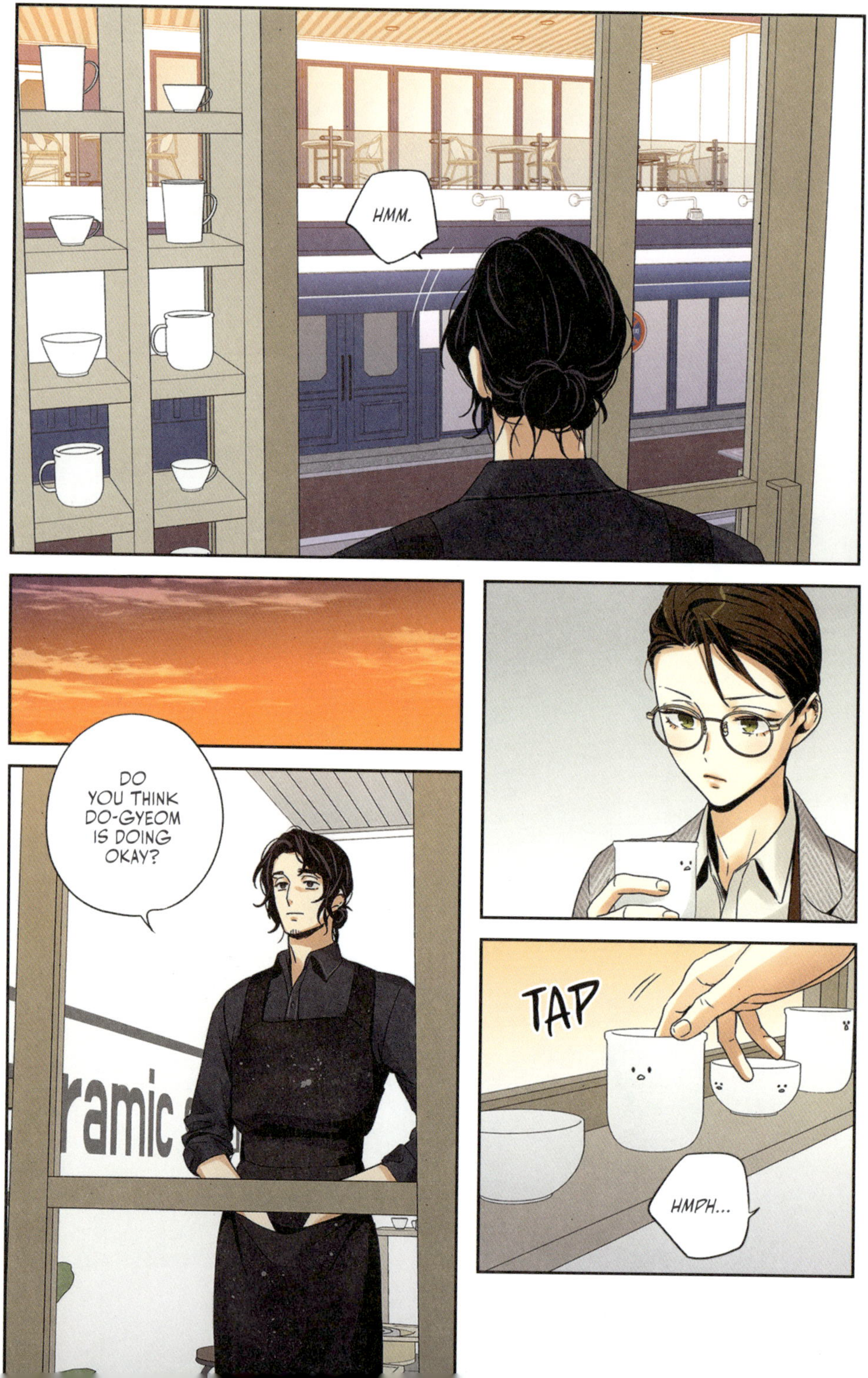
HMM.
DO YOU THINK DO-GYEOM IS DOING OKAY?
TAP
HMPH...

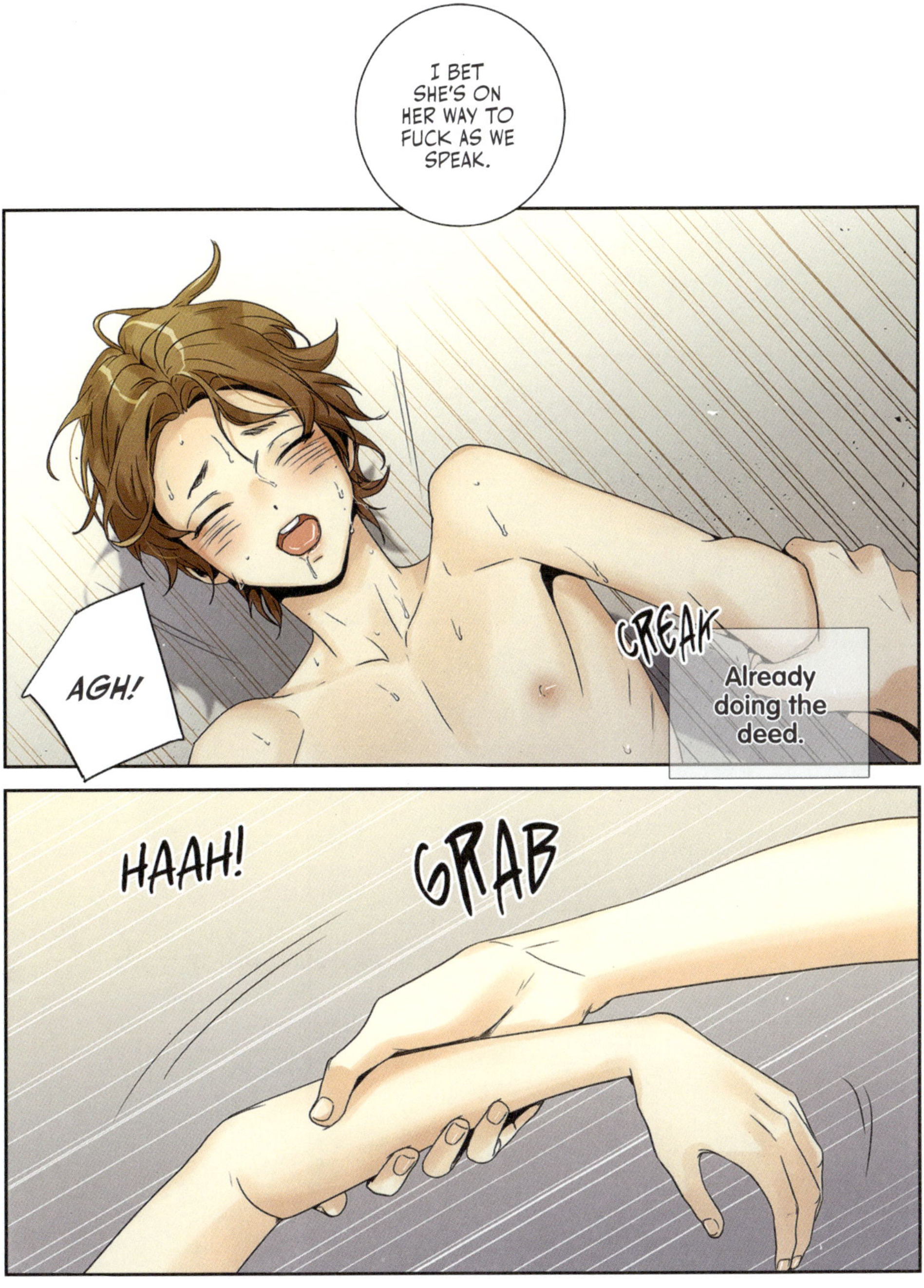
I BET SHE'S ON HER WAY TO FUCK AS WE SPEAK.
AGH!
CREAK
Already doing the deed.
HAAH!
GRAB

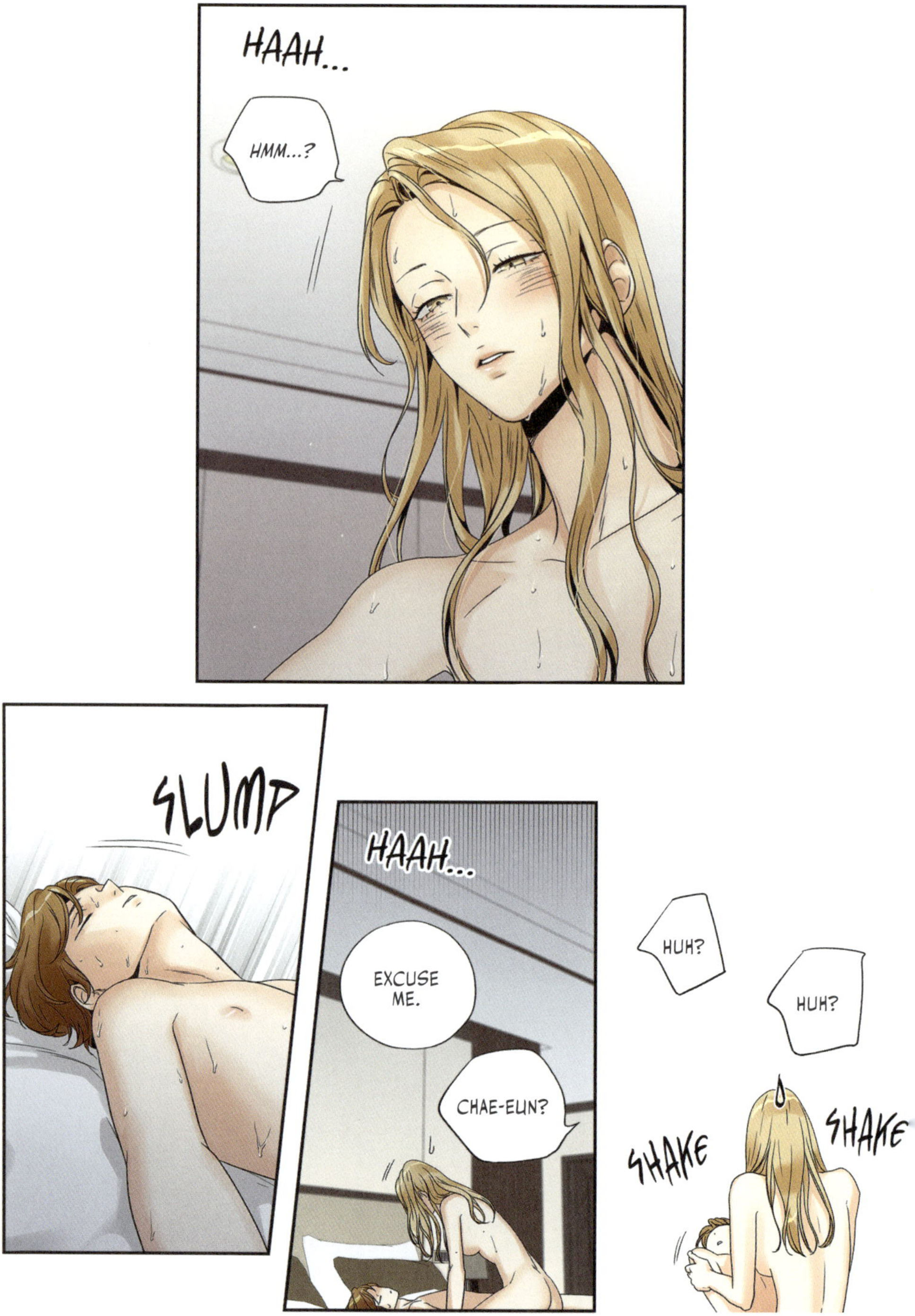
HAAH...
HMM...?
SLUMP
HAAH...
EXCUSE ME.
CHAE-EUN?
HUH?
HUH?
SHAKE
SHAKE

HMM...
SCRATCH

NOT BREATHING, HUH...

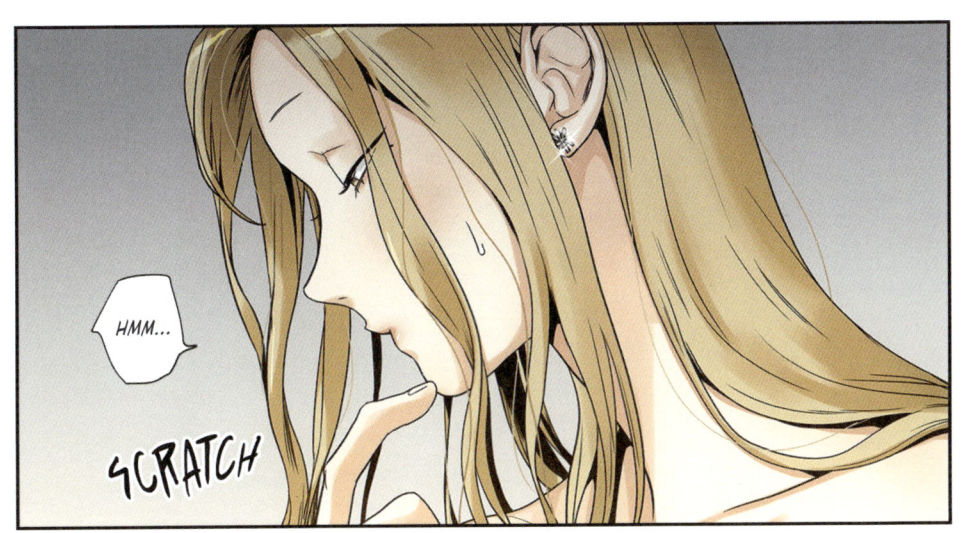

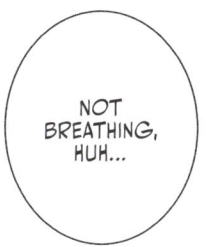

Love is an Illusion!
The Queen

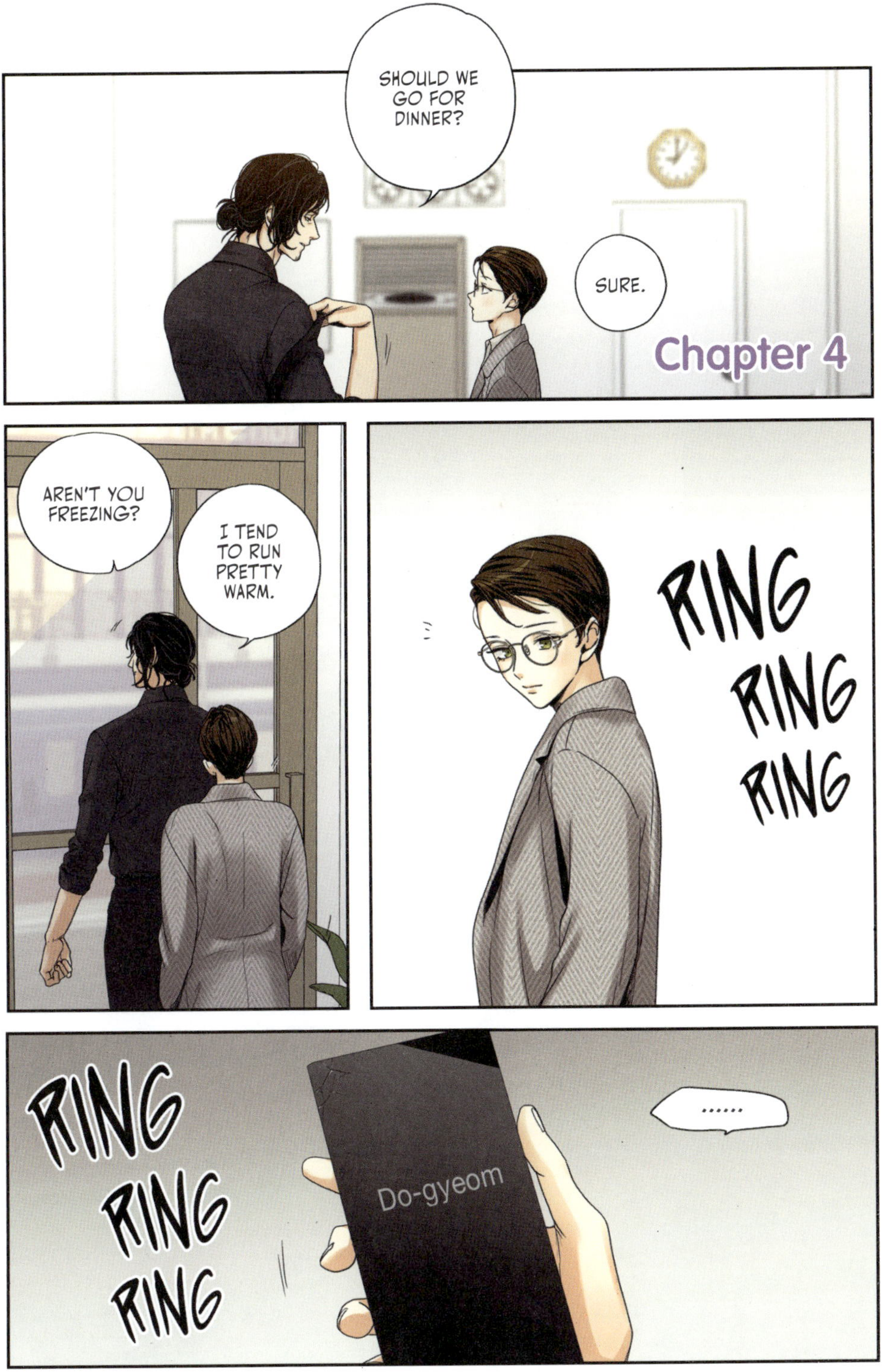
SHOULD WE GO FOR DINNER?
SURE.
Chapter 4
AREN'T YOU FREEZING?
I TEND TO RUN PRETTY WARM.
RING RING RING
RING RING RING
Do-gyeom
......

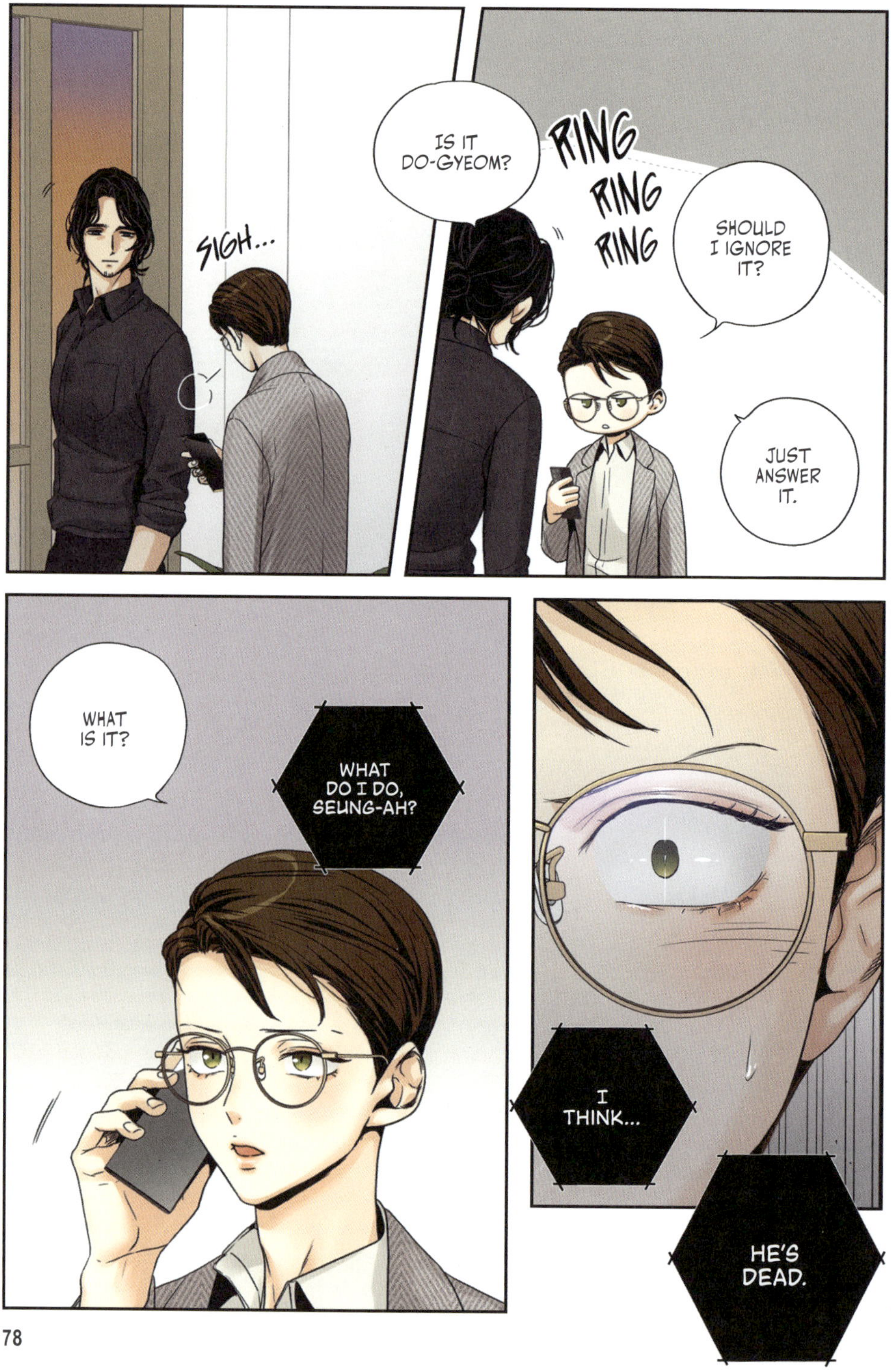
SIGH...
IS IT DO-GYEOM?
RING
RING
RING
SHOULD I IGNORE IT?
JUST ANSWER IT.
WHAT IS IT?
WHAT DO I DO, SEUNG-AH?
I THINK...
HE'S DEAD.

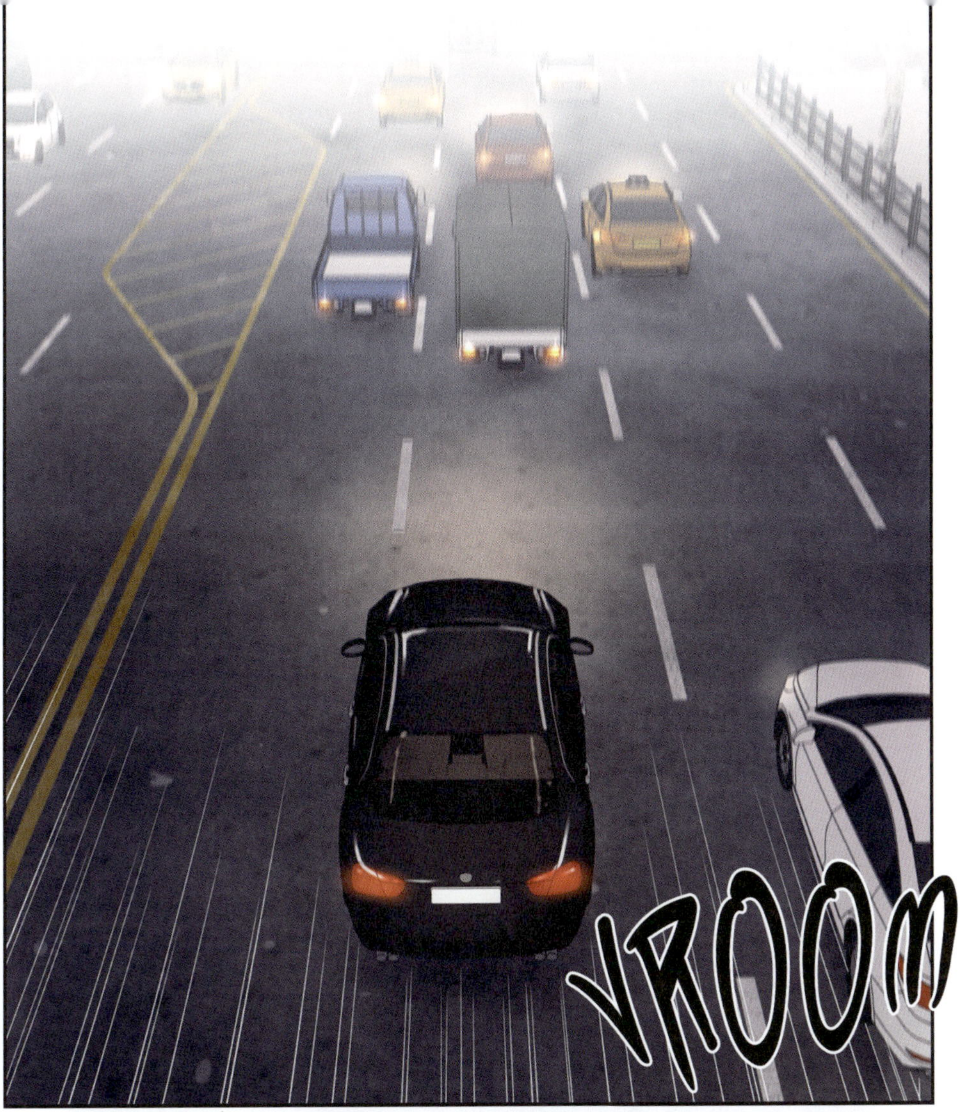
VROOM

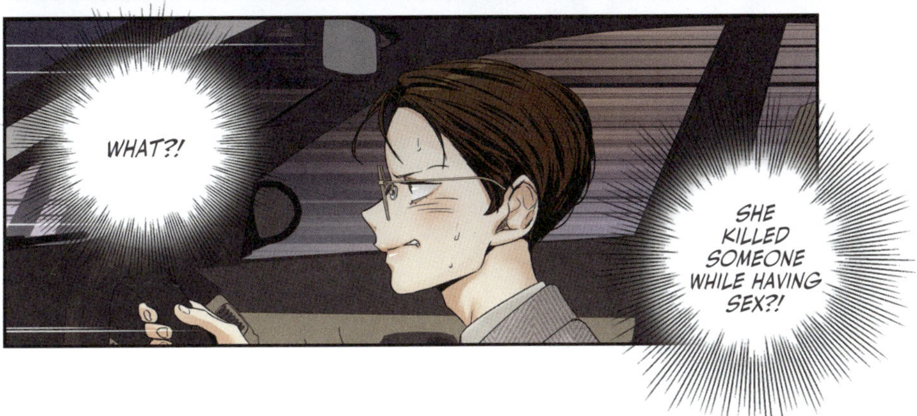
WHAT?!
SHE KILLED SOMEONE WHILE HAVING SEX?!

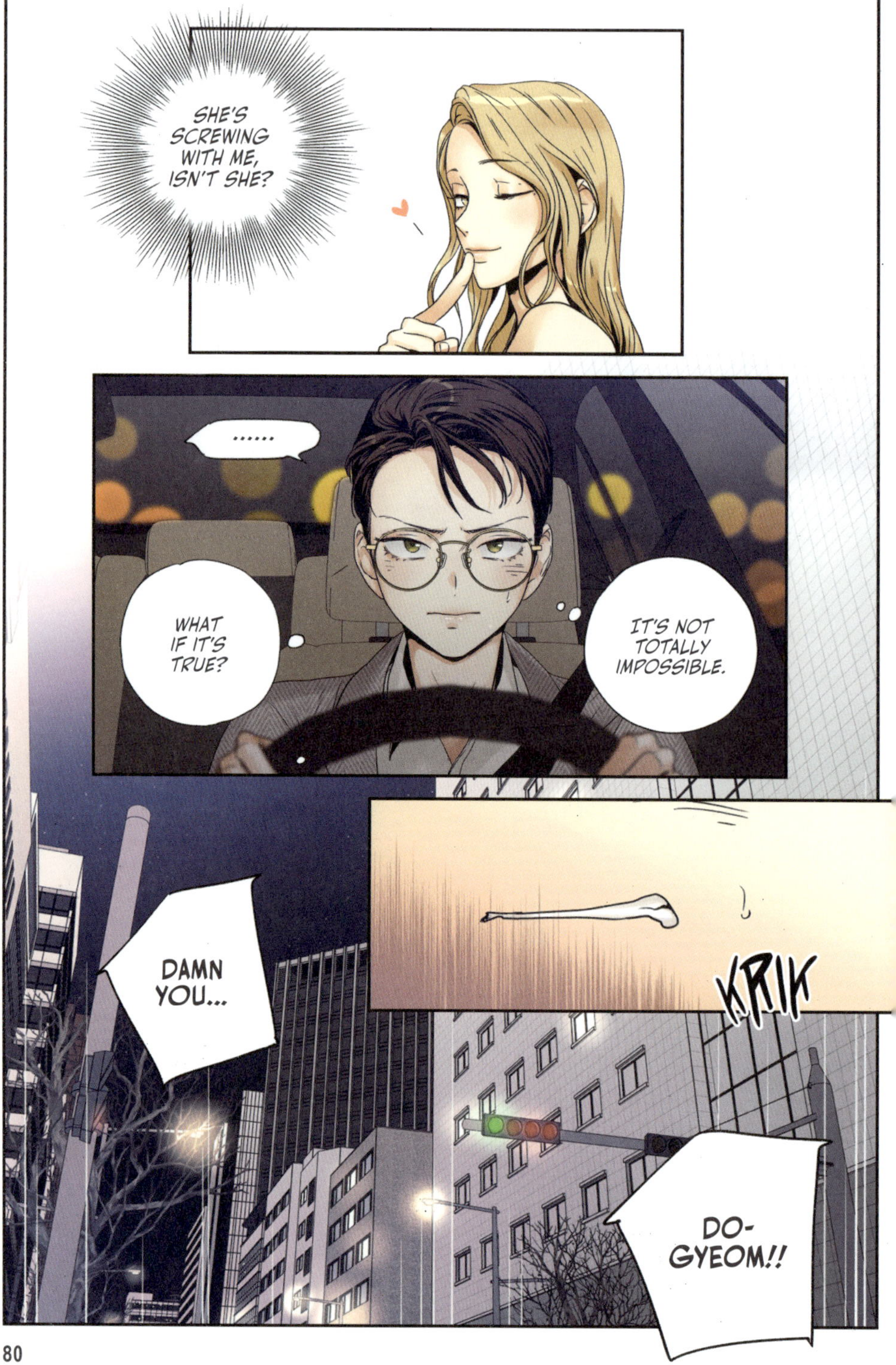

SHE'S SCREWING WITH ME, ISN'T SHE?
......
WHAT IF IT'S TRUE?
IT'S NOT TOTALLY IMPOSSIBLE.
DAMN YOU...
KRIK
DO-GYEOM!!

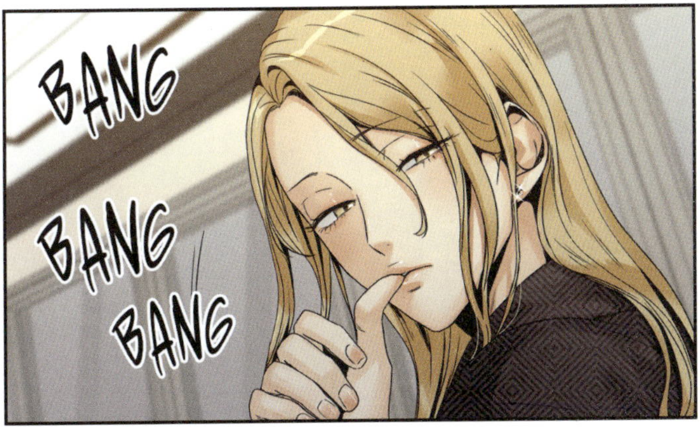
BANG
BANG
BANG
BANG

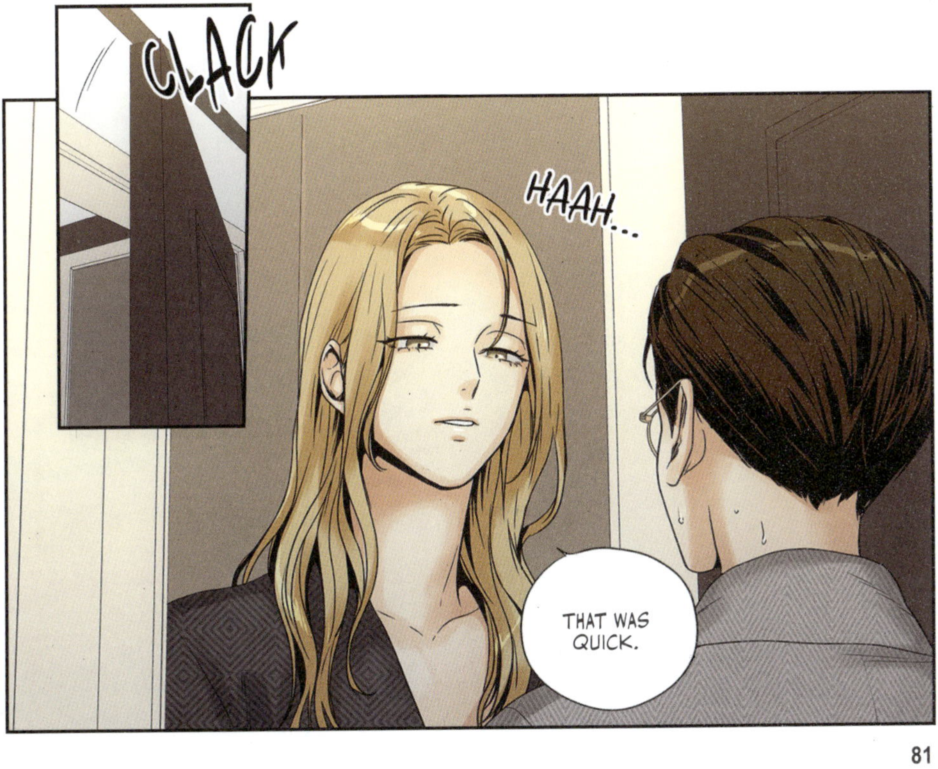
CLACK
HAAH...
THAT WAS QUICK.

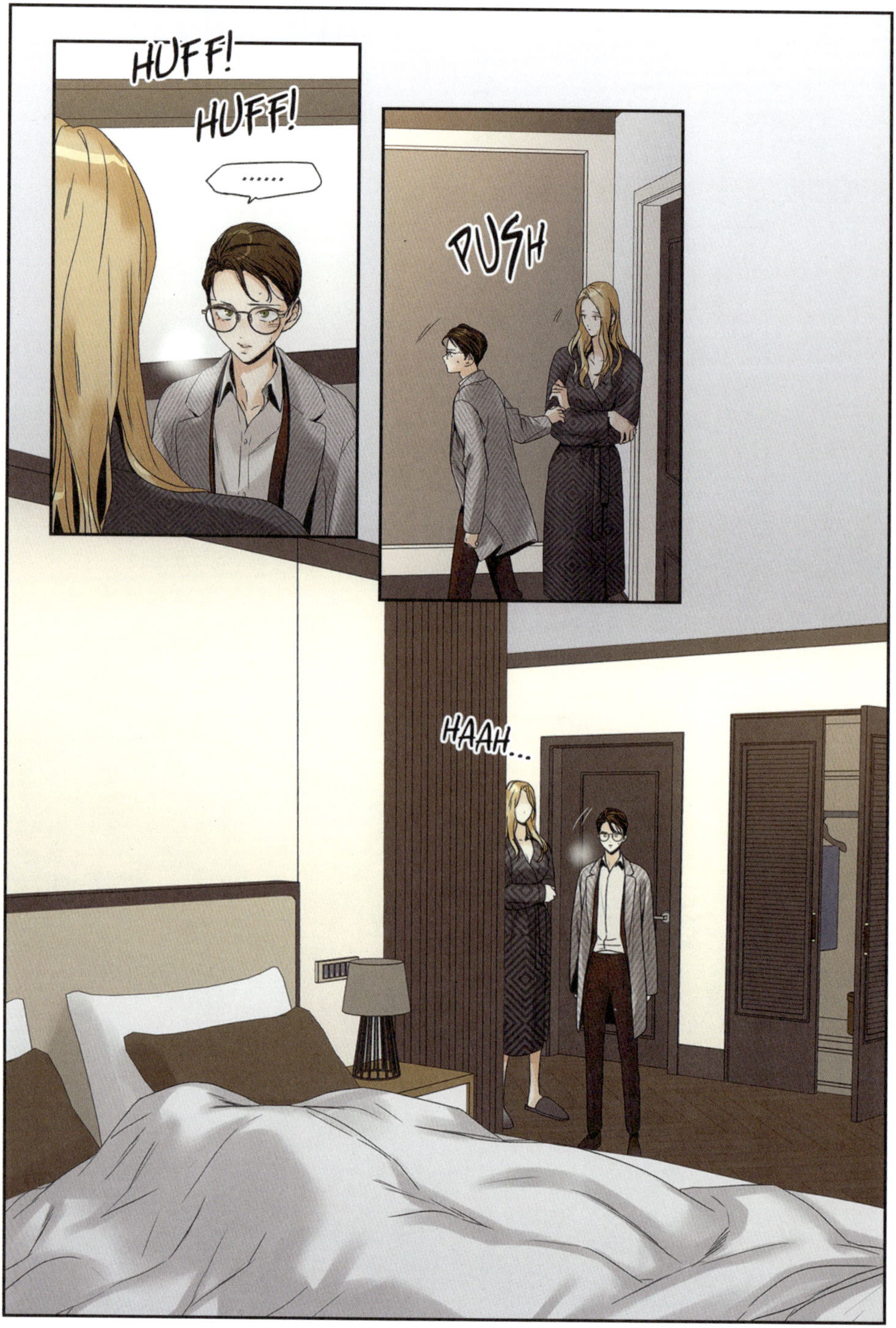
HUFF!
HUFF!
......
PUSH
HAAH...

HAAH...
HAAH...
SLIDE
HAAH...
......
HAAH...
WAIT...
HE'S JUST SLEEPING!!
REALLY?

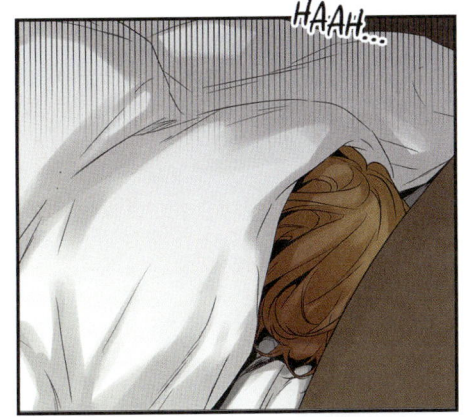

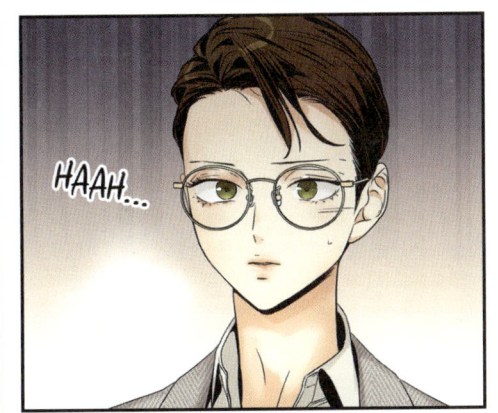

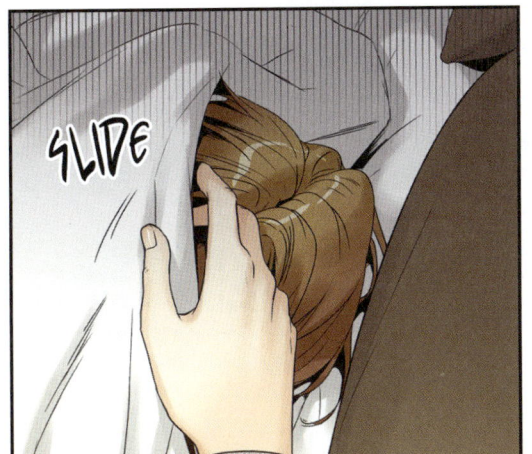

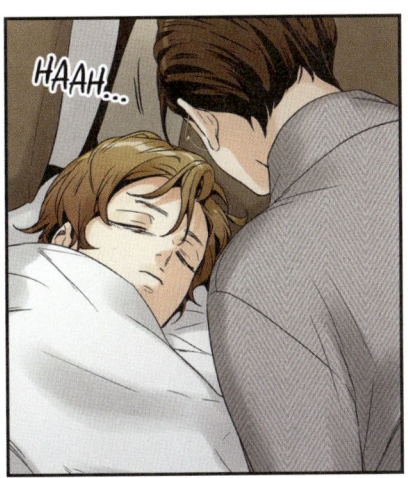

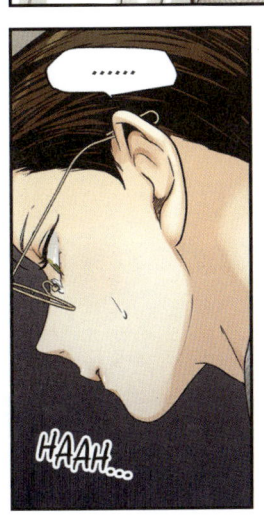

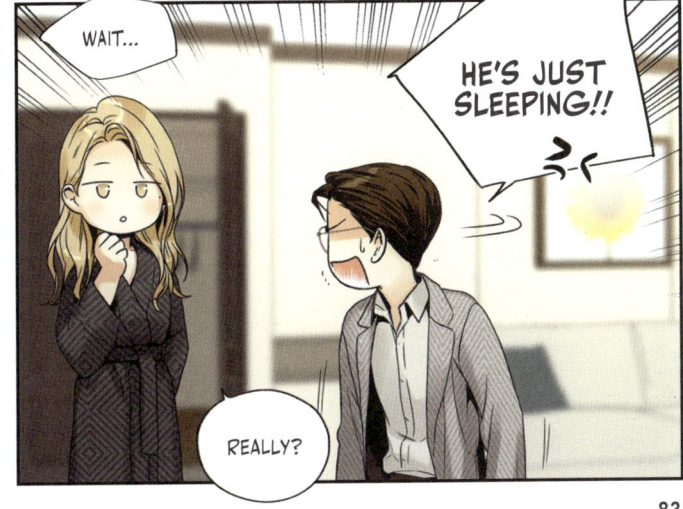

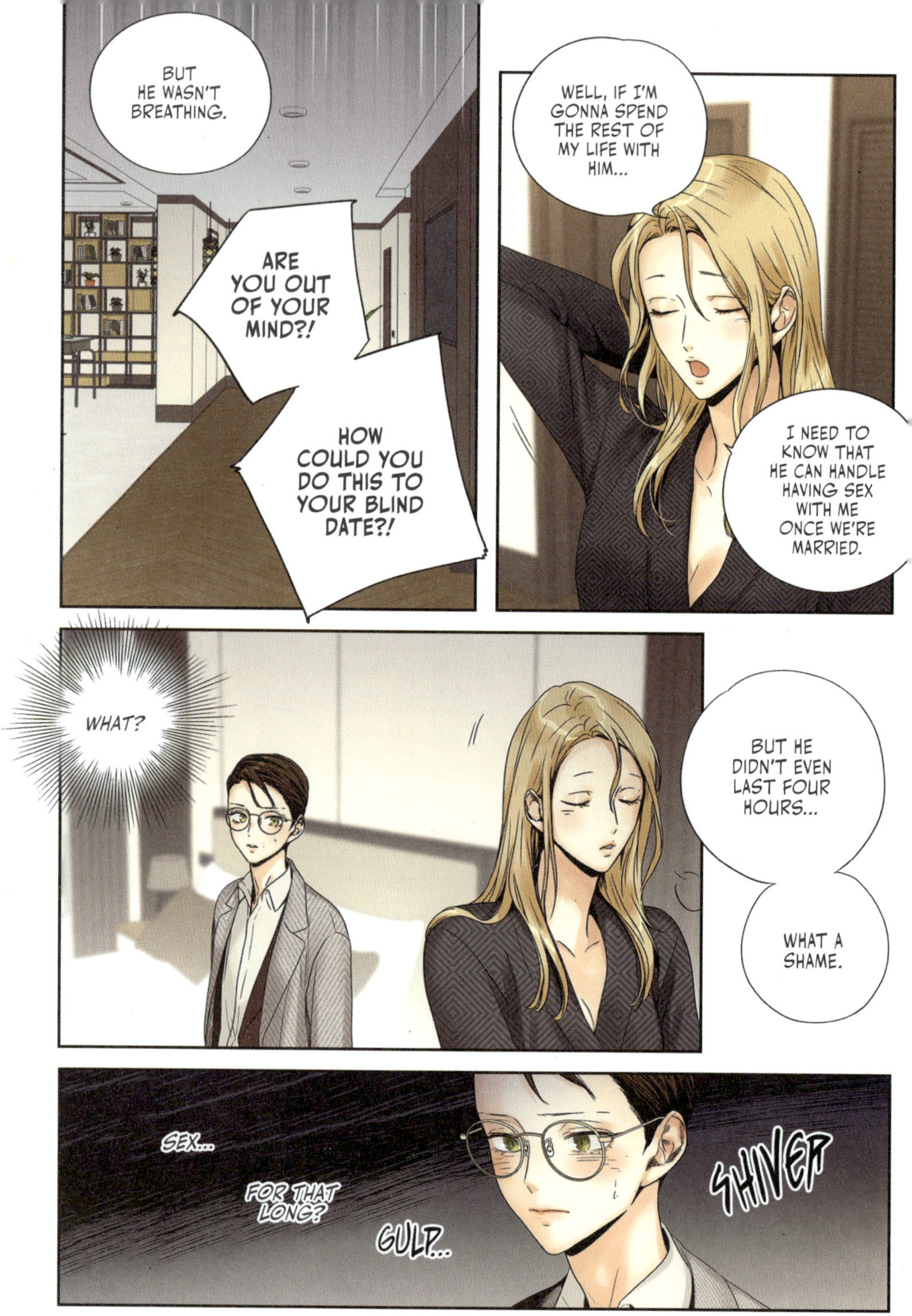
BUT HE WASN'T BREATHING.
ARE YOU OUT OF YOUR MIND?!
HOW COULD YOU DO THIS TO YOUR BLIND DATE?!
WELL, IF I'M GONNA SPEND THE REST OF MY LIFE WITH HIM...
I NEED TO KNOW THAT HE CAN HANDLE HAVING SEX WITH ME ONCE WE'RE MARRIED.
WHAT?
BUT HE DIDN'T EVEN LAST FOUR HOURS...
WHAT A SHAME.
SEX...
FOR THAT LONG?
GULP...
SHIVER

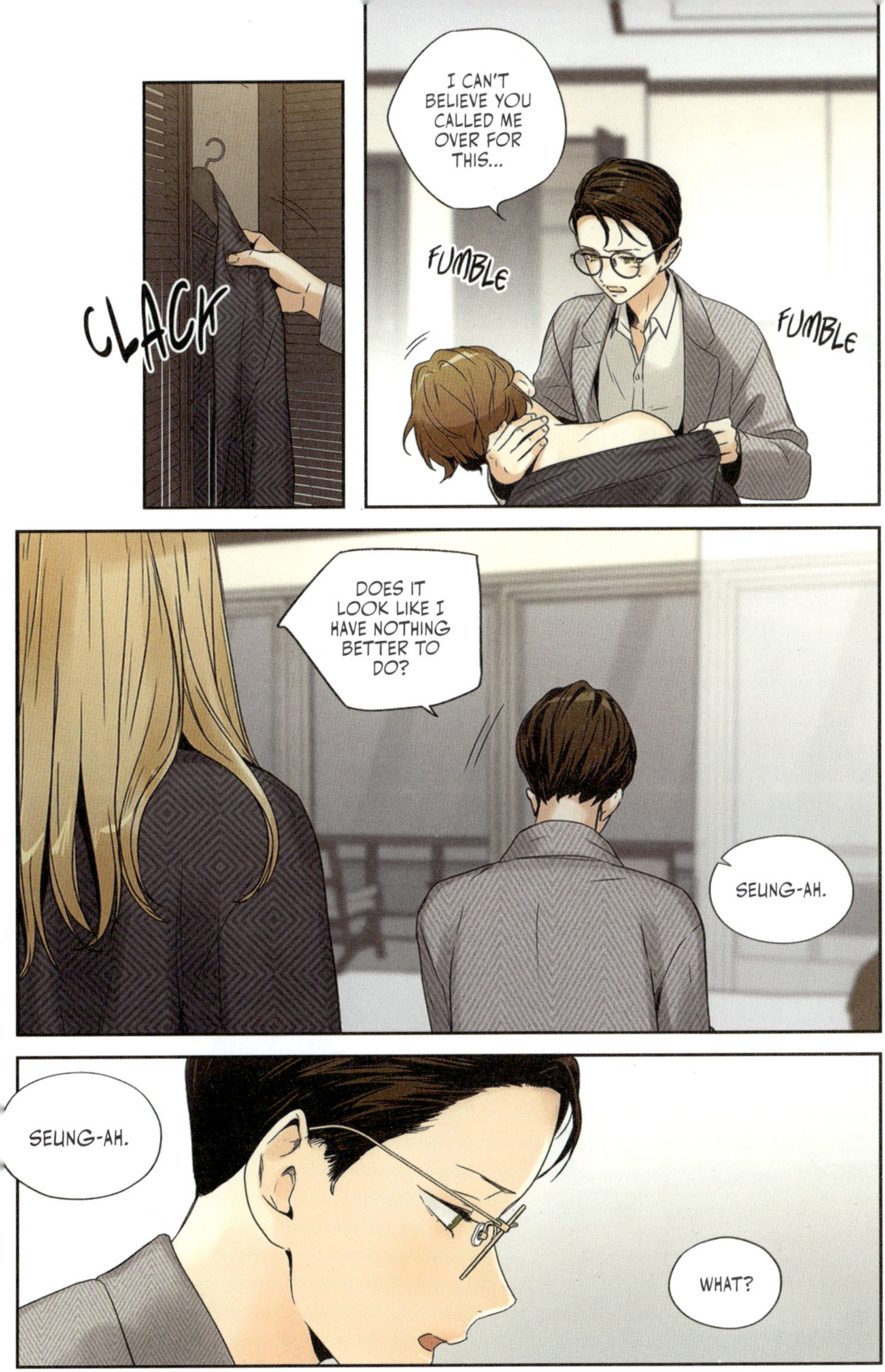
CLACK
I CAN'T BELIEVE YOU CALLED ME OVER FOR THIS...
FUMBLE
FUMBLE
DOES IT LOOK LIKE I HAVE NOTHING BETTER TO DO?
SEUNG-AH.
SEUNG-AH.
WHAT?

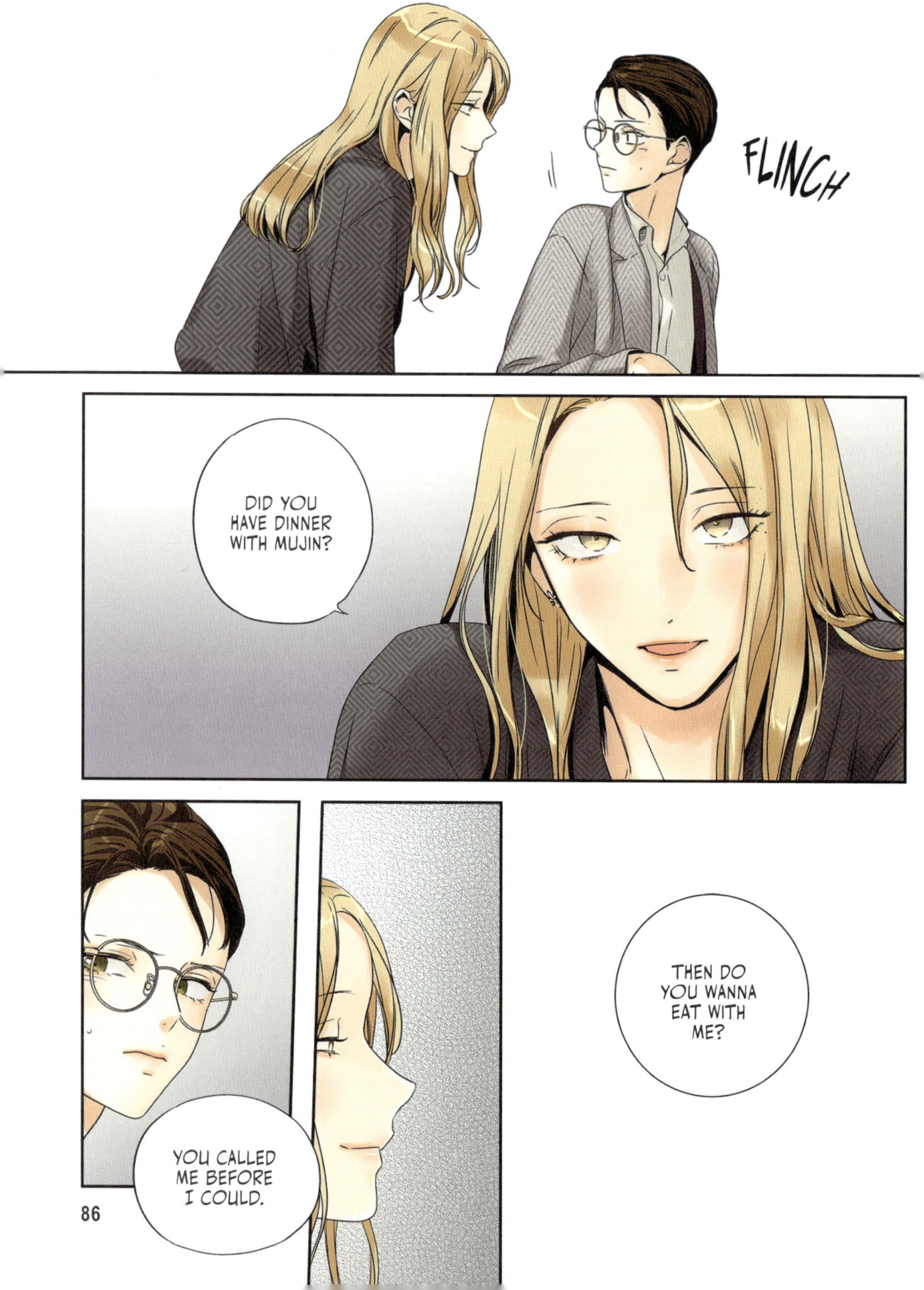
FLINCH
DID YOU HAVE DINNER WITH MUJIN?
YOU CALLED ME BEFORE I COULD.
THEN DO YOU WANNA EAT WITH ME?

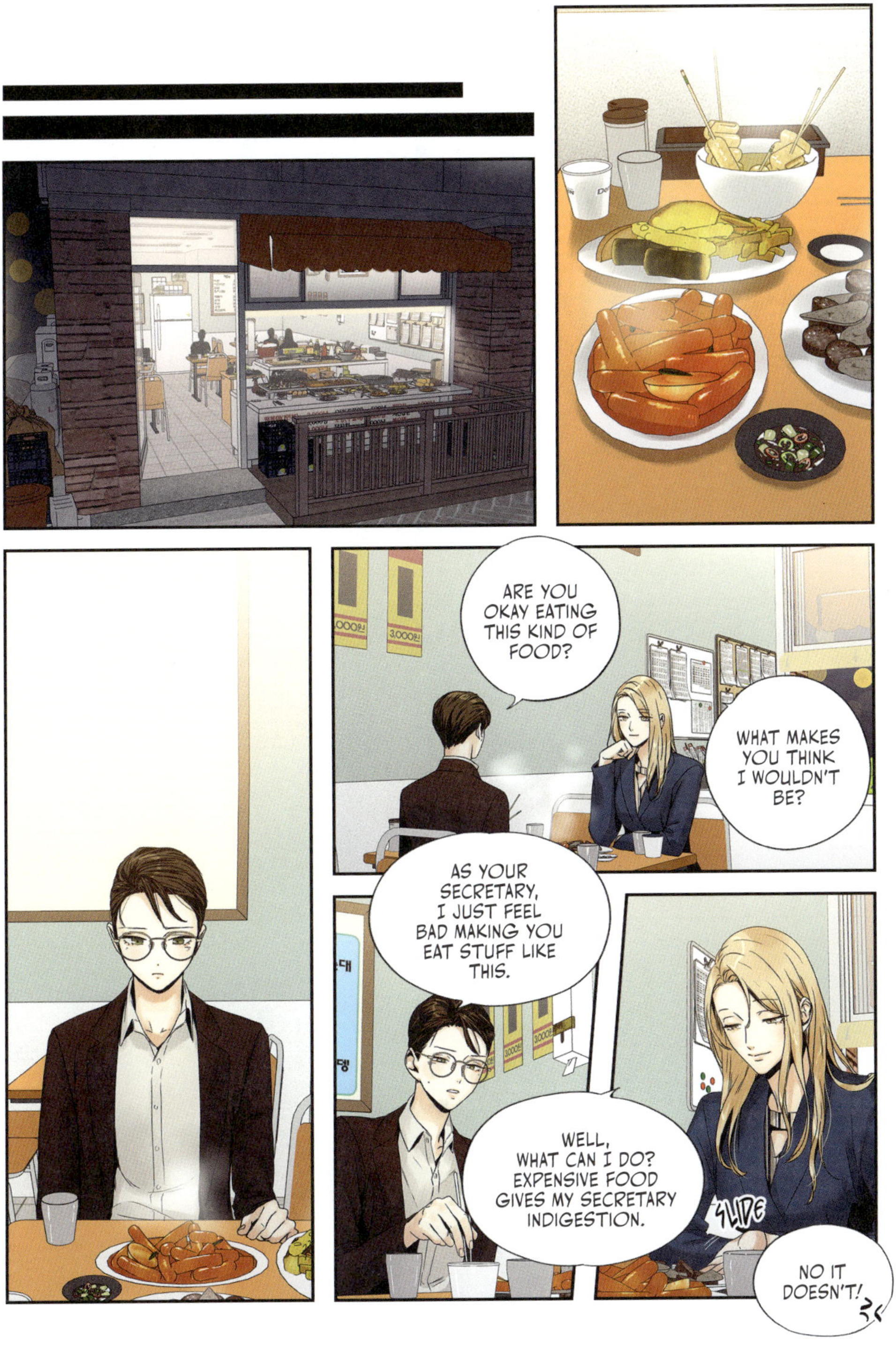
ARE YOU OKAY EATING THIS KIND OF FOOD?
WHAT MAKES YOU THINK I WOULDN'T BE?
AS YOUR SECRETARY, I JUST FEEL BAD MAKING YOU EAT STUFF LIKE THIS.
WELL, WHAT CAN I DO? EXPENSIVE FOOD GIVES MY SECRETARY INDIGESTION.
SLIDE
NO IT DOESN'T!

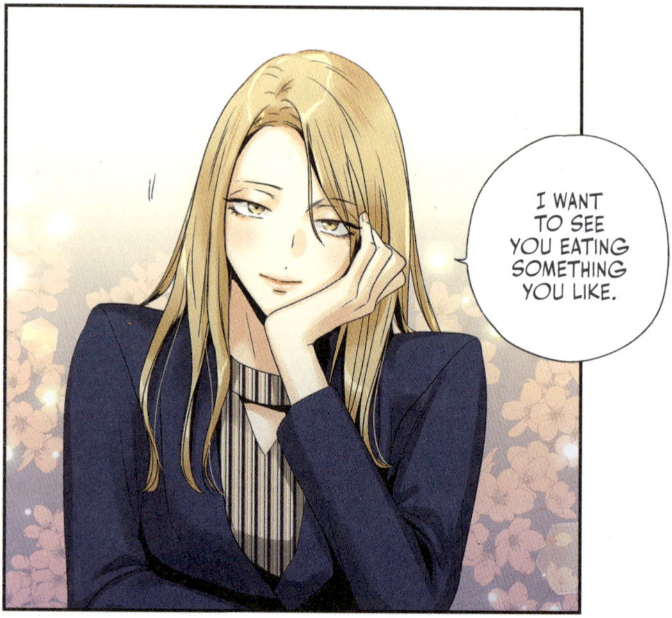
I WANT TO SEE YOU EATING SOMETHING YOU LIKE.

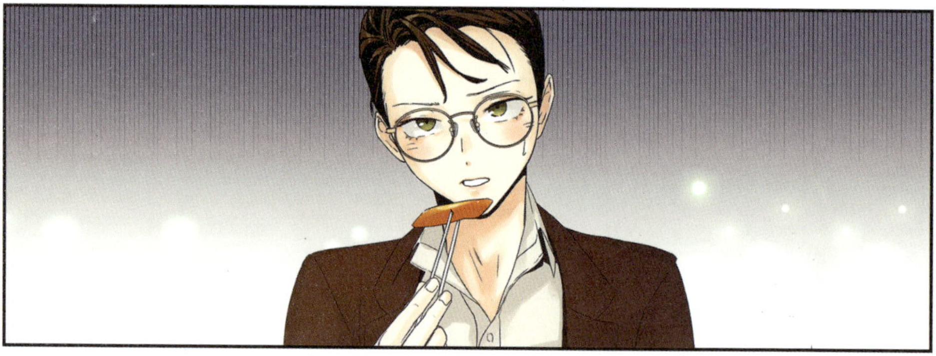

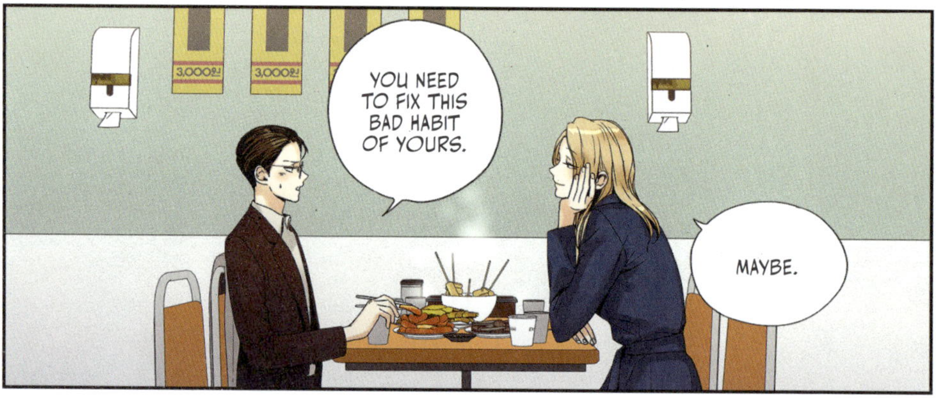
3,000원
3,000원
YOU NEED TO FIX THIS BAD HABIT OF YOURS.
MAYBE.

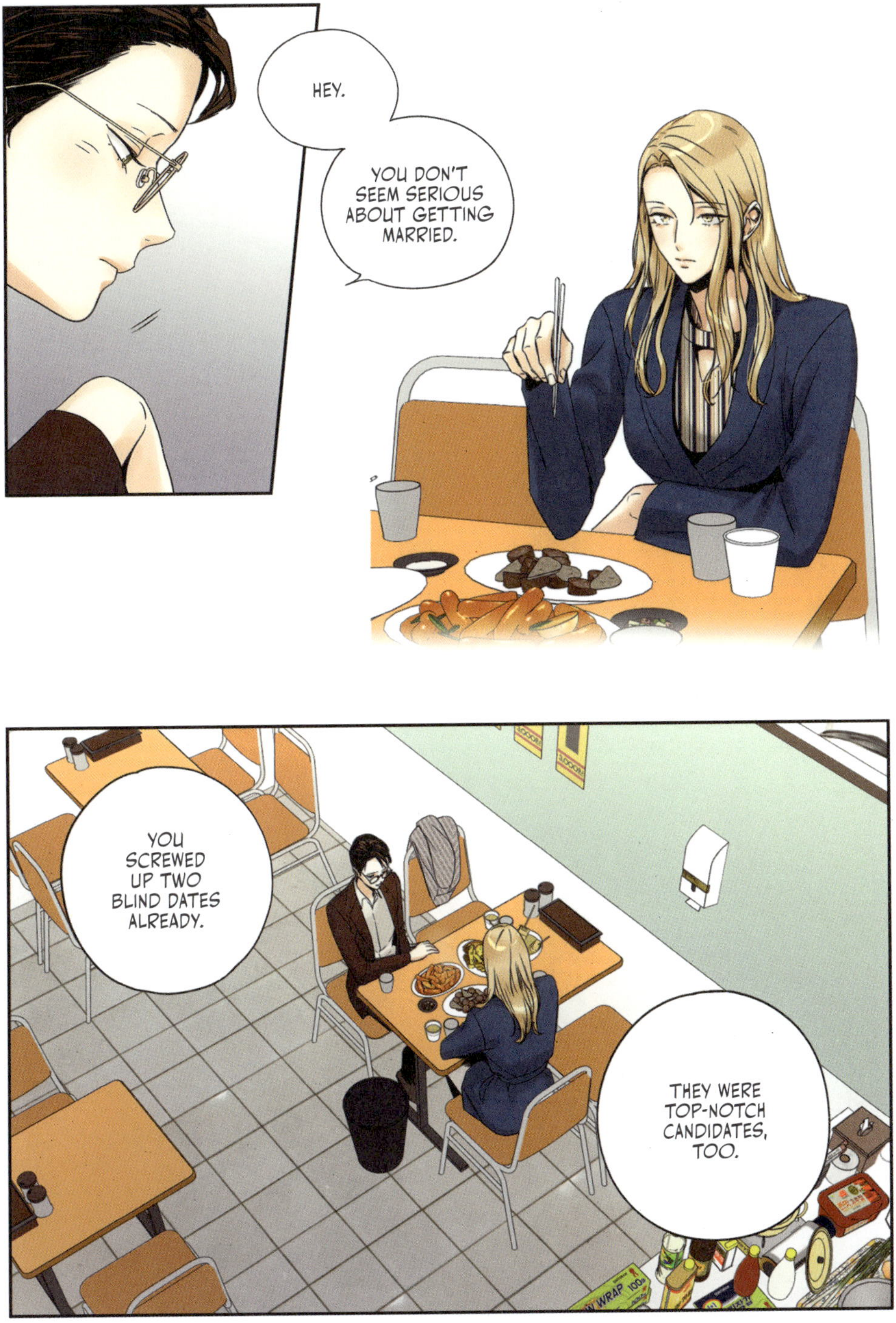
HEY.
YOU DON'T SEEM SERIOUS ABOUT GETTING MARRIED.
YOU SCREWED UP TWO BLIND DATES ALREADY.
THEY WERE TOP-NOTCH CANDIDATES, TOO.

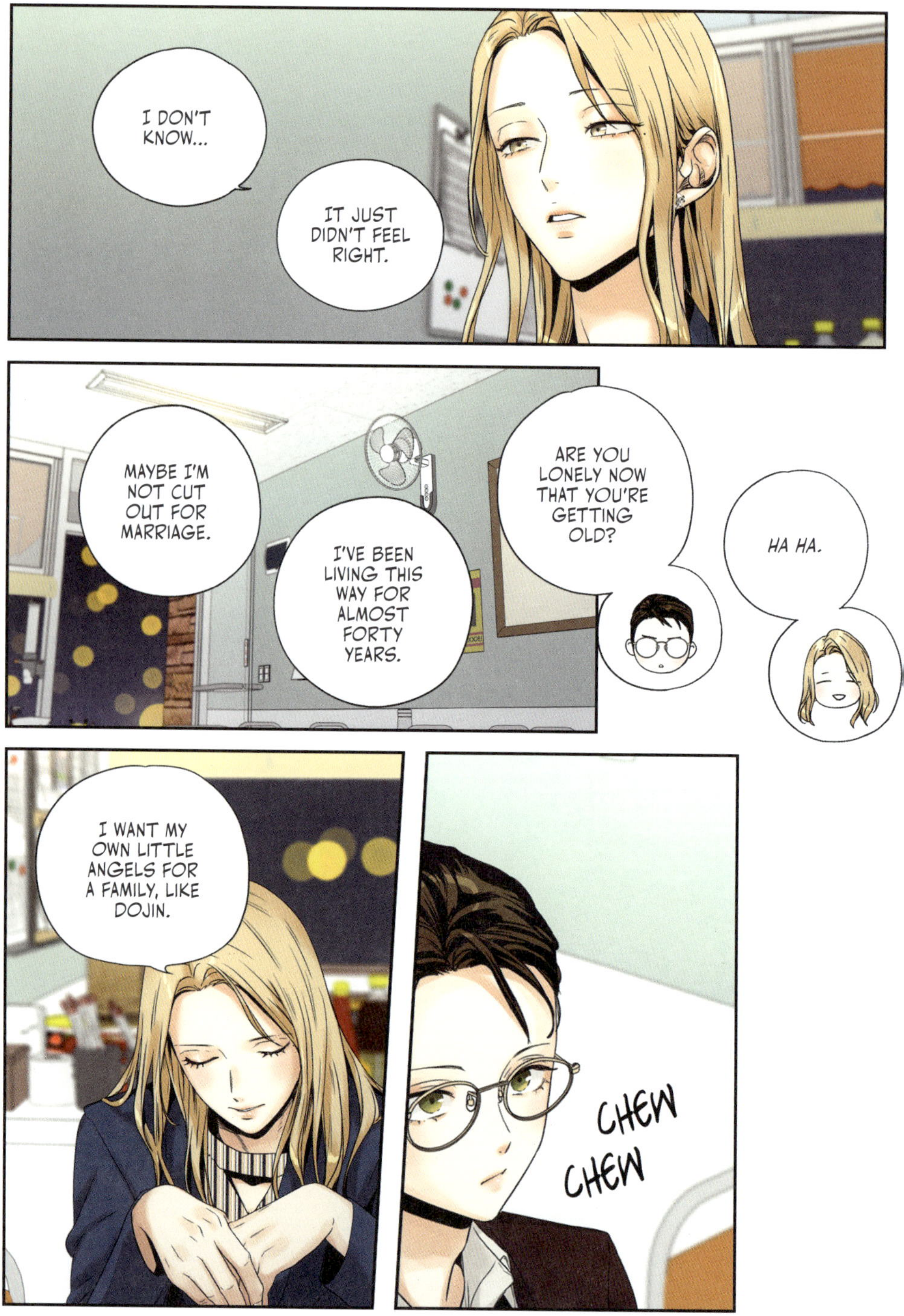
I DON'T KNOW...
IT JUST DIDN'T FEEL RIGHT.
MAYBE I'M NOT CUT OUT FOR MARRIAGE.
I'VE BEEN LIVING THIS WAY FOR ALMOST FORTY YEARS.
ARE YOU LONELY NOW THAT YOU'RE GETTING OLD?
HA HA.
I WANT MY OWN LITTLE ANGELS FOR A FAMILY, LIKE DOJIN.
CHEW CHEW

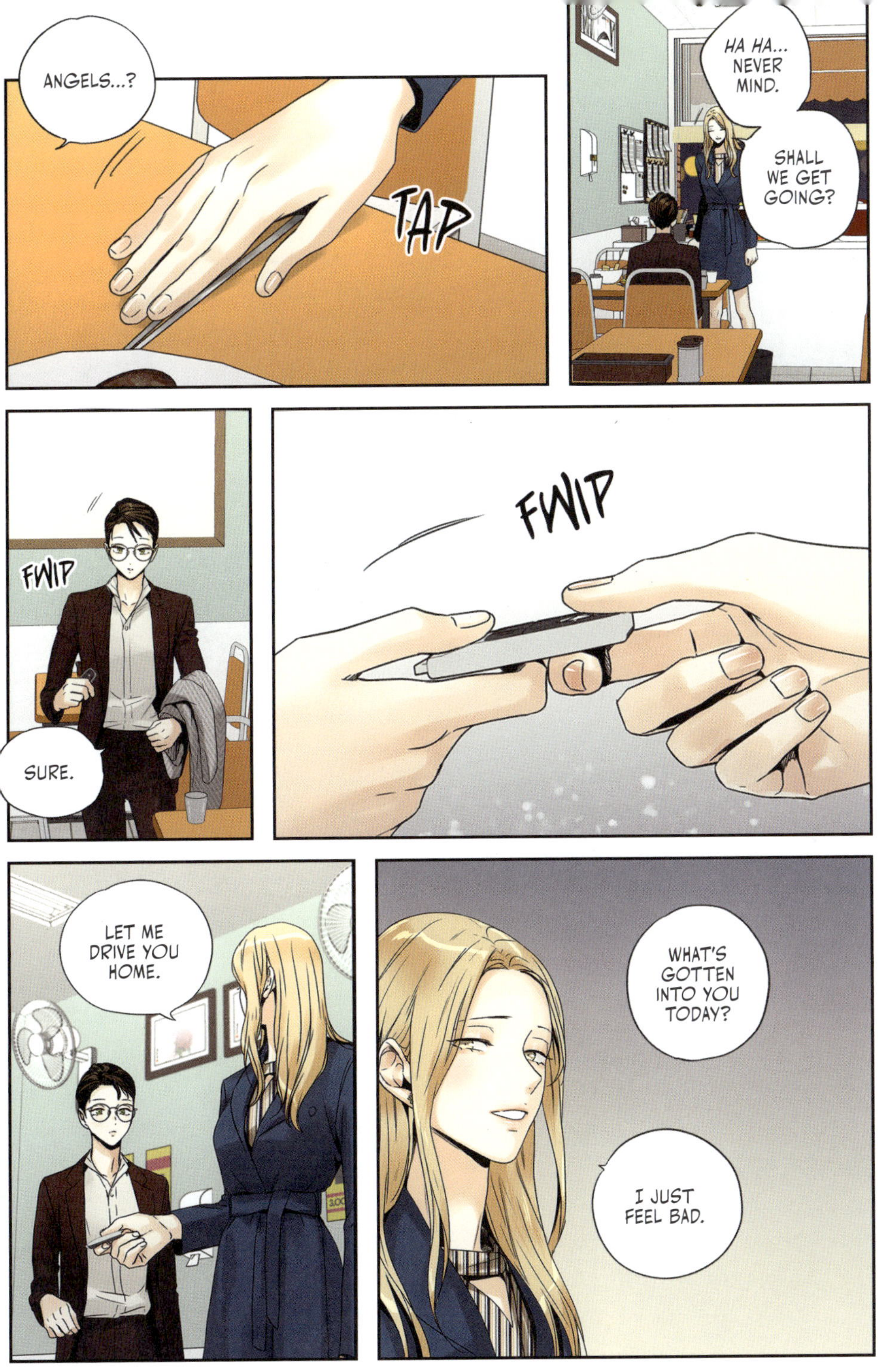
ANGELS...?
TAP
HA HA... NEVER MIND.
SHALL WE GET GOING?
FWIP
SURE.
FWIP
LET ME DRIVE YOU HOME.
WHAT'S GOTTEN INTO YOU TODAY?
I JUST FEEL BAD.

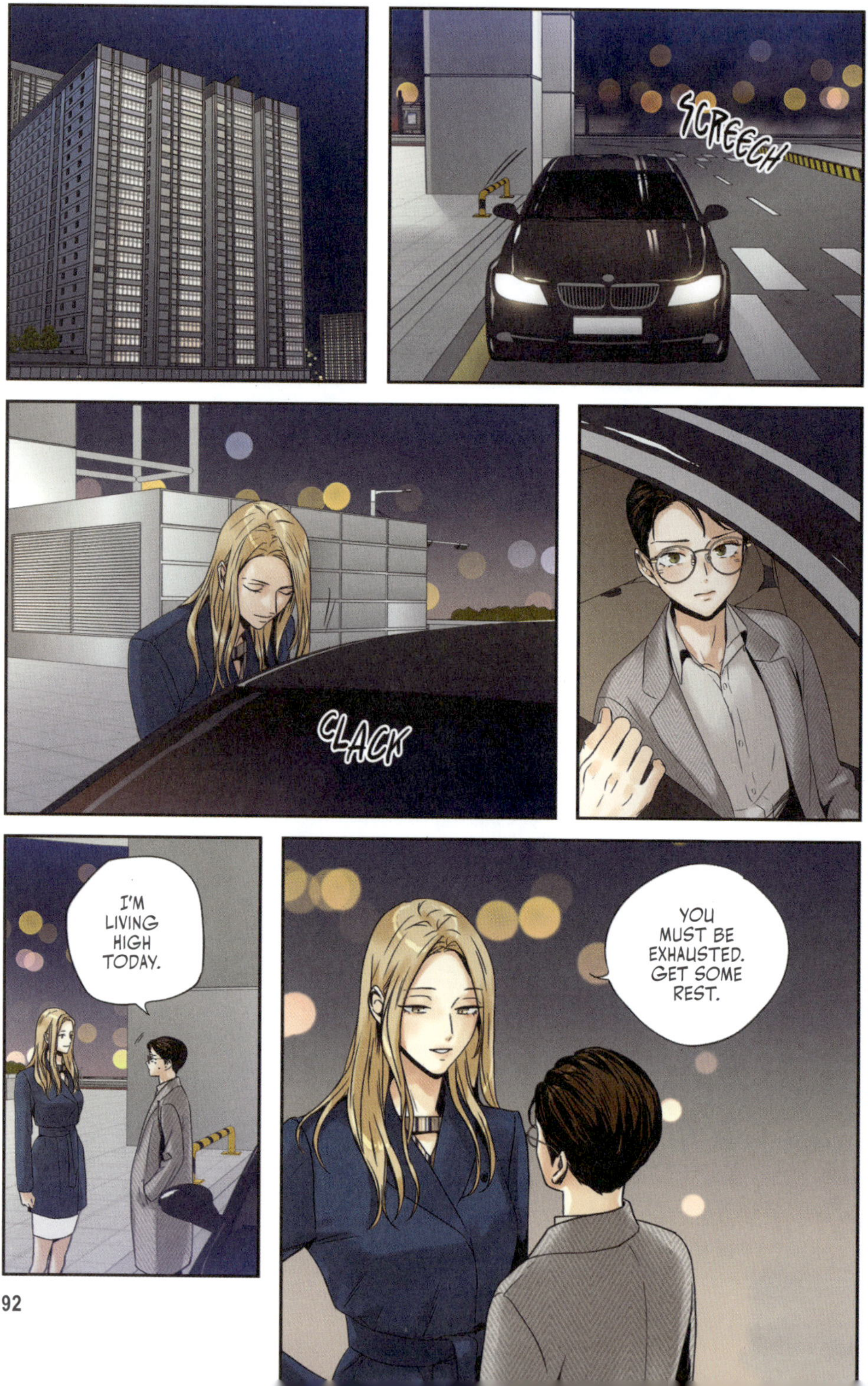
SCREECH
CLACK
I'M LIVING HIGH TODAY.
YOU MUST BE EXHAUSTED. GET SOME REST.

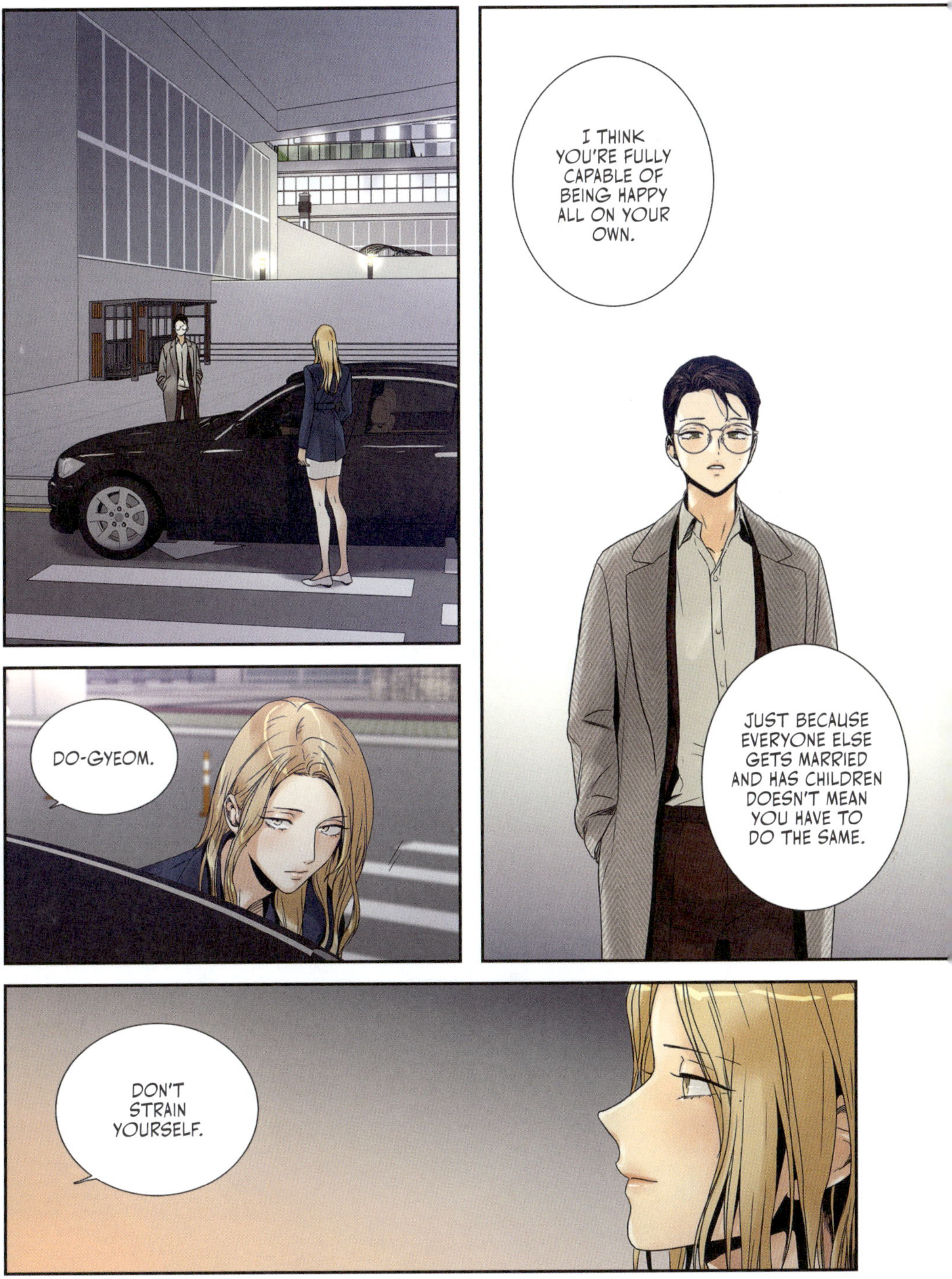
DO-GYEOM.
I THINK YOU'RE FULLY CAPABLE OF BEING HAPPY ALL ON YOUR OWN.
JUST BECAUSE EVERYONE ELSE GETS MARRIED AND HAS CHILDREN DOESN'T MEAN YOU HAVE TO DO THE SAME.
DON'T STRAIN YOURSELF.

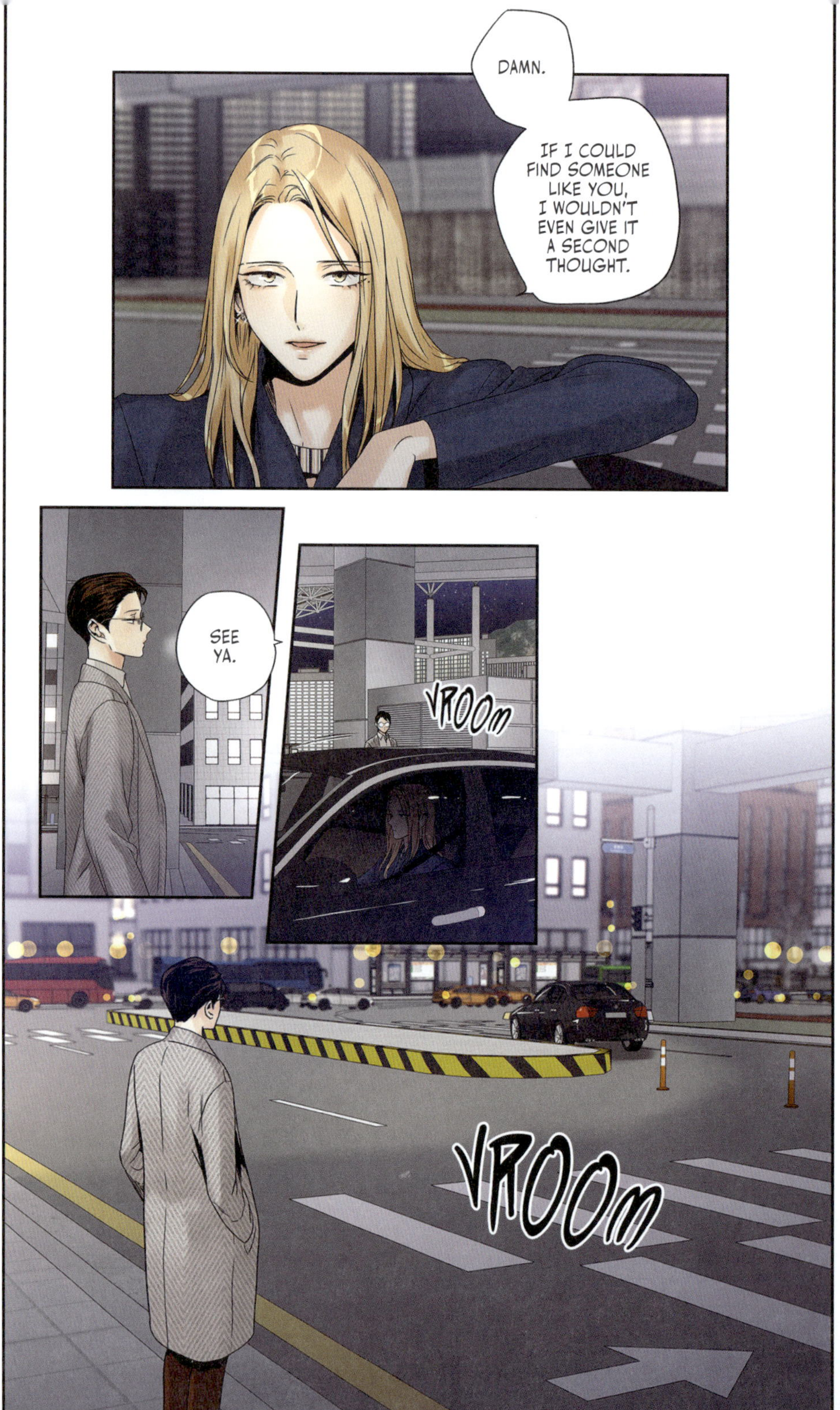
DAMN.
IF I COULD FIND SOMEONE LIKE YOU, I WOULDN'T EVEN GIVE IT A SECOND THOUGHT.
SEE YA.
VROOM
VROOM

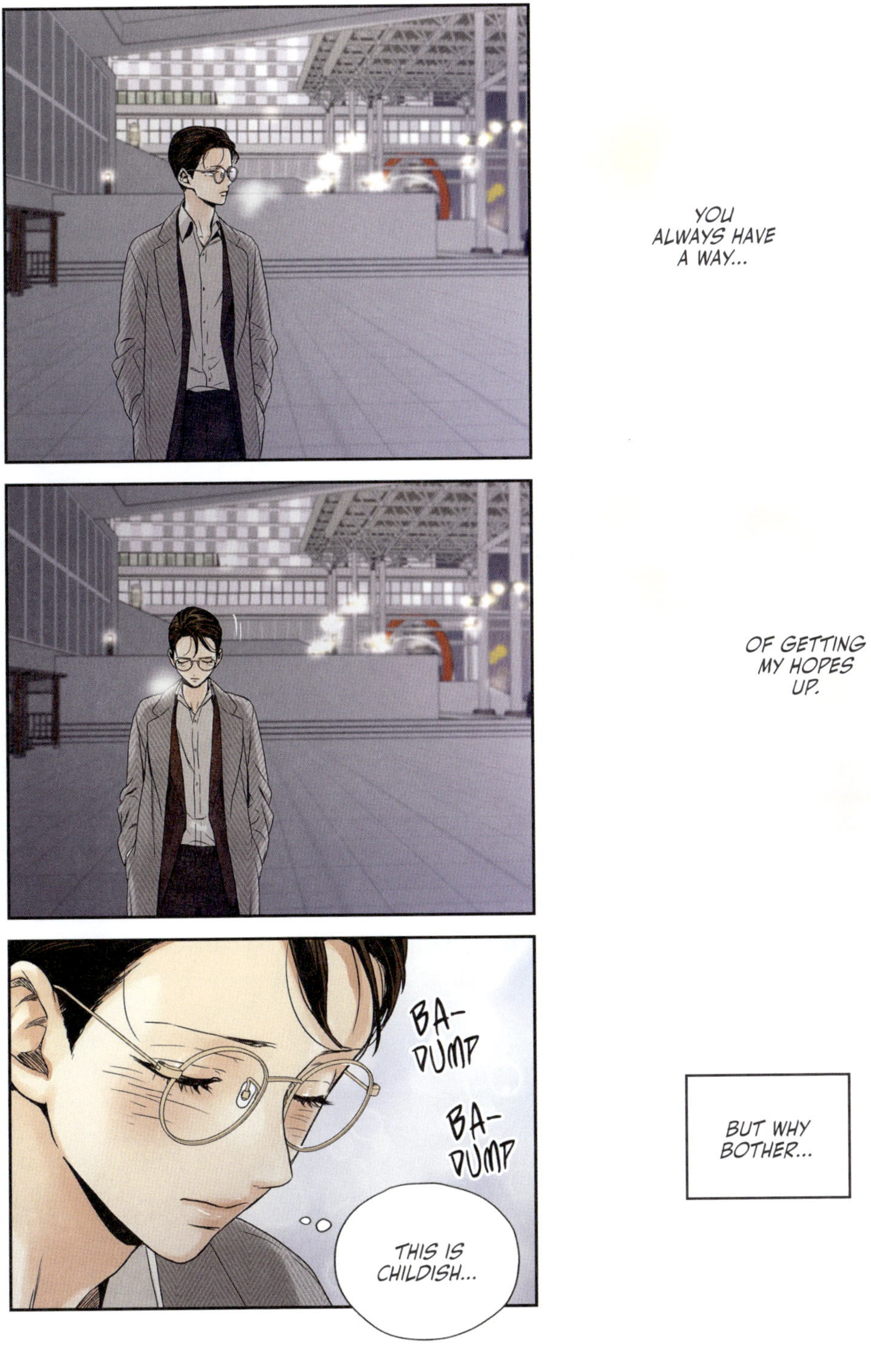
YOU ALWAYS HAVE A WAY...
OF GETTING MY HOPES UP.
BA-DUMP
BA-DUMP
THIS IS CHILDISH...
BUT WHY BOTHER...

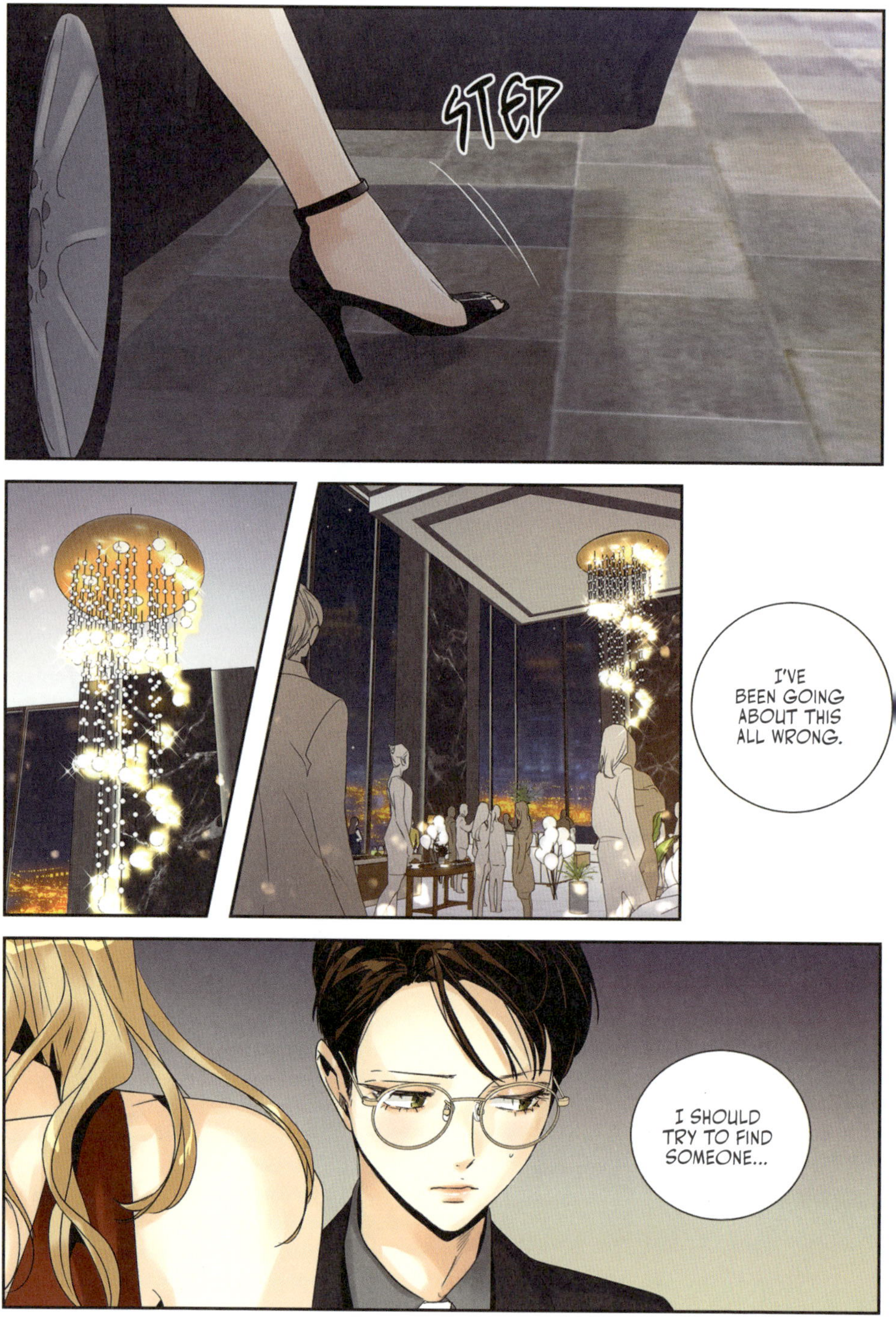
STEP
I'VE BEEN GOING ABOUT THIS ALL WRONG.
I SHOULD TRY TO FIND SOMEONE...

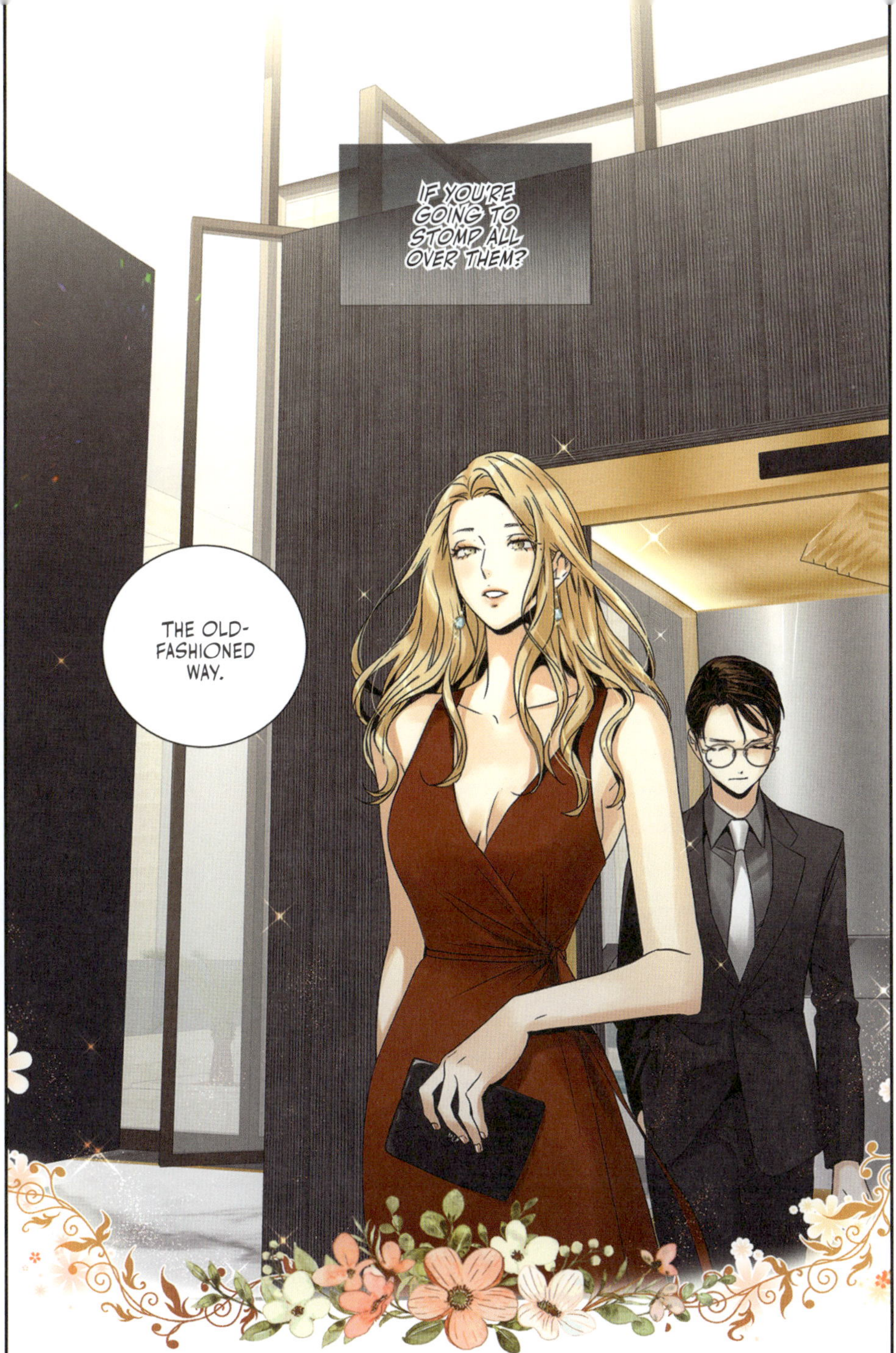
IF YOU'RE GOING TO STOMP ALL OVER THEM?
THE OLD-FASHIONED WAY.

Love is an Illusion!
The Queen

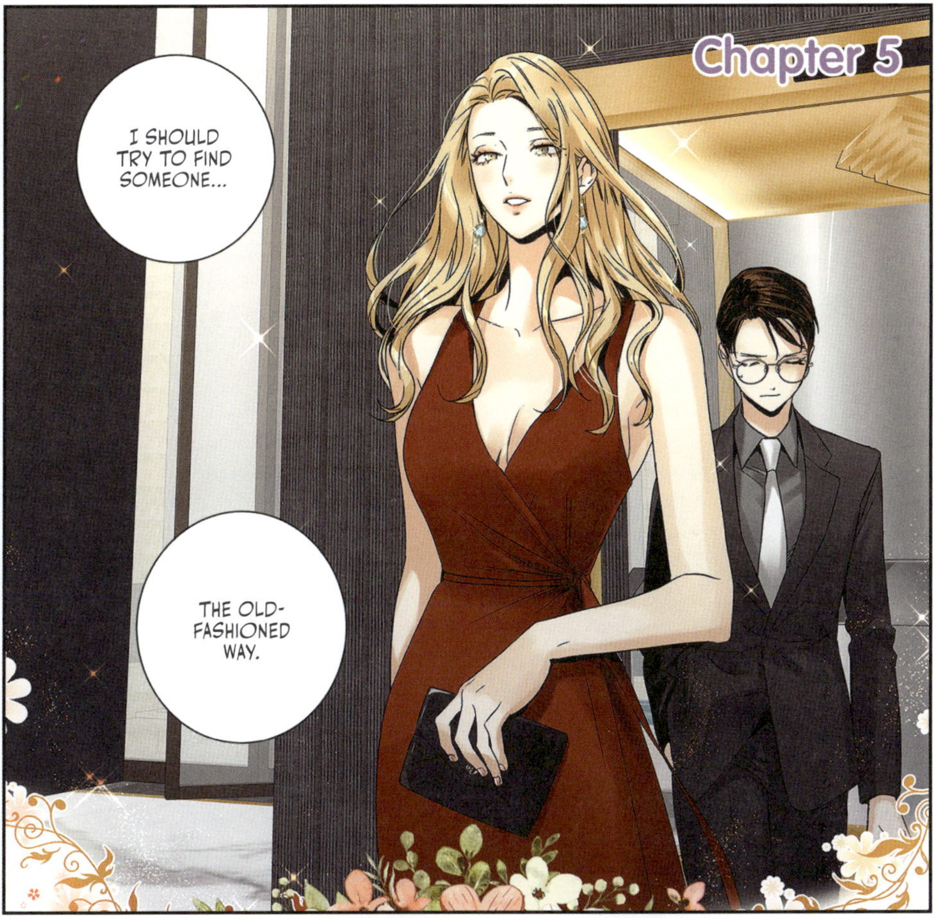
Chapter 5
I SHOULD TRY TO FIND SOMEONE...
THE OLD-FASHIONED WAY.

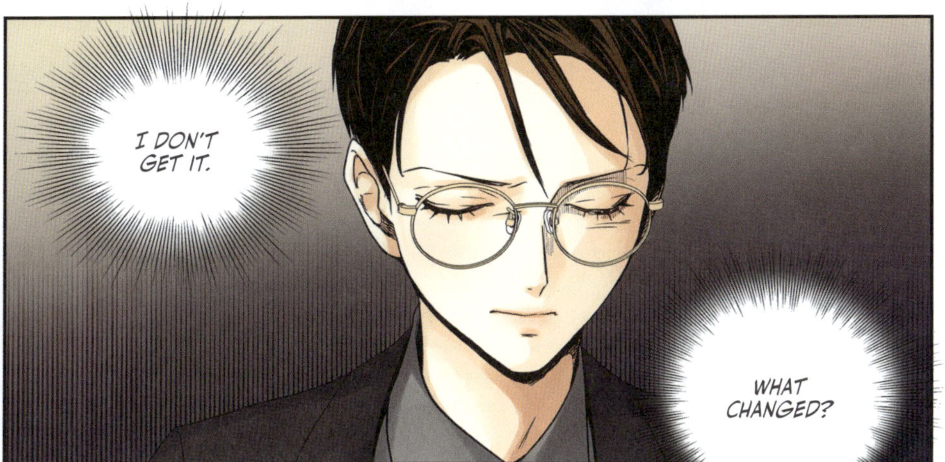
I DON'T GET IT.
WHAT CHANGED?

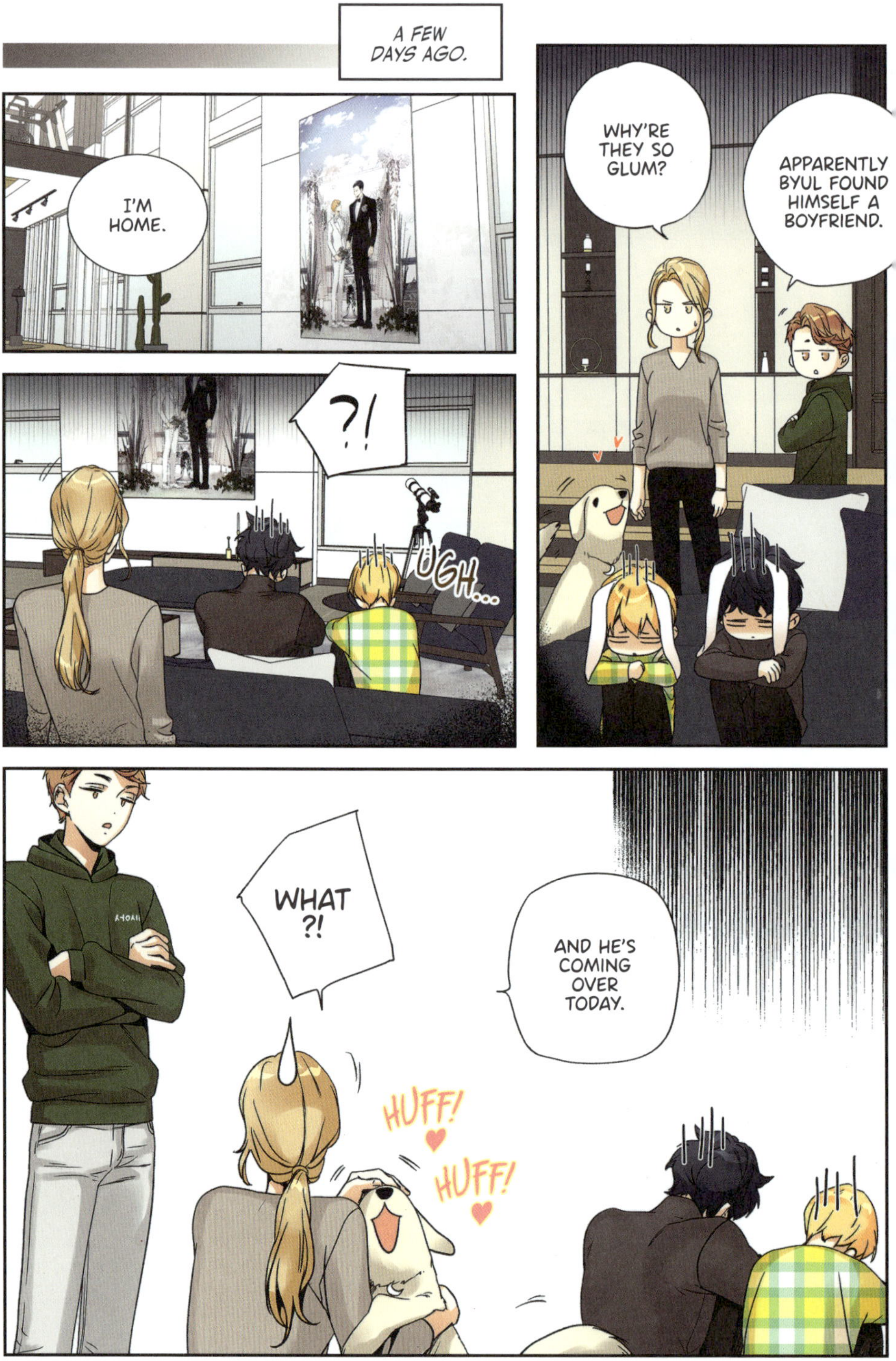
A FEW DAYS AGO.
I'M HOME.
?!
UGH...
WHY'RE THEY SO GLUM?
APPARENTLY BYUL FOUND HIMSELF A BOYFRIEND.
WHAT?!
AND HE'S COMING OVER TODAY.
HUFF!
HUFF!

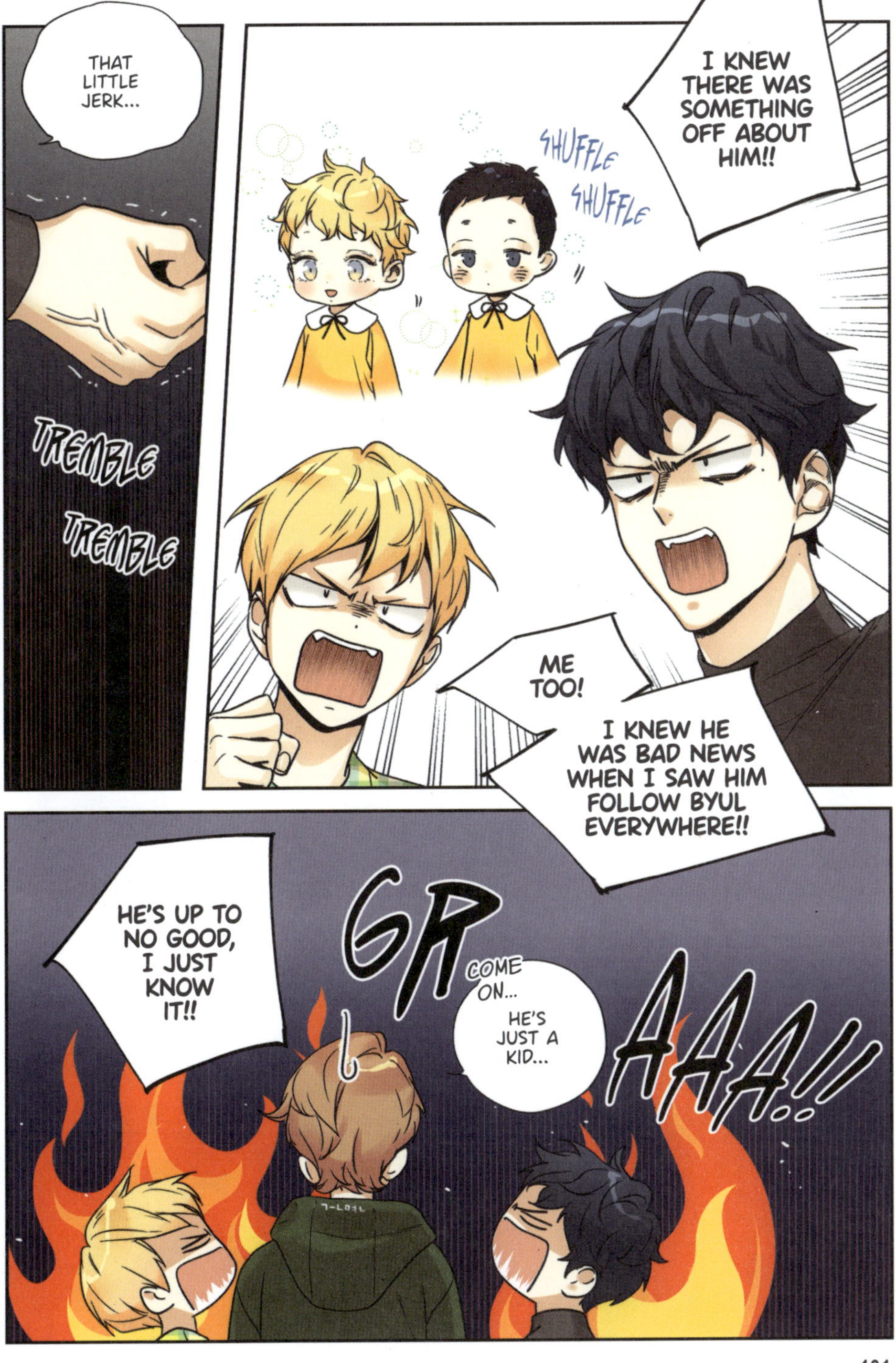
THAT LITTLE JERK...
TREMBLE
TREMBLE
SHUFFLE
SHUFFLE
I KNEW THERE WAS SOMETHING OFF ABOUT HIM!!
ME TOO!
I KNEW HE WAS BAD NEWS WHEN I SAW HIM FOLLOW BYUL EVERYWHERE!!
HE'S UP TO NO GOOD, I JUST KNOW IT!!
GR
COME ON...
HE'S JUST A KID...
AAA!!

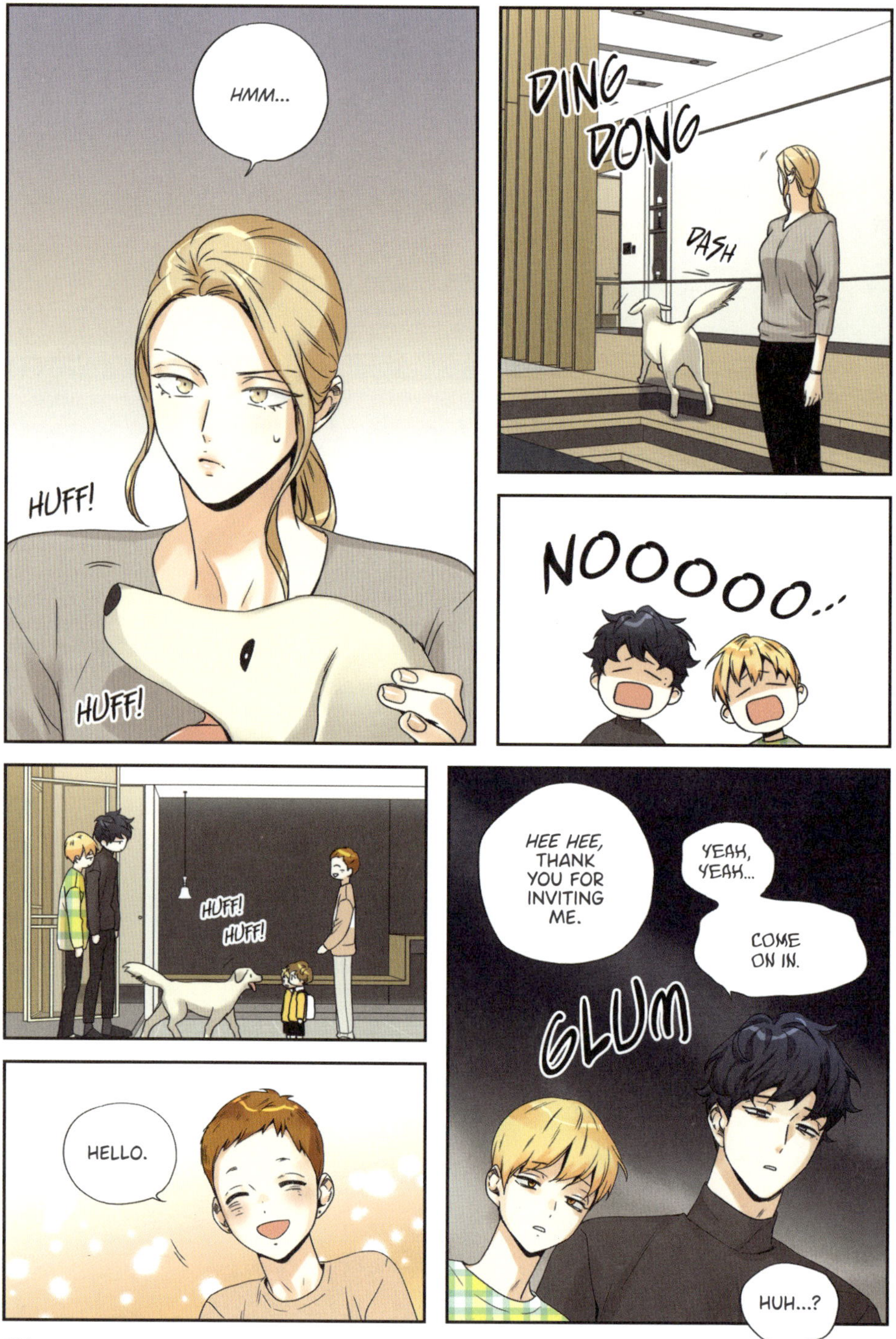
HMM...
HUFF!
HUFF!
DING DONG
DASH
NOOOOO...
HUFF!
HUFF!
HELLO.
HEE HEE, THANK YOU FOR INVITING ME.
YEAH, YEAH...
COME ON IN.
GLUM
HUH...?

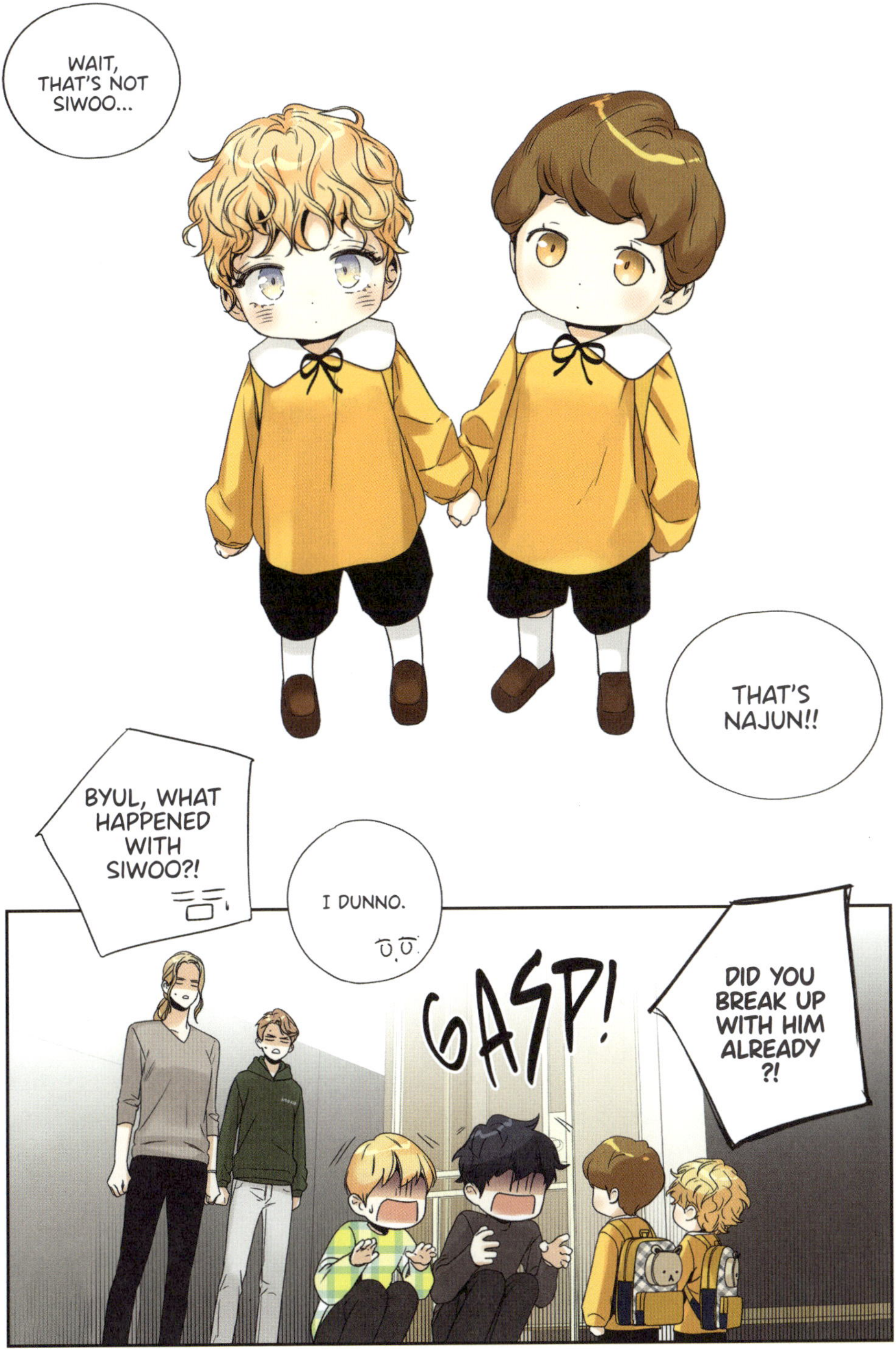

WAIT, THAT'S NOT SIWOO...
THAT'S NAJUN!!
BYUL, WHAT HAPPENED WITH SIWOO?!
I DUNNO.
GASP!
DID YOU BREAK UP WITH HIM ALREADY ?!

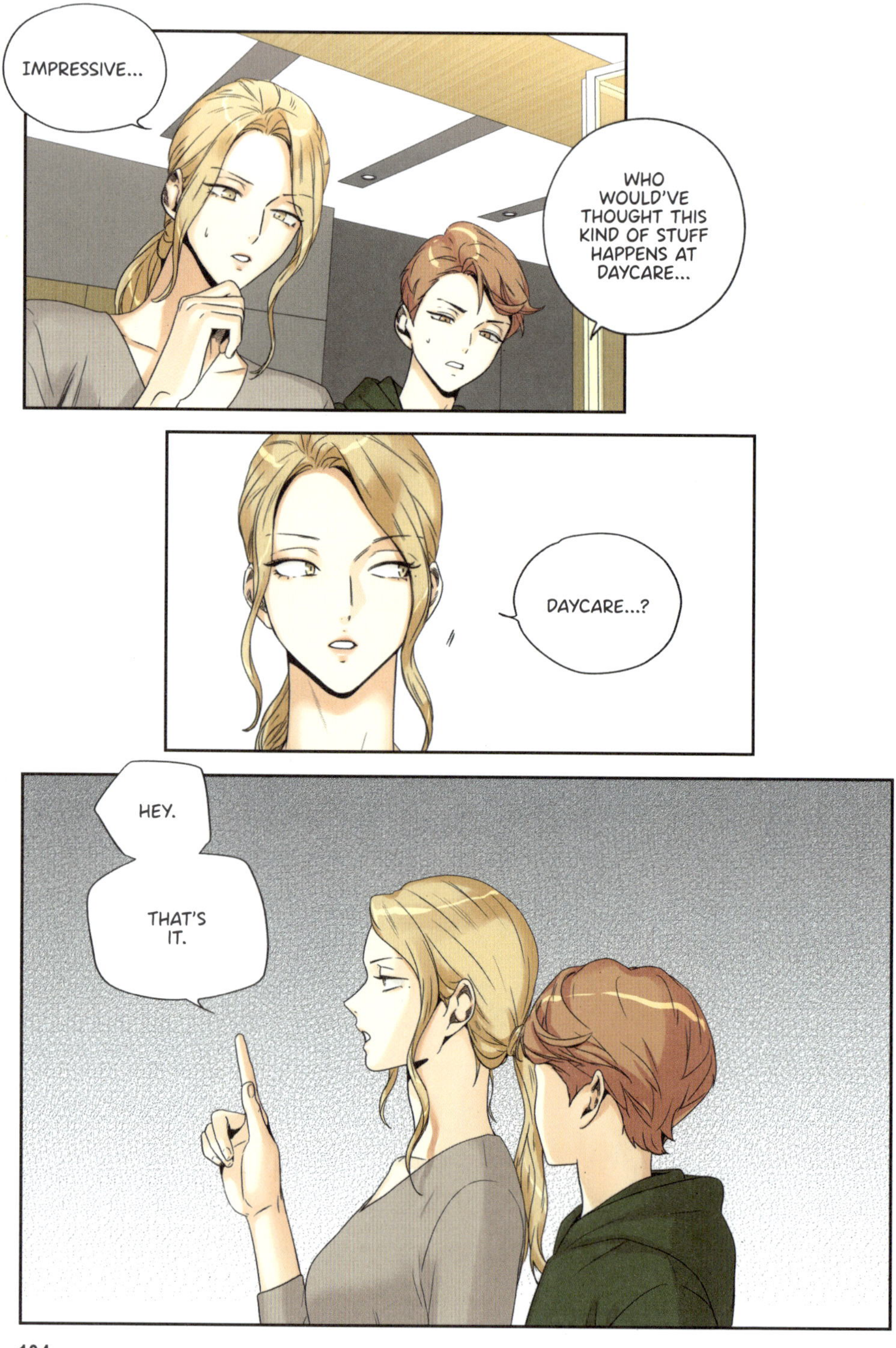
IMPRESSIVE...
WHO WOULD'VE THOUGHT THIS KIND OF STUFF HAPPENS AT DAYCARE...
DAYCARE...?
HEY.
THAT'S IT.

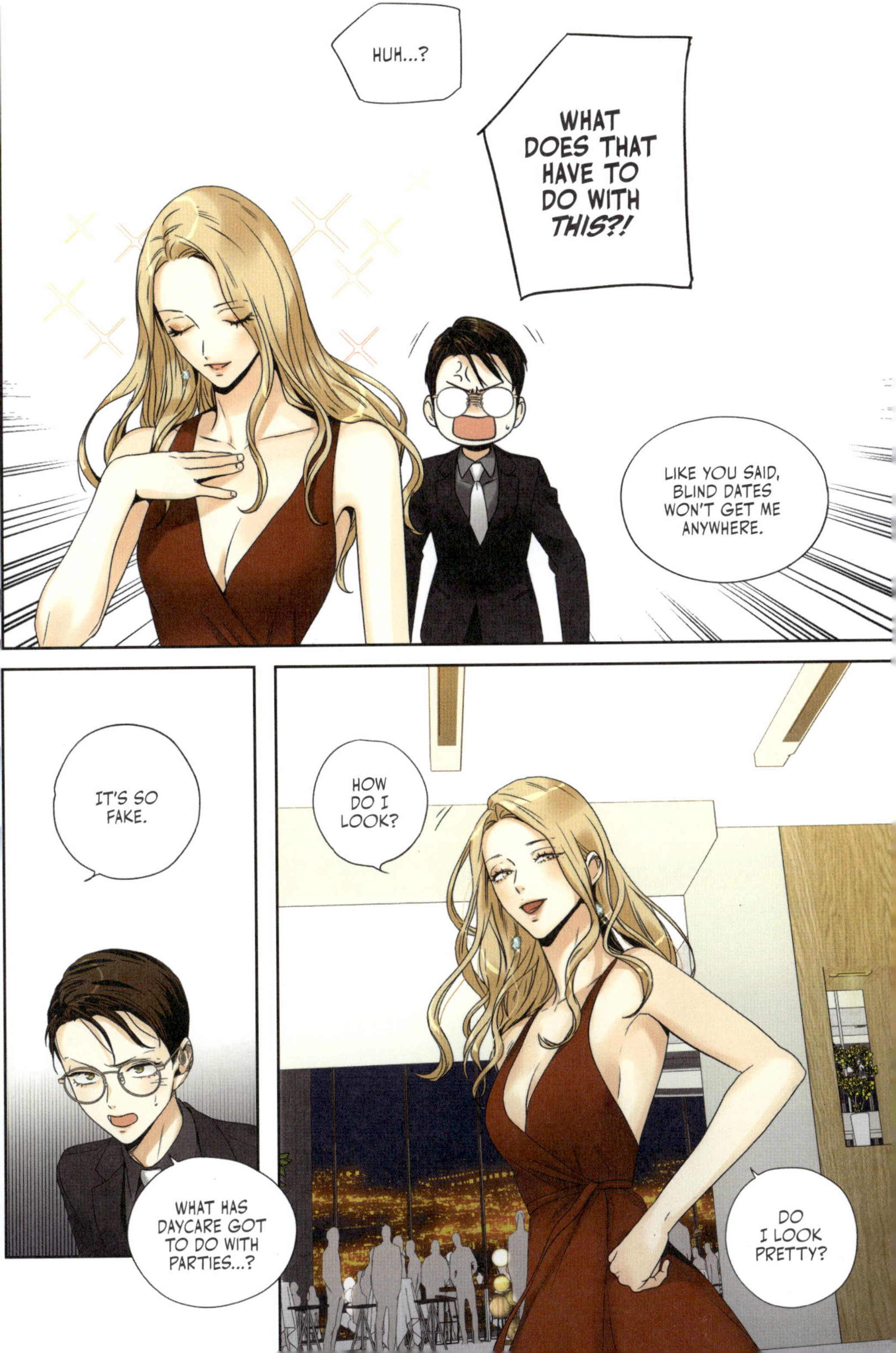
HUH...?
WHAT DOES THAT HAVE TO DO WITH *THIS?!*
LIKE YOU SAID, BLIND DATES WON'T GET ME ANYWHERE.
IT'S SO FAKE.
WHAT HAS DAYCARE GOT TO DO WITH PARTIES...?
HOW DO I LOOK?
DO I LOOK PRETTY?

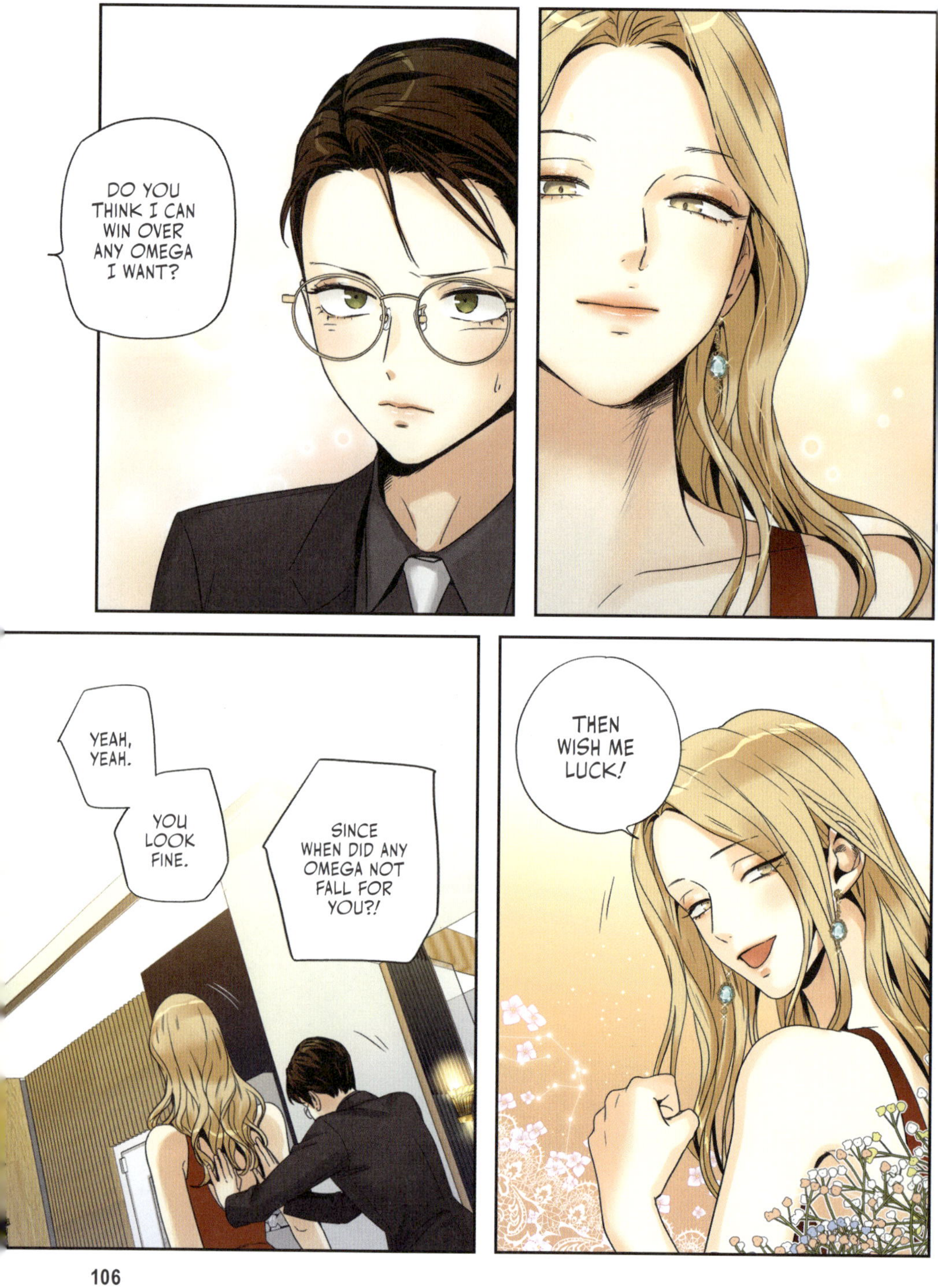
DO YOU THINK I CAN WIN OVER ANY OMEGA I WANT?
YEAH, YEAH.
YOU LOOK FINE.
SINCE WHEN DID ANY OMEGA NOT FALL FOR YOU?!
THEN WISH ME LUCK!

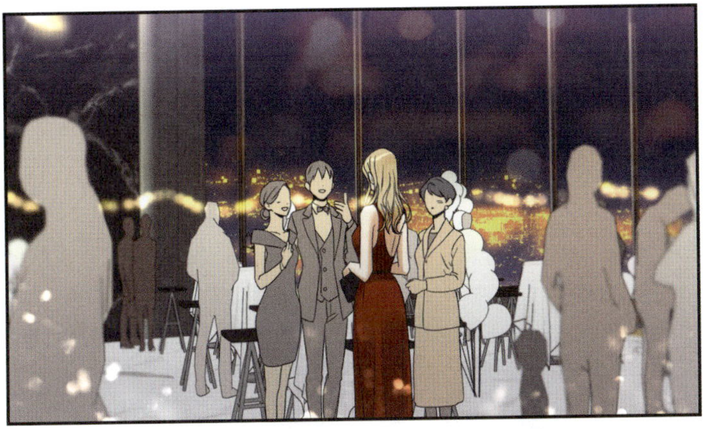

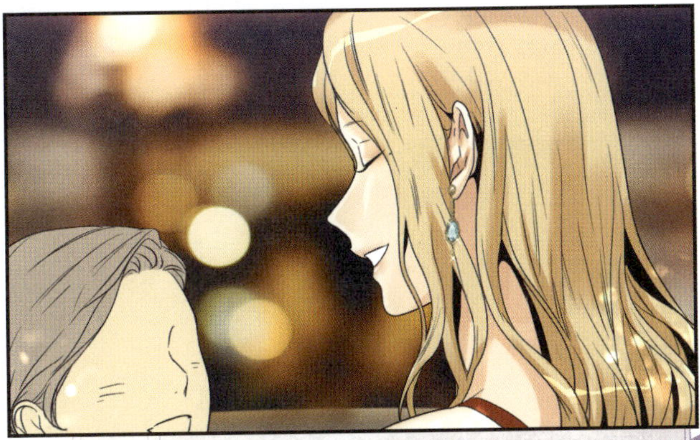

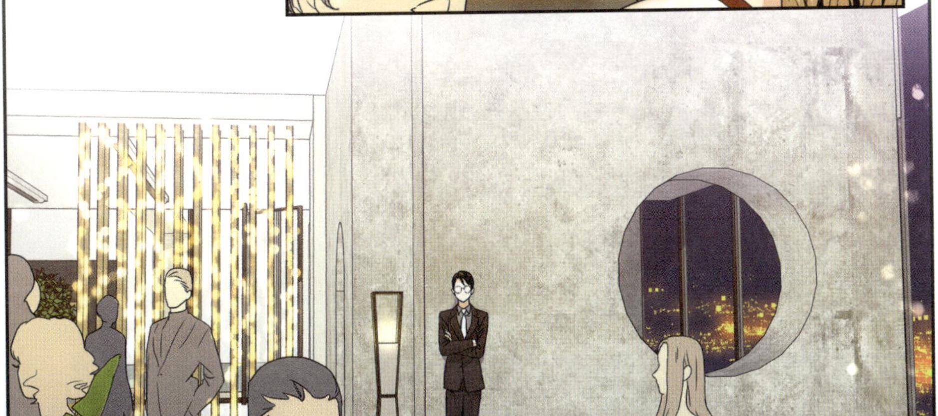

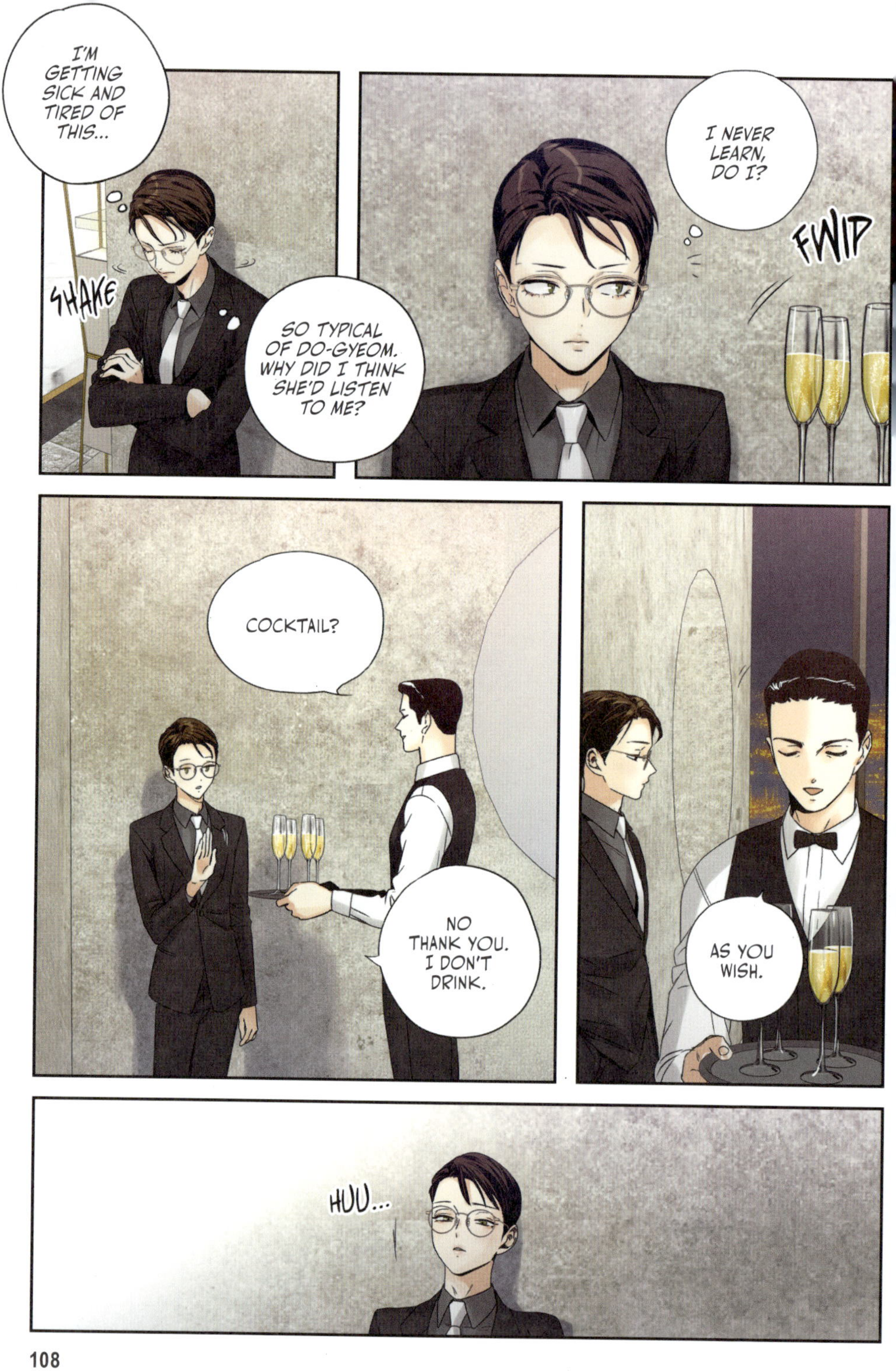
I'M GETTING SICK AND TIRED OF THIS...
SHAKE
SO TYPICAL OF DO-GYEOM. WHY DID I THINK SHE'D LISTEN TO ME?
I NEVER LEARN, DO I?
FWIP
COCKTAIL?
NO THANK YOU. I DON'T DRINK.
AS YOU WISH.
HUU...

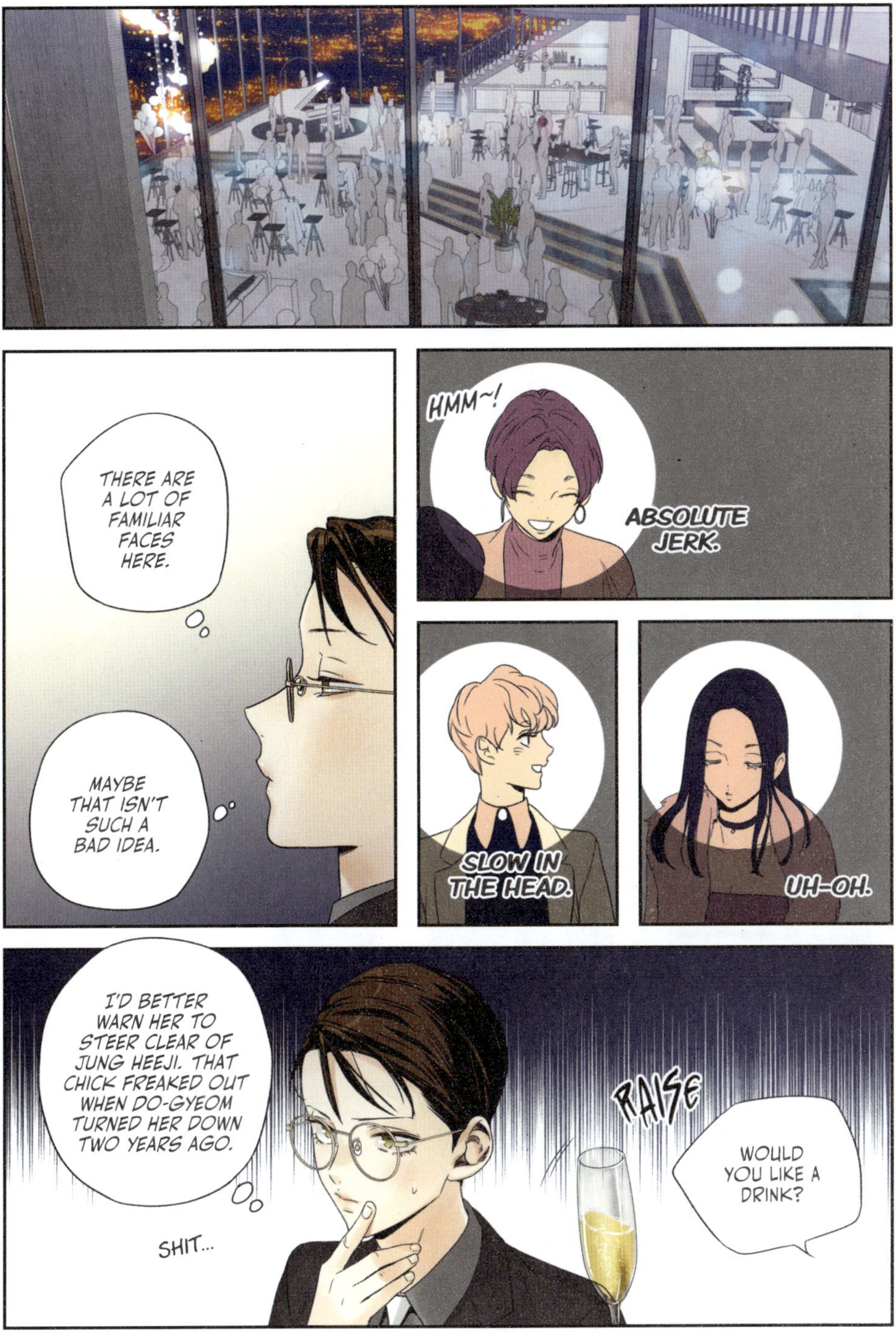
THERE ARE A LOT OF FAMILIAR FACES HERE.
MAYBE THAT ISN'T SUCH A BAD IDEA.
HMM~!
ABSOLUTE JERK.
SLOW IN THE HEAD.
UH-OH.
I'D BETTER WARN HER TO STEER CLEAR OF JUNG HEEJI. THAT CHICK FREAKED OUT WHEN DO-GYEOM TURNED HER DOWN TWO YEARS AGO.
SHIT...
RAISE
WOULD YOU LIKE A DRINK?

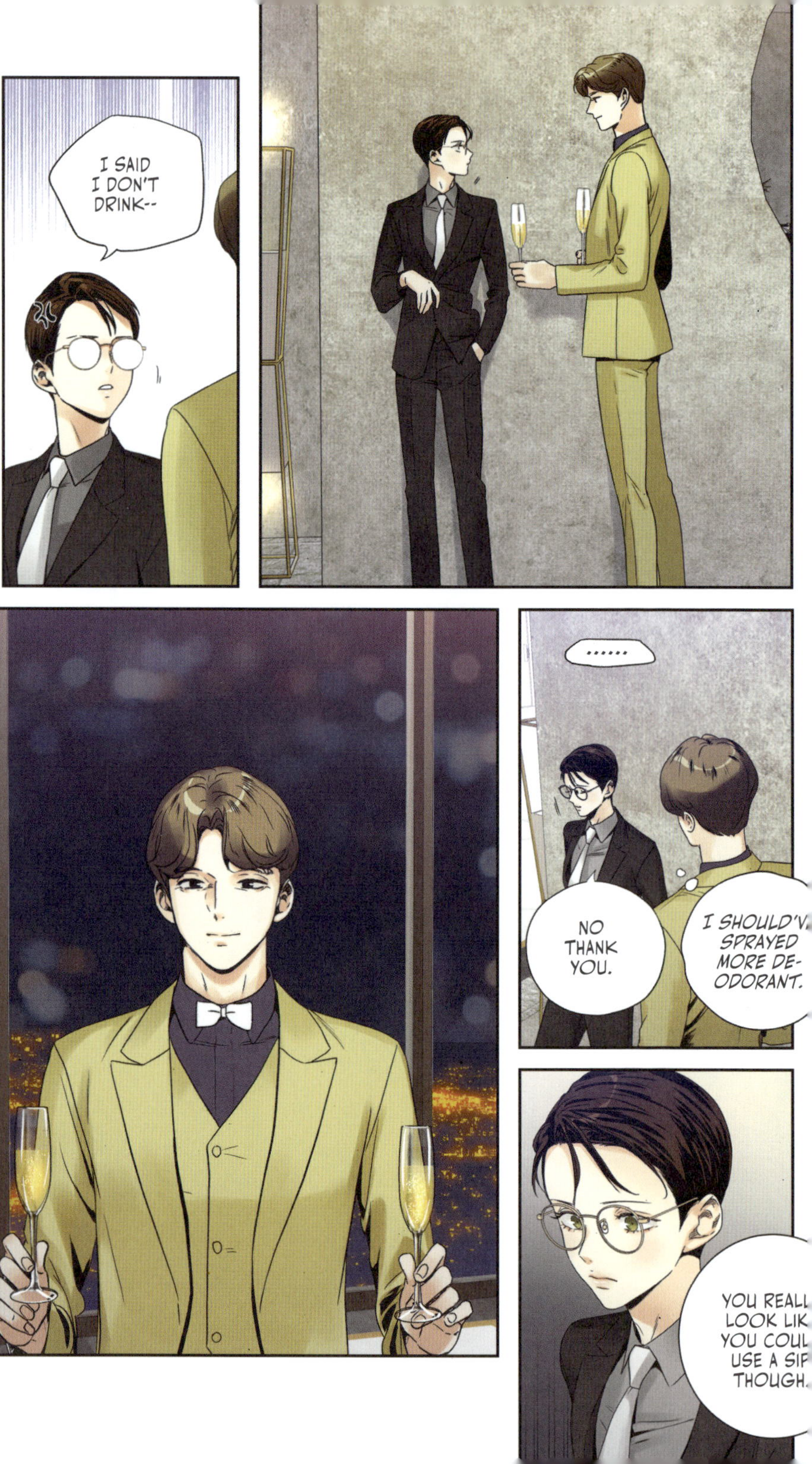
I SAID I DON'T DRINK--
......
NO THANK YOU.
I SHOULD'V SPRAYED MORE DE-ODORANT.
YOU REALL LOOK LIK YOU COUL USE A SIF THOUGH.

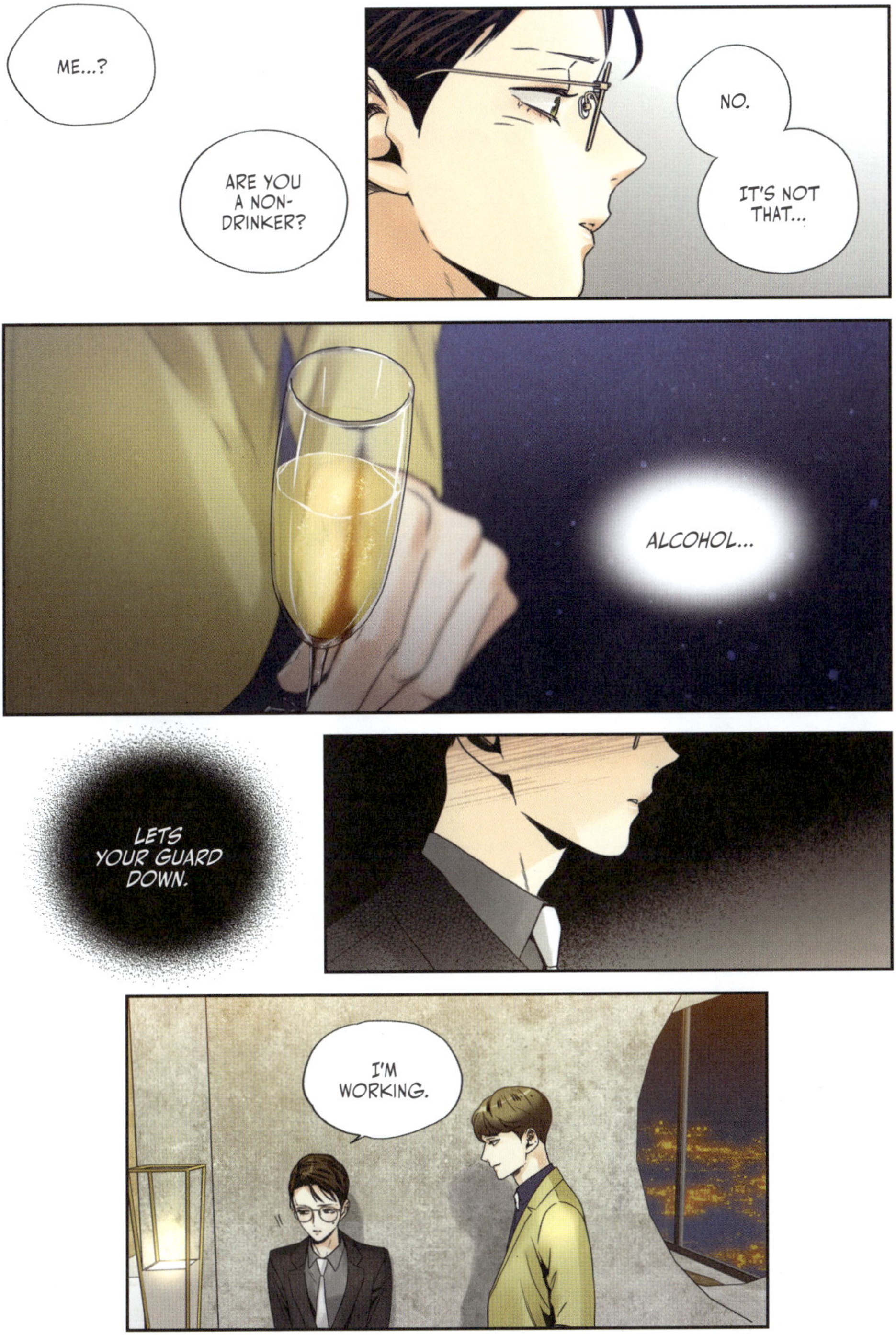
ME...?
ARE YOU A NON-DRINKER?
NO.
IT'S NOT THAT...
ALCOHOL...
LETS YOUR GUARD DOWN.
I'M WORKING.

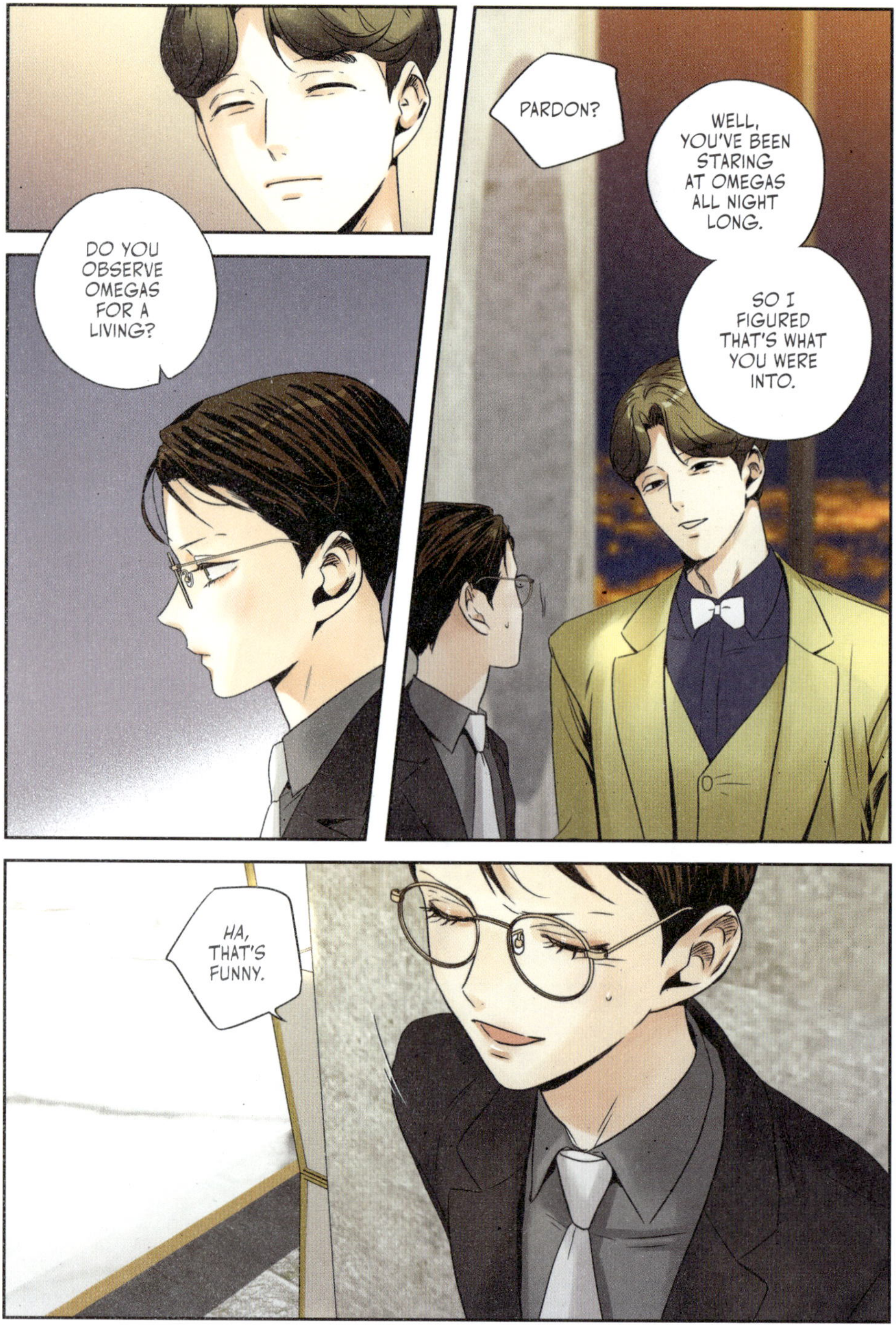
DO YOU OBSERVE OMEGAS FOR A LIVING?
PARDON?
WELL, YOU'VE BEEN STARING AT OMEGAS ALL NIGHT LONG.
SO I FIGURED THAT'S WHAT YOU WERE INTO.
HA, THAT'S FUNNY.

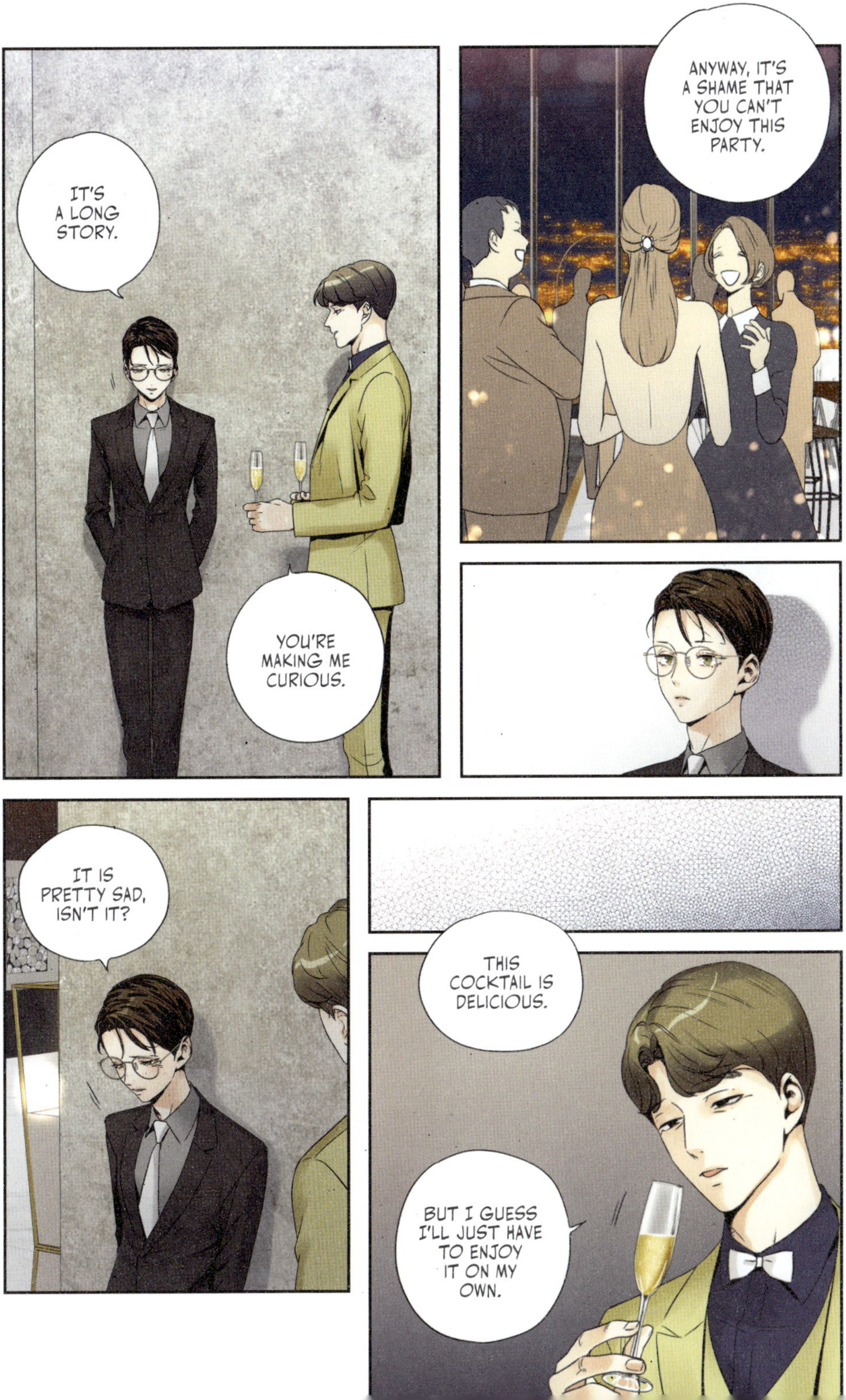
IT'S A LONG STORY.
YOU'RE MAKING ME CURIOUS.
ANYWAY, IT'S A SHAME THAT YOU CAN'T ENJOY THIS PARTY.
IT IS PRETTY SAD, ISN'T IT?
THIS COCKTAIL IS DELICIOUS.
BUT I GUESS I'LL JUST HAVE TO ENJOY IT ON MY OWN.

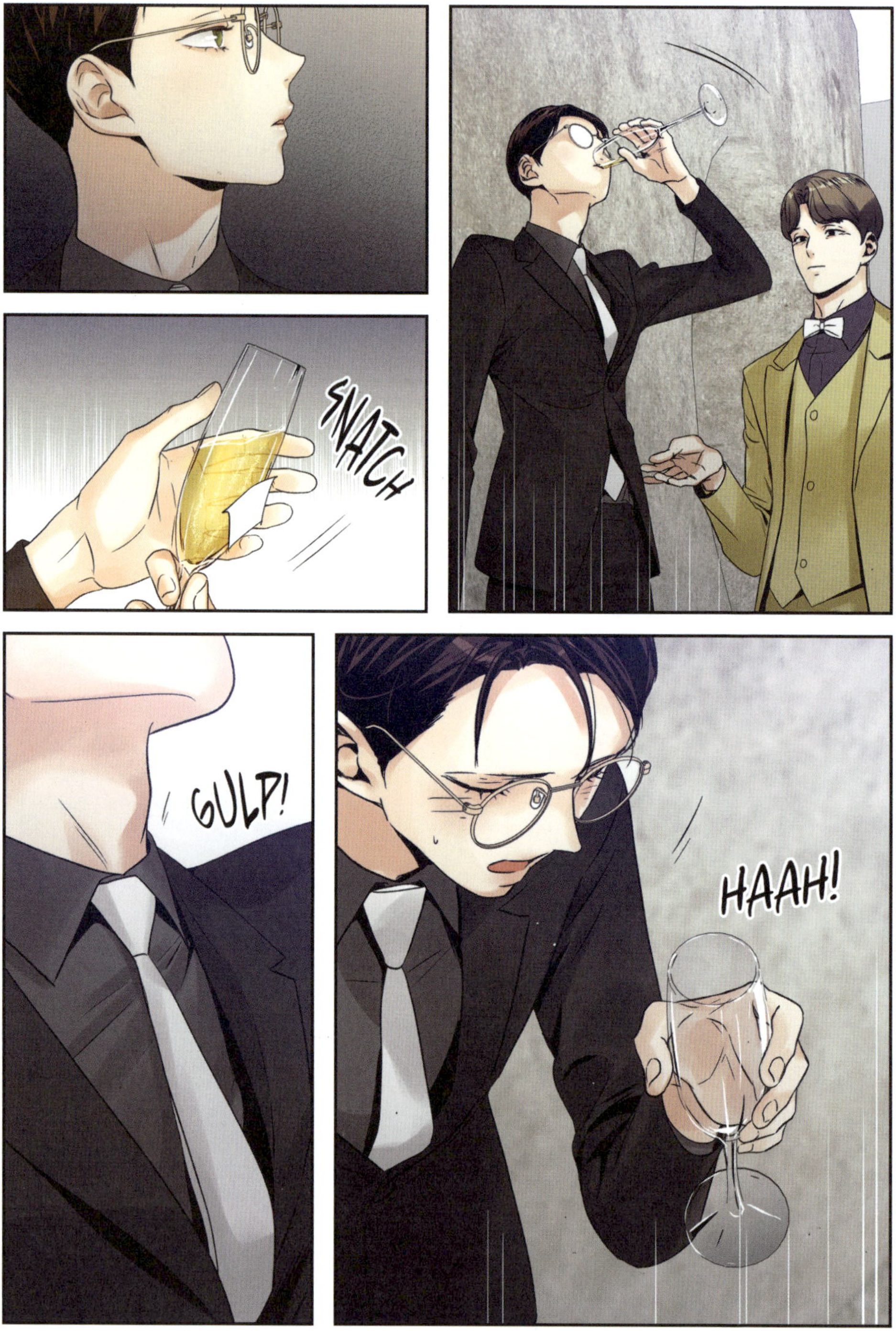
SNATCH
GULP!
HAAH!

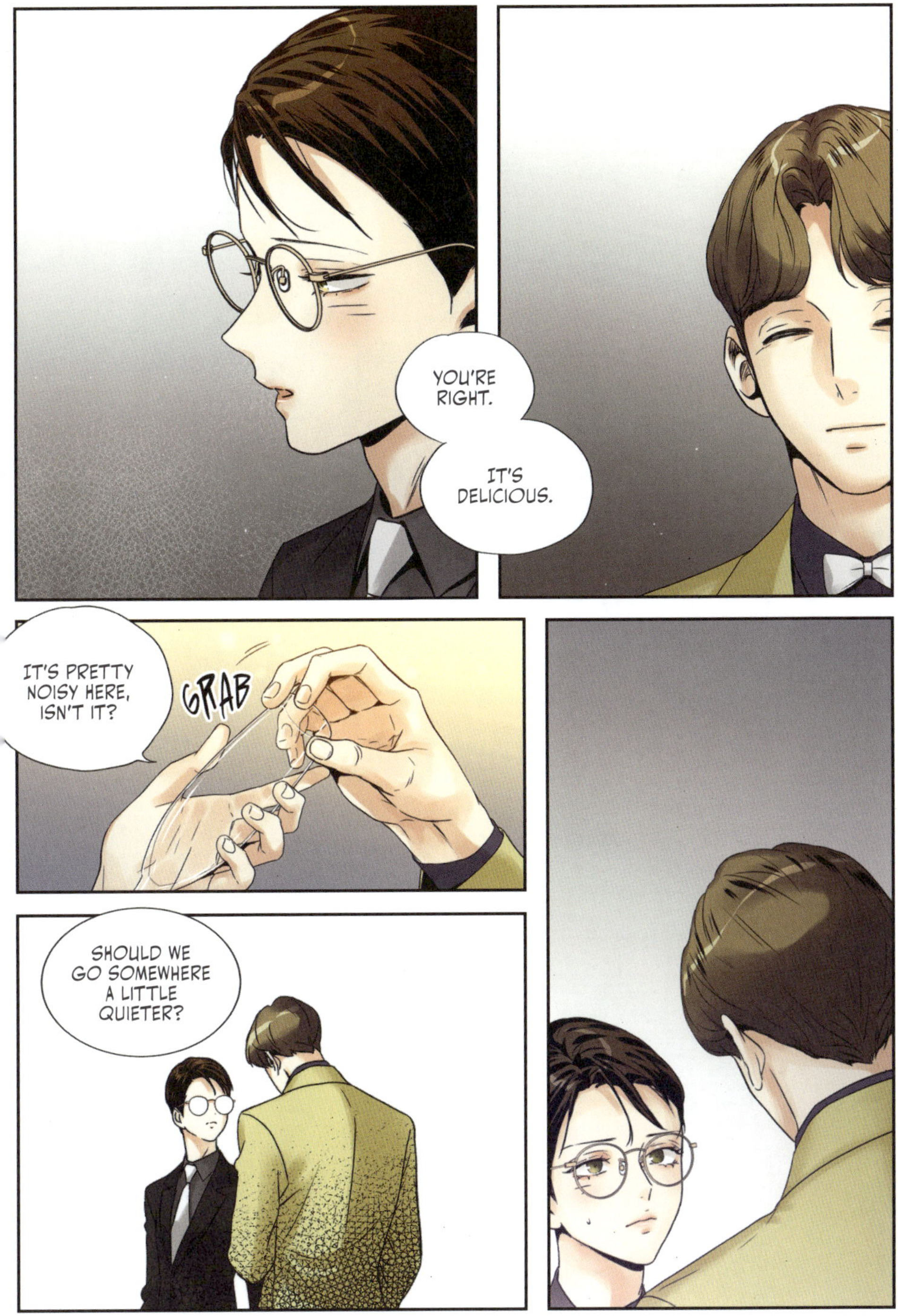
YOU'RE RIGHT.
IT'S DELICIOUS.
IT'S PRETTY NOISY HERE, ISN'T IT?
GRAB
SHOULD WE GO SOMEWHERE A LITTLE QUIETER?

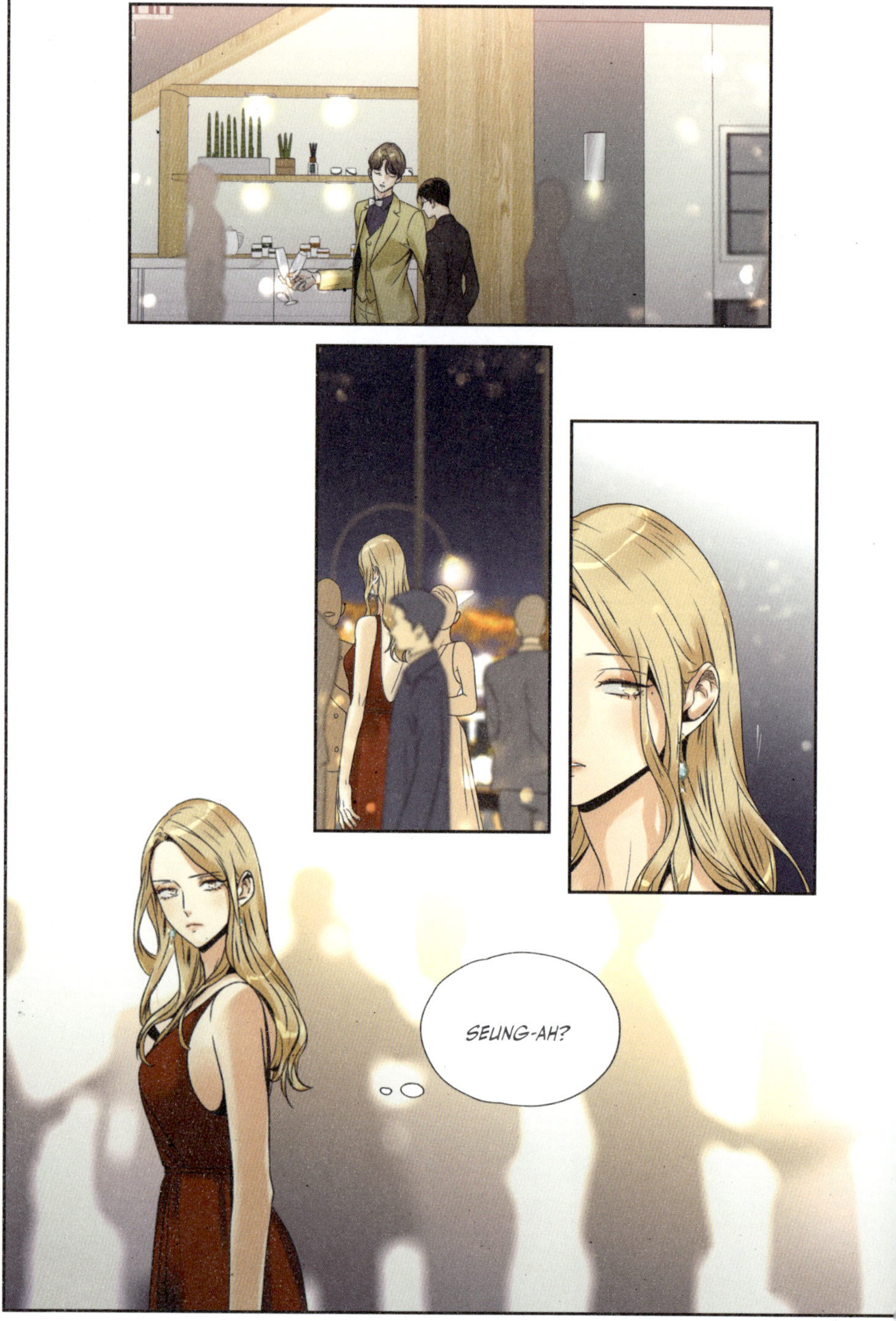
SEUNG-AH?

Love is an Illusion!
The Queen

Love is an Illusion!
The Queen

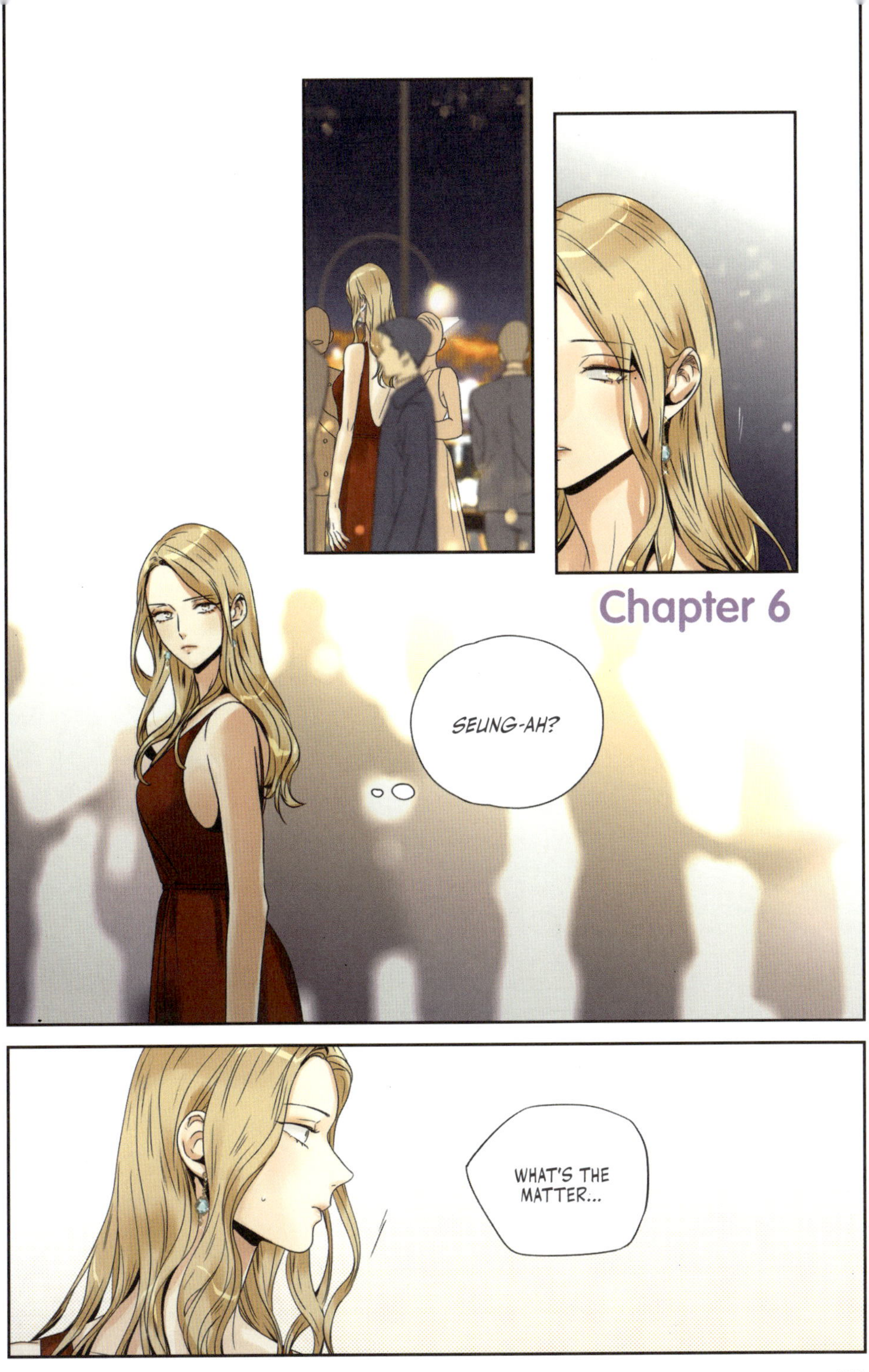
Chapter 6
SEUNG-AH?
WHAT'S THE MATTER...

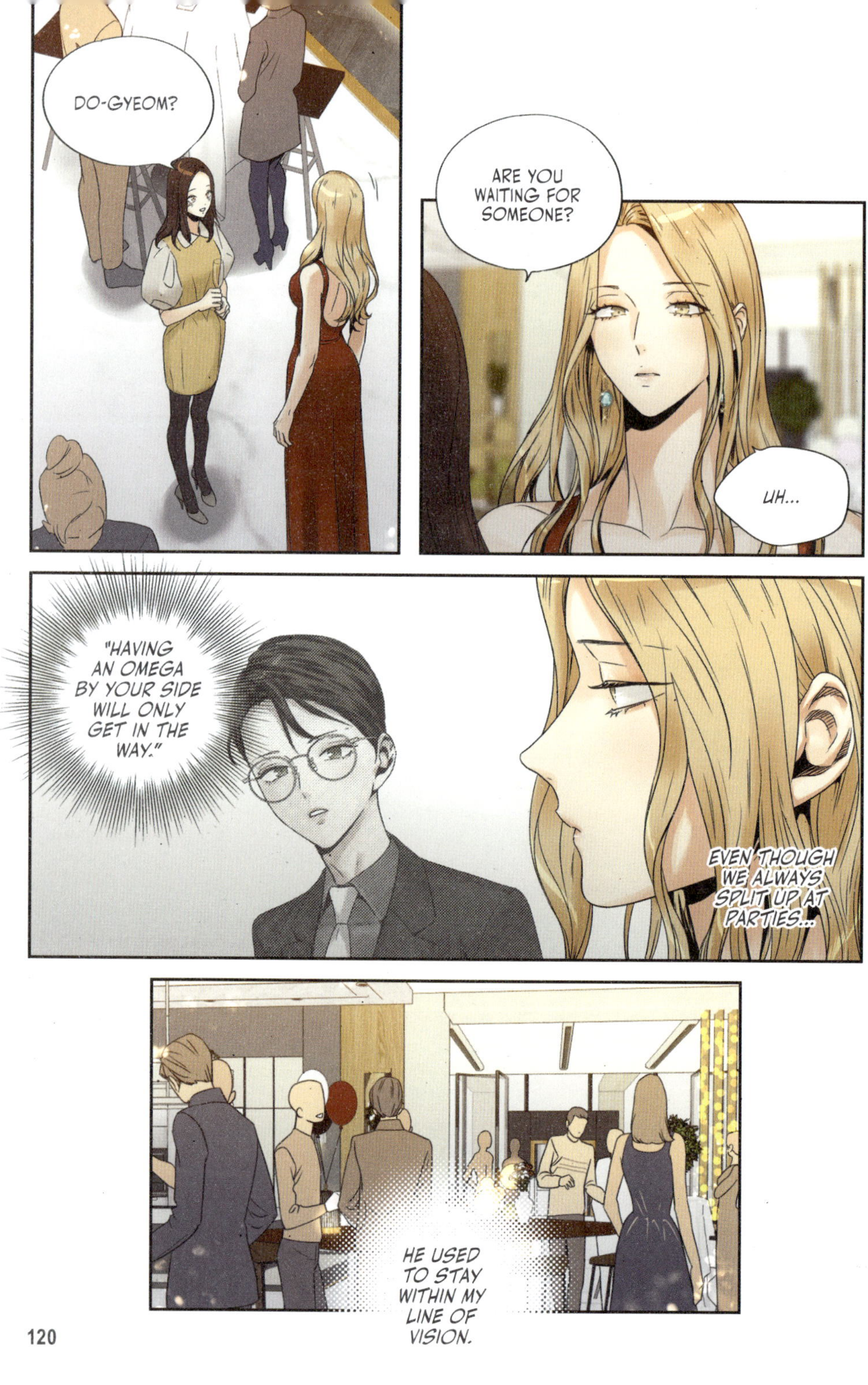
DO-GYEOM?
ARE YOU WAITING FOR SOMEONE?
UH...
"HAVING AN OMEGA BY YOUR SIDE WILL ONLY GET IN THE WAY."
EVEN THOUGH WE ALWAYS SPLIT UP AT PARTIES...
HE USED TO STAY WITHIN MY LINE OF VISION.

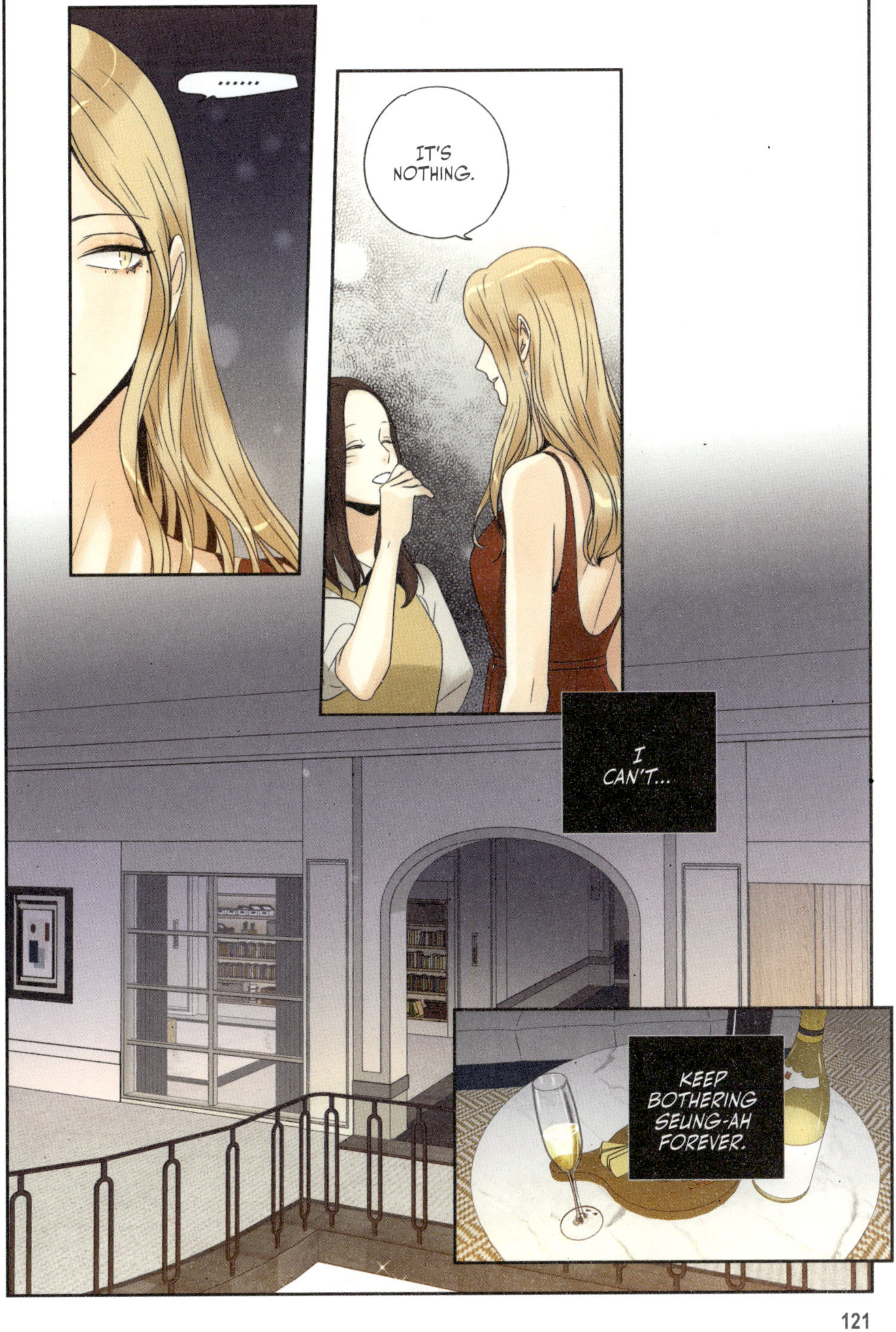
......
IT'S NOTHING.
I CAN'T...
KEEP BOTHERING SEUNG-AH FOREVER.

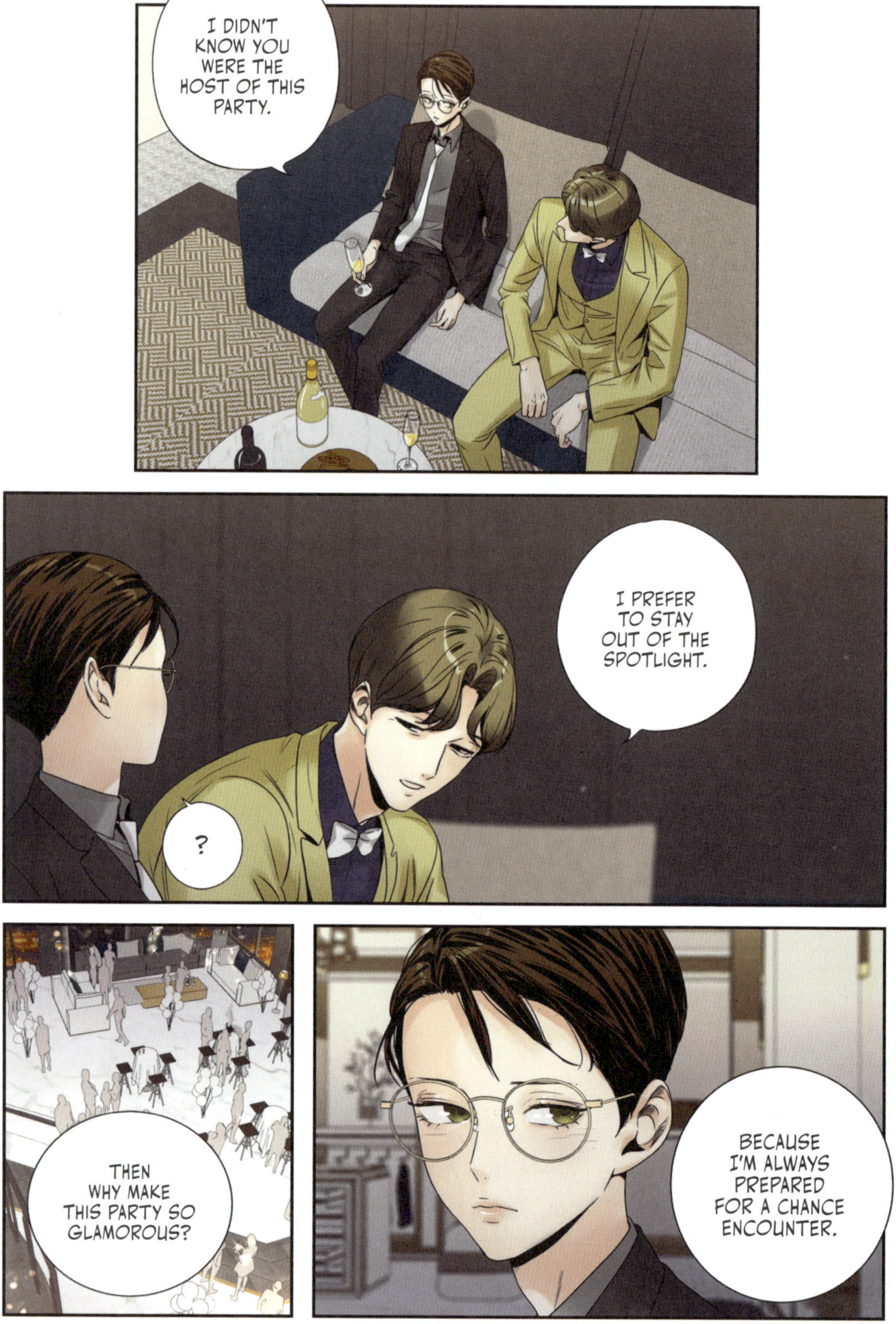
I DIDN'T KNOW YOU WERE THE HOST OF THIS PARTY.
I PREFER TO STAY OUT OF THE SPOTLIGHT.
?
THEN WHY MAKE THIS PARTY SO GLAMOROUS?
BECAUSE I'M ALWAYS PREPARED FOR A CHANCE ENCOUNTER.

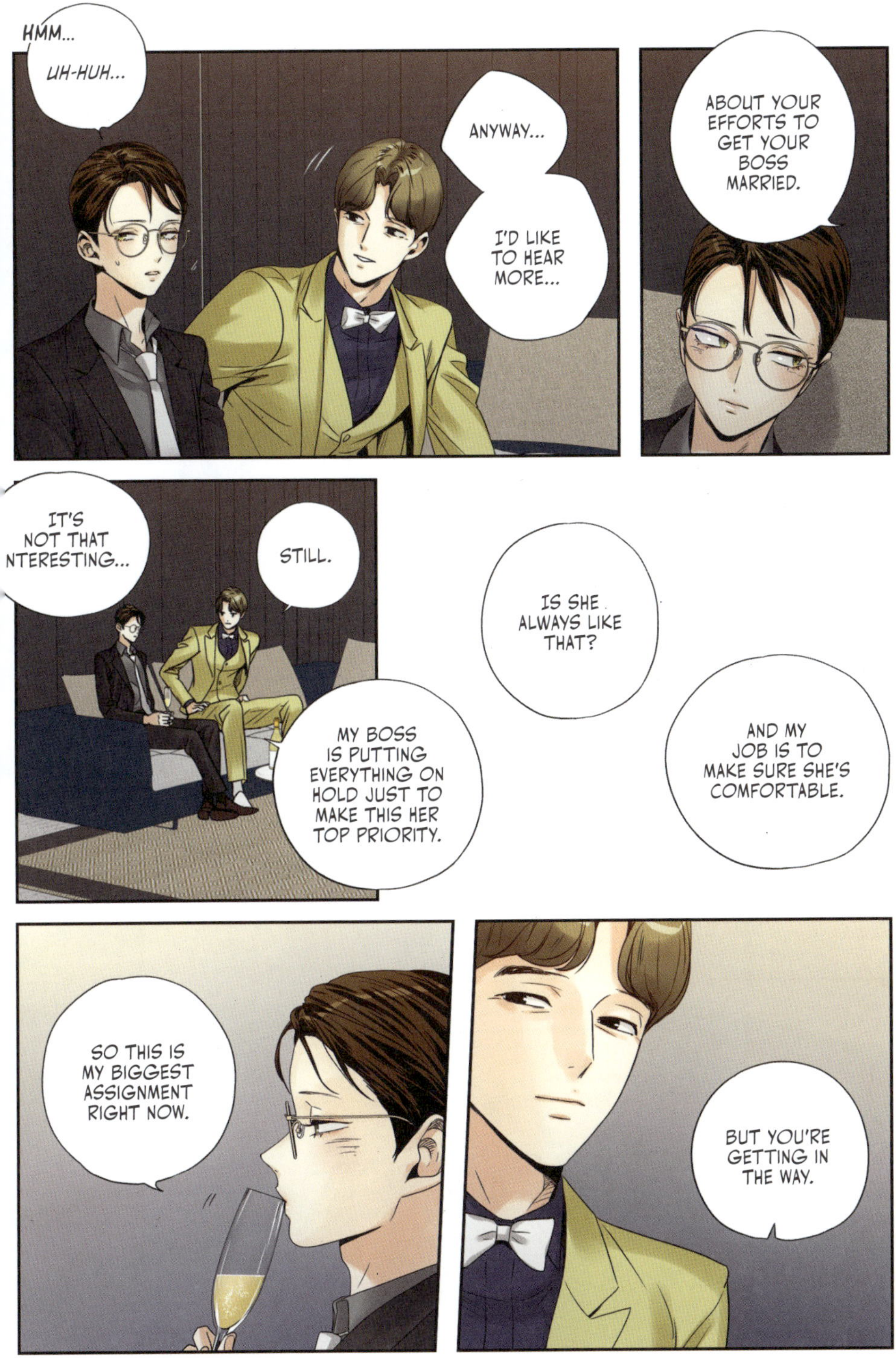
HMM...
UH-HUH...
ANYWAY...
I'D LIKE TO HEAR MORE...
ABOUT YOUR EFFORTS TO GET YOUR BOSS MARRIED.
IT'S NOT THAT NTERESTING...
STILL.
IS SHE ALWAYS LIKE THAT?
MY BOSS IS PUTTING EVERYTHING ON HOLD JUST TO MAKE THIS HER TOP PRIORITY.
AND MY JOB IS TO MAKE SURE SHE'S COMFORTABLE.
SO THIS IS MY BIGGEST ASSIGNMENT RIGHT NOW.
BUT YOU'RE GETTING IN THE WAY.

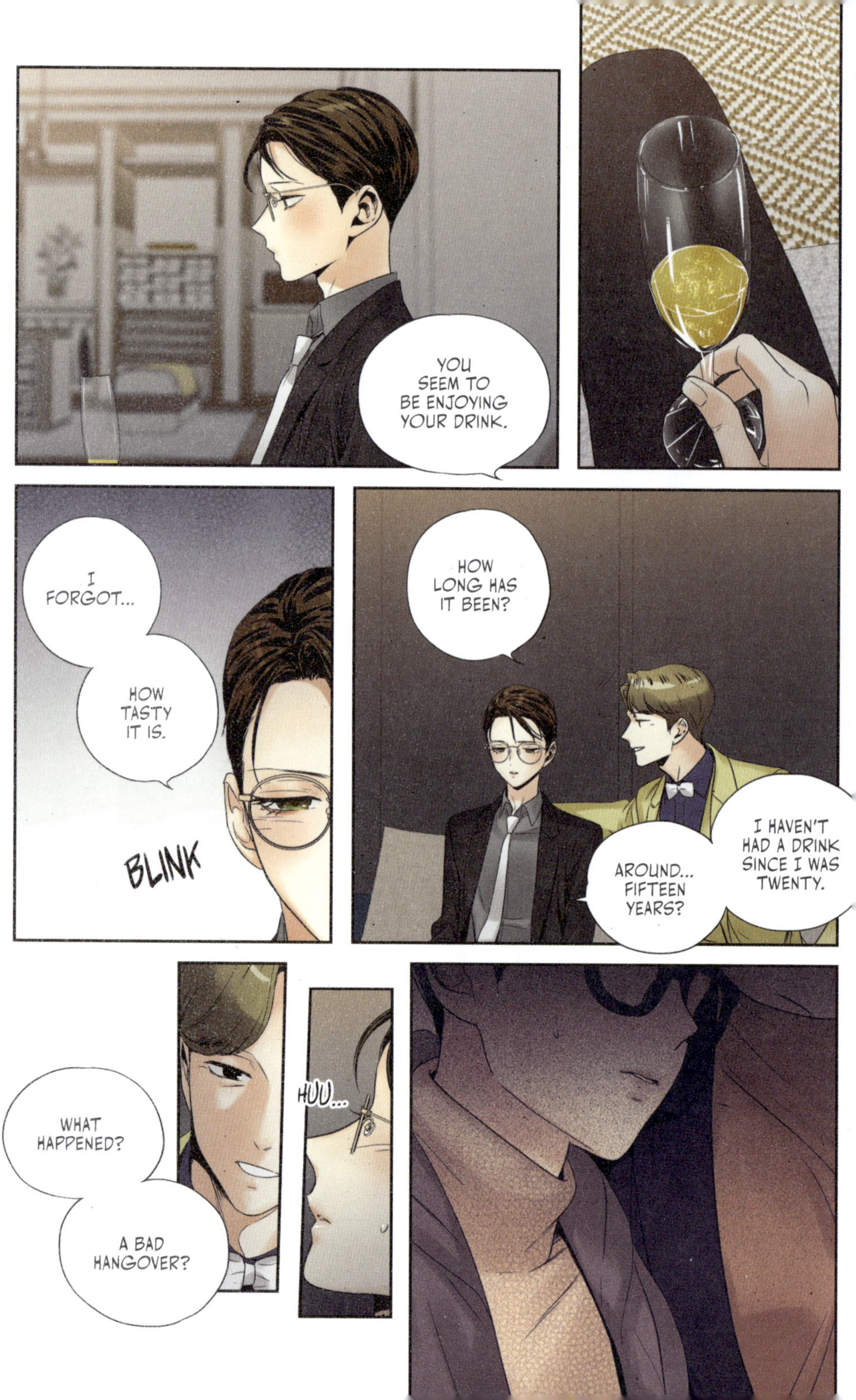
YOU SEEM TO BE ENJOYING YOUR DRINK.
I FORGOT...
HOW TASTY IT IS.
BLINK
HOW LONG HAS IT BEEN?
I HAVEN'T HAD A DRINK SINCE I WAS TWENTY.
AROUND... FIFTEEN YEARS?
WHAT HAPPENED?
A BAD HANGOVER?
HUU...

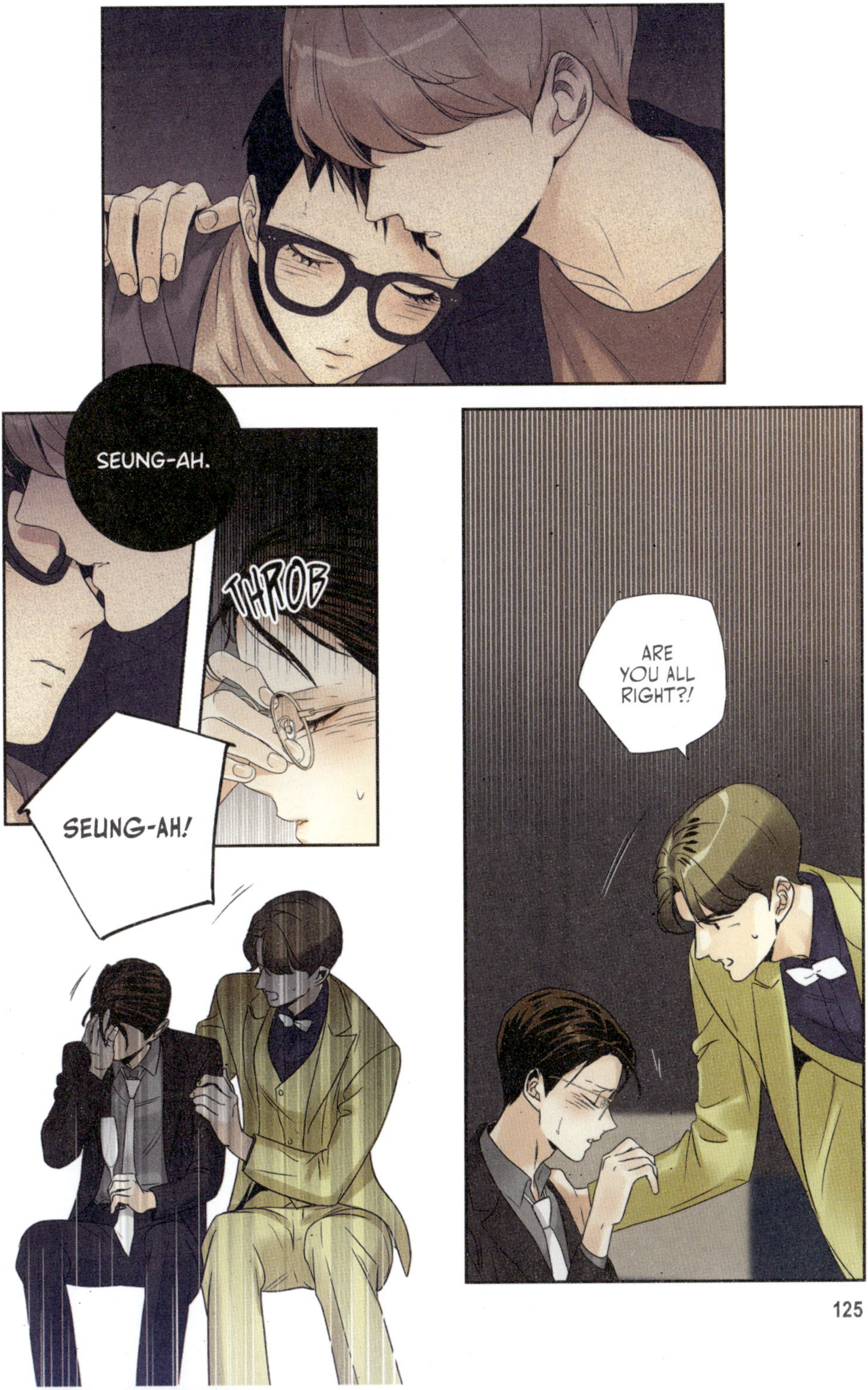
SEUNG-AH.
THROB
SEUNG-AH!
ARE YOU ALL RIGHT?!

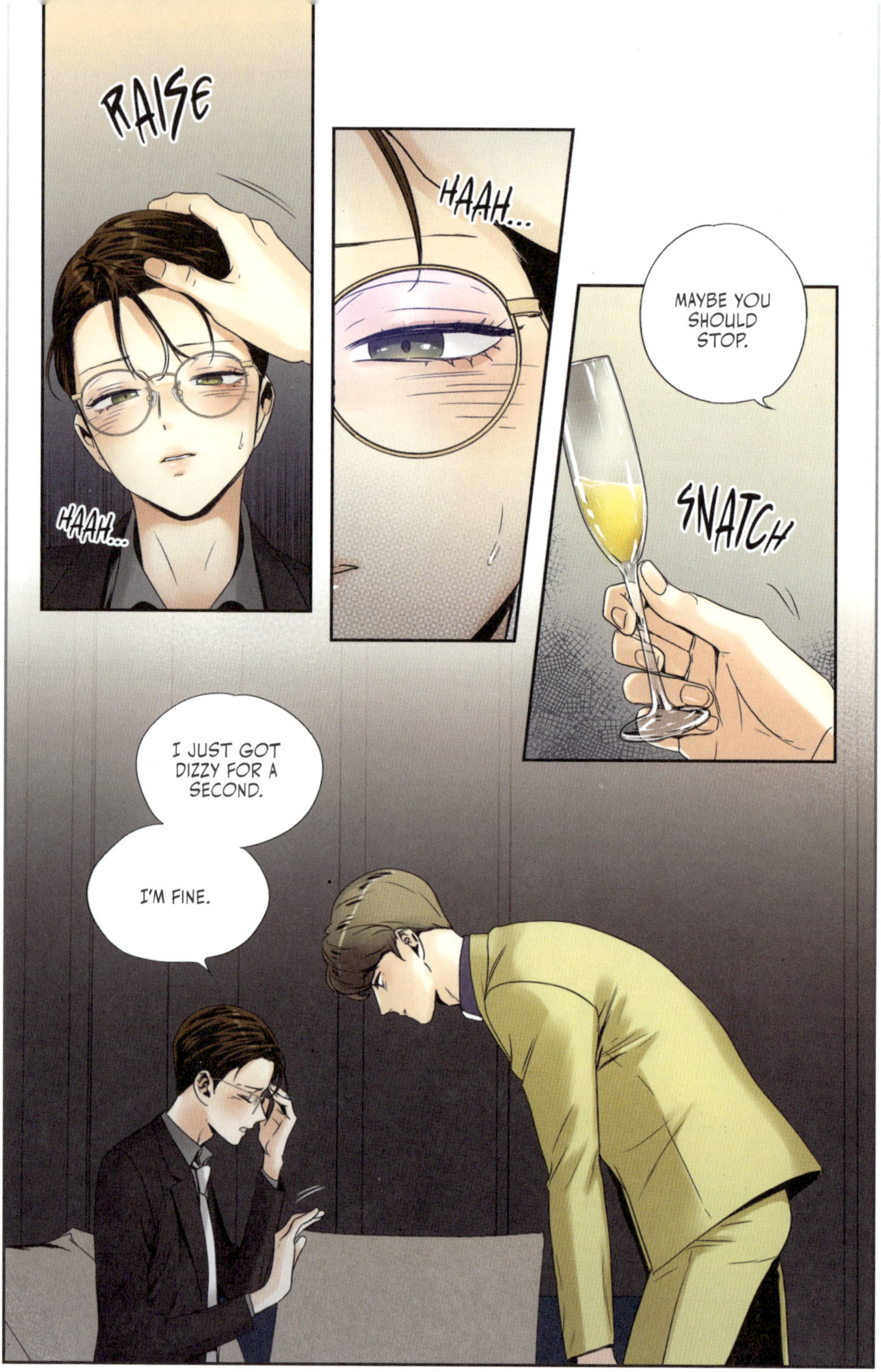
RAISE
HAAH...
HAAH...
MAYBE YOU SHOULD STOP.
SNATCH
I JUST GOT DIZZY FOR A SECOND.
I'M FINE.

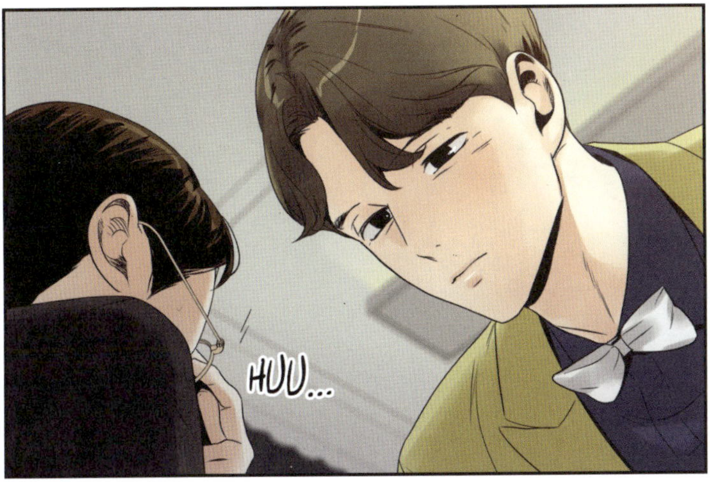
HUU...

I DON'T UNDERSTAND THAT BOSS OF YOURS.

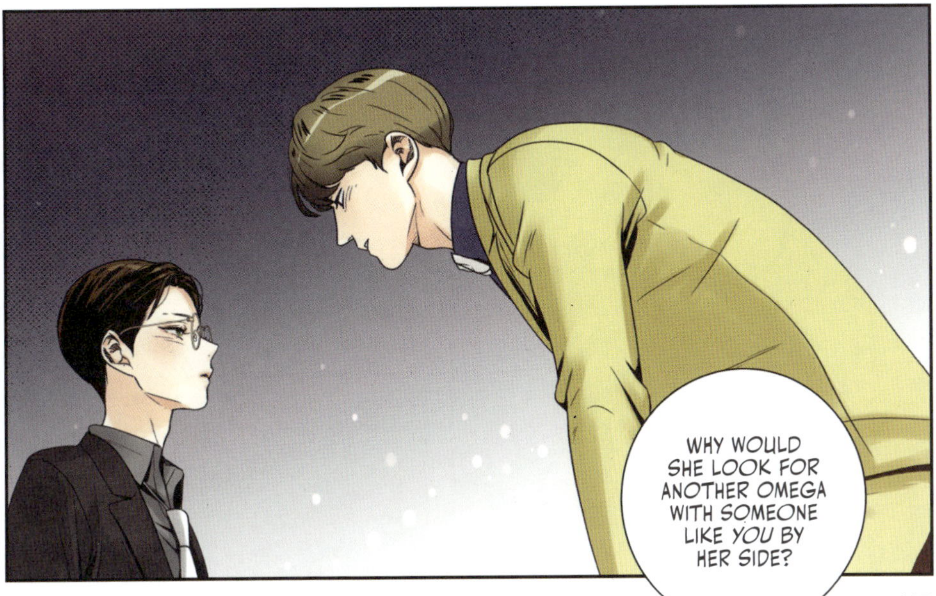
WHY WOULD SHE LOOK FOR ANOTHER OMEGA WITH SOMEONE LIKE *YOU* BY HER SIDE?

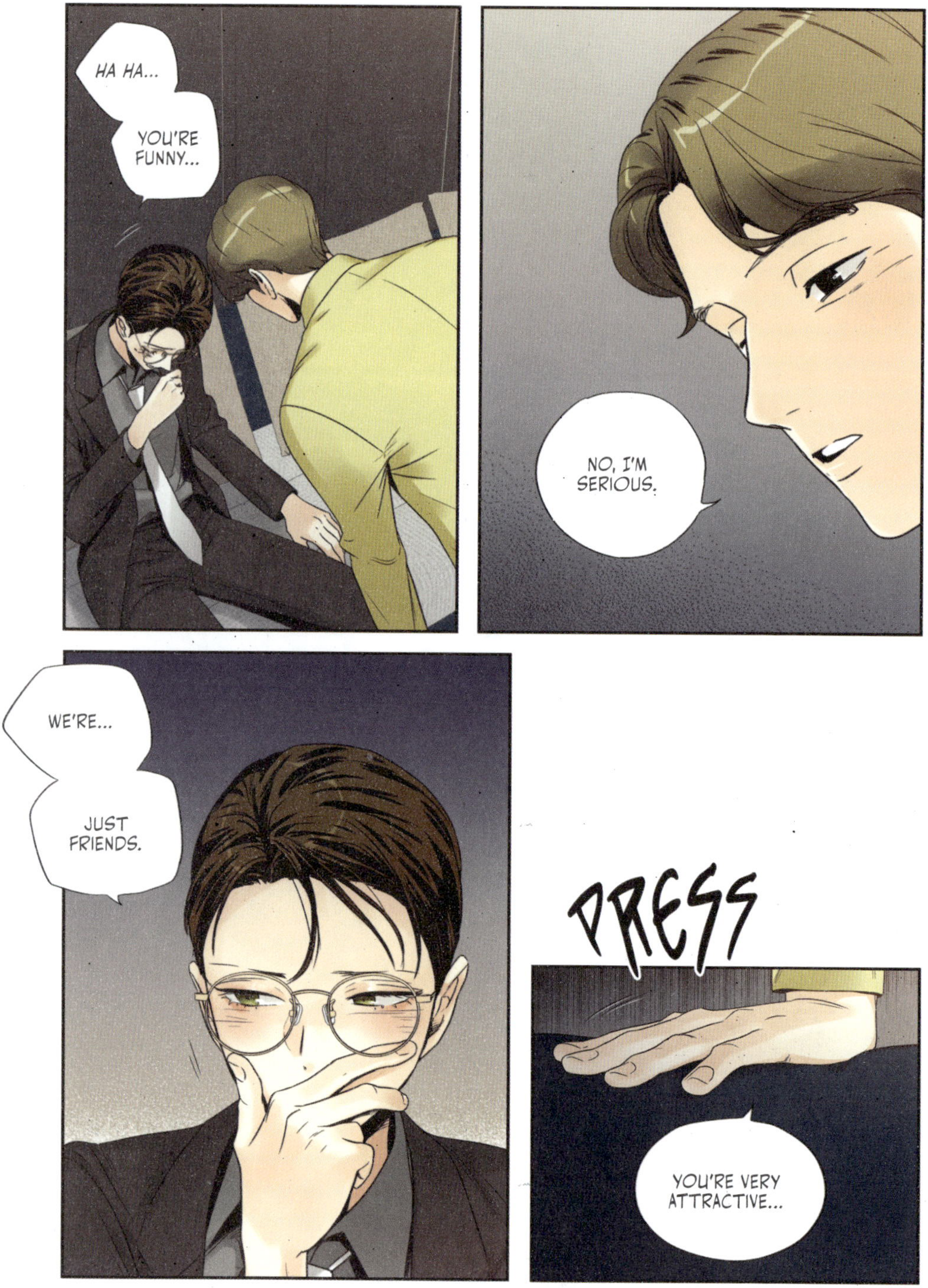
HA HA...
YOU'RE FUNNY...
NO, I'M SERIOUS.
WE'RE...
JUST FRIENDS.
PRESS
YOU'RE VERY ATTRACTIVE...

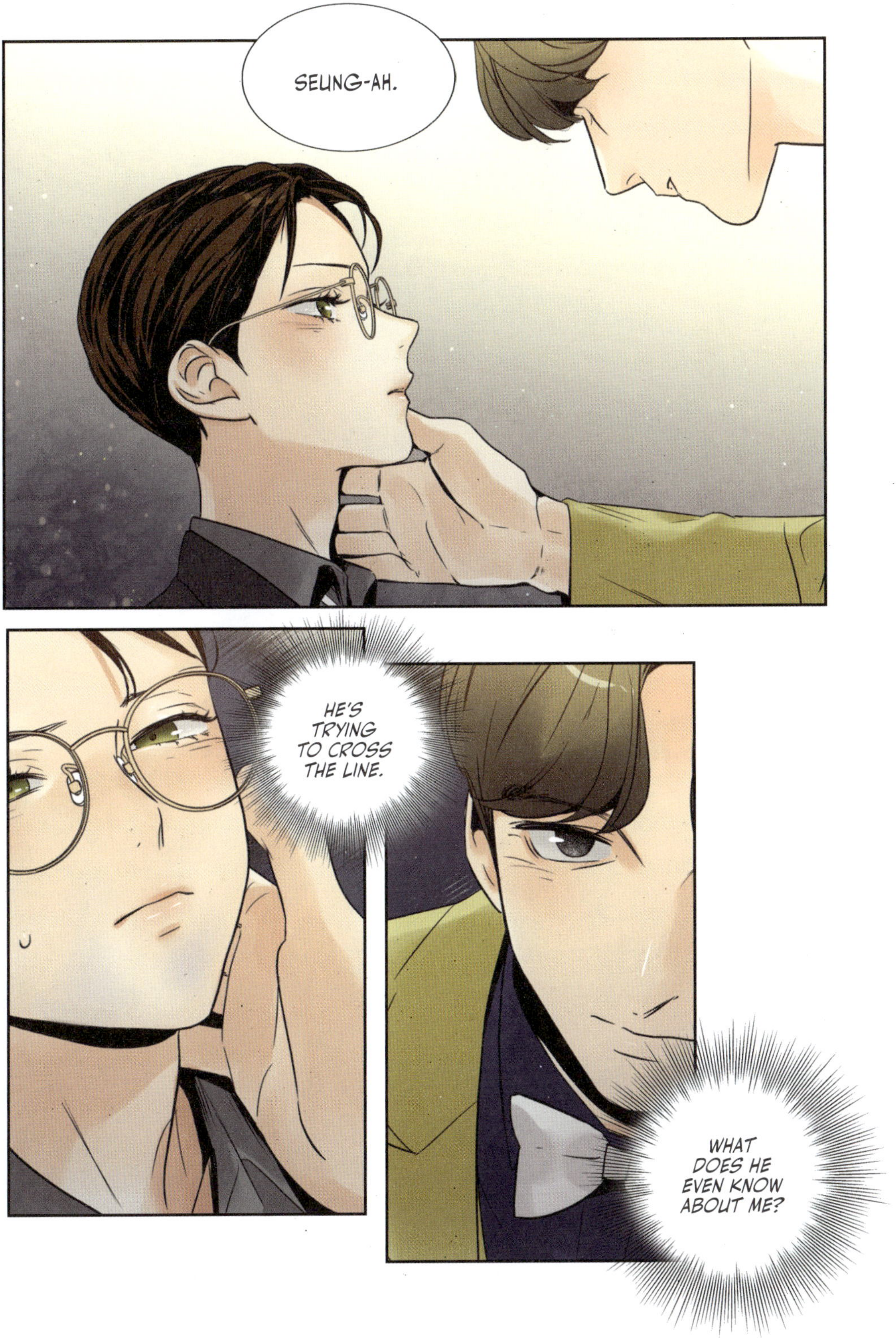
SEUNG-AH.
HE'S TRYING TO CROSS THE LINE.
WHAT DOES HE EVEN KNOW ABOUT ME?

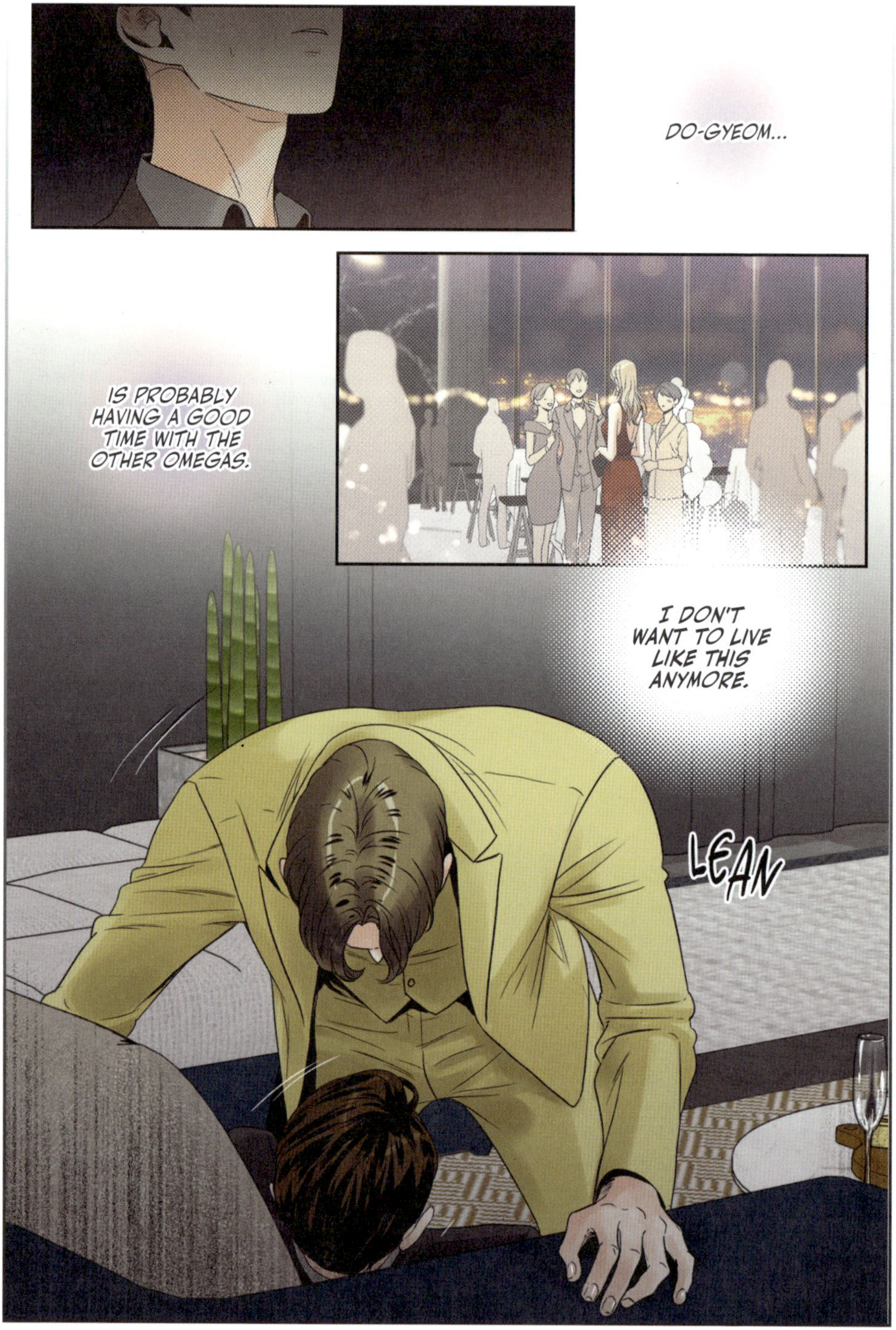

DO-GYEOM...
IS PROBABLY HAVING A GOOD TIME WITH THE OTHER OMEGAS.
I DON'T WANT TO LIVE LIKE THIS ANYMORE.
LEAN

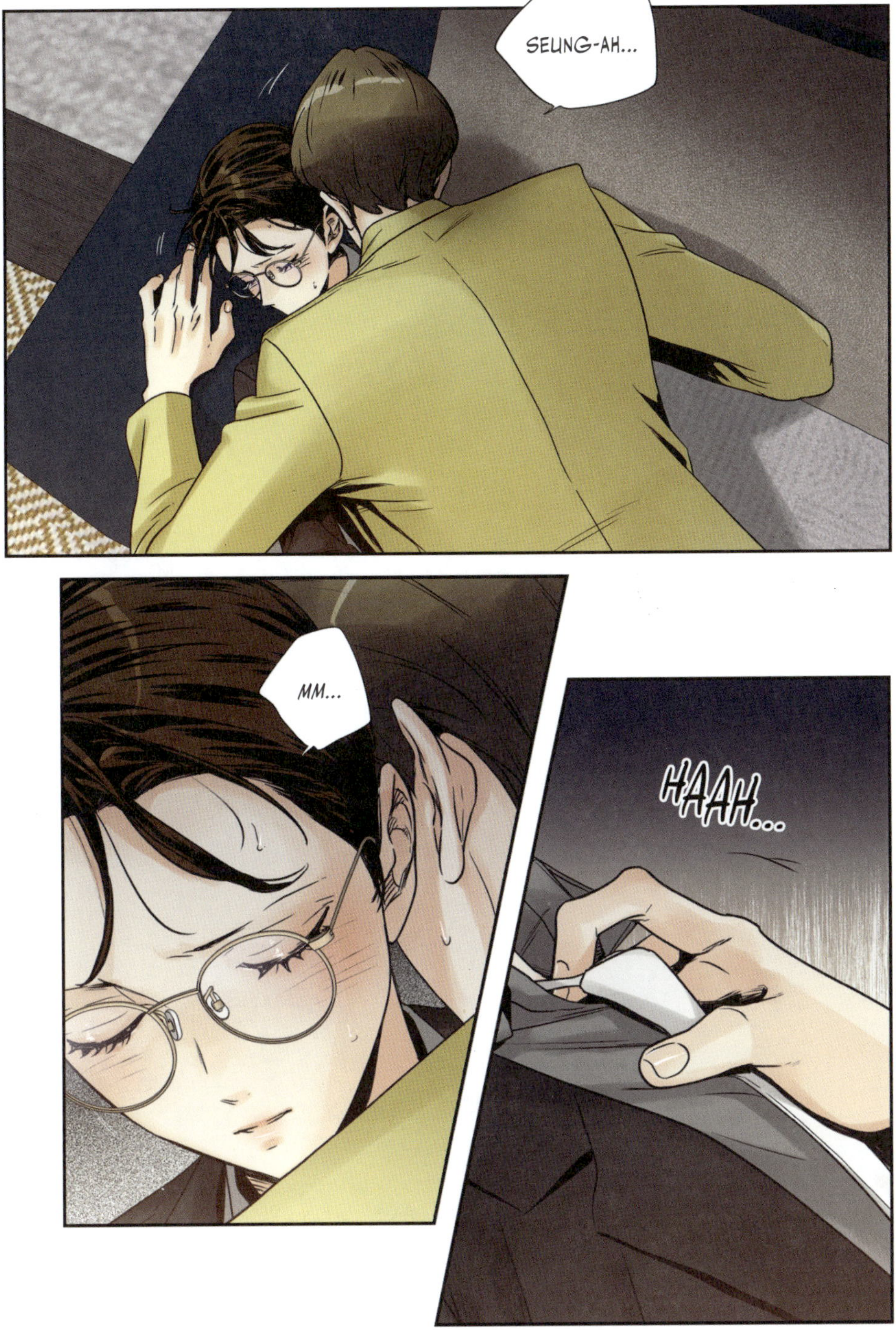
SEUNG-AH...
MM...
HAAH...

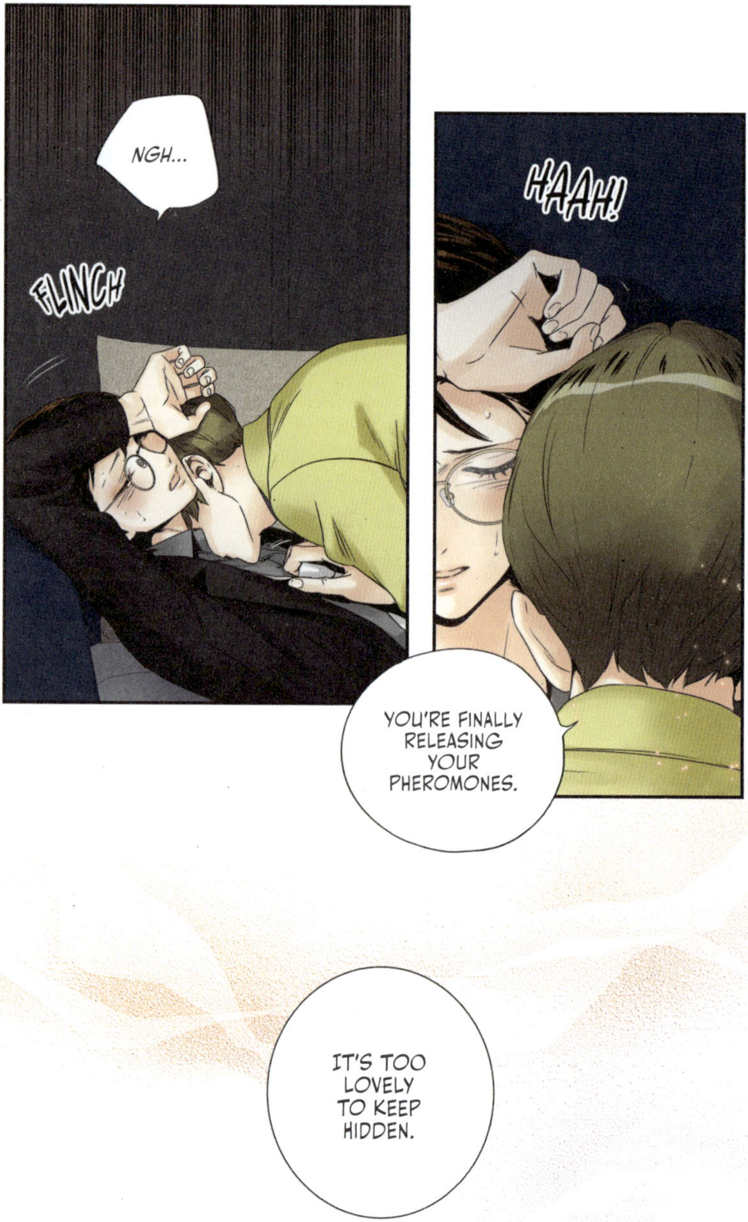
NGH...
FLINCH
HAAAH!
YOU'RE FINALLY RELEASING YOUR PHEROMONES.
IT'S TOO LOVELY TO KEEP HIDDEN.

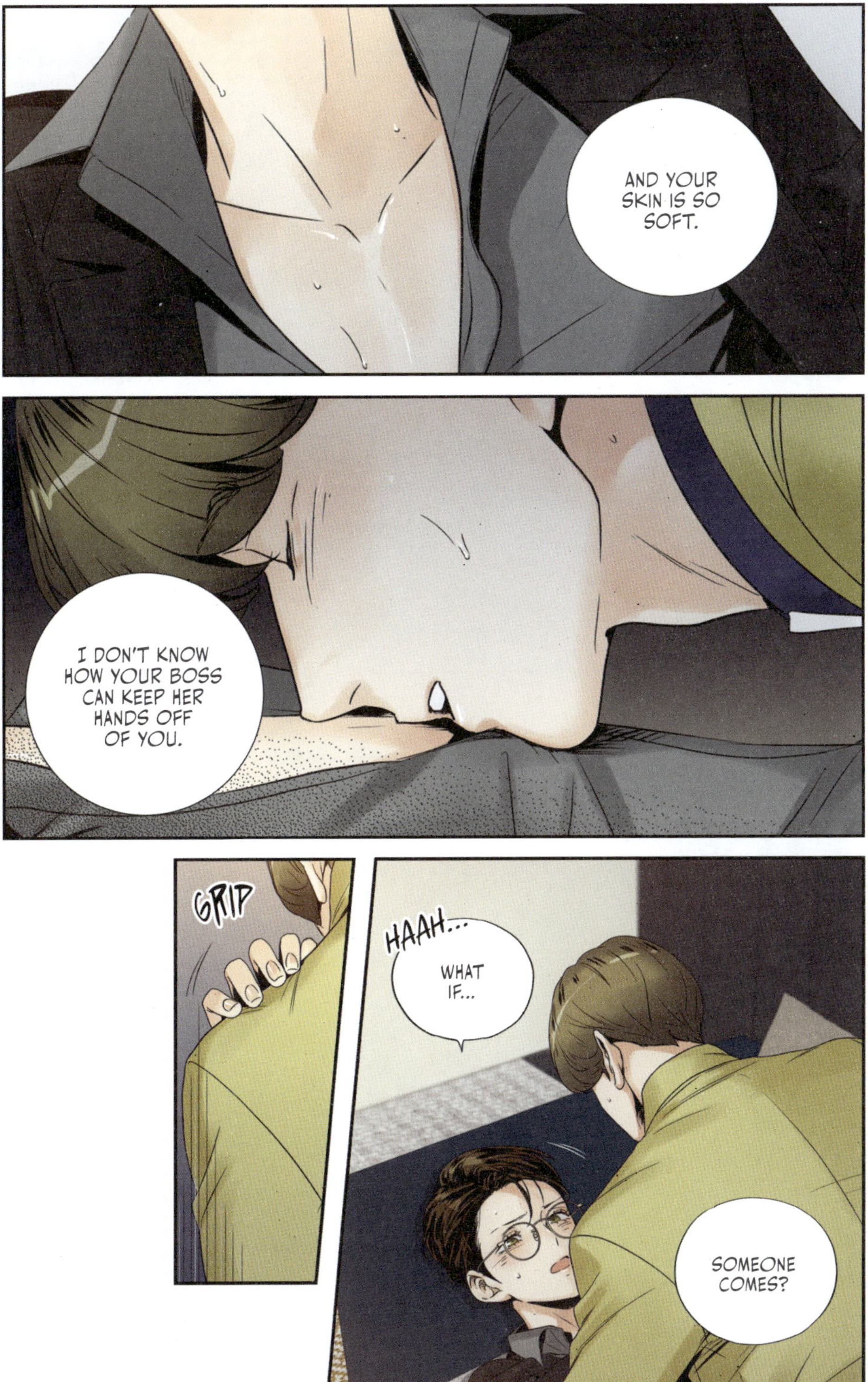
AND YOUR SKIN IS SO SOFT.
I DON'T KNOW HOW YOUR BOSS CAN KEEP HER HANDS OFF OF YOU.
GRIP
HAAH...
WHAT IF...
SOMEONE COMES?

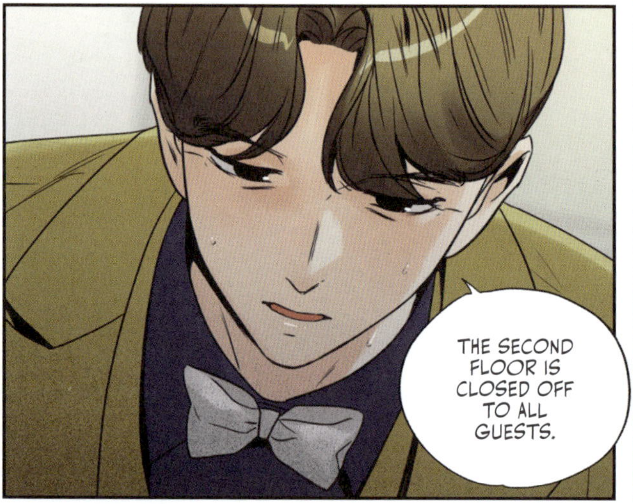
THE SECOND FLOOR IS CLOSED OFF TO ALL GUESTS.

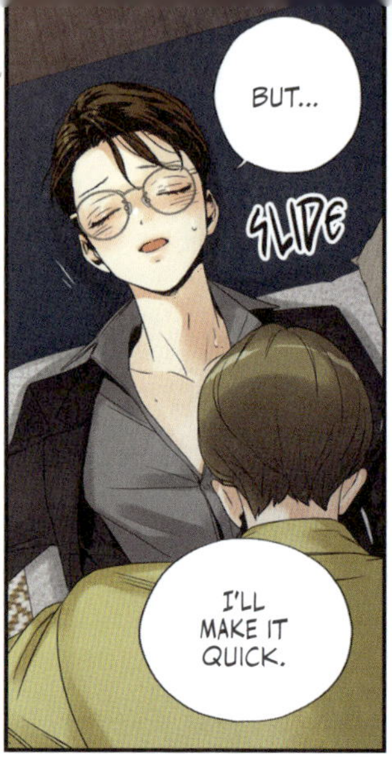
BUT...
SLIDE
I'LL MAKE IT QUICK.

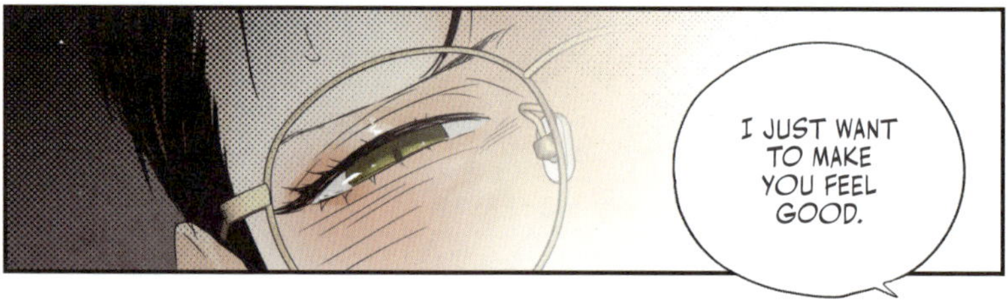
I JUST WANT TO MAKE YOU FEEL GOOD.

BUT WHY HERE...?

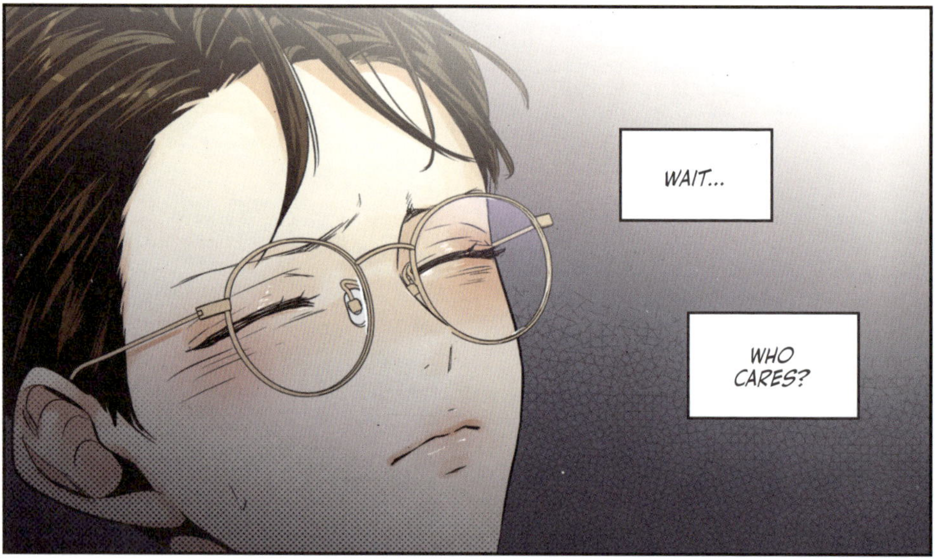
WAIT...
WHO CARES?

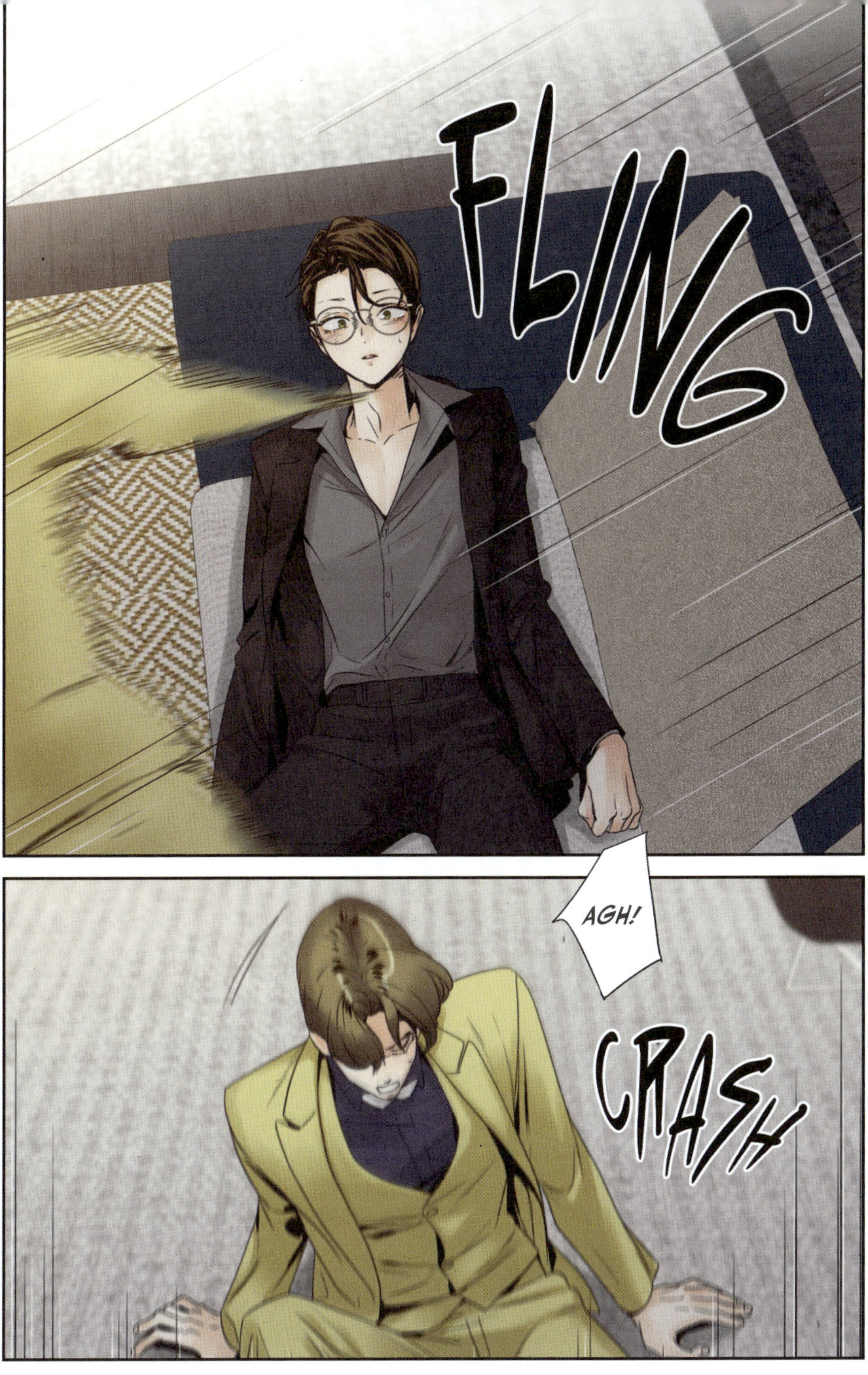
FLING
AGH!
CRASH

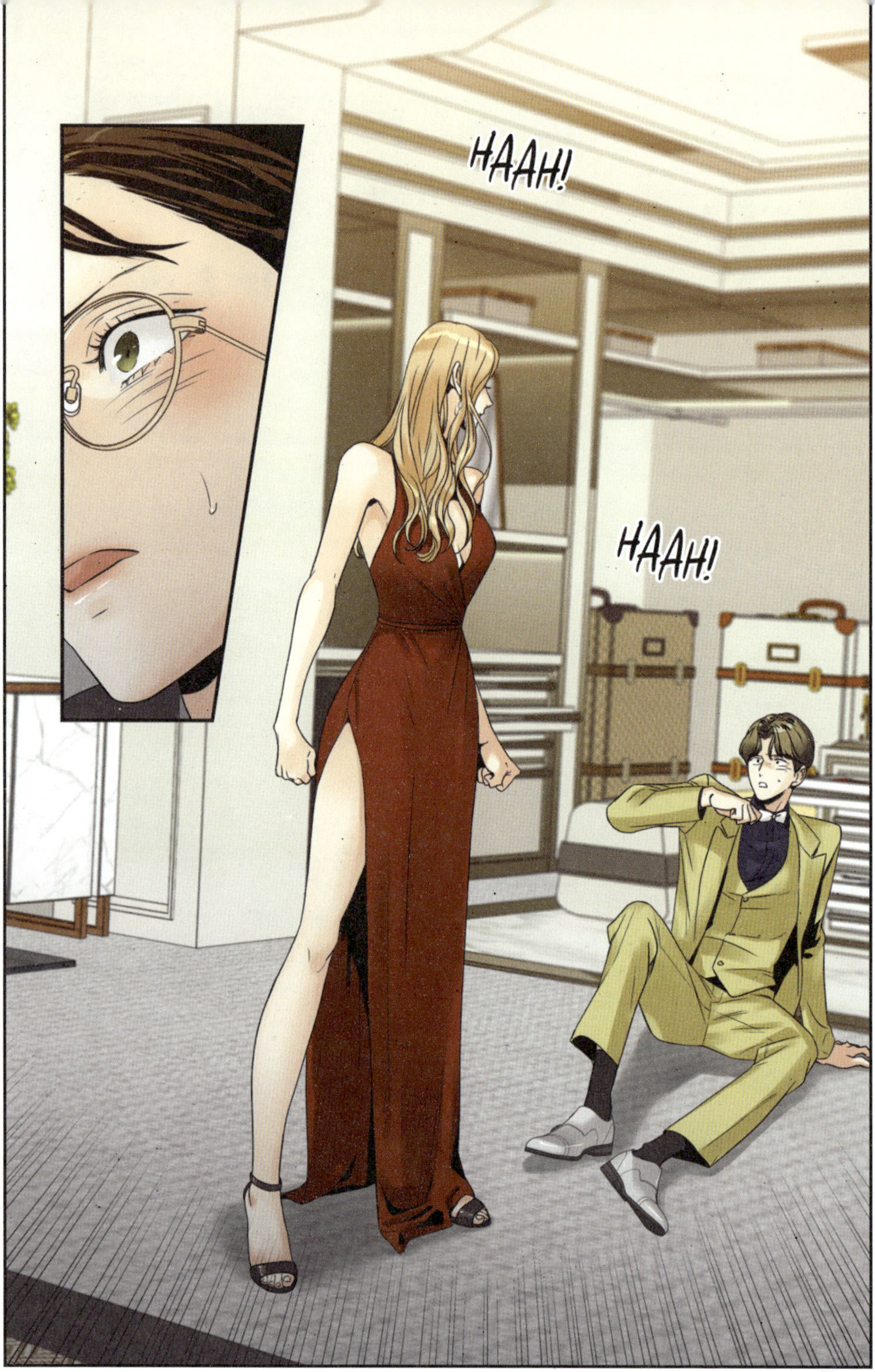
HAAH!
HAAH!

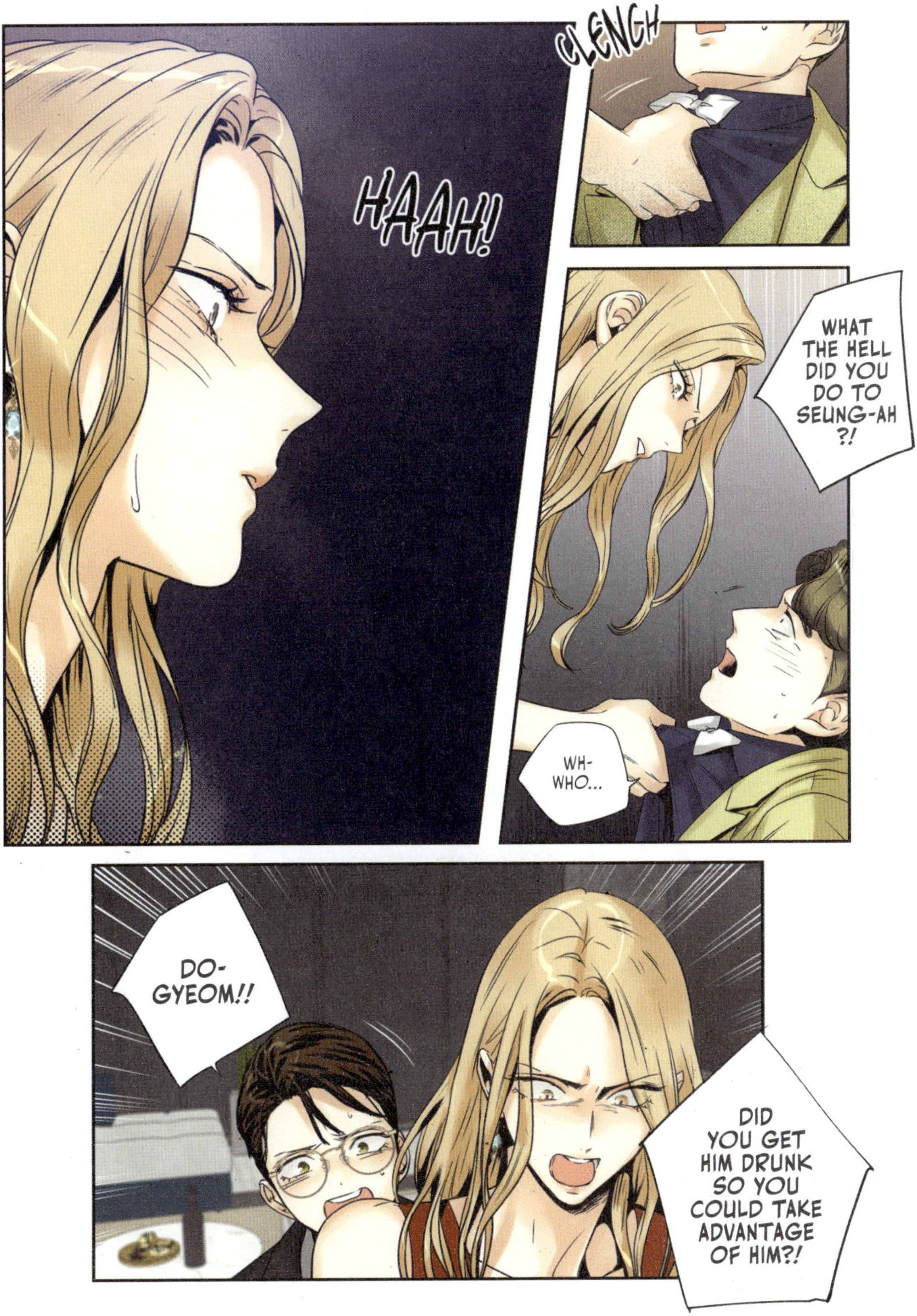
HAAAH!
CLENCH
WHAT THE HELL DID YOU DO TO SEUNG-AH?!
WH- WHO...
DO- GYEOM!!
DID YOU GET HIM DRUNK SO YOU COULD TAKE ADVANTAGE OF HIM?!

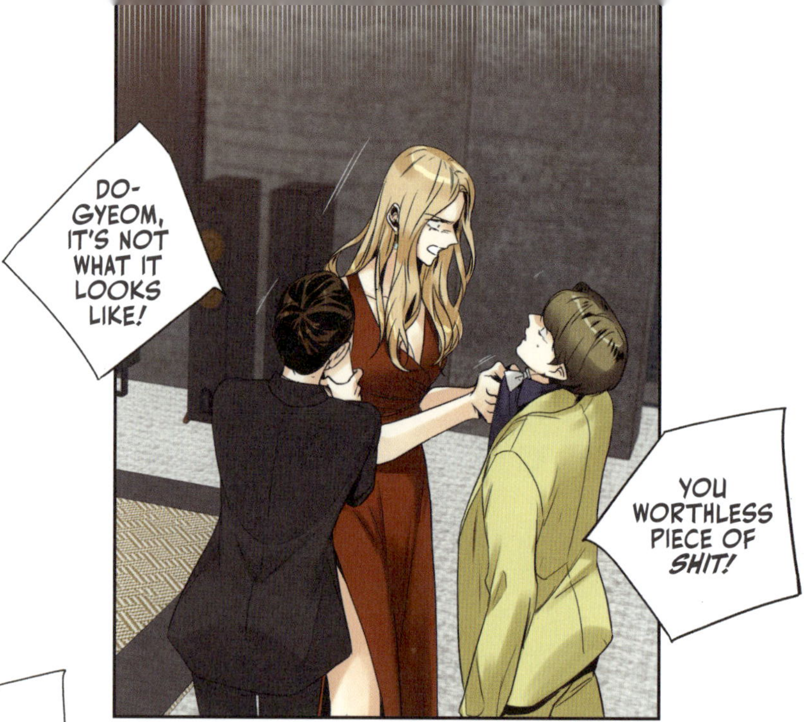
DO-GYEOM, IT'S NOT WHAT IT LOOKS LIKE!
YOU WORTHLESS PIECE OF SHIT!
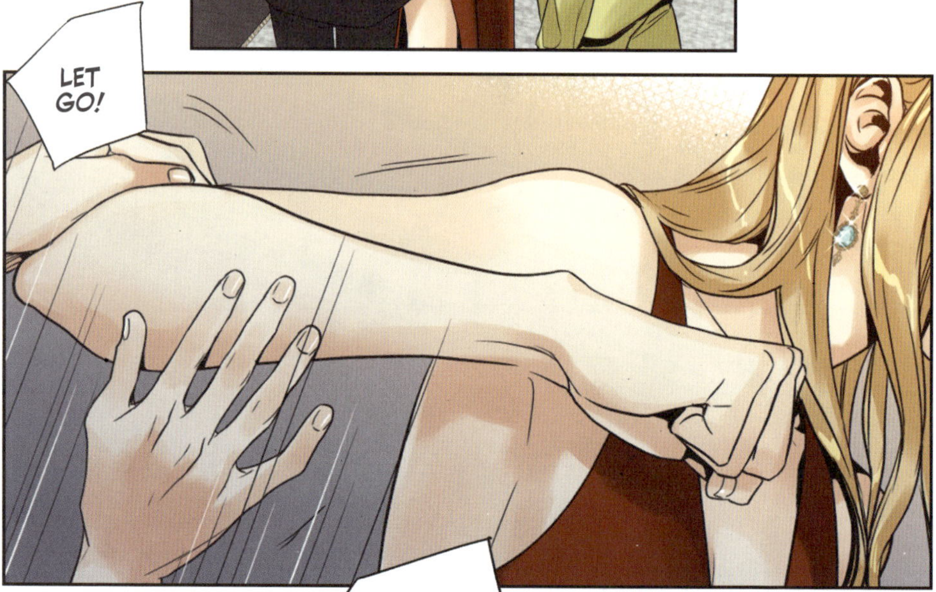
LET GO!
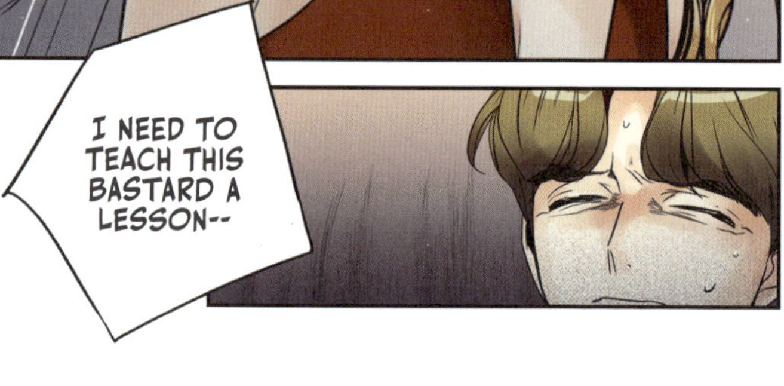
I NEED TO TEACH THIS BASTARD A LESSON--

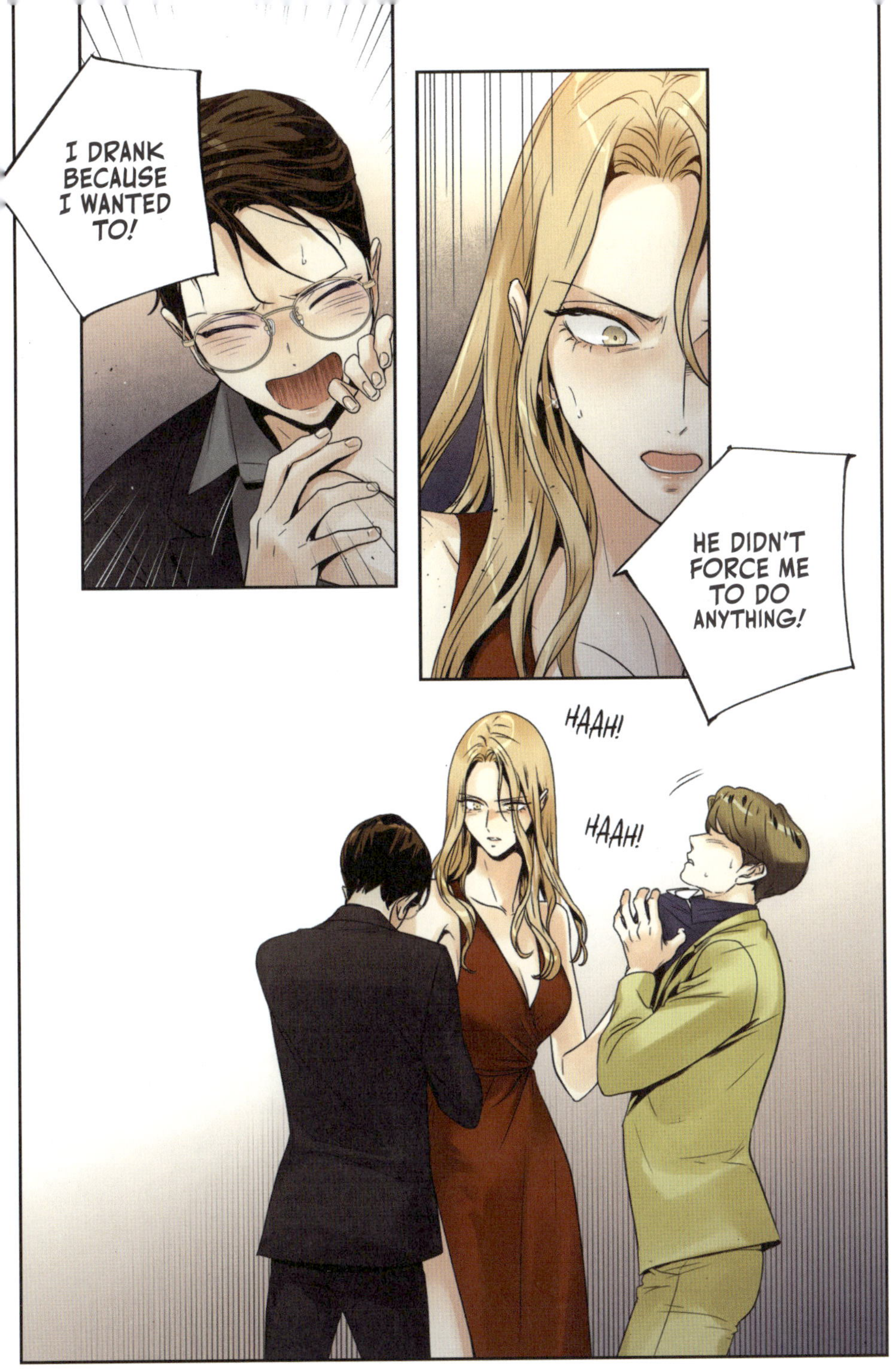
I DRANK BECAUSE I WANTED TO!
HE DIDN'T FORCE ME TO DO ANYTHING!
HAAH!
HAAH!

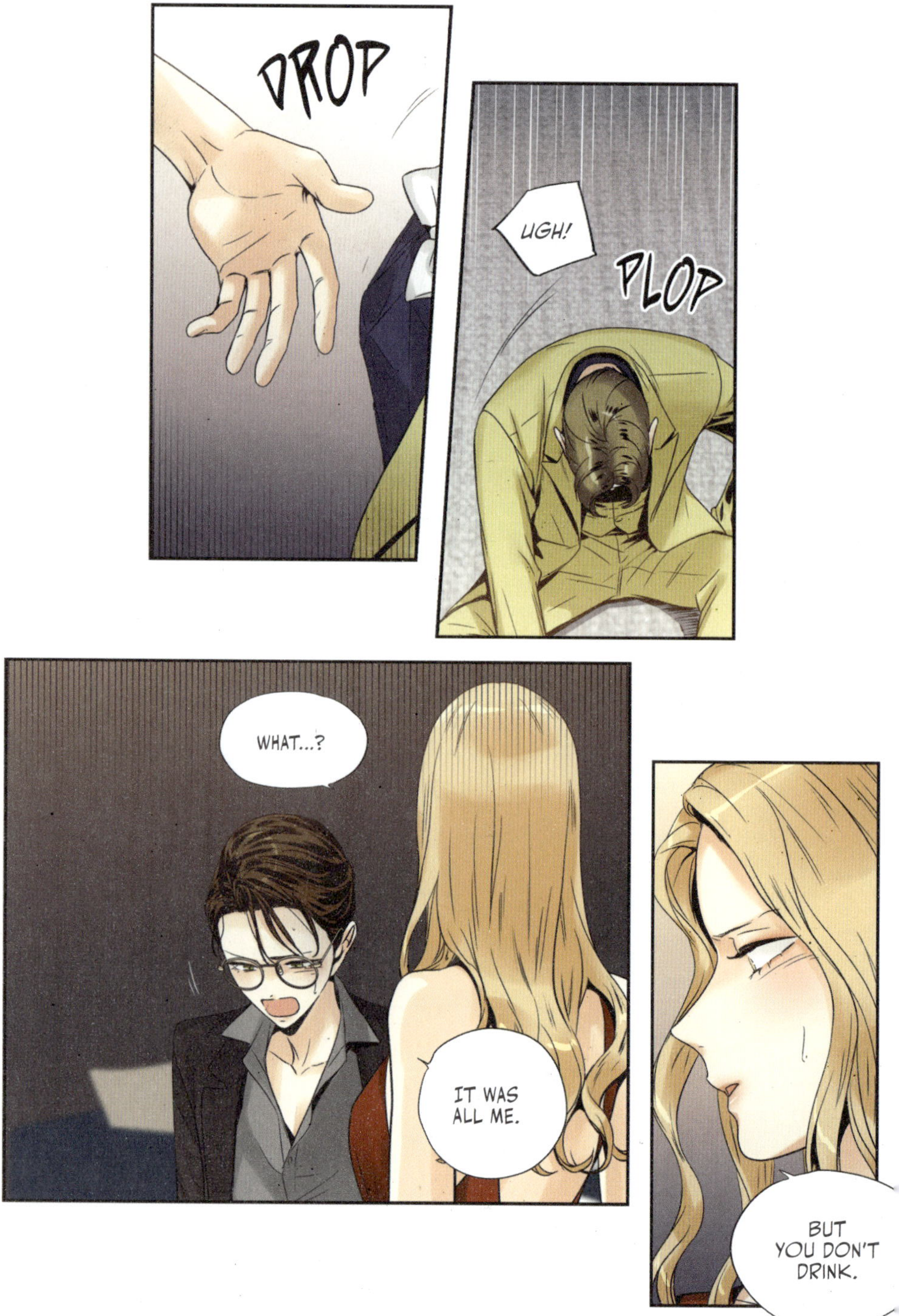
DROP
UGH!
PLOP
WHAT...?
IT WAS ALL ME.
BUT YOU DON'T DRINK.

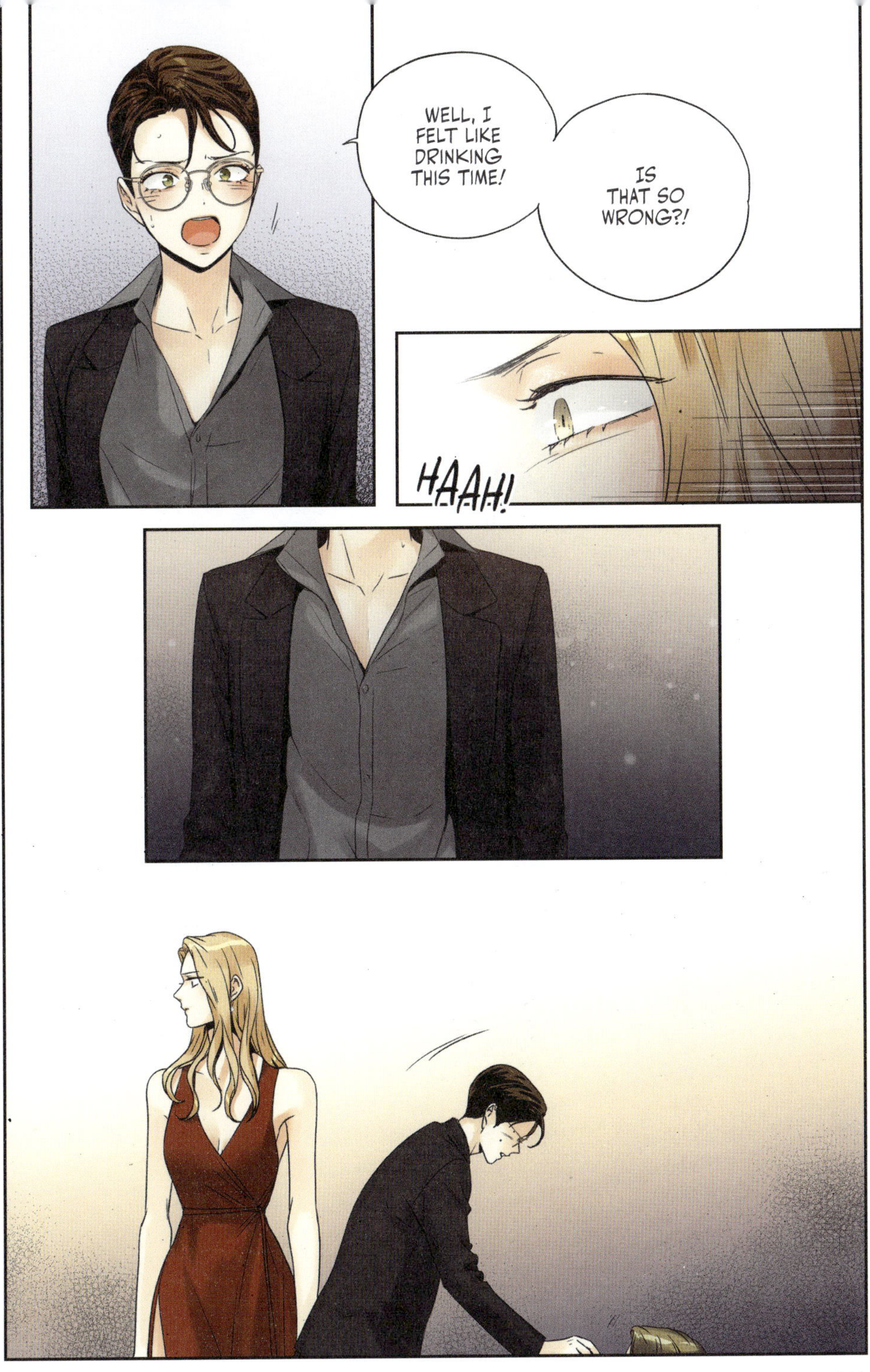
WELL, I FELT LIKE DRINKING THIS TIME!
IS THAT SO WRONG?!
HAAAH!

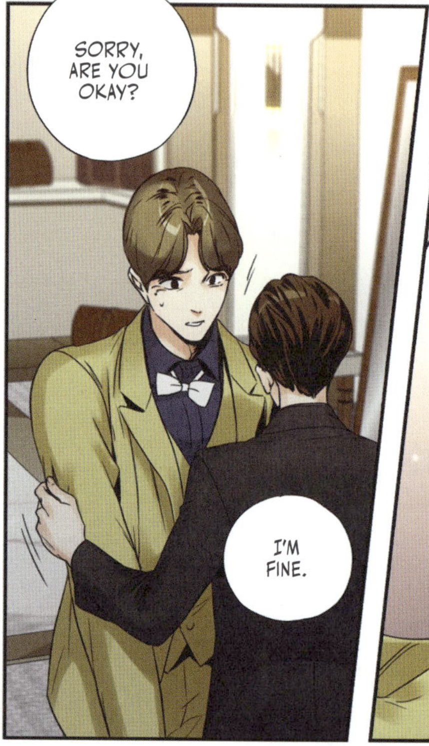
SORRY, ARE YOU OKAY?
I'M FINE.

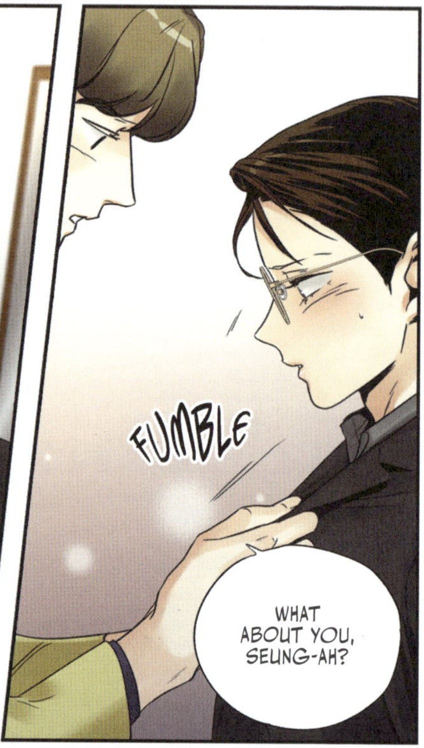
FUMBLE
WHAT ABOUT YOU, SEUNG-AH?

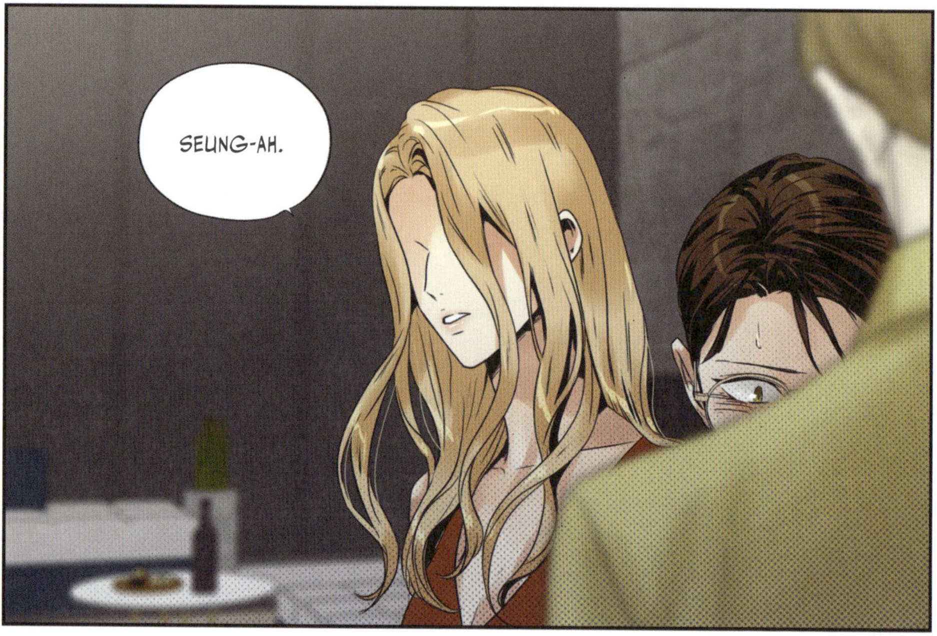
SEUNG-AH.

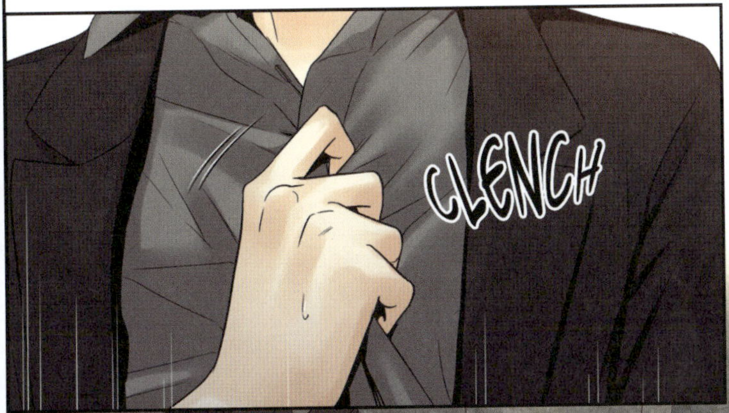
CLENCH

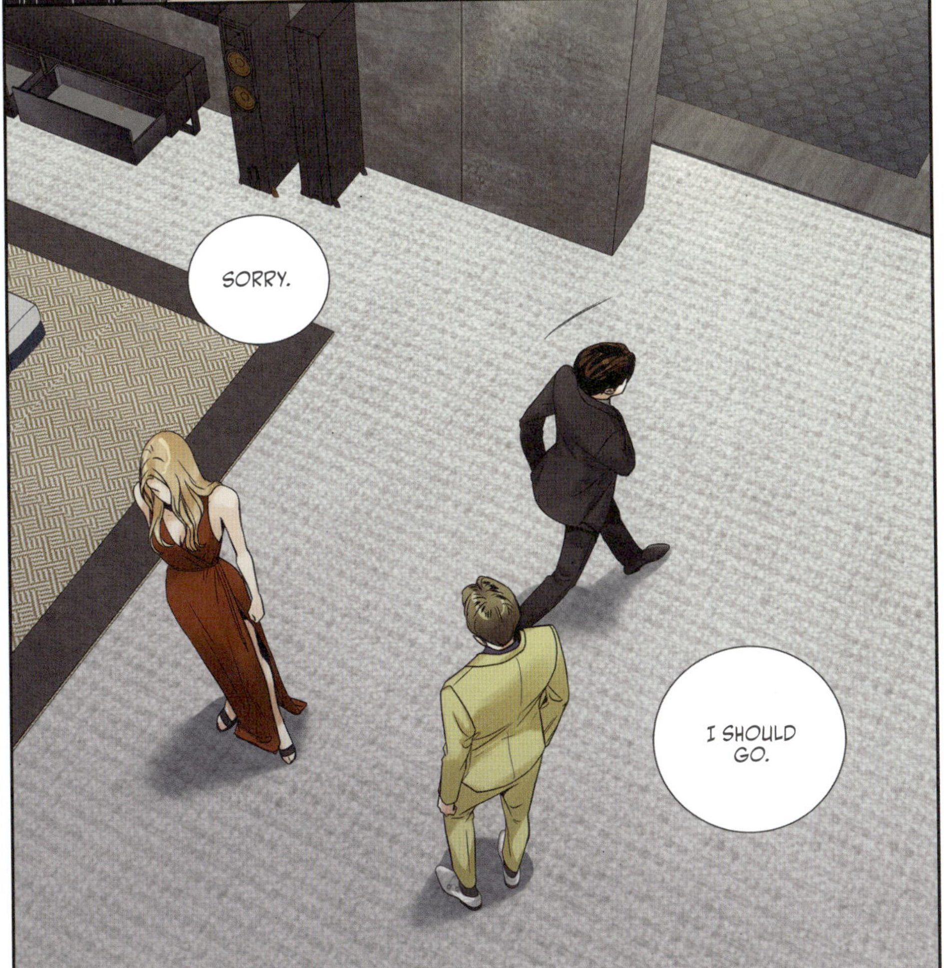
SORRY.
I SHOULD GO.

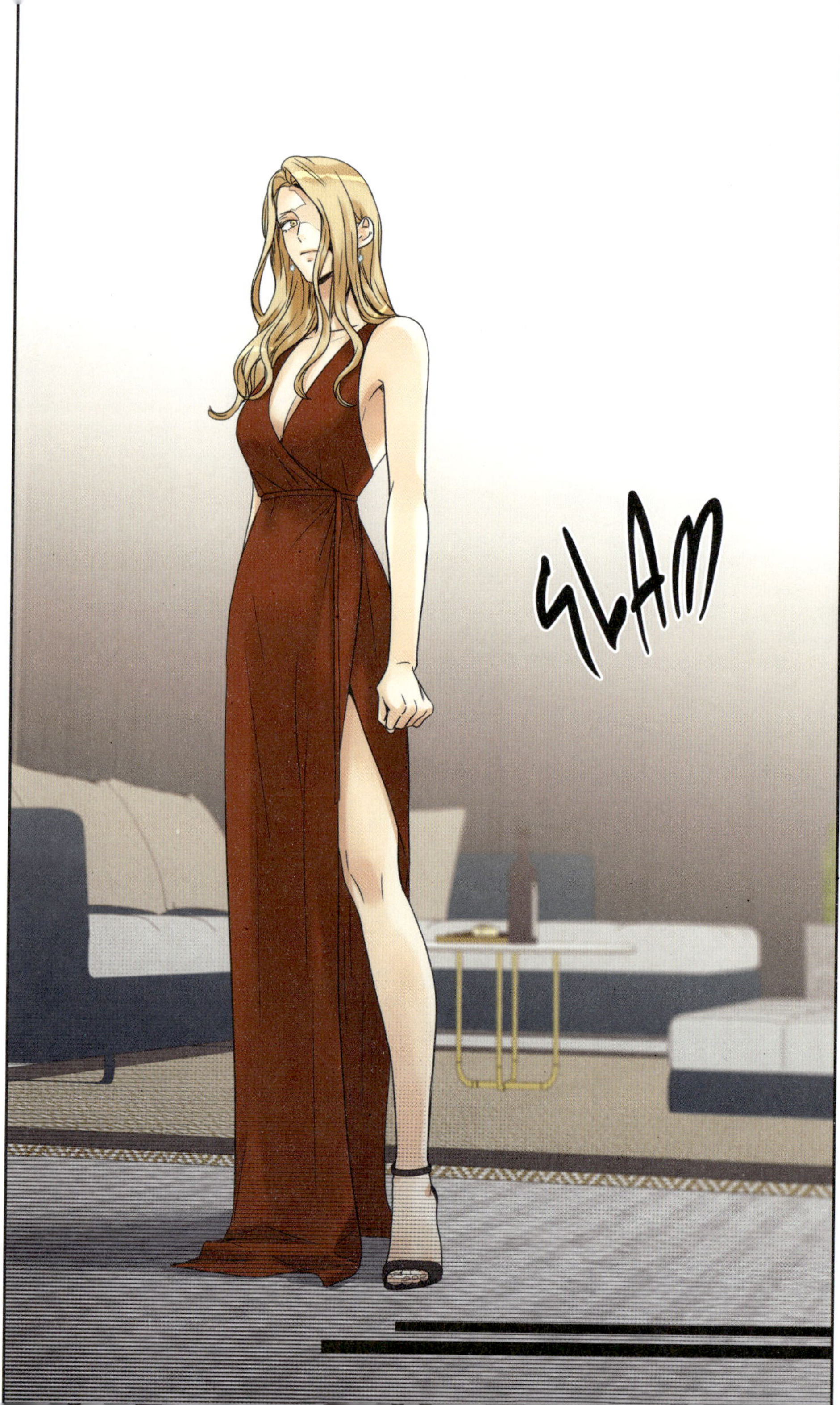
SLAM

Love is an Illusion!
The Queen

Love is an Illusion!
The Queen

THE DOWNSIDE OF WORKING WITH A FRIEND...

IS THAT YOU HAVE NO CHOICE BUT TO FACE THEM EVEN AFTER A FIGHT.

Chapter 7

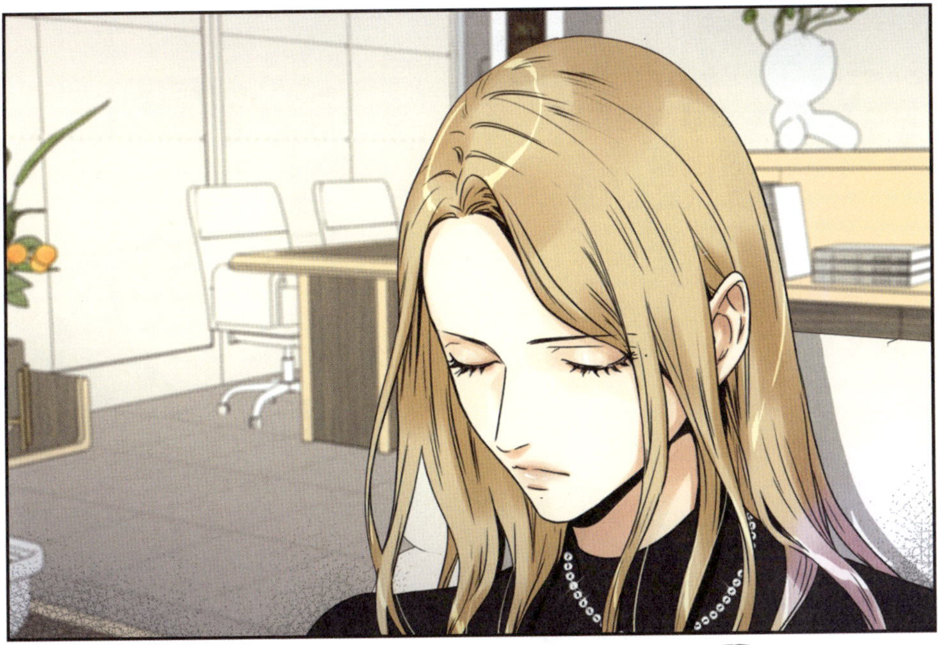

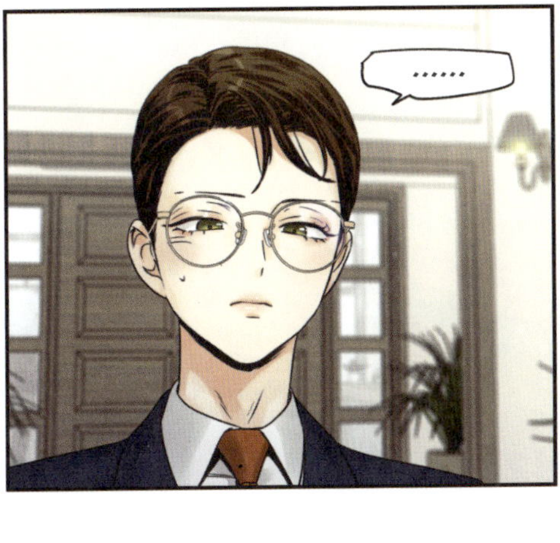
......

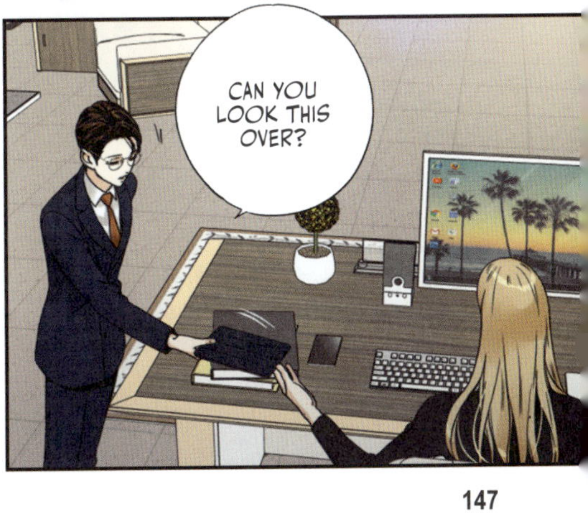
CAN YOU LOOK THIS OVER?

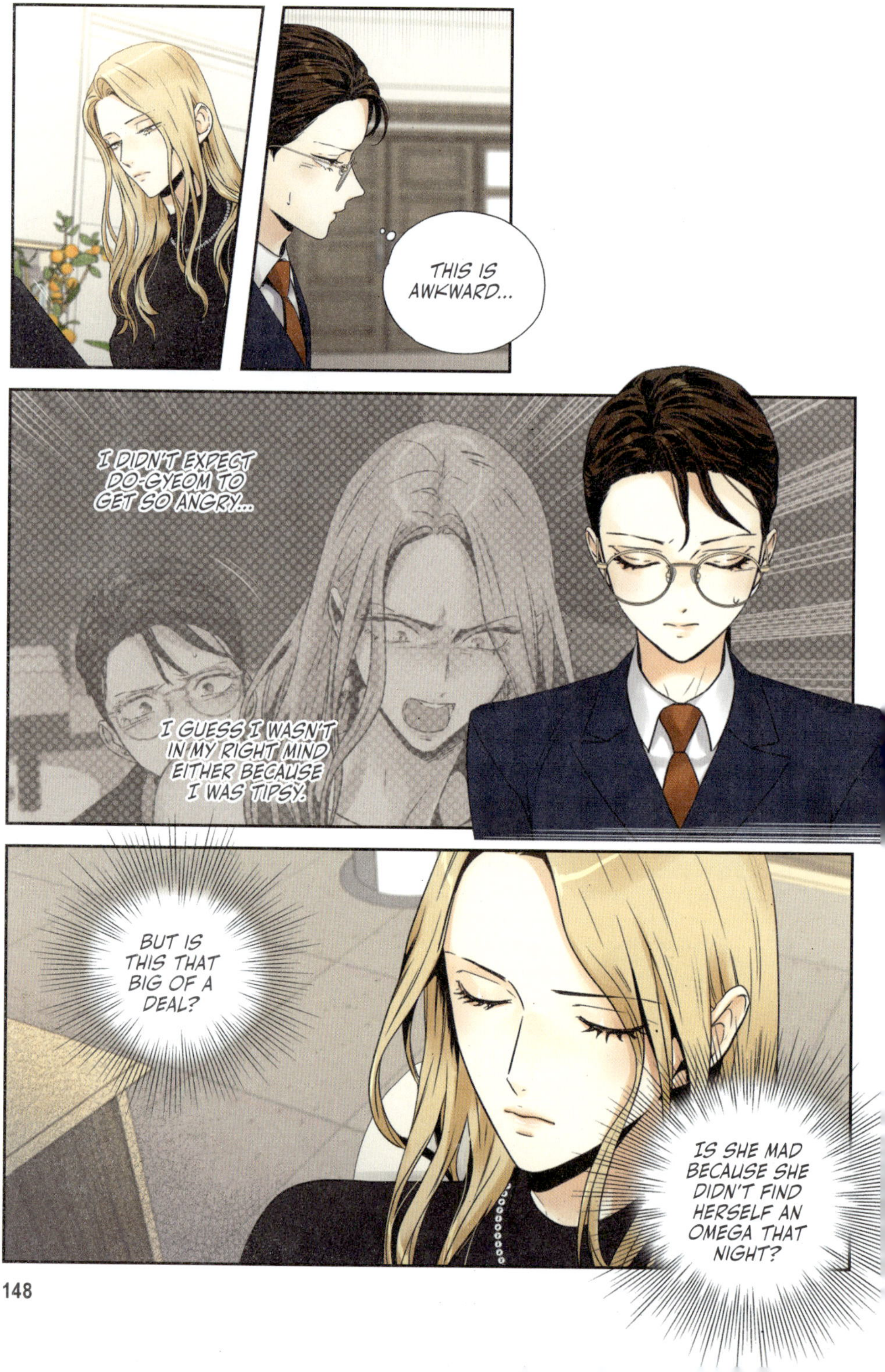
THIS IS AWKWARD...
I DIDN'T EXPECT DO-GYEOM TO GET SO ANGRY...
I GUESS I WASN'T IN MY RIGHT MIND EITHER BECAUSE I WAS TIPSY.
BUT IS THIS THAT BIG OF A DEAL?
IS SHE MAD BECAUSE SHE DIDN'T FIND HERSELF AN OMEGA THAT NIGHT?

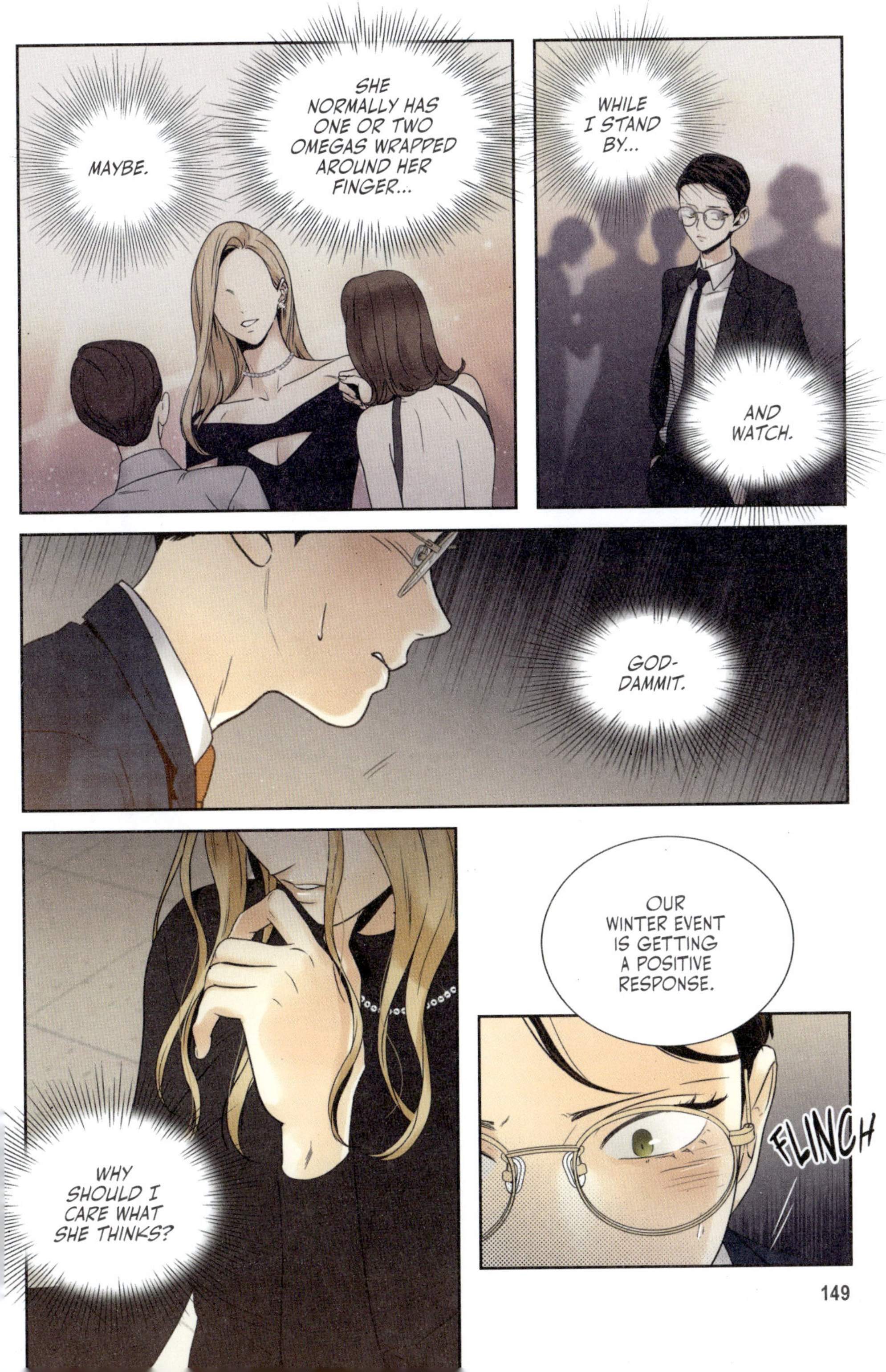
MAYBE.
SHE NORMALLY HAS ONE OR TWO OMEGAS WRAPPED AROUND HER FINGER...
WHILE I STAND BY...
AND WATCH.
GOD-DAMMIT.
WHY SHOULD I CARE WHAT SHE THINKS?
OUR WINTER EVENT IS GETTING A POSITIVE RESPONSE.
FLINCH

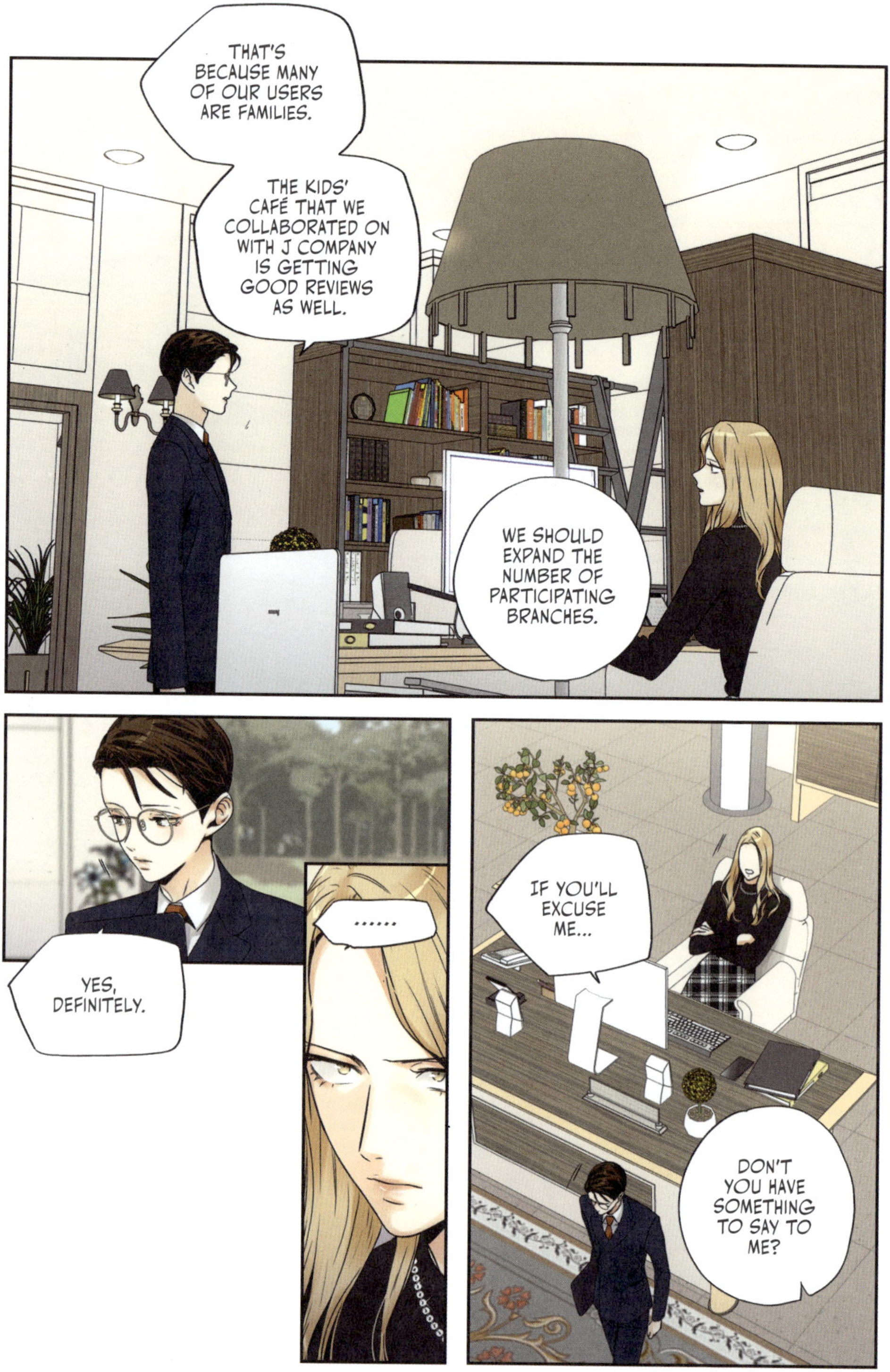
THAT'S BECAUSE MANY OF OUR USERS ARE FAMILIES.
THE KIDS' CAFÉ THAT WE COLLABORATED ON WITH J COMPANY IS GETTING GOOD REVIEWS AS WELL.
WE SHOULD EXPAND THE NUMBER OF PARTICIPATING BRANCHES.
YES, DEFINITELY.
......
IF YOU'LL EXCUSE ME...
DON'T YOU HAVE SOMETHING TO SAY TO ME?

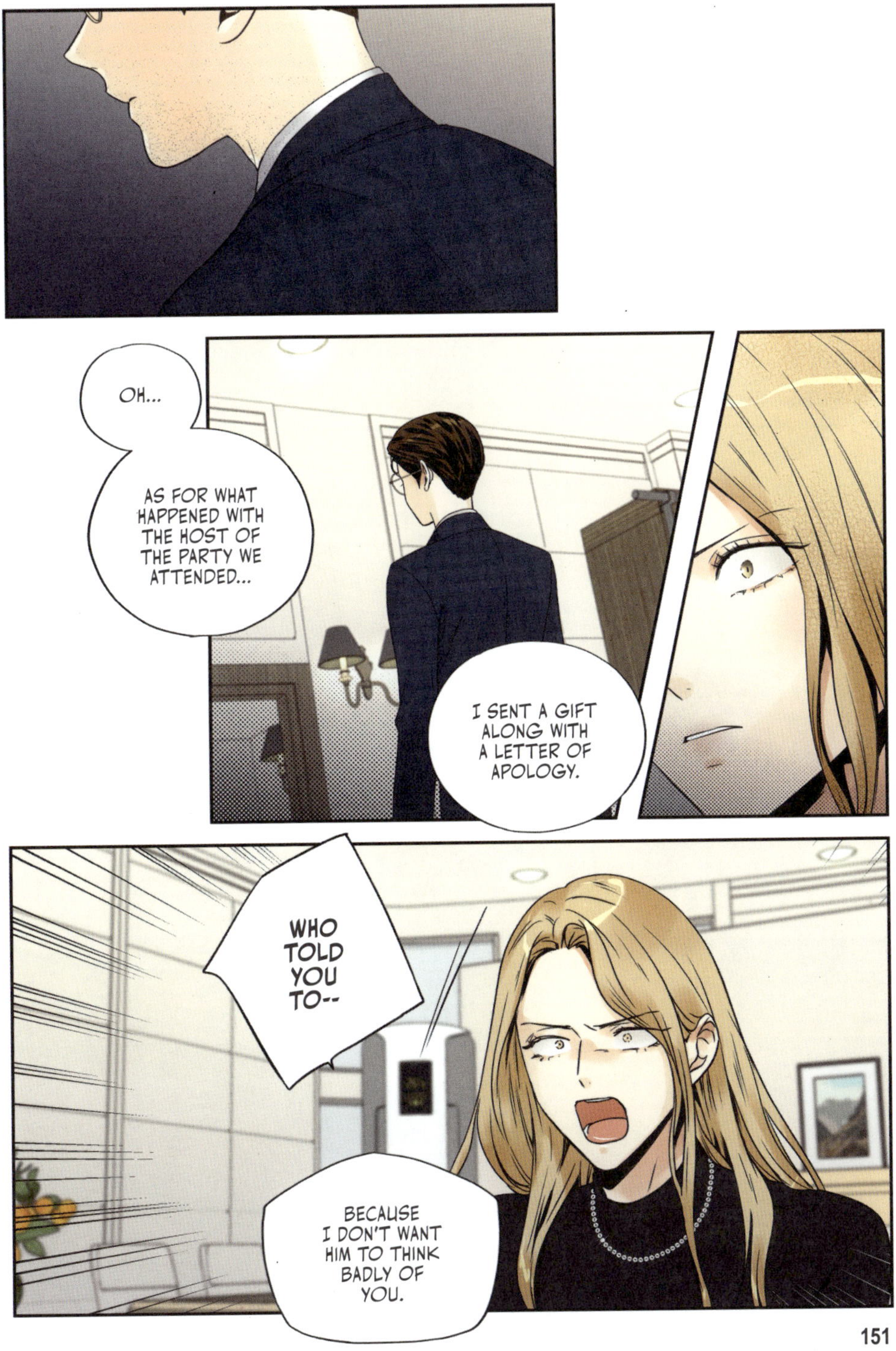

OH...
AS FOR WHAT HAPPENED WITH THE HOST OF THE PARTY WE ATTENDED...
I SENT A GIFT ALONG WITH A LETTER OF APOLOGY.
WHO TOLD YOU TO--
BECAUSE I DON'T WANT HIM TO THINK BADLY OF YOU.

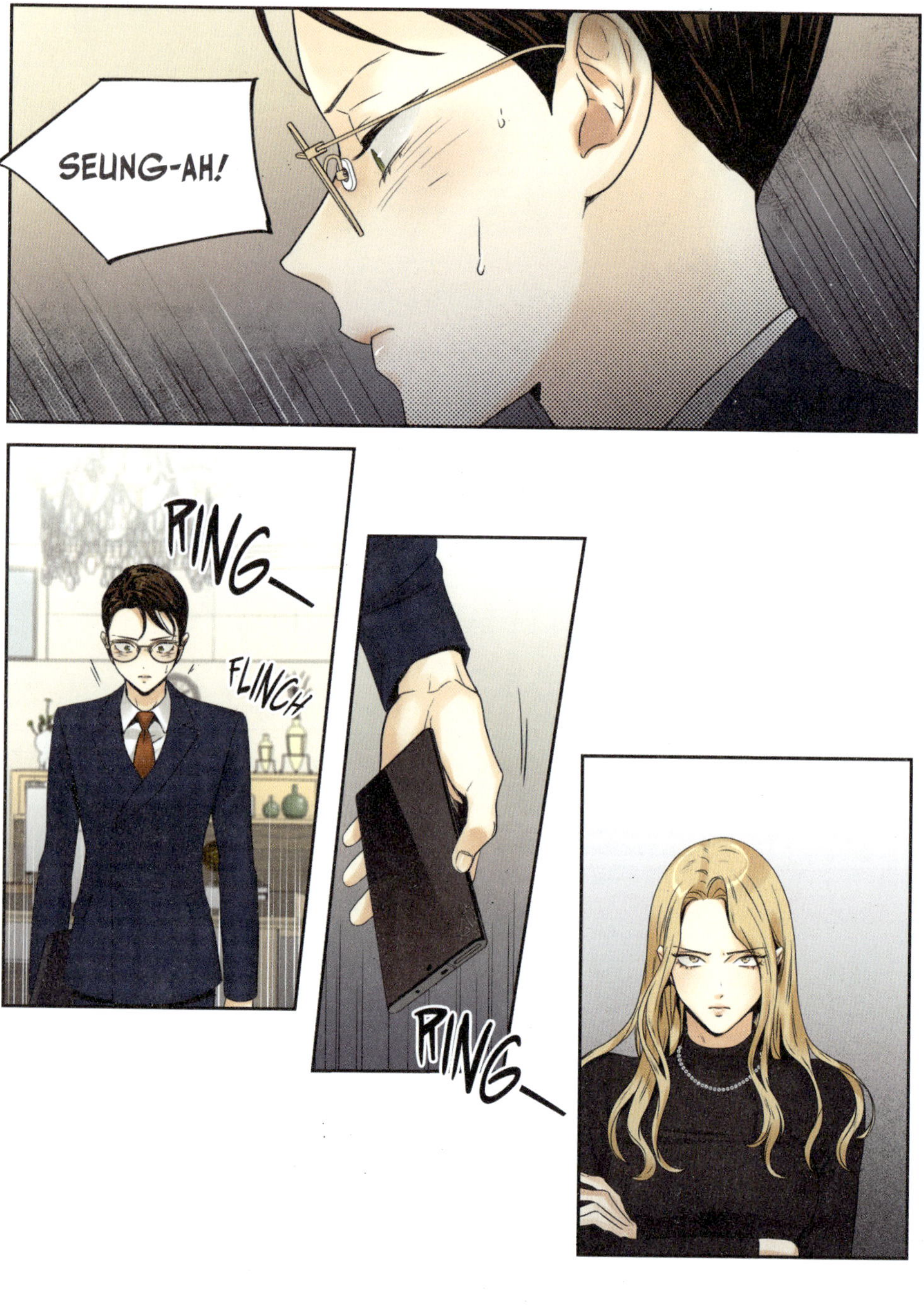
SEUNG-AH!
RING-
FLINCH
RING-

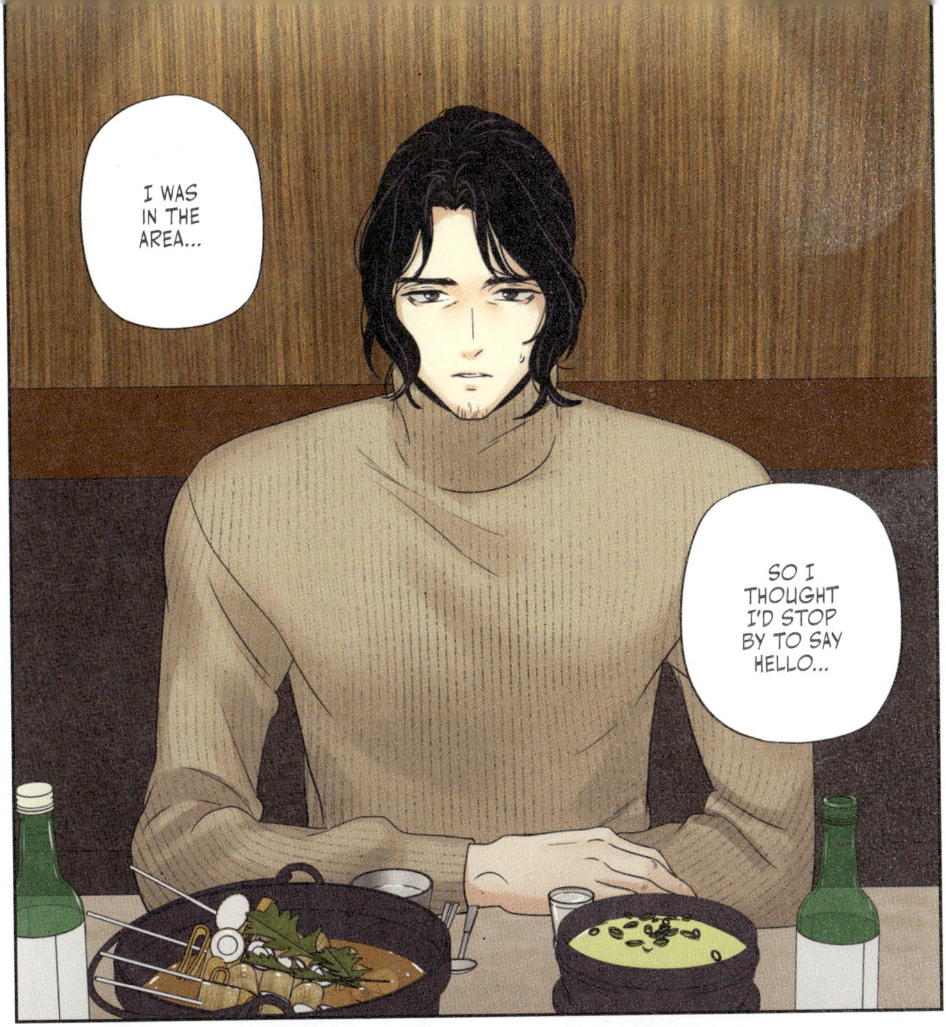
I WAS IN THE AREA...
SO I THOUGHT I'D STOP BY TO SAY HELLO...
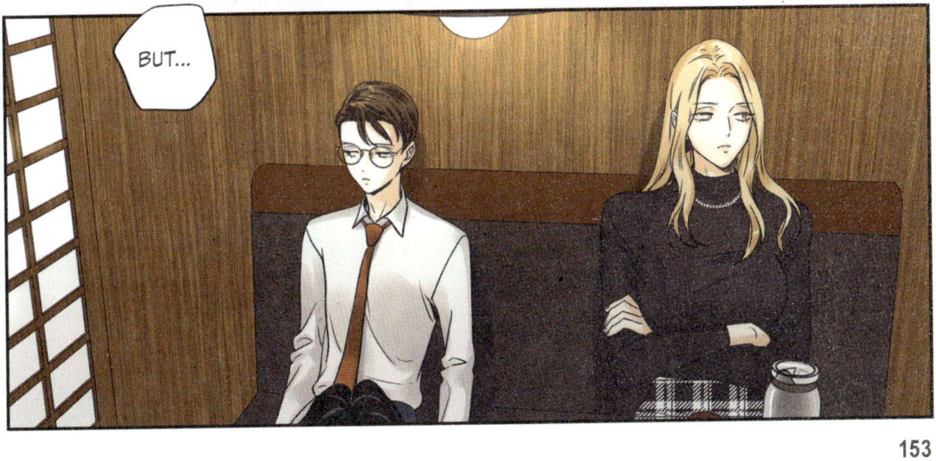
BUT...

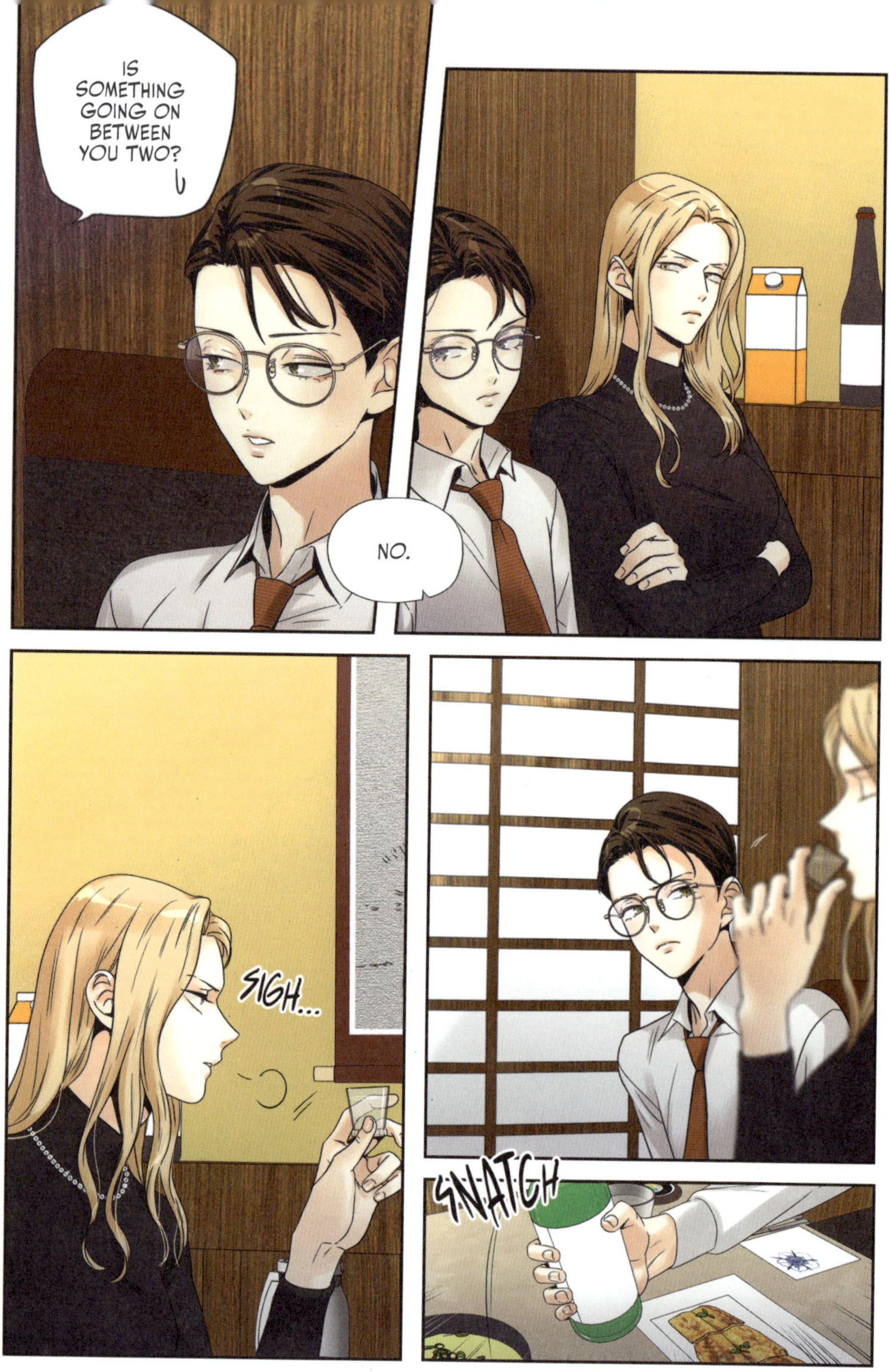
IS SOMETHING GOING ON BETWEEN YOU TWO?
NO.
SIGH...
SNATCH

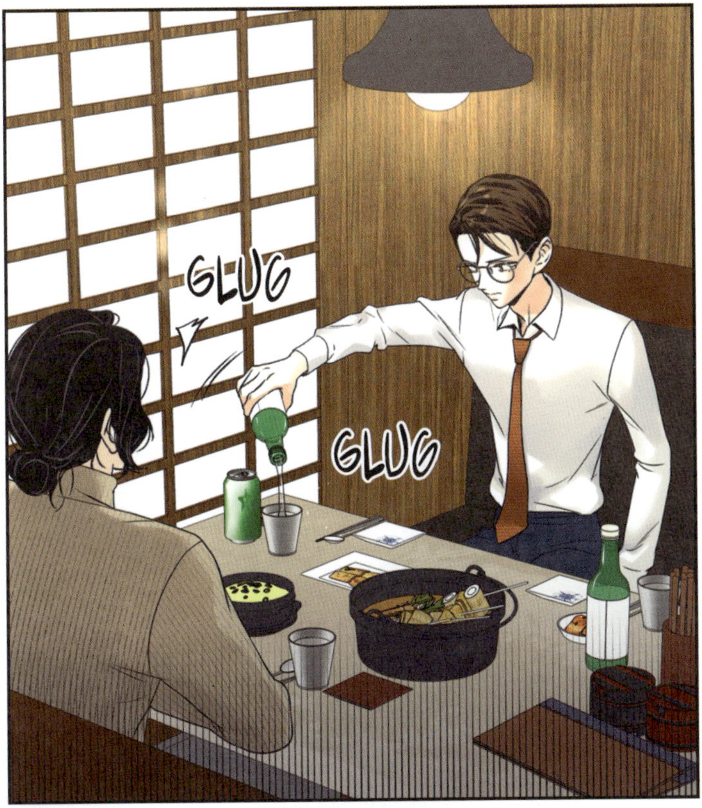
GLUG
GLUG

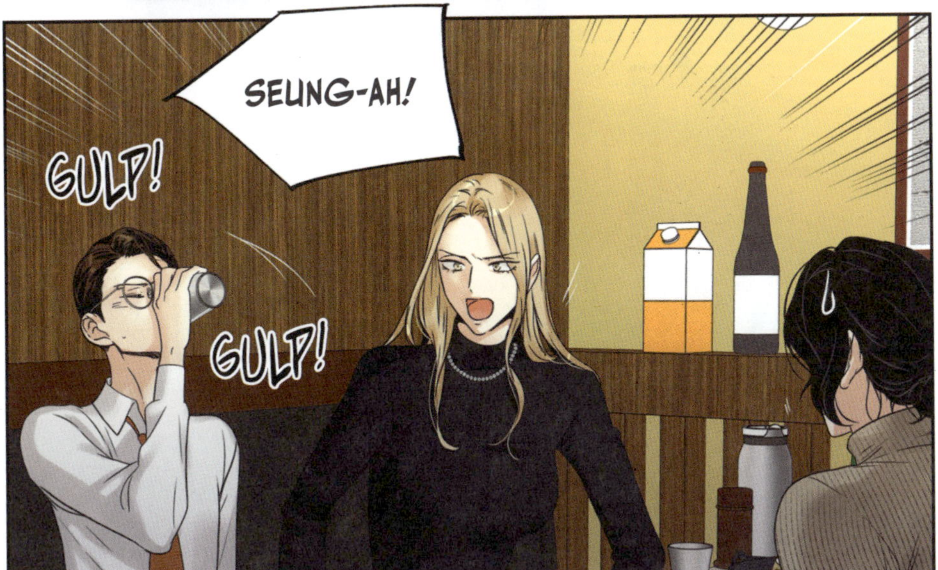
GULP!
SEUNG-AH!
GULP!

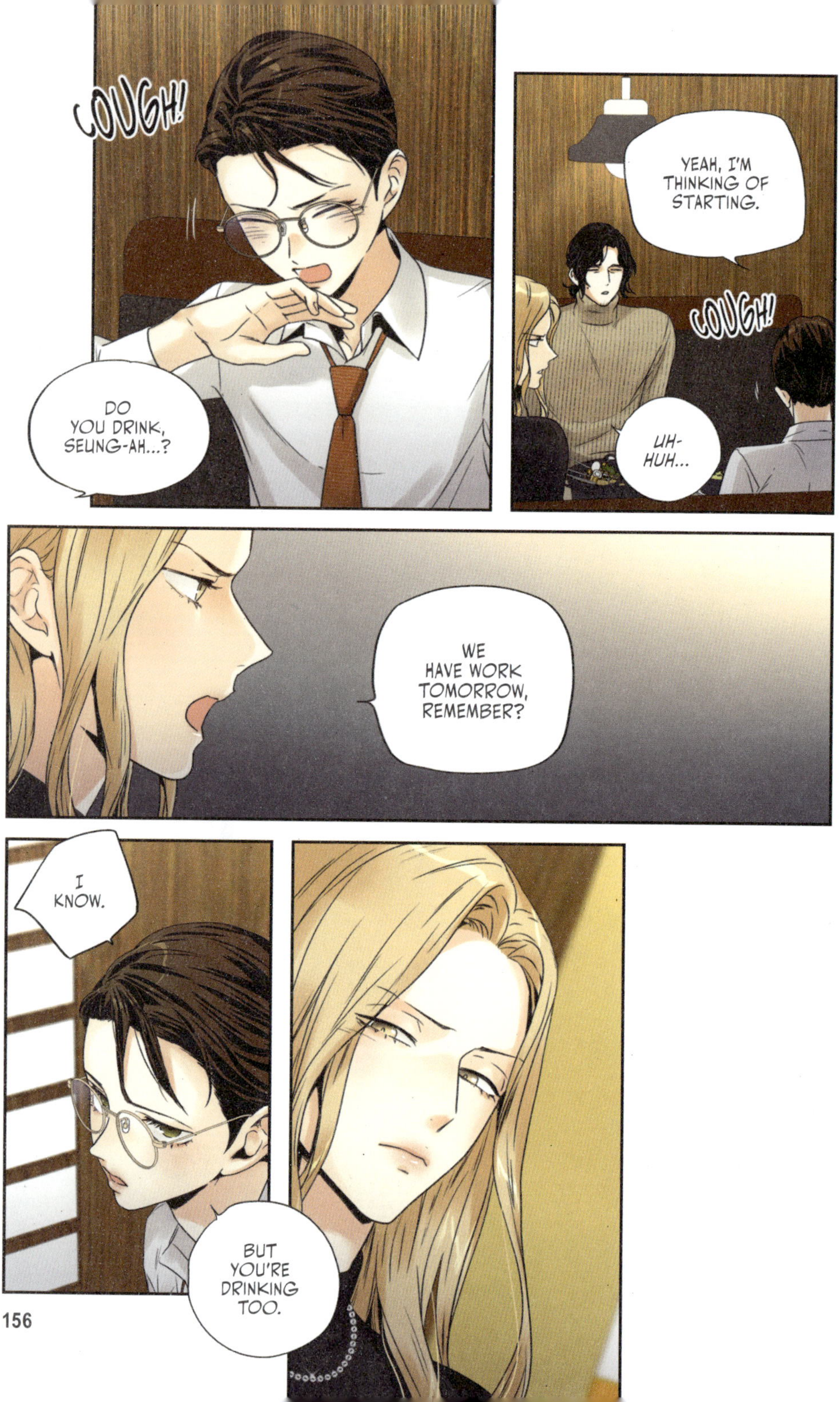
COUGH!
DO YOU DRINK, SEUNG-AH...?
YEAH, I'M THINKING OF STARTING.
COUGH!
UH-HUH...
WE HAVE WORK TOMORROW, REMEMBER?
I KNOW.
BUT YOU'RE DRINKING TOO.

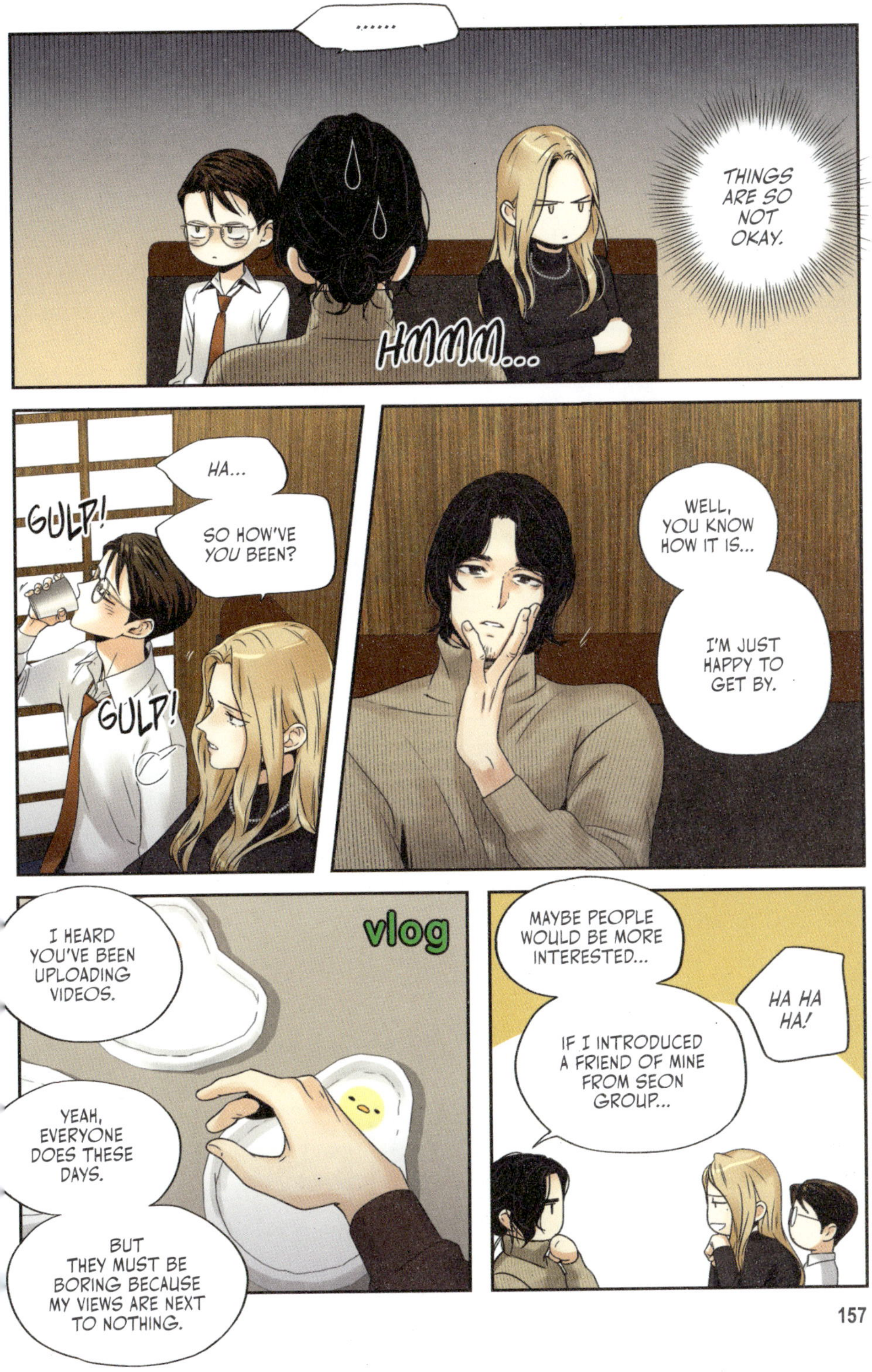
......
HMMM...
THINGS ARE SO NOT OKAY.
HA...
GULP!
SO HOW'VE YOU BEEN?
GULP!
WELL, YOU KNOW HOW IT IS...
I'M JUST HAPPY TO GET BY.
vlog
I HEARD YOU'VE BEEN UPLOADING VIDEOS.
YEAH, EVERYONE DOES THESE DAYS.
BUT THEY MUST BE BORING BECAUSE MY VIEWS ARE NEXT TO NOTHING.
MAYBE PEOPLE WOULD BE MORE INTERESTED...
HA HA HA!
IF I INTRODUCED A FRIEND OF MINE FROM SEON GROUP...

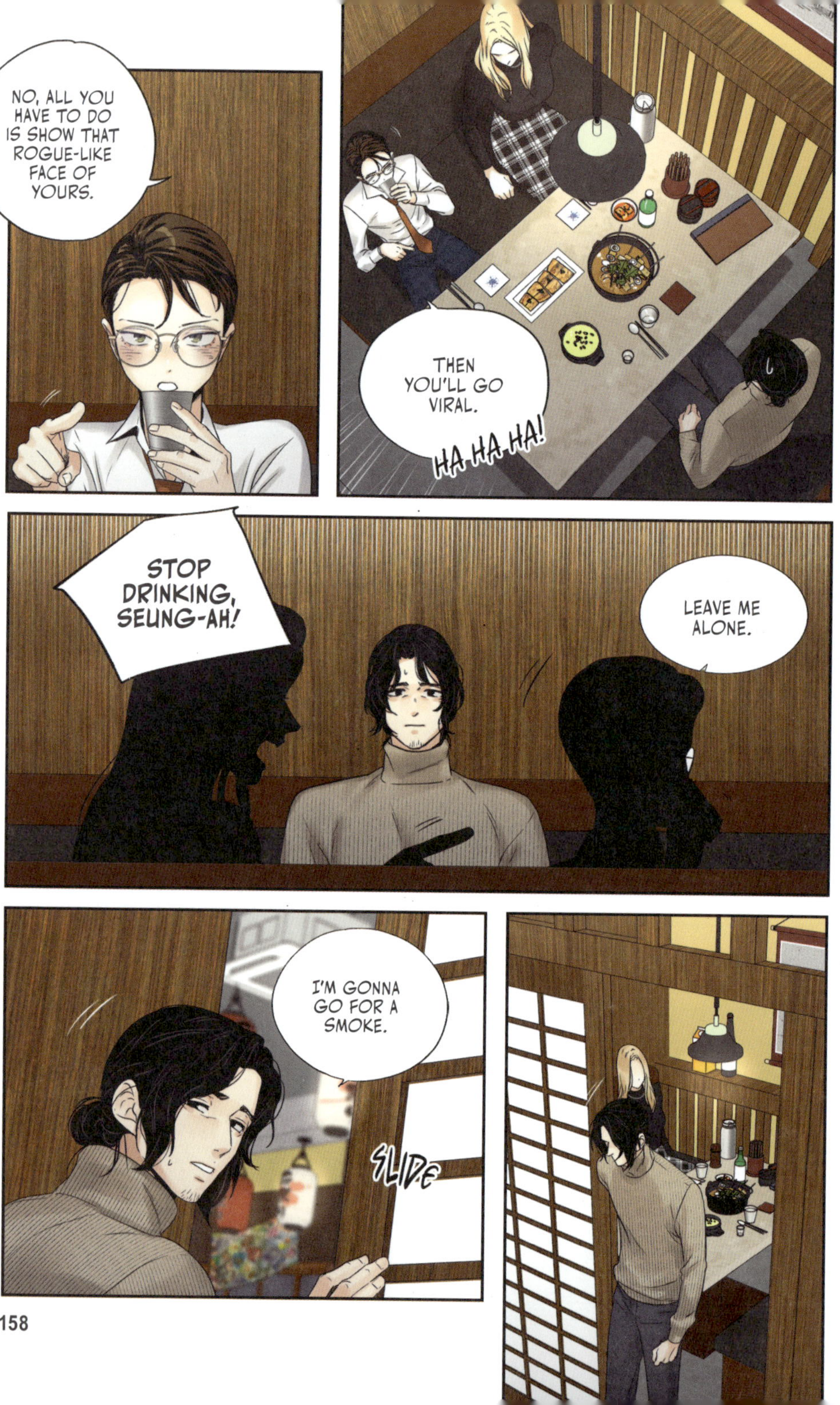
NO, ALL YOU HAVE TO DO IS SHOW THAT ROGUE-LIKE FACE OF YOURS.
THEN YOU'LL GO VIRAL.
HA HA HA!
STOP DRINKING, SEUNG-AH!
LEAVE ME ALONE.
I'M GONNA GO FOR A SMOKE.
SLIDE

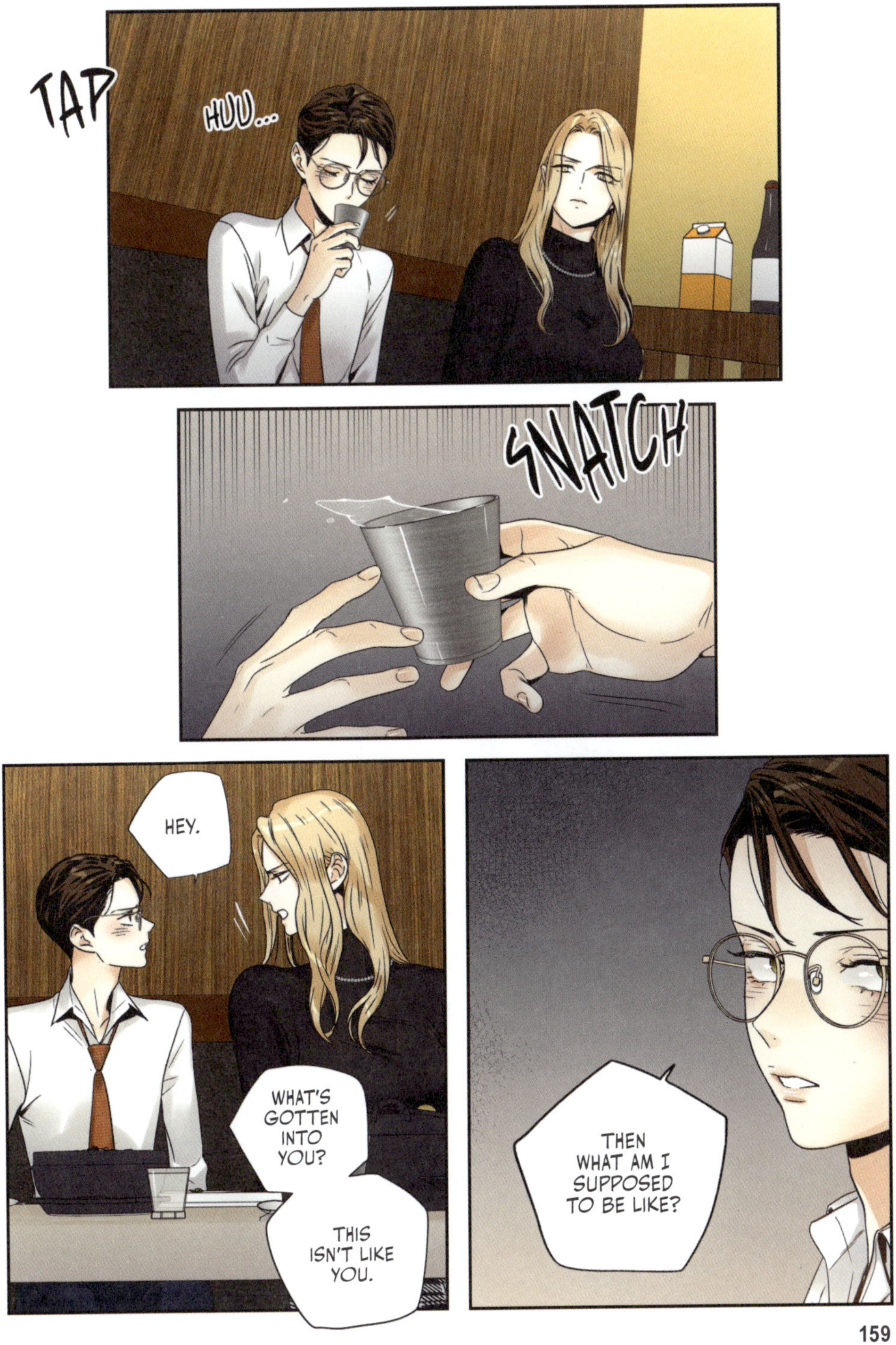
TAP
HUU...
SNATCH
HEY.
WHAT'S GOTTEN INTO YOU?
THIS ISN'T LIKE YOU.
THEN WHAT AM I SUPPOSED TO BE LIKE?

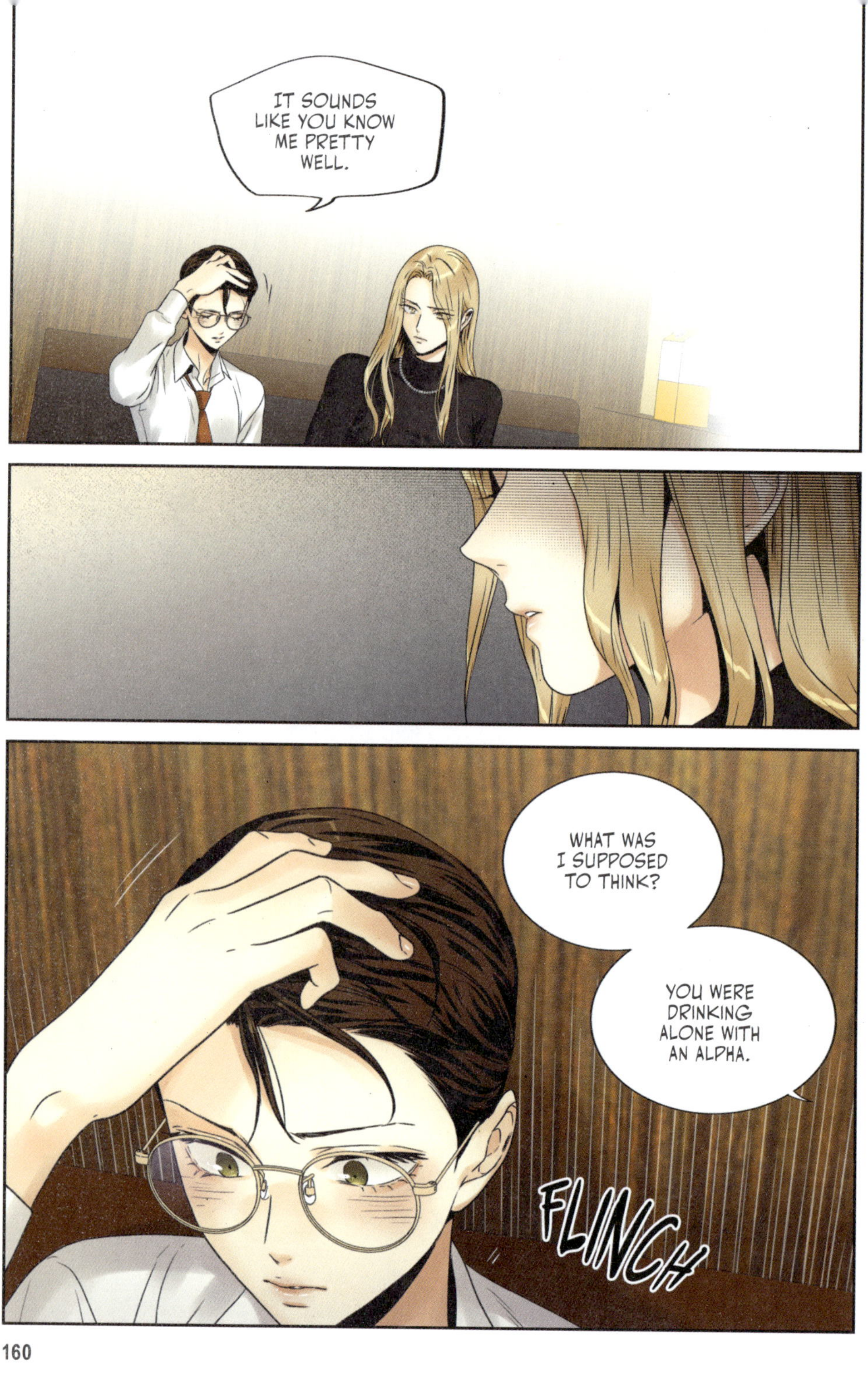
IT SOUNDS LIKE YOU KNOW ME PRETTY WELL.
WHAT WAS I SUPPOSED TO THINK?
YOU WERE DRINKING ALONE WITH AN ALPHA.
FLINCH

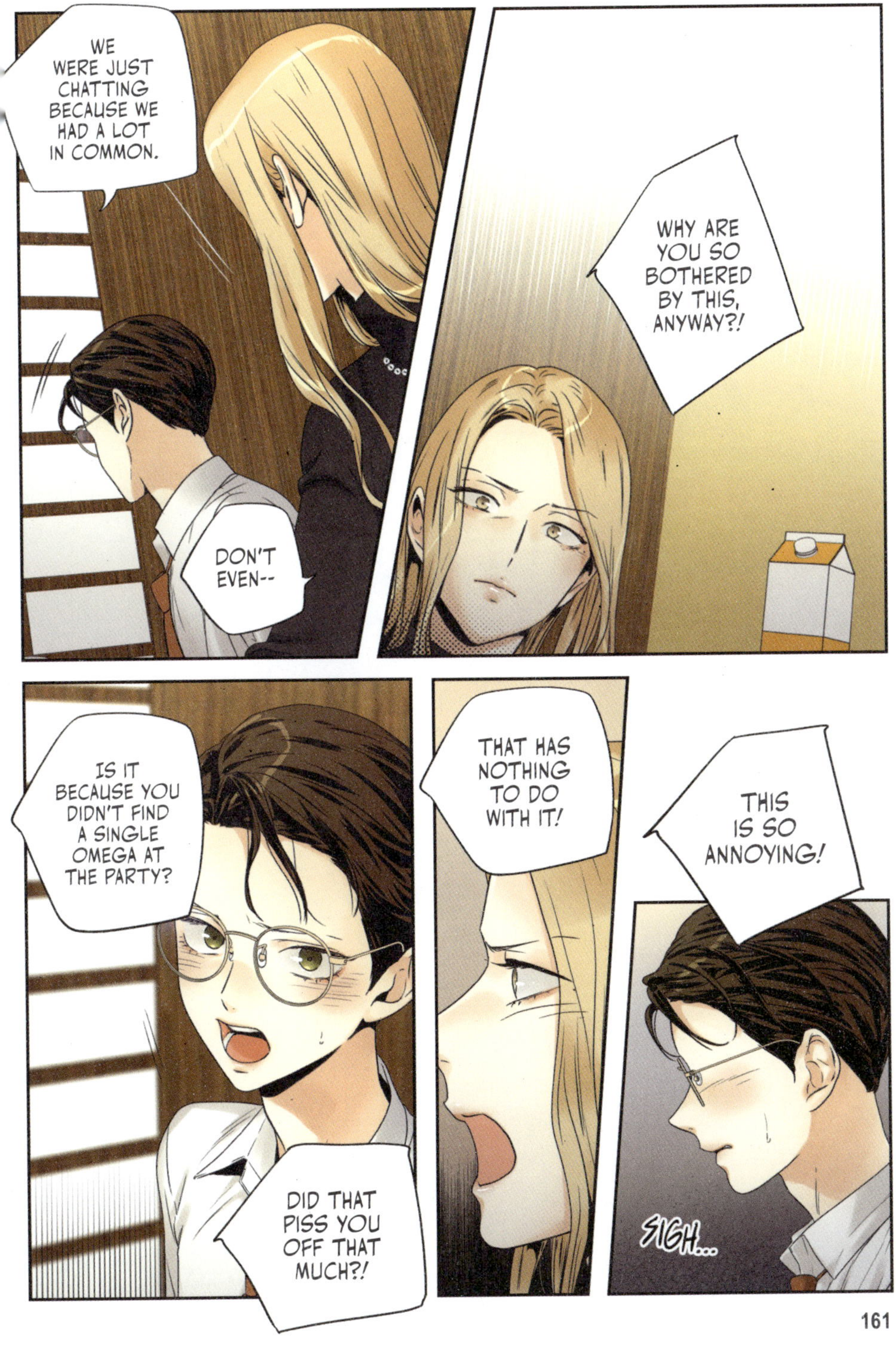
WE WERE JUST CHATTING BECAUSE WE HAD A LOT IN COMMON.
DON'T EVEN--
WHY ARE YOU SO BOTHERED BY THIS, ANYWAY?!
IS IT BECAUSE YOU DIDN'T FIND A SINGLE OMEGA AT THE PARTY?
DID THAT PISS YOU OFF THAT MUCH?!
THAT HAS NOTHING TO DO WITH IT!
THIS IS SO ANNOYING!
SIGH...

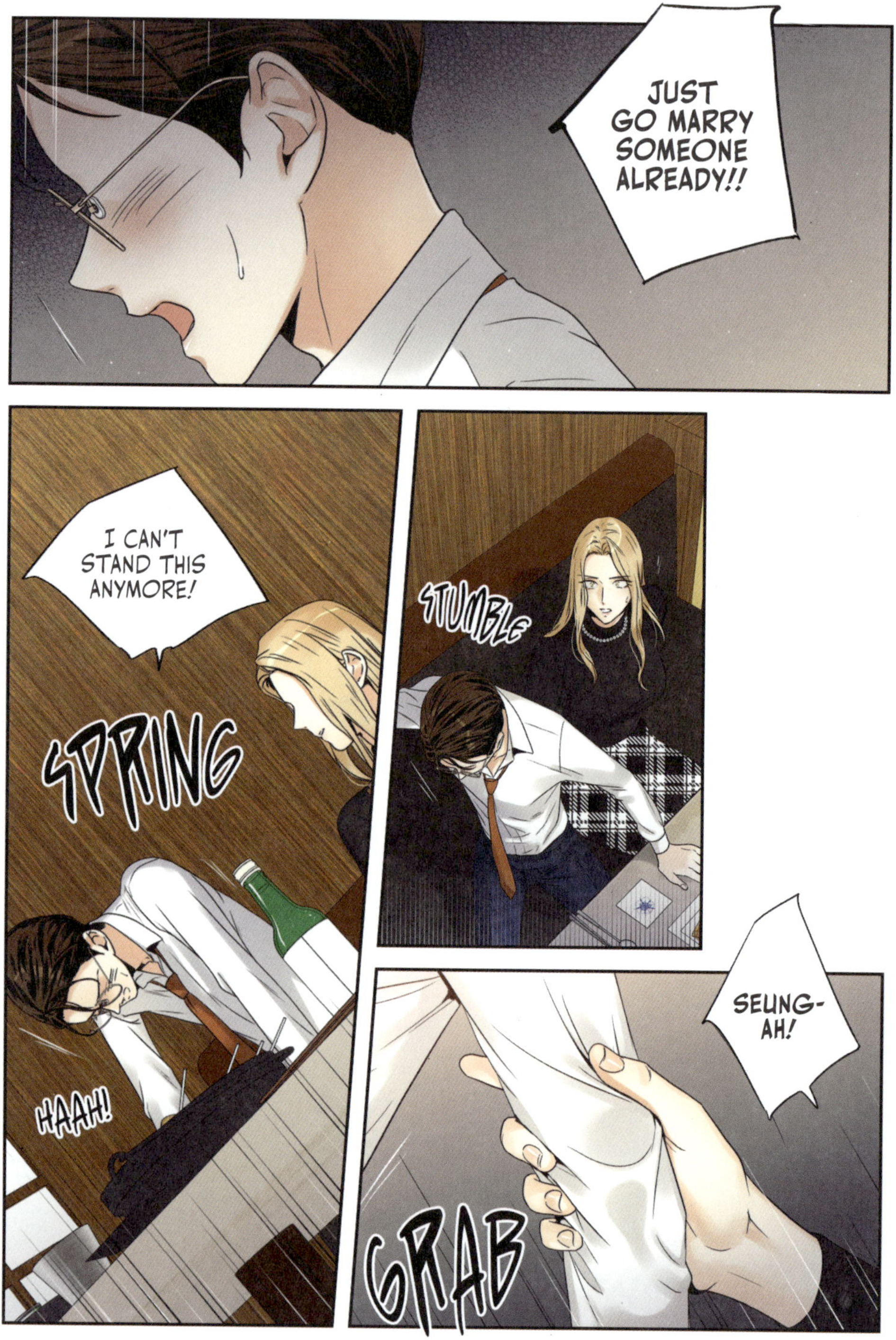
JUST GO MARRY SOMEONE ALREADY!!
I CAN'T STAND THIS ANYMORE!
SPRING
HAAAH!
STUMBLE
SEUNG-AH!
GRAB

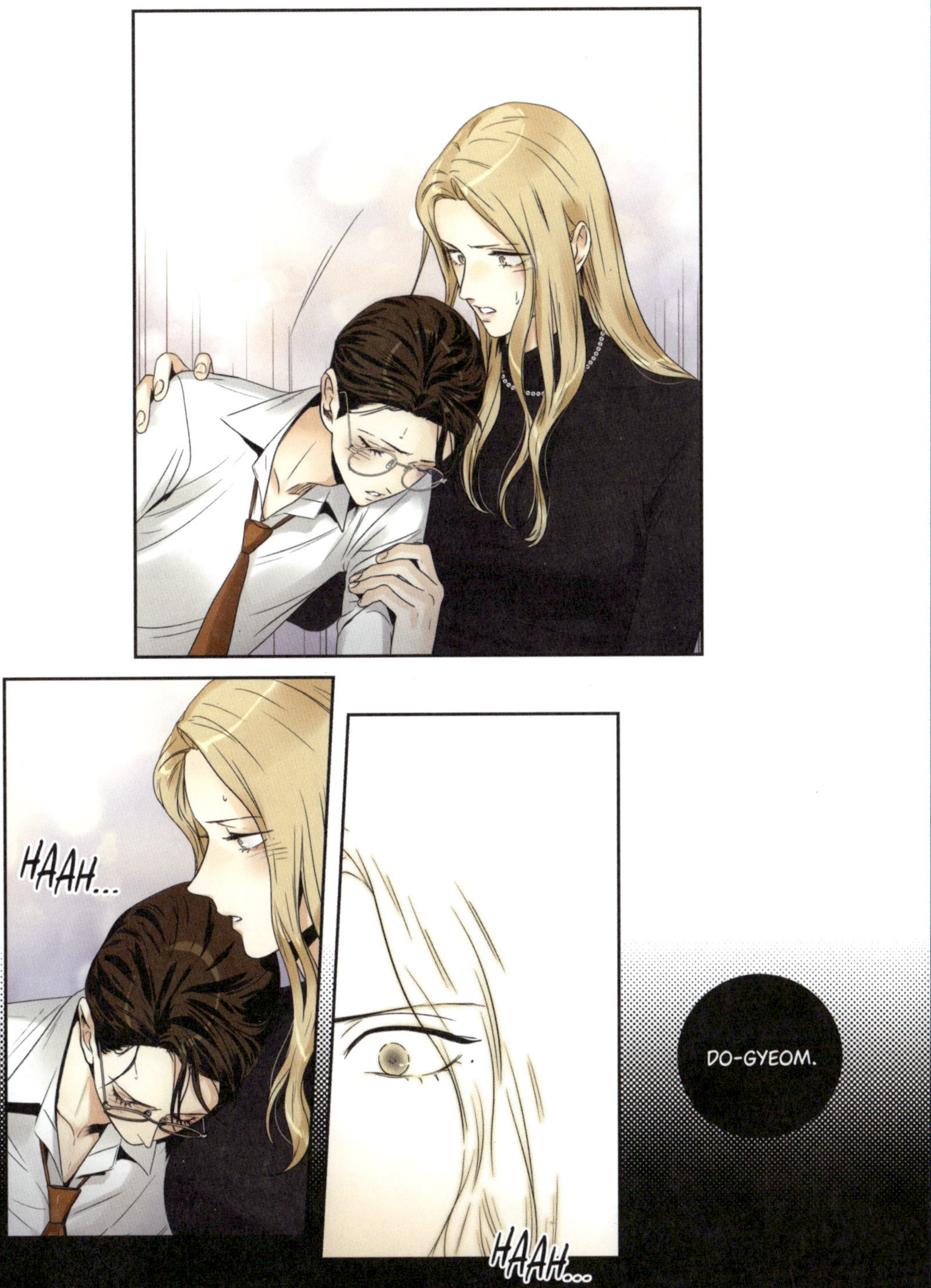
HAAH...
DO-GYEOM.
HAAH...

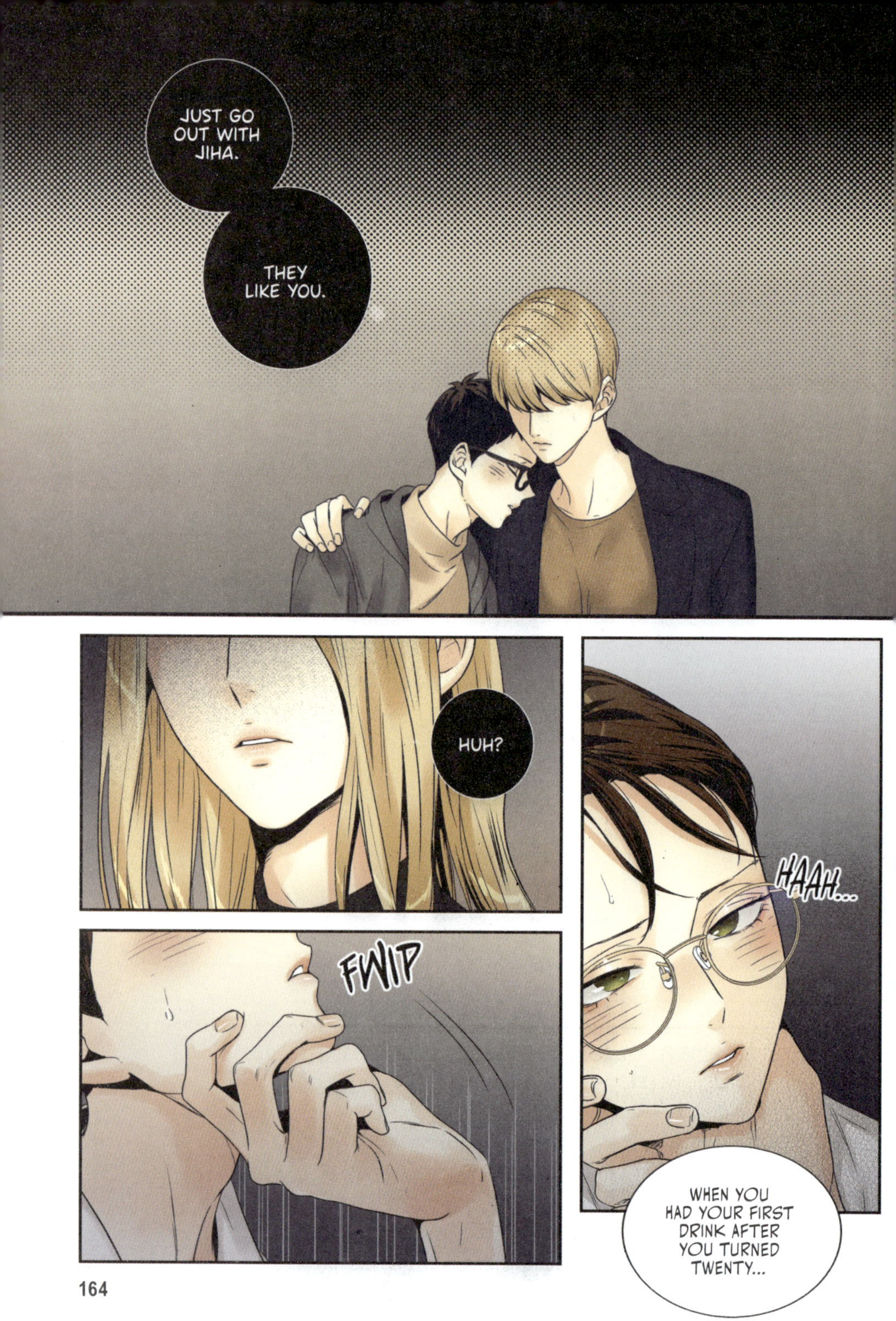
JUST GO OUT WITH JIHA.
THEY LIKE YOU.
HUH?
FWIP
HAAH...
WHEN YOU HAD YOUR FIRST DRINK AFTER YOU TURNED TWENTY...

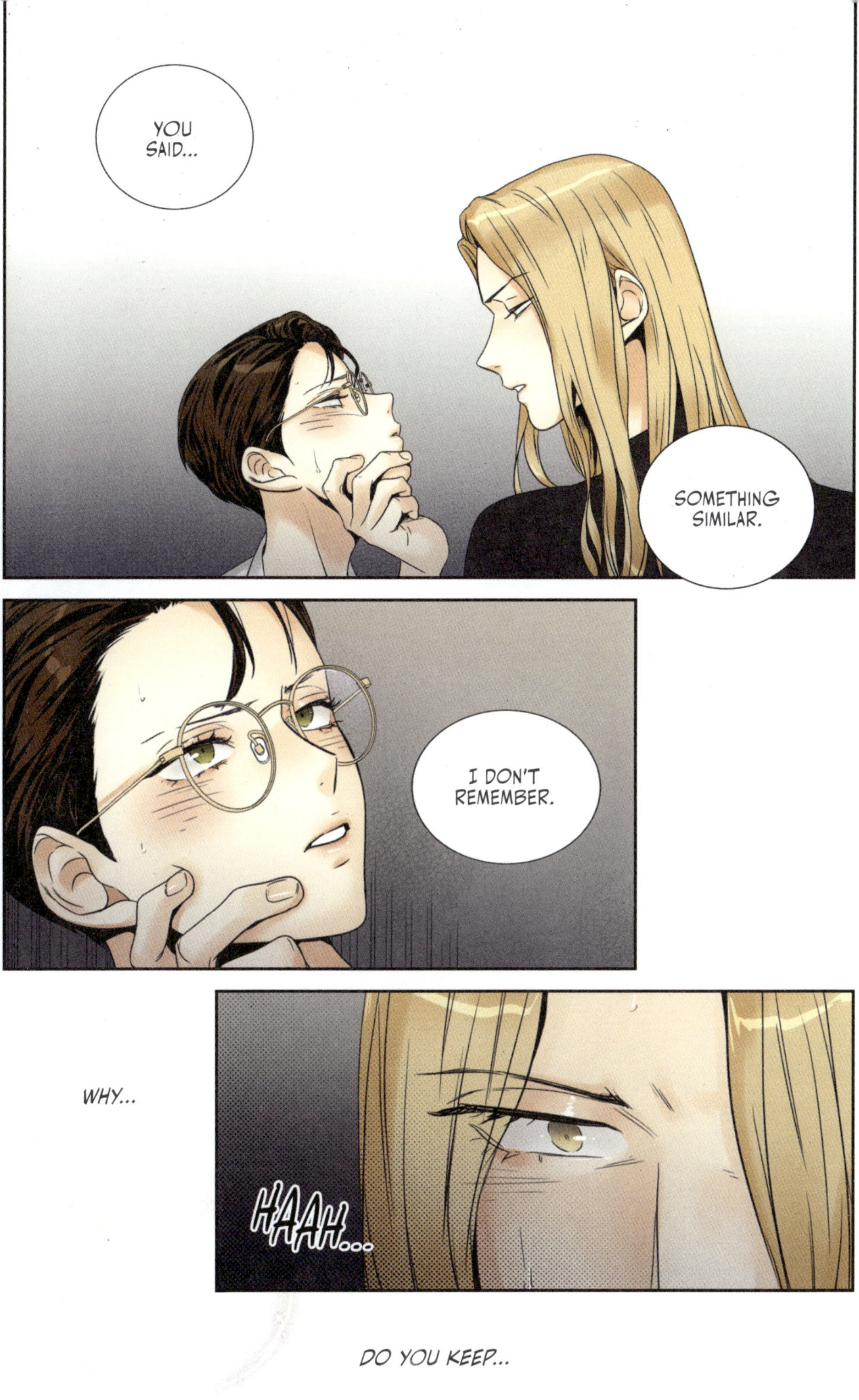
YOU SAID...
SOMETHING SIMILAR.
I DON'T REMEMBER.
WHY...
HAAH...
DO YOU KEEP...

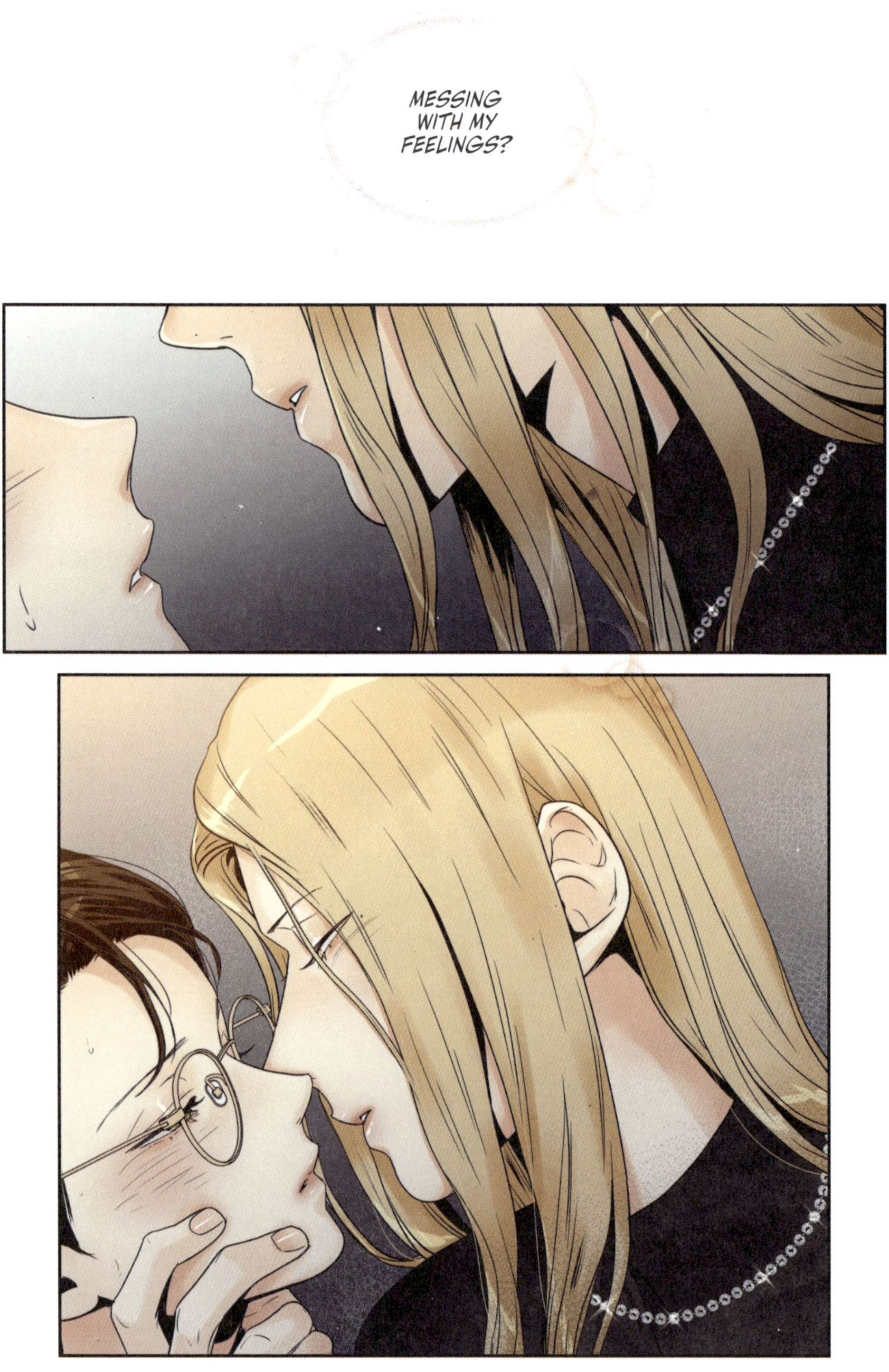
MESSING WITH MY FEELINGS?

Love is an Illusion!
The Queen

Love is an Illusion!
The Queen

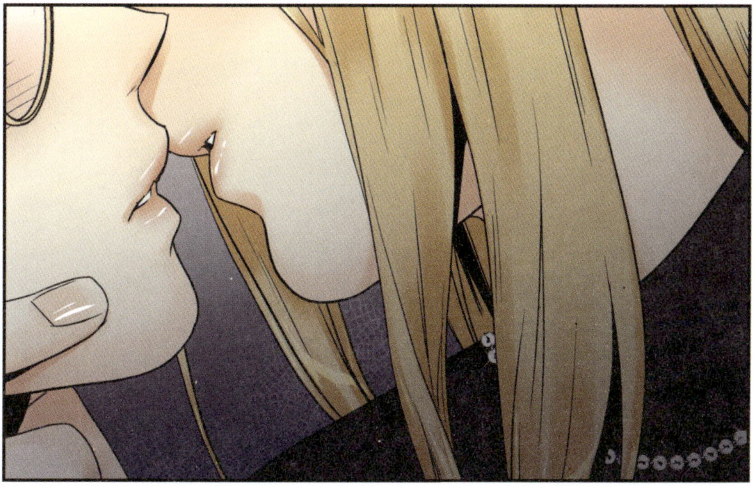

Chapter 8

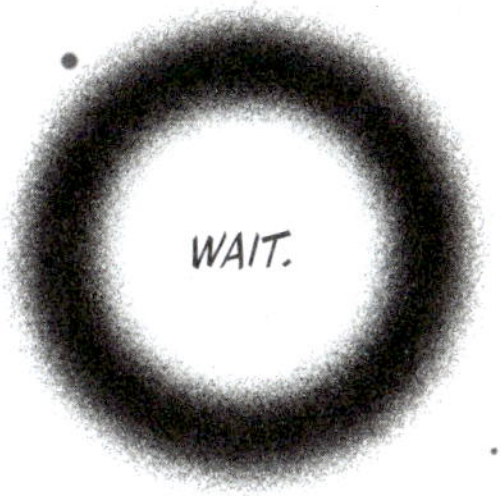
WAIT.

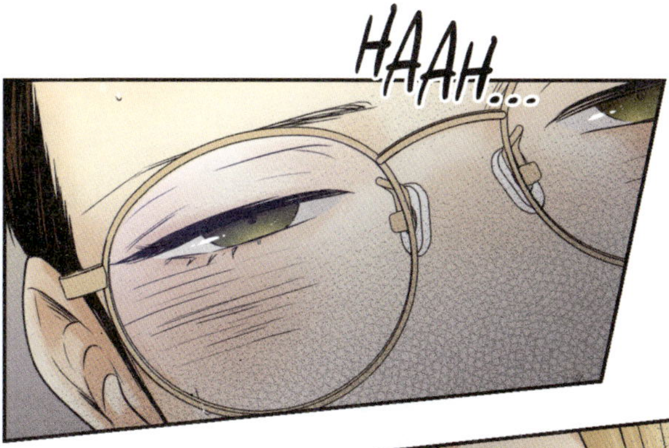
HAAH...

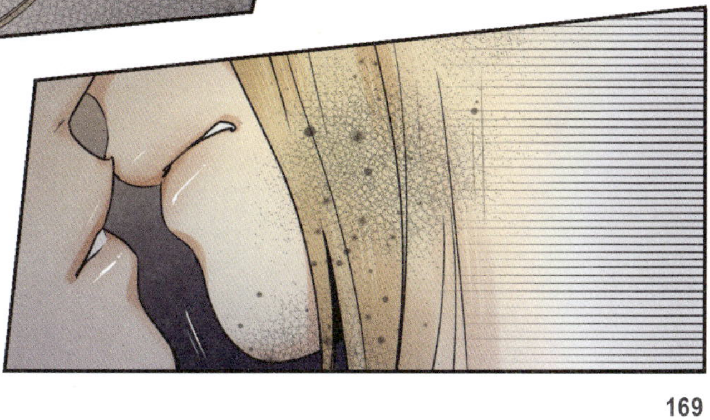

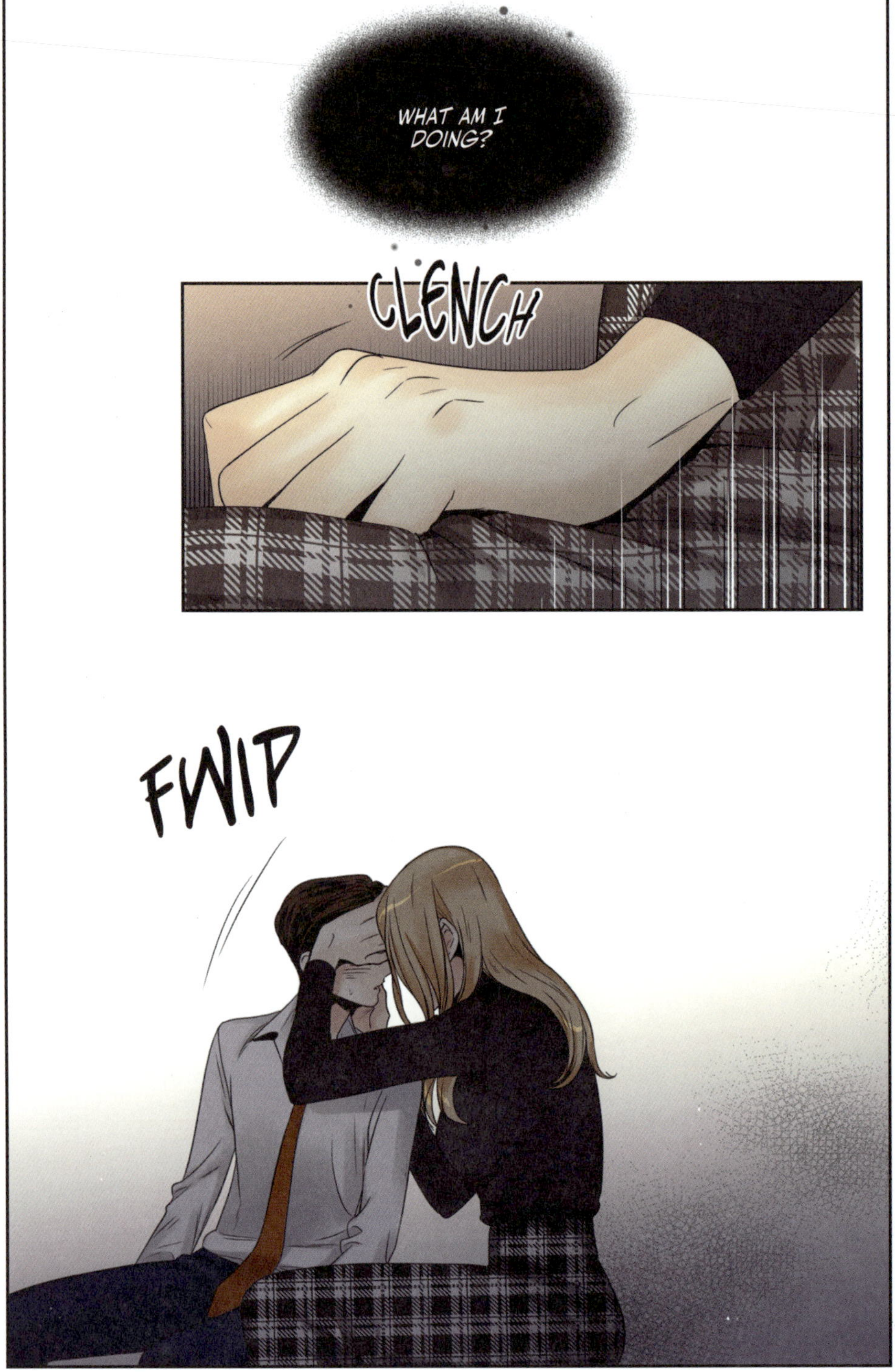
WHAT AM I DOING?
CLENCH
FWIP

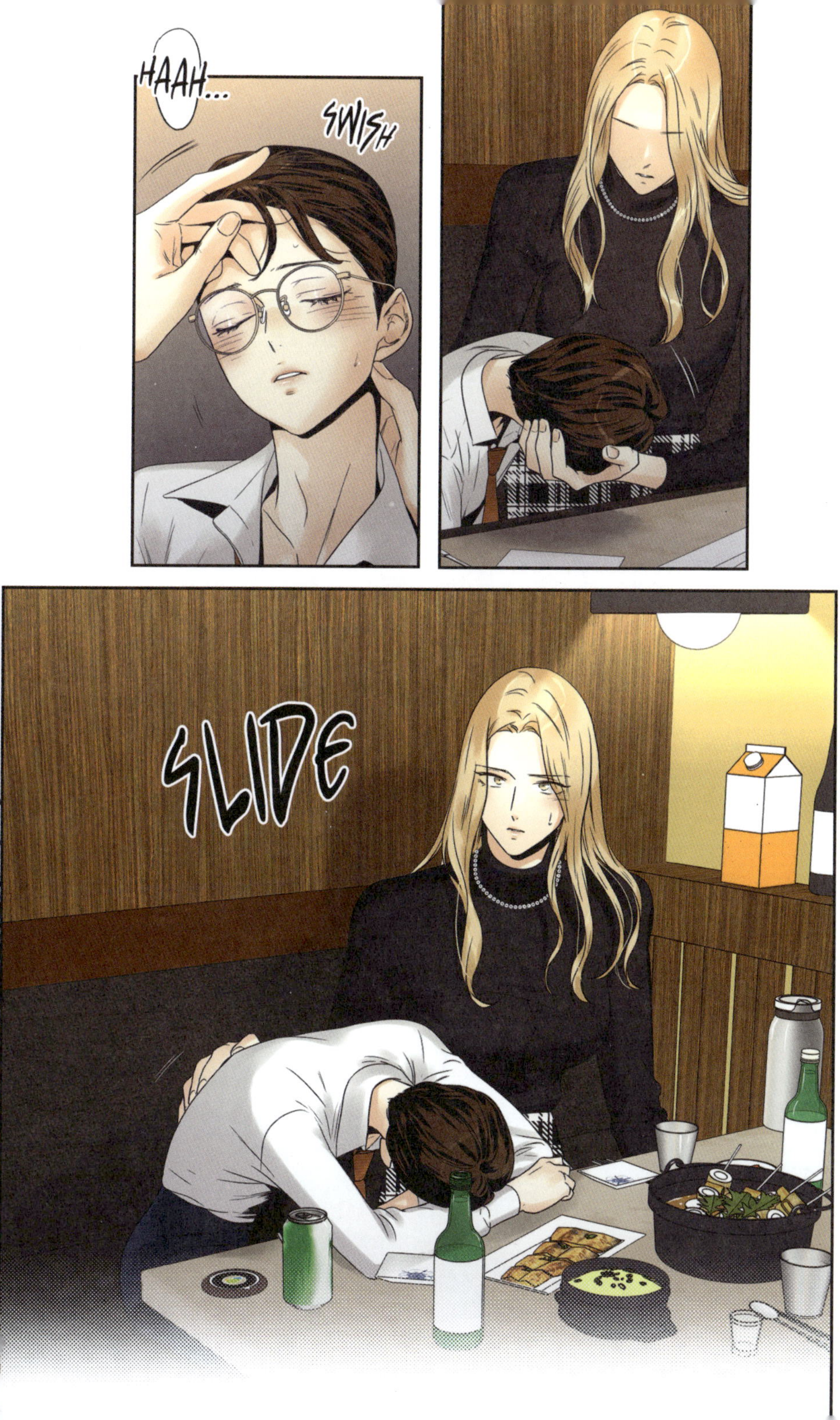
HAAH...
SWISH
SLIDE

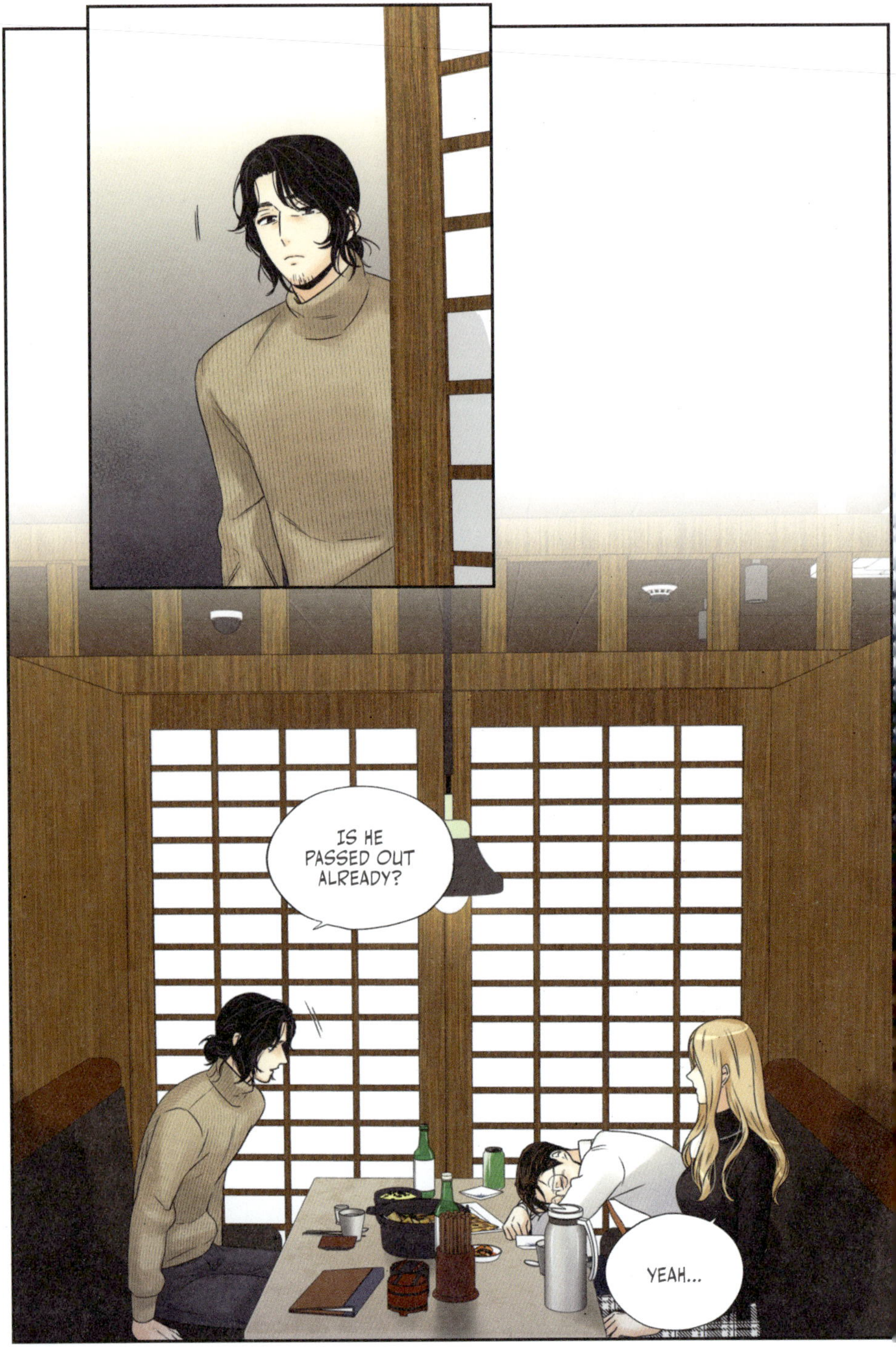
IS HE PASSED OUT ALREADY?
YEAH...

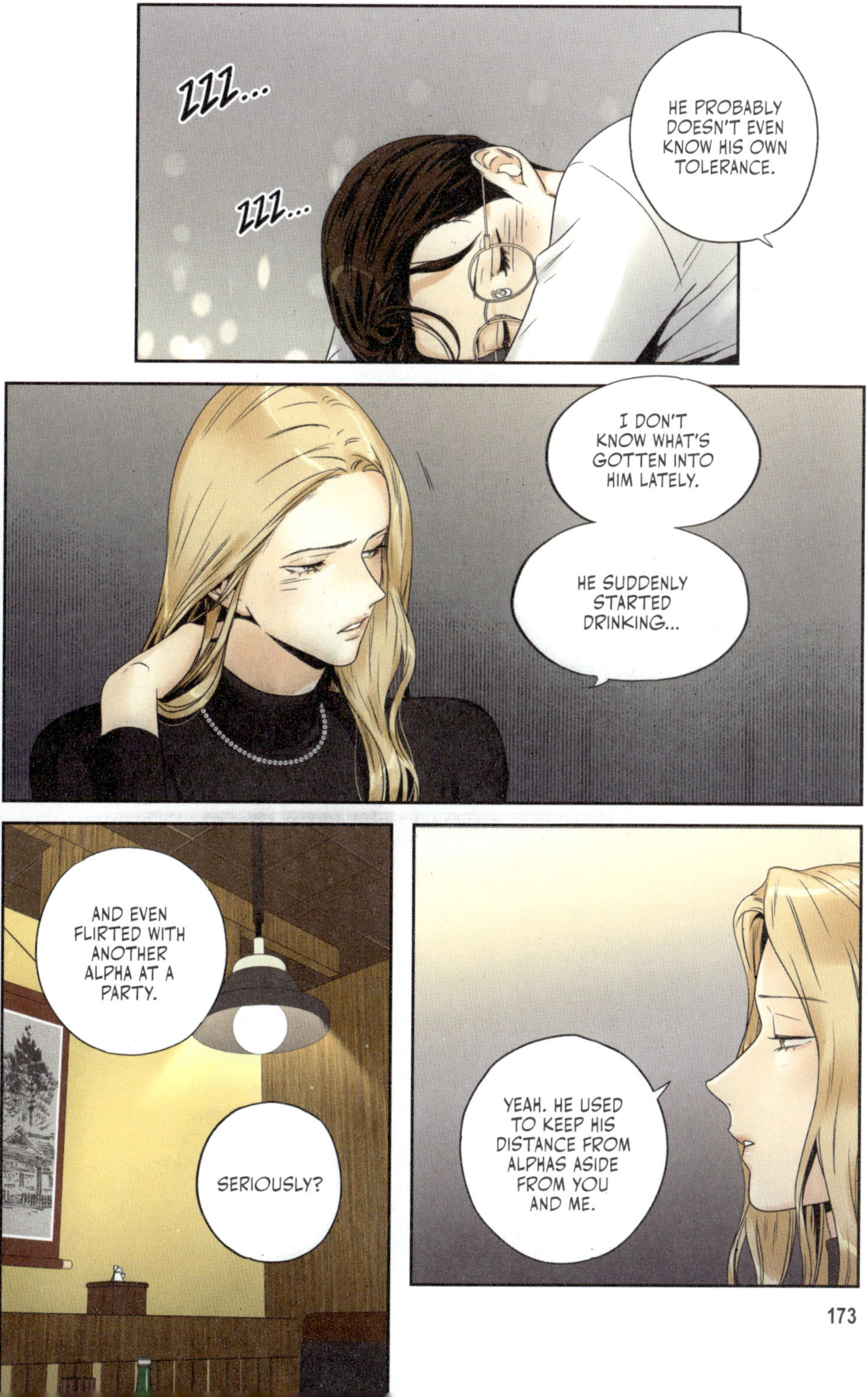

ZZZ...
ZZZ...
HE PROBABLY DOESN'T EVEN KNOW HIS OWN TOLERANCE.
I DON'T KNOW WHAT'S GOTTEN INTO HIM LATELY.
HE SUDDENLY STARTED DRINKING...
AND EVEN FLIRTED WITH ANOTHER ALPHA AT A PARTY.
SERIOUSLY?
YEAH. HE USED TO KEEP HIS DISTANCE FROM ALPHAS ASIDE FROM YOU AND ME.

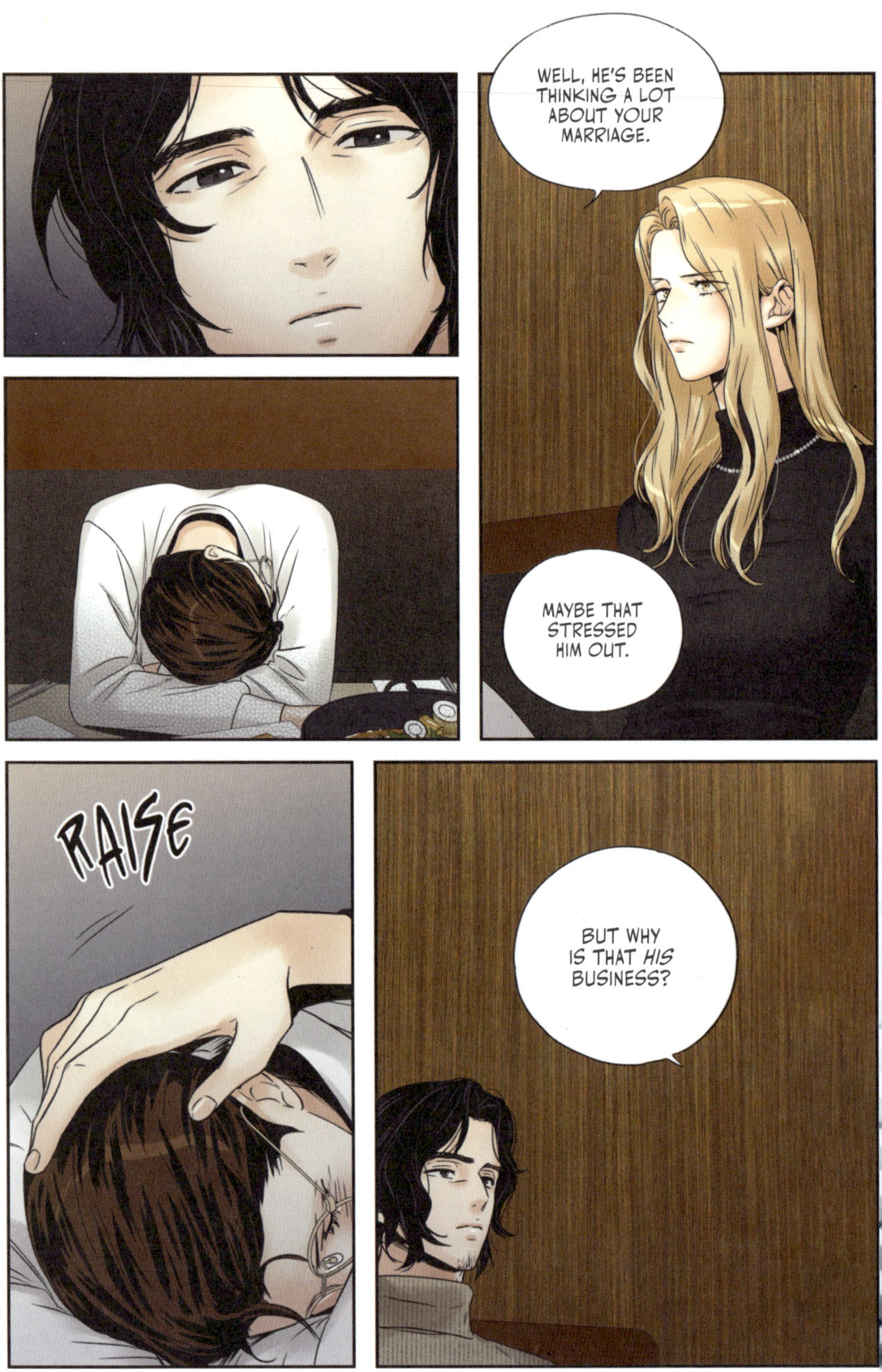
WELL, HE'S BEEN THINKING A LOT ABOUT YOUR MARRIAGE.
MAYBE THAT STRESSED HIM OUT.
RAISE
BUT WHY IS THAT *HIS* BUSINESS?

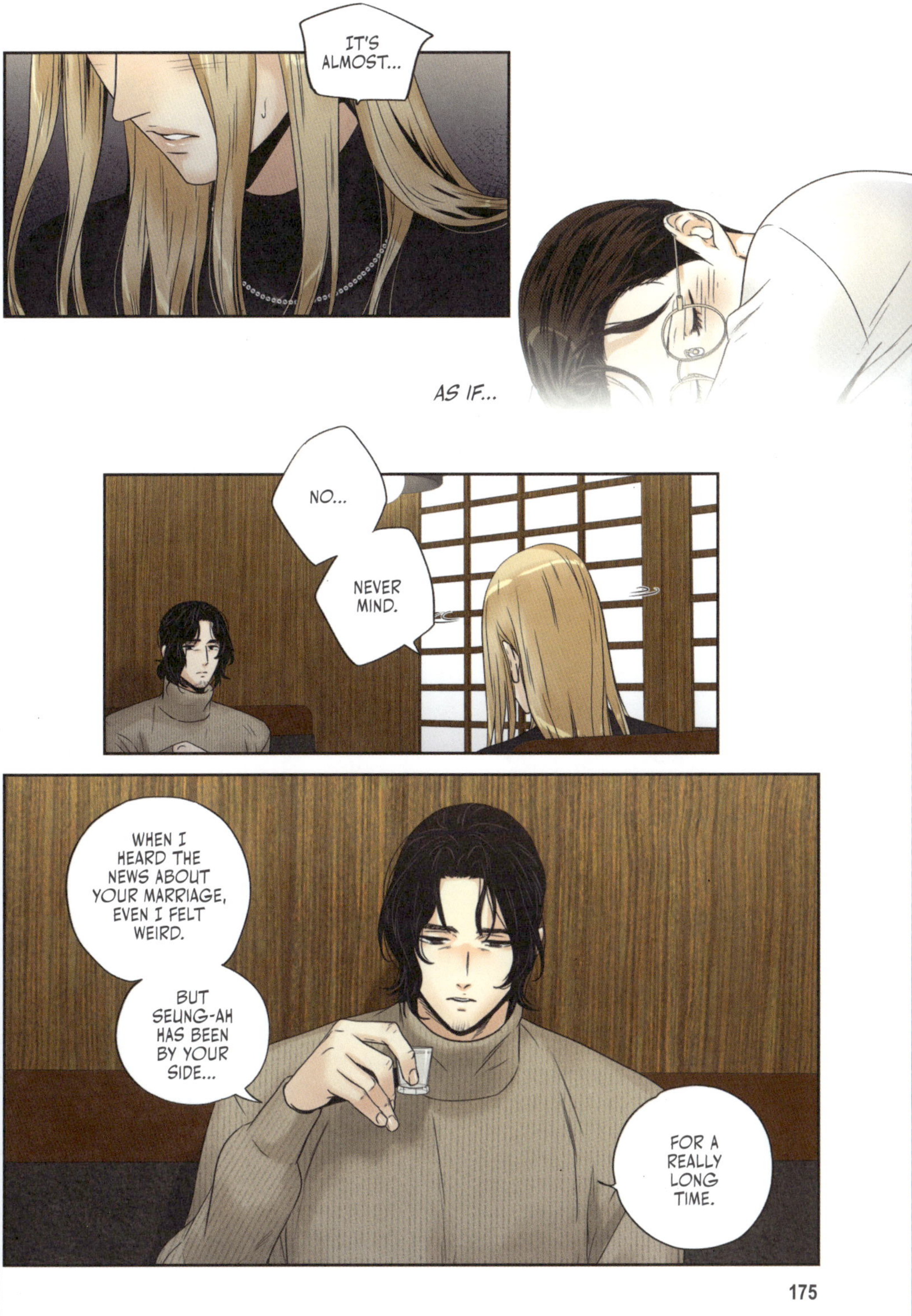
IT'S ALMOST...
AS IF...
NO...
NEVER MIND.
WHEN I HEARD THE NEWS ABOUT YOUR MARRIAGE, EVEN I FELT WEIRD.
BUT SEUNG-AH HAS BEEN BY YOUR SIDE...
FOR A REALLY LONG TIME.

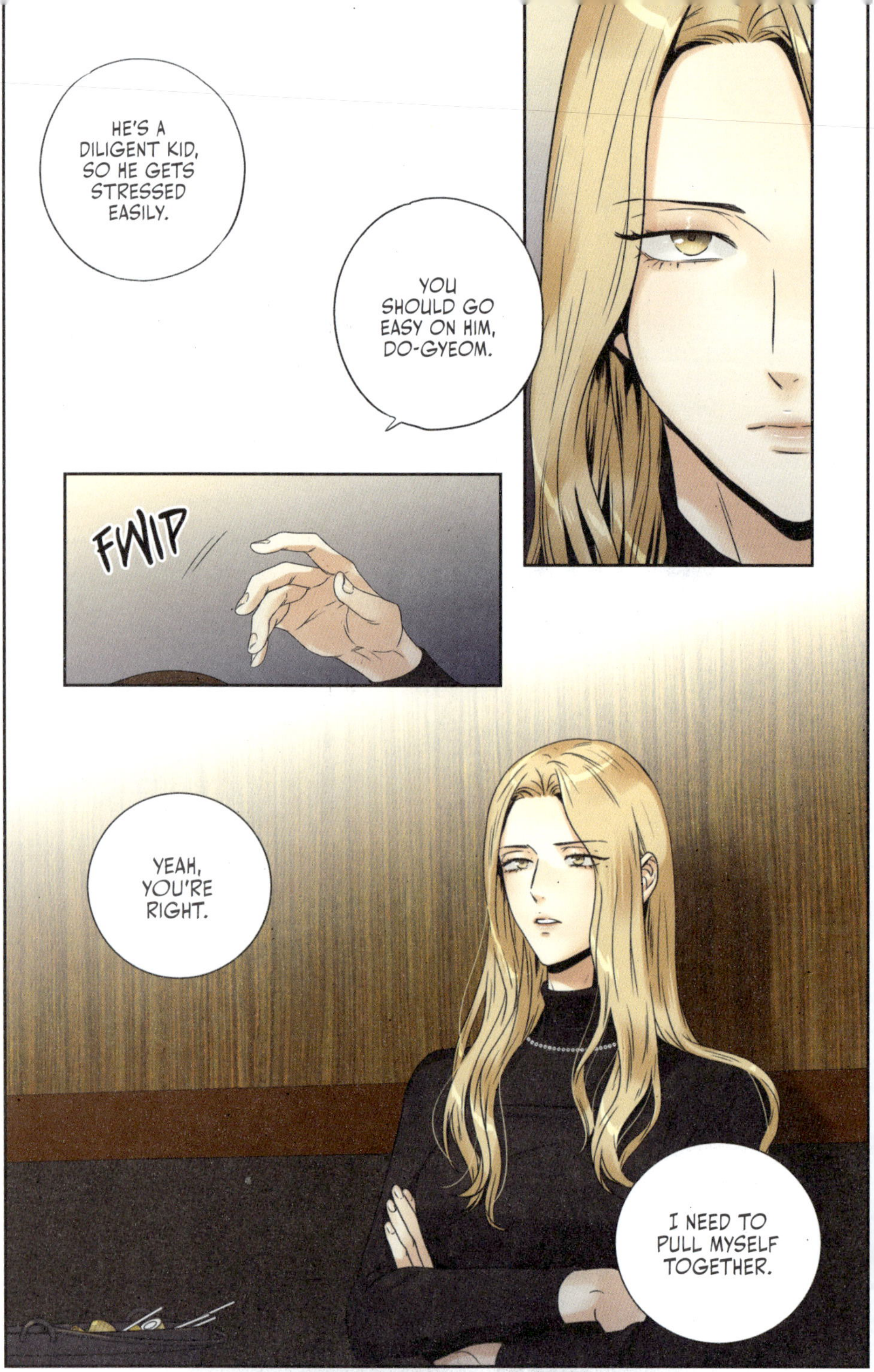
HE'S A DILIGENT KID, SO HE GETS STRESSED EASILY.
YOU SHOULD GO EASY ON HIM, DO-GYEOM.
FWIP
YEAH, YOU'RE RIGHT.
I NEED TO PULL MYSELF TOGETHER.

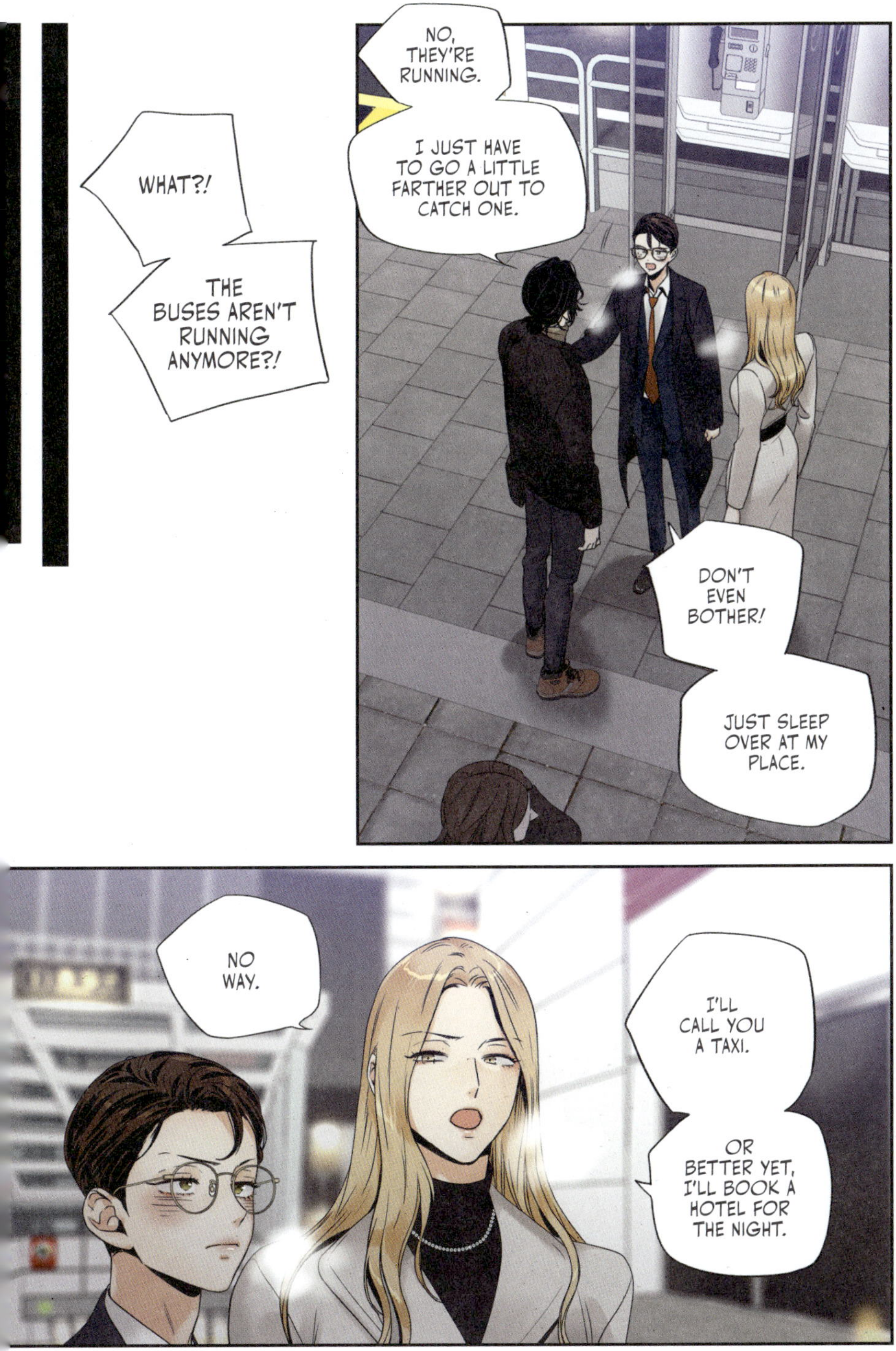
WHAT?!
THE BUSES AREN'T RUNNING ANYMORE?!
NO, THEY'RE RUNNING.
I JUST HAVE TO GO A LITTLE FARTHER OUT TO CATCH ONE.
DON'T EVEN BOTHER!
JUST SLEEP OVER AT MY PLACE.
NO WAY.
I'LL CALL YOU A TAXI.
OR BETTER YET, I'LL BOOK A HOTEL FOR THE NIGHT.

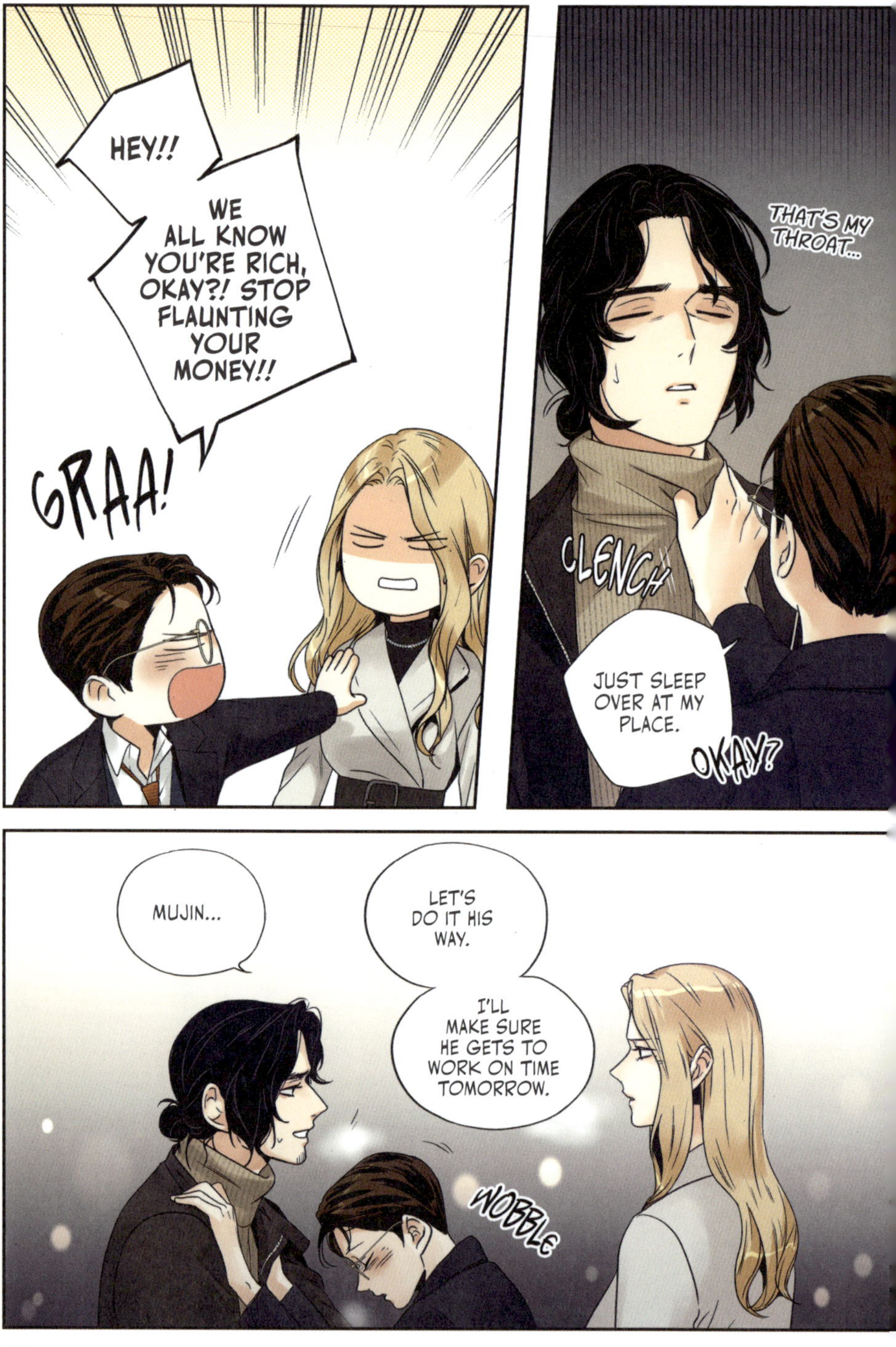
HEY!!
WE ALL KNOW YOU'RE RICH, OKAY?! STOP FLAUNTING YOUR MONEY!!
GRAA!
THAT'S MY THROAT...
CLENCH
JUST SLEEP OVER AT MY PLACE.
OKAY?
MUJIN...
LET'S DO IT HIS WAY.
I'LL MAKE SURE HE GETS TO WORK ON TIME TOMORROW.
WOBBLE

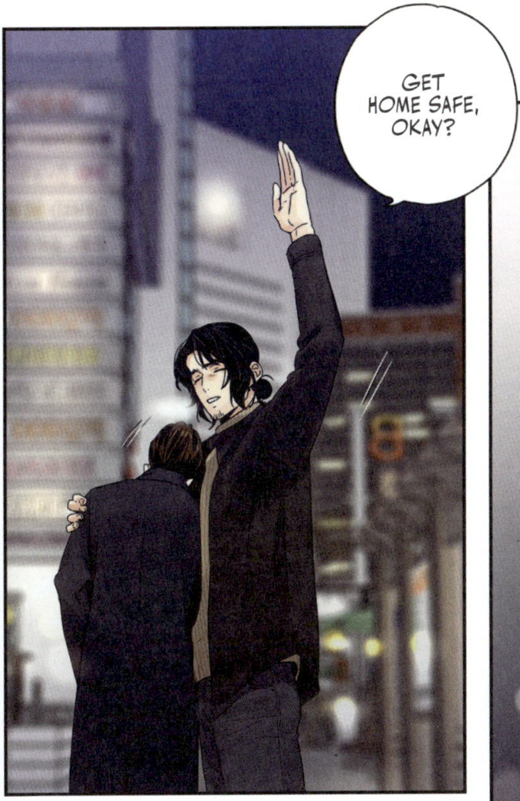
GET HOME SAFE, OKAY?

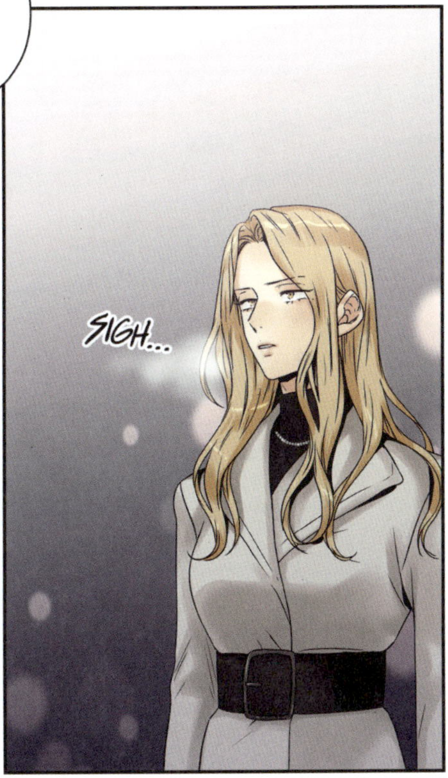
SIGH...

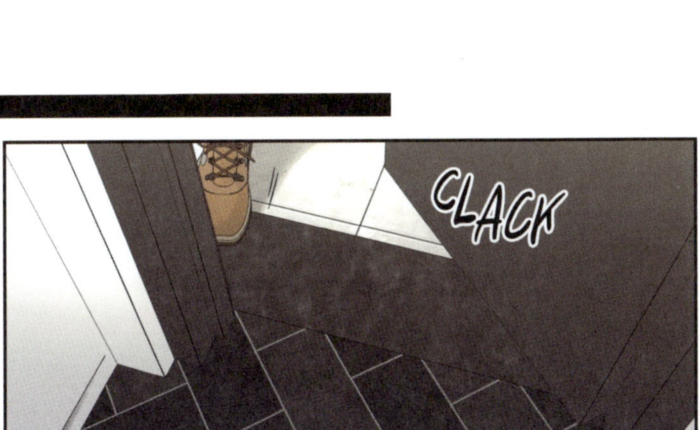
CLACK

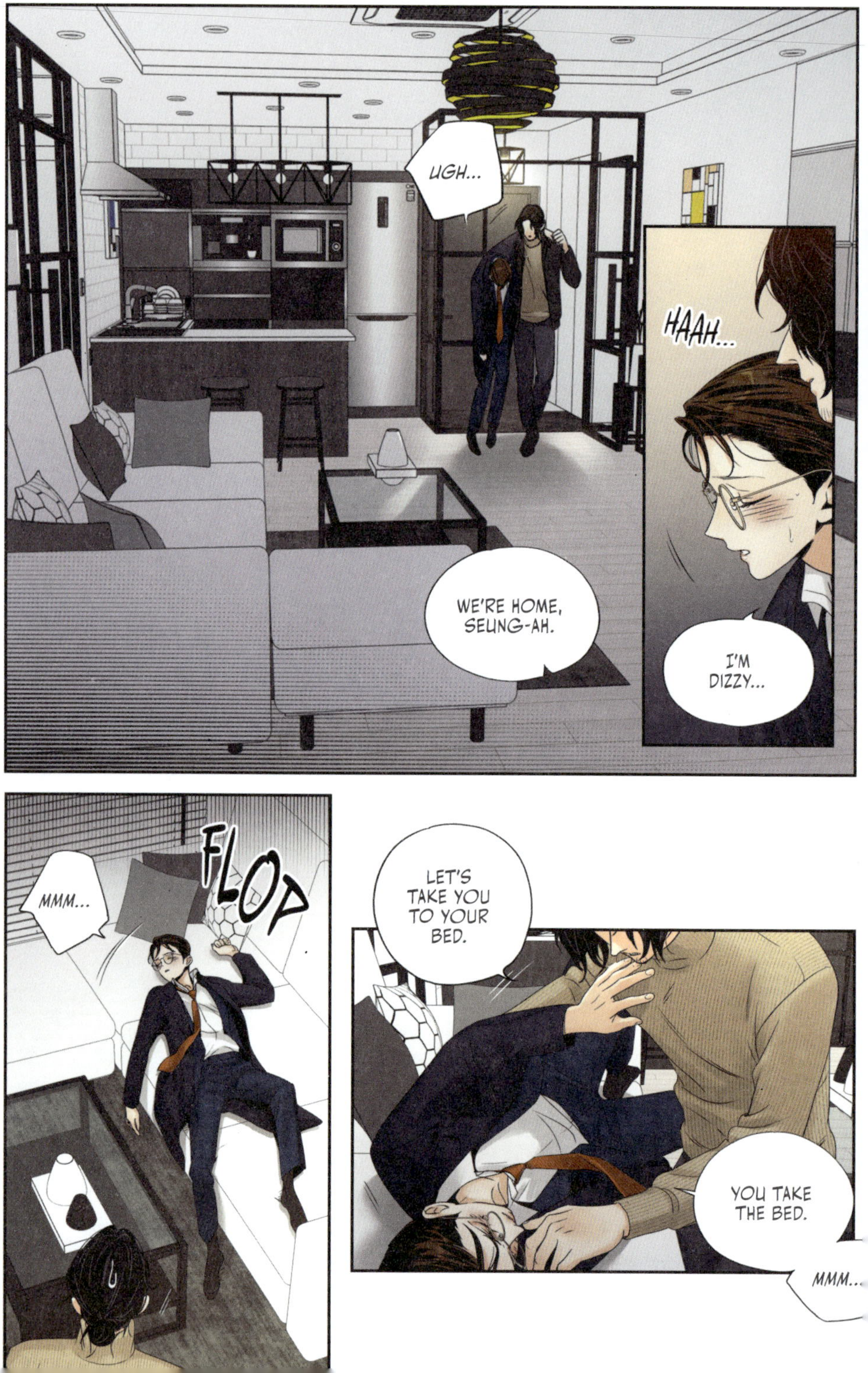
UGH...
WE'RE HOME, SEUNG-AH.
HAAH...
I'M DIZZY...
MMM...
FLOP
LET'S TAKE YOU TO YOUR BED.
YOU TAKE THE BED.
MMM...

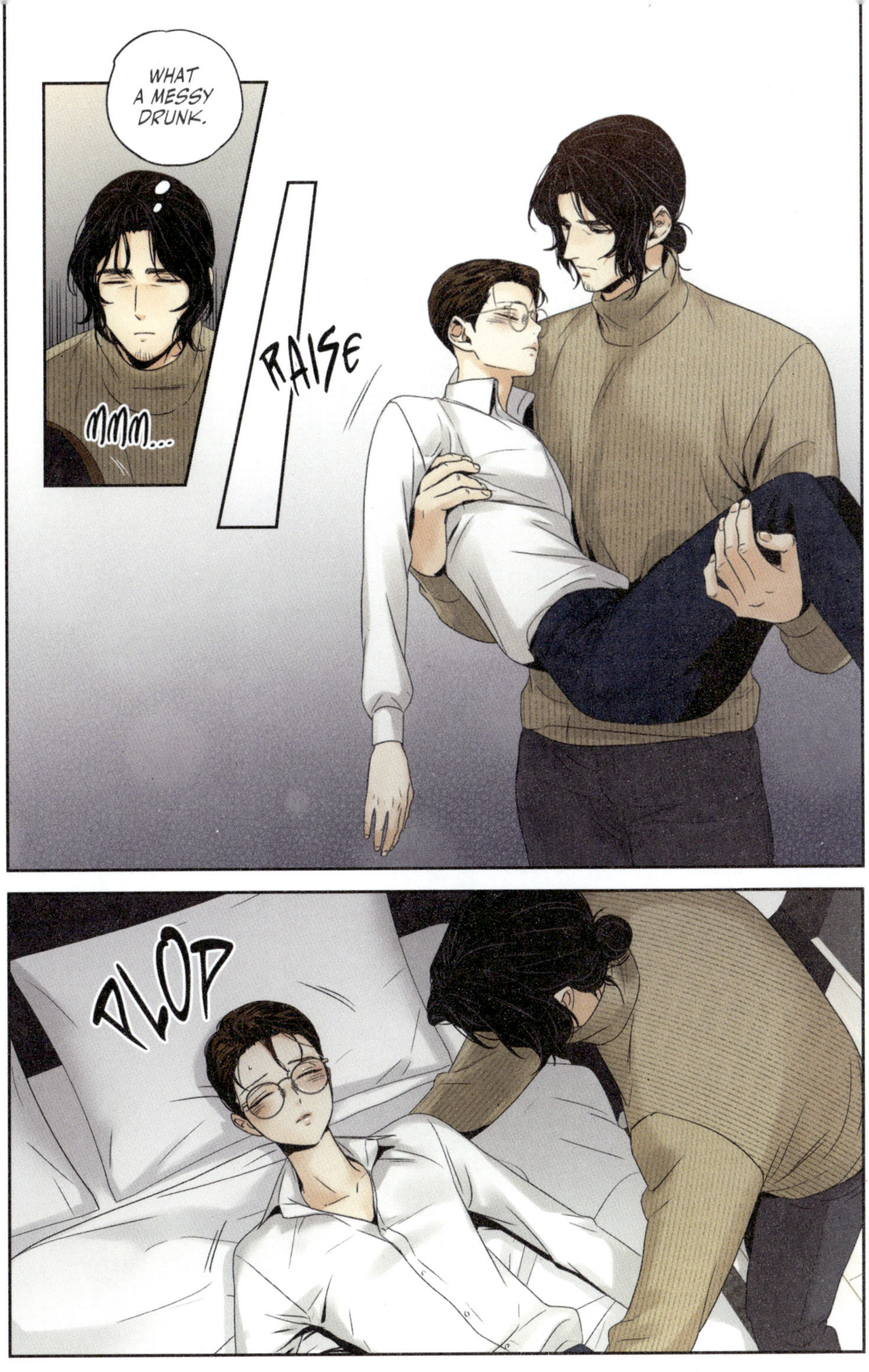
WHAT A MESSY DRUNK.
MMM...
RAISE
PLOP

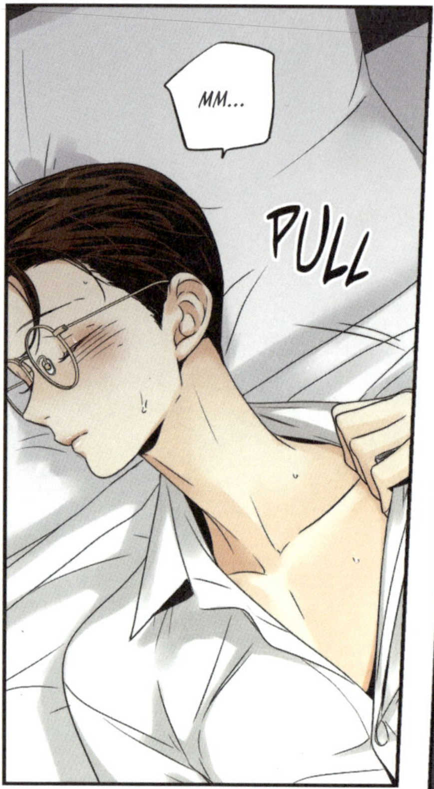
MM...
PULL

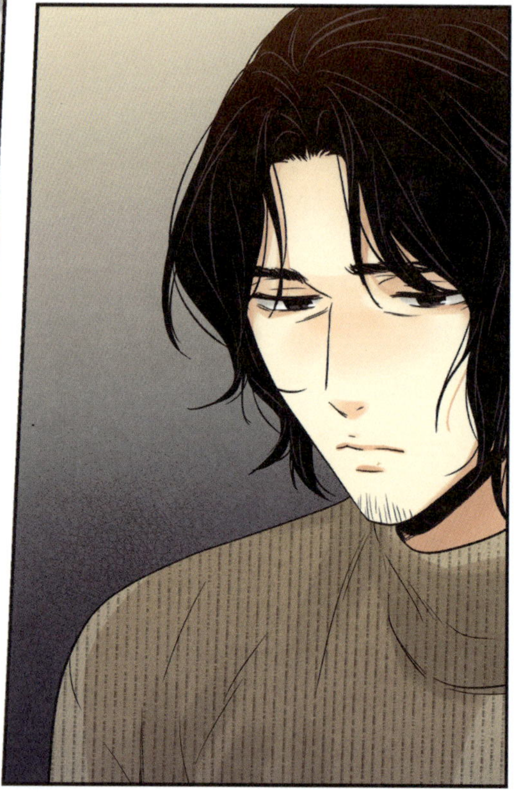

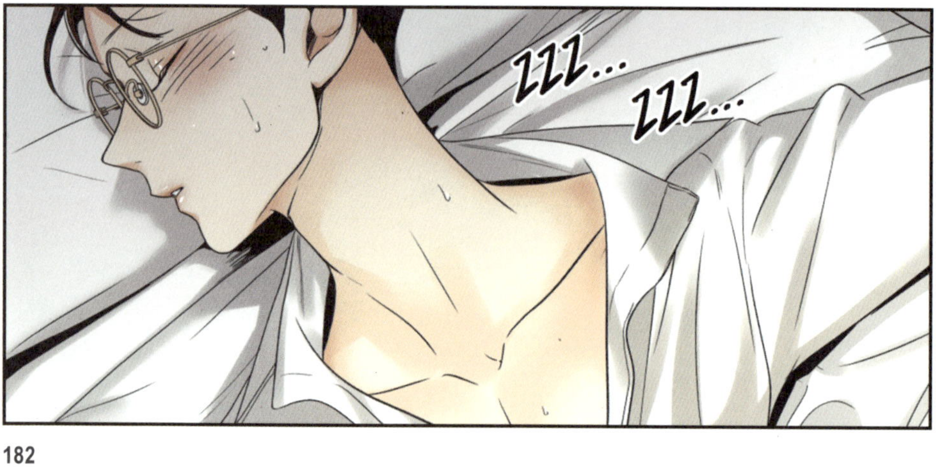
ZZZ...
ZZZ...

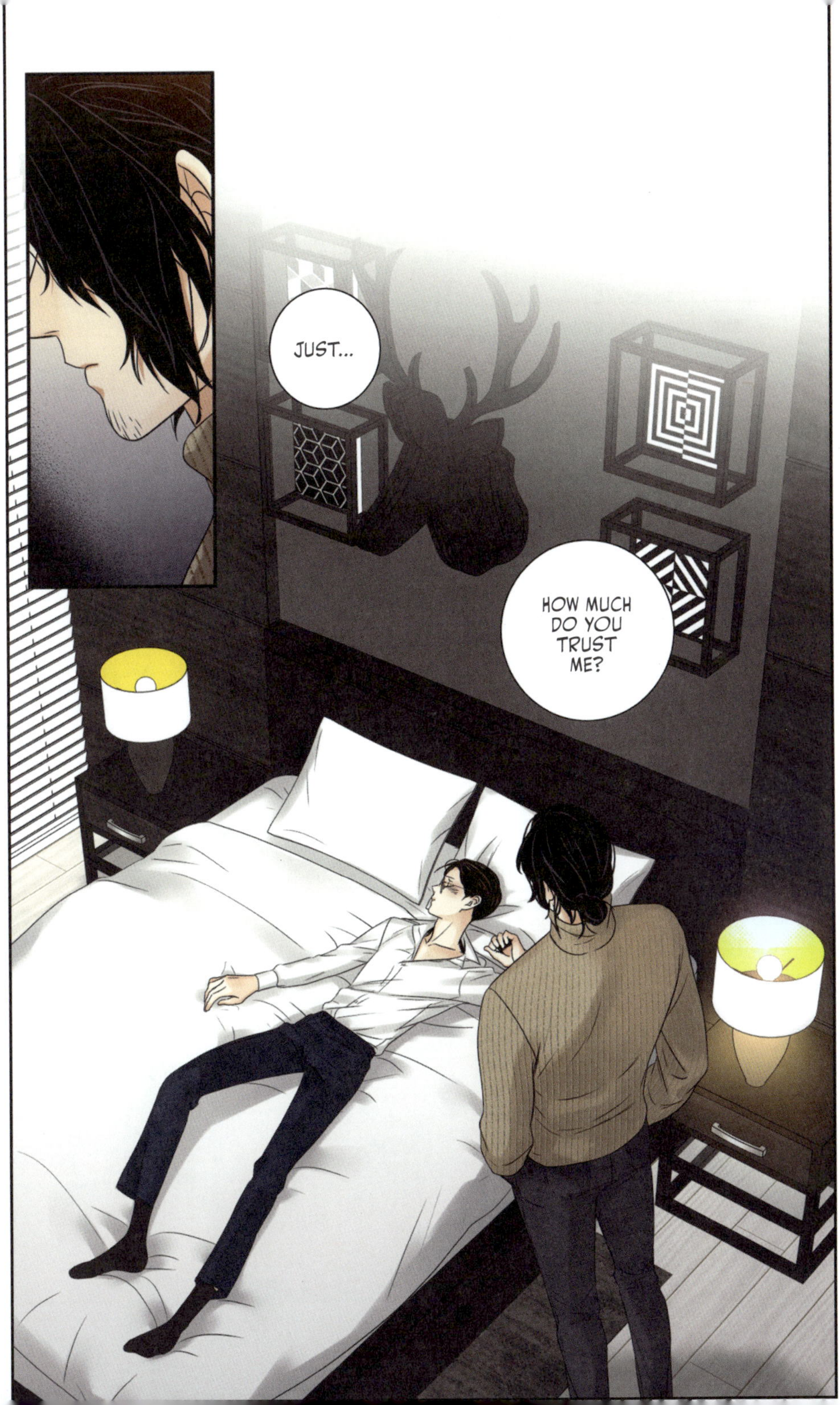
JUST...
HOW MUCH DO YOU TRUST ME?

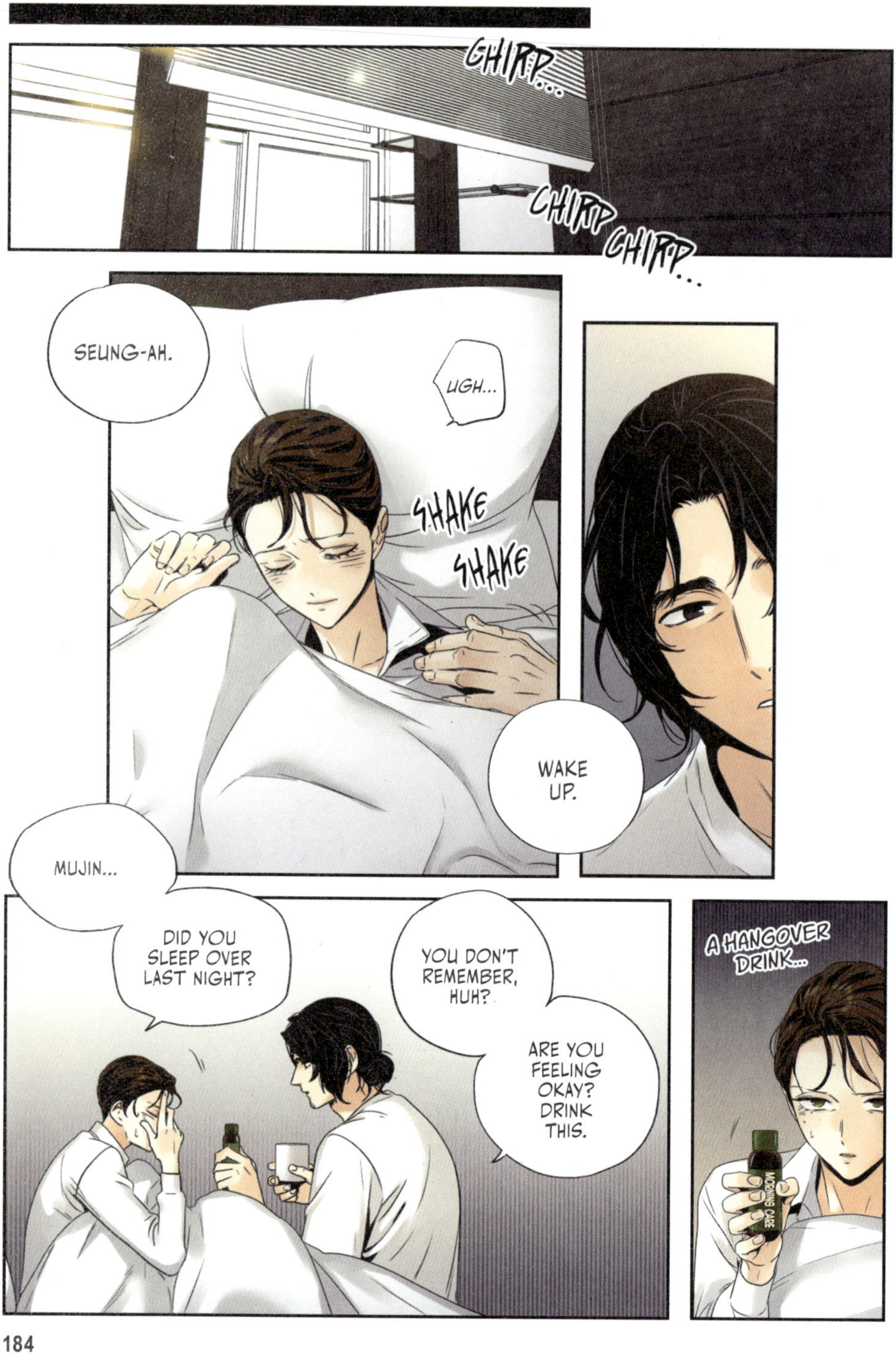

CHIRP...
CHIRP CHIRP...
SEUNG-AH.
UGH...
SHAKE SHAKE
WAKE UP.
MUJIN...
DID YOU SLEEP OVER LAST NIGHT?
YOU DON'T REMEMBER, HUH?
ARE YOU FEELING OKAY? DRINK THIS.
A HANGOVER DRINK...
MORNING CARE

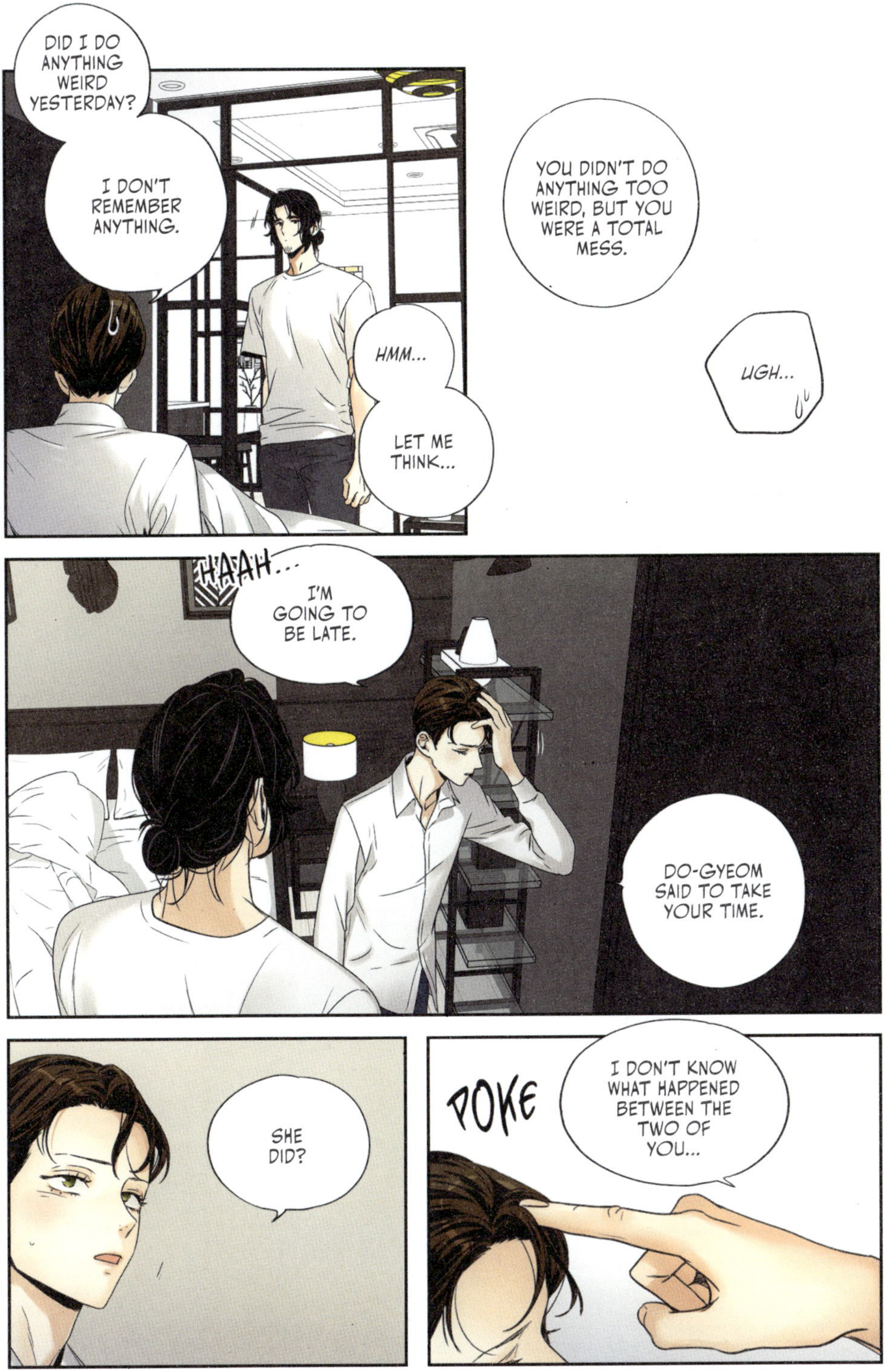
DID I DO ANYTHING WEIRD YESTERDAY?
I DON'T REMEMBER ANYTHING.
HMM...
LET ME THINK...
YOU DIDN'T DO ANYTHING TOO WEIRD, BUT YOU WERE A TOTAL MESS.
UGH...
HAAAH...
I'M GOING TO BE LATE.
DO-GYEOM SAID TO TAKE YOUR TIME.
SHE DID?
POKE
I DON'T KNOW WHAT HAPPENED BETWEEN THE TWO OF YOU...

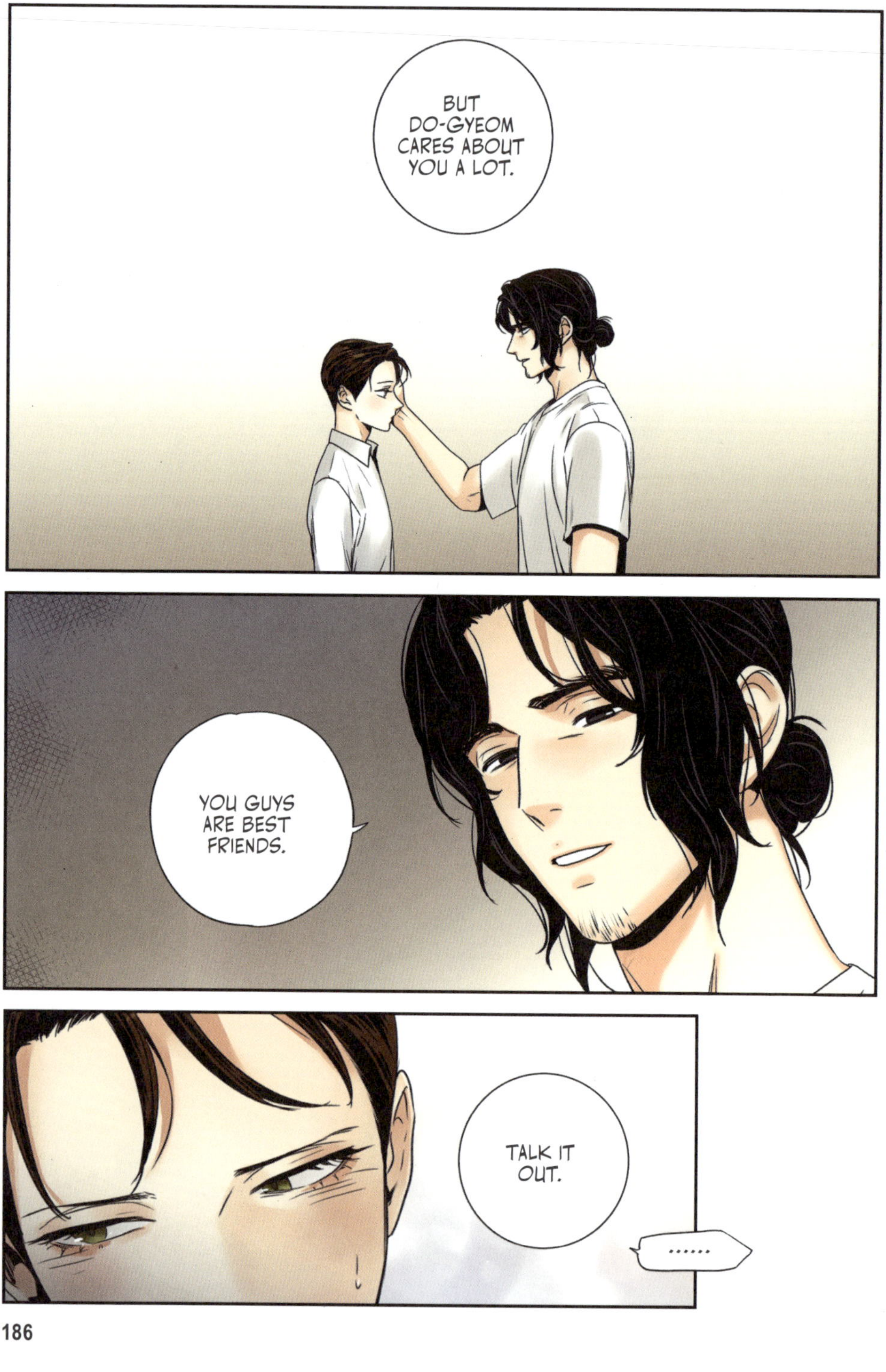
BUT DO-GYEOM CARES ABOUT YOU A LOT.
YOU GUYS ARE BEST FRIENDS.
TALK IT OUT.
......

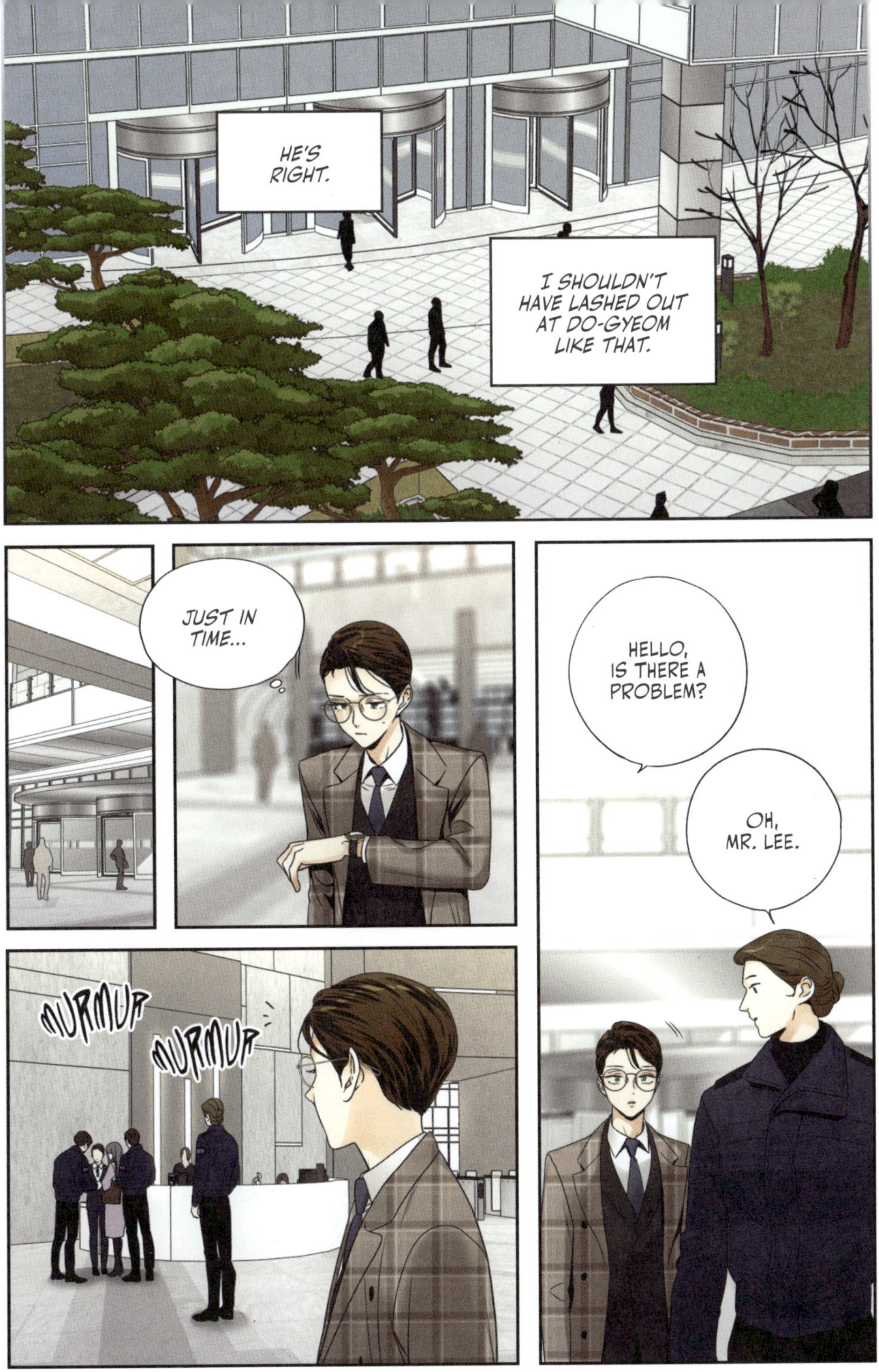

HE'S RIGHT.
I SHOULDN'T HAVE LASHED OUT AT DO-GYEOM LIKE THAT.
JUST IN TIME...
HELLO, IS THERE A PROBLEM?
OH, MR. LEE.
MURMUR
MURMUR

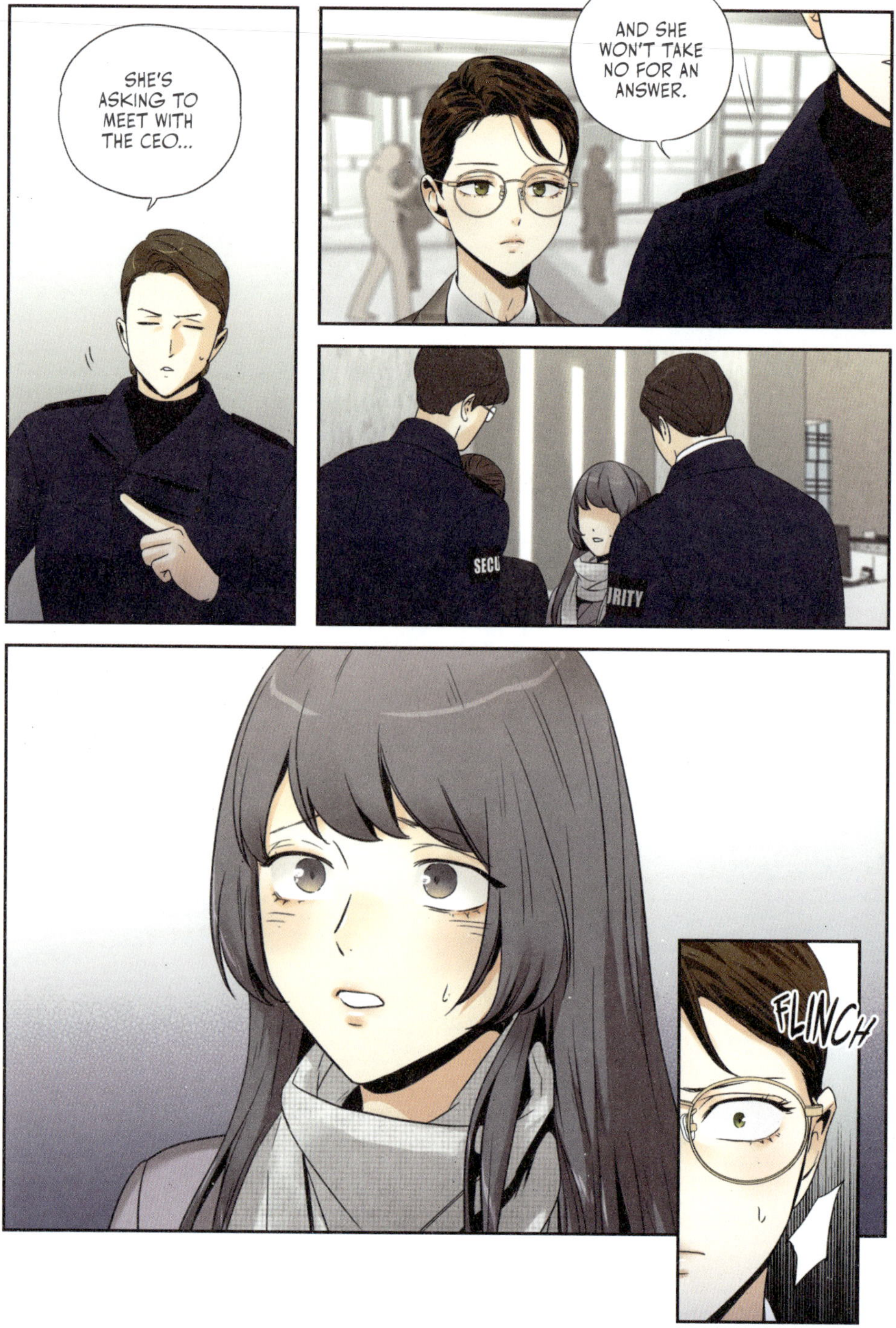
SHE'S ASKING TO MEET WITH THE CEO...
AND SHE WON'T TAKE NO FOR AN ANSWER.
SECU
RITY
FLINCH

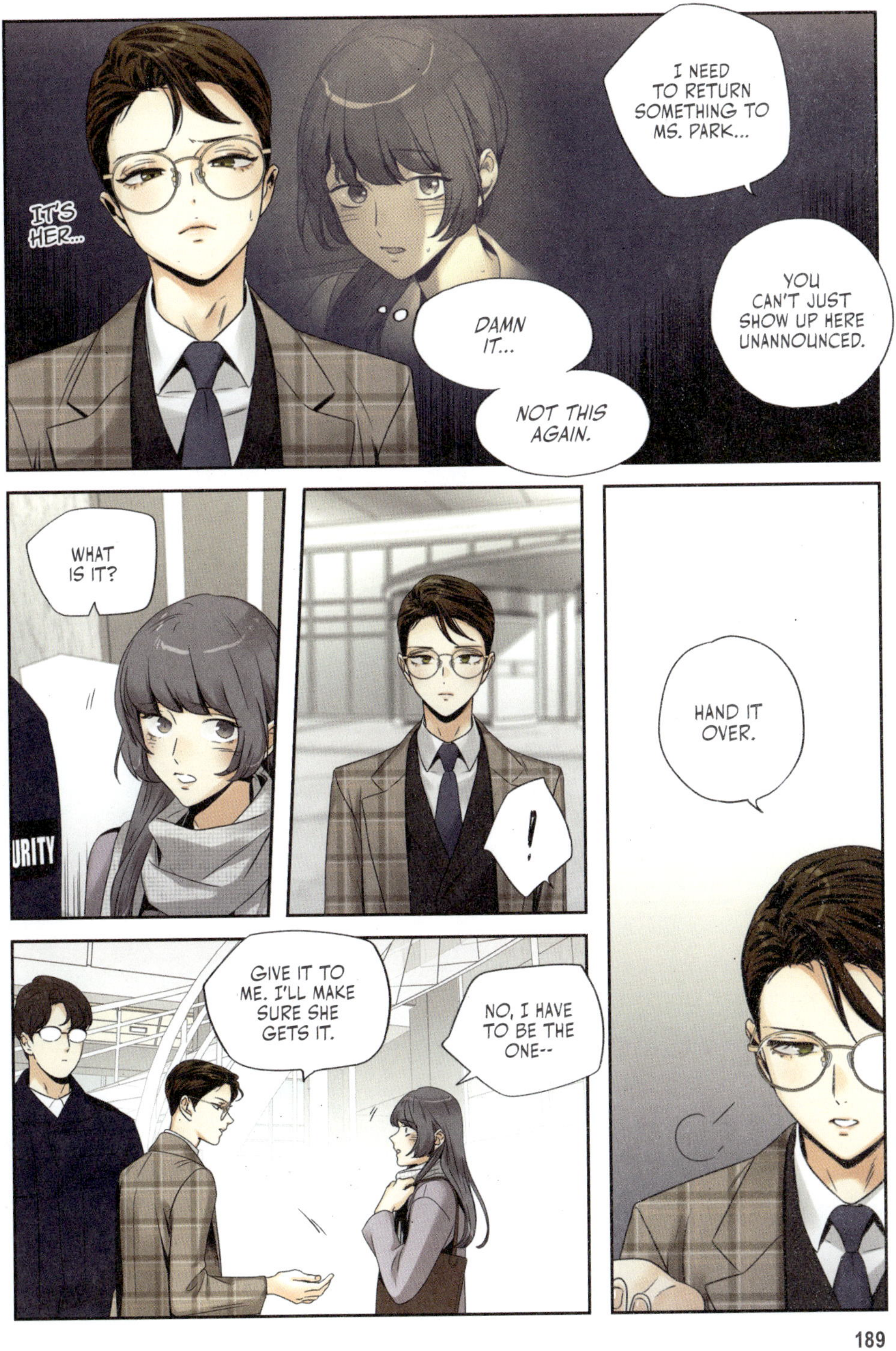
I NEED TO RETURN SOMETHING TO MS. PARK...
IT'S HER...
DAMN IT...
NOT THIS AGAIN.
YOU CAN'T JUST SHOW UP HERE UNANNOUNCED.
WHAT IS IT?
URITY
!
GIVE IT TO ME. I'LL MAKE SURE SHE GETS IT.
NO, I HAVE TO BE THE ONE--
HAND IT OVER.

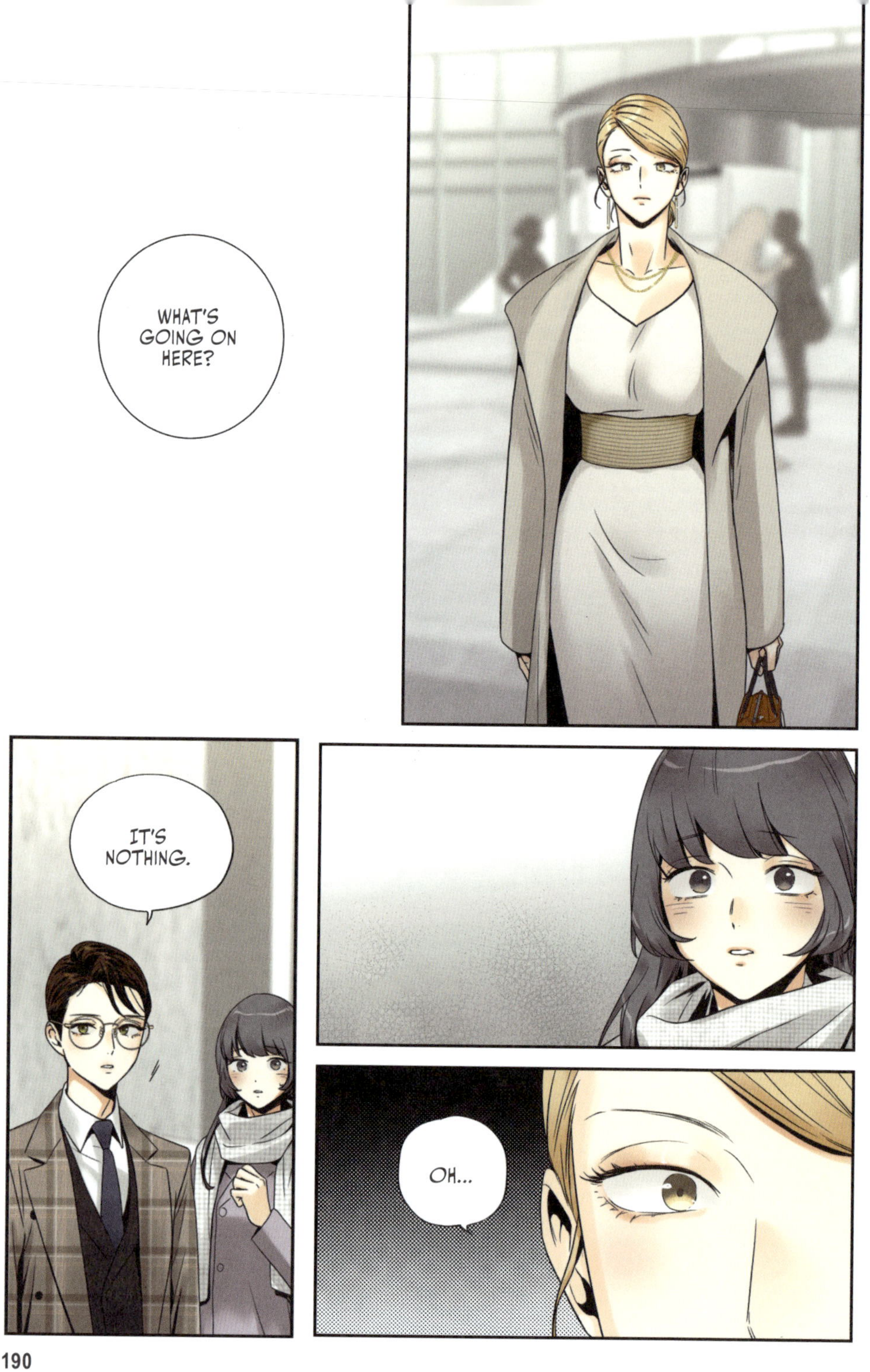
WHAT'S GOING ON HERE?
IT'S NOTHING.
OH...

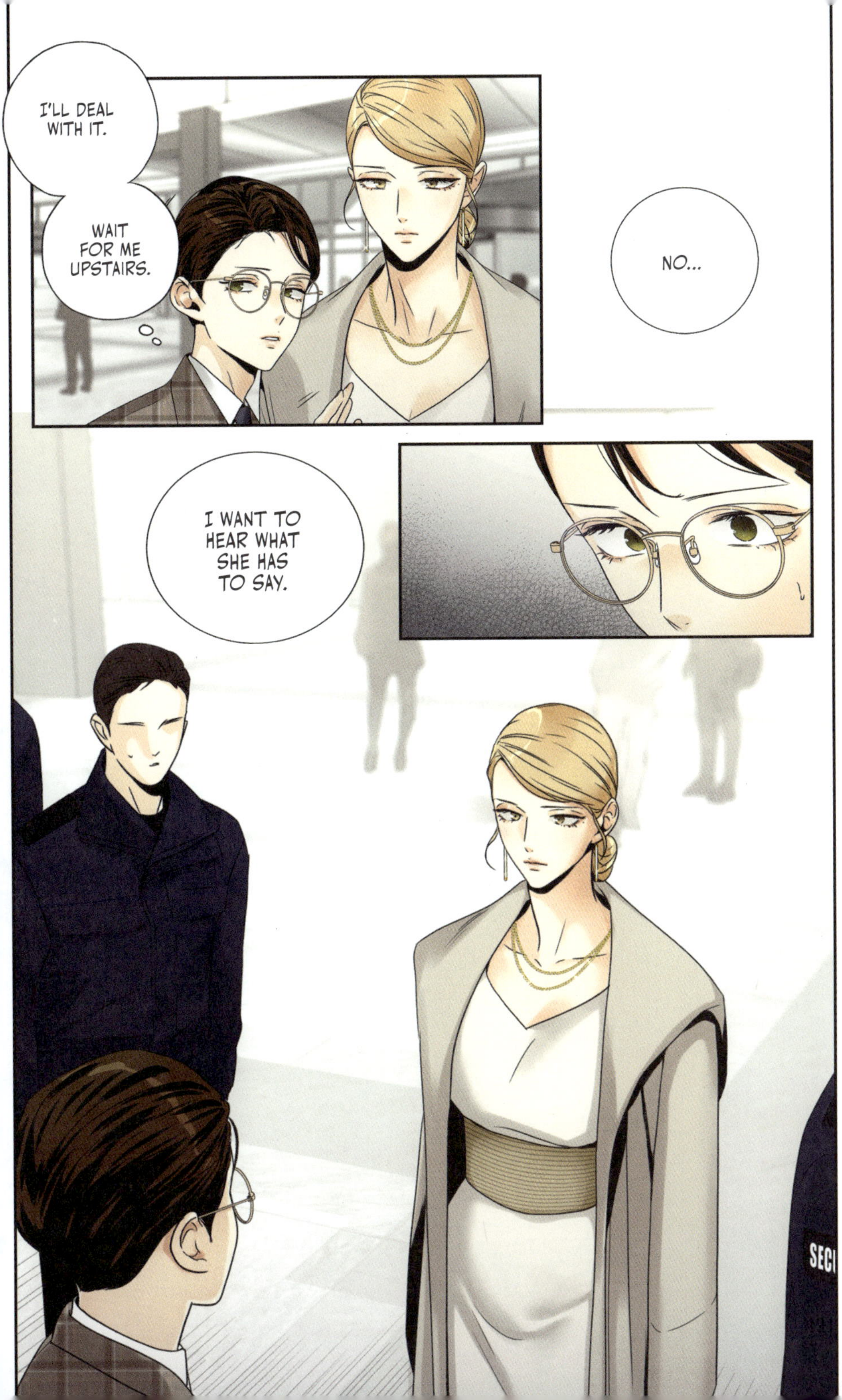
I'LL DEAL WITH IT.
WAIT FOR ME UPSTAIRS.
NO...
I WANT TO HEAR WHAT SHE HAS TO SAY.
SECI

WHAT?

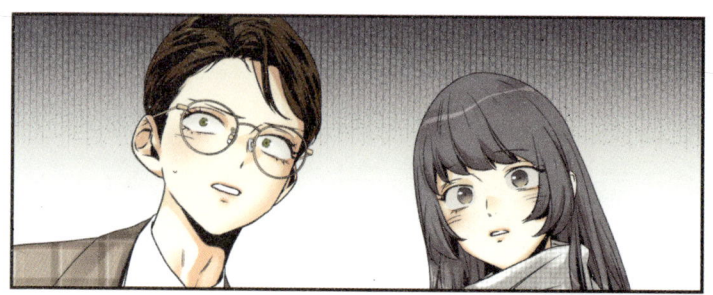

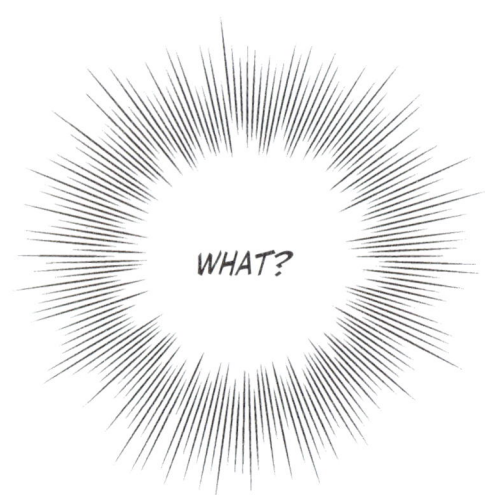

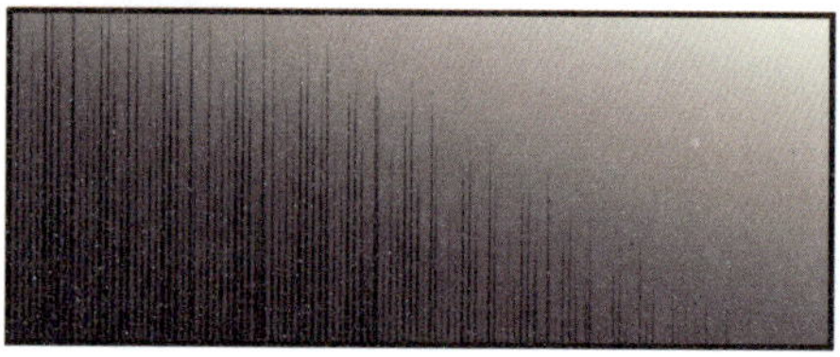

Love is an Illusion!
The Queen

Love is an Illusion!
The Queen

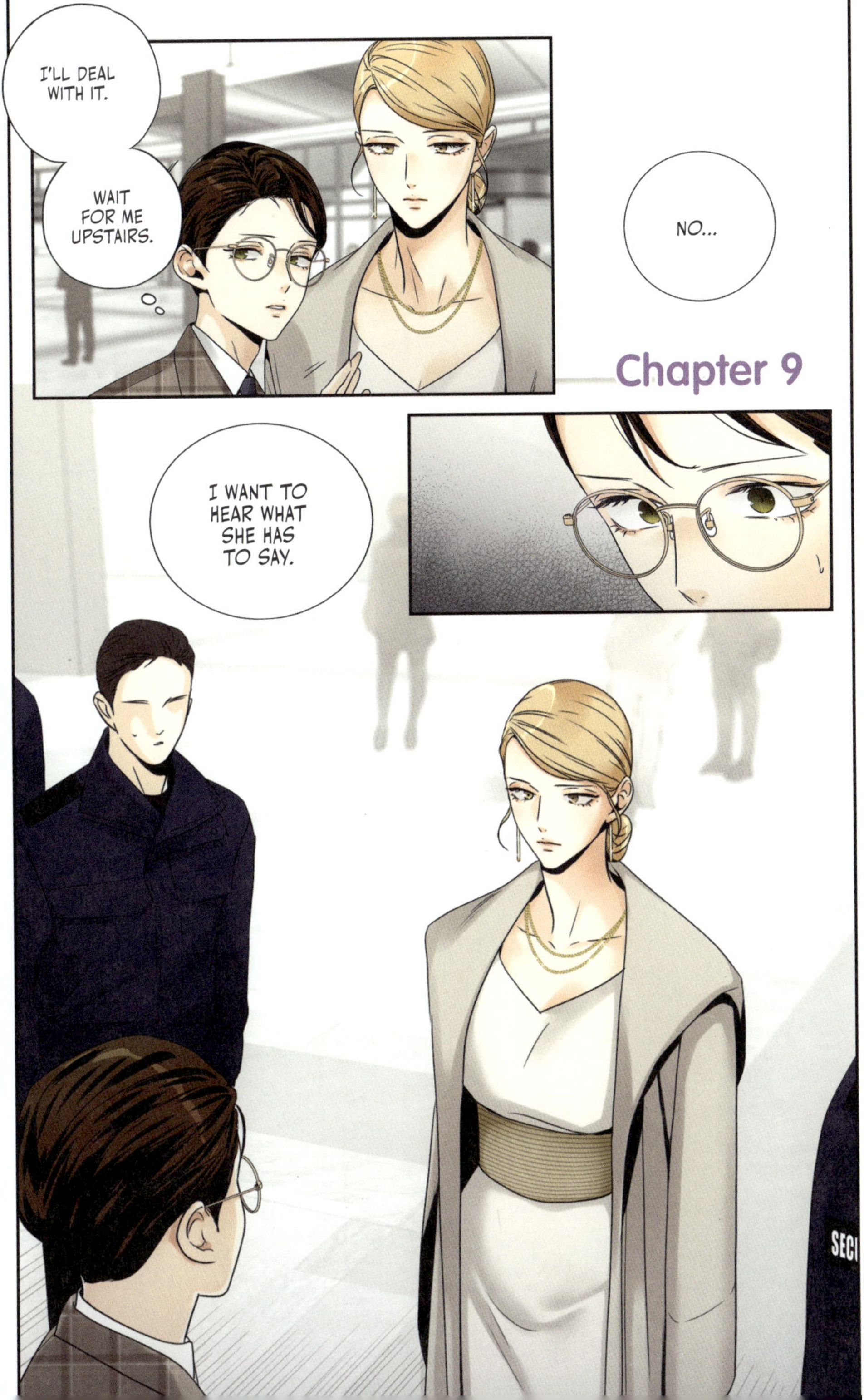
I'LL DEAL WITH IT.
WAIT FOR ME UPSTAIRS.
NO...
Chapter 9
I WANT TO HEAR WHAT SHE HAS TO SAY.
SECI

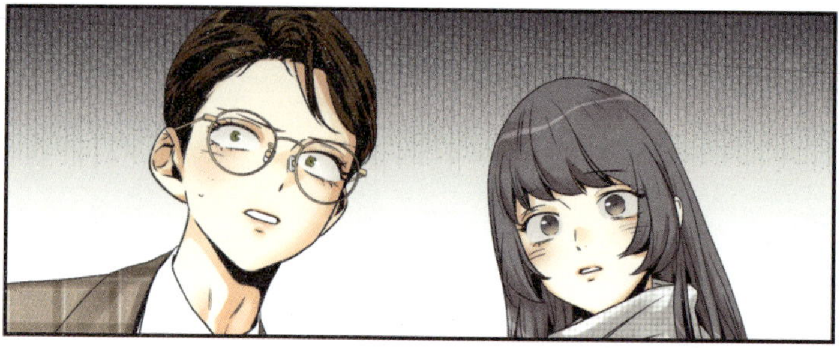

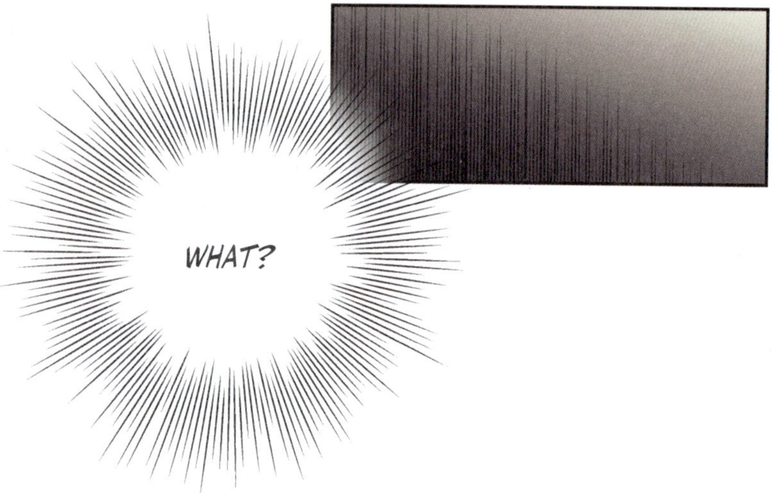
WHAT?

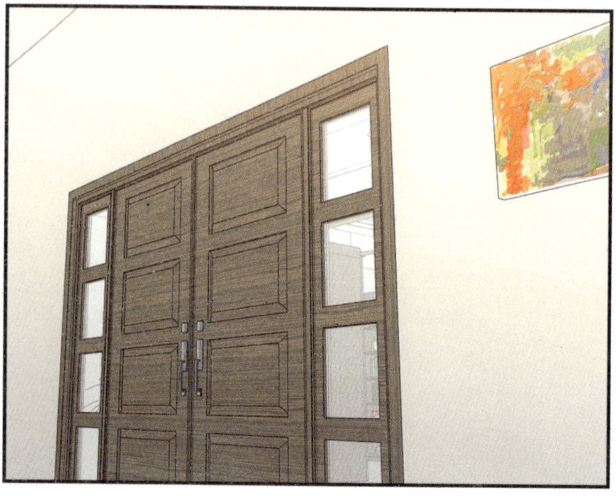

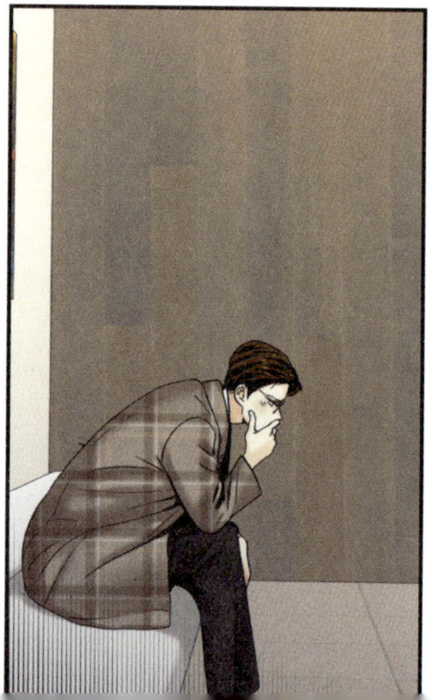

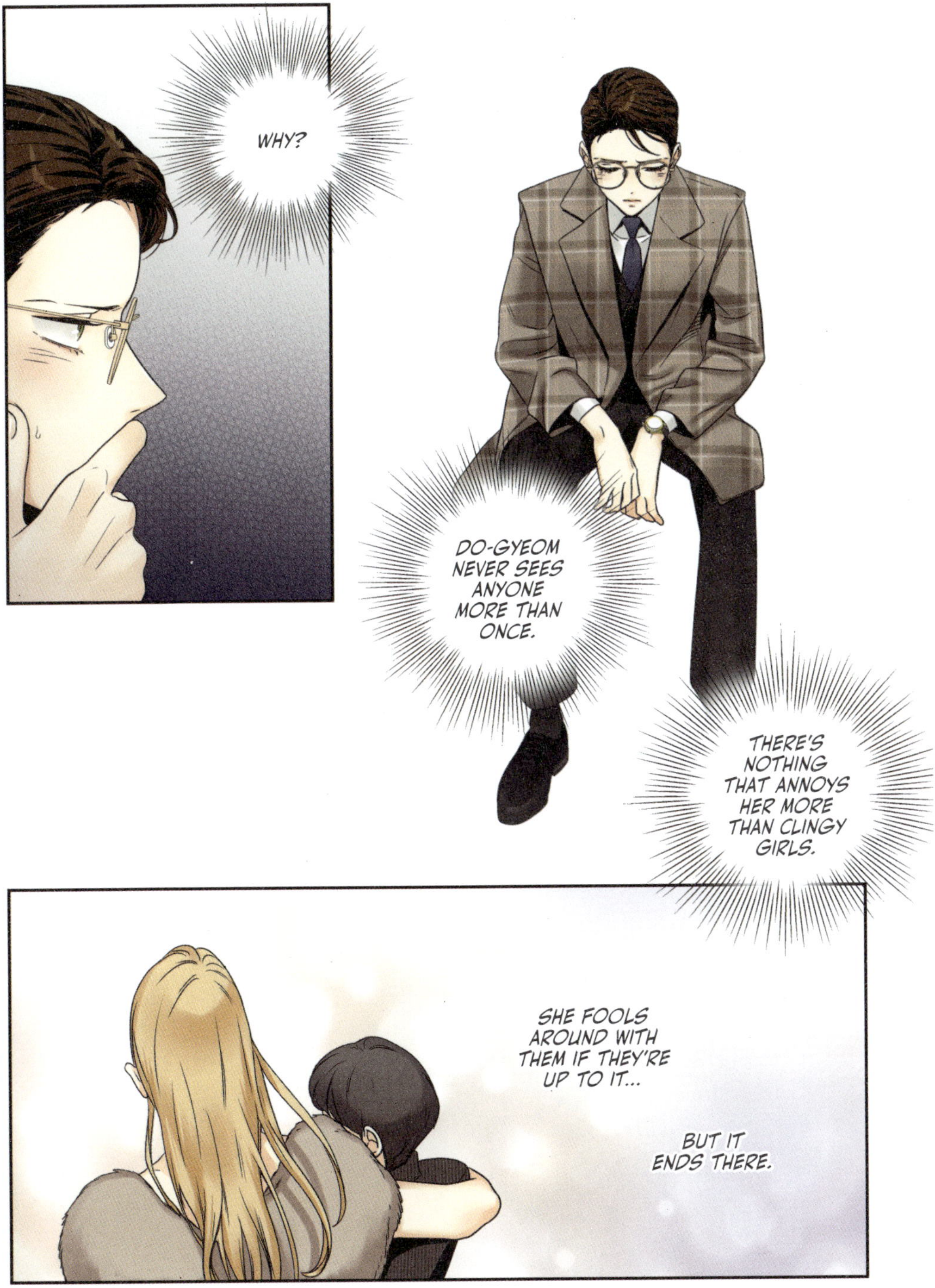
WHY?
DO-GYEOM NEVER SEES ANYONE MORE THAN ONCE.
THERE'S NOTHING THAT ANNOYS HER MORE THAN CLINGY GIRLS.
SHE FOOLS AROUND WITH THEM IF THEY'RE UP TO IT...
BUT IT ENDS THERE.

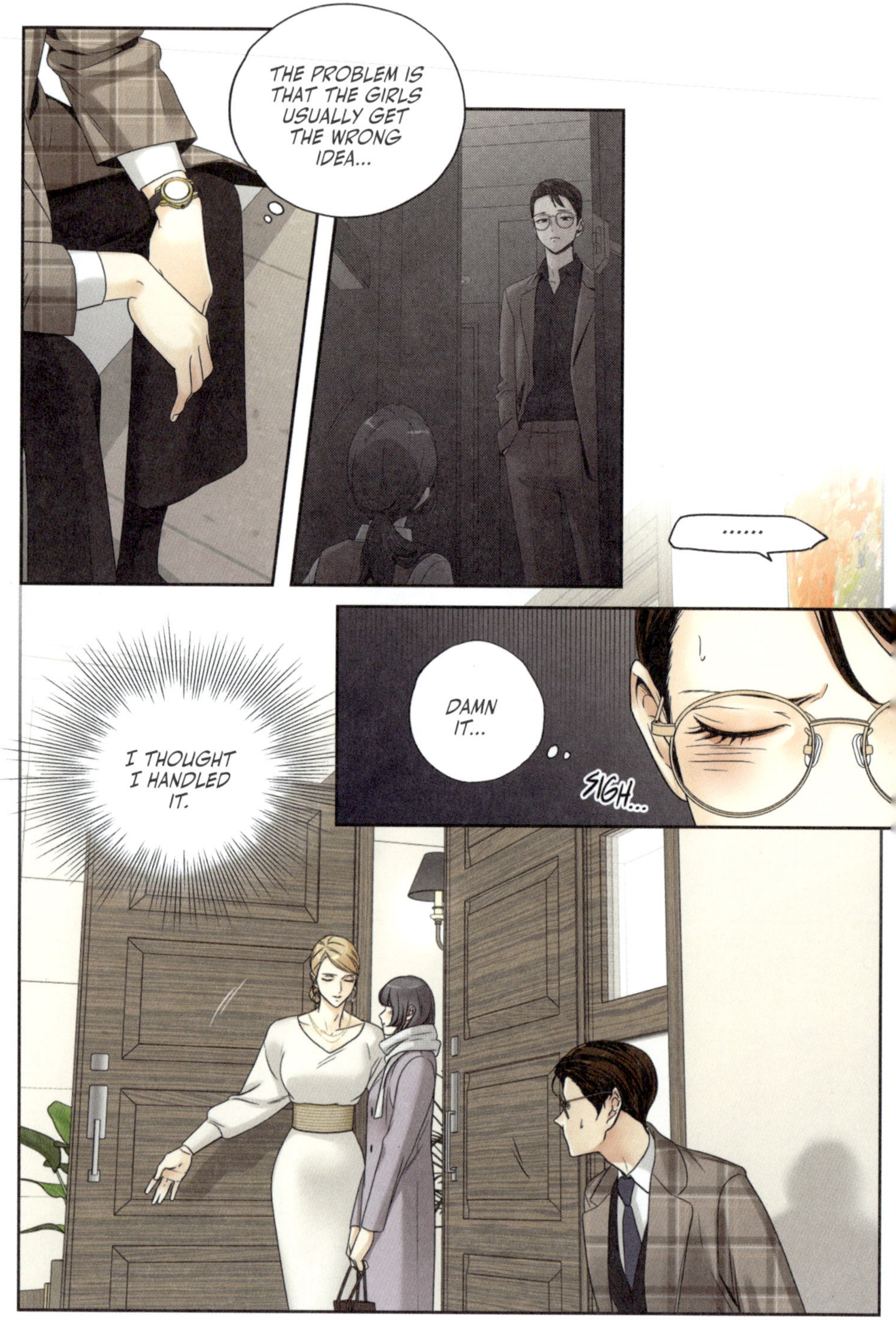
THE PROBLEM IS THAT THE GIRLS USUALLY GET THE WRONG IDEA...
......
DAMN IT...
SIGH...
I THOUGHT I HANDLED IT.

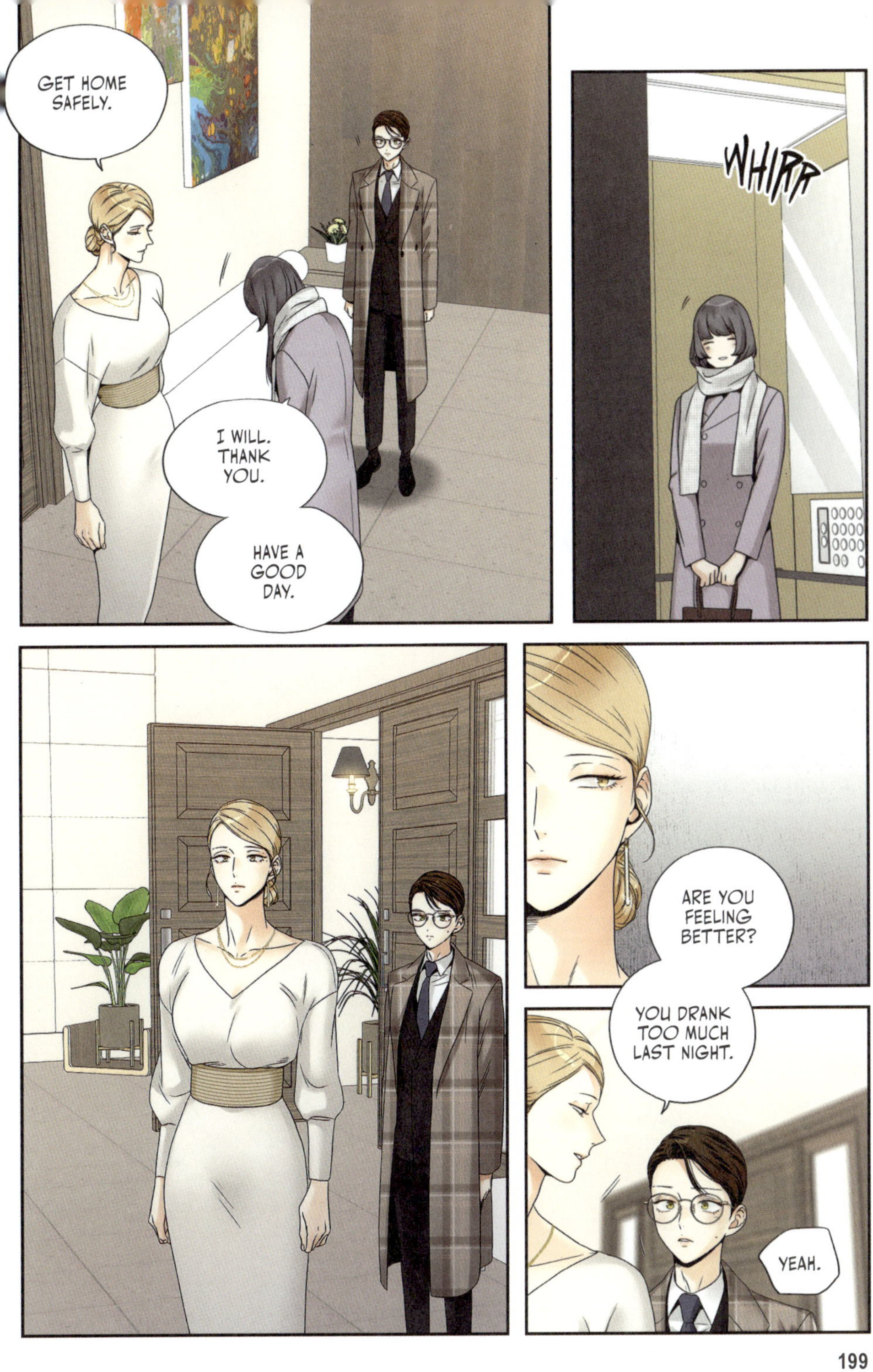
GET HOME SAFELY.
I WILL. THANK YOU.
HAVE A GOOD DAY.
WHIRR
ARE YOU FEELING BETTER?
YOU DRANK TOO MUCH LAST NIGHT.
YEAH.

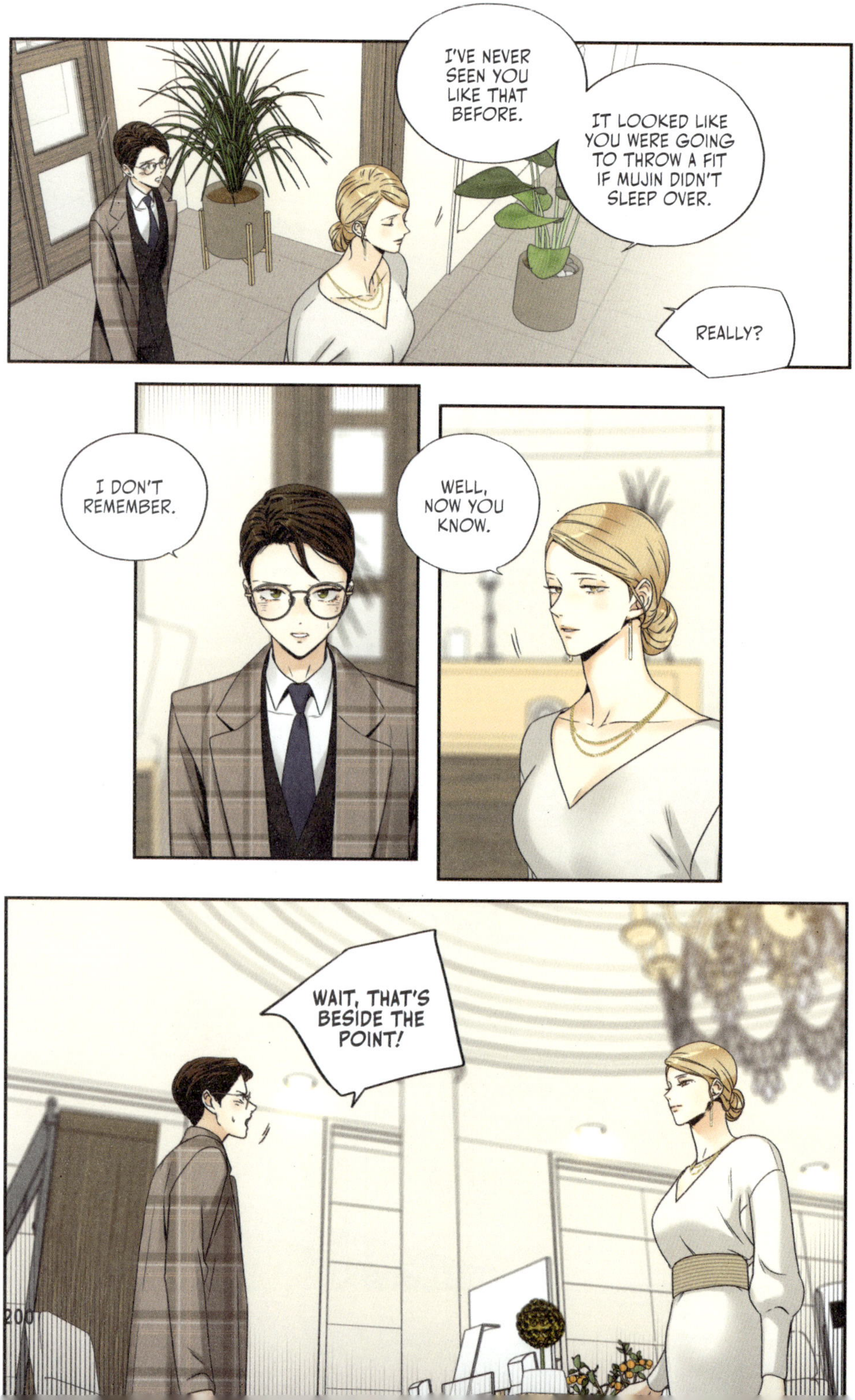
I'VE NEVER SEEN YOU LIKE THAT BEFORE.
IT LOOKED LIKE YOU WERE GOING TO THROW A FIT IF MUJIN DIDN'T SLEEP OVER.
REALLY?
I DON'T REMEMBER.
WELL, NOW YOU KNOW.
WAIT, THAT'S BESIDE THE POINT!

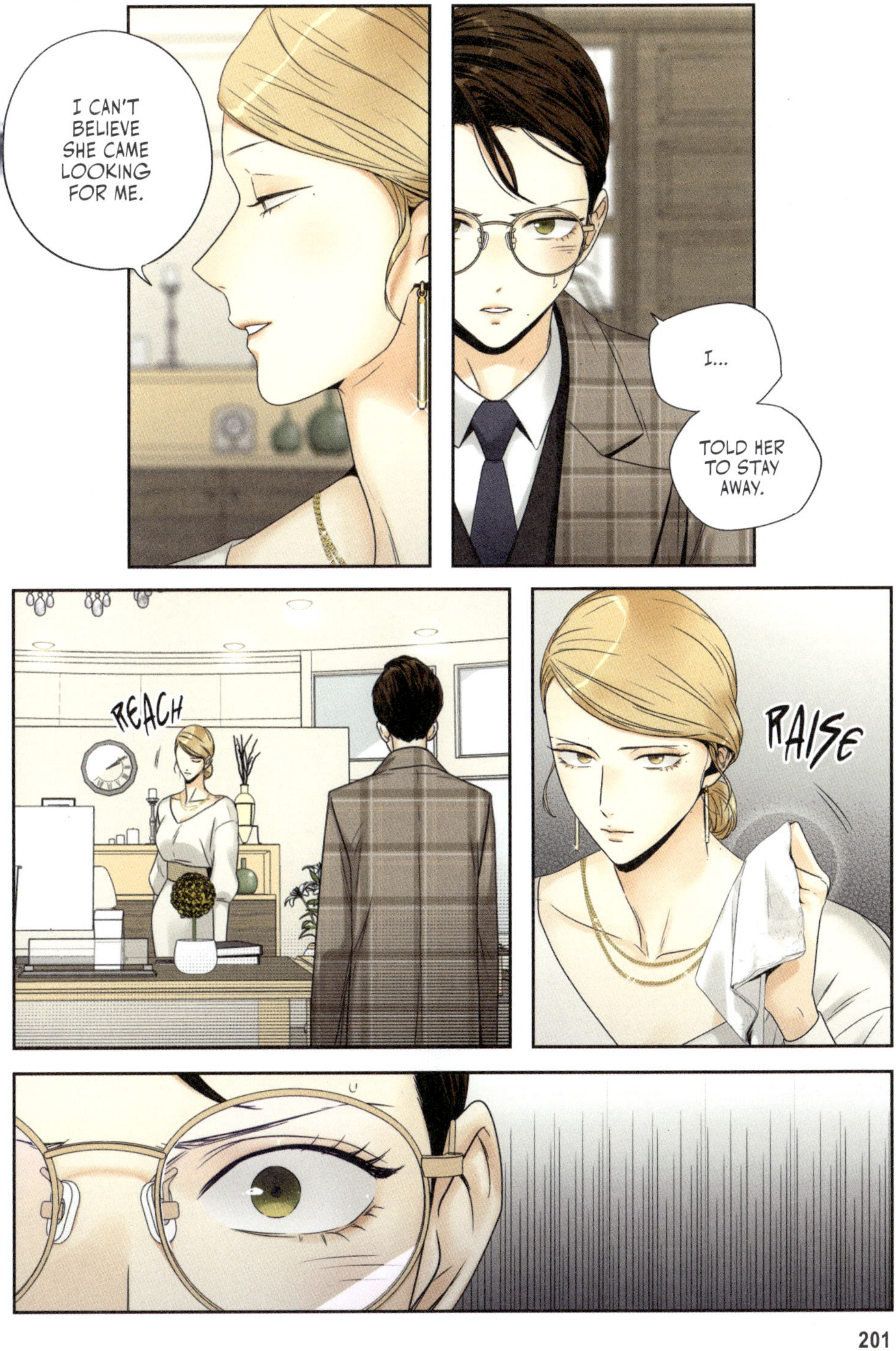
I CAN'T BELIEVE SHE CAME LOOKING FOR ME.
I...
TOLD HER TO STAY AWAY.
REACH
RAISE

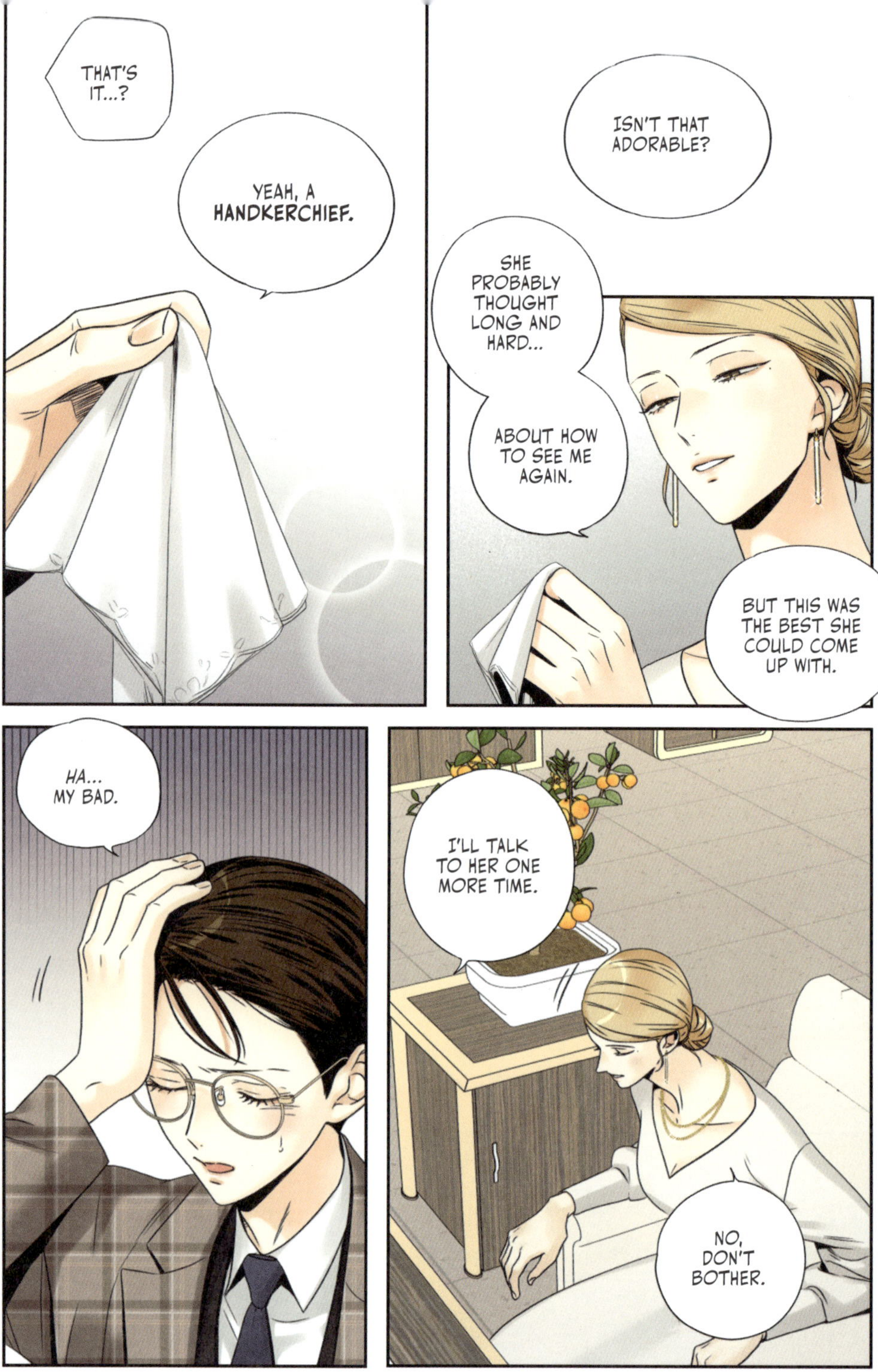
THAT'S IT...?
YEAH, A HANDKERCHIEF.
ISN'T THAT ADORABLE?
SHE PROBABLY THOUGHT LONG AND HARD...
ABOUT HOW TO SEE ME AGAIN.
BUT THIS WAS THE BEST SHE COULD COME UP WITH.
HA... MY BAD.
I'LL TALK TO HER ONE MORE TIME.
NO, DON'T BOTHER.

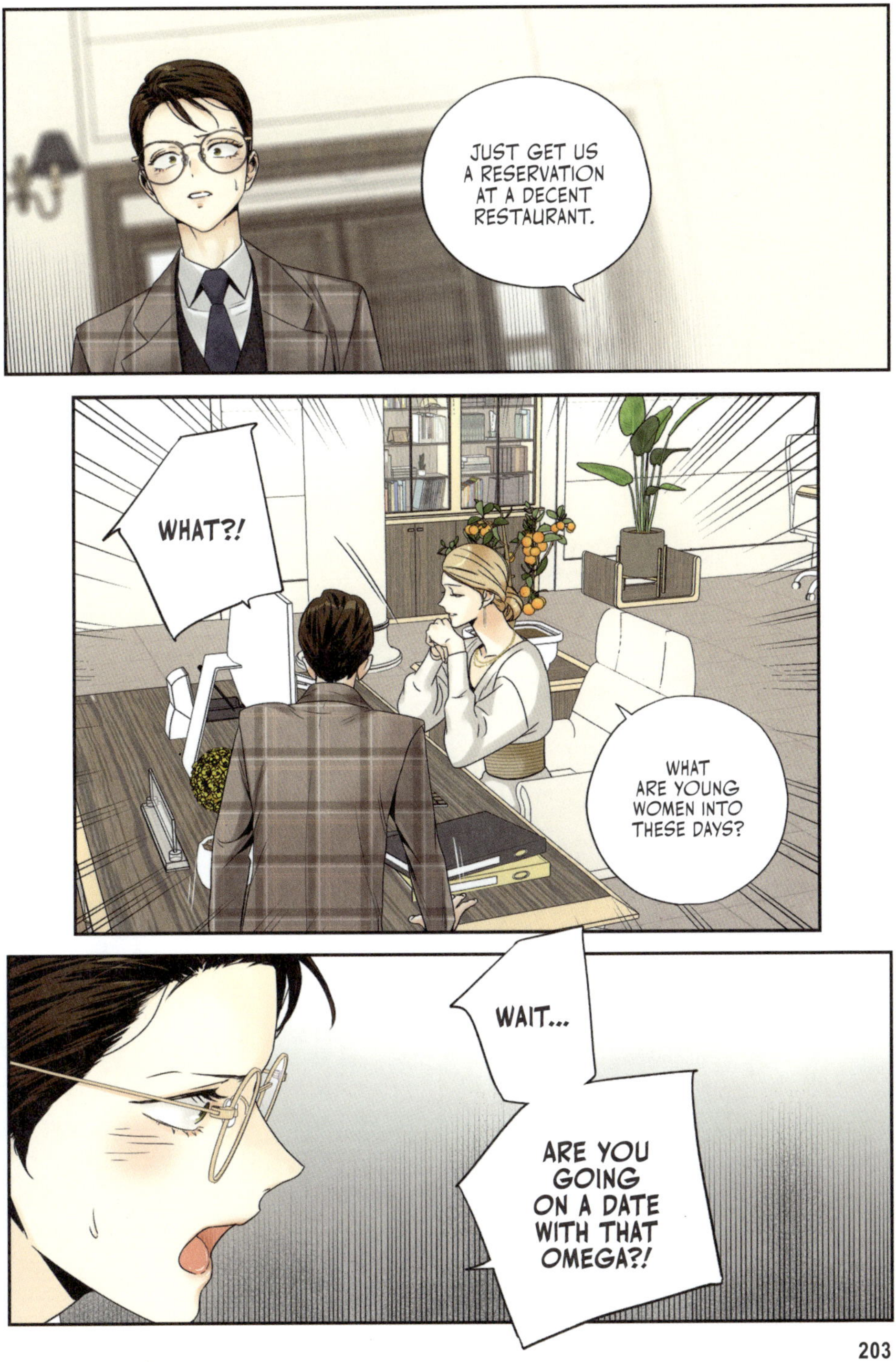
JUST GET US A RESERVATION AT A DECENT RESTAURANT.
WHAT?!
WHAT ARE YOUNG WOMEN INTO THESE DAYS?
WAIT...
ARE YOU GOING ON A DATE WITH THAT OMEGA?!

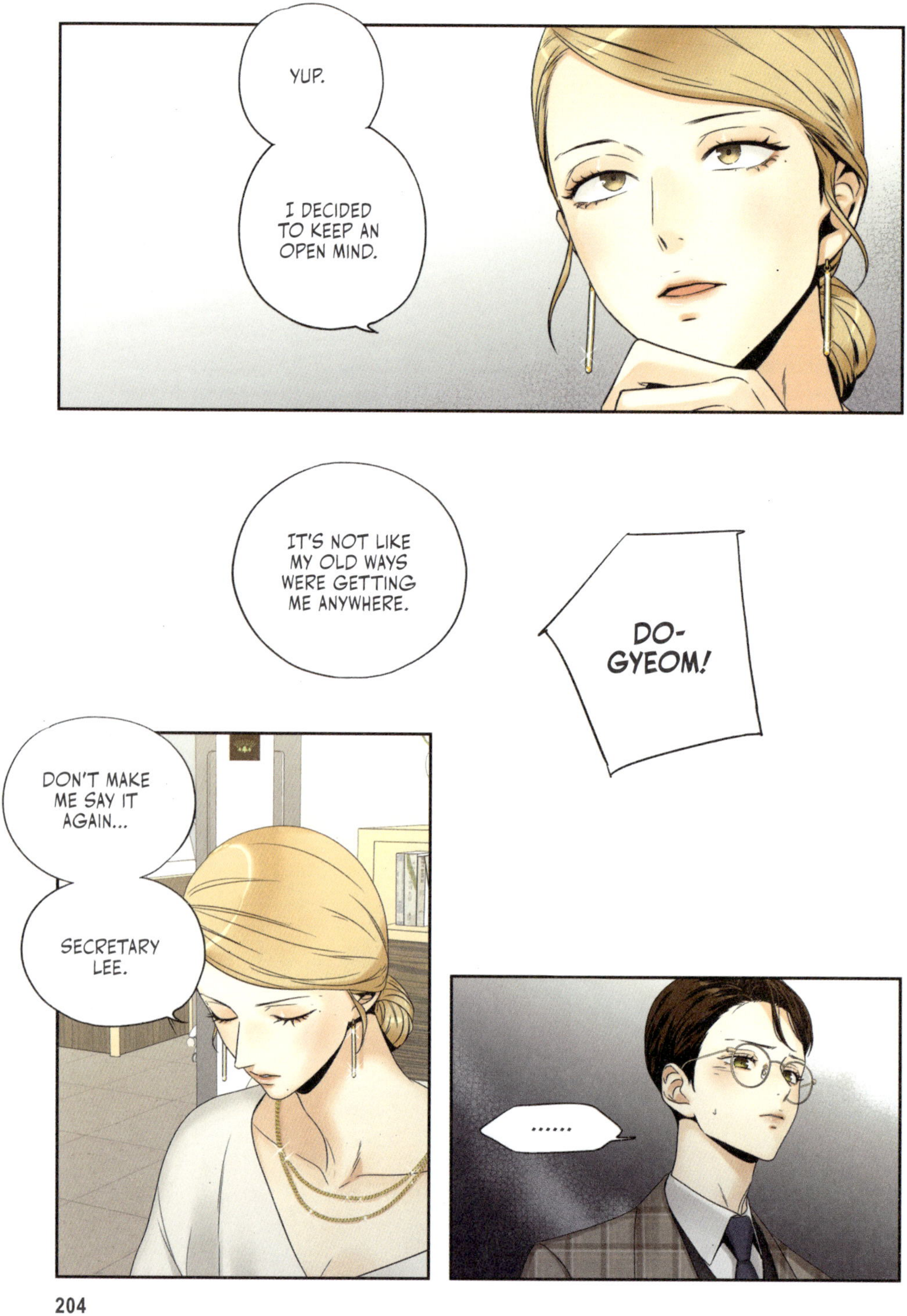
YUP.
I DECIDED TO KEEP AN OPEN MIND.
IT'S NOT LIKE MY OLD WAYS WERE GETTING ME ANYWHERE.
DO-GYEOM!
DON'T MAKE ME SAY IT AGAIN...
SECRETARY LEE.
......

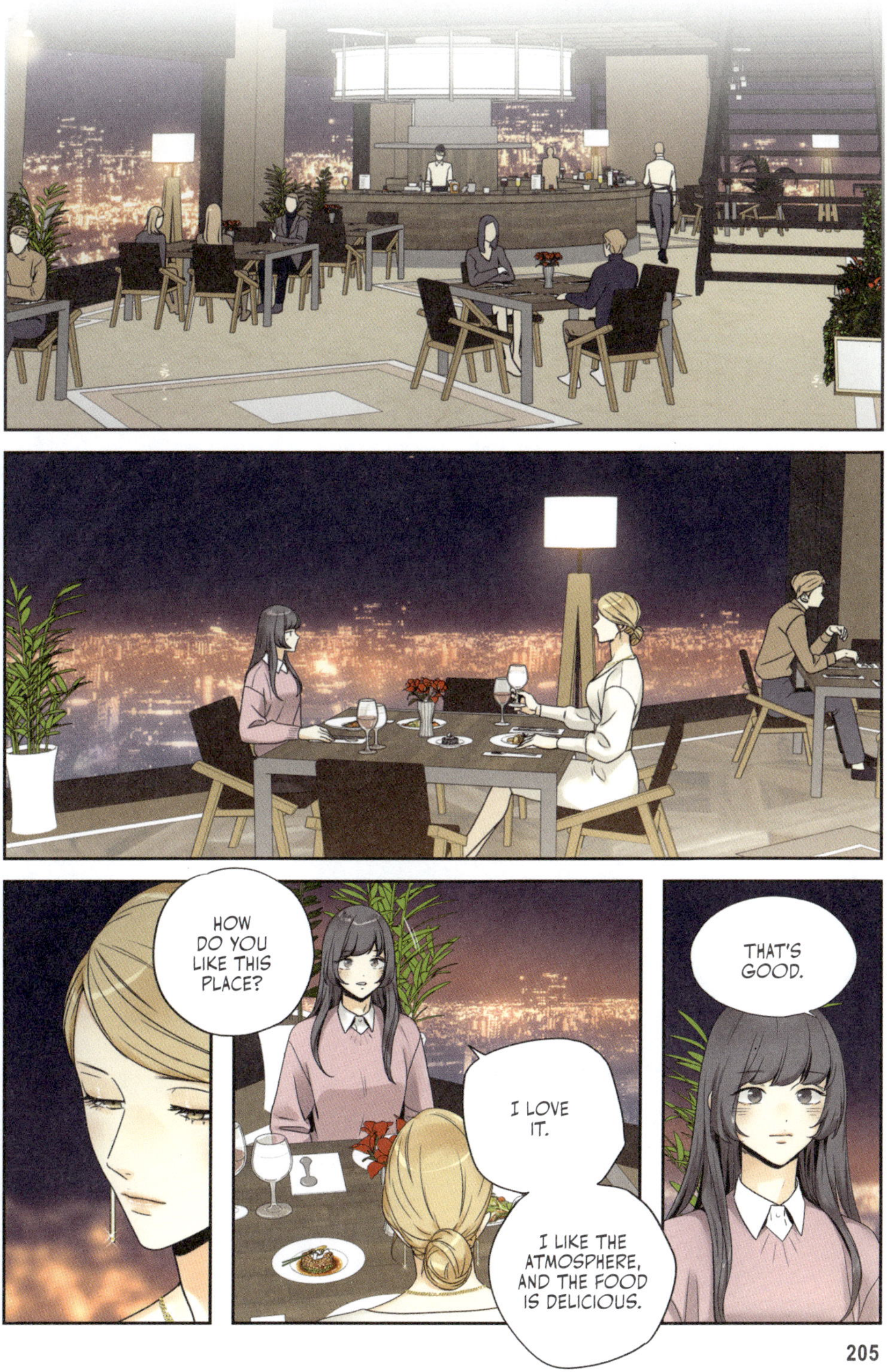
HOW DO YOU LIKE THIS PLACE?
I LOVE IT.
I LIKE THE ATMOSPHERE, AND THE FOOD IS DELICIOUS.
THAT'S GOOD.

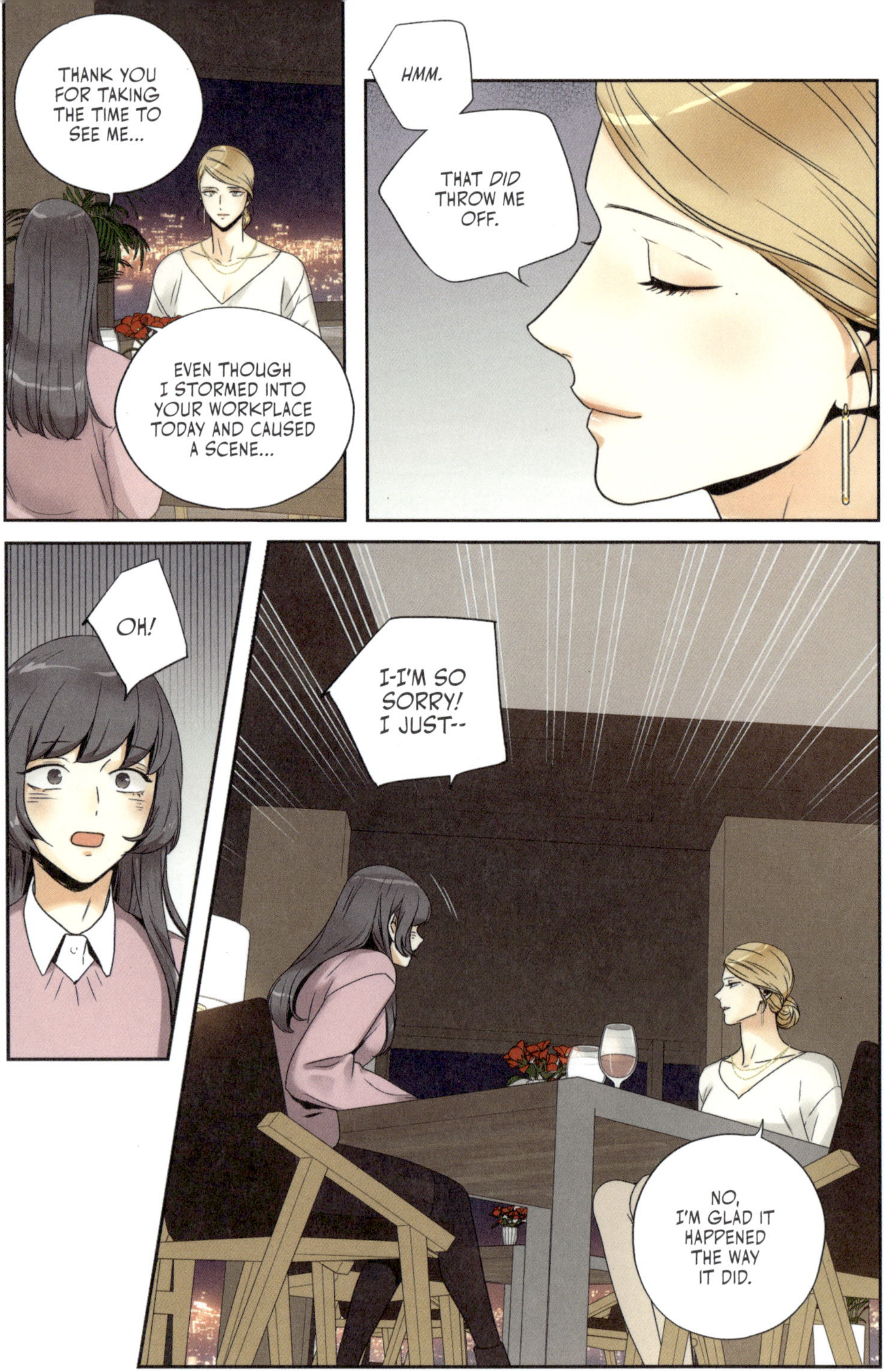
THANK YOU FOR TAKING THE TIME TO SEE ME...
EVEN THOUGH I STORMED INTO YOUR WORKPLACE TODAY AND CAUSED A SCENE...
HMM.
THAT *DID* THROW ME OFF.
OH!
I-I'M SO SORRY! I JUST--
NO, I'M GLAD IT HAPPENED THE WAY IT DID.

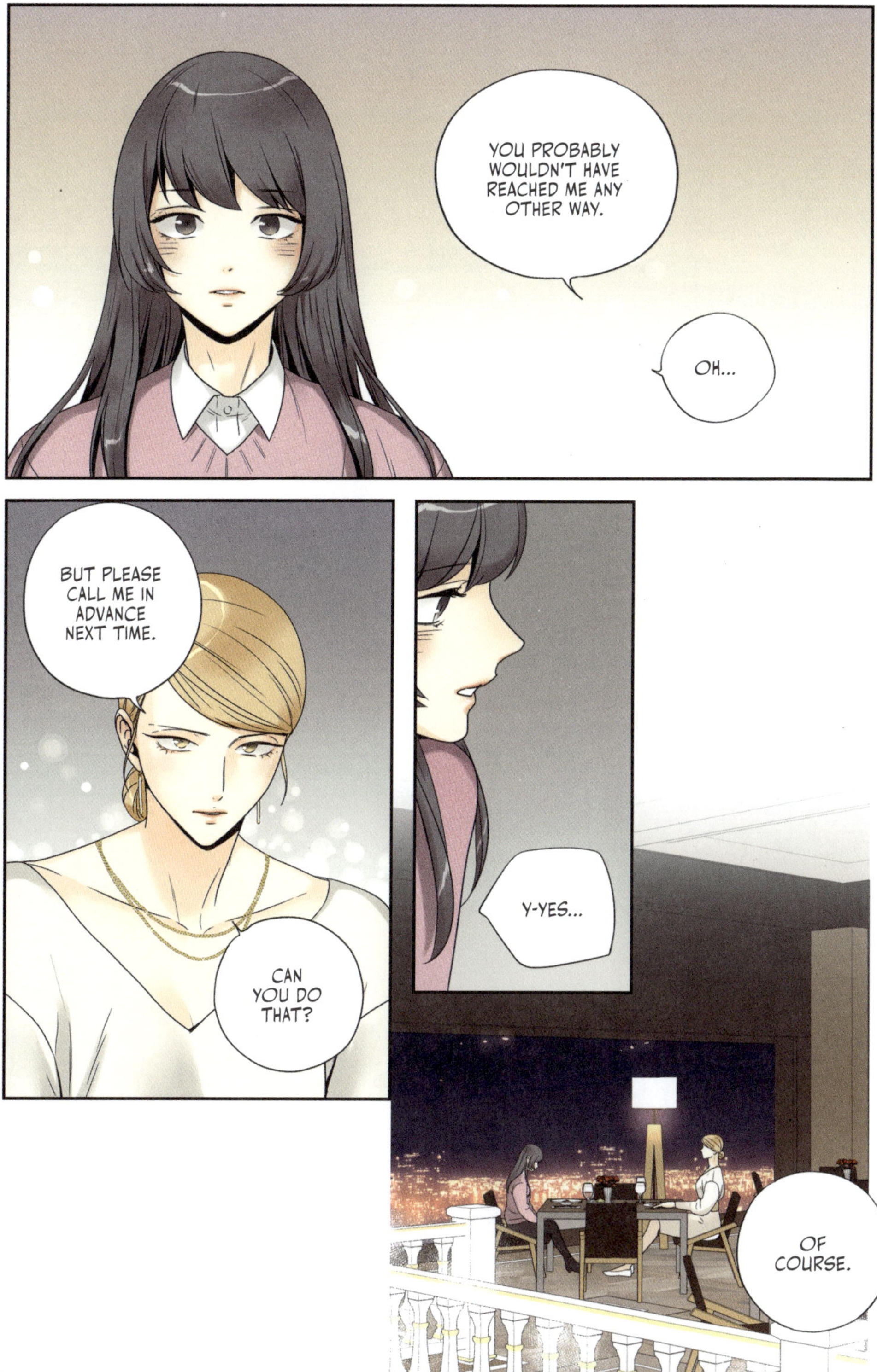
YOU PROBABLY WOULDN'T HAVE REACHED ME ANY OTHER WAY.
OH...
BUT PLEASE CALL ME IN ADVANCE NEXT TIME.
CAN YOU DO THAT?
Y-YES...
OF COURSE.

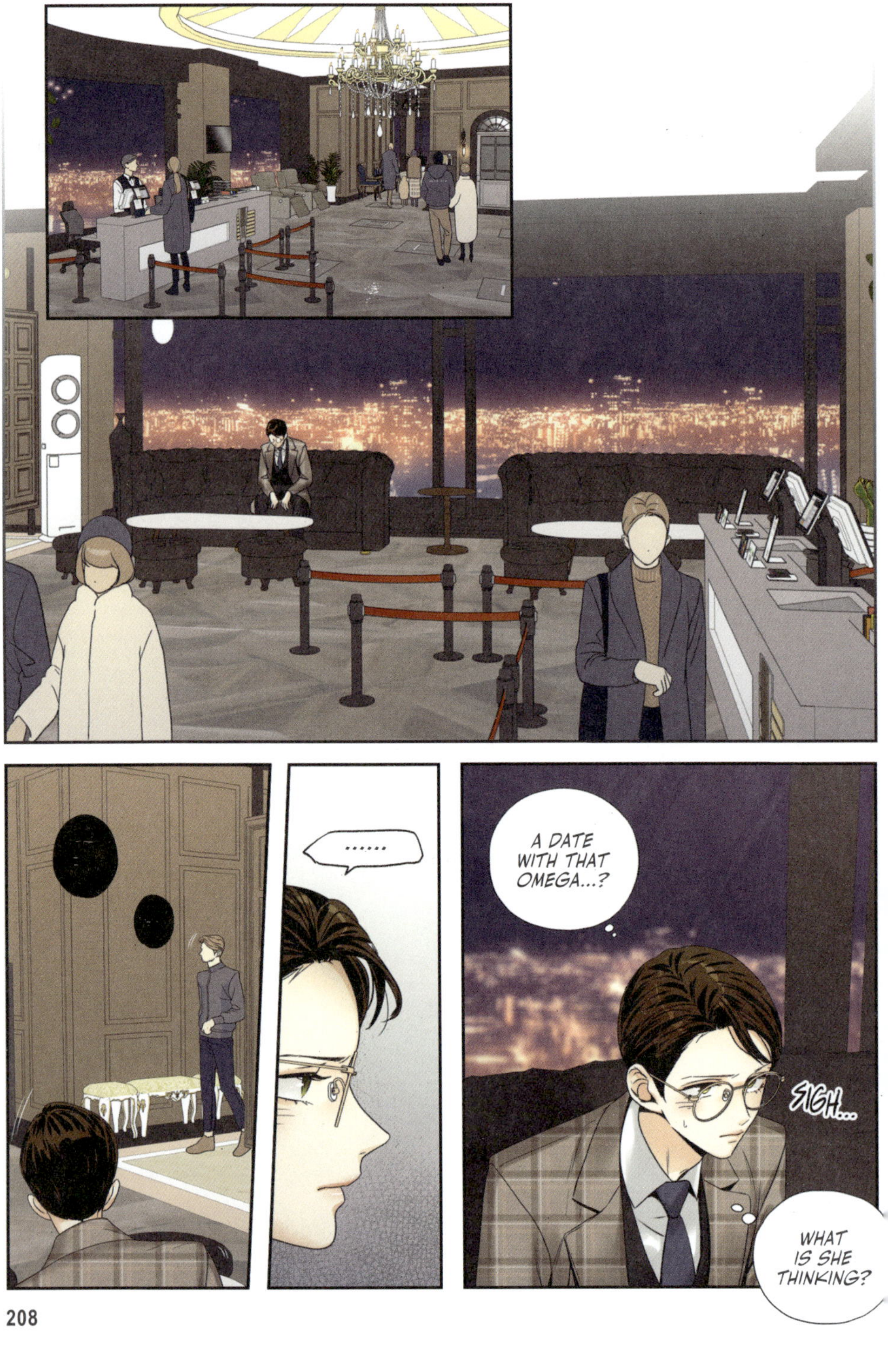

....
A DATE WITH THAT OMEGA...?
SIGH...
WHAT IS SHE THINKING?

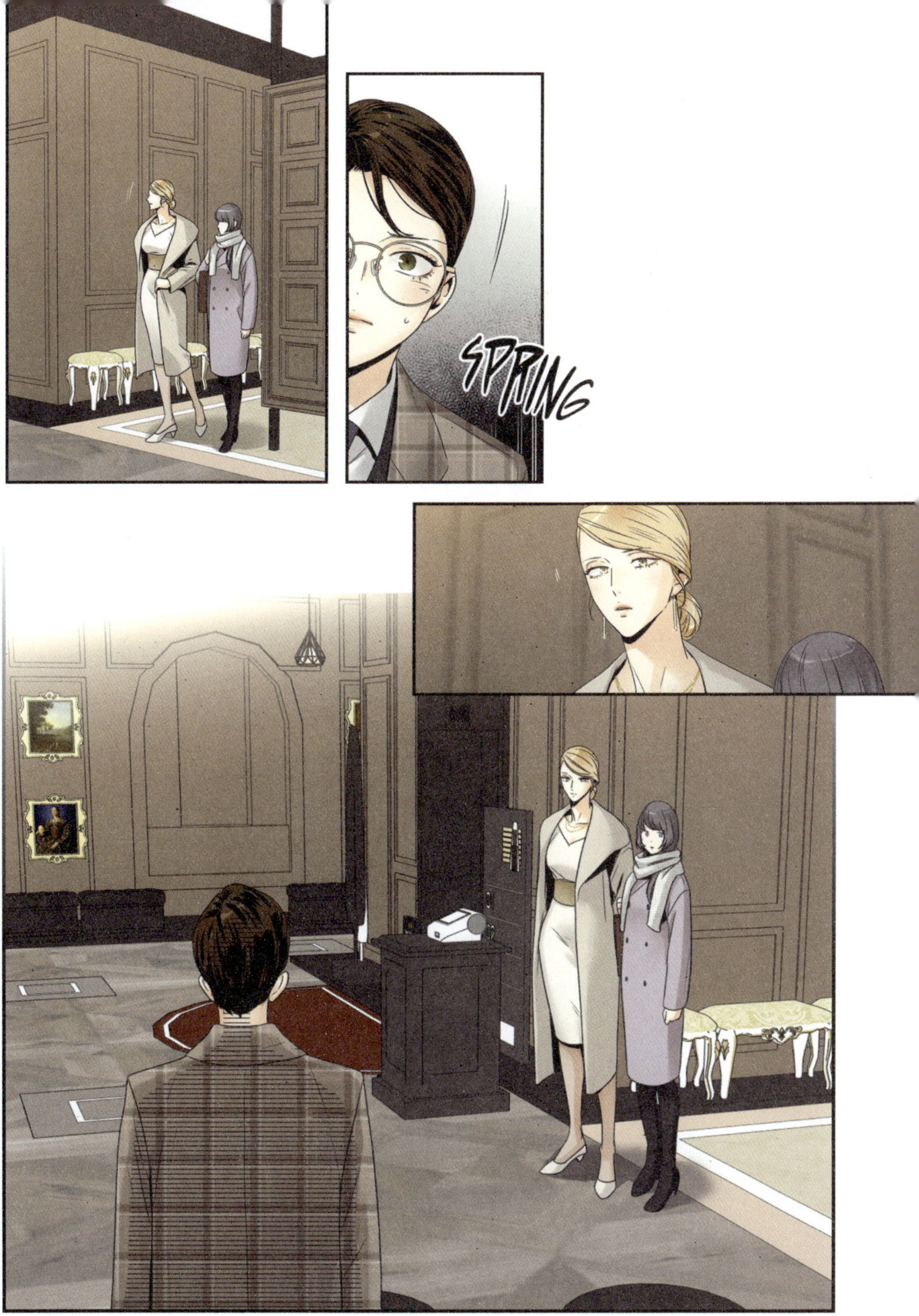
SPRING

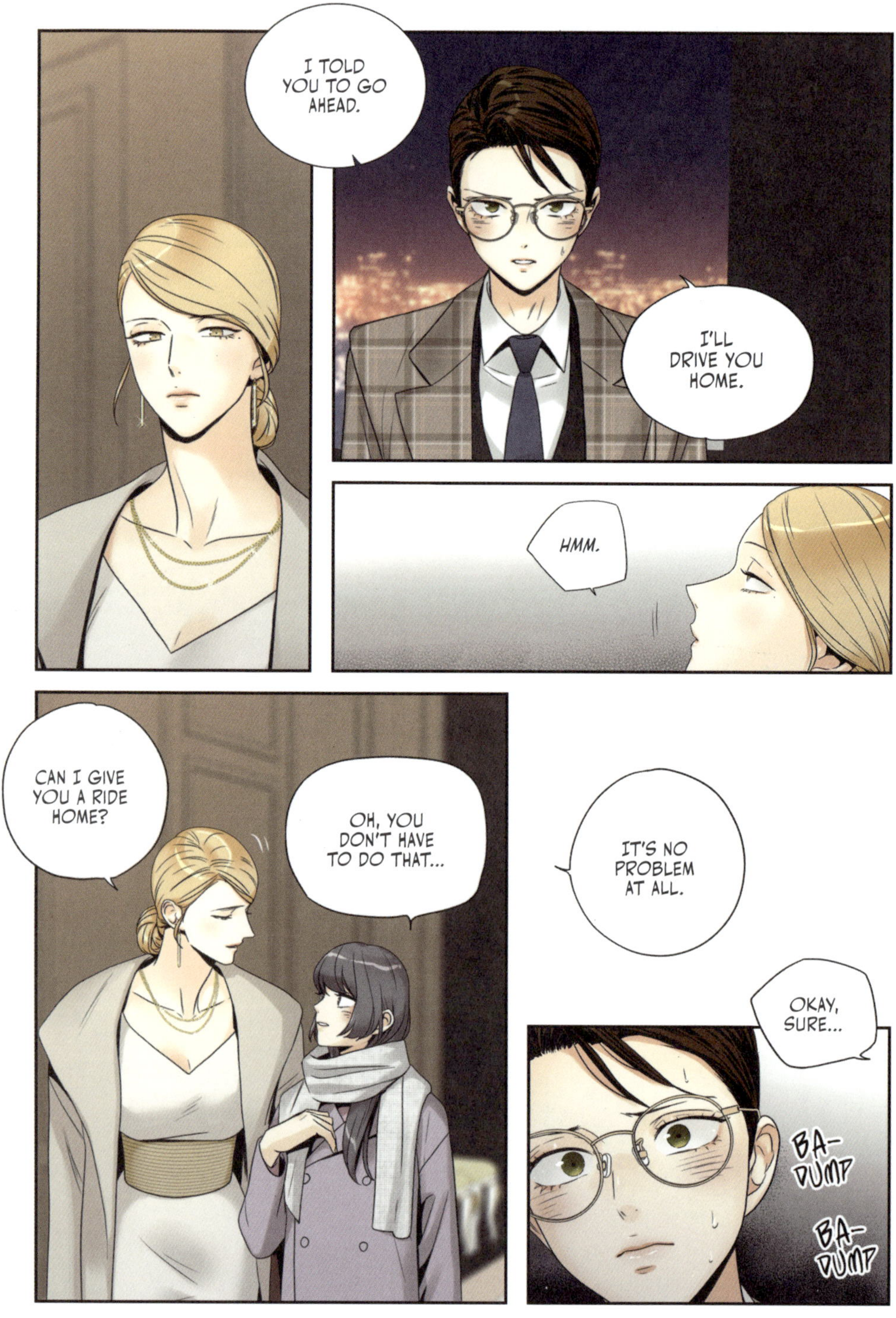
I TOLD YOU TO GO AHEAD.
I'LL DRIVE YOU HOME.
HMM.
CAN I GIVE YOU A RIDE HOME?
OH, YOU DON'T HAVE TO DO THAT...
IT'S NO PROBLEM AT ALL.
OKAY, SURE...
BA-DUMP
BA-DUMP

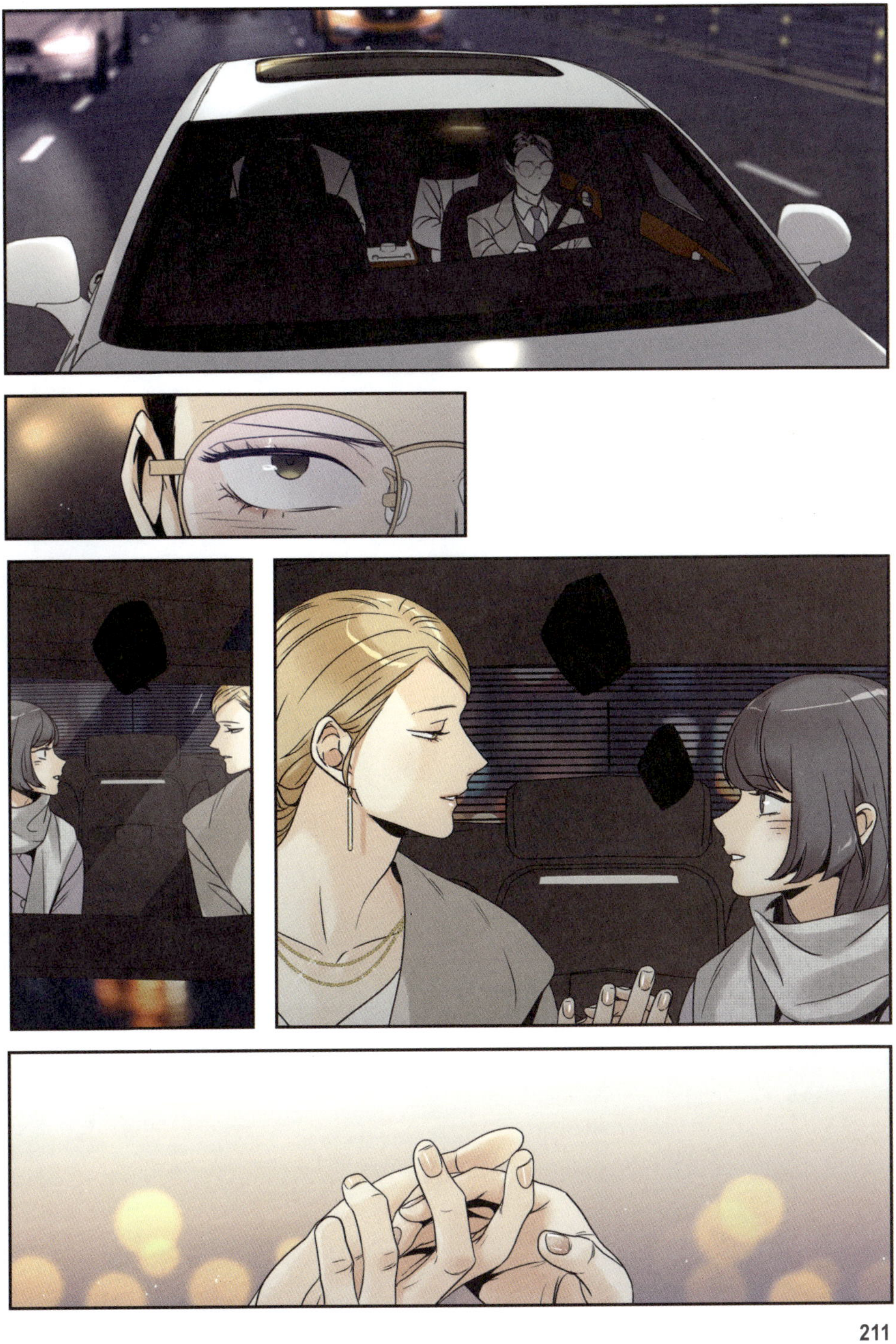

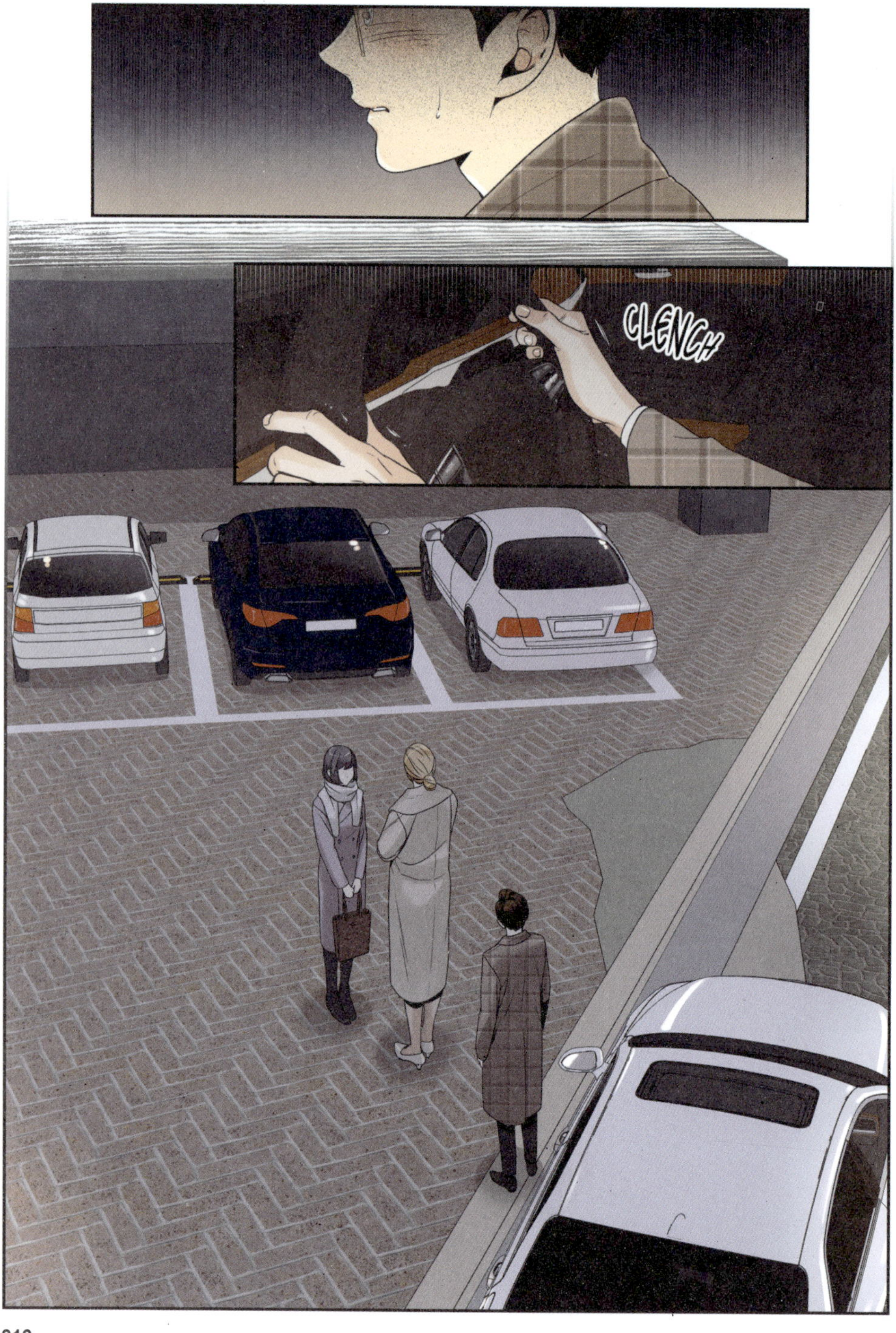
CLENCH

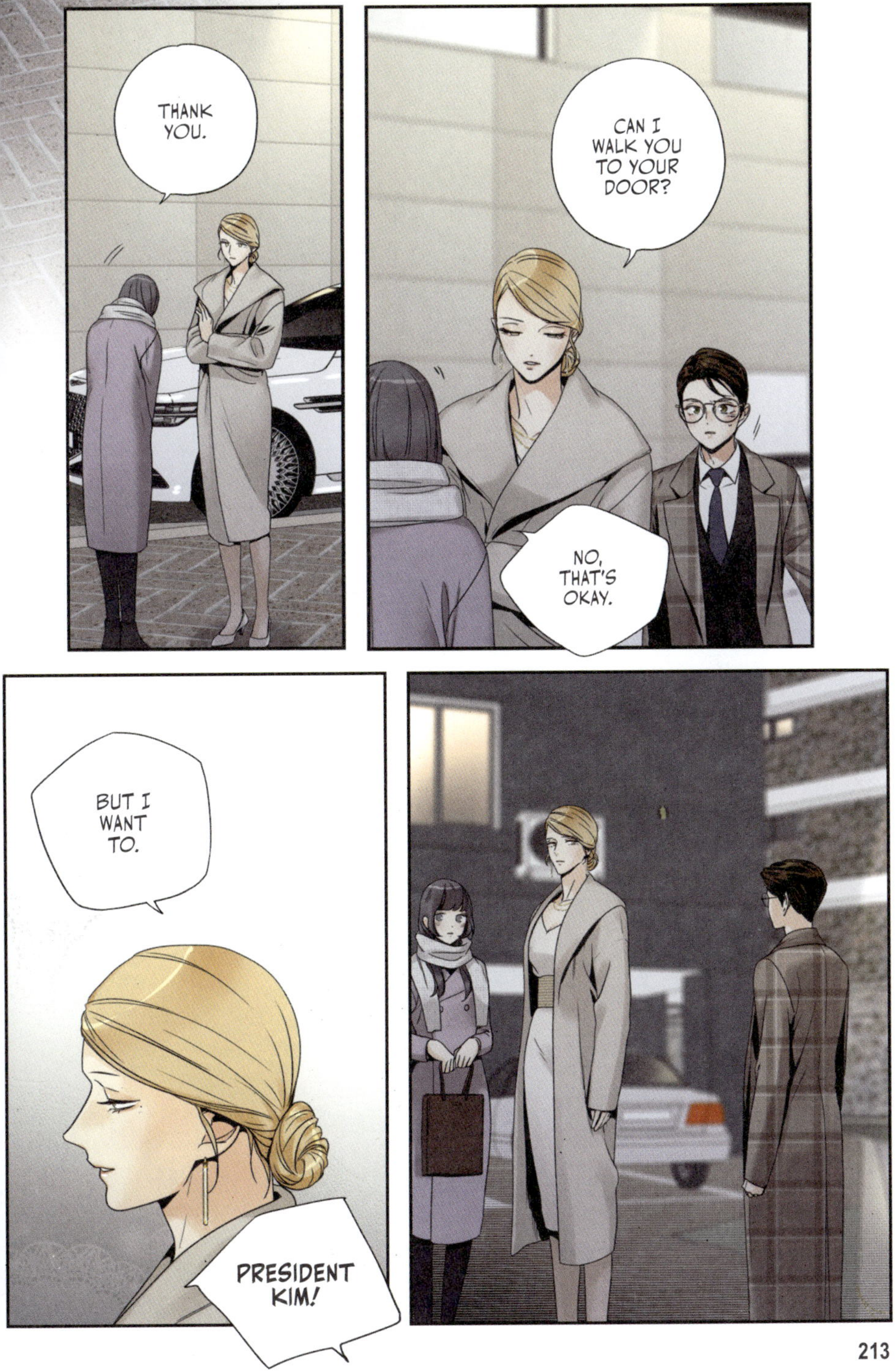
THANK YOU.
CAN I WALK YOU TO YOUR DOOR?
NO, THAT'S OKAY.
BUT I WANT TO.
PRESIDENT KIM!

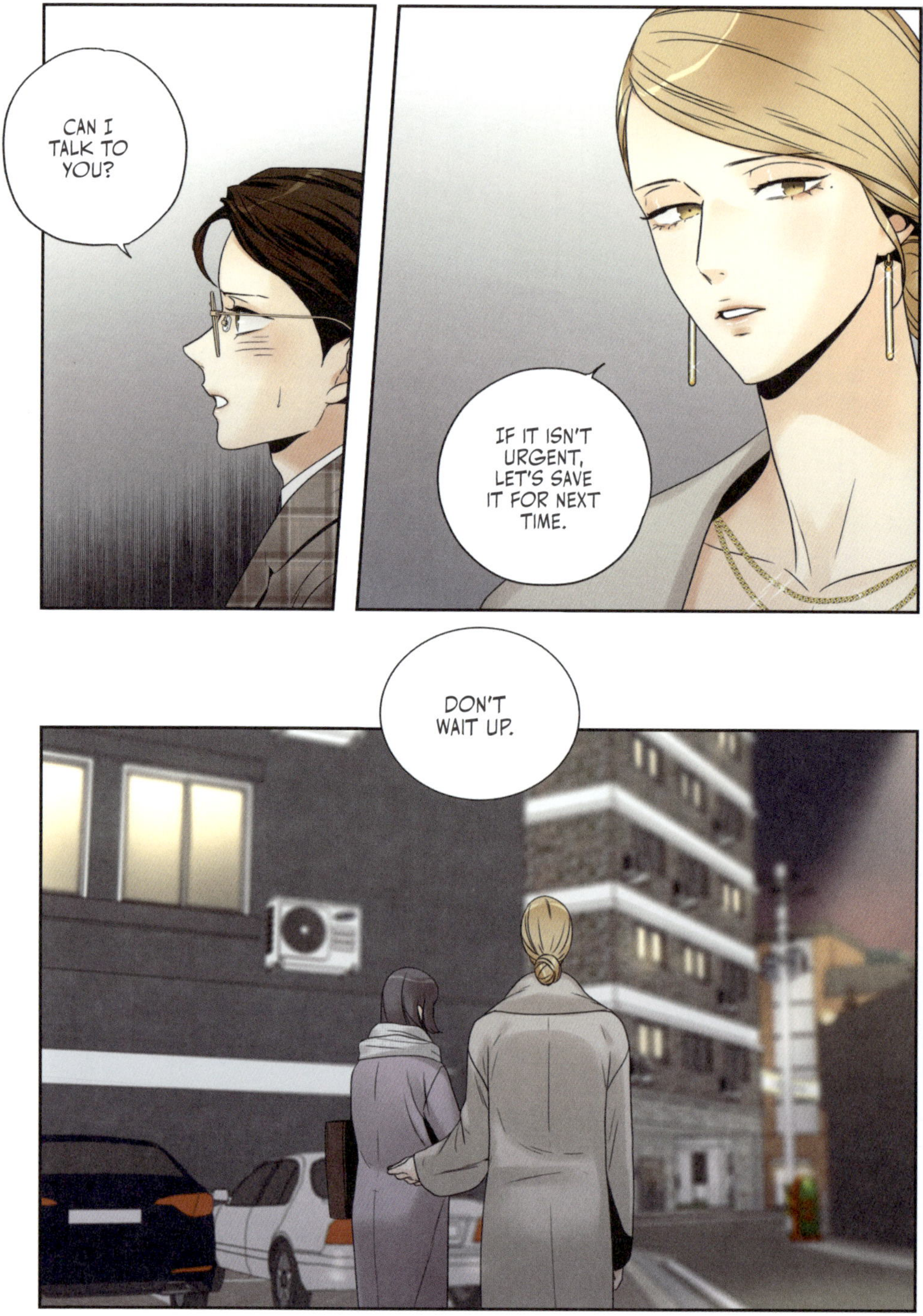
CAN I TALK TO YOU?
IF IT ISN'T URGENT, LET'S SAVE IT FOR NEXT TIME.
DON'T WAIT UP.

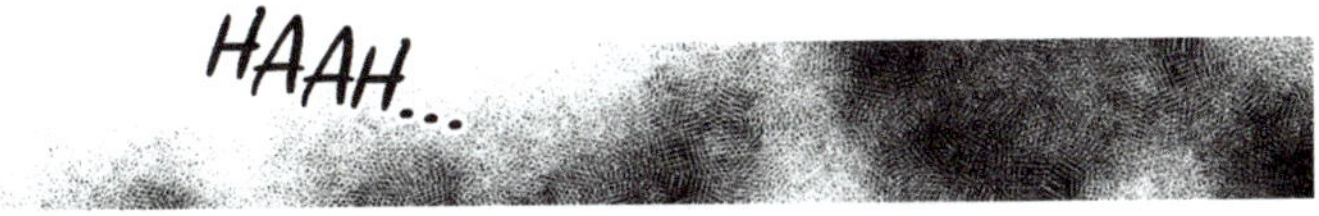
HAAH...

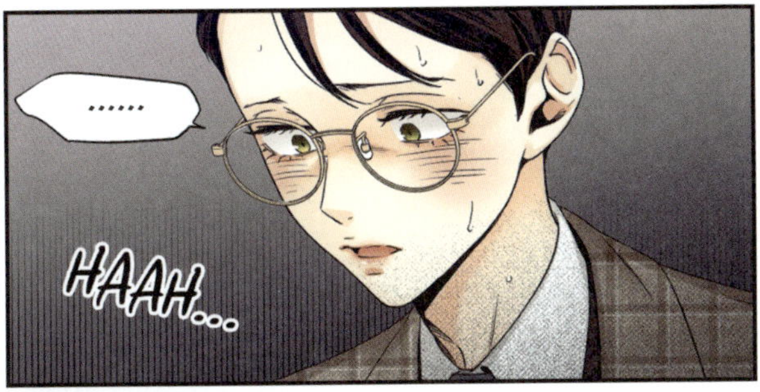
......
HAAH...

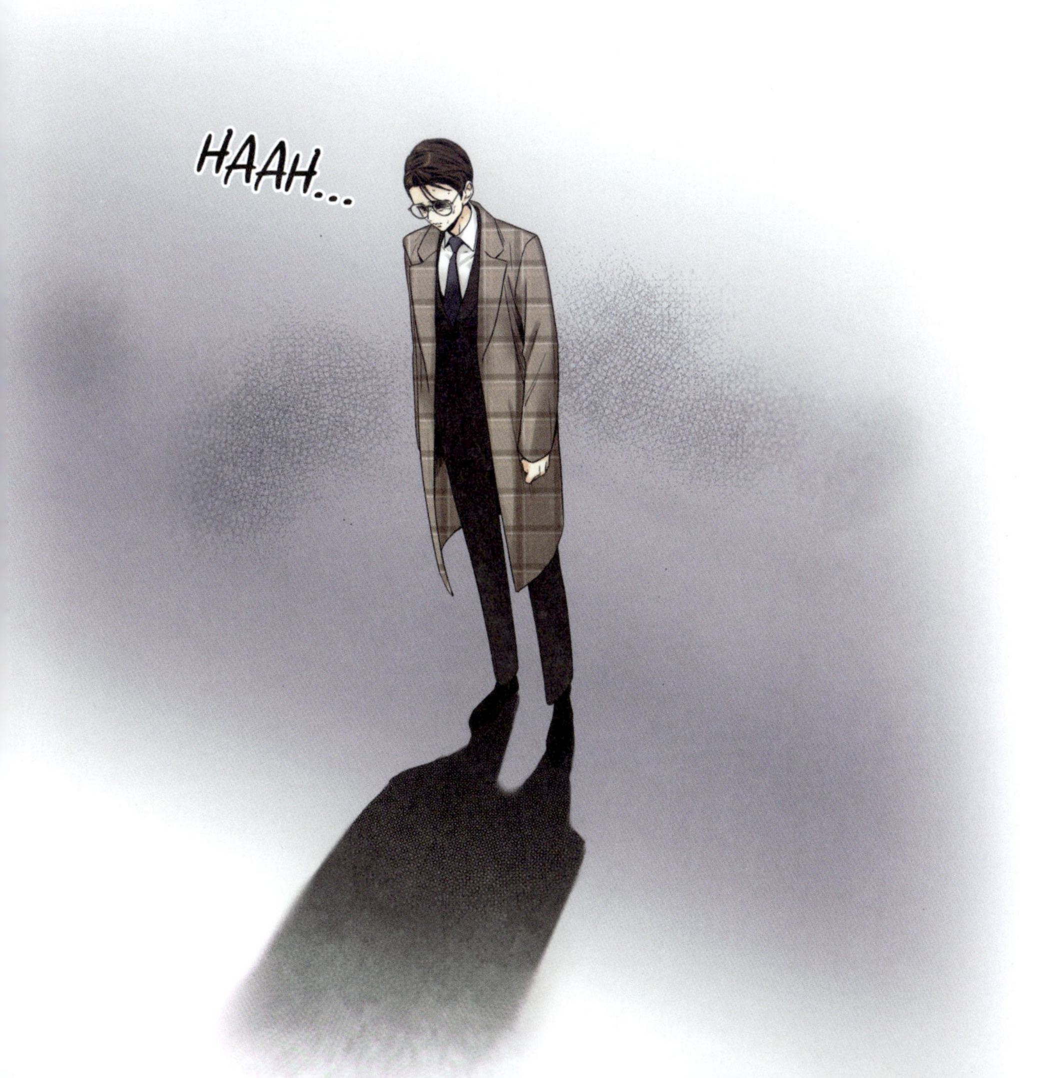
HAAH...

Love is an Illusion!
The Queen

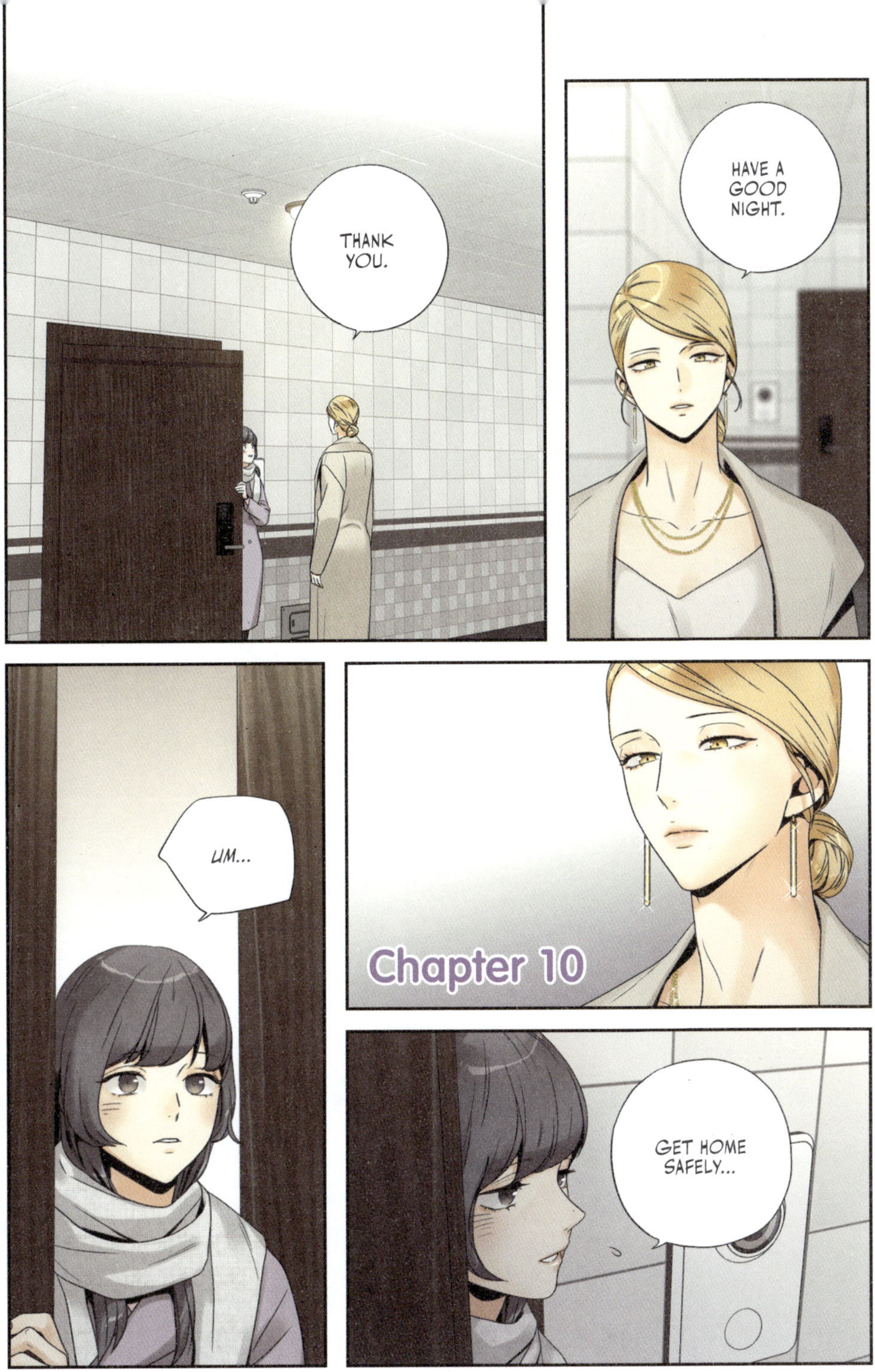
THANK YOU.
HAVE A GOOD NIGHT.
UM...
Chapter 10
GET HOME SAFELY...

CLUNK

I THOUGHT SHE WAS GOING TO COME IN...

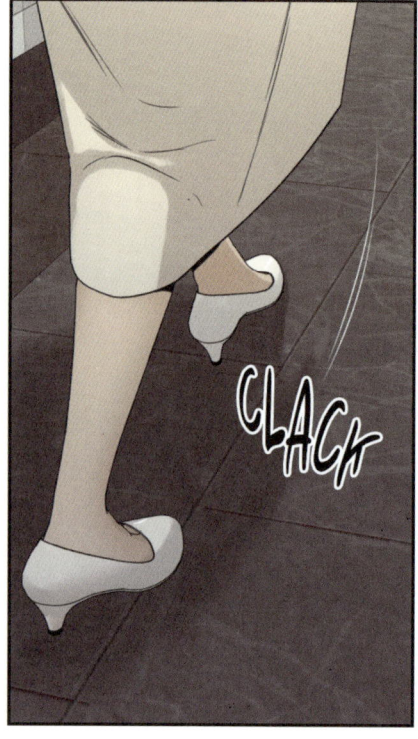
CLACK

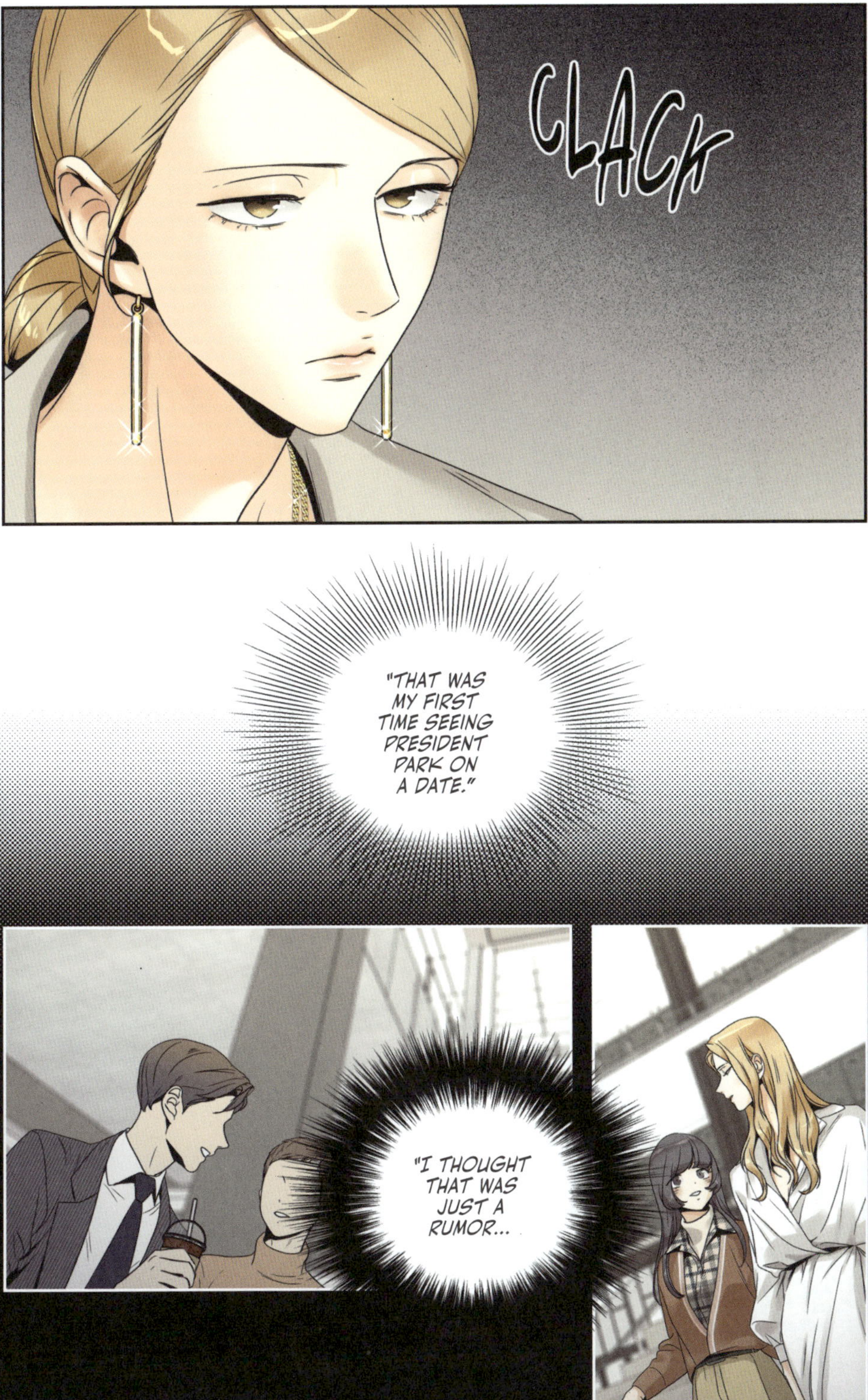
CLACK
"THAT WAS MY FIRST TIME SEEING PRESIDENT PARK ON A DATE."
"I THOUGHT THAT WAS JUST A RUMOR...

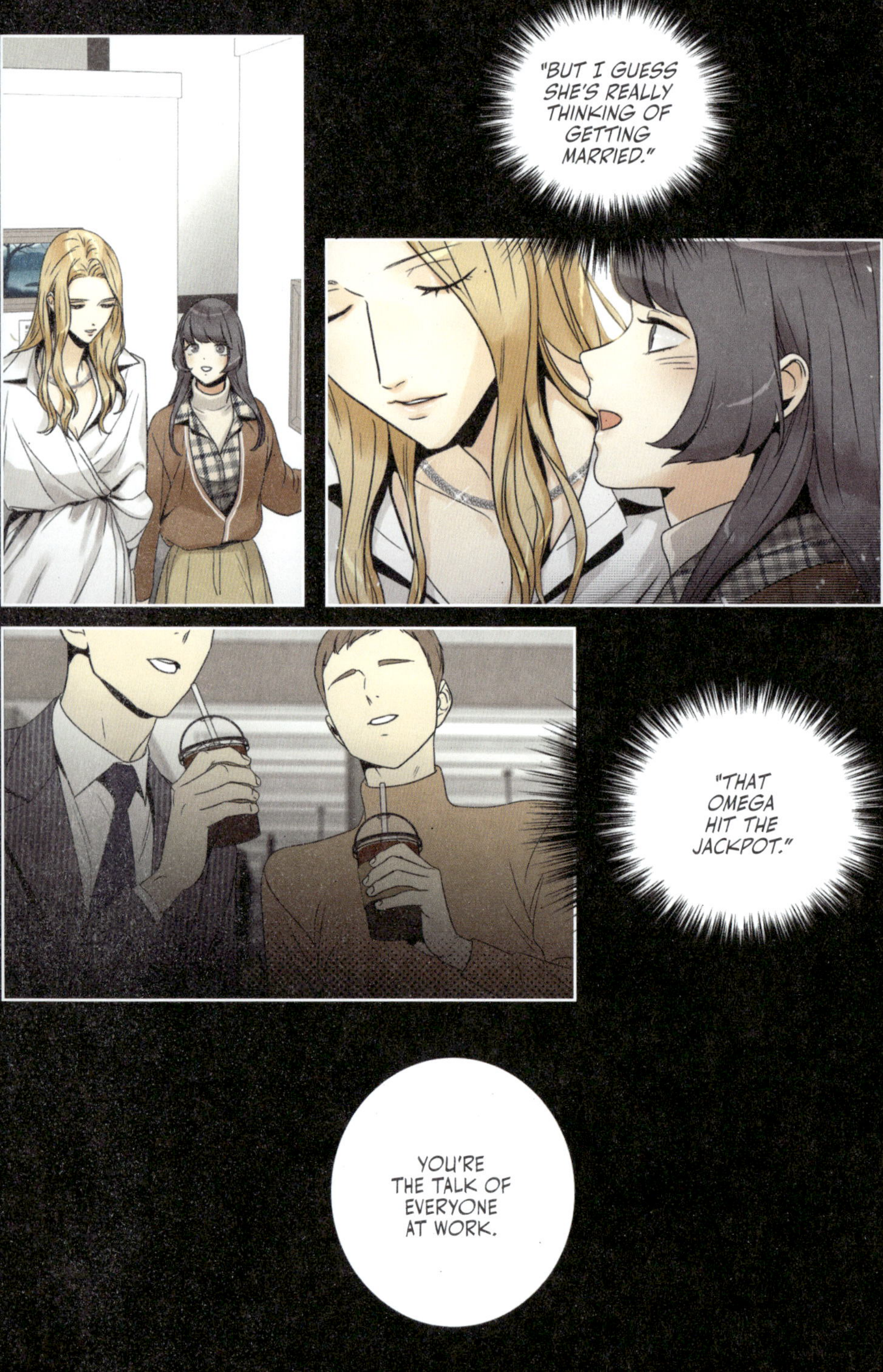
"BUT I GUESS SHE'S REALLY THINKING OF GETTING MARRIED."
"THAT OMEGA HIT THE JACKPOT."
YOU'RE THE TALK OF EVERYONE AT WORK.

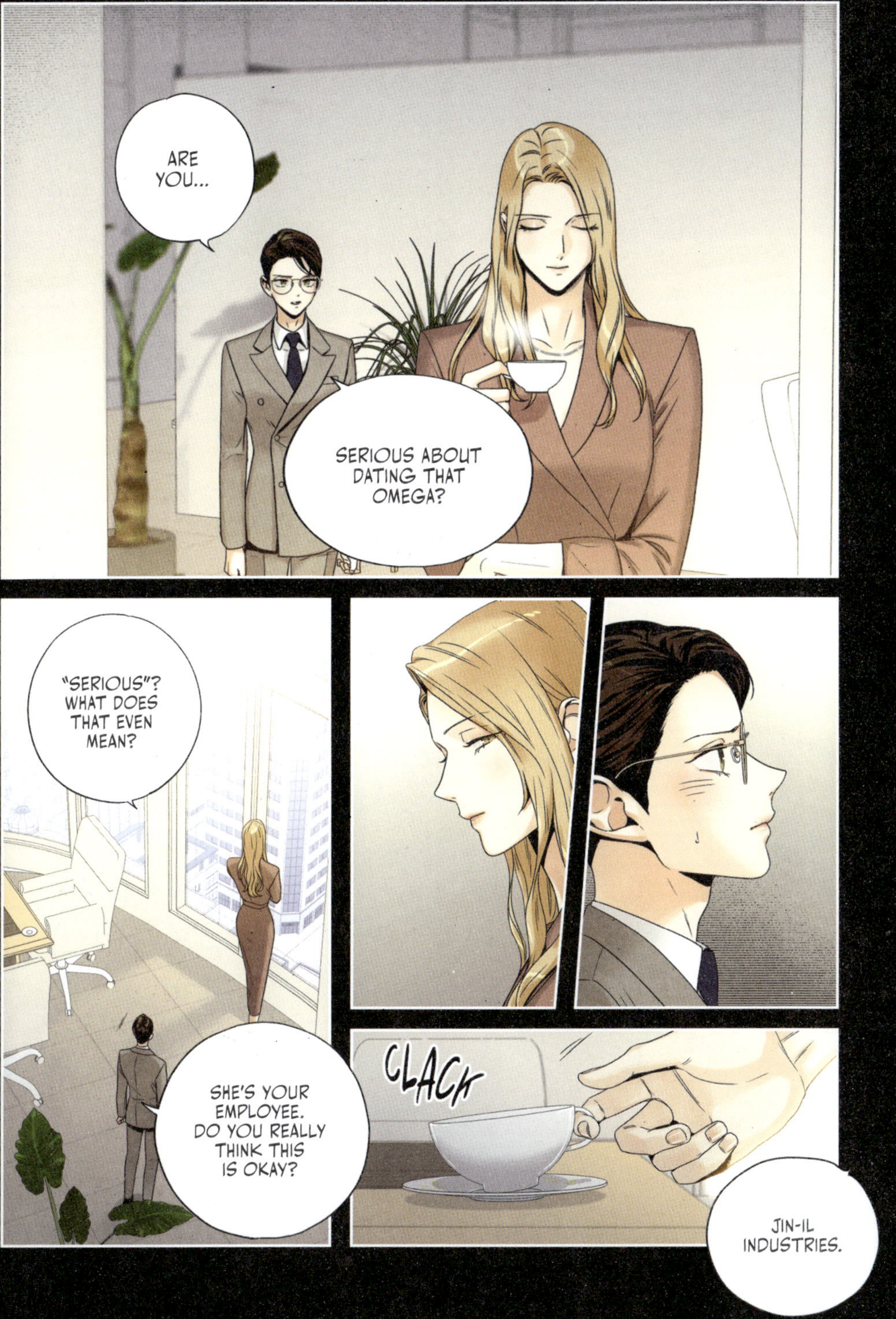
ARE YOU...
SERIOUS ABOUT DATING THAT OMEGA?
"SERIOUS"? WHAT DOES THAT EVEN MEAN?
SHE'S YOUR EMPLOYEE. DO YOU REALLY THINK THIS IS OKAY?
CLACK
JIN-IL INDUSTRIES.

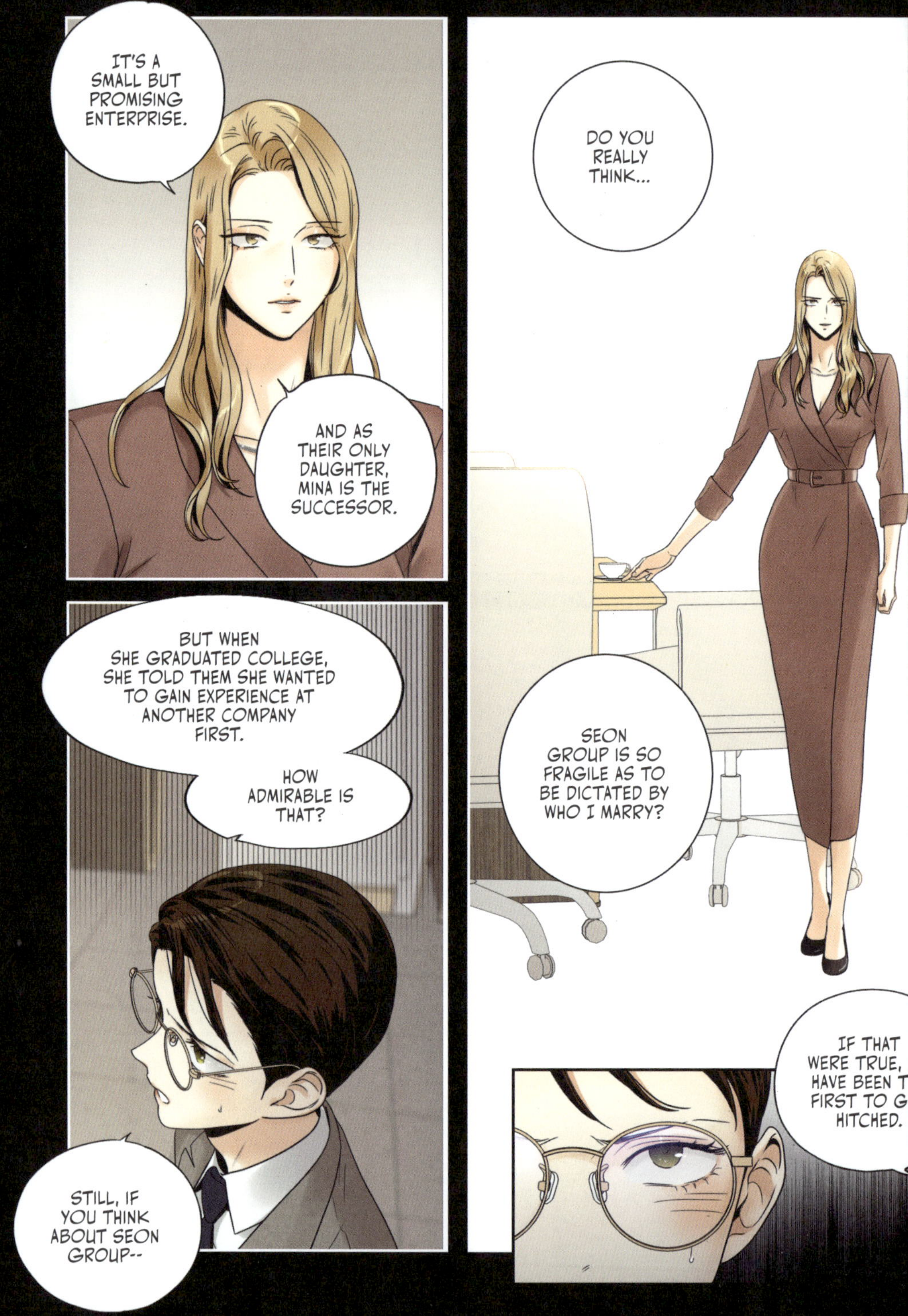
IT'S A SMALL BUT PROMISING ENTERPRISE.
AND AS THEIR ONLY DAUGHTER, MINA IS THE SUCCESSOR.
BUT WHEN SHE GRADUATED COLLEGE, SHE TOLD THEM SHE WANTED TO GAIN EXPERIENCE AT ANOTHER COMPANY FIRST.
HOW ADMIRABLE IS THAT?
STILL, IF YOU THINK ABOUT SEON GROUP--
DO YOU REALLY THINK...
SEON GROUP IS SO FRAGILE AS TO BE DICTATED BY WHO I MARRY?
IF THAT WERE TRUE, HAVE BEEN T FIRST TO G HITCHED.

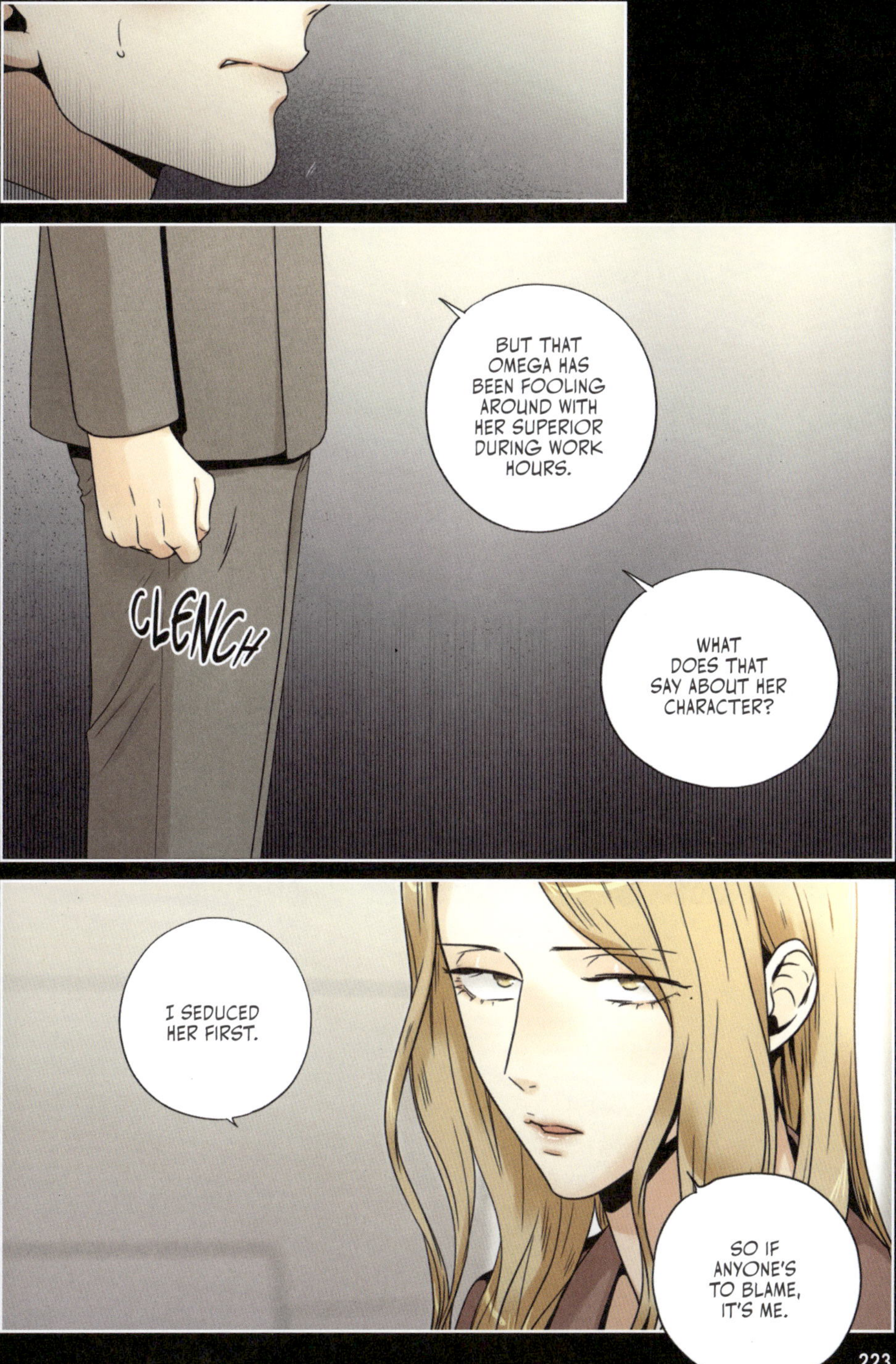
BUT THAT OMEGA HAS BEEN FOOLING AROUND WITH HER SUPERIOR DURING WORK HOURS.
CLENCH
WHAT DOES THAT SAY ABOUT HER CHARACTER?
I SEDUCED HER FIRST.
SO IF ANYONE'S TO BLAME, IT'S ME.

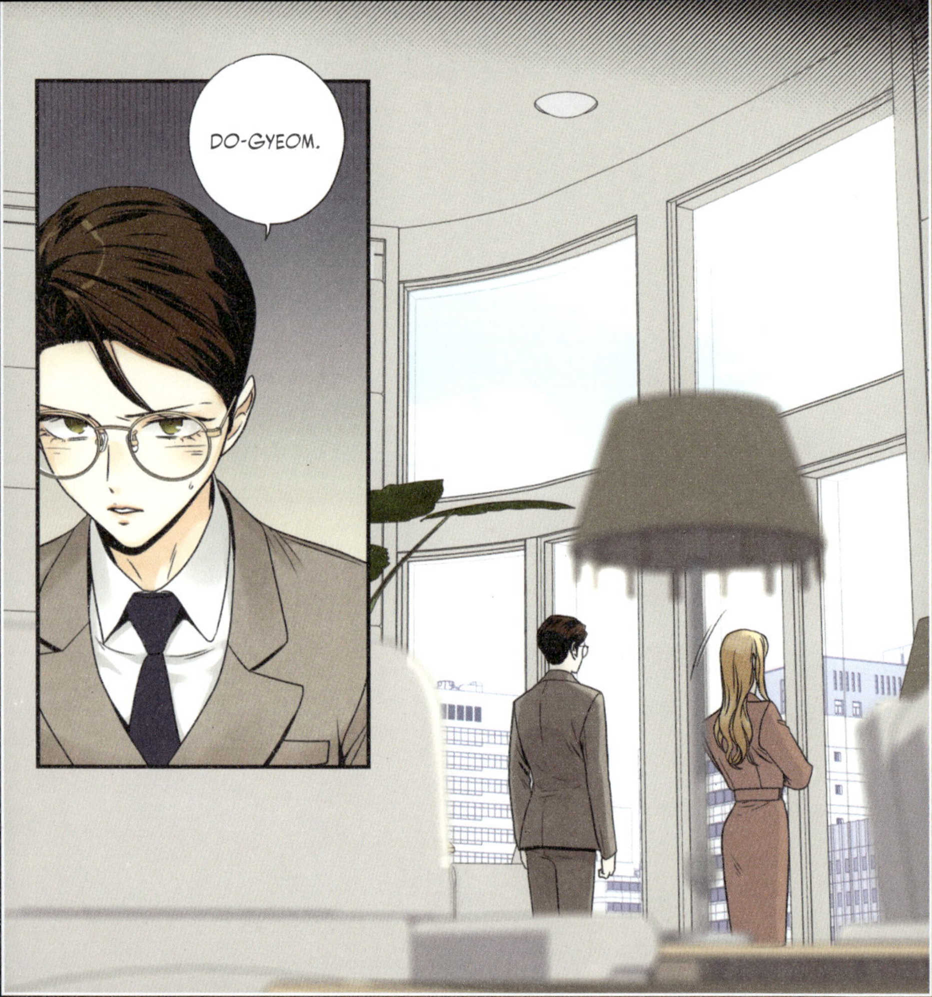
DO-GYEOM.

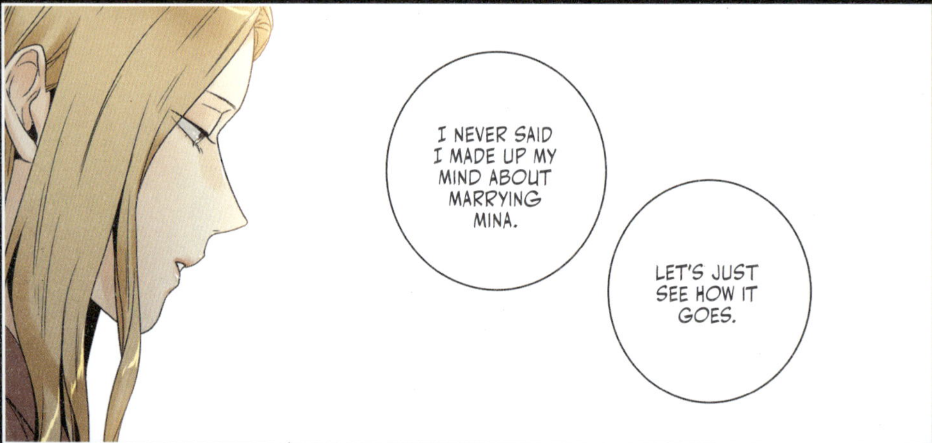
I NEVER SAID I MADE UP MY MIND ABOUT MARRYING MINA.
LET'S JUST SEE HOW IT GOES.

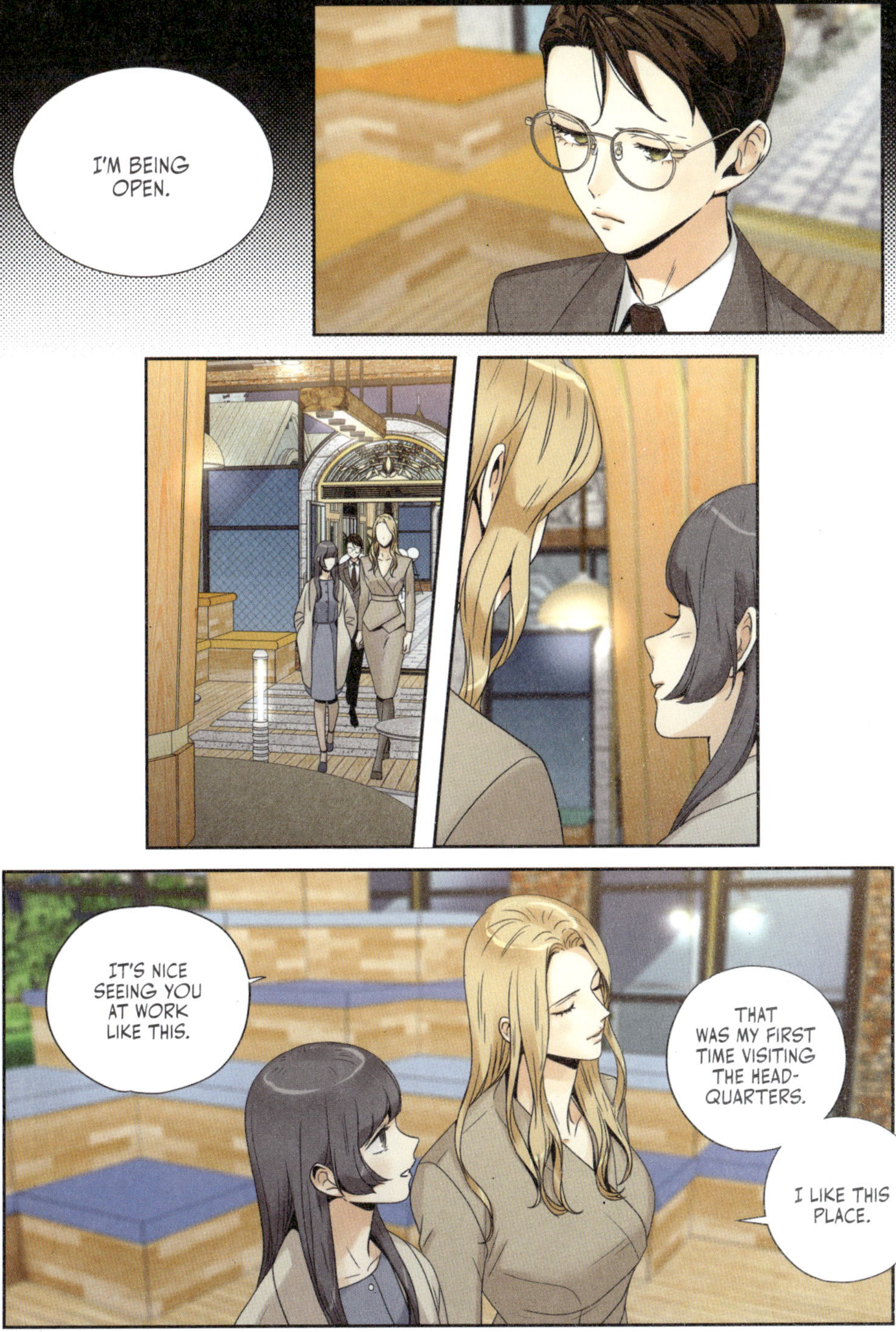
I'M BEING OPEN.
IT'S NICE SEEING YOU AT WORK LIKE THIS.
THAT WAS MY FIRST TIME VISITING THE HEAD-QUARTERS.
I LIKE THIS PLACE.

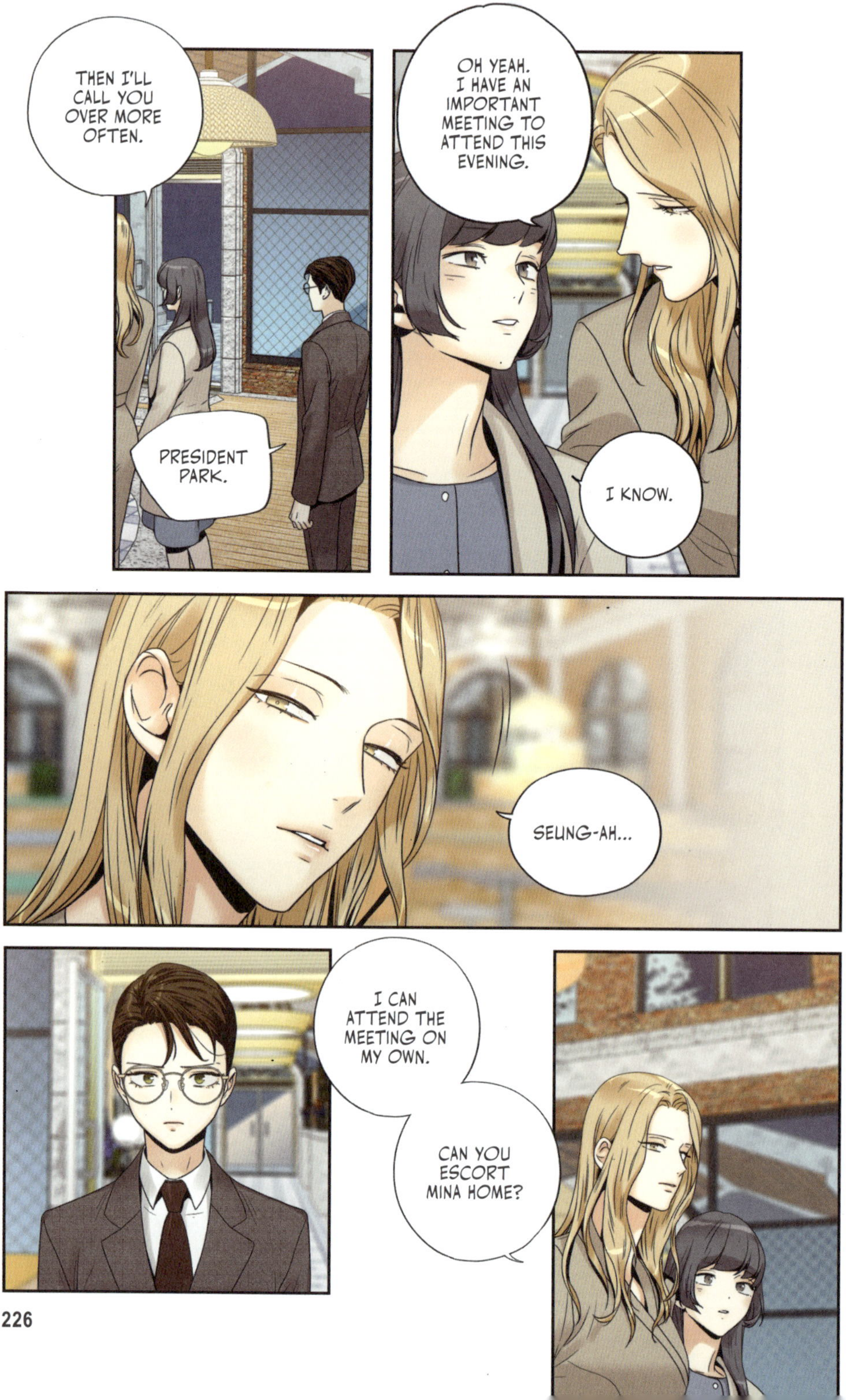
THEN I'LL CALL YOU OVER MORE OFTEN.
PRESIDENT PARK.
OH YEAH. I HAVE AN IMPORTANT MEETING TO ATTEND THIS EVENING.
I KNOW.
SEUNG-AH...
I CAN ATTEND THE MEETING ON MY OWN.
CAN YOU ESCORT MINA HOME?

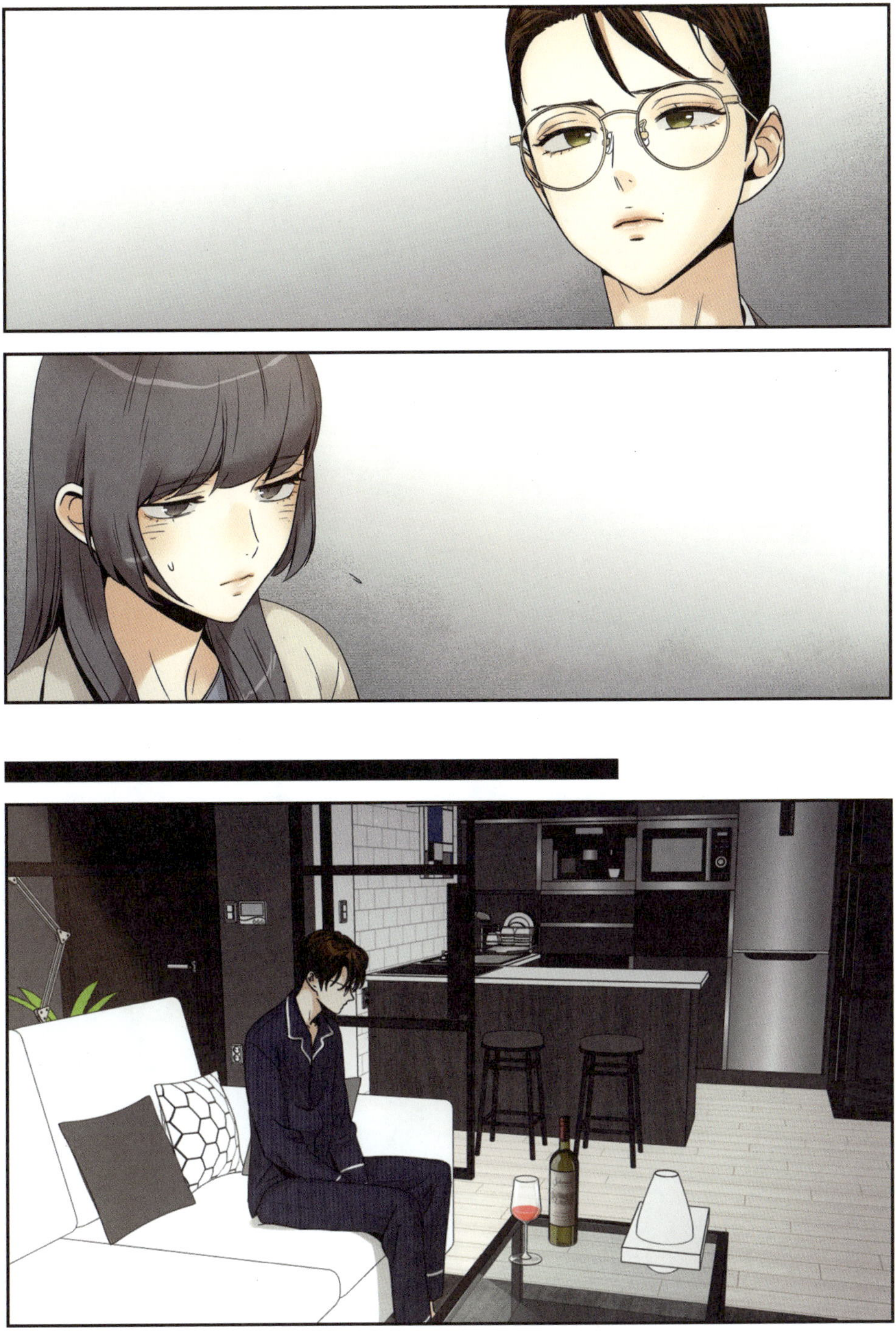

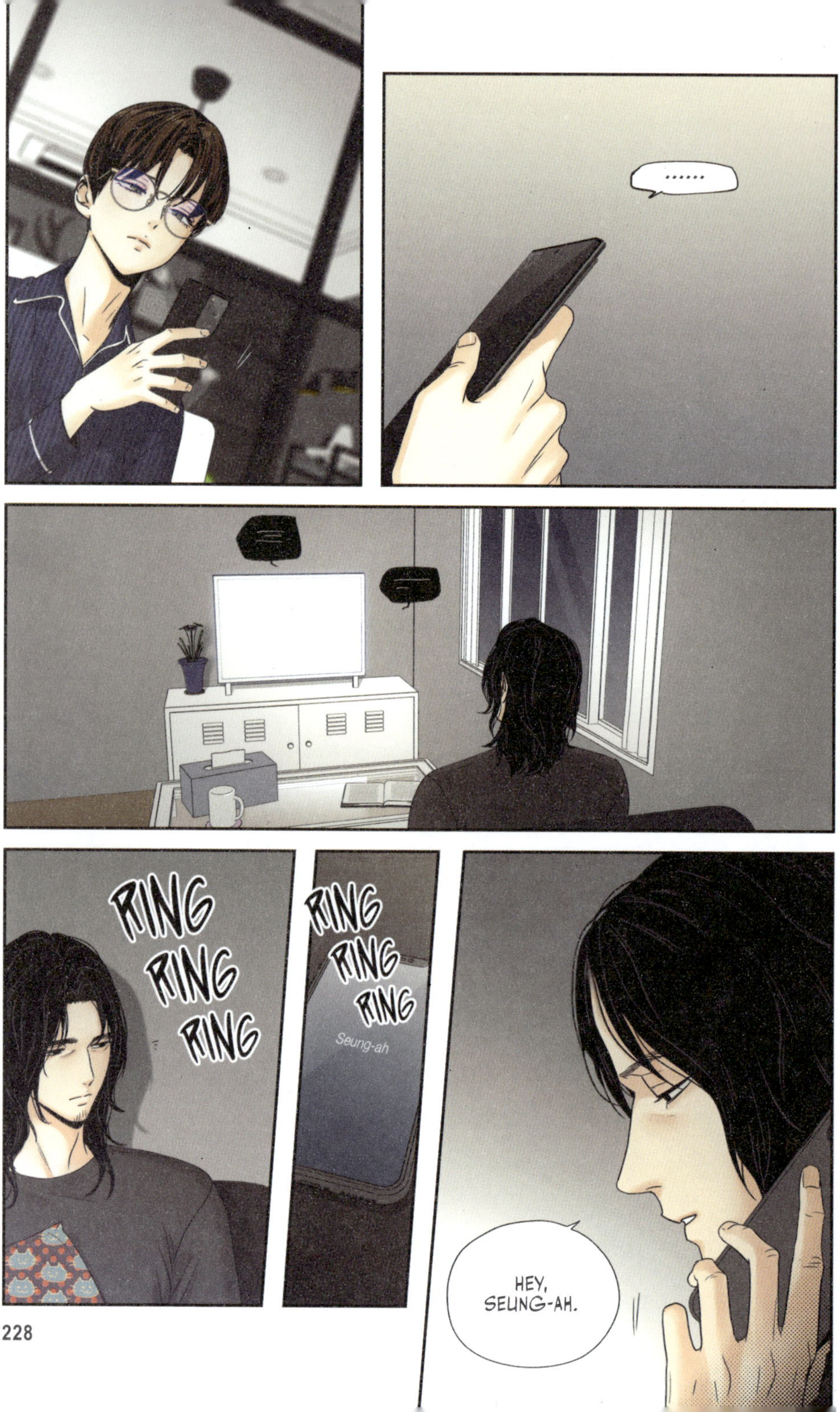
......
RING RING RING
RING RING RING
Seung-ah
HEY, SEUNG-AH.

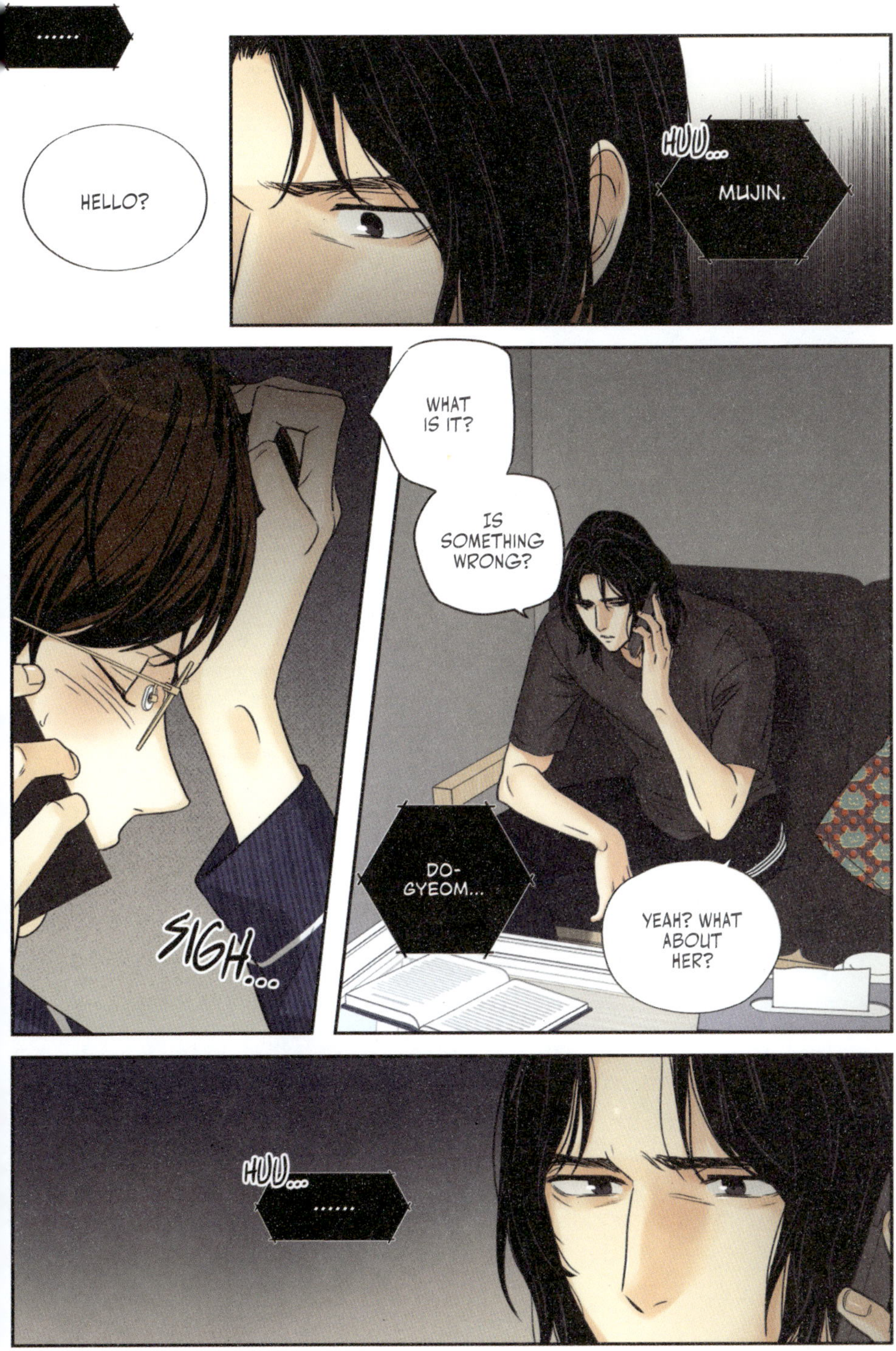
....
HELLO?
HUU...
MUJIN.
WHAT IS IT?
IS SOMETHING WRONG?
SIGH...
DO-GYEOM...
YEAH? WHAT ABOUT HER?
HUU...
....

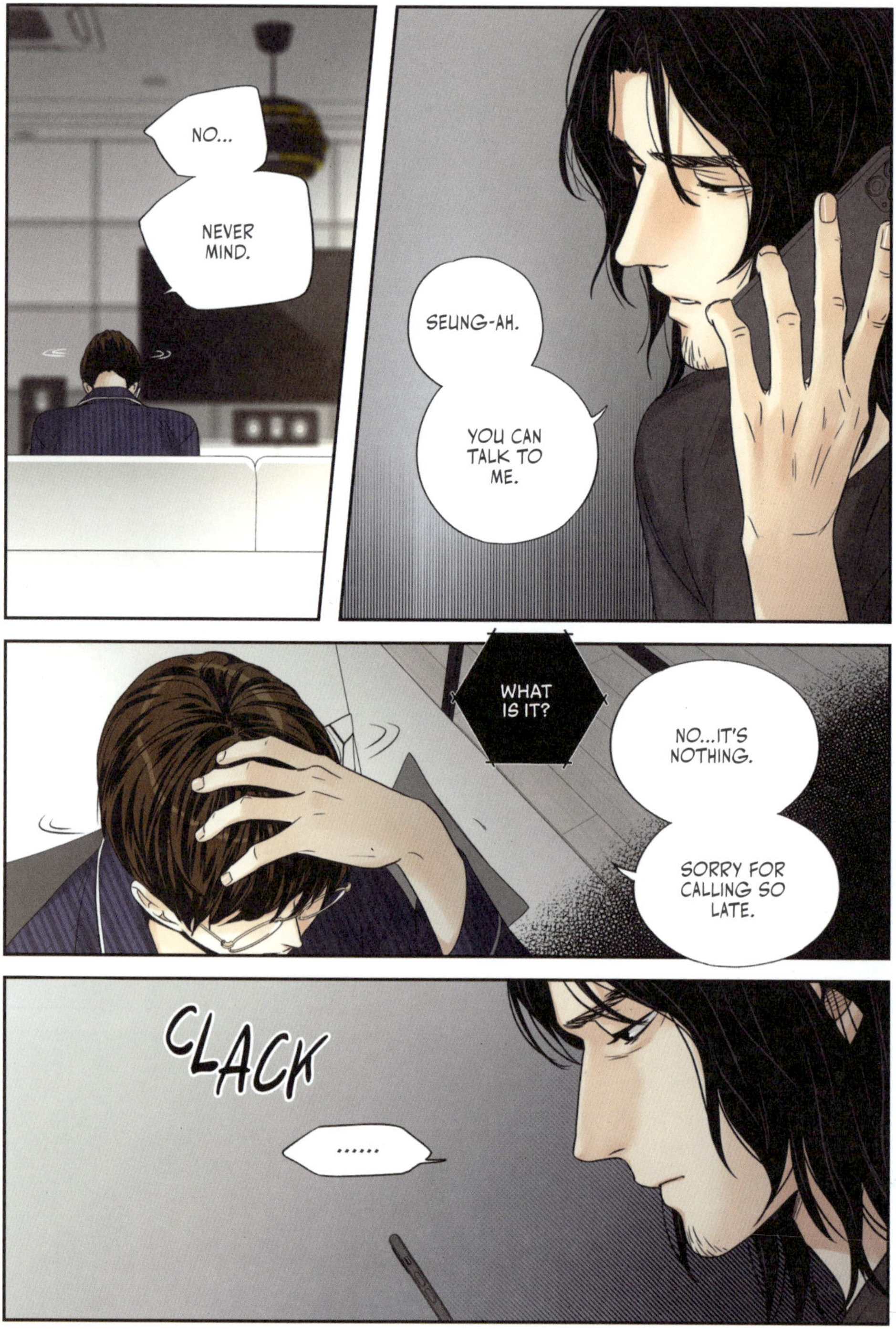
NO...
NEVER MIND.
SEUNG-AH.
YOU CAN TALK TO ME.
WHAT IS IT?
NO...IT'S NOTHING.
SORRY FOR CALLING SO LATE.
CLACK
....

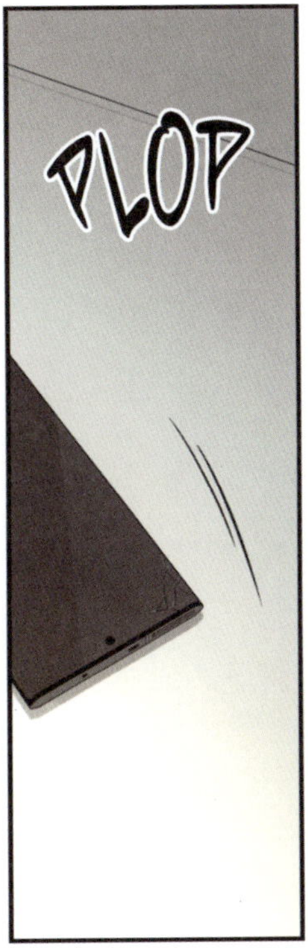
PLOP
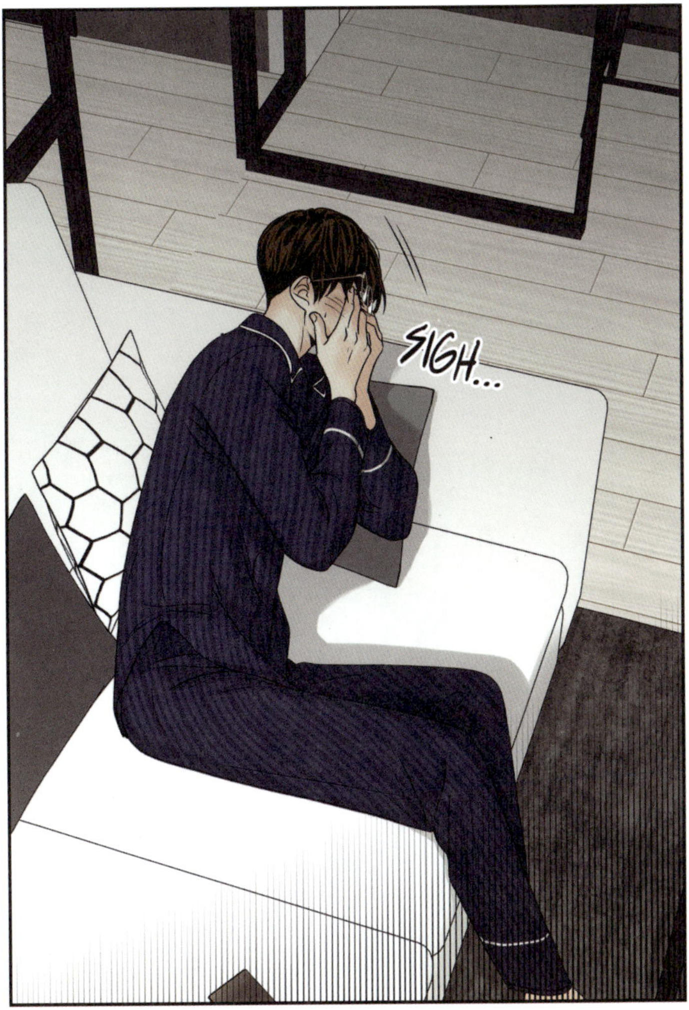
SIGH...

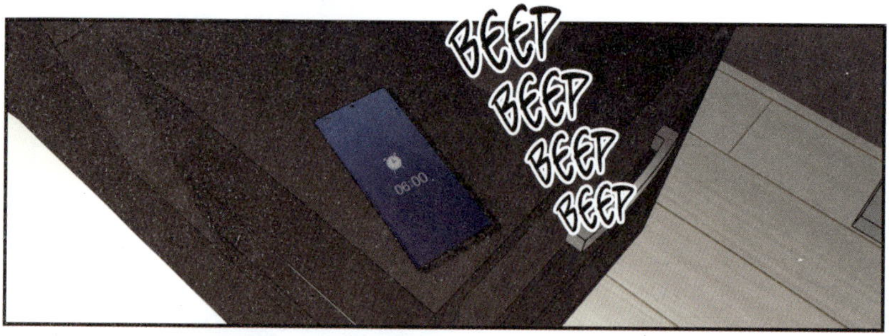
06:00
BEEP
BEEP
BEEP
BEEP
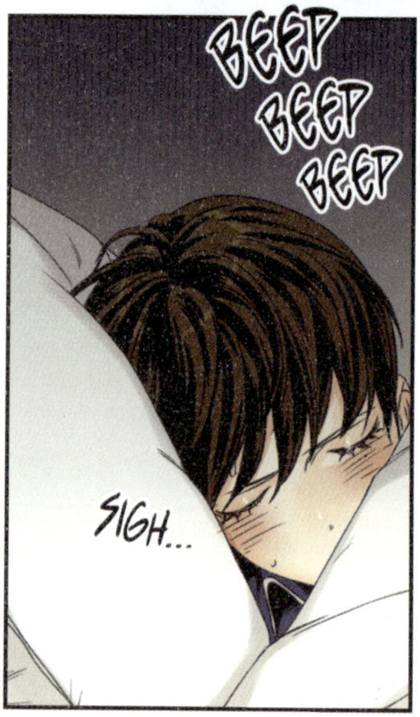
BEEP
BEEP
BEEP
SIGH...
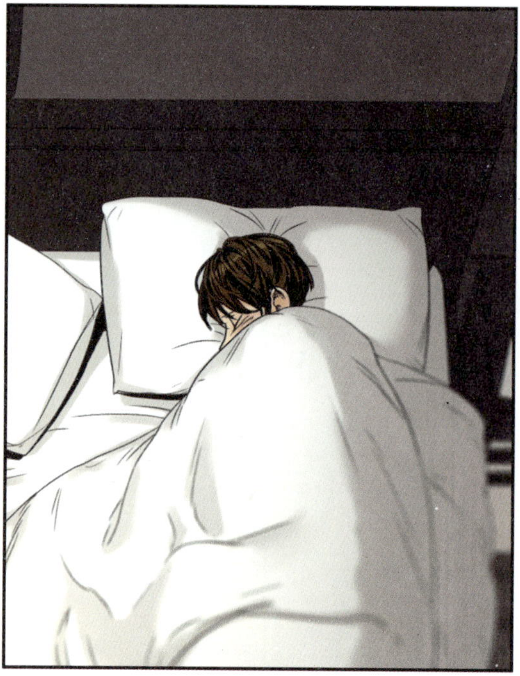

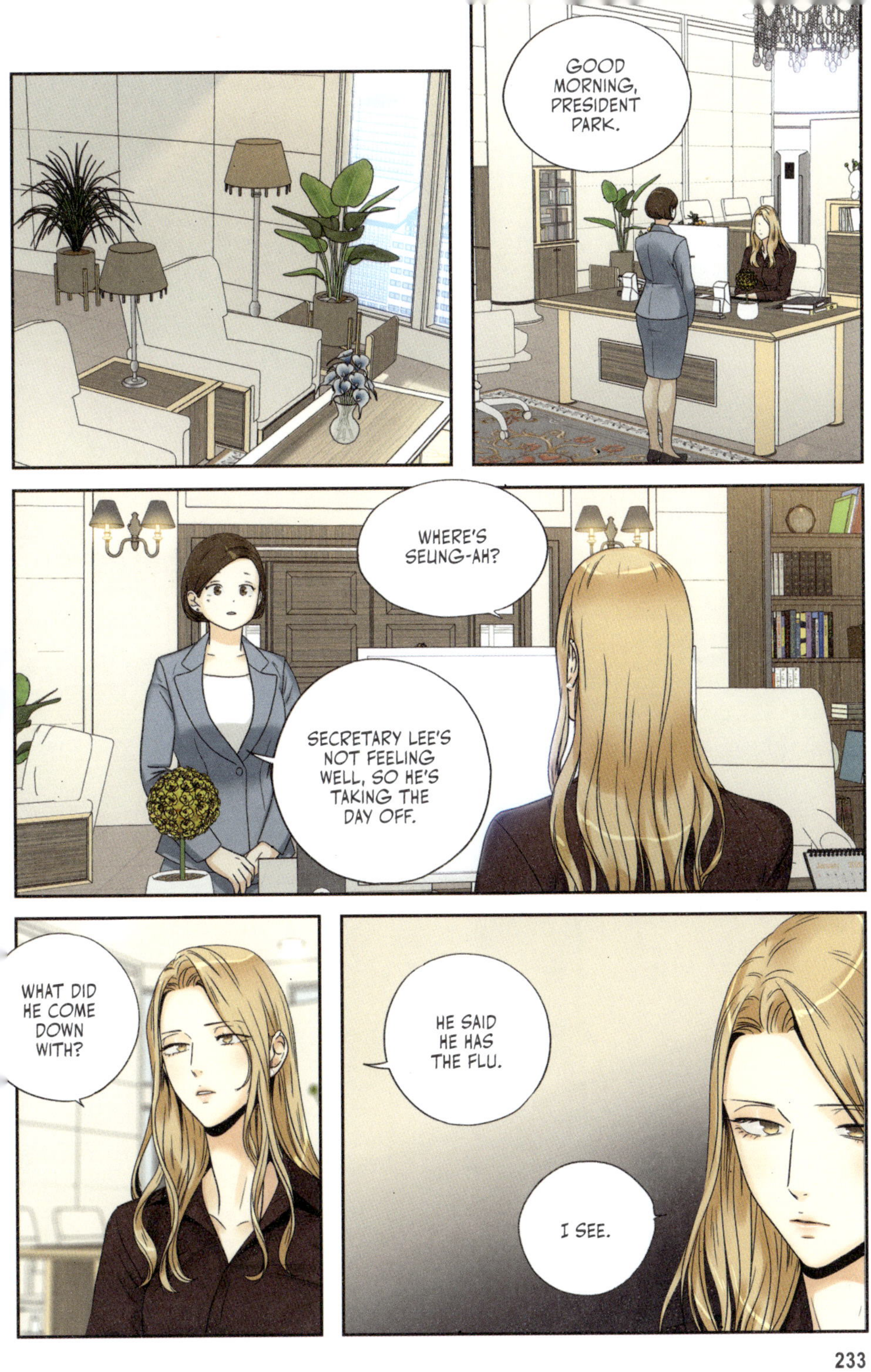
GOOD MORNING, PRESIDENT PARK.
WHERE'S SEUNG-AH?
SECRETARY LEE'S NOT FEELING WELL, SO HE'S TAKING THE DAY OFF.
WHAT DID HE COME DOWN WITH?
HE SAID HE HAS THE FLU.
I SEE.

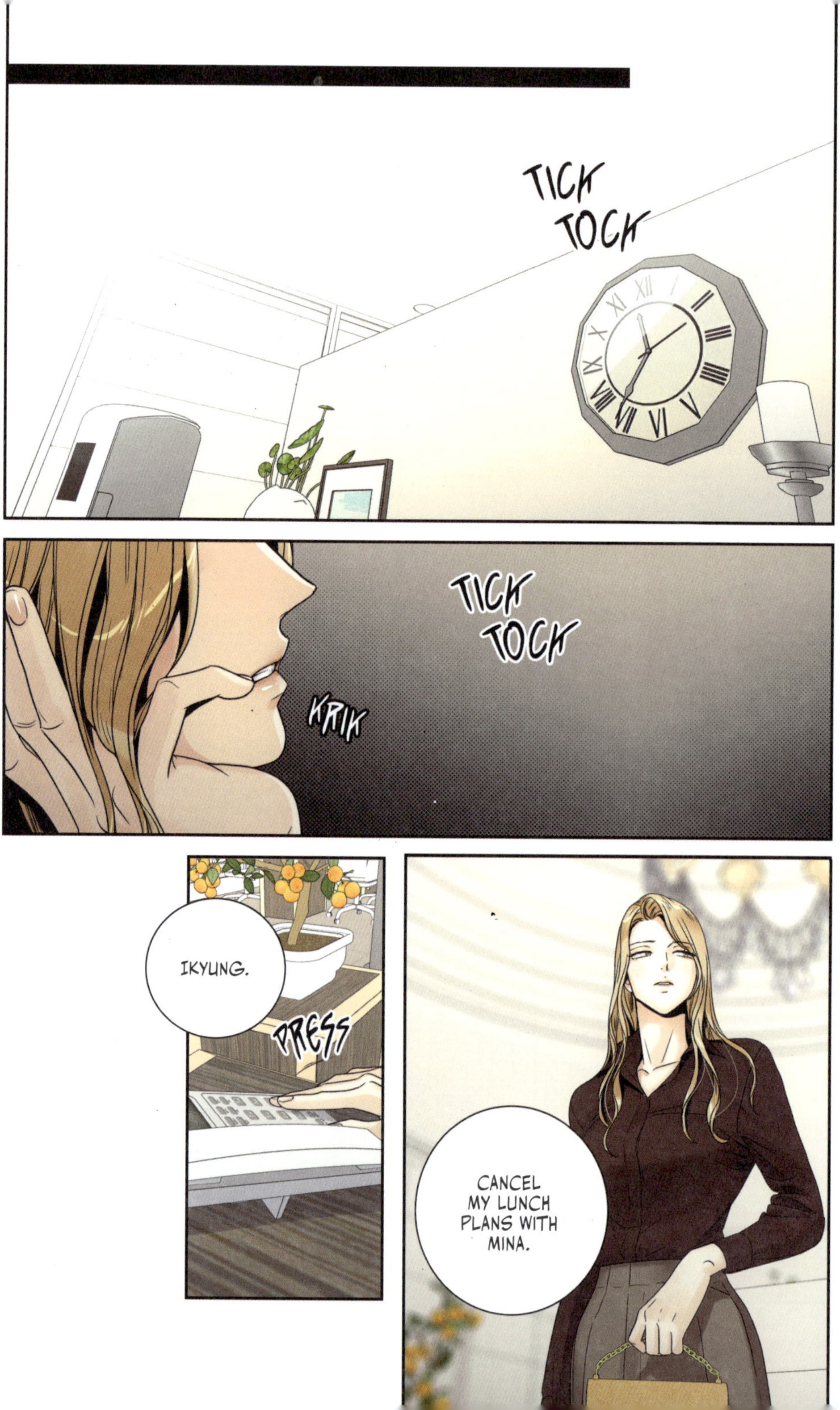
TICK
TOCK
TICK
TOCK
KRIK
IKYUNG.
PRESS
CANCEL MY LUNCH PLANS WITH MINA.

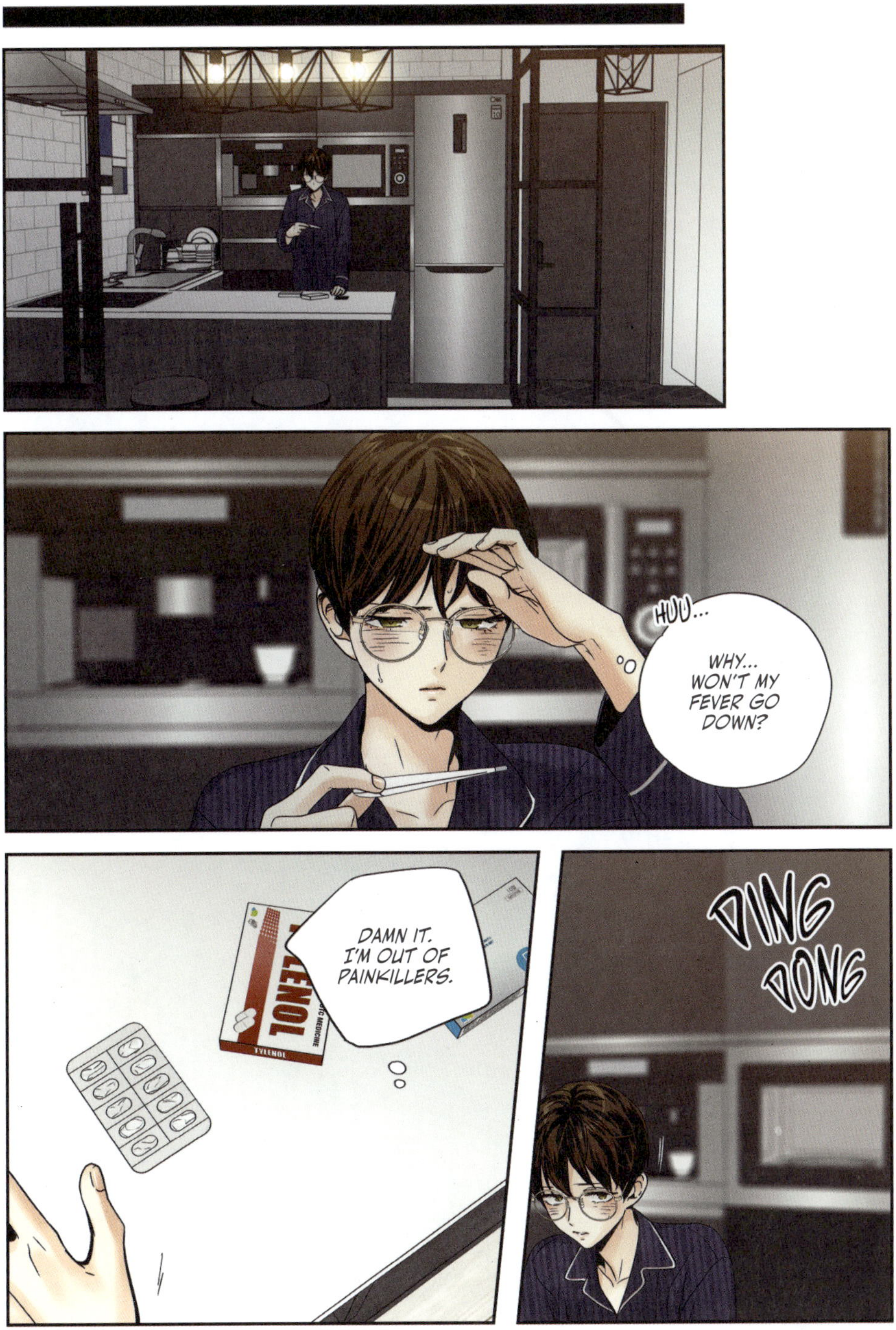
HUU...
WHY... WON'T MY FEVER GO DOWN?
DAMN IT. I'M OUT OF PAINKILLERS.
TYLENOL
DING DONG

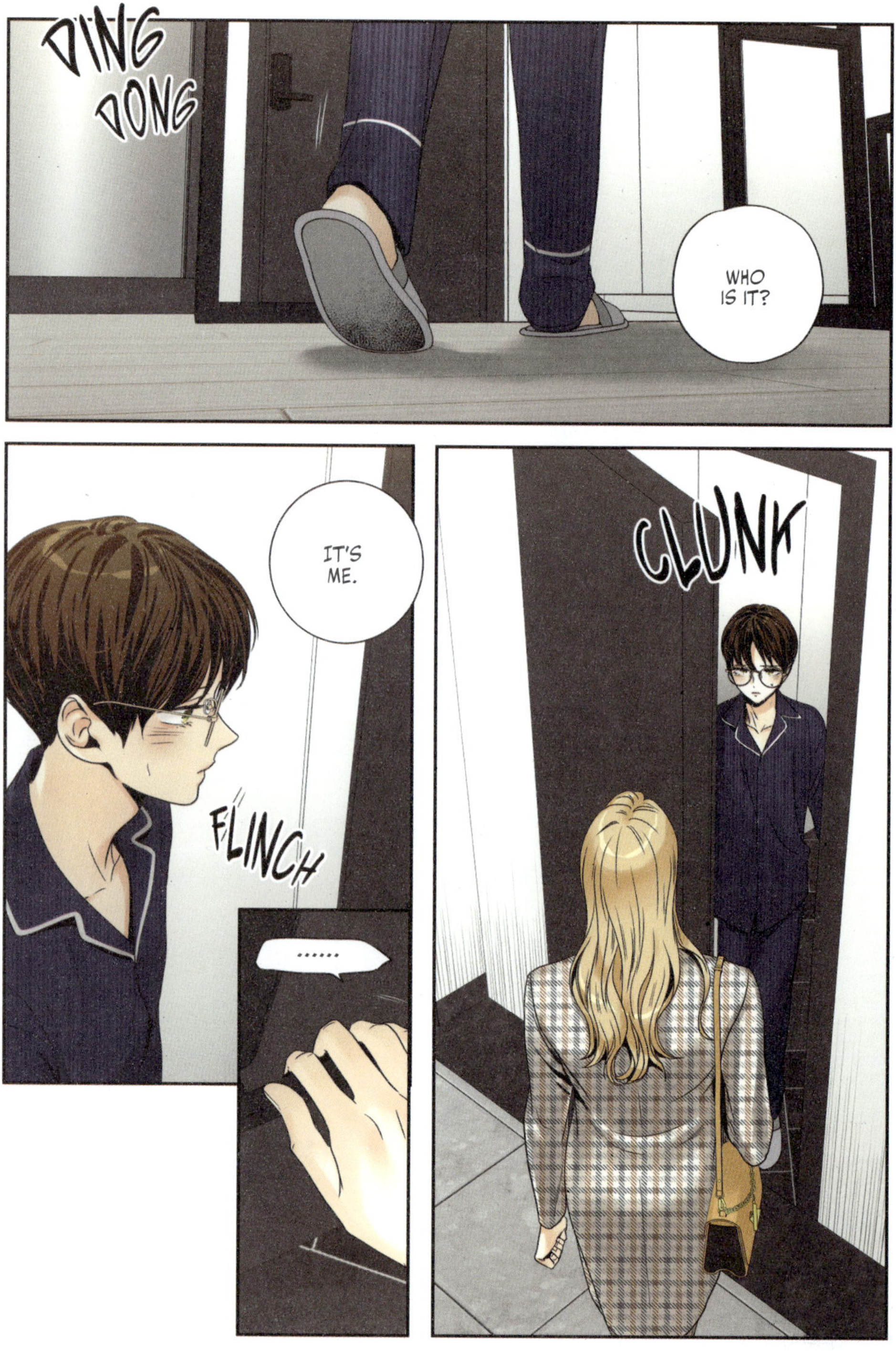

DING DONG
WHO IS IT?
IT'S ME.
FLINCH
......
CLUNK

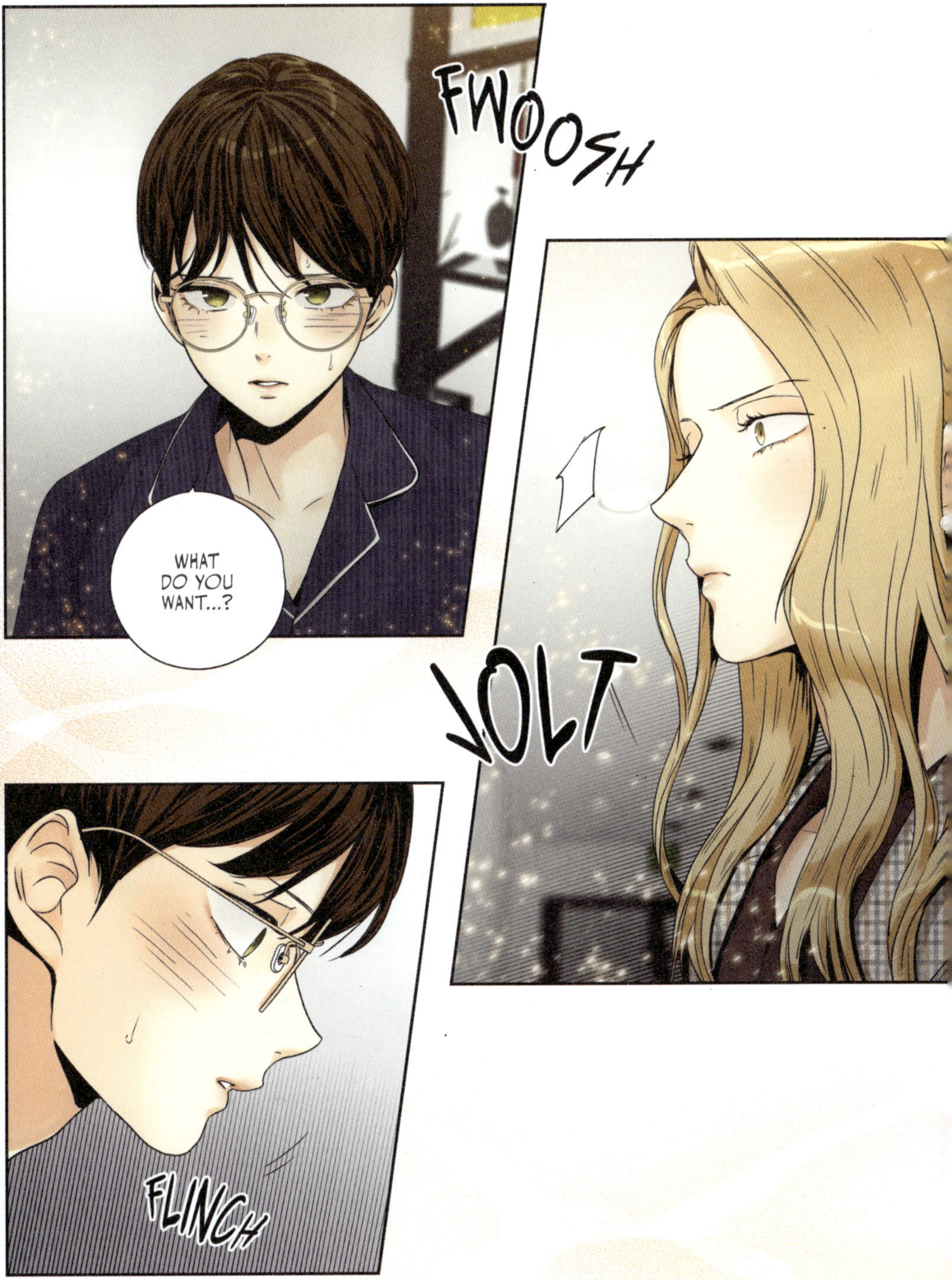
WHAT DO YOU WANT...?
FWOOSH
JOLT
FLINCH

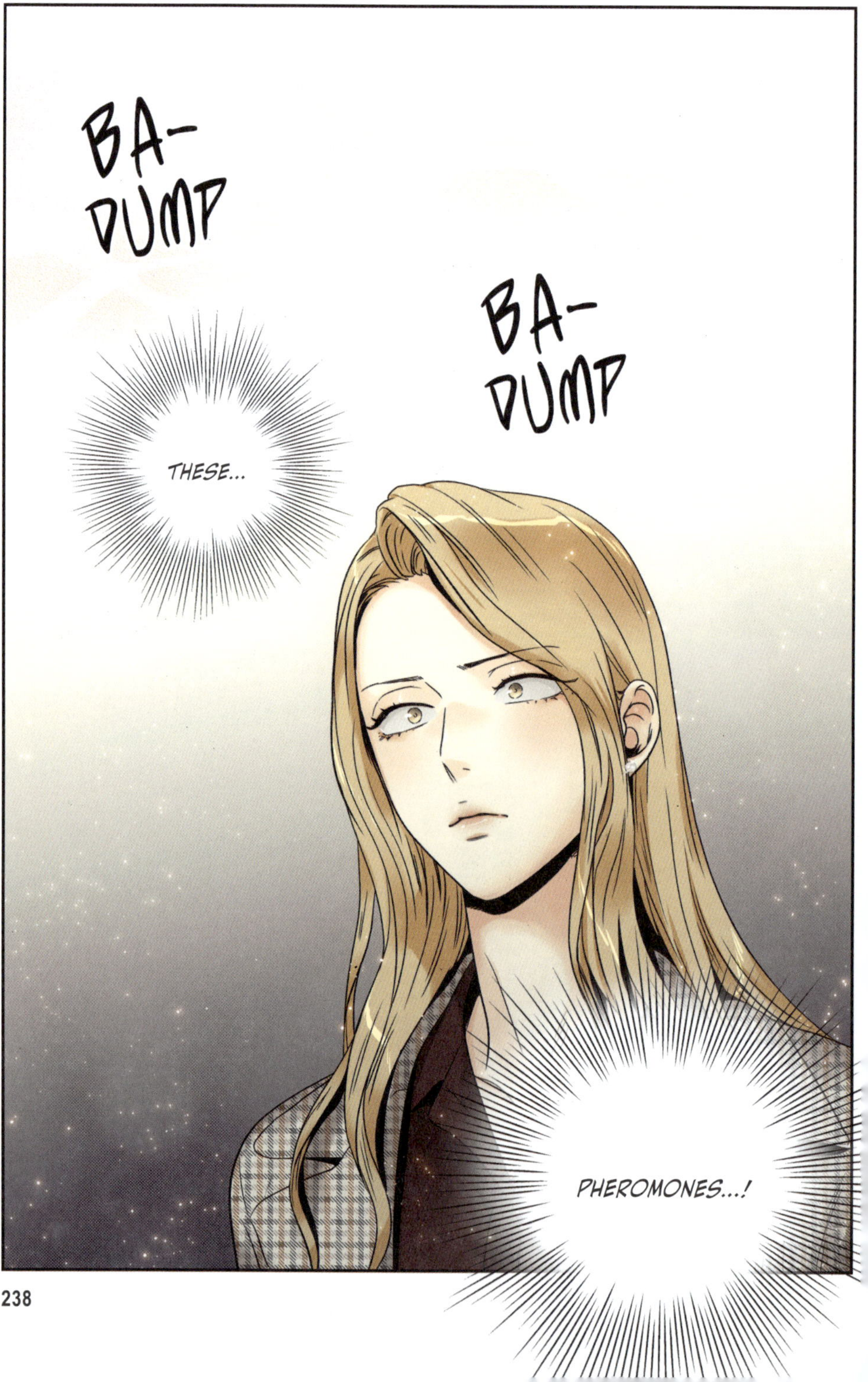
BA-DUMP
BA-DUMP
THESE...
PHEROMONES...!

Love is an Illusion!
The Queen

Love is an Illusion!
The Queen

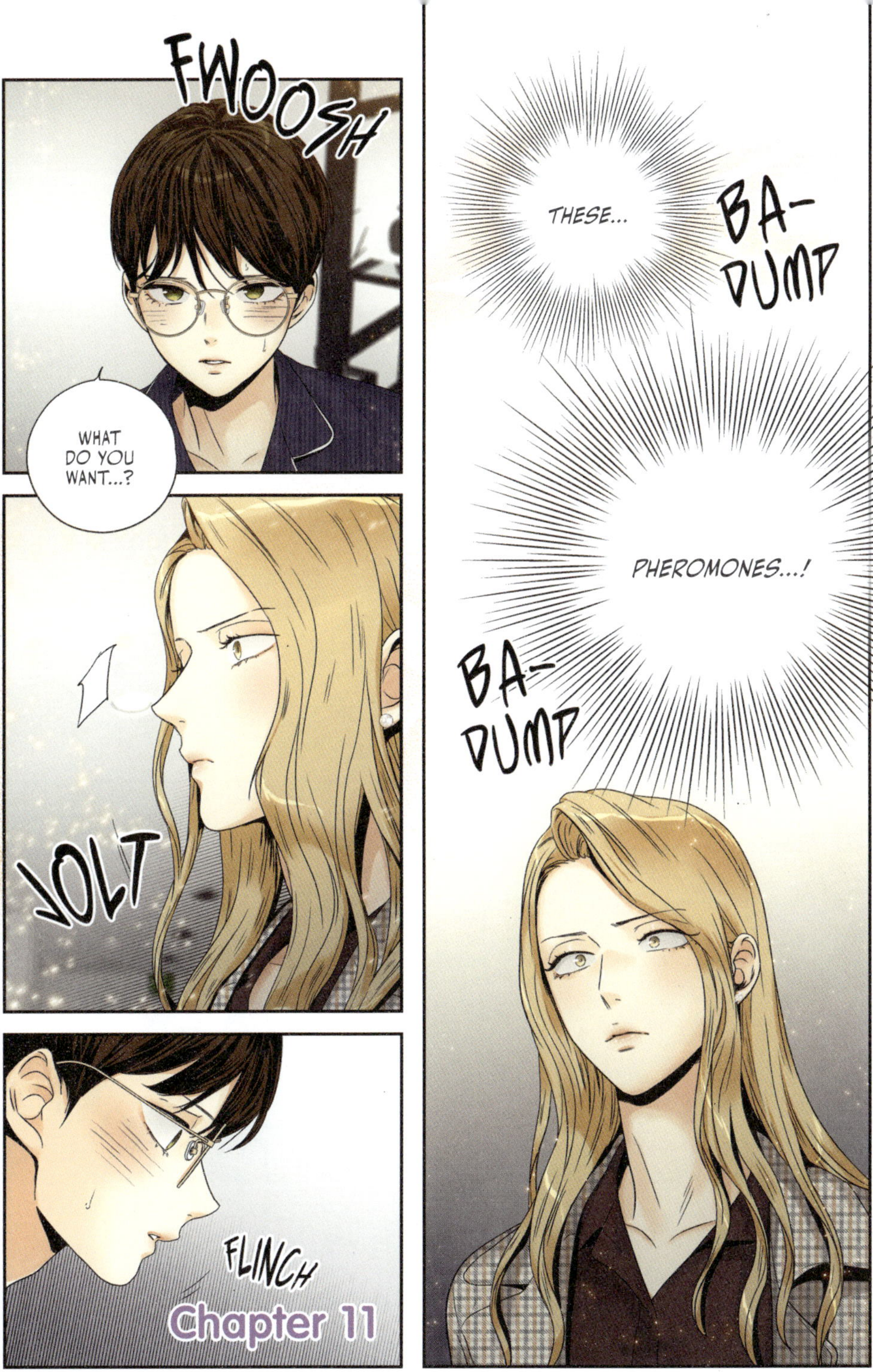
FWOOSH
WHAT DO YOU WANT...?
JOLT
FLINCH
Chapter 11
THESE...
BA-DUMP
PHEROMONES...!
BA-DUMP

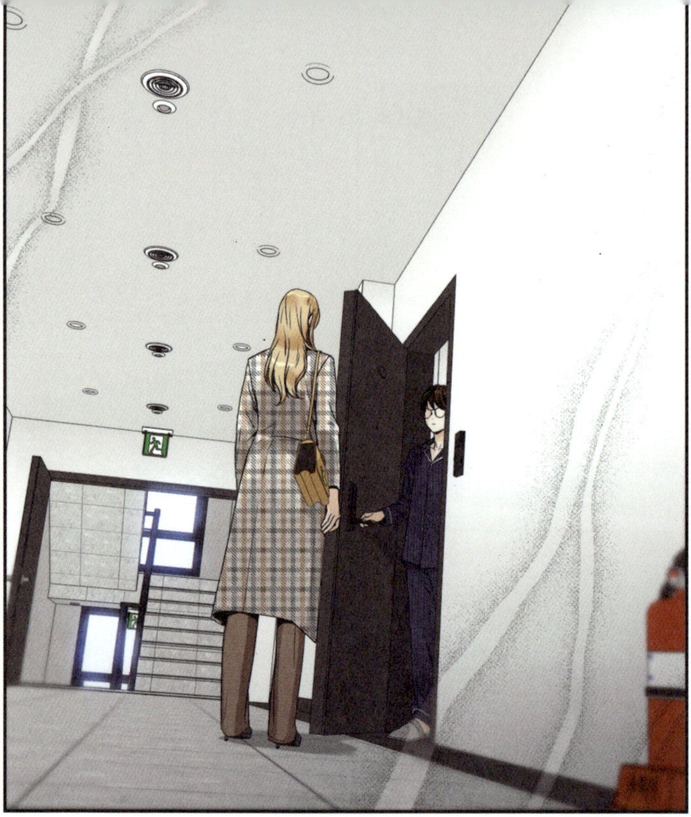

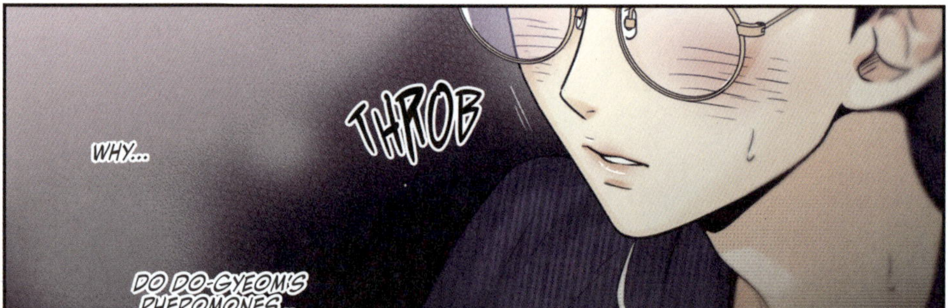
WHY...
THROB
DO DO-GYEOM'S PHEROMONES...
THROB

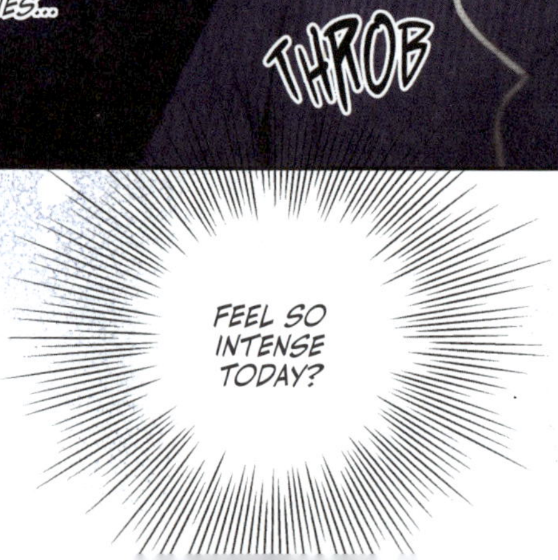
FEEL SO INTENSE TODAY?

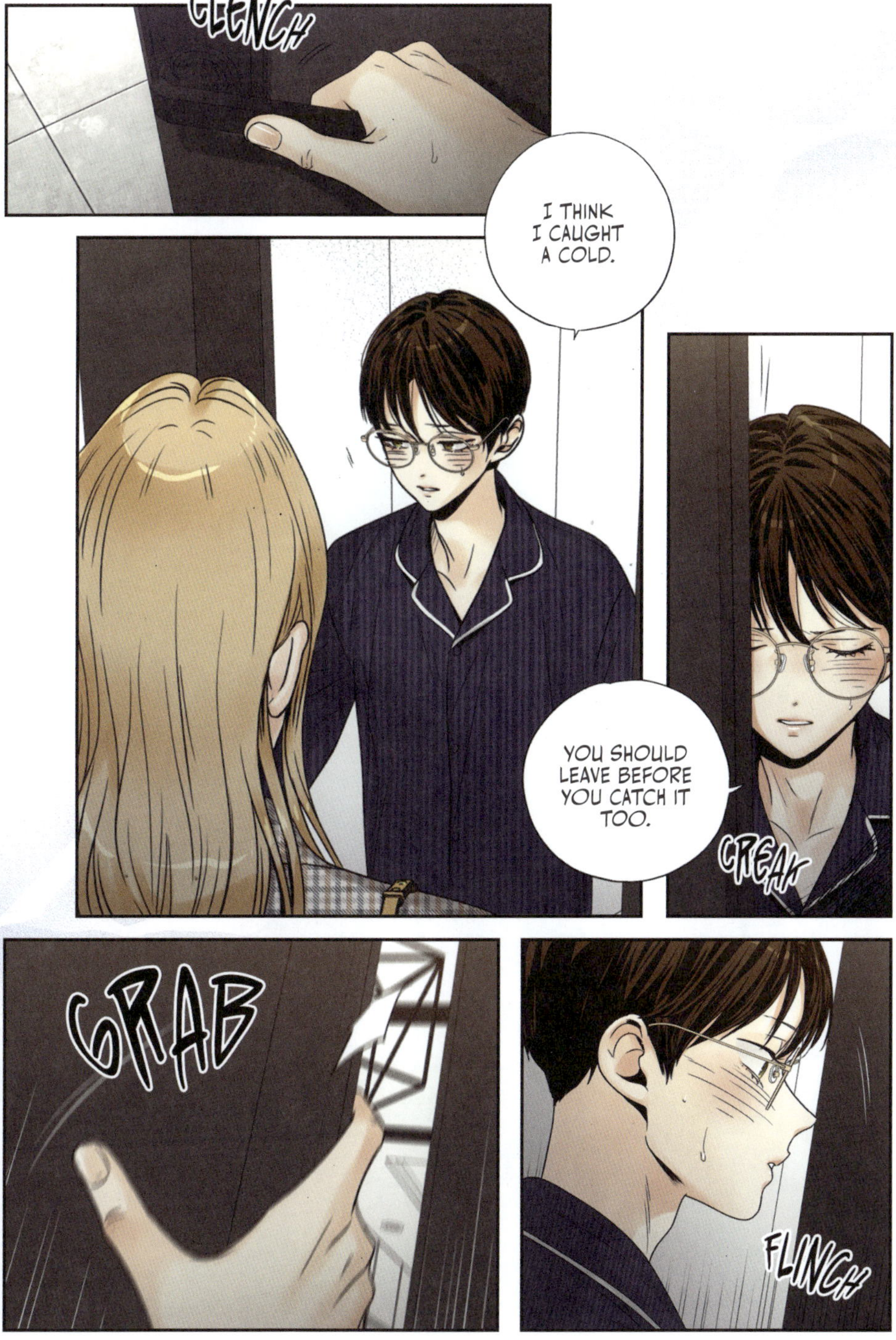
CLENCH
I THINK I CAUGHT A COLD.
YOU SHOULD LEAVE BEFORE YOU CATCH IT TOO.
CREAK
GRAB
FLINCH

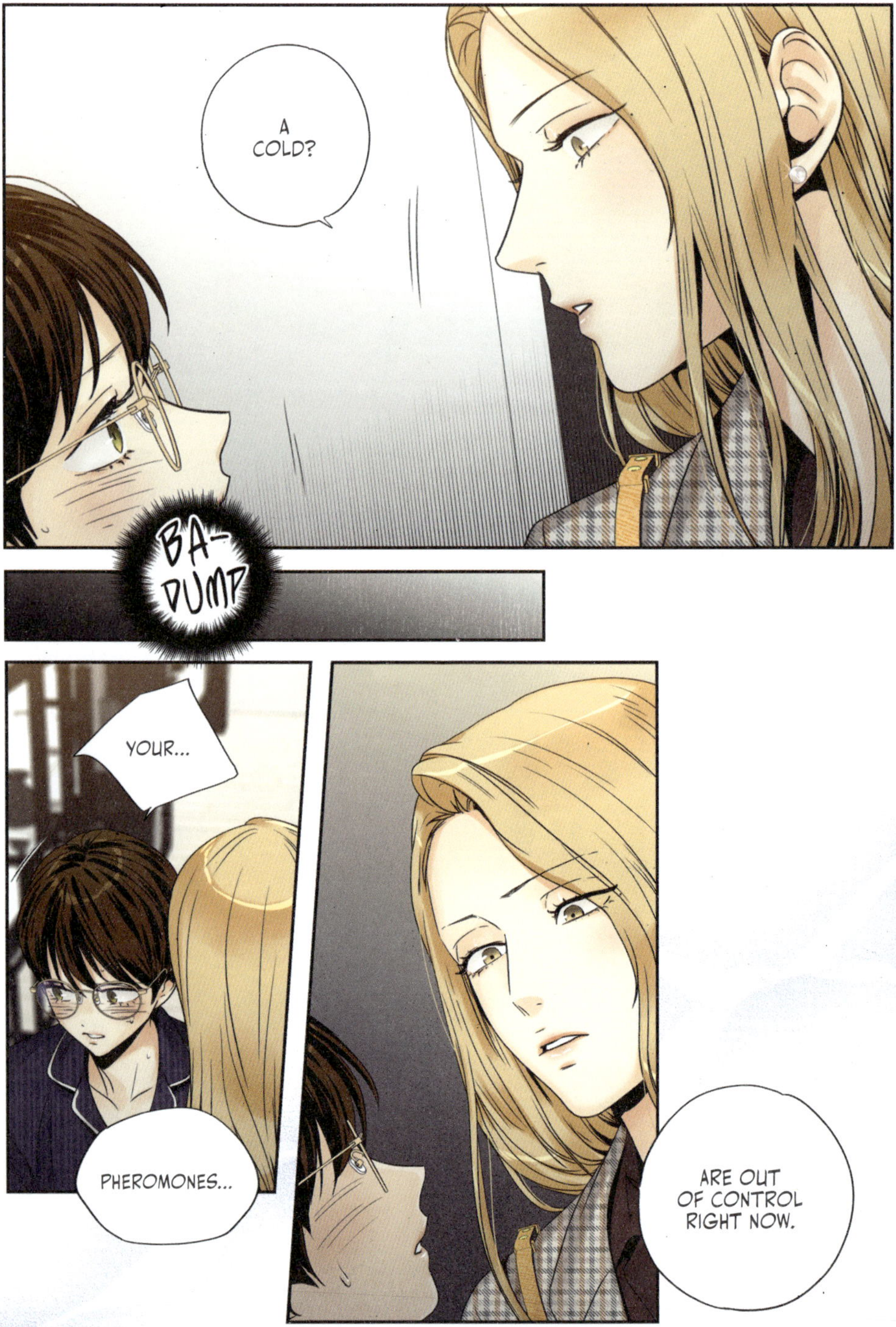
A COLD?
BA-DUMP
YOUR...
PHEROMONES...
ARE OUT OF CONTROL RIGHT NOW.

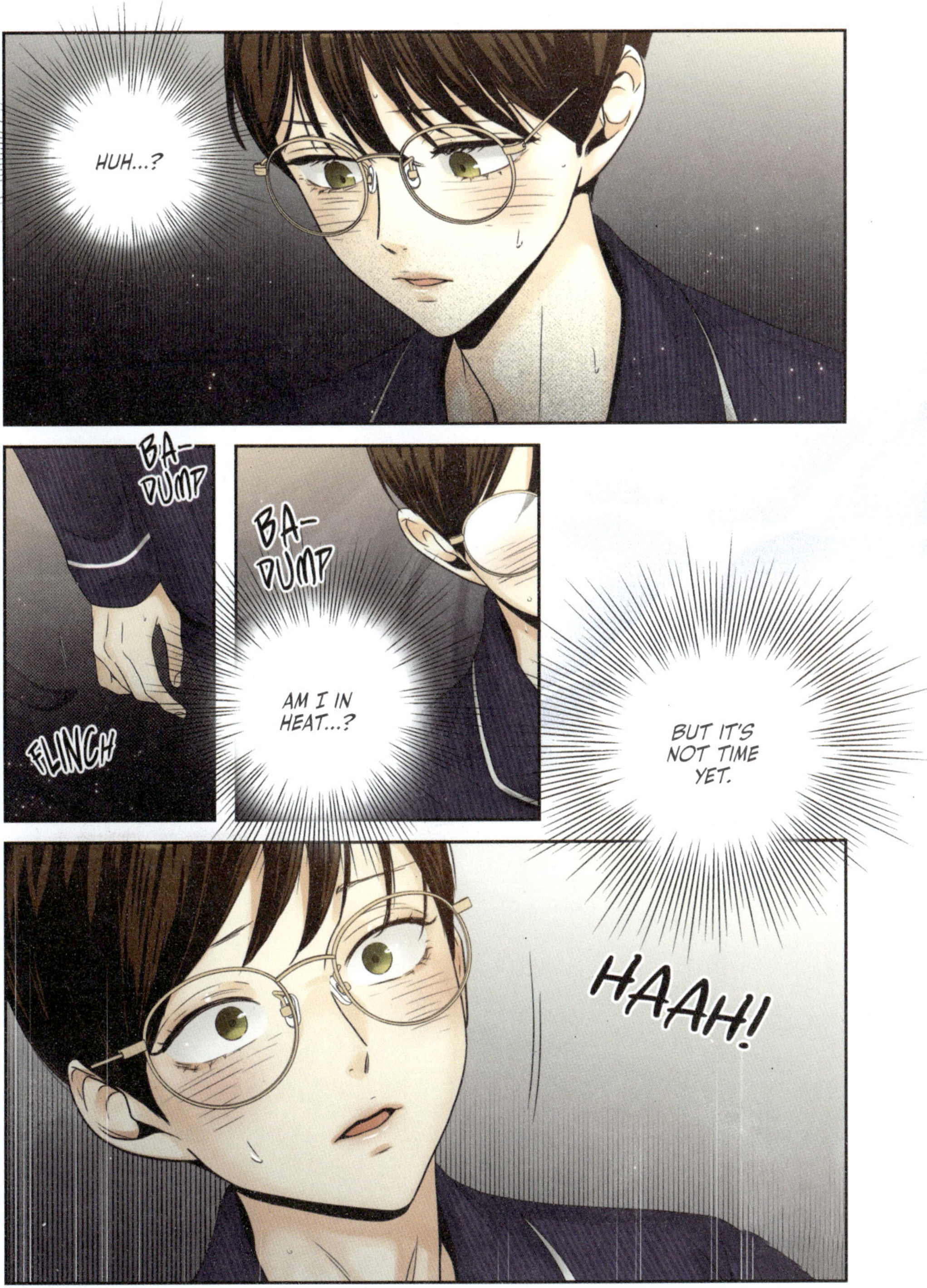
HUH...?
BA-DUMP
FLINCH
BA-DUMP
AM I IN HEAT...?
BUT IT'S NOT TIME YET.
HAAH!

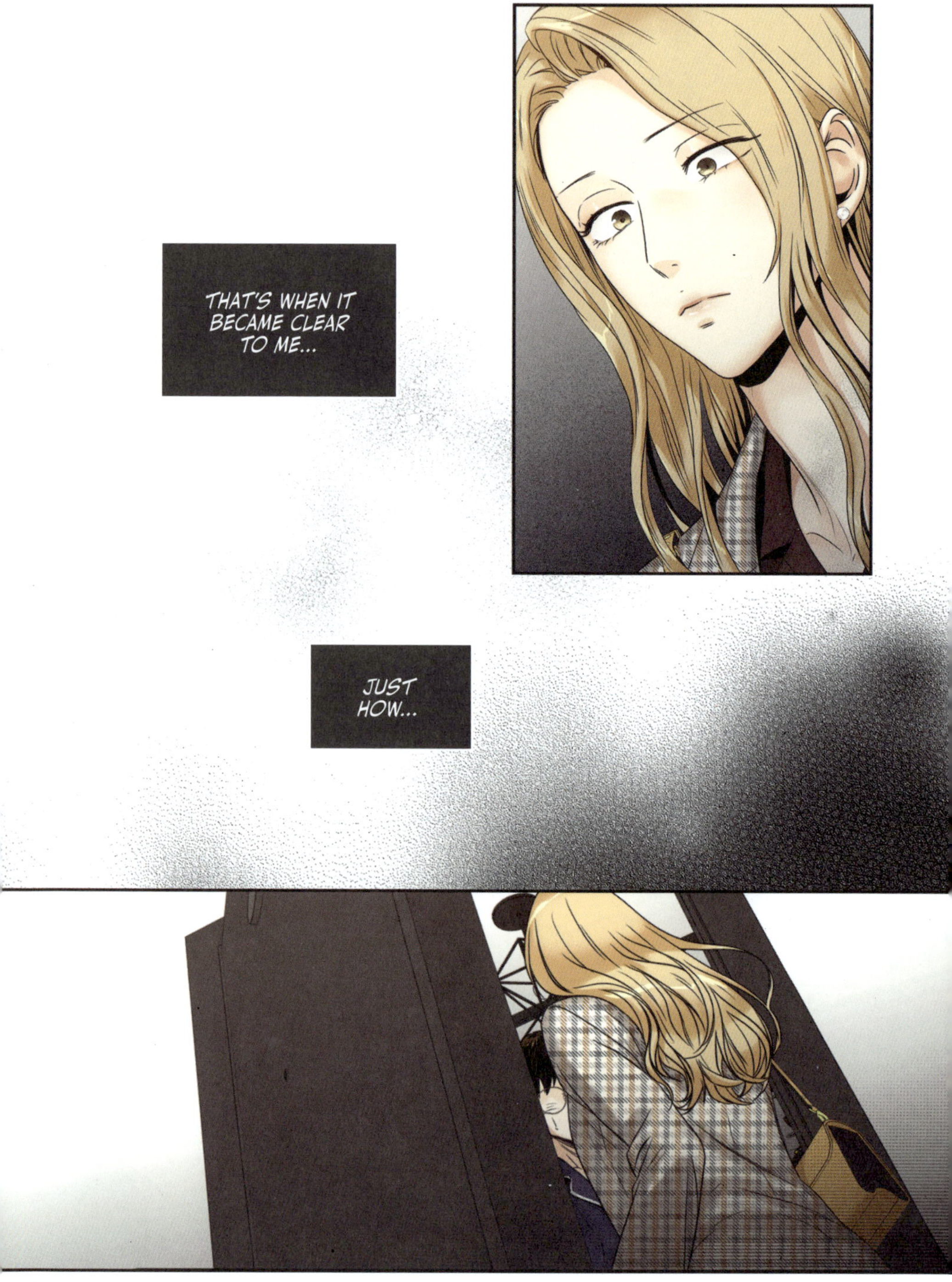
THAT'S WHEN IT BECAME CLEAR TO ME...
JUST HOW...

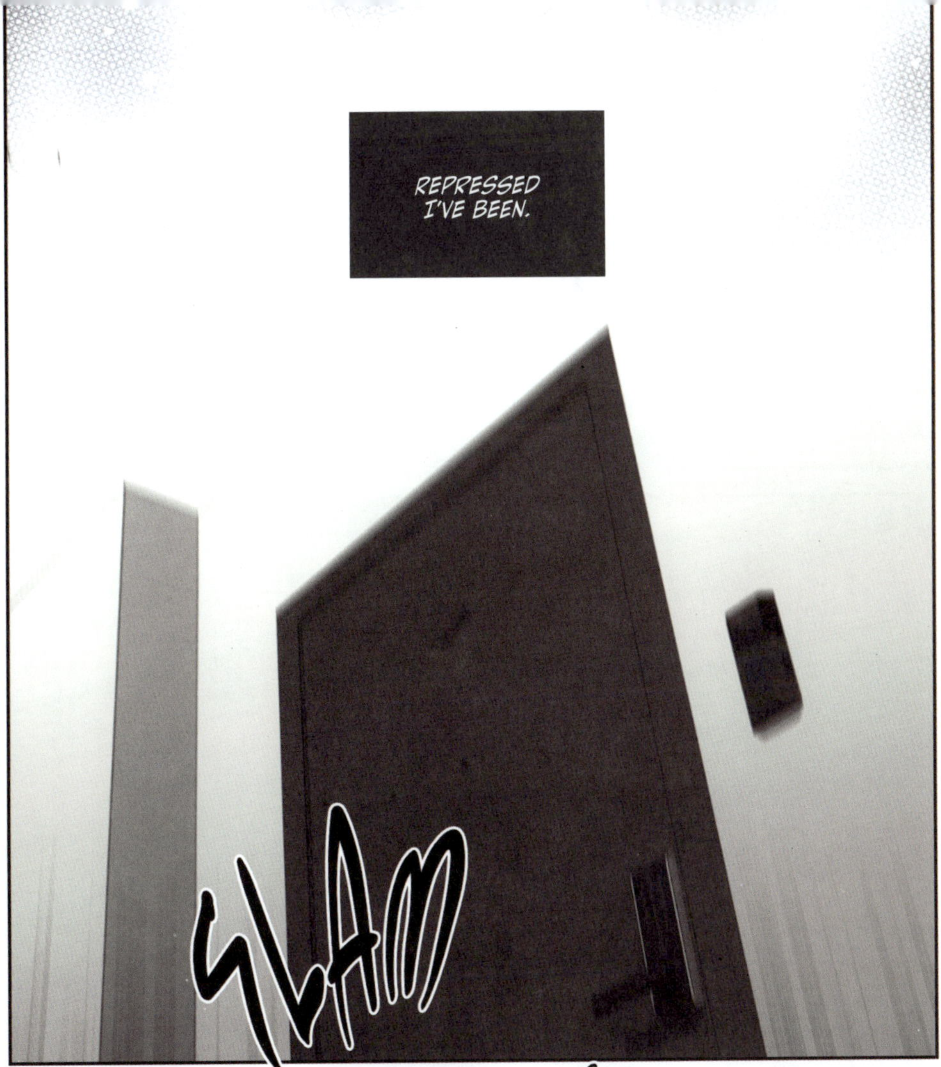
REPRESSED
I'VE BEEN.
SLAM
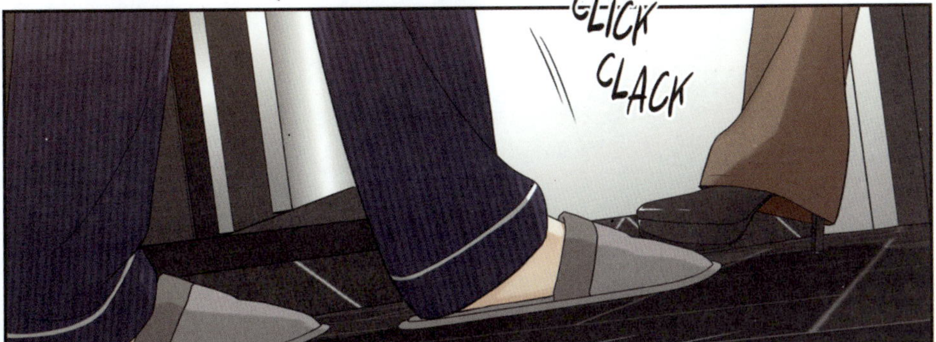
CLICK
CLACK

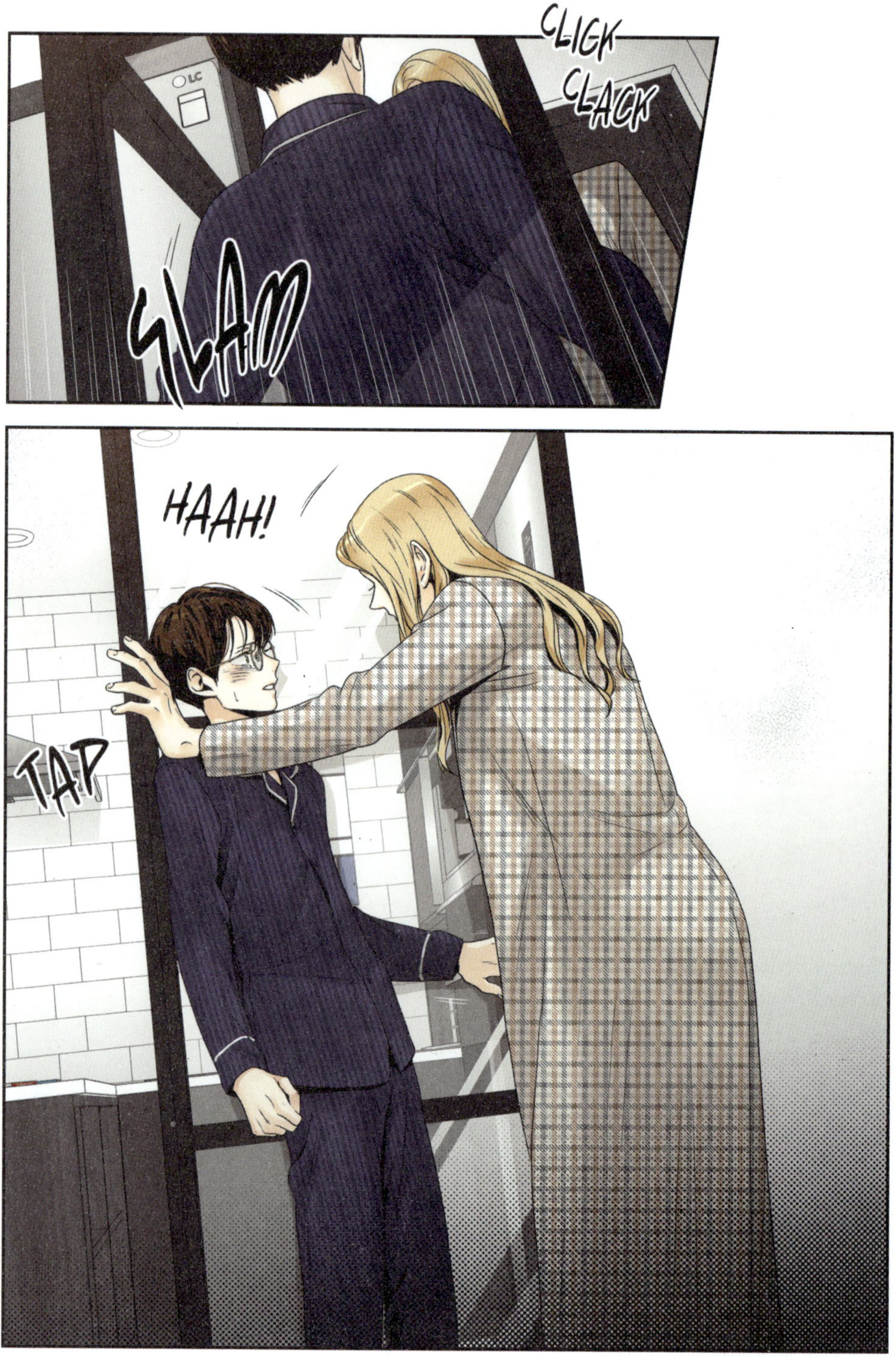
CLICK
CLACK
SLAM
HAAH!
TAP

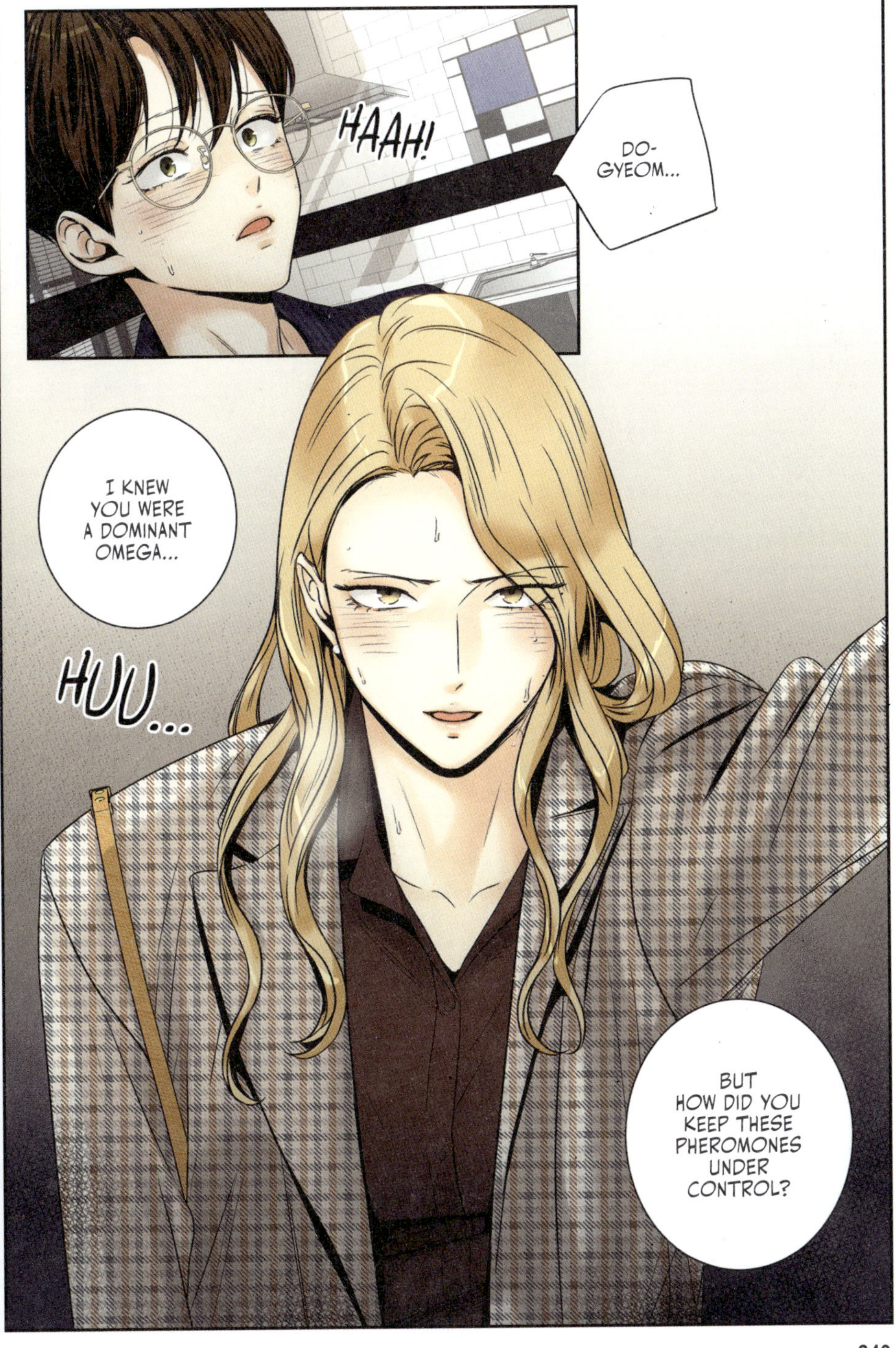
HAAAH!
DO-GYEOM...
I KNEW YOU WERE A DOMINANT OMEGA...
HUU...
BUT HOW DID YOU KEEP THESE PHEROMONES UNDER CONTROL?

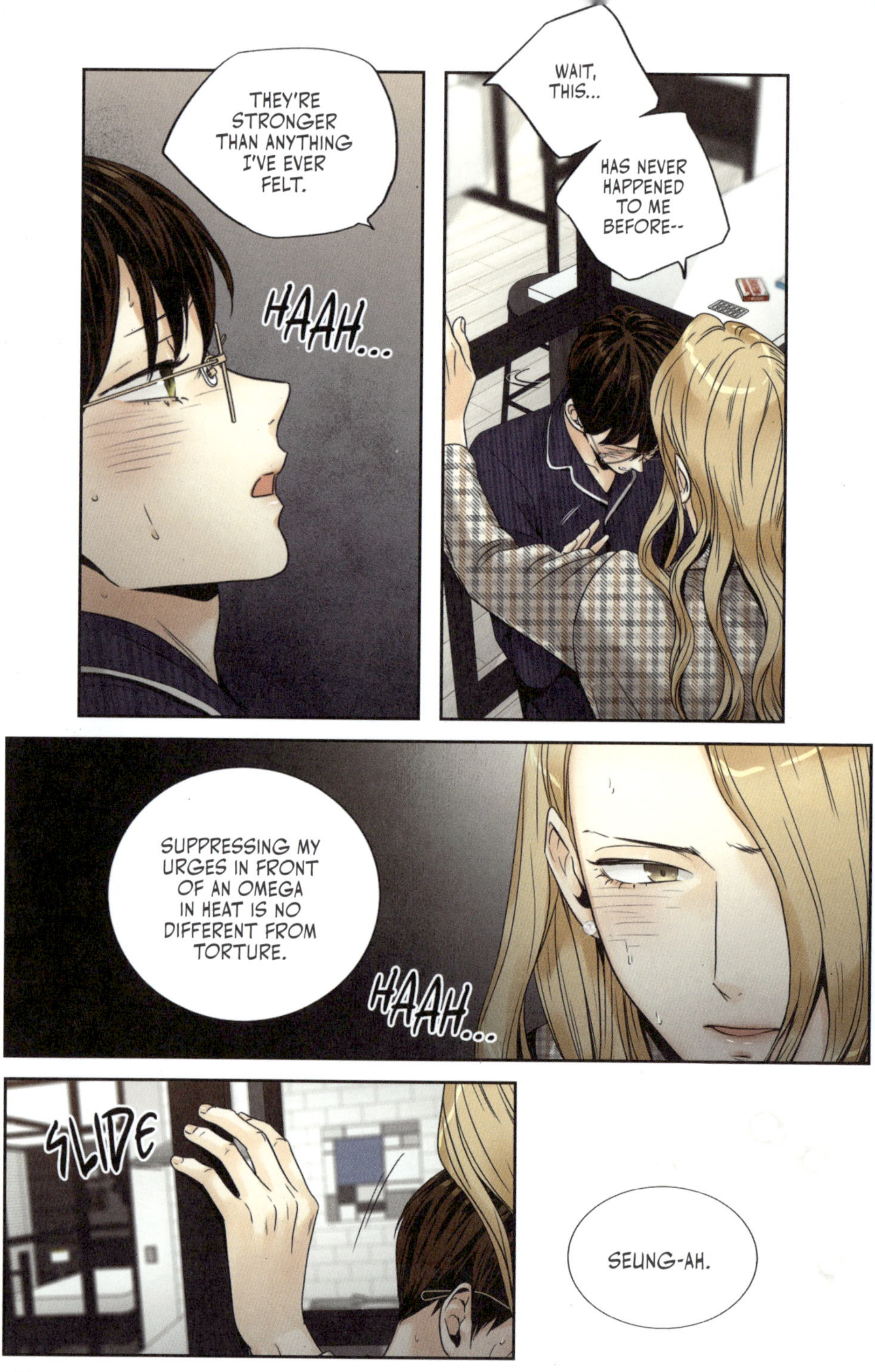
THEY'RE STRONGER THAN ANYTHING I'VE EVER FELT.
HAAH...
WAIT, THIS...
HAS NEVER HAPPENED TO ME BEFORE--
SUPPRESSING MY URGES IN FRONT OF AN OMEGA IN HEAT IS NO DIFFERENT FROM TORTURE.
HAAH...
SLIDE
SEUNG-AH.

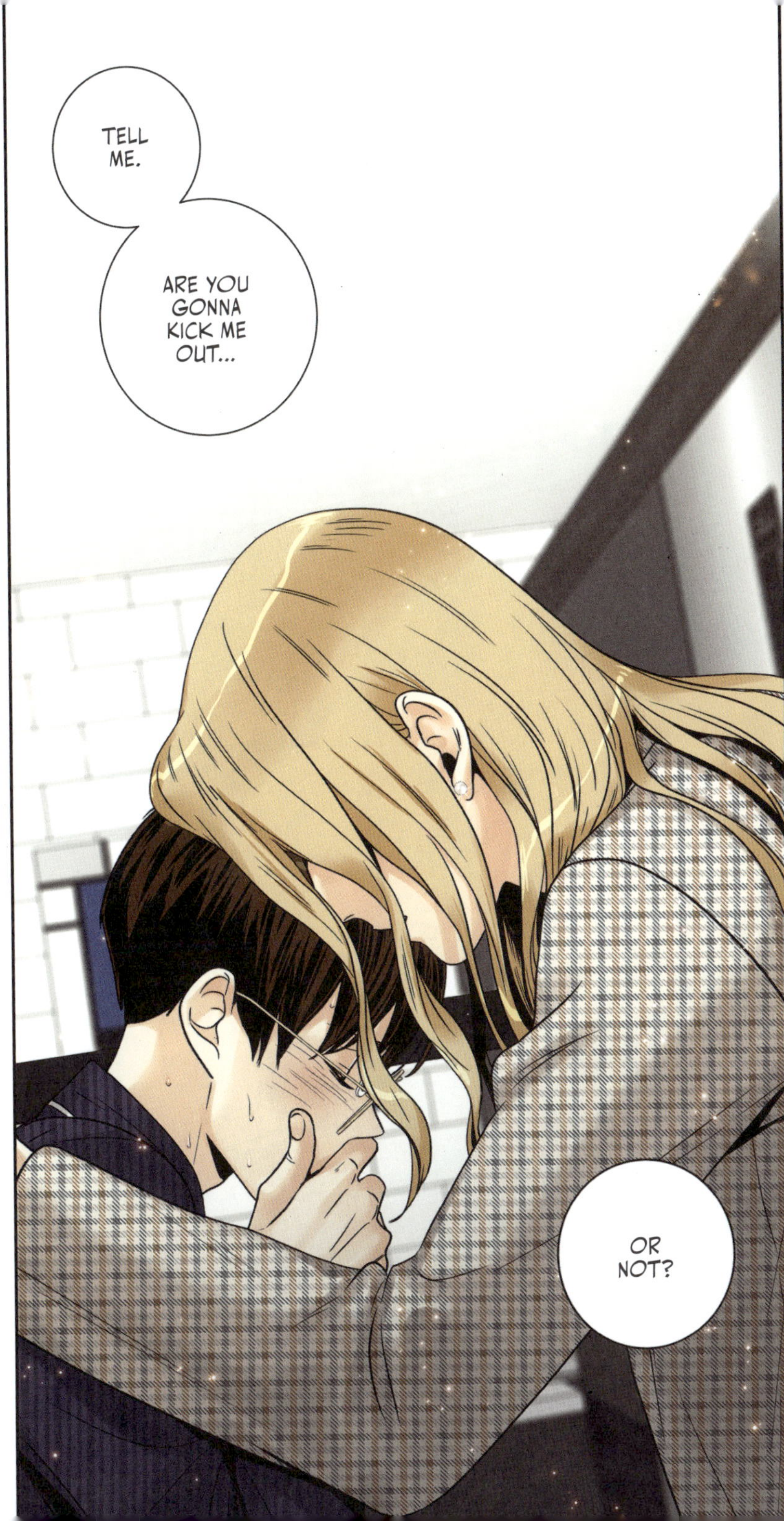
TELL ME.
ARE YOU GONNA KICK ME OUT...
OR NOT?

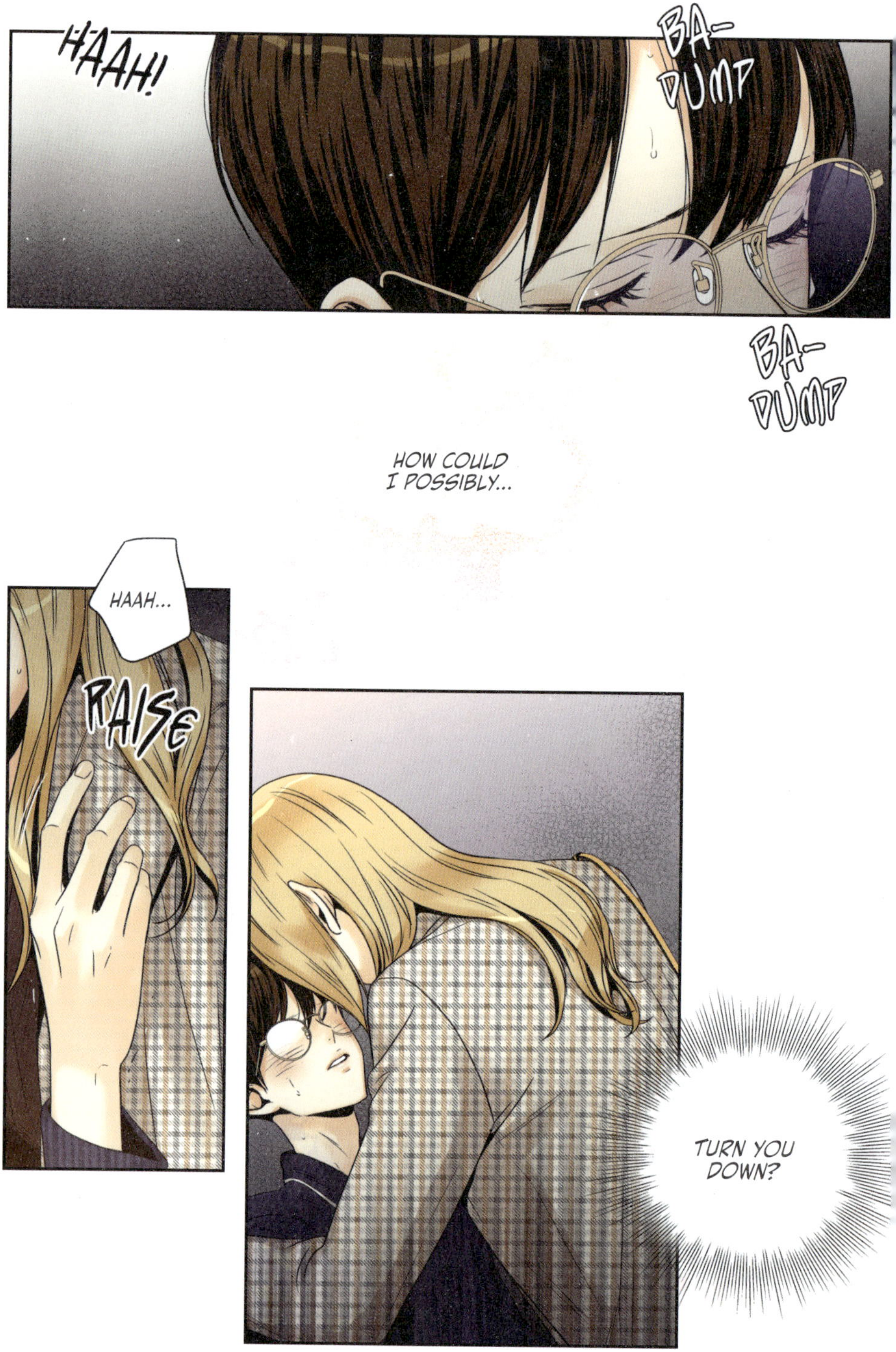
HAAAH!
BA-DUMP
BA-DUMP
HOW COULD I POSSIBLY...
HAAH...
RAISE
TURN YOU DOWN?

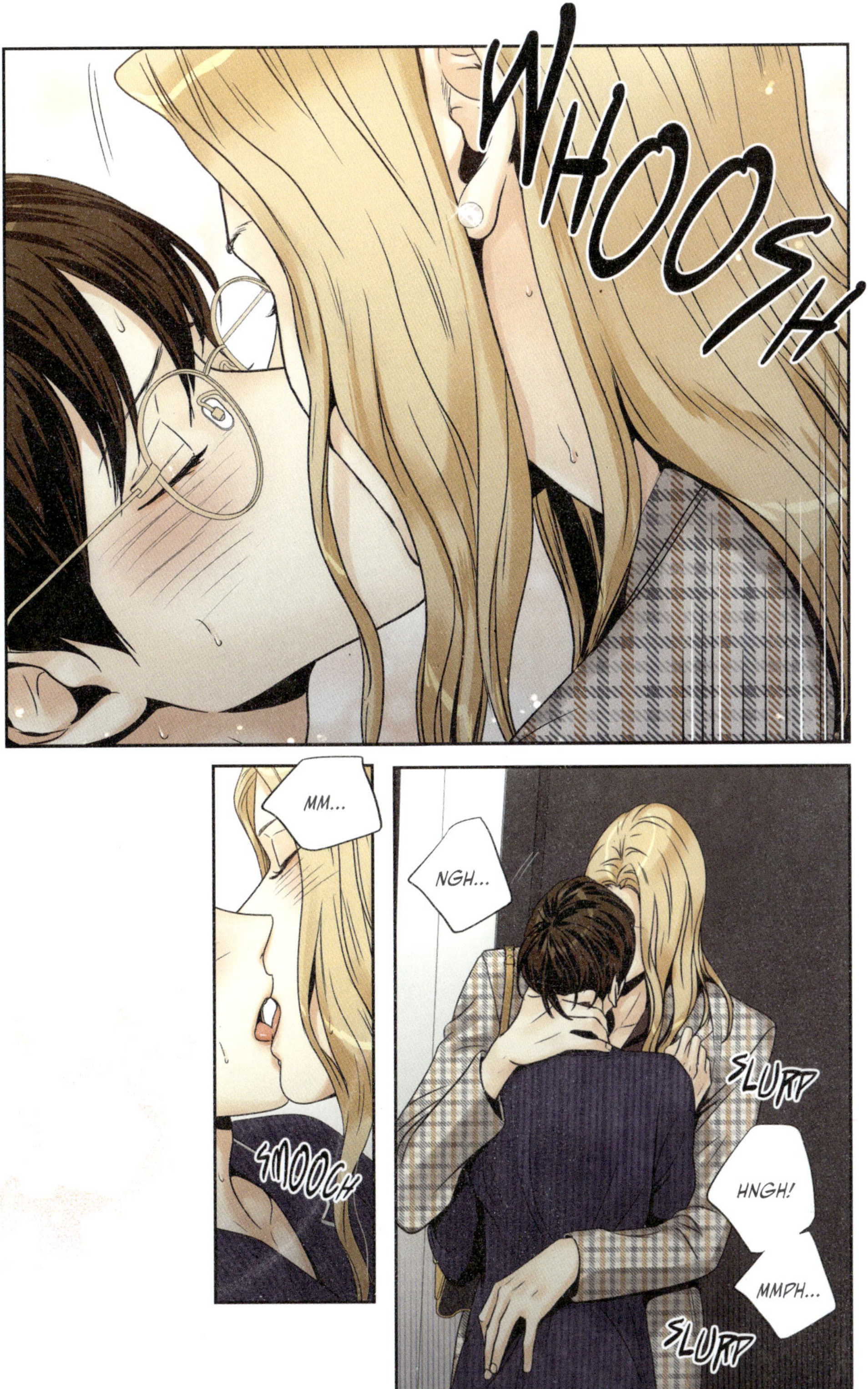
WHOOSH
MM...
SMOOCH
NGH...
SLURP
HNGH!
MMPH...
SLURP

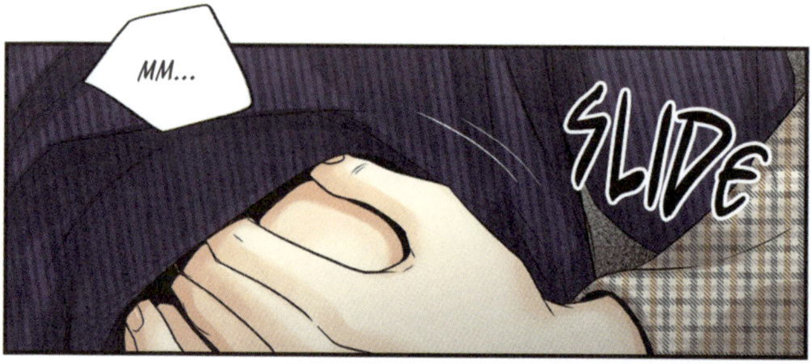
MM...
SLIDE
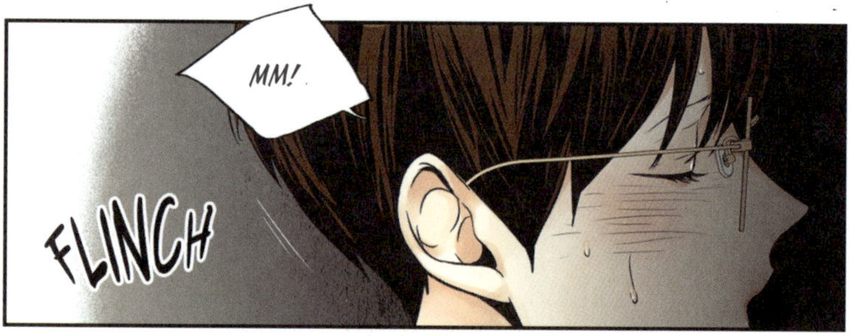
MM!
FLINCH
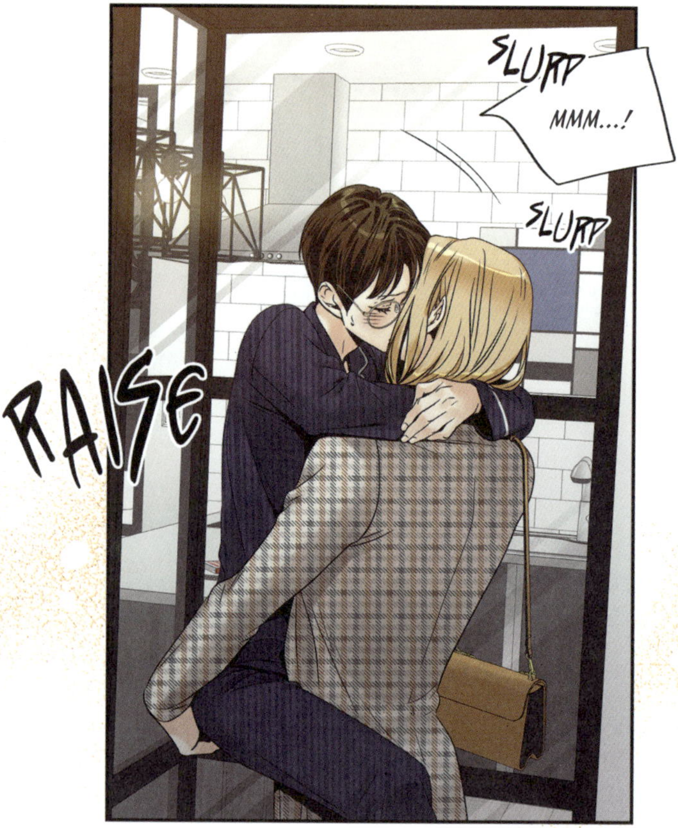
SLURP
MMM...!
SLURP
RAISE

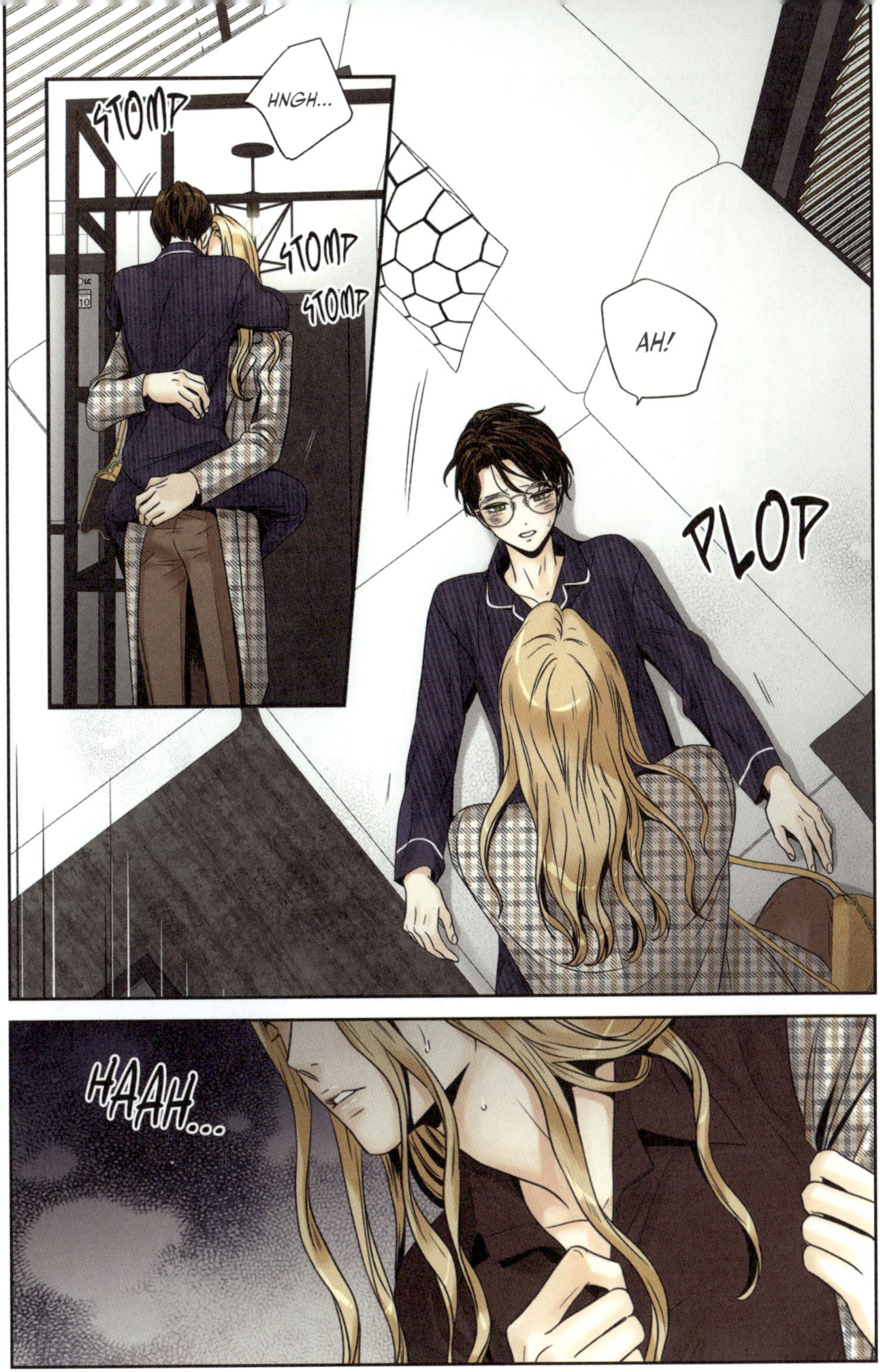
STOMP
HNGH...
STOMP
STOMP
AH!
PLOP
HAAH...

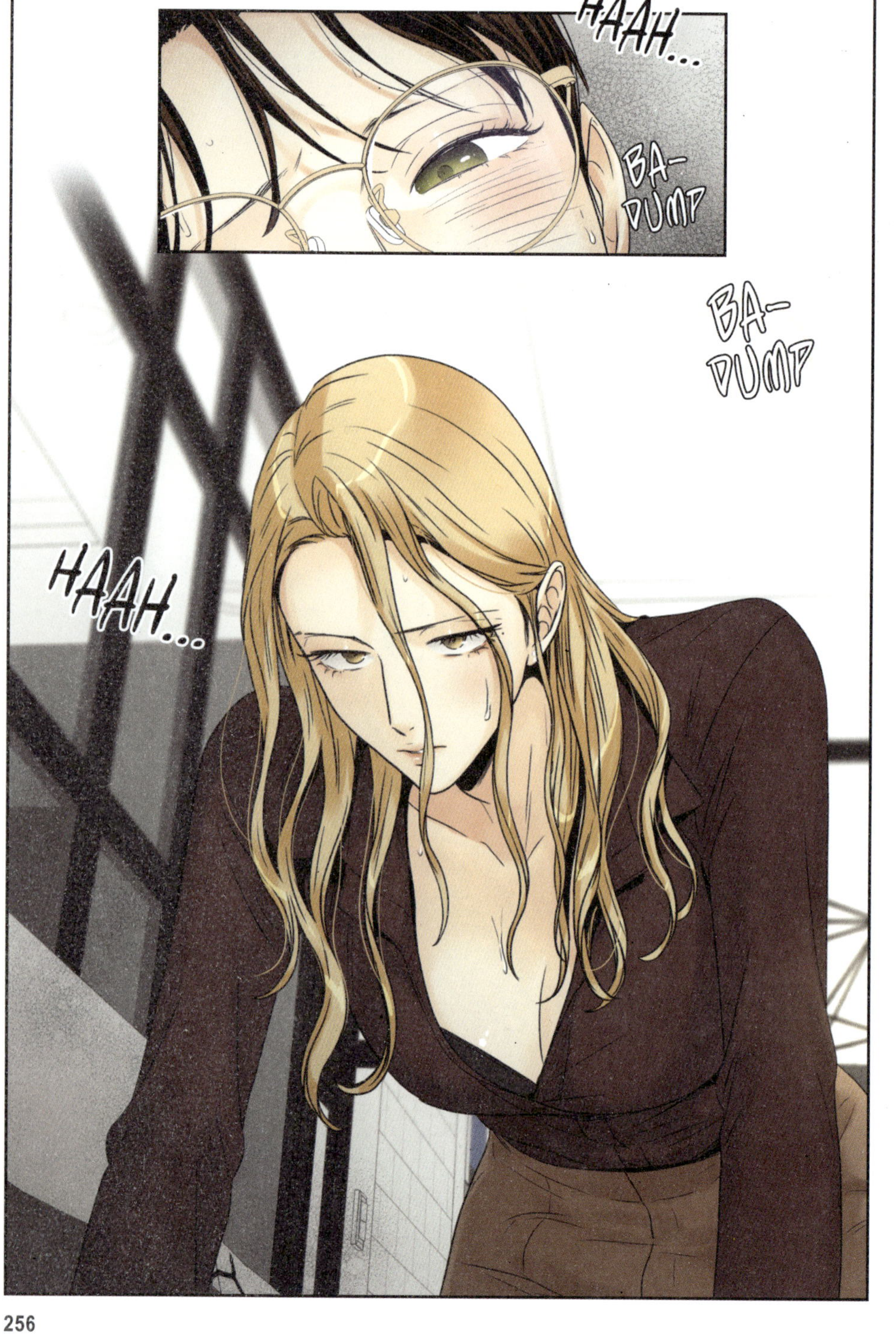
HAAAH...
BA-
DUMP
BA-
DUMP
HAAAH...

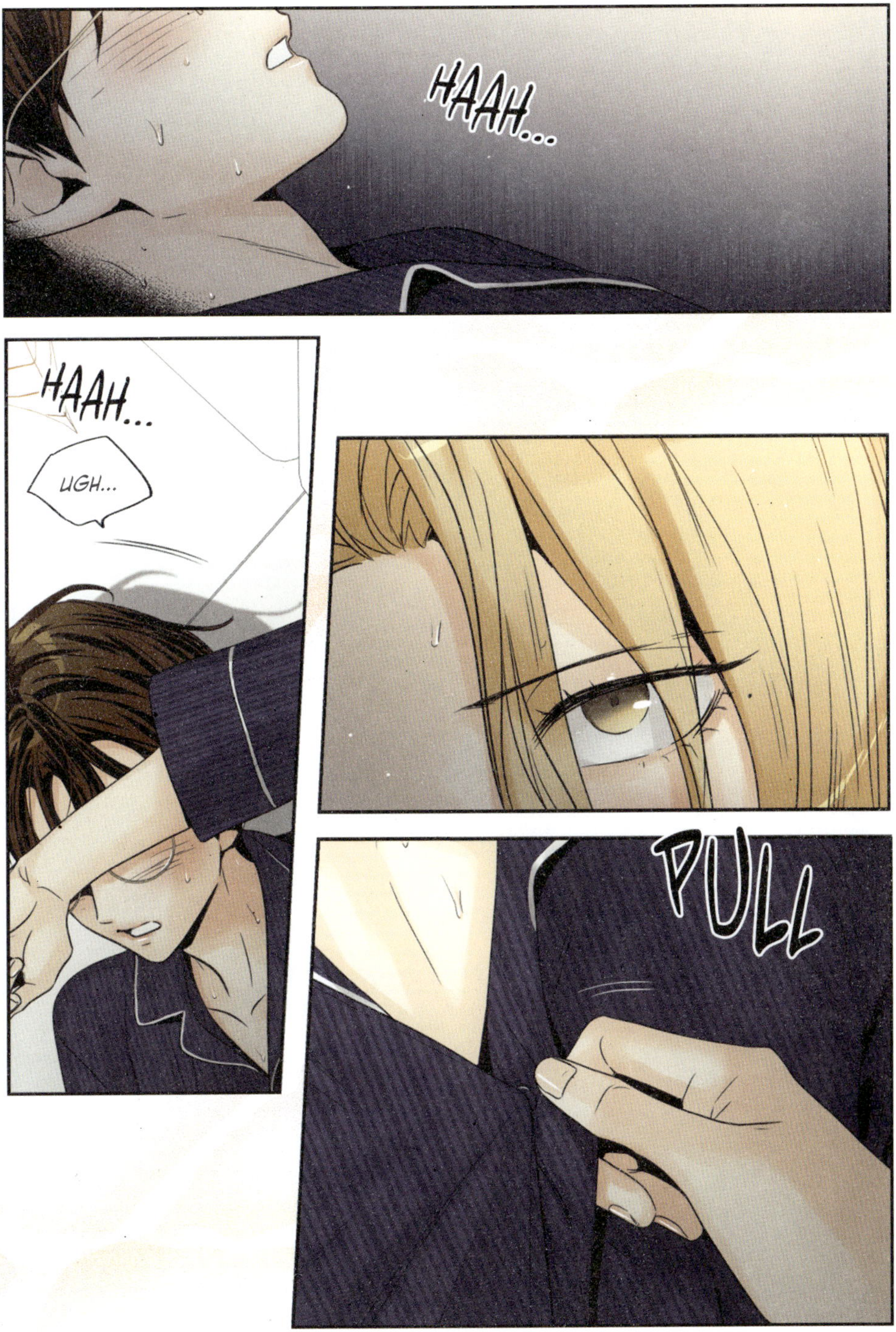
HAAAH...
HAAAH...
UGH...
PULL

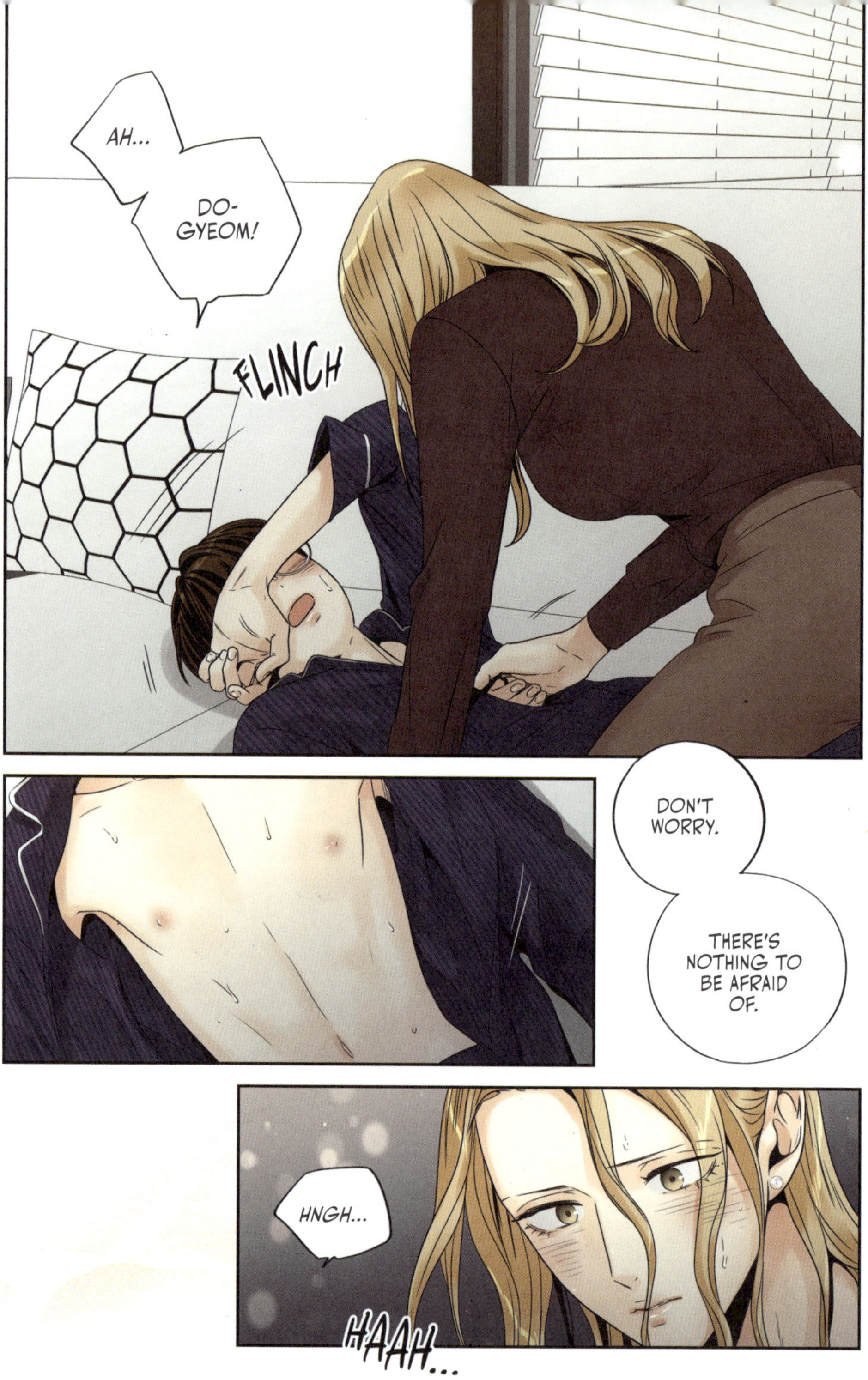
AH...
DO-GYEOM!
FLINCH
DON'T WORRY.
THERE'S NOTHING TO BE AFRAID OF.
HNGH...
HAAH...

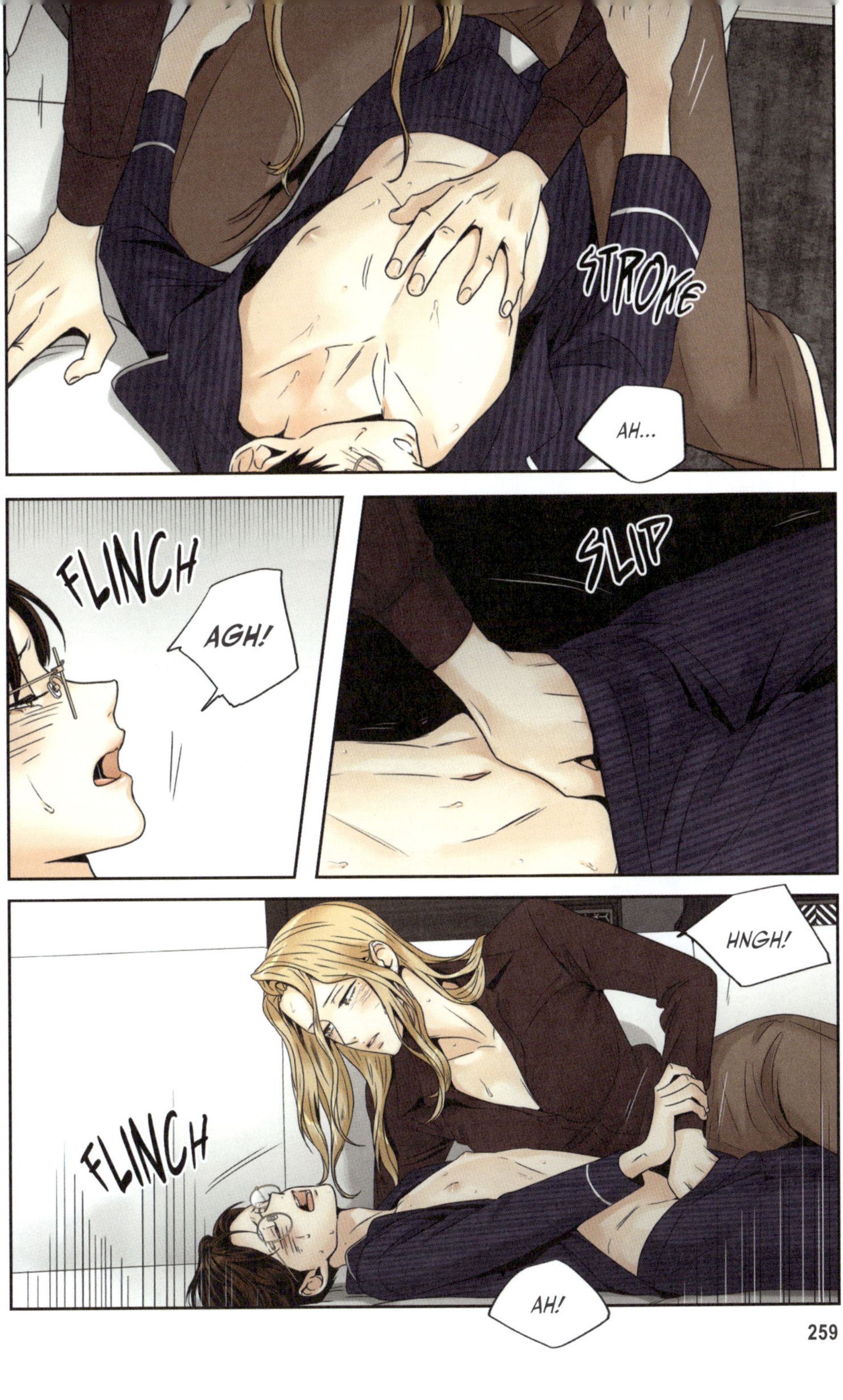
STROKE
AH...
FLINCH
AGH!
SLIP
HNGH!
FLINCH
AH!

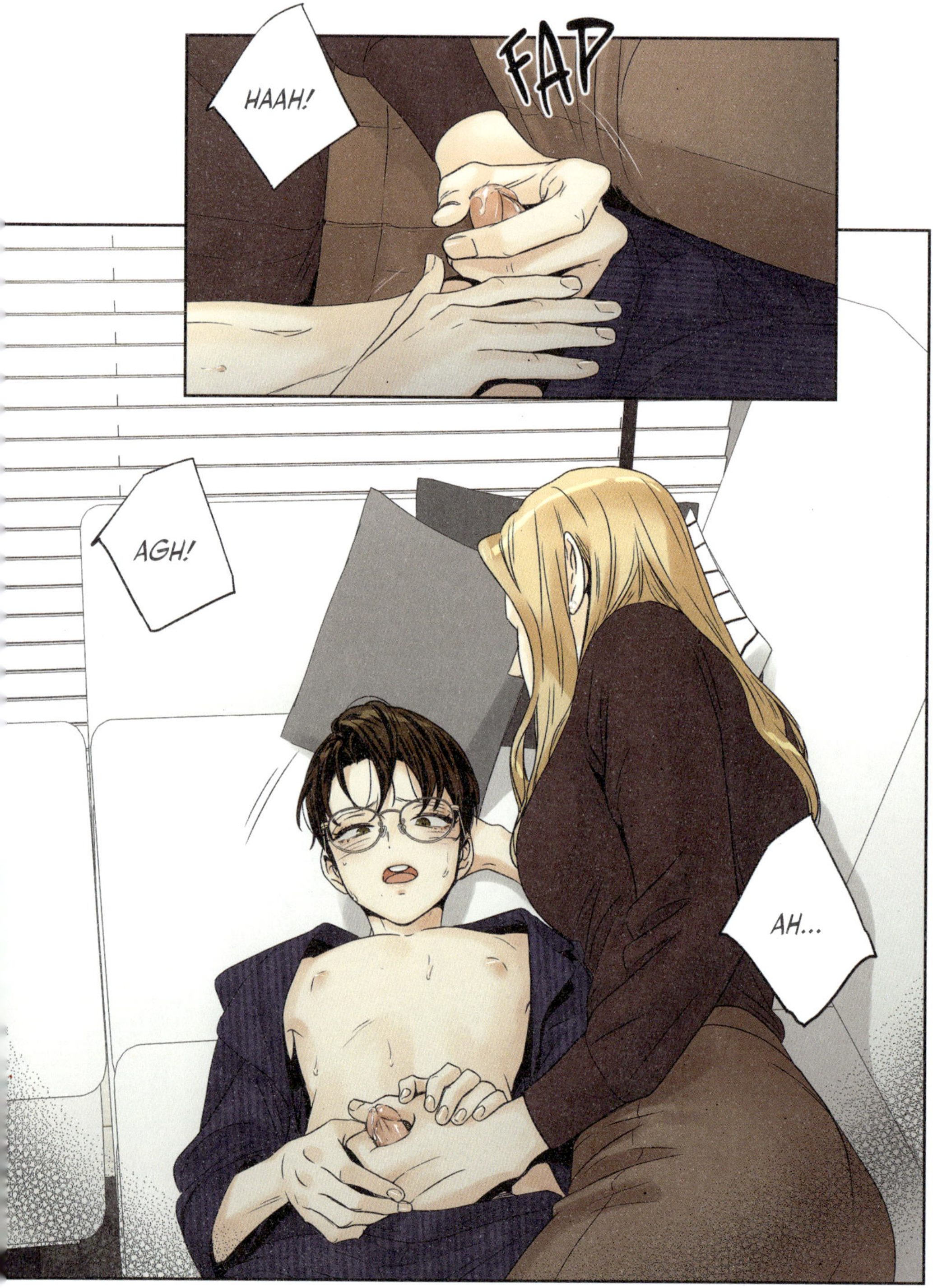
HAAH!
FAP
AGH!
AH...

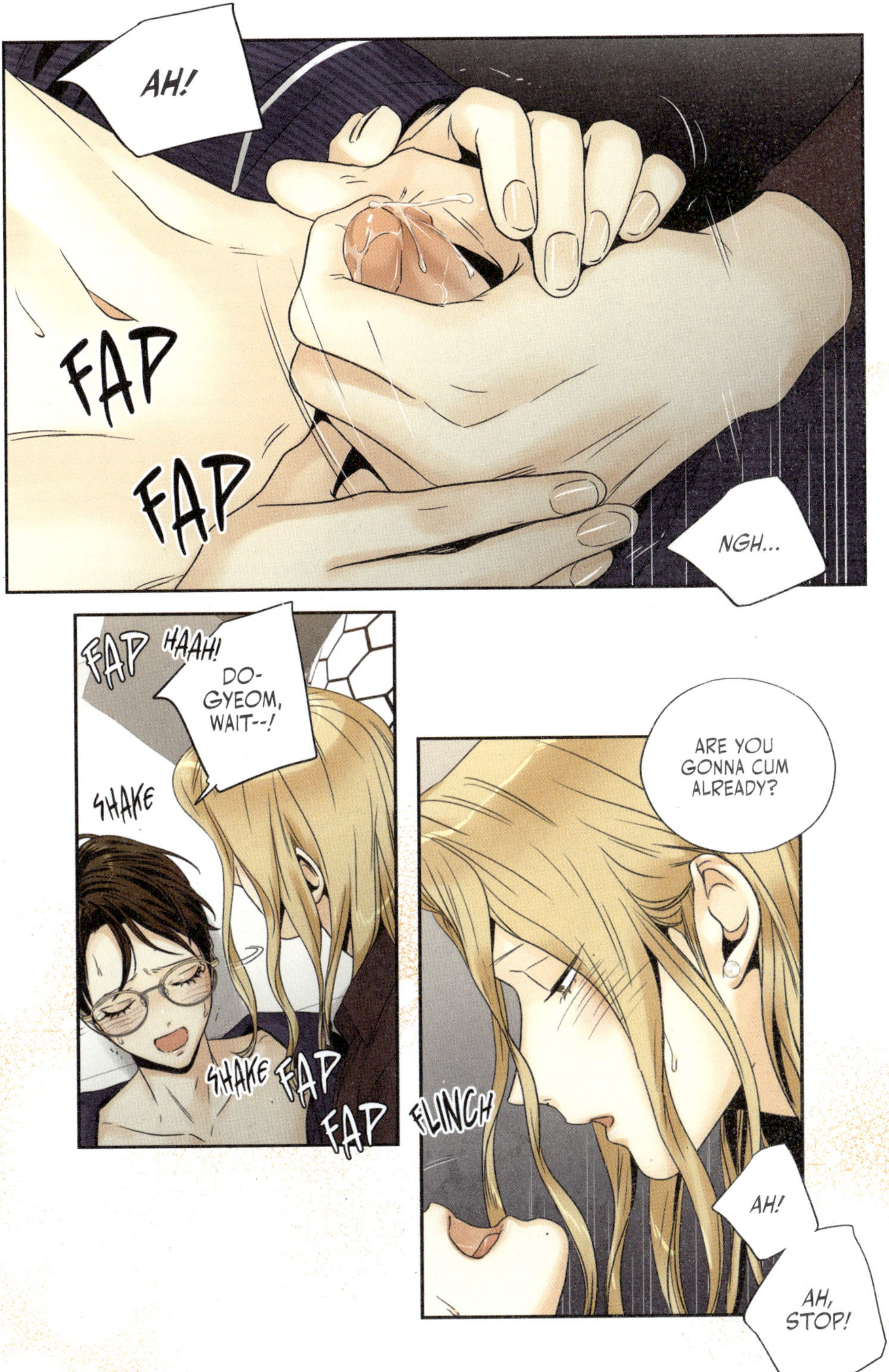
AH!
FAP
FAP
NGH...
FAP
HAAH!
DO-GYEOM, WAIT--!
SHAKE
SHAKE
FAP
FAP
FLINCH
ARE YOU GONNA CUM ALREADY?
AH!
AH, STOP!

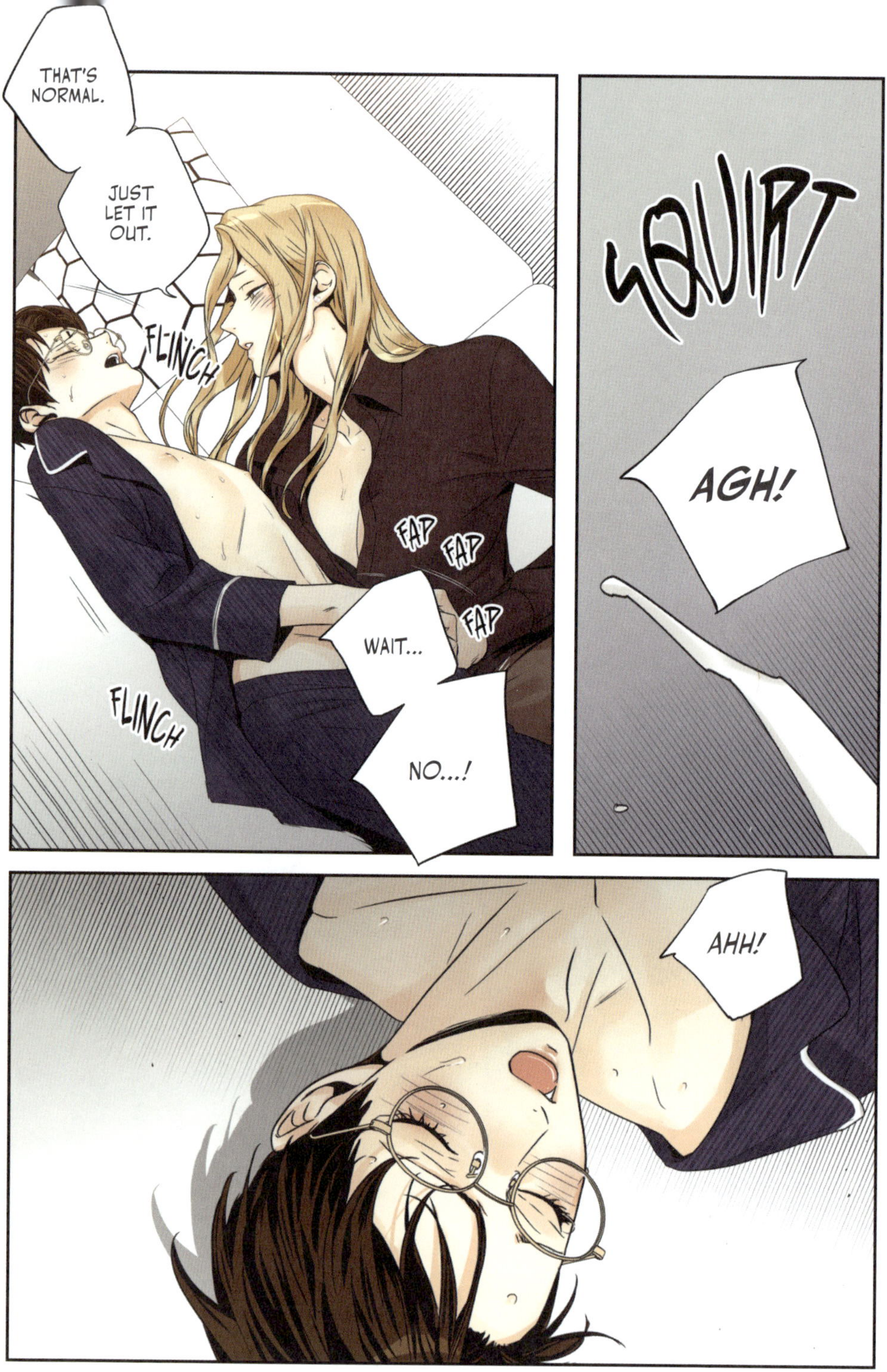
THAT'S NORMAL.
JUST LET IT OUT.
FLINCH
FAP
FAP
FAP
WAIT...
FLINCH
NO...!
SQUIRT
AGH!
AHH!

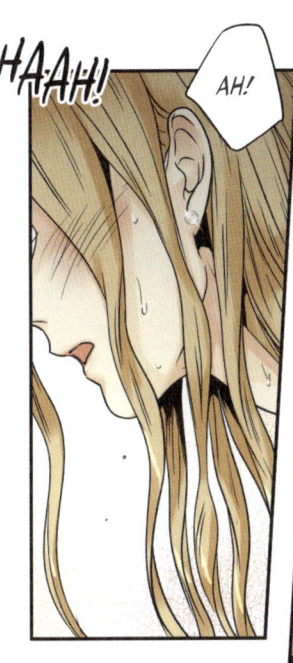

NOT ONLY IS SEUNG-AH IN HEAT...

BUT HE'S REALLY, REALLY AROUSED.

I DIDN'T KNOW THAT WAS POSSIBLE.

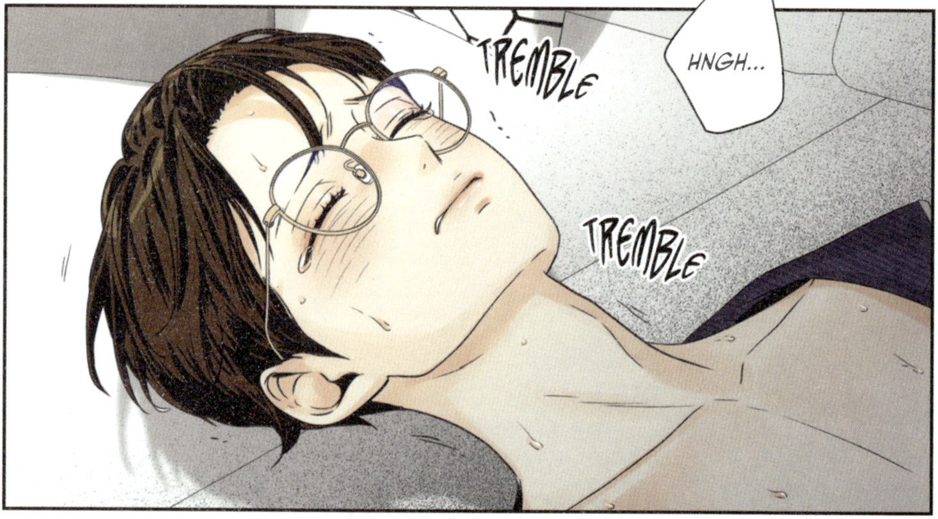
TREMBLE
HNGH...
TREMBLE

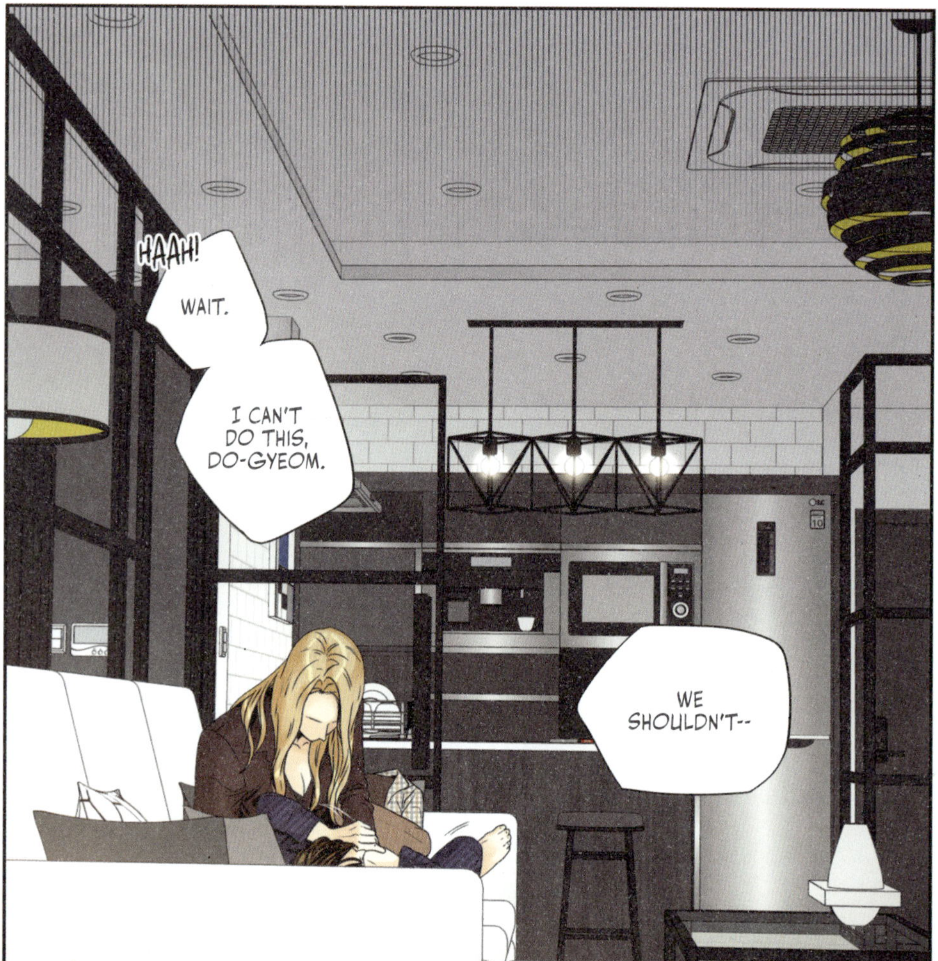
HAAH!
WAIT.
I CAN'T DO THIS, DO-GYEOM.
WE SHOULDN'T--

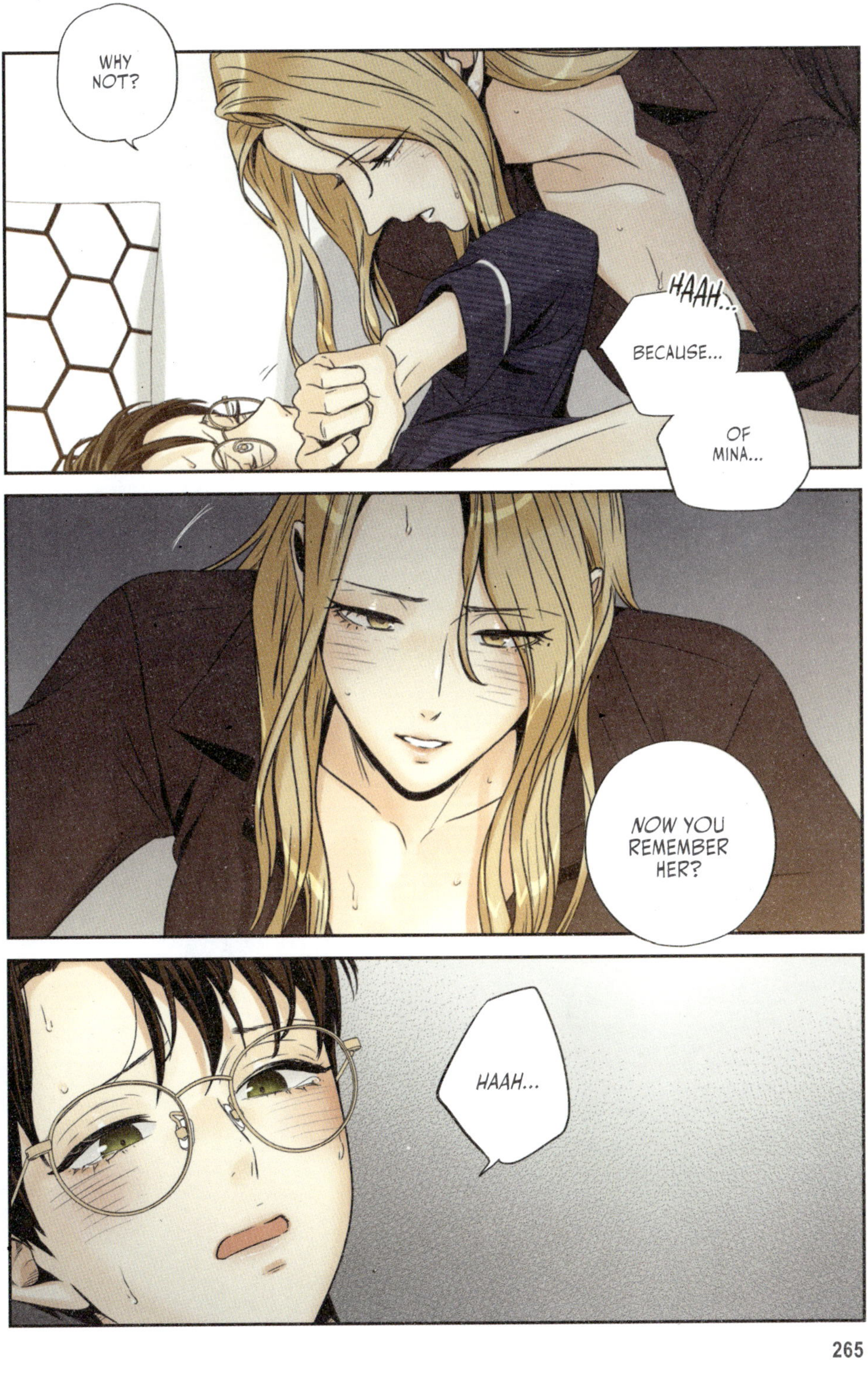
WHY NOT?
HAAH...
BECAUSE...
OF MINA...
NOW YOU REMEMBER HER?
HAAH...

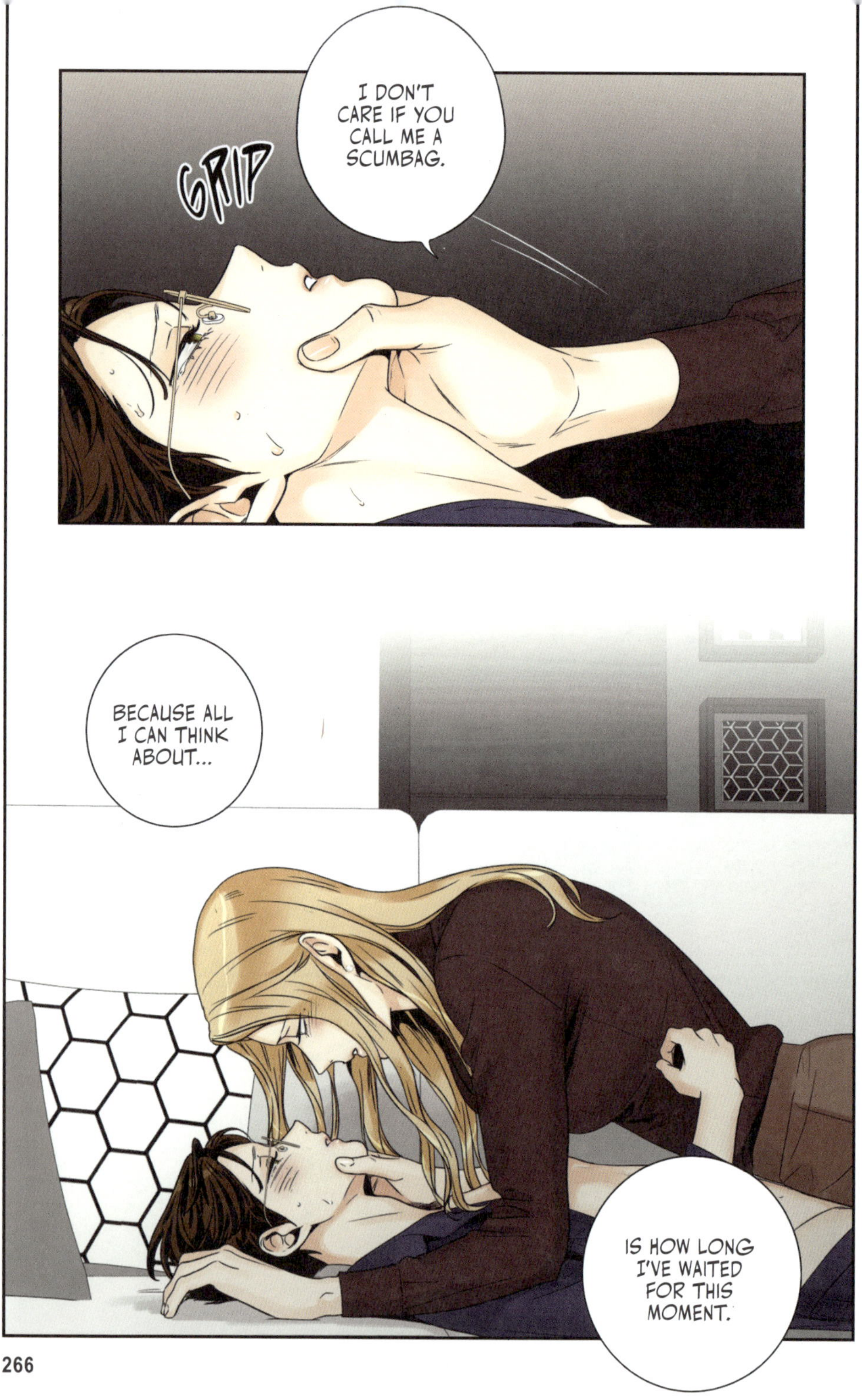
GRIP
I DON'T CARE IF YOU CALL ME A SCUMBAG.
BECAUSE ALL I CAN THINK ABOUT...
IS HOW LONG I'VE WAITED FOR THIS MOMENT.

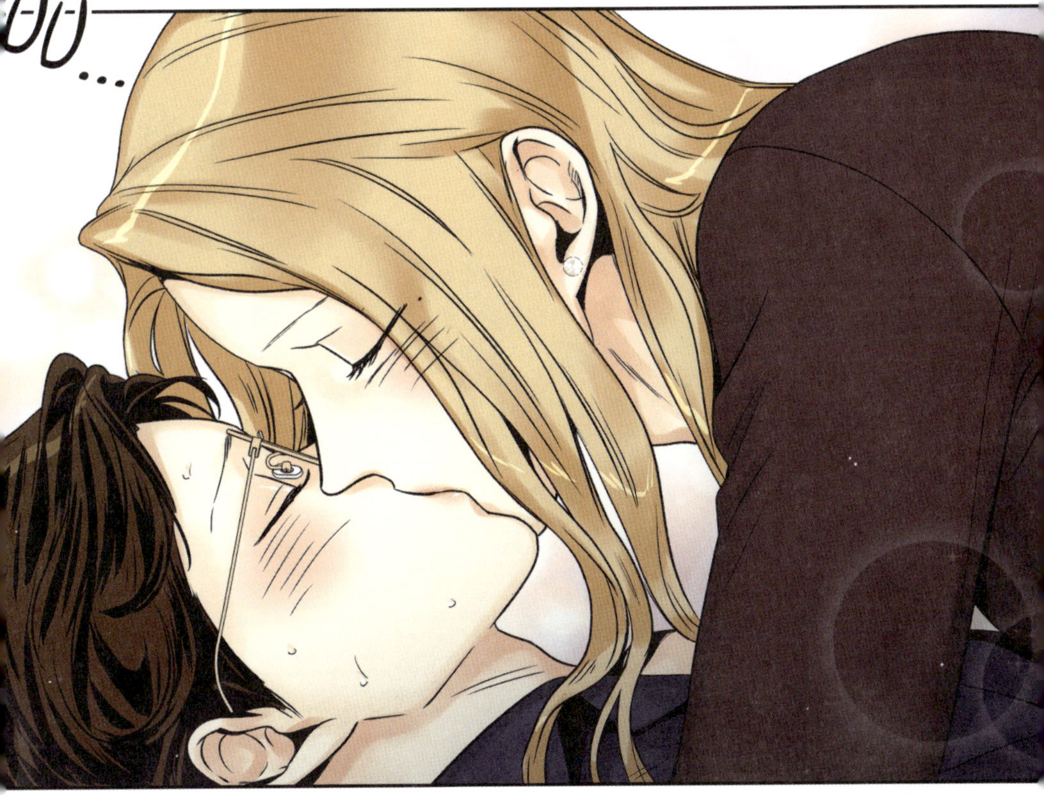
UU...

Love is an Illusion!
The Queen

Chapter 12

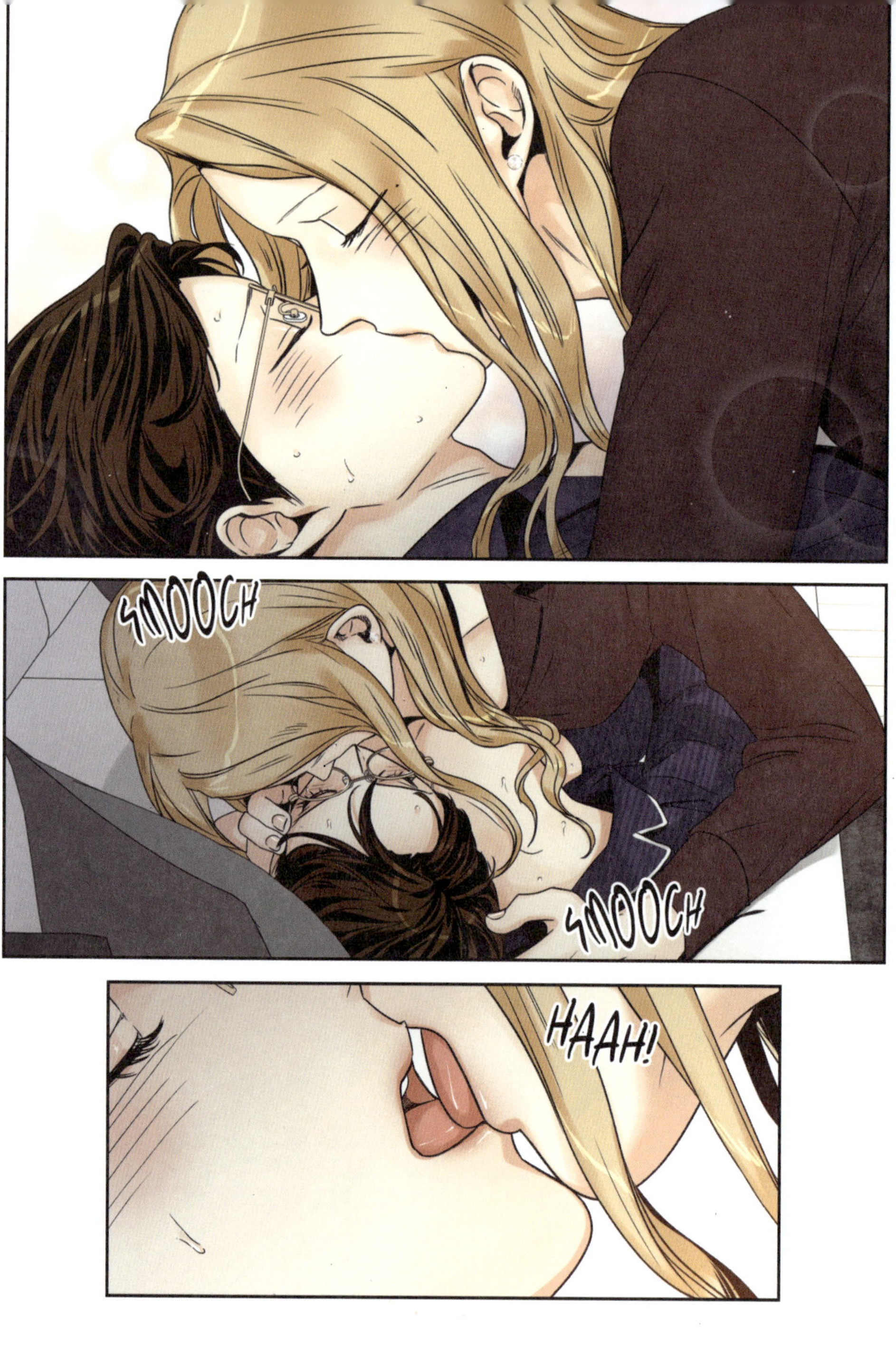
SMOOCH
SMOOCH
HAAH!

I'VE IMAGINED THIS...

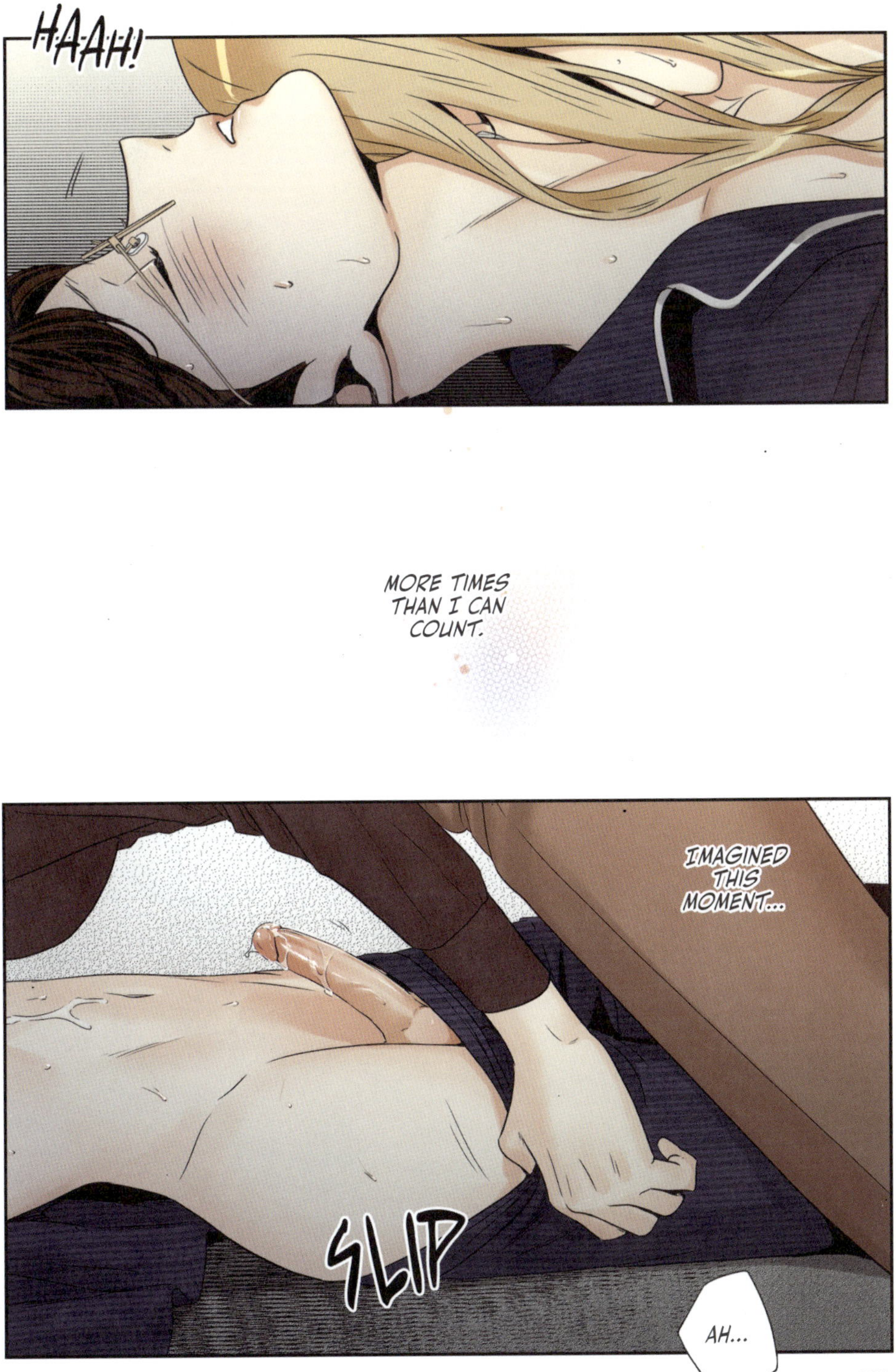
HAAAH!
MORE TIMES THAN I CAN COUNT.
IMAGINED THIS MOMENT...
SLIP
AH...

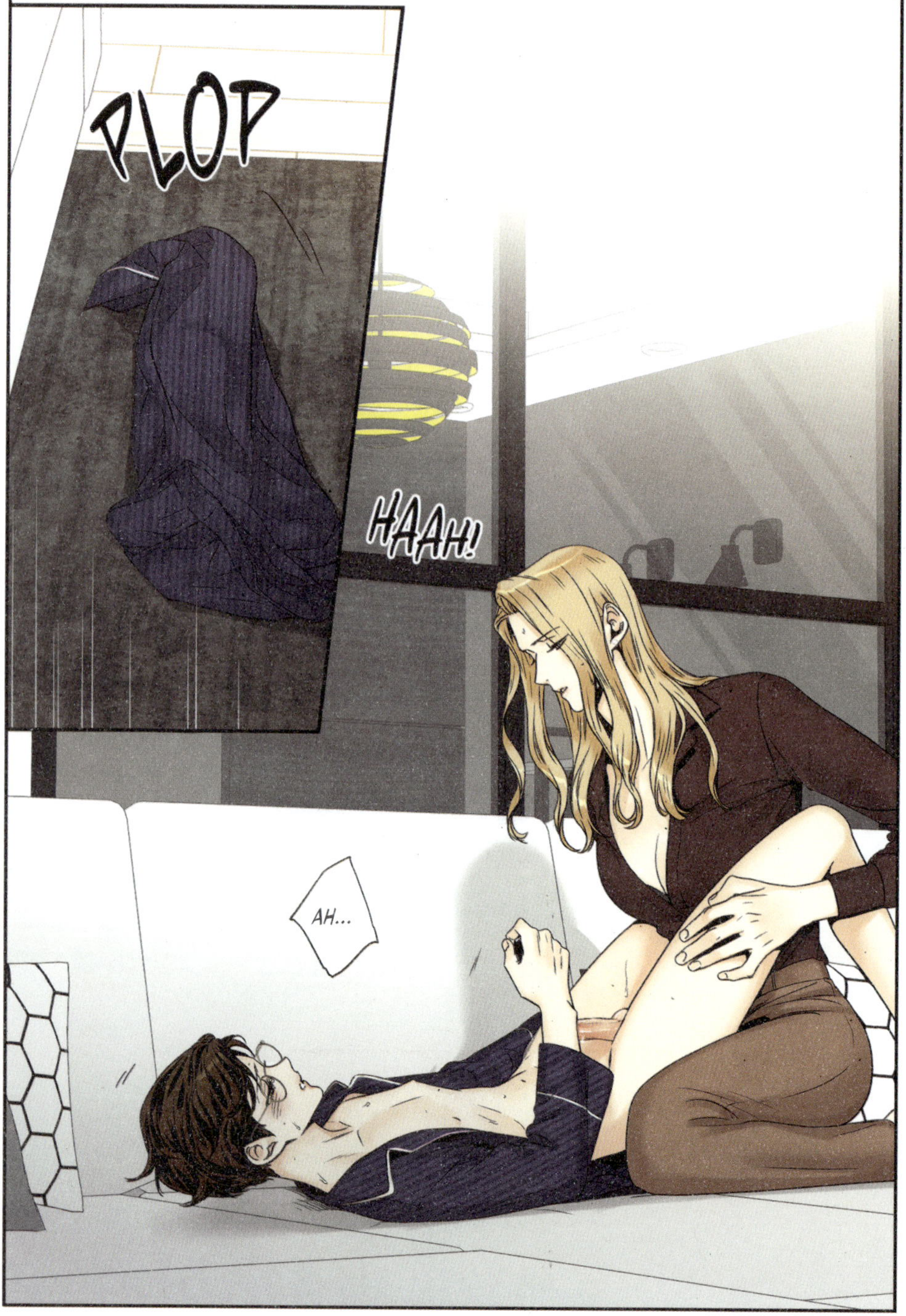
PLOP
HAAAH!
AH...

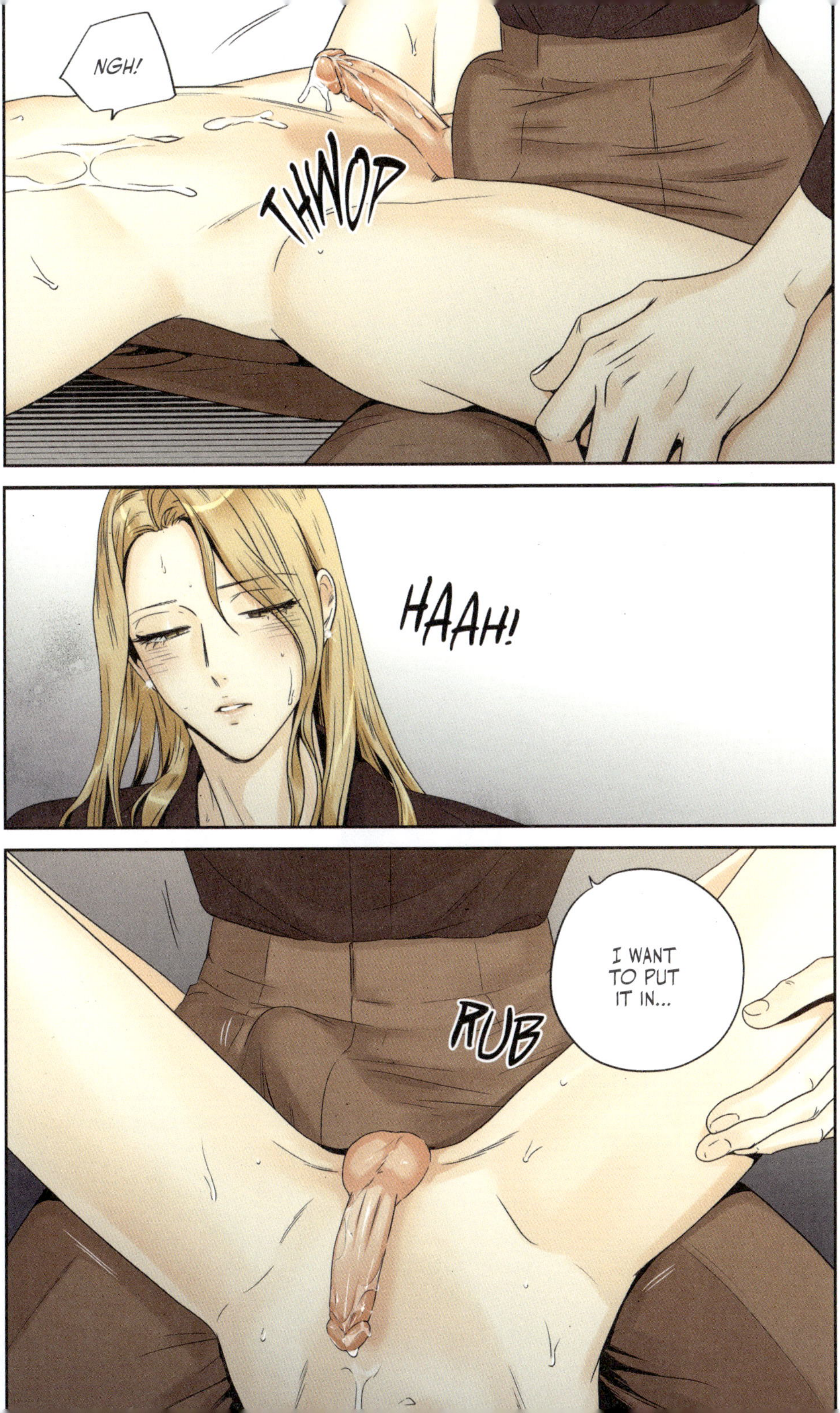
NGH!
THWOP
HAAH!
I WANT TO PUT IT IN...
RUB

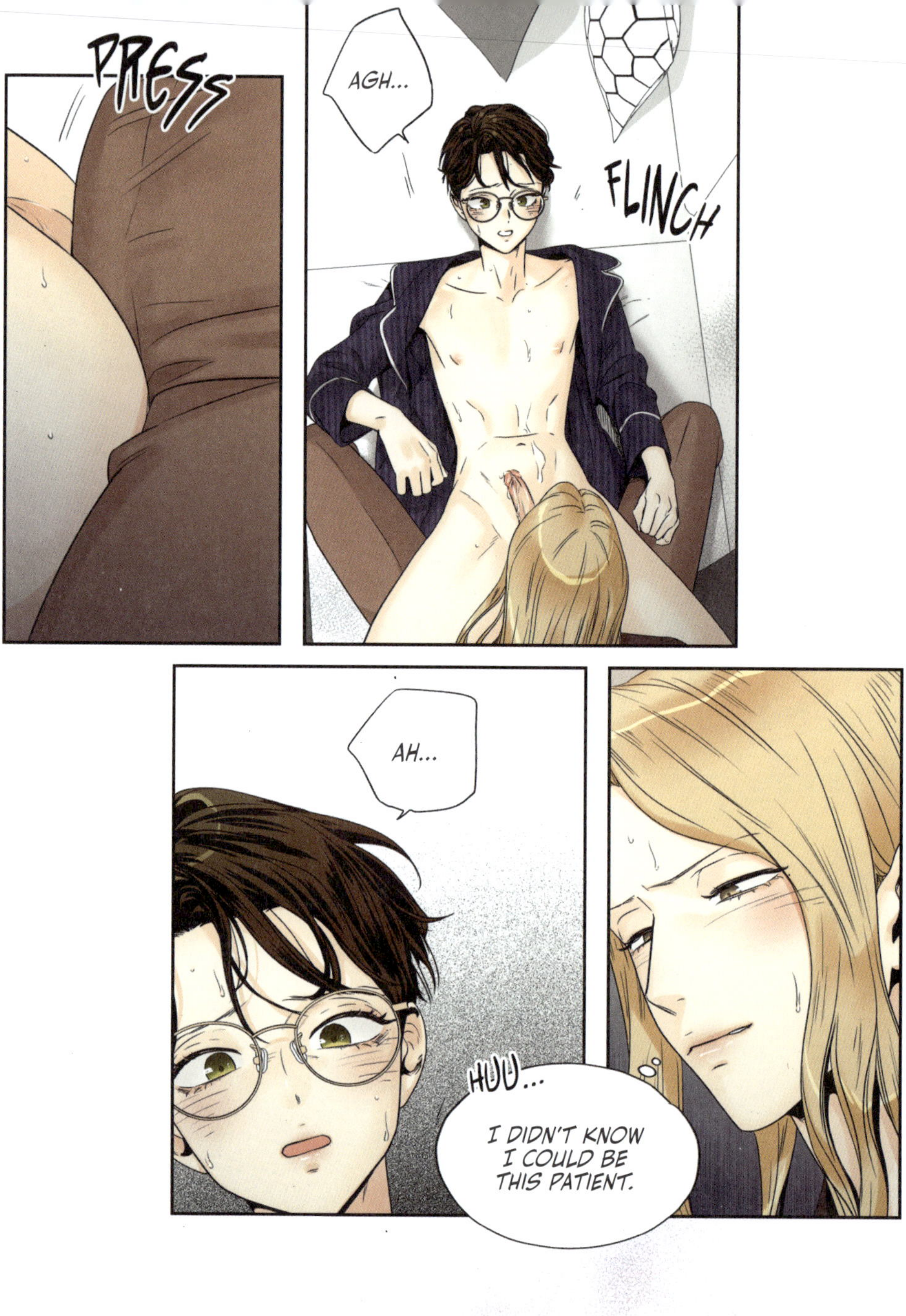
PRESS
AGH...
FLINCH
AH...
HUU...
I DIDN'T KNOW I COULD BE THIS PATIENT.
I SHOULDN'T SCARE HIM OFF.

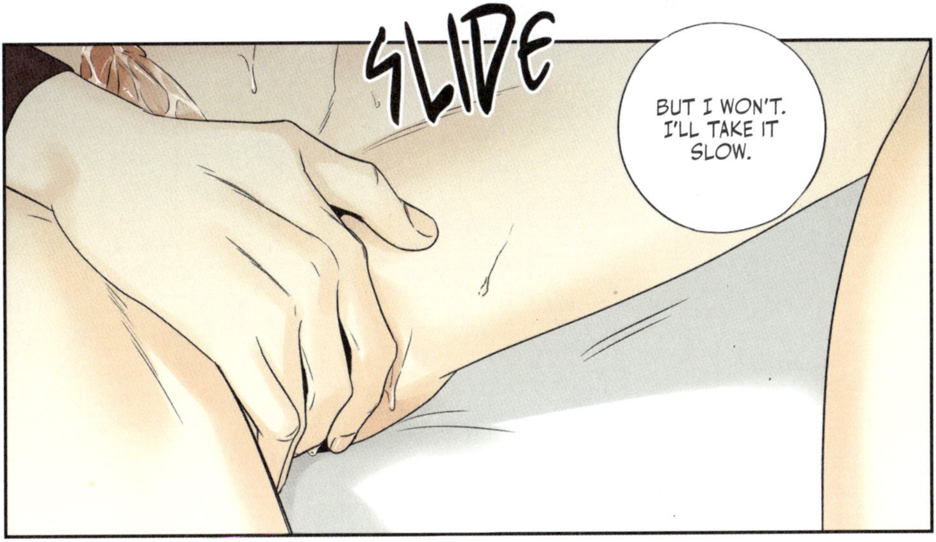
SLIDE
BUT I WON'T. I'LL TAKE IT SLOW.

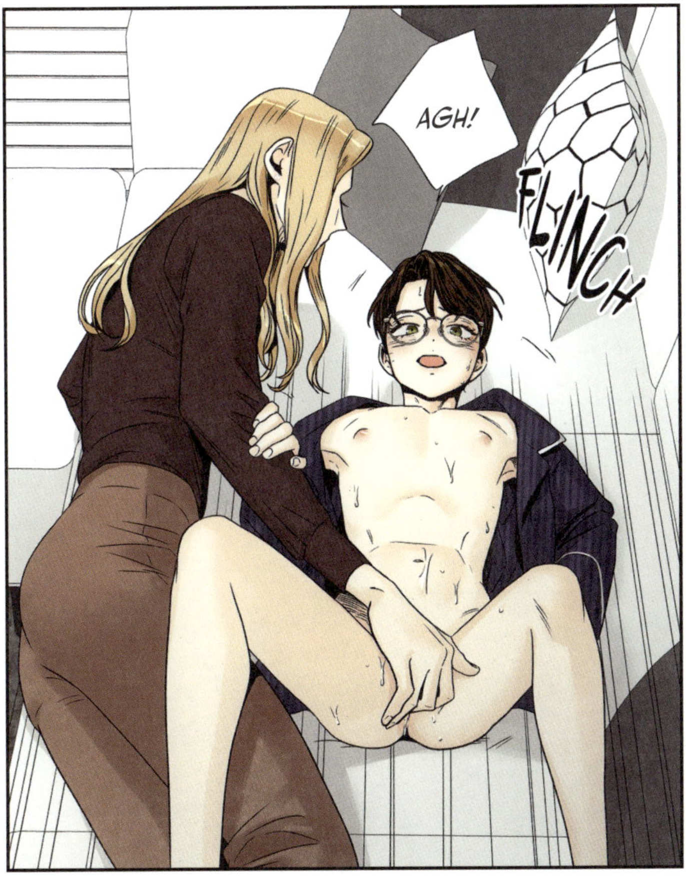
AGH!
FLINCH

NGH!
SQUELCH
SQUEEZE
YOU'RE SOAKING WET.
TH- THAT'S BECAUSE...
AH!
SQUELCH
I'M IN HEAT!
SQUEEZE
I'M IN...!!
AGH!
I KNOW, I KNOW.
SQUEEZE
AGH!
FLINCH

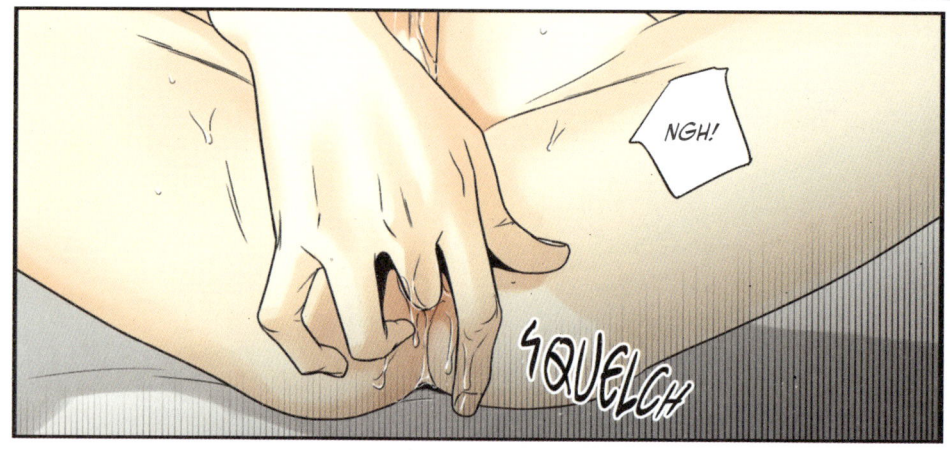

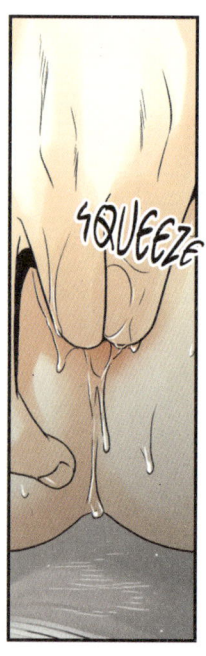

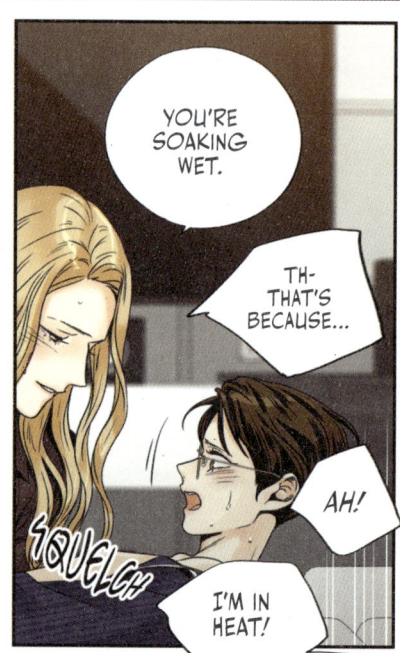

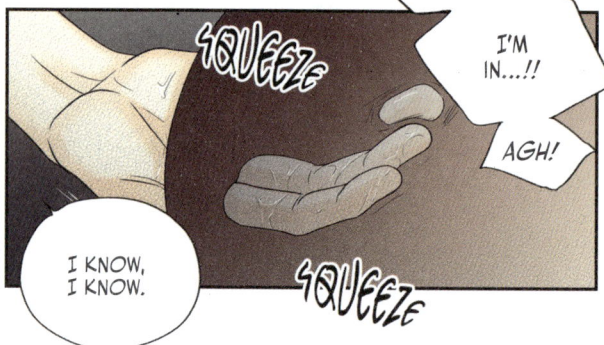

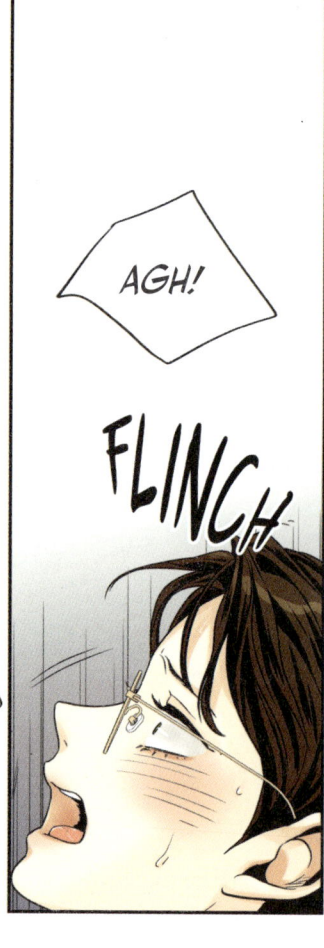

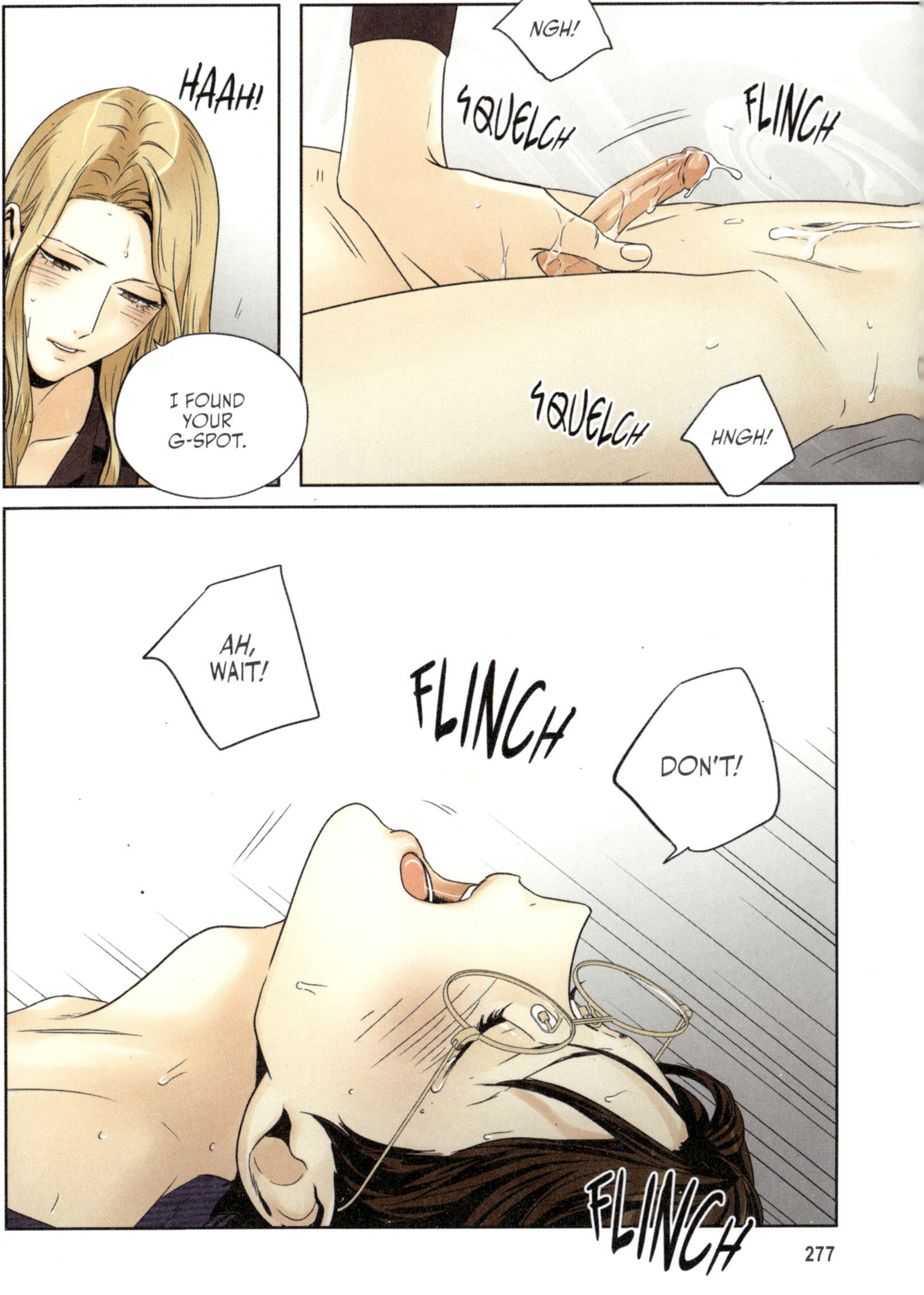
HAAH!
I FOUND YOUR G-SPOT.
NGH!
SQUELCH
FLINCH
SQUELCH
HNGH!
AH, WAIT!
FLINCH
DON'T!
FLINCH

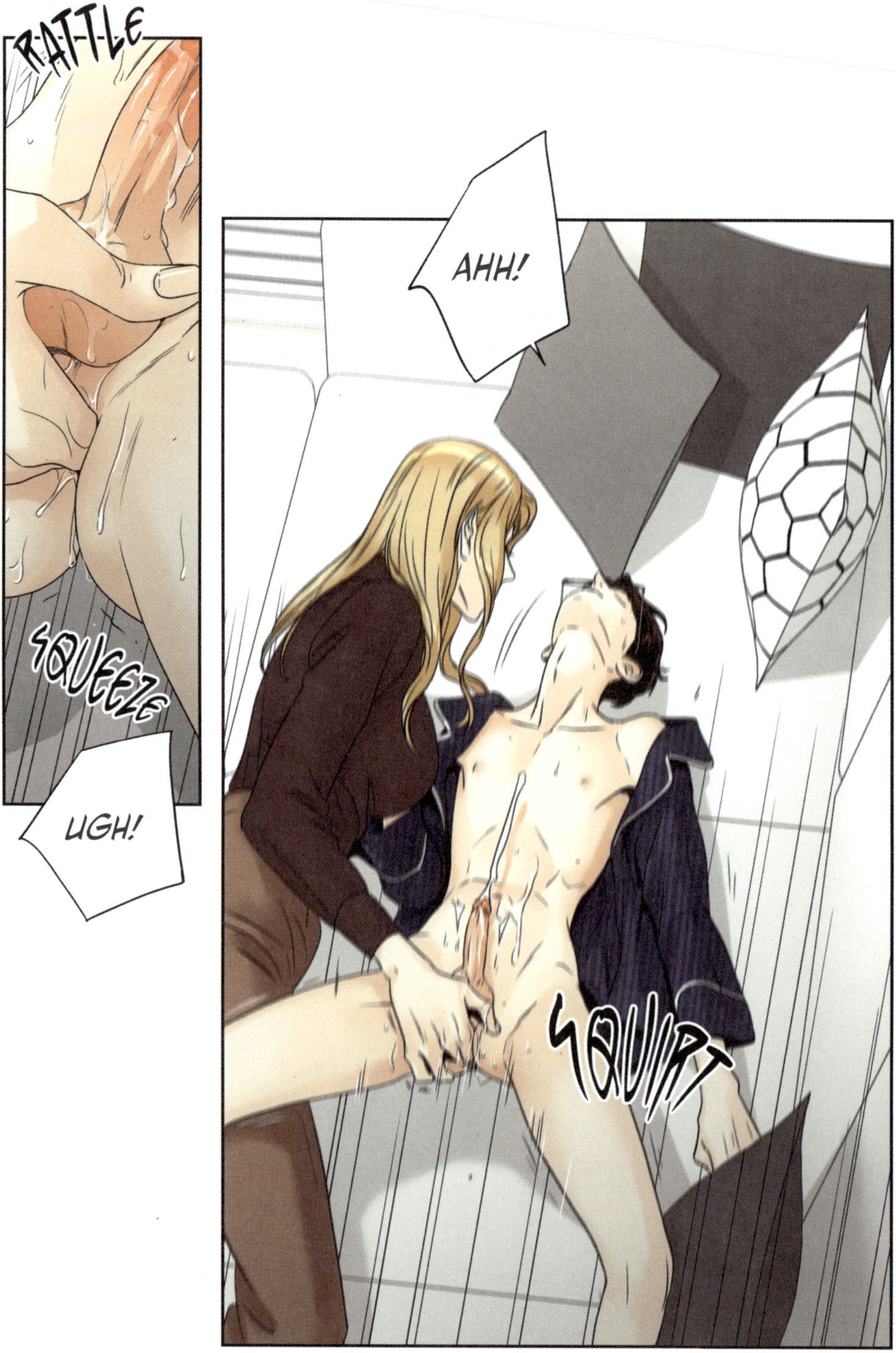
RATTLE
SQUEEZE
UGH!
AHH!
SQUIRT

HAAAH!
UGH...
YOU DID GOOD.
HAAH...
HAAH...
I CAN'T STOP CUMMING IN FRONT OF DO-GYEOM.
CLACK

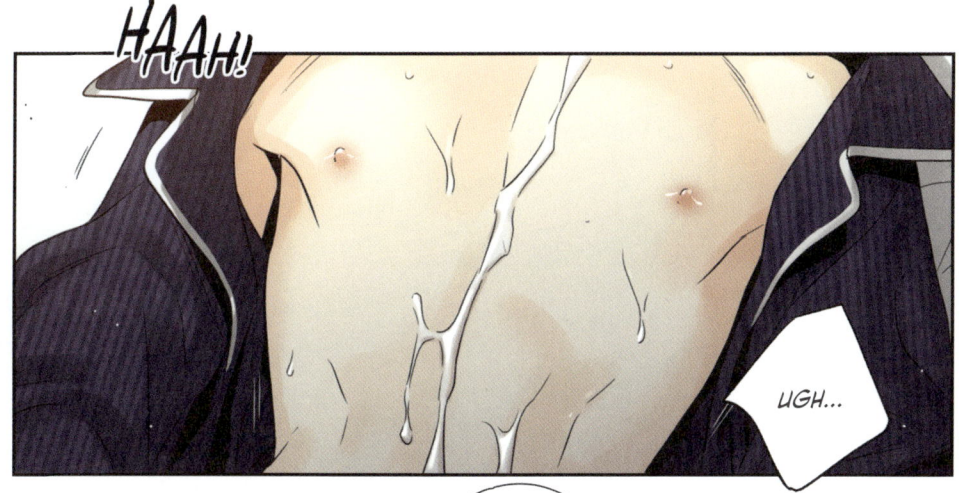

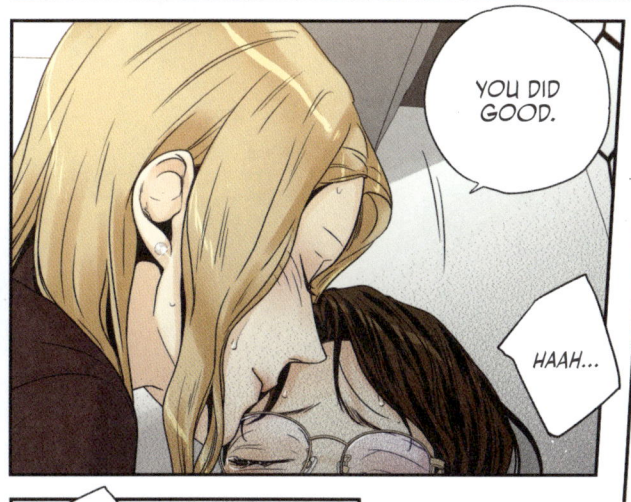

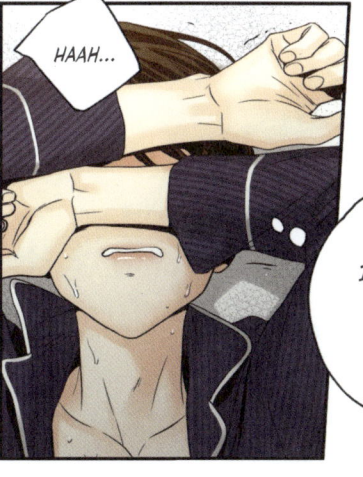

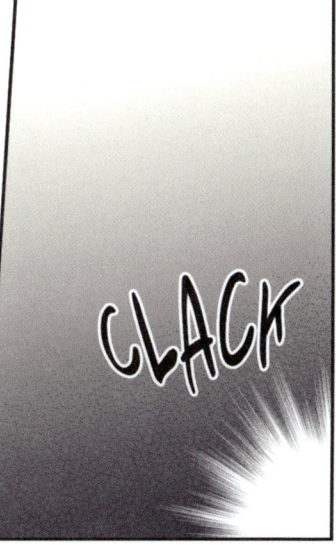

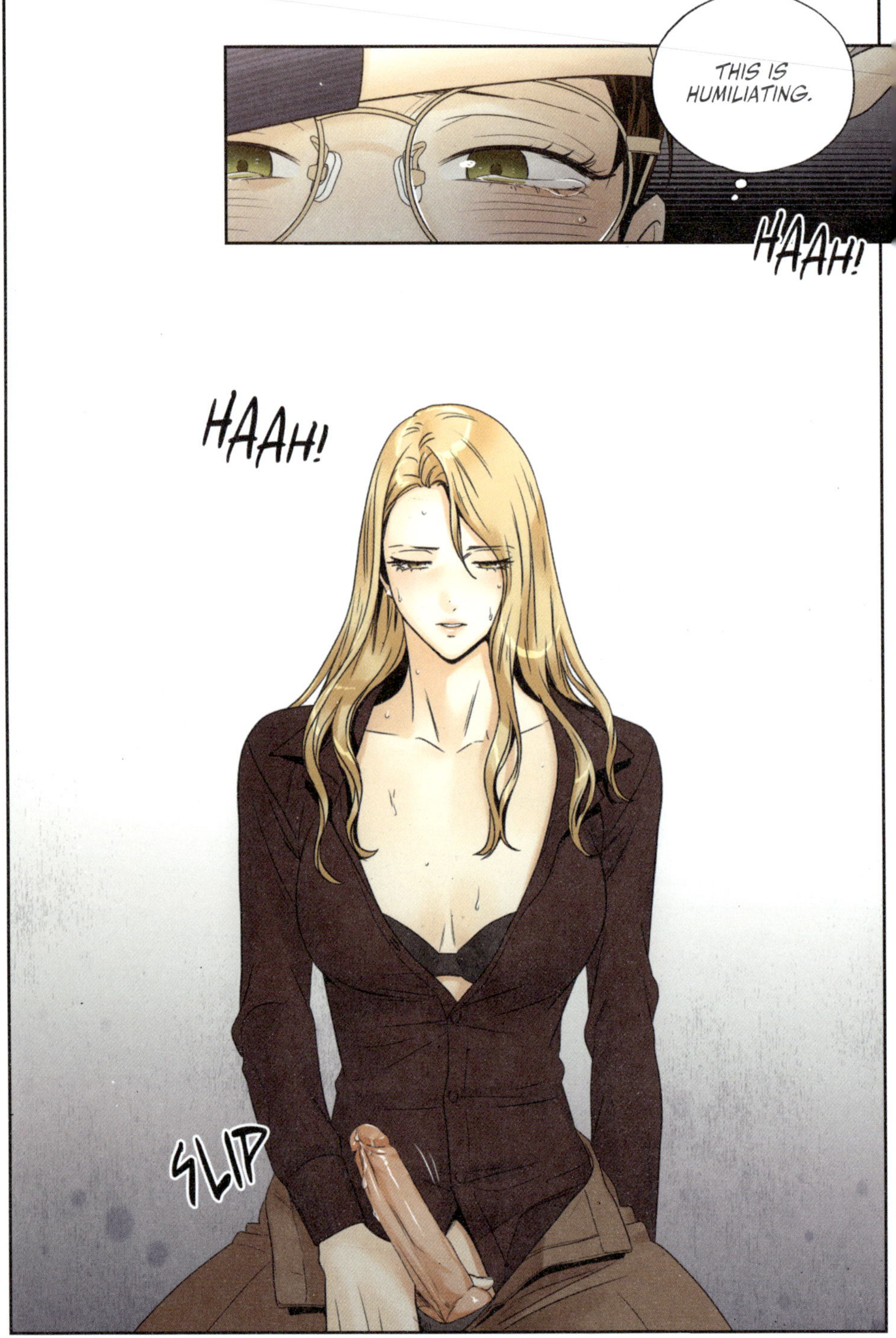
THIS IS HUMILIATING.
HAAAH!
HAAAH!
SLIP

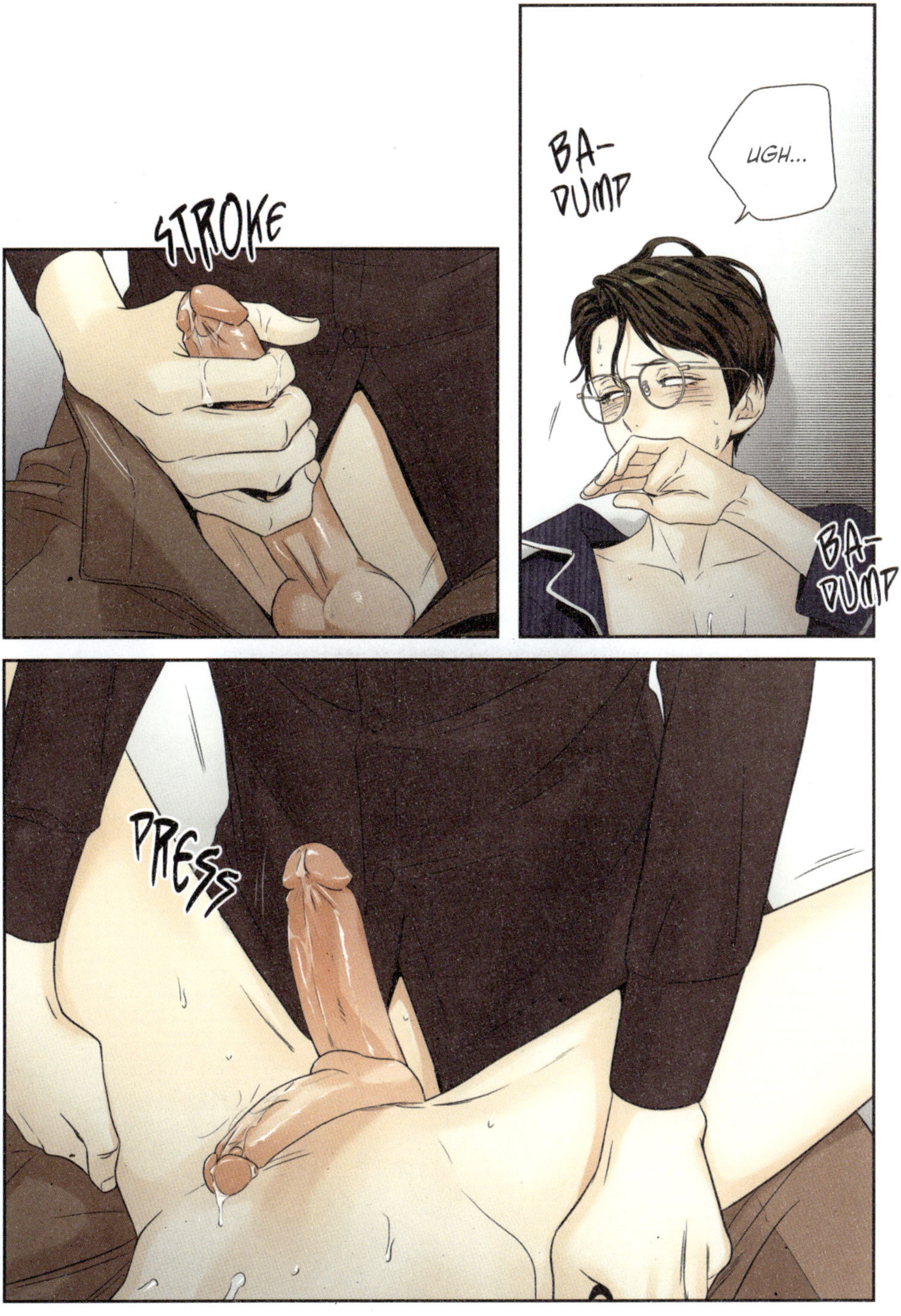
STROKE
BA-DUMP
UGH...
BA-DUMP
PRESS

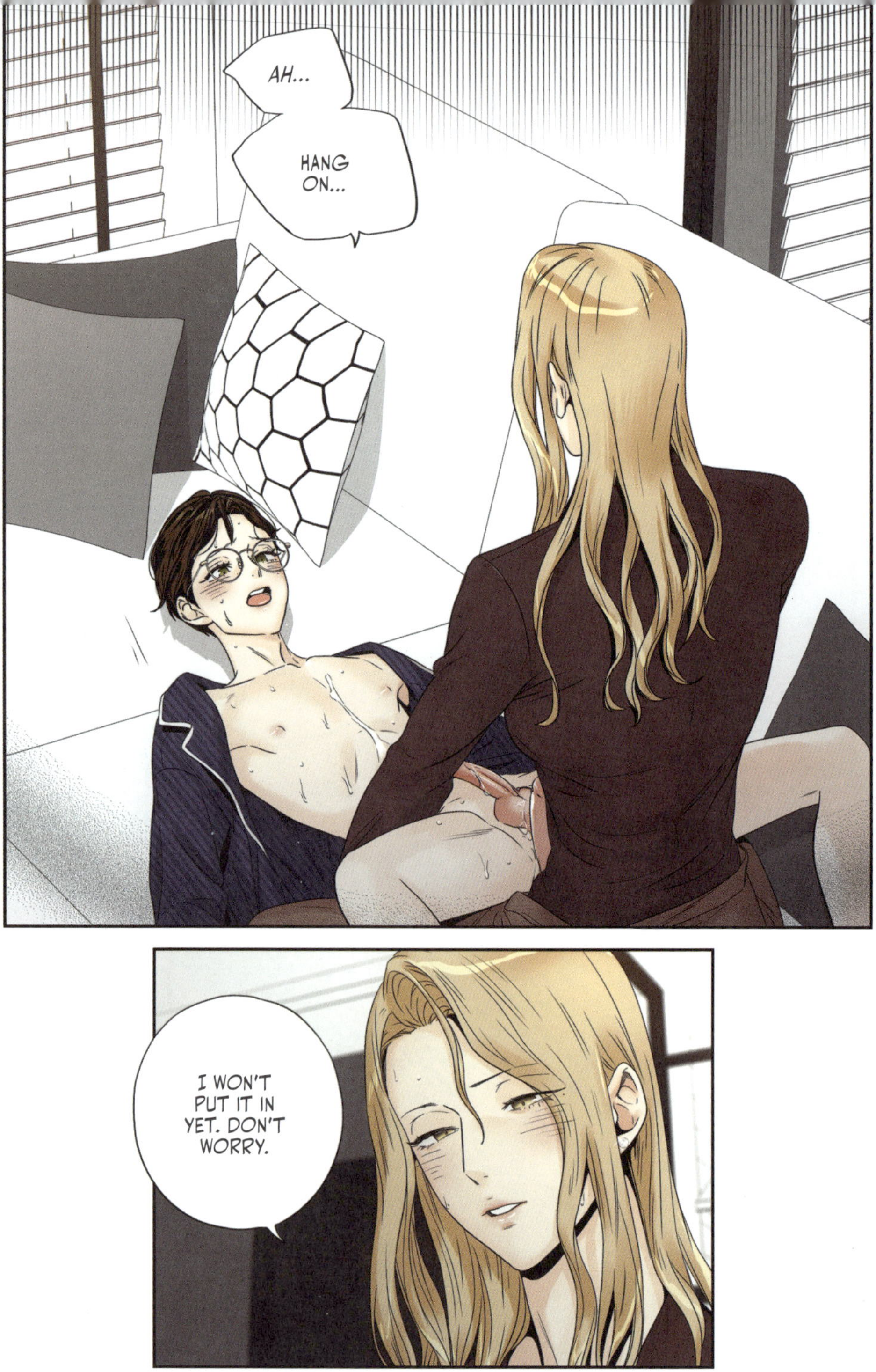
AH...
HANG ON...
I WON'T PUT IT IN YET. DON'T WORRY.

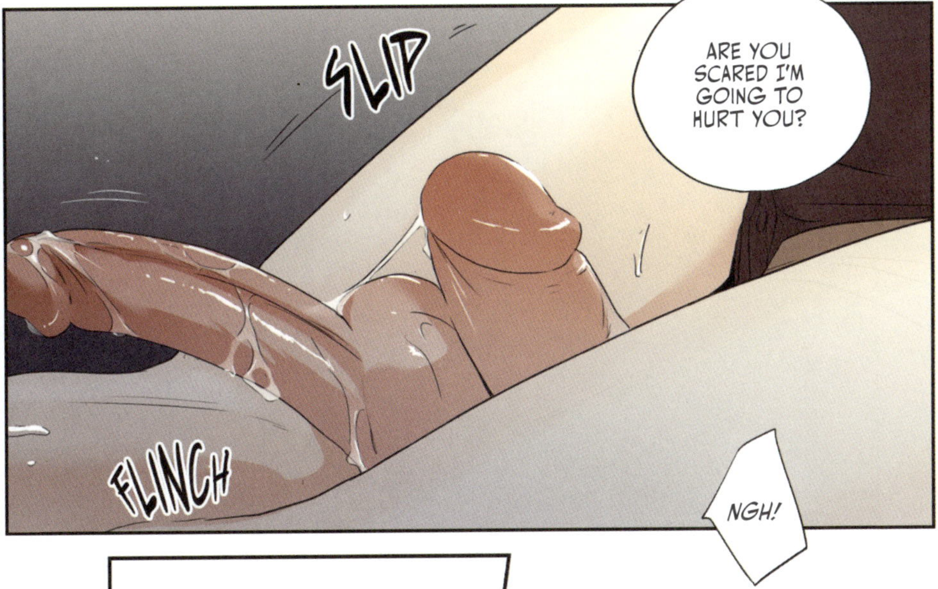
SLIP
ARE YOU SCARED I'M GOING TO HURT YOU?
FLINCH
NGH!

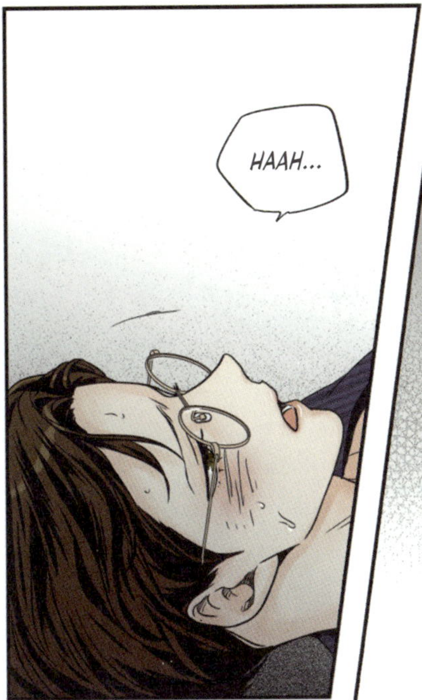
HAAH...

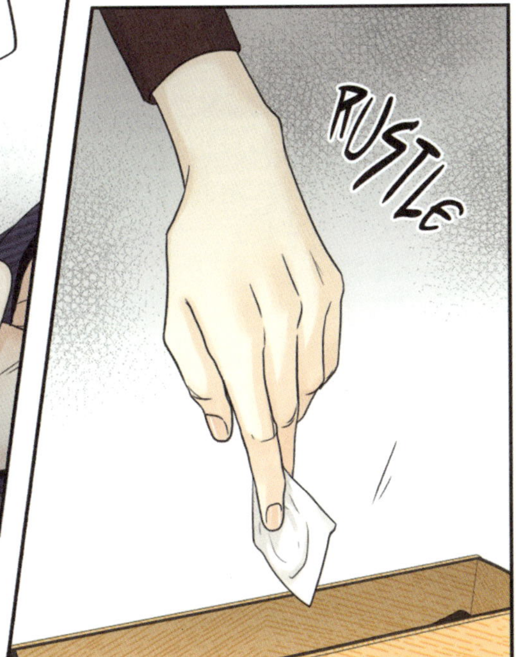
RUSTLE

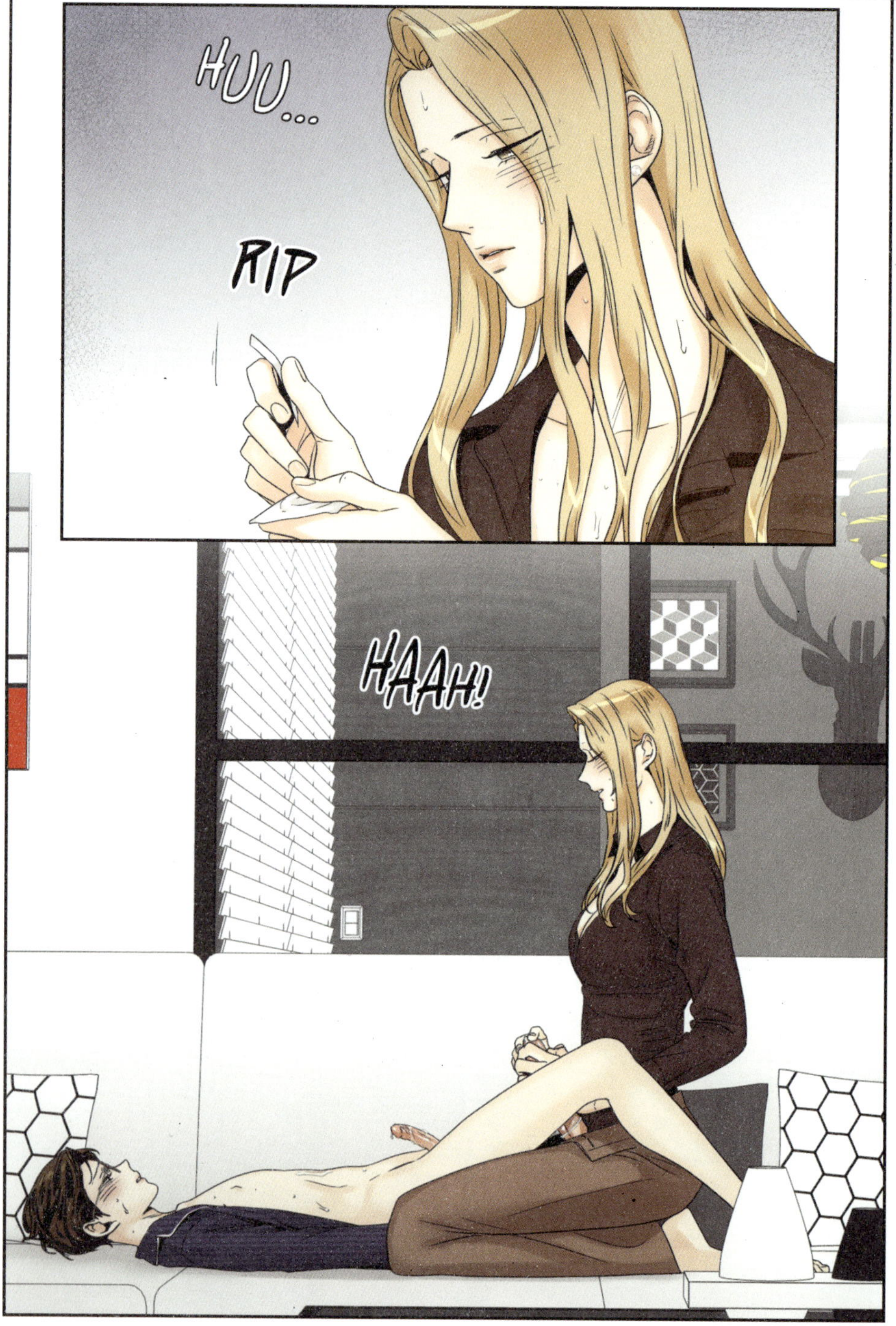
HUU...
RIP
HAAH!

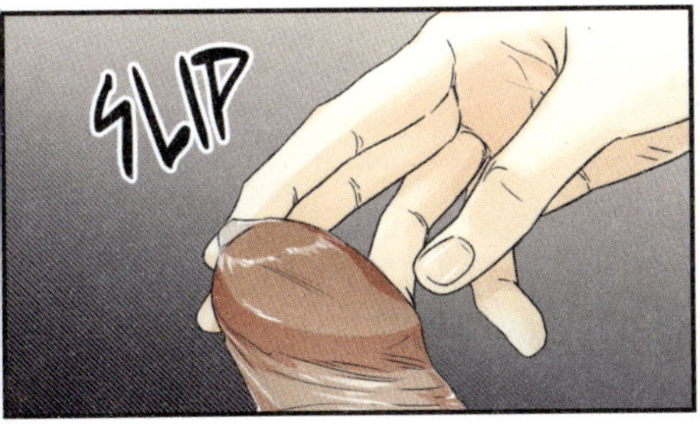
SLIP

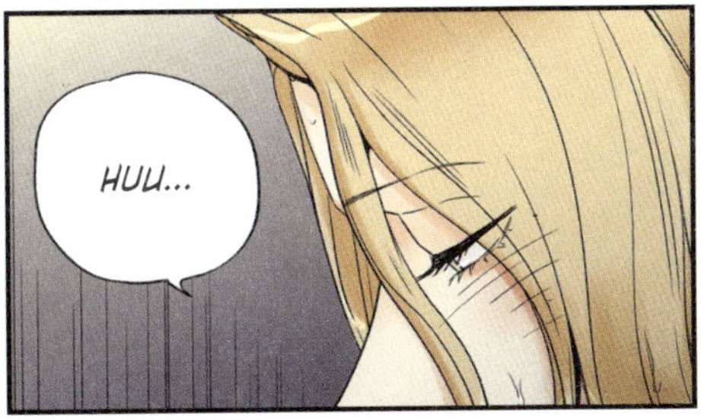
HUU...

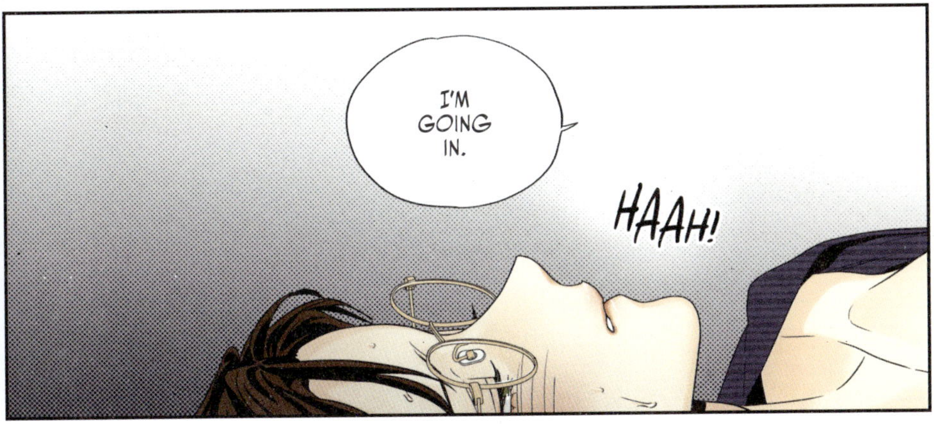
I'M GOING IN.
HAAH!

AM I...

AM I REALLY...

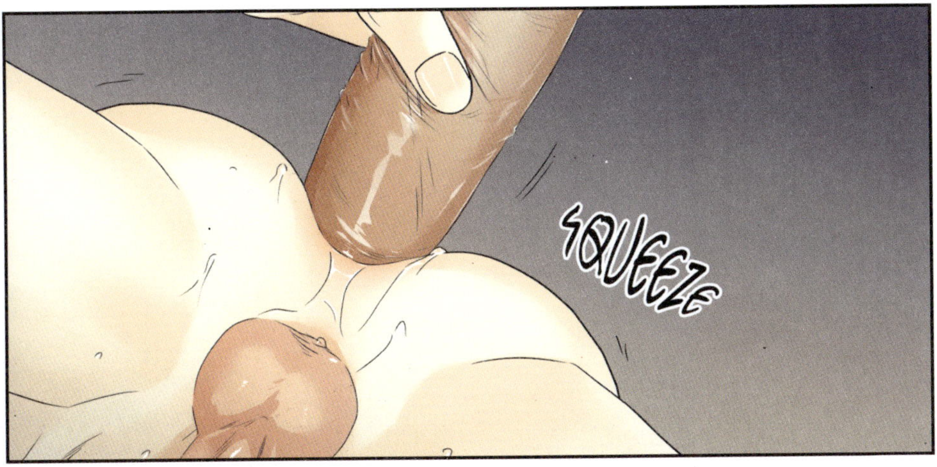
SQUEEZE

DOING THIS WITH
DO-GYEOM...?

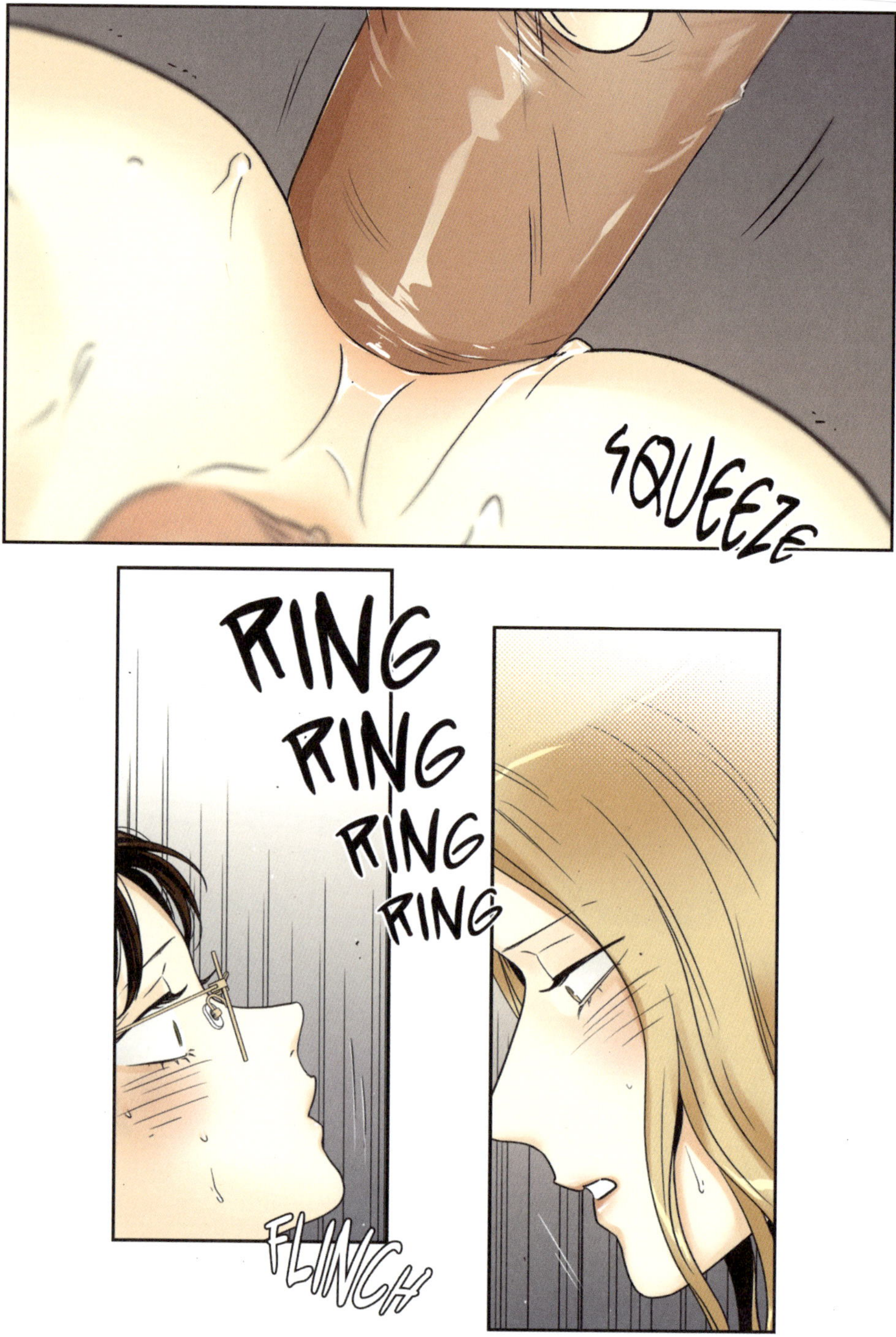
SQUEEZE
RING
RING
RING
RING
FLINCH

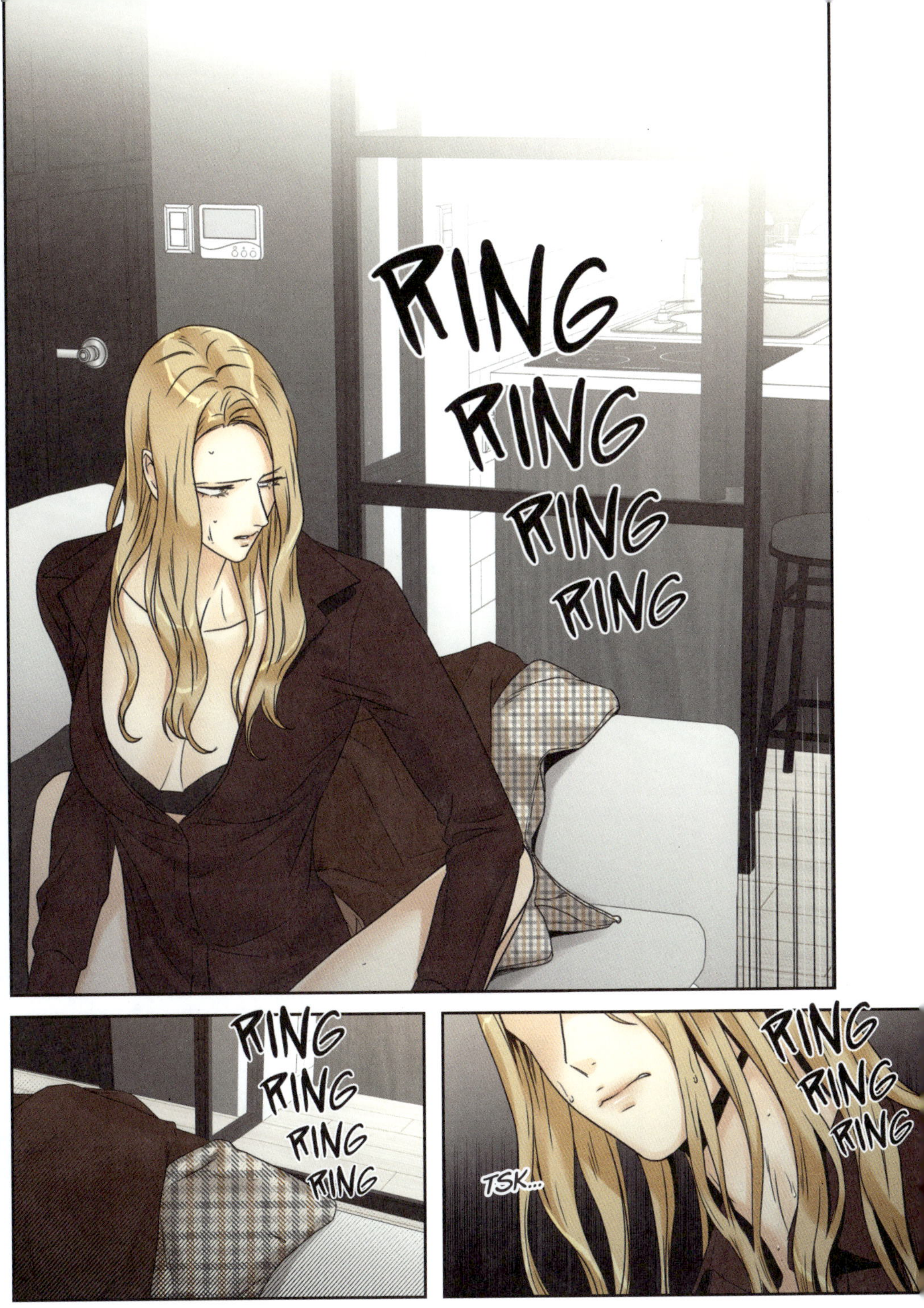
RING
RING
RING
RING
RING
RING
RING
RING
RING
RING
RING
TSK...

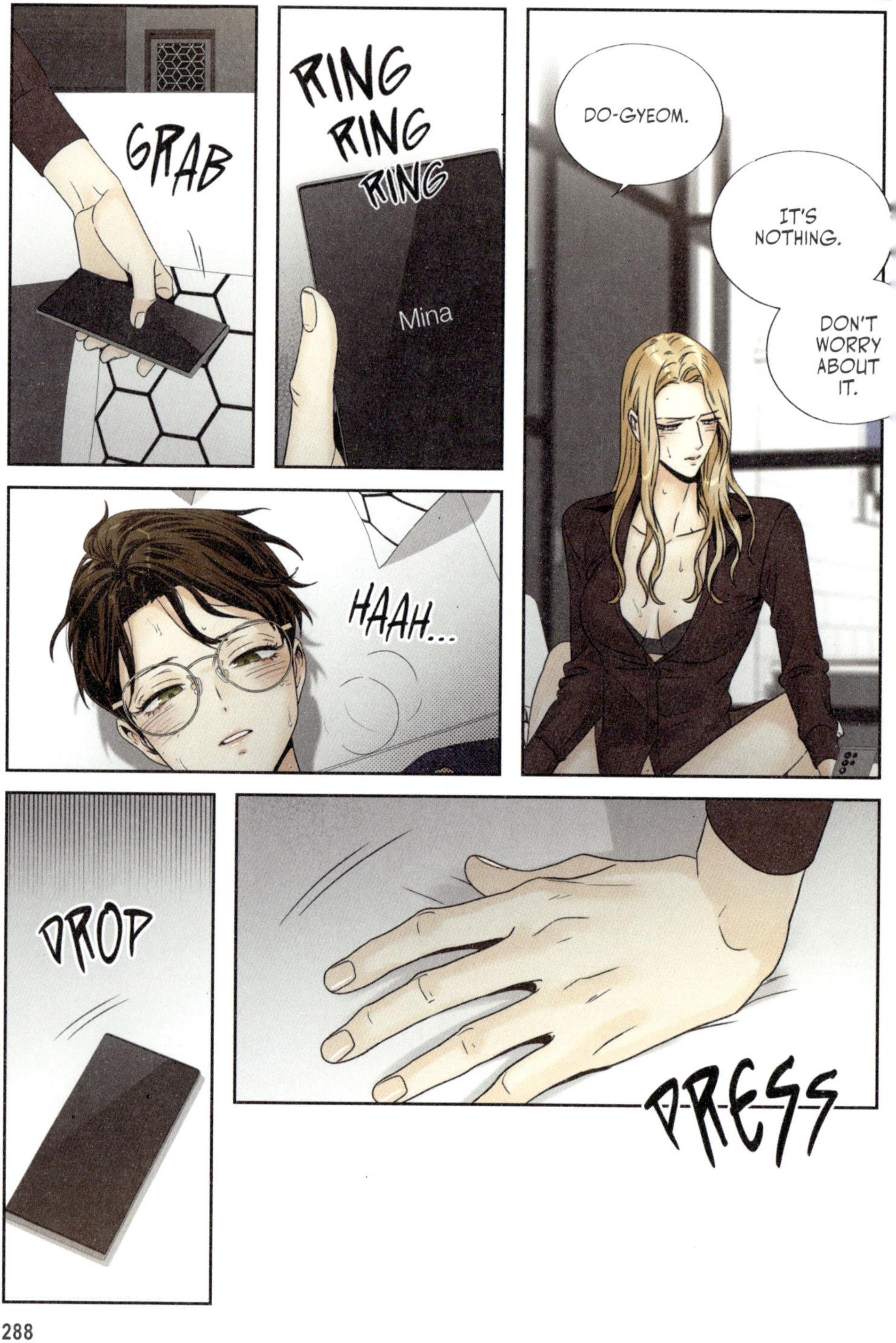
GRAB
RING
RING
RING
Mina
HAAAH...
DO-GYEOM.
IT'S NOTHING.
DON'T WORRY ABOUT IT.
DROP
PRESS

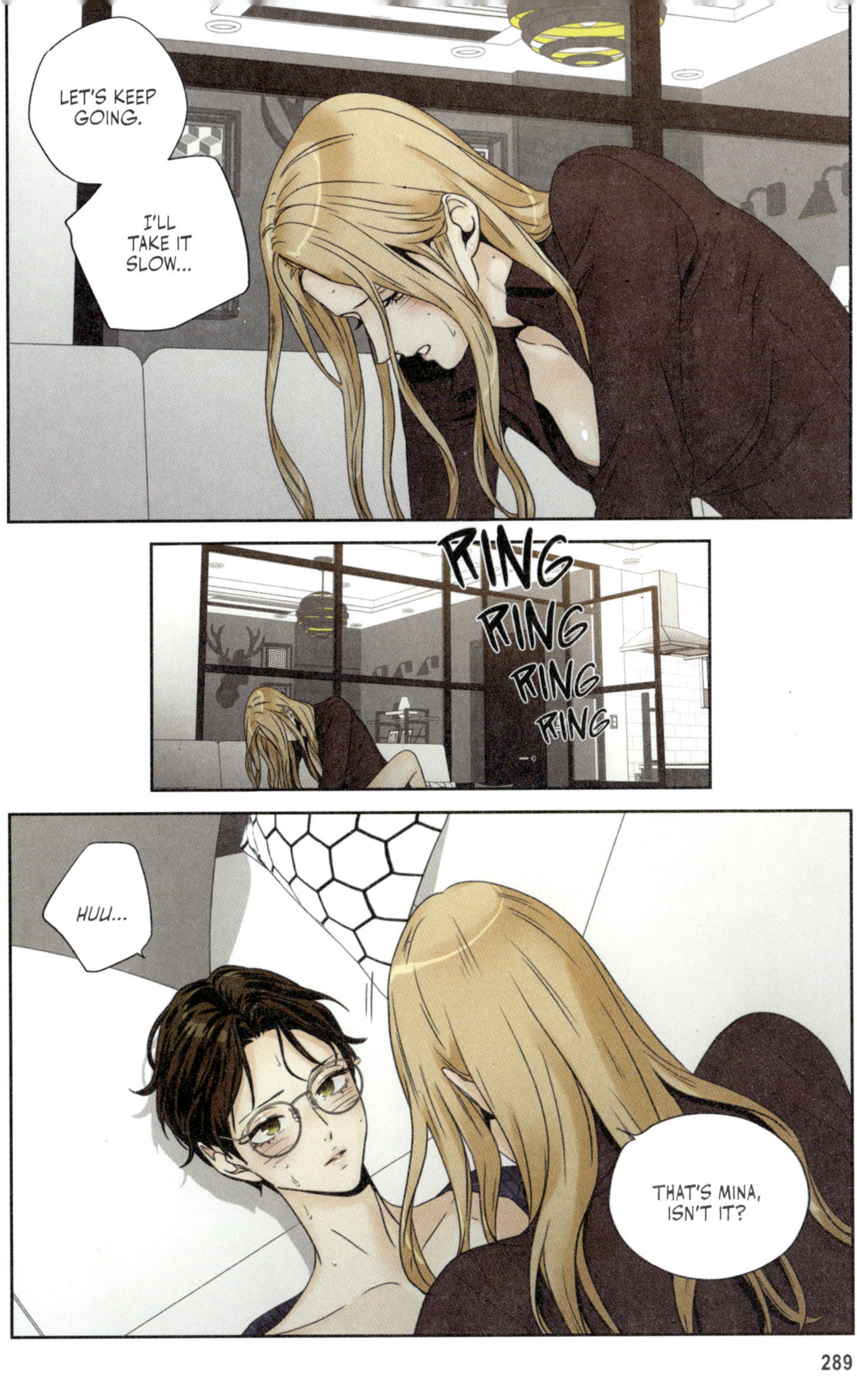
LET'S KEEP GOING.
I'LL TAKE IT SLOW...
RING RING RING RING
HUU...
THAT'S MINA, ISN'T IT?

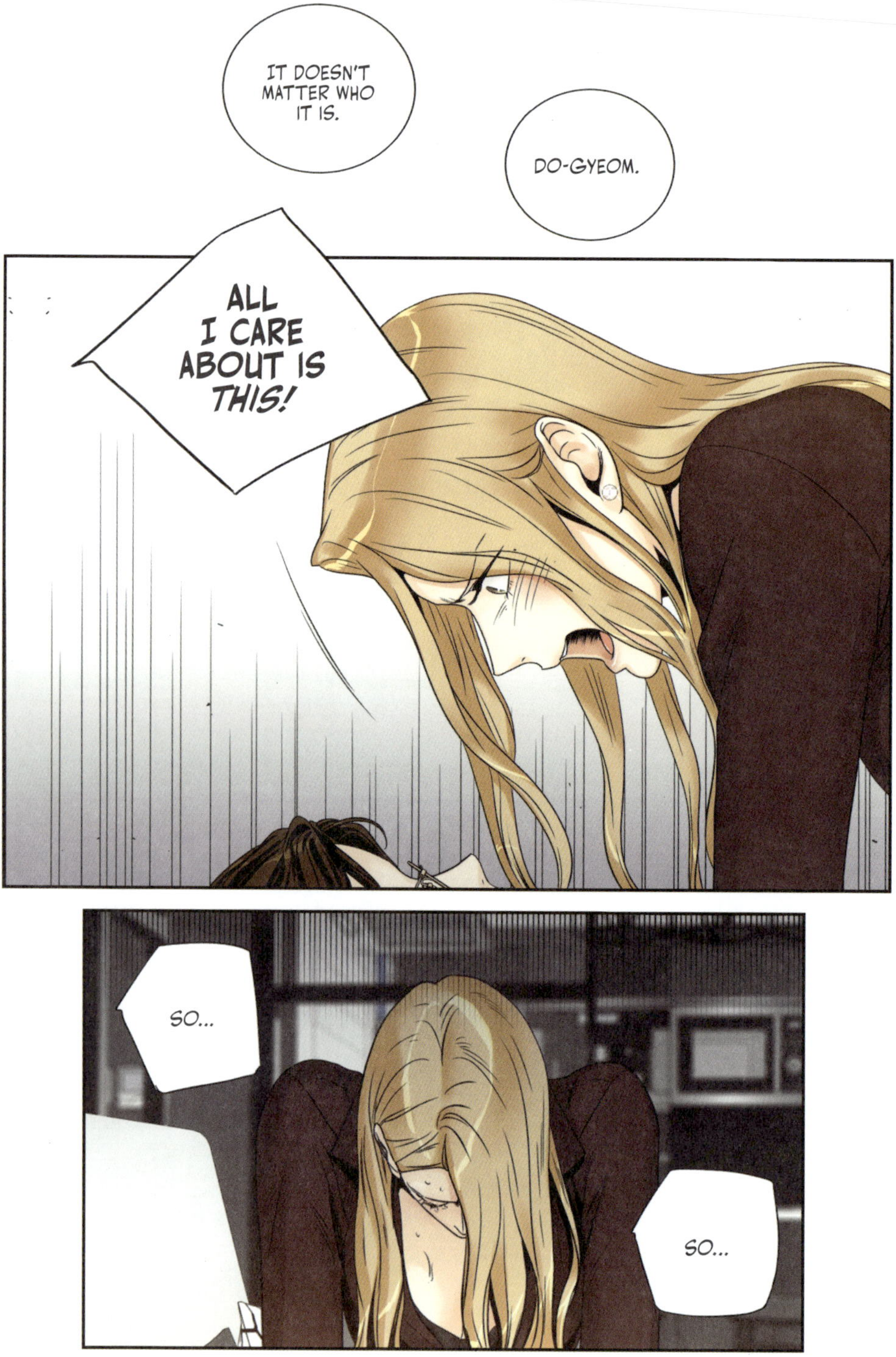
IT DOESN'T MATTER WHO IT IS.
DO-GYEOM.
ALL I CARE ABOUT IS THIS!
SO...
SO...

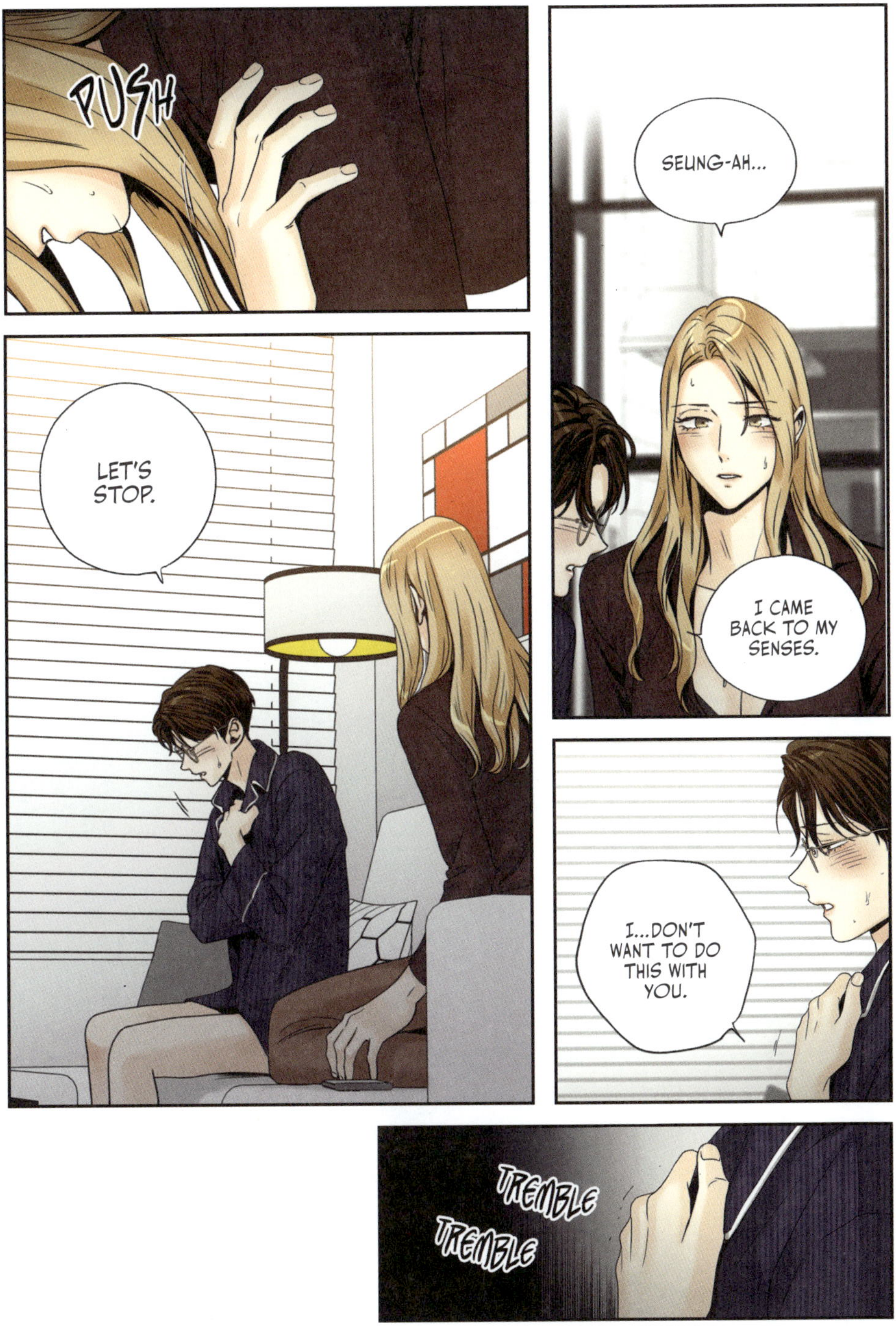
PUSH
SEUNG-AH...
I CAME BACK TO MY SENSES.
LET'S STOP.
I...DON'T WANT TO DO THIS WITH YOU.
TREMBLE
TREMBLE

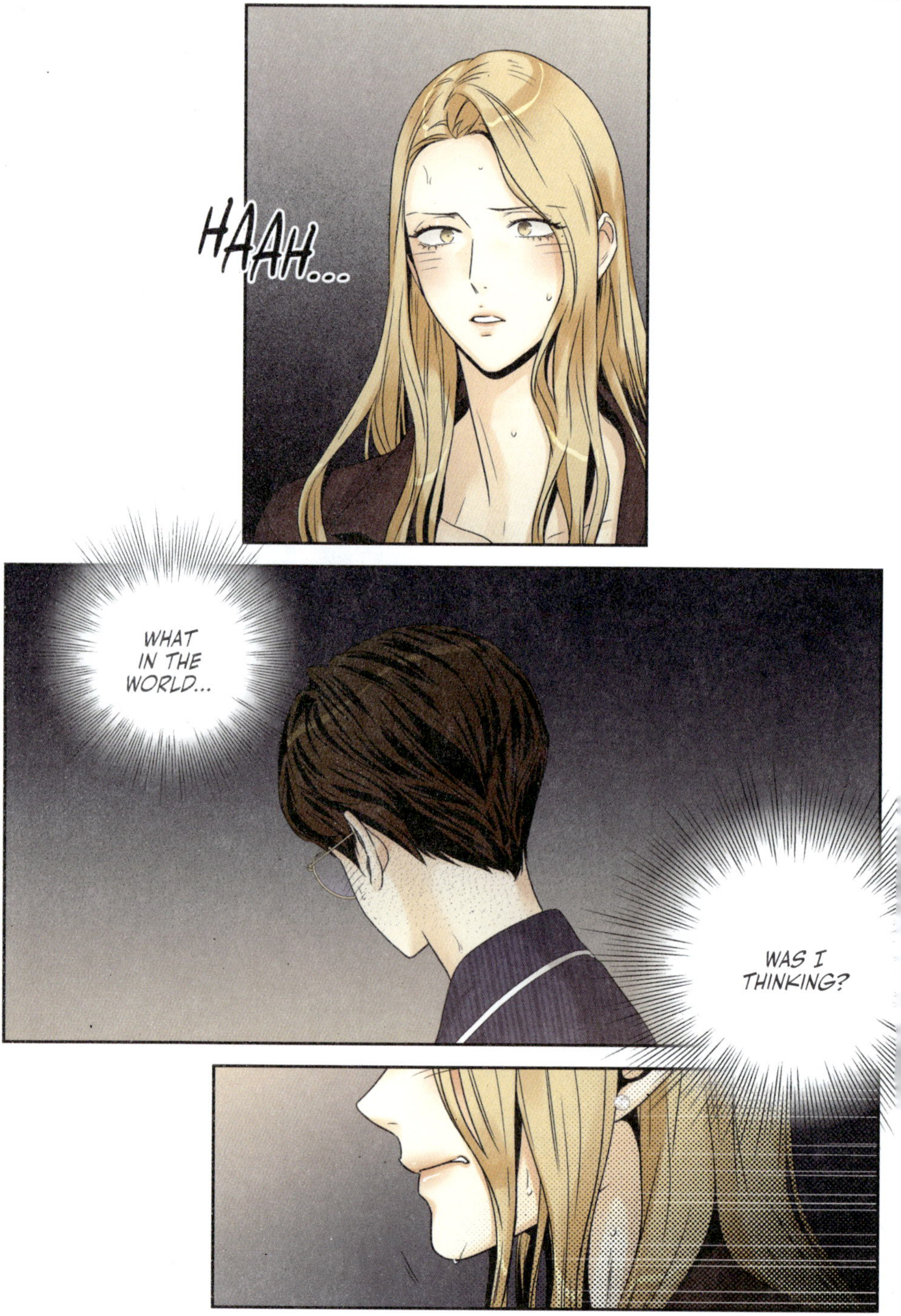
HAAH...
WHAT IN THE WORLD...
WAS I THINKING?

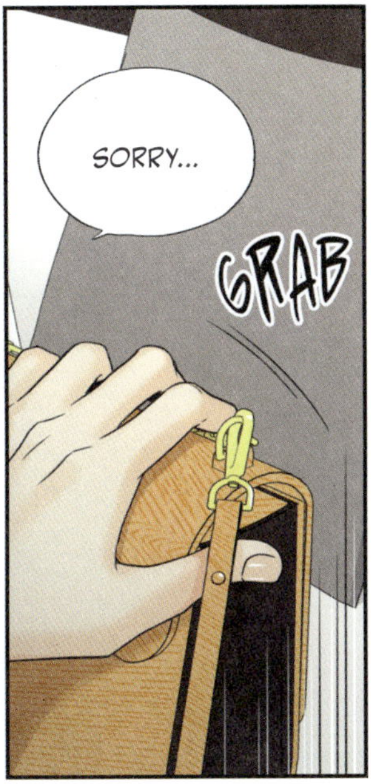
SORRY...
GRAB

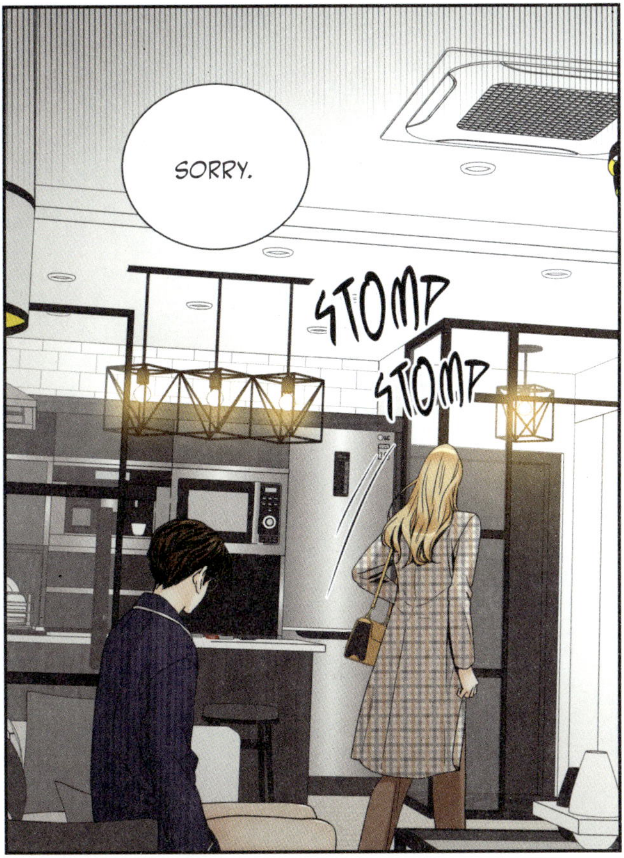
SORRY.
STOMP
STOMP

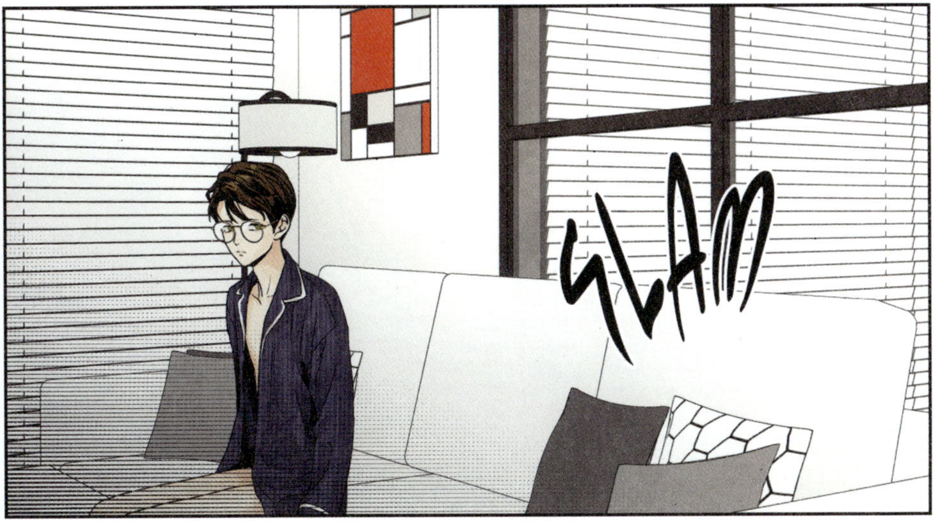
SLAM

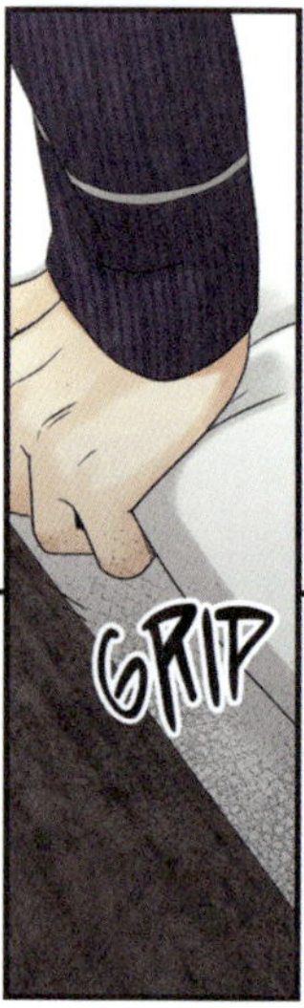
GRIP

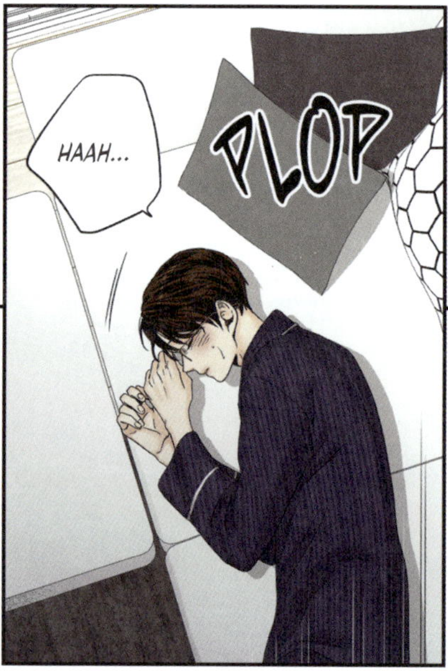
HAAH...
PLOP

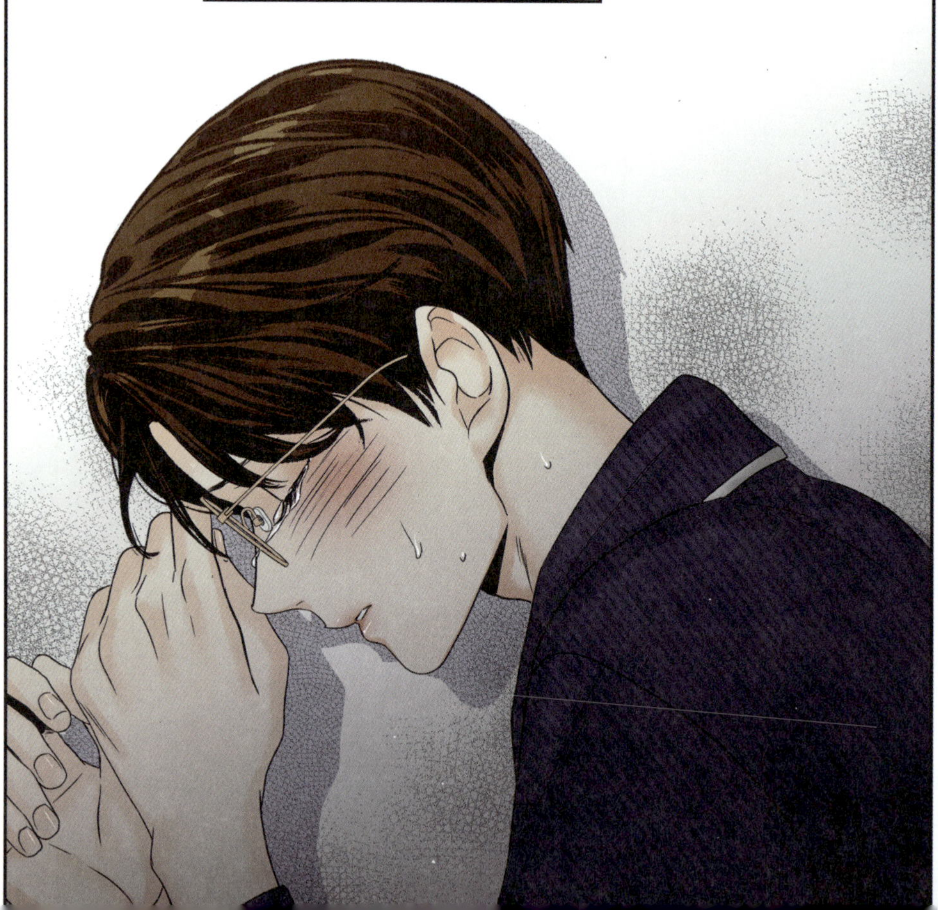

Love is an Illusion!
The Queen

Love is an Illusion!
The Queen

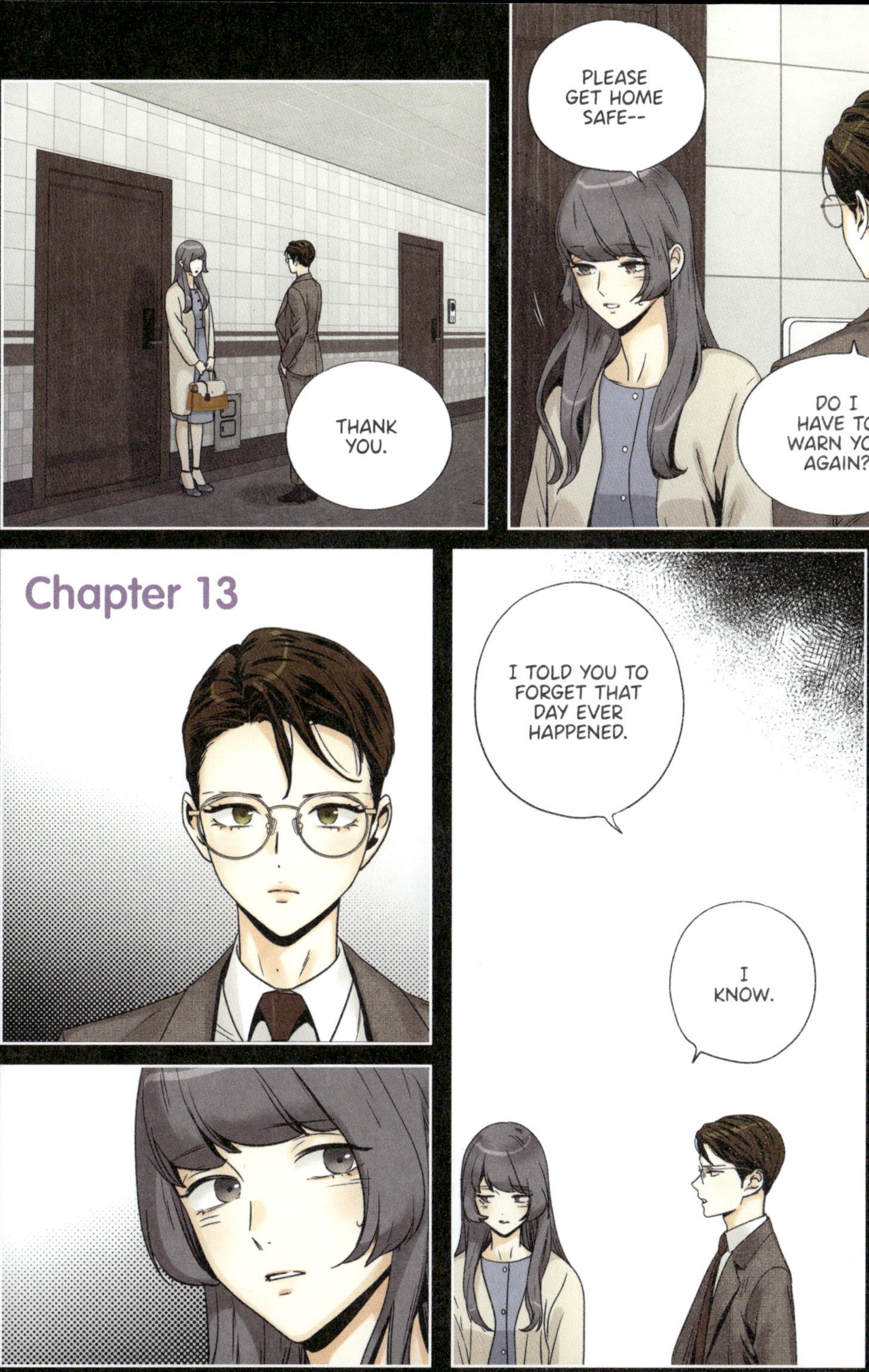
THANK YOU.
PLEASE GET HOME SAFE--
DO I HAVE TO WARN YOU AGAIN?
Chapter 13
I TOLD YOU TO FORGET THAT DAY EVER HAPPENED.
I KNOW.

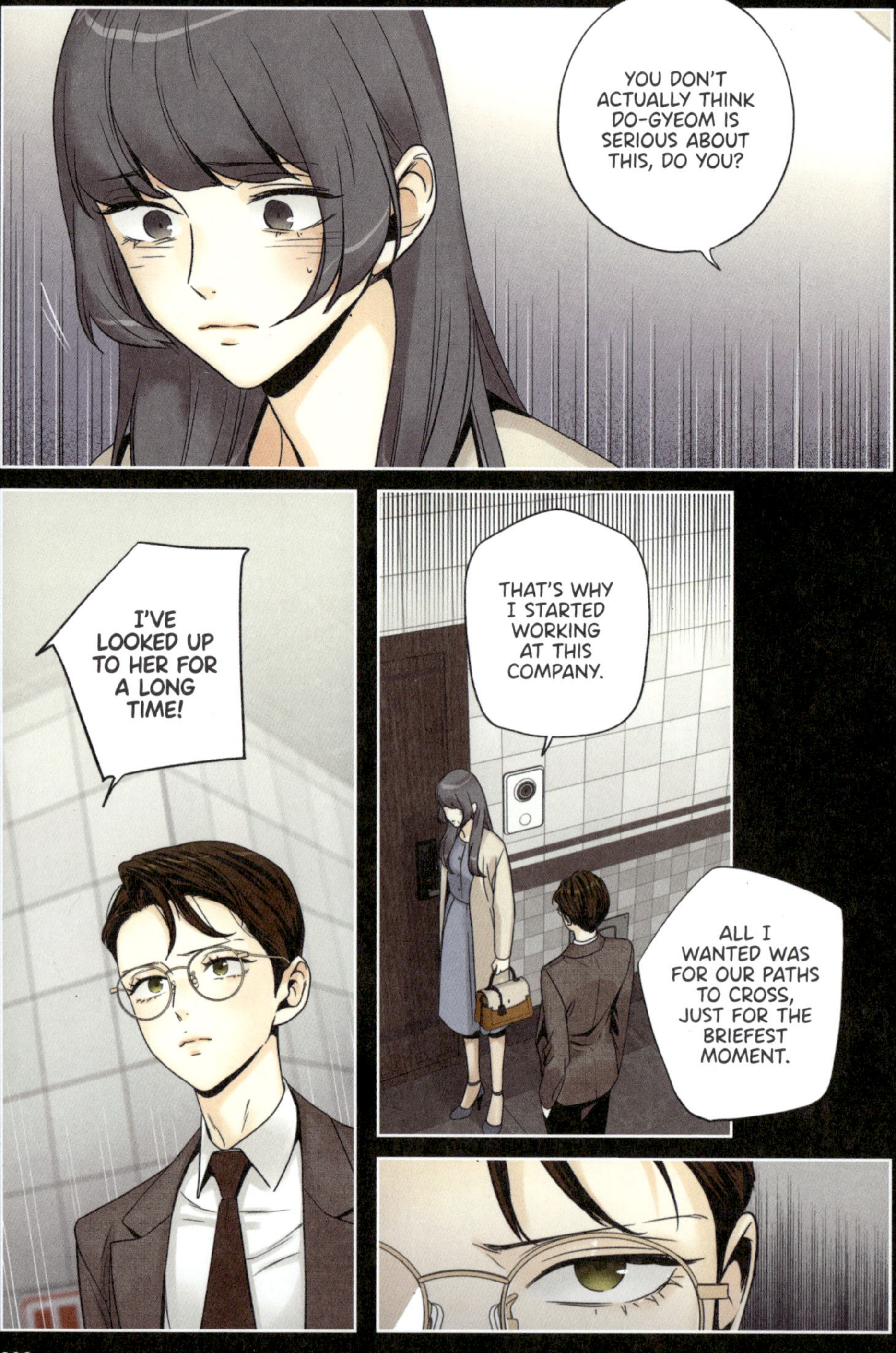
YOU DON'T ACTUALLY THINK DO-GYEOM IS SERIOUS ABOUT THIS, DO YOU?
I'VE LOOKED UP TO HER FOR A LONG TIME!
THAT'S WHY I STARTED WORKING AT THIS COMPANY.
ALL I WANTED WAS FOR OUR PATHS TO CROSS, JUST FOR THE BRIEFEST MOMENT.

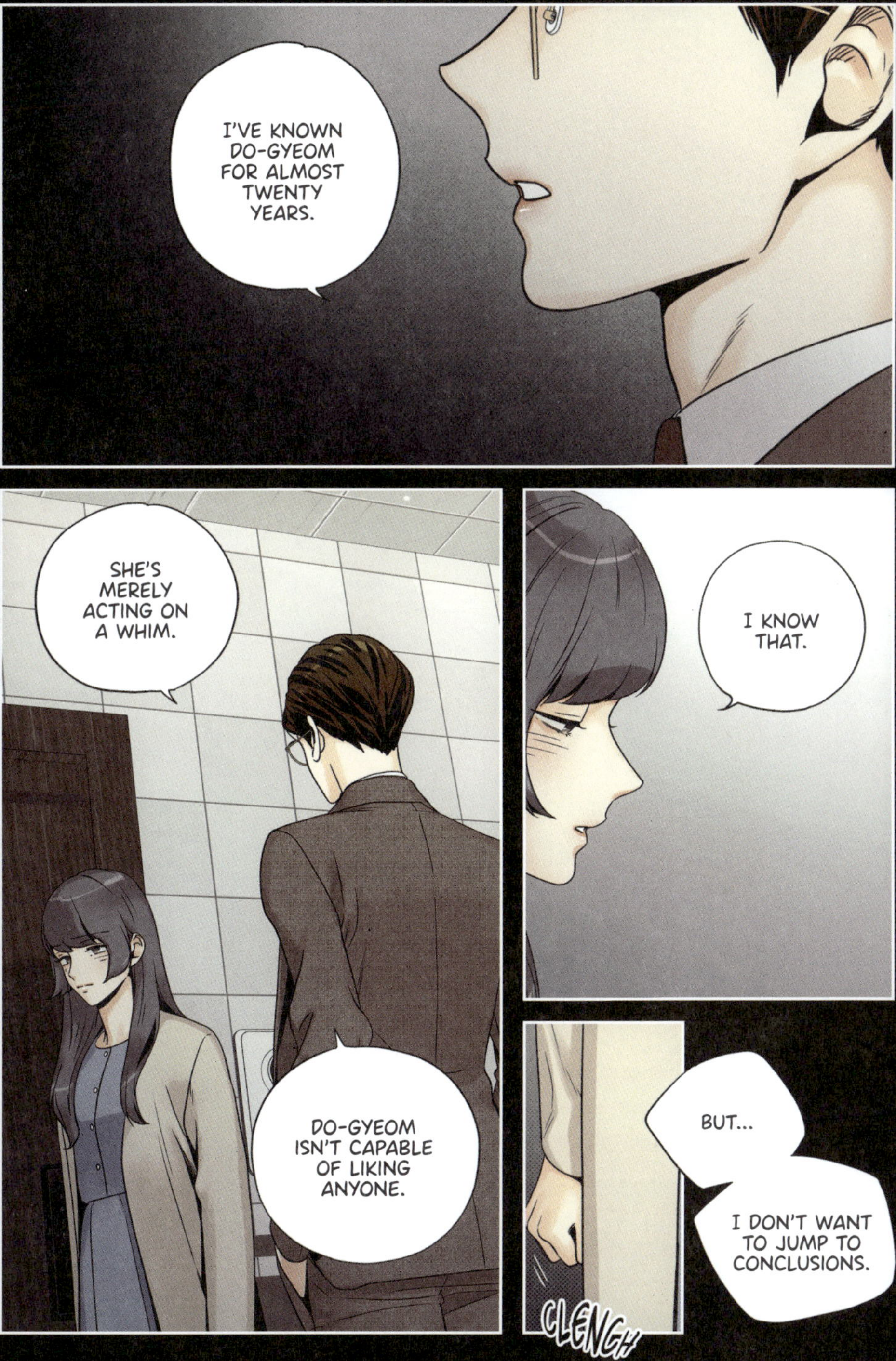
I'VE KNOWN DO-GYEOM FOR ALMOST TWENTY YEARS.
SHE'S MERELY ACTING ON A WHIM.
DO-GYEOM ISN'T CAPABLE OF LIKING ANYONE.
I KNOW THAT.
BUT...
I DON'T WANT TO JUMP TO CONCLUSIONS.
CLENCH

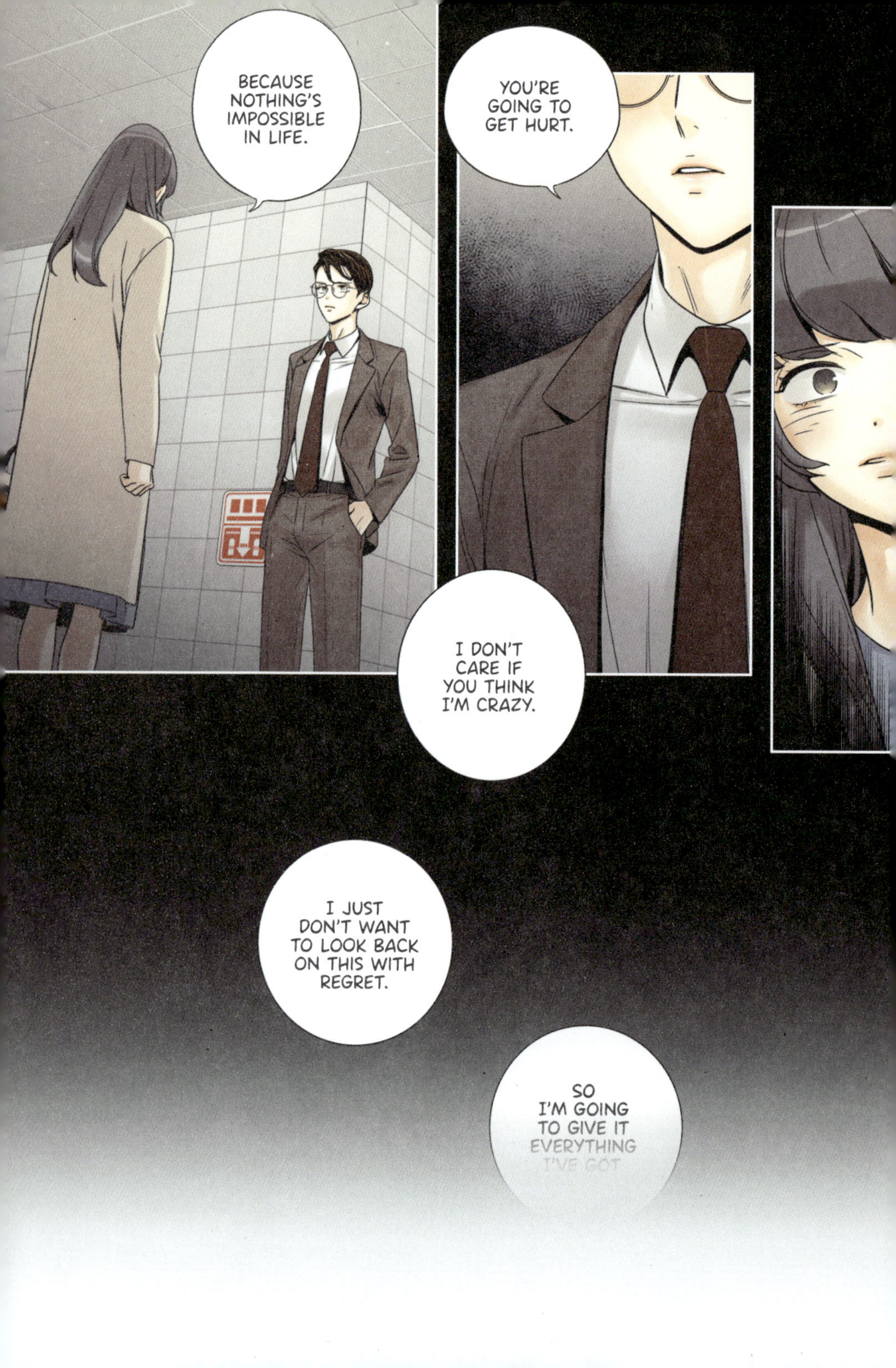
BECAUSE NOTHING'S IMPOSSIBLE IN LIFE.
YOU'RE GOING TO GET HURT.
I DON'T CARE IF YOU THINK I'M CRAZY.
I JUST DON'T WANT TO LOOK BACK ON THIS WITH REGRET.
SO I'M GOING TO GIVE IT EVERYTHING I'VE GOT

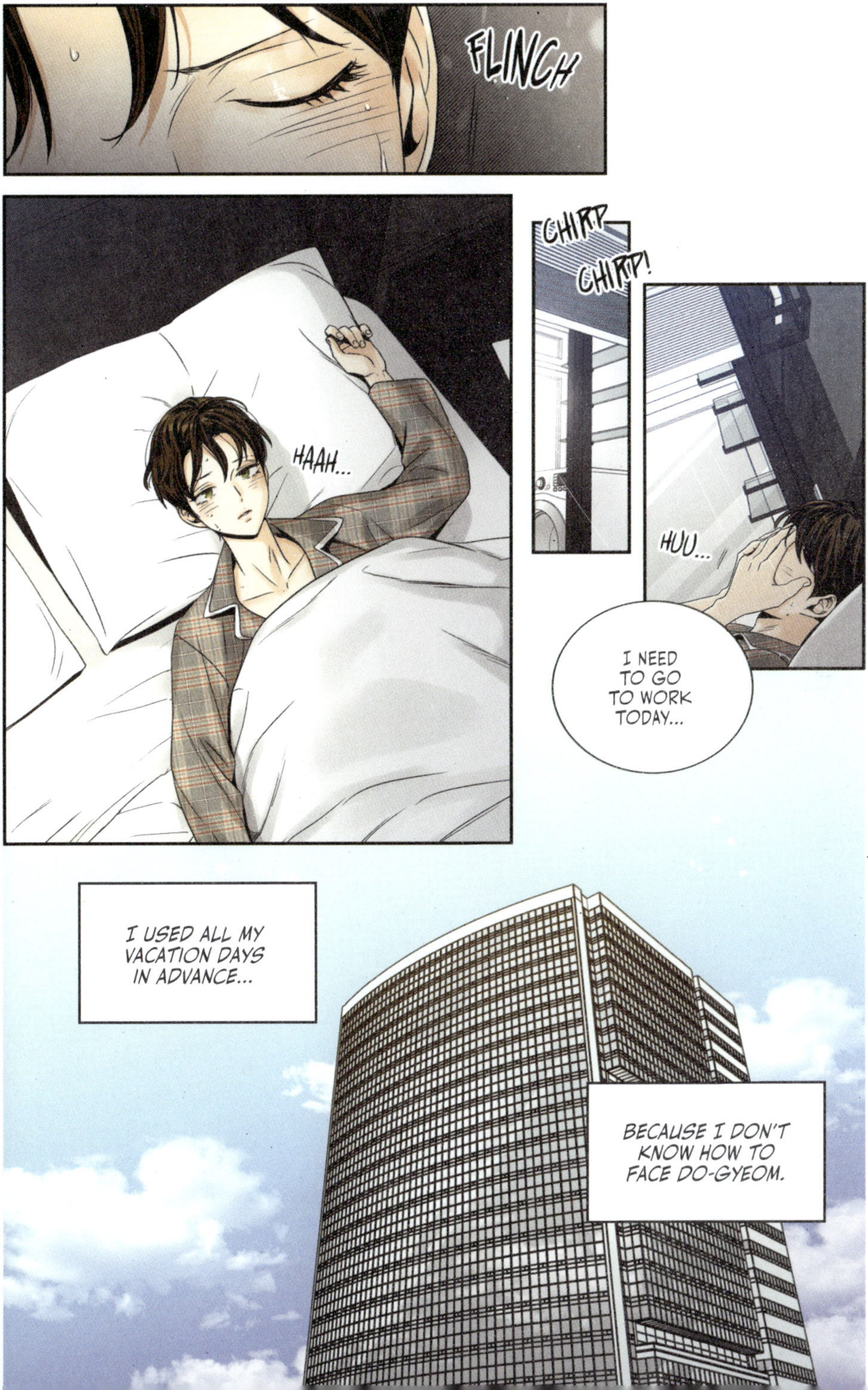
FLINCH
HAAH...
CHIRP
CHIRP!
HUU...
I NEED TO GO TO WORK TODAY...
I USED ALL MY VACATION DAYS IN ADVANCE...
BECAUSE I DON'T KNOW HOW TO FACE DO-GYEOM.

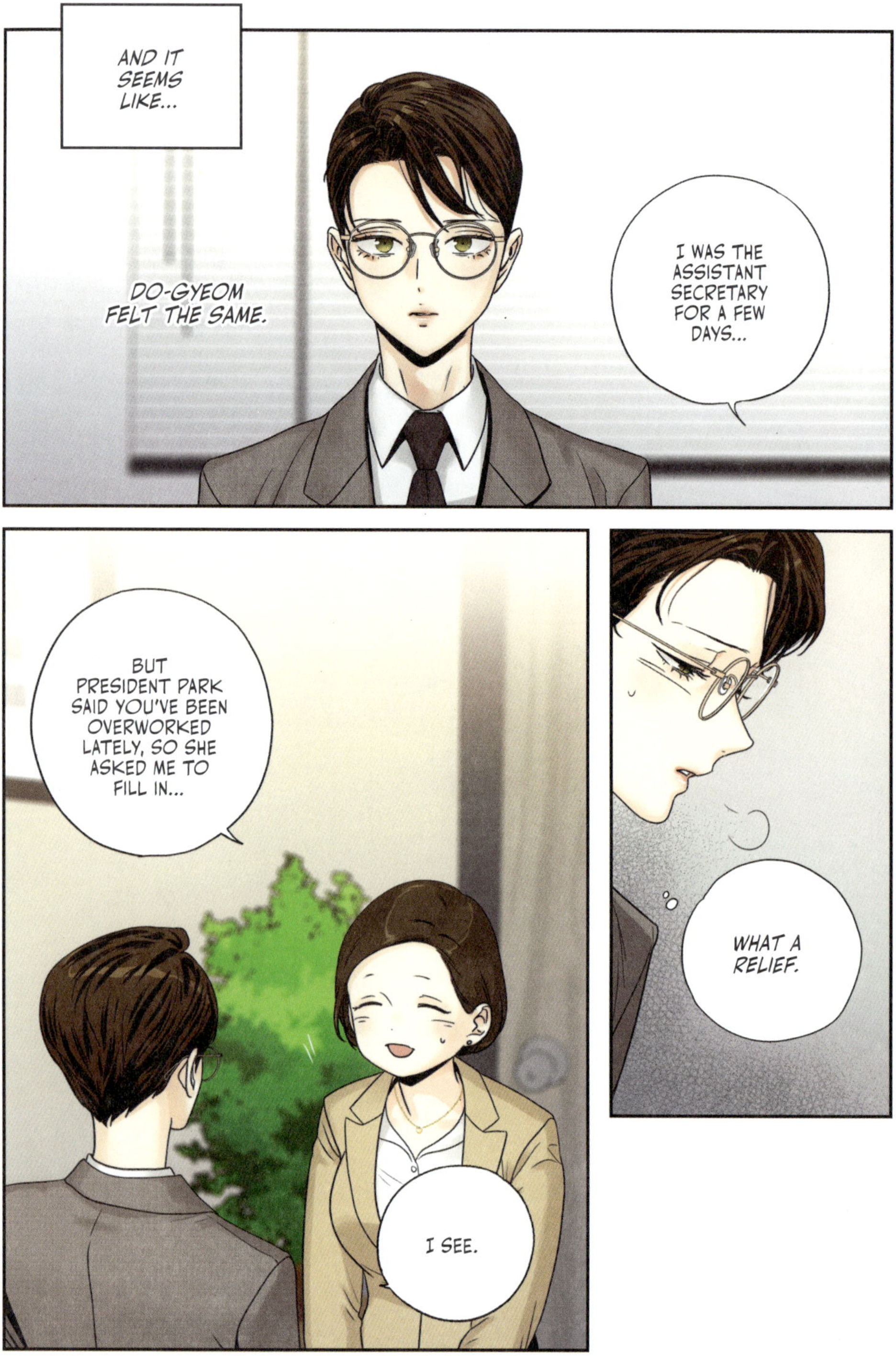
AND IT SEEMS LIKE...
DO-GYEOM FELT THE SAME.
I WAS THE ASSISTANT SECRETARY FOR A FEW DAYS...
BUT PRESIDENT PARK SAID YOU'VE BEEN OVERWORKED LATELY, SO SHE ASKED ME TO FILL IN...
I SEE.
WHAT A RELIEF.

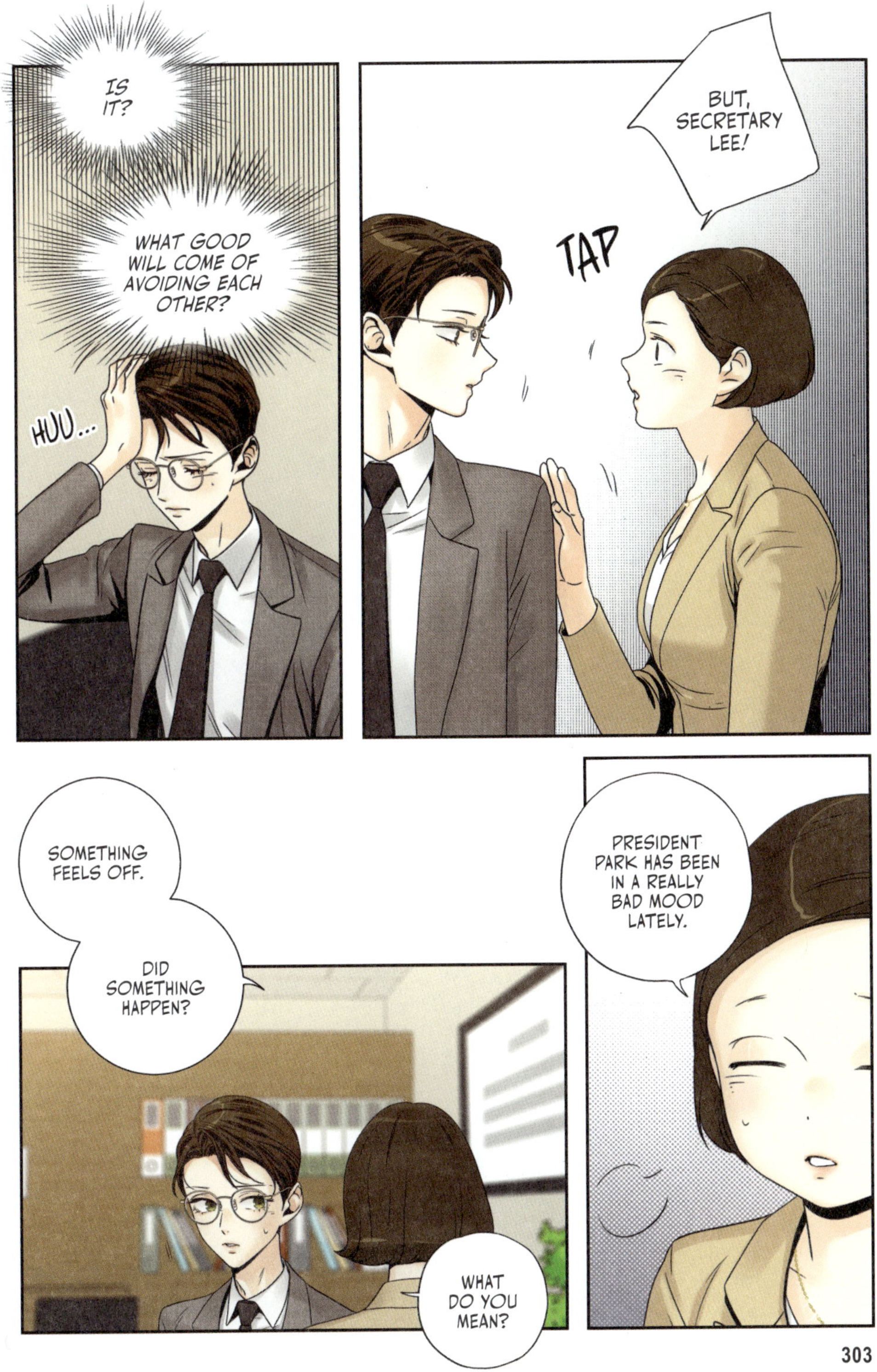
IS IT?
WHAT GOOD WILL COME OF AVOIDING EACH OTHER?
HUU...
BUT, SECRETARY LEE!
TAP
SOMETHING FEELS OFF.
DID SOMETHING HAPPEN?
WHAT DO YOU MEAN?
PRESIDENT PARK HAS BEEN IN A REALLY BAD MOOD LATELY.

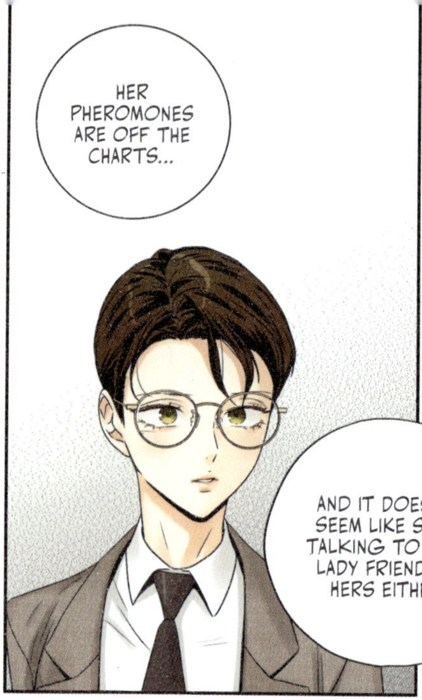
HER PHEROMONES ARE OFF THE CHARTS...
AND IT DOESN'T SEEM LIKE SHE'S TALKING TO THAT LADY FRIEND OF HERS EITHER.
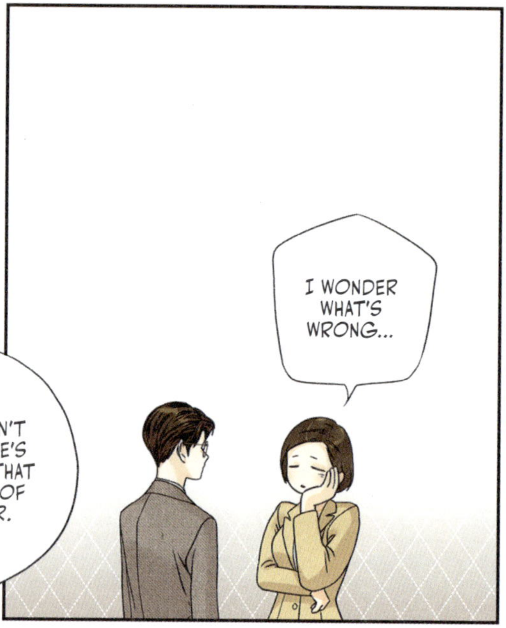
I WONDER WHAT'S WRONG...
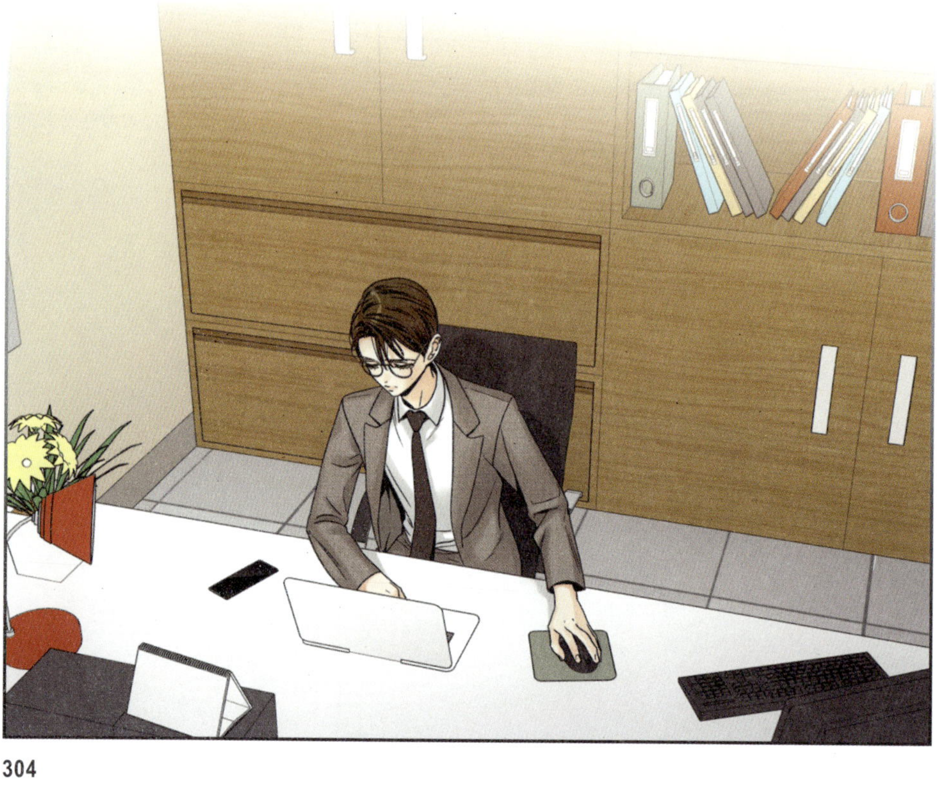

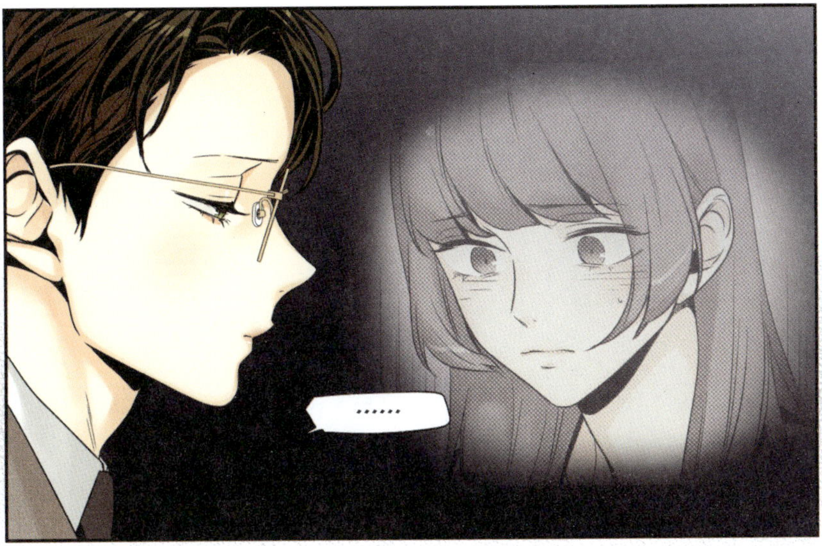
......

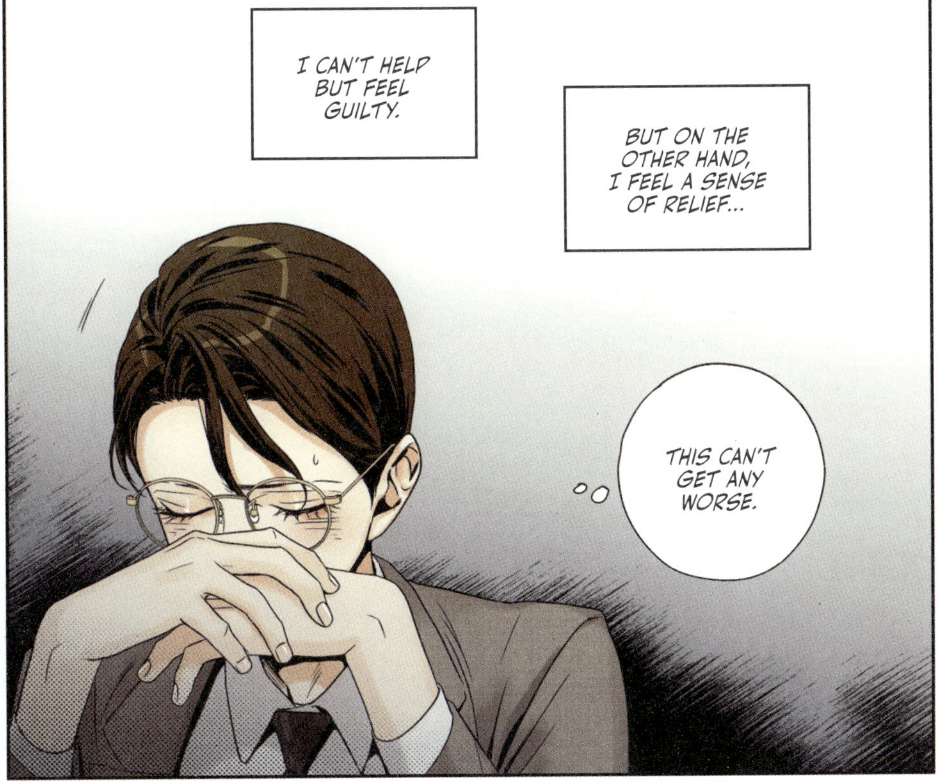
I CAN'T HELP BUT FEEL GUILTY.
BUT ON THE OTHER HAND, I FEEL A SENSE OF RELIEF...
THIS CAN'T GET ANY WORSE.

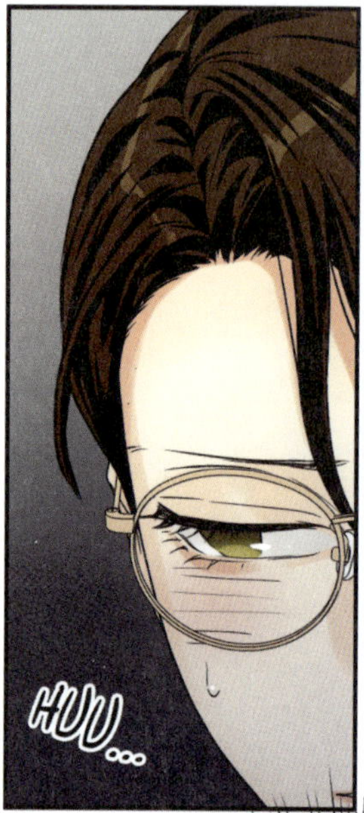
HUU...

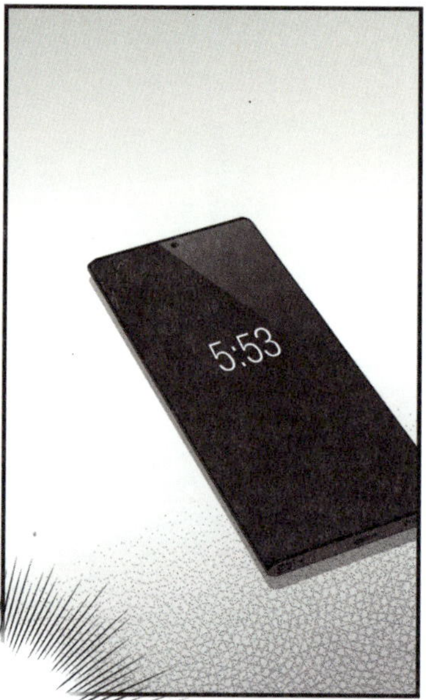
5:53

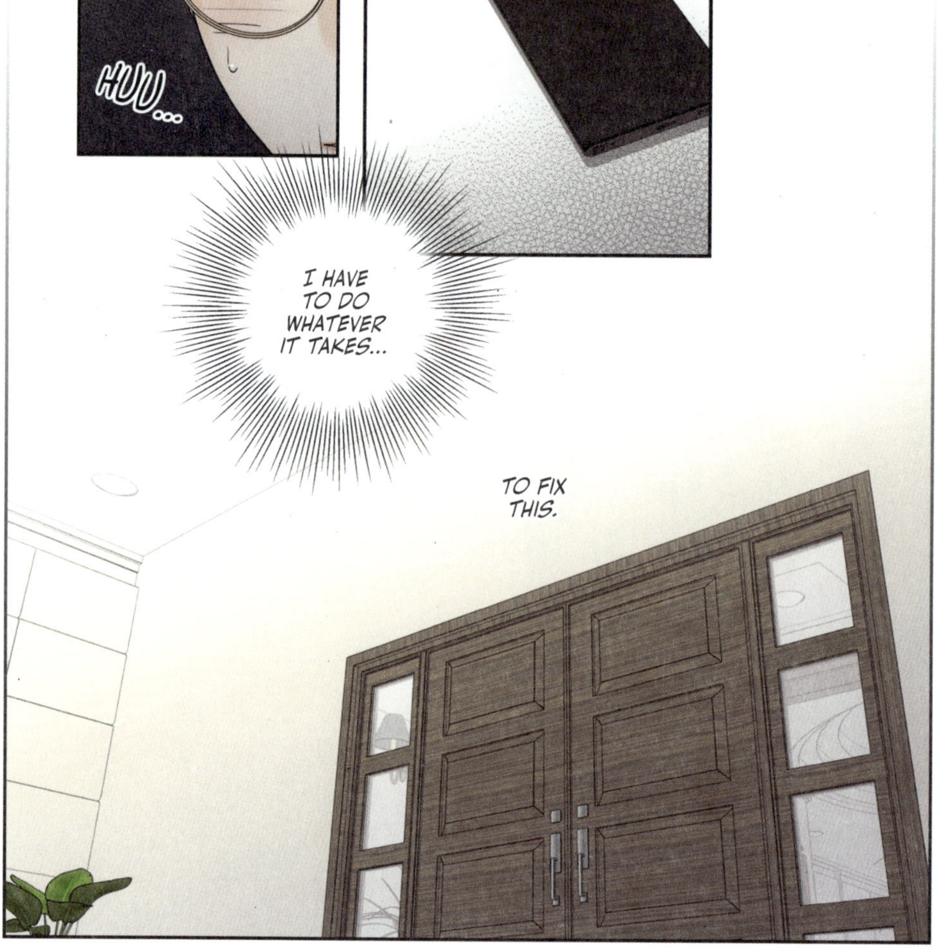
I HAVE TO DO WHATEVER IT TAKES...
TO FIX THIS.

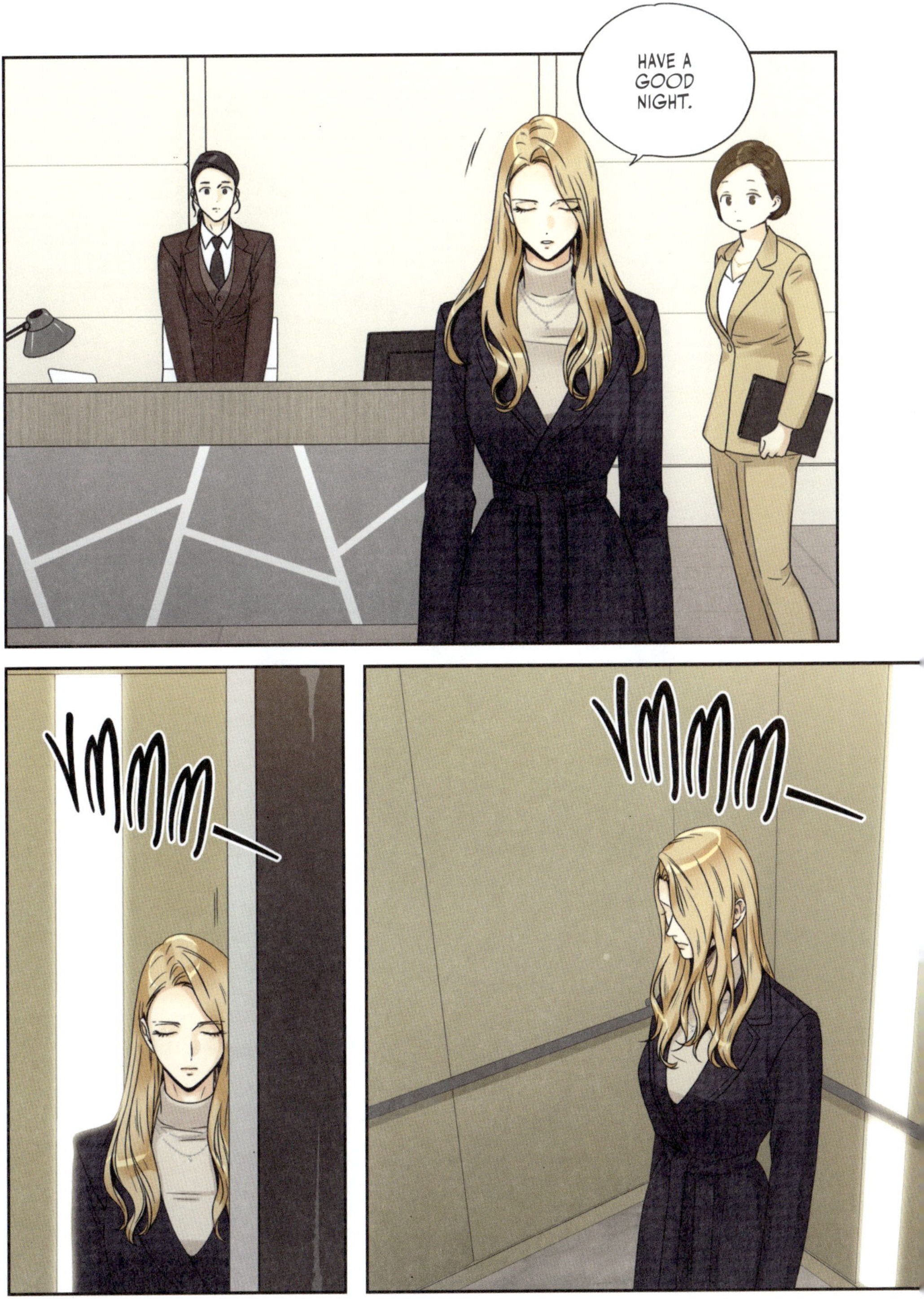
HAVE A GOOD NIGHT.
VMMM—
VMMM—

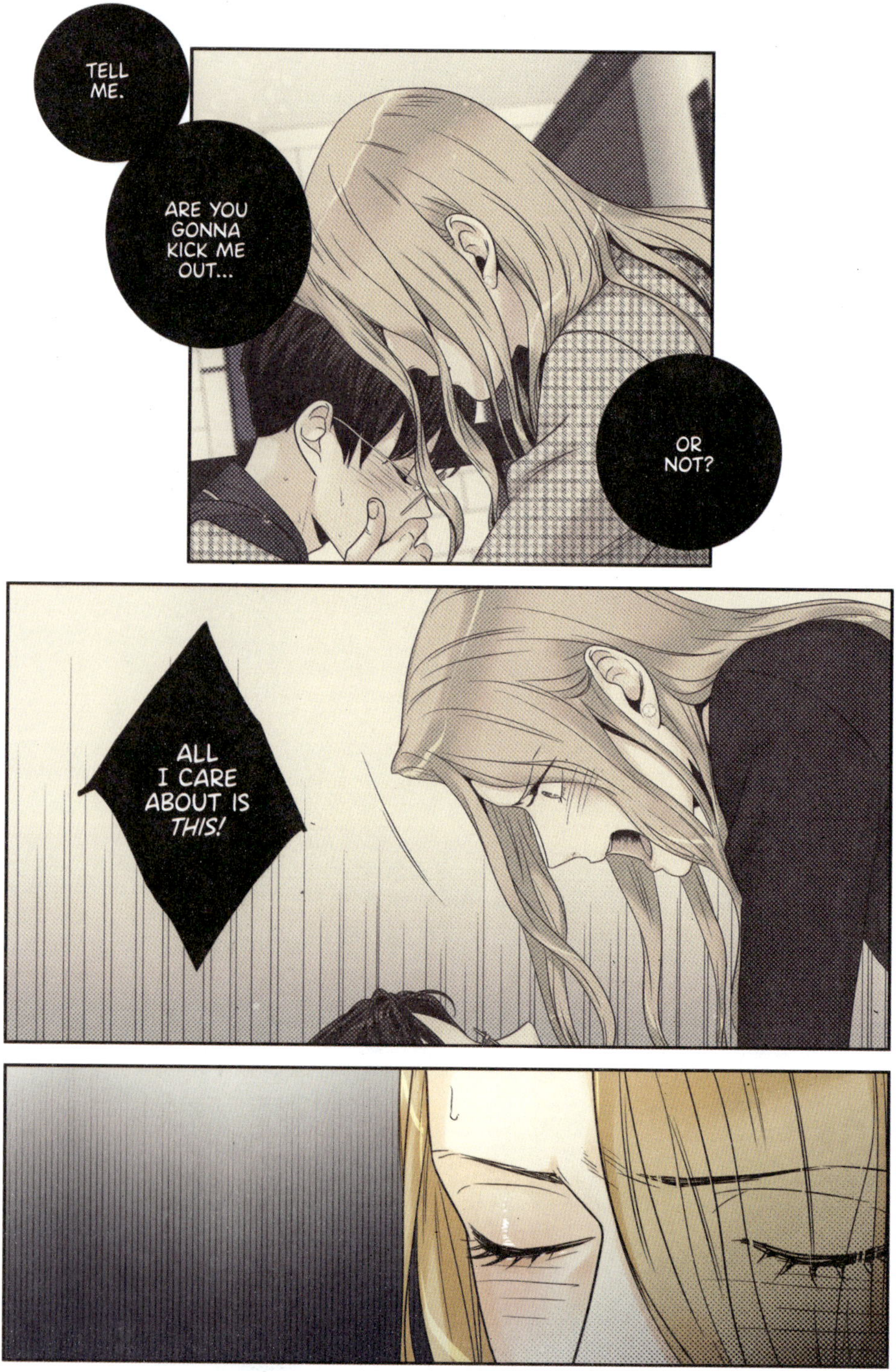
TELL ME.
ARE YOU GONNA KICK ME OUT...
OR NOT?
ALL I CARE ABOUT IS *THIS!*

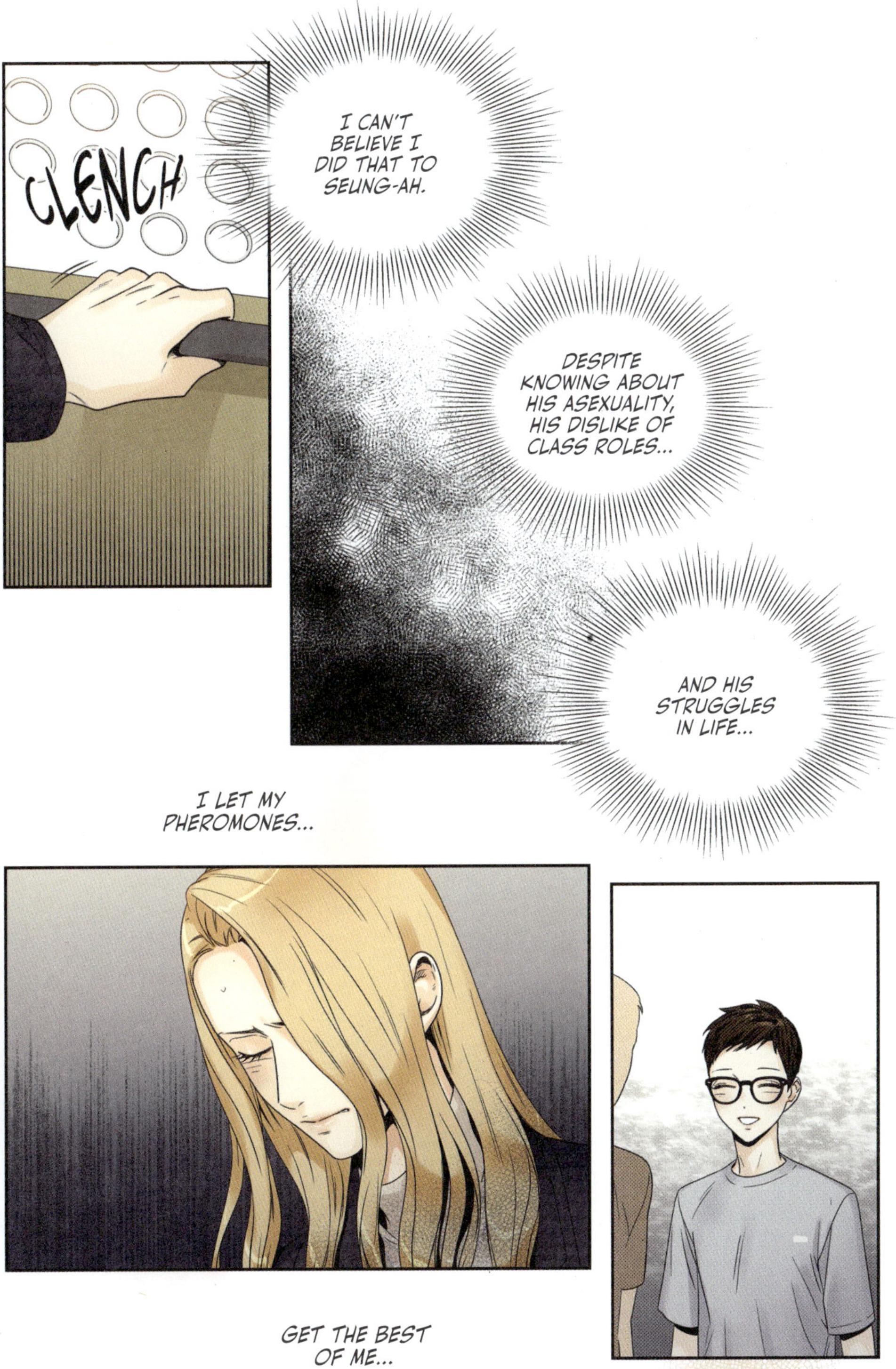
CLENCH
I CAN'T BELIEVE I DID THAT TO SEUNG-AH.
DESPITE KNOWING ABOUT HIS ASEXUALITY, HIS DISLIKE OF CLASS ROLES...
AND HIS STRUGGLES IN LIFE...
I LET MY PHEROMONES...
GET THE BEST OF ME...

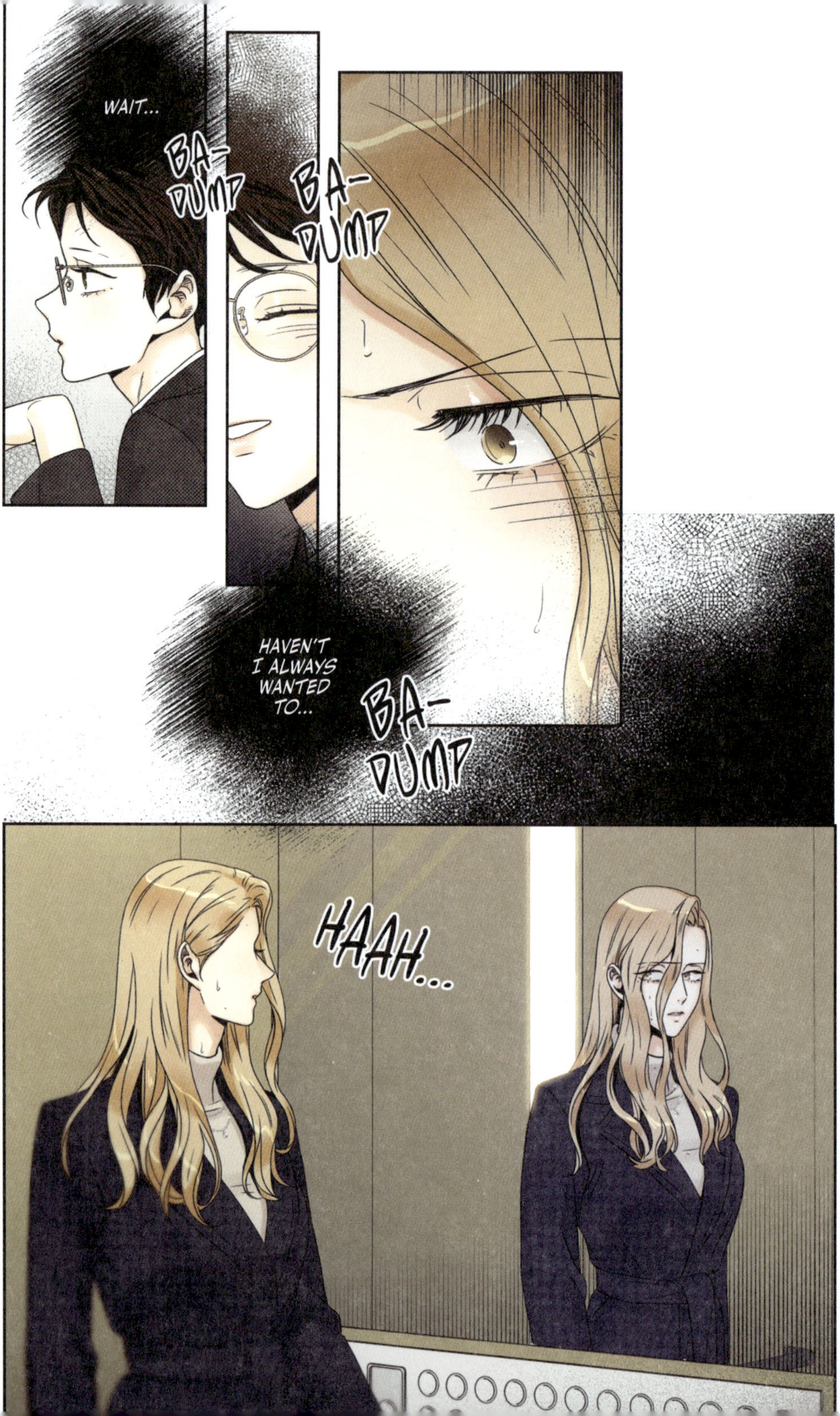
WAIT...
BA-DUMP
BA-DUMP
HAVEN'T I ALWAYS WANTED TO...
BA-DUMP
HAAAH...

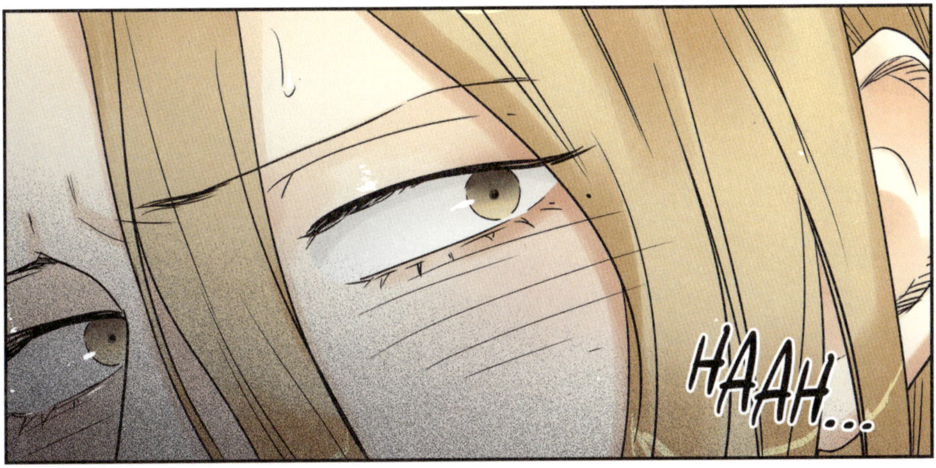
HAAH...
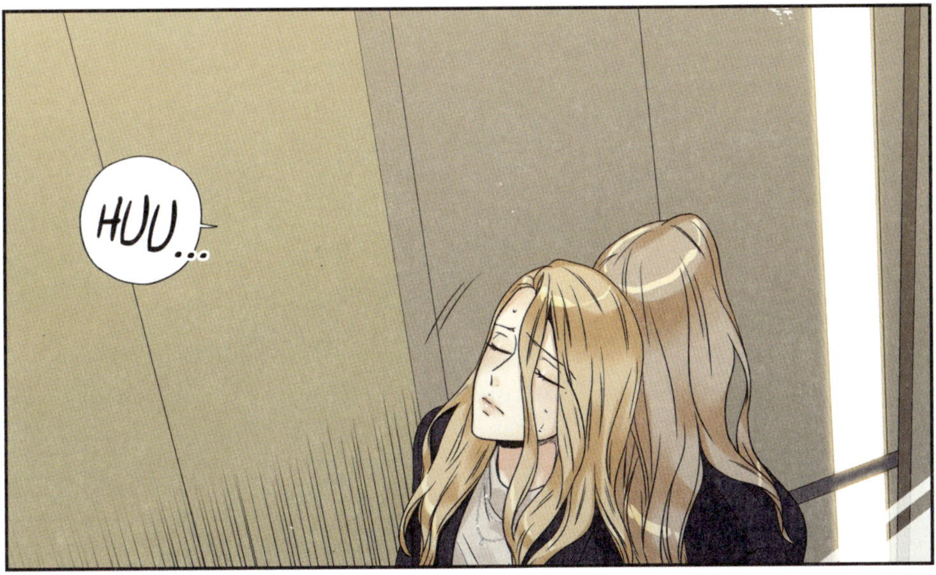
HUU...

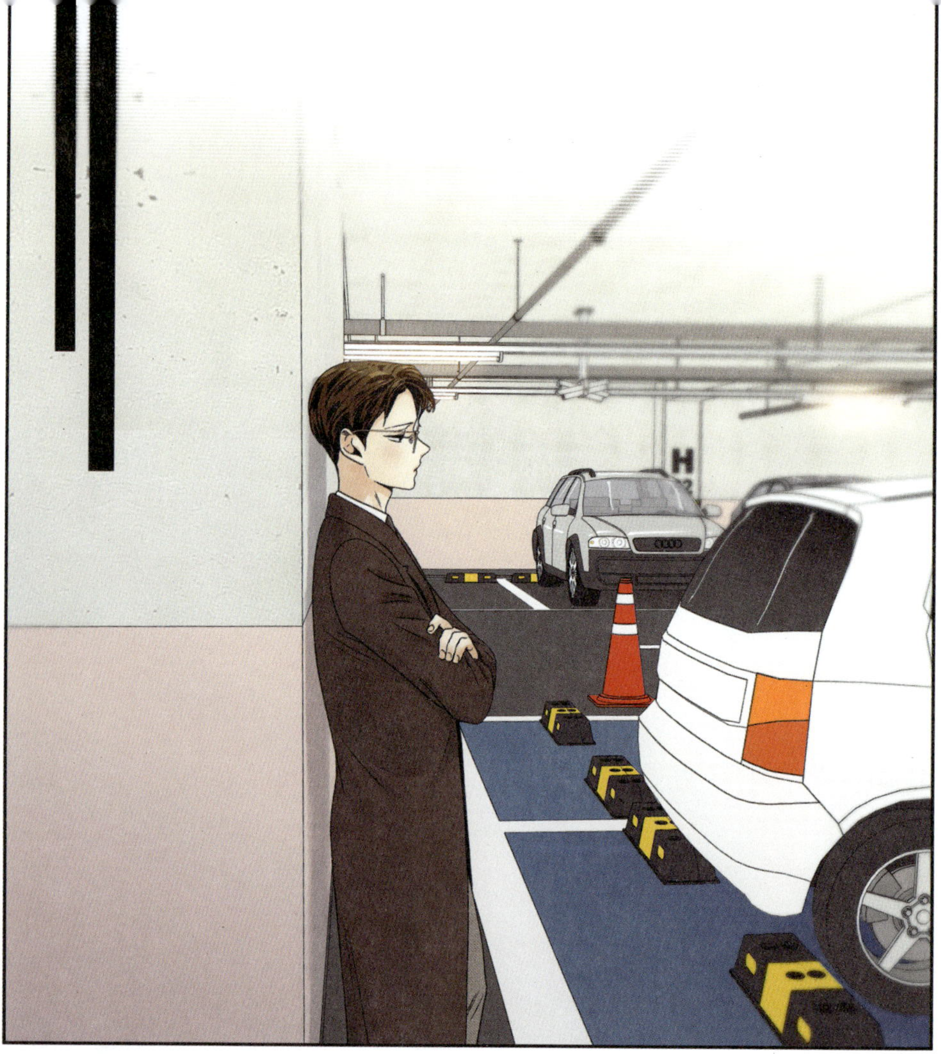

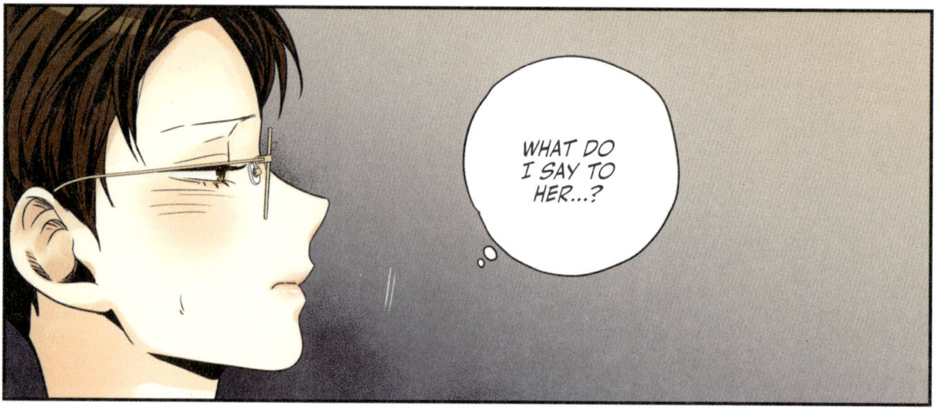
WHAT DO I SAY TO HER...?

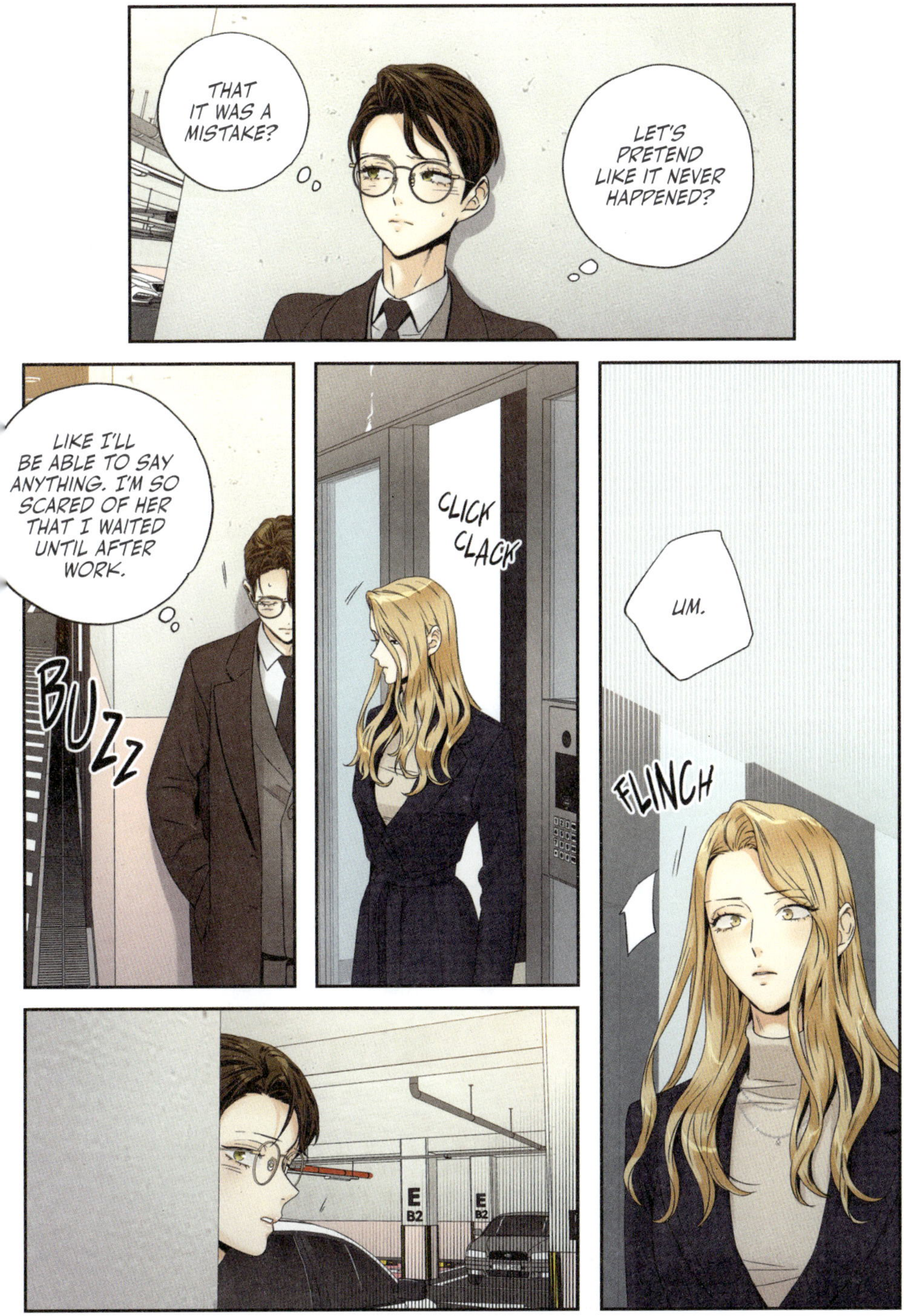
THAT IT WAS A MISTAKE?
LET'S PRETEND LIKE IT NEVER HAPPENED?
LIKE I'LL BE ABLE TO SAY ANYTHING. I'M SO SCARED OF HER THAT I WAITED UNTIL AFTER WORK.
BUZZ
CLICK
CLACK
UM.
FLINCH
E
B2
E
B2

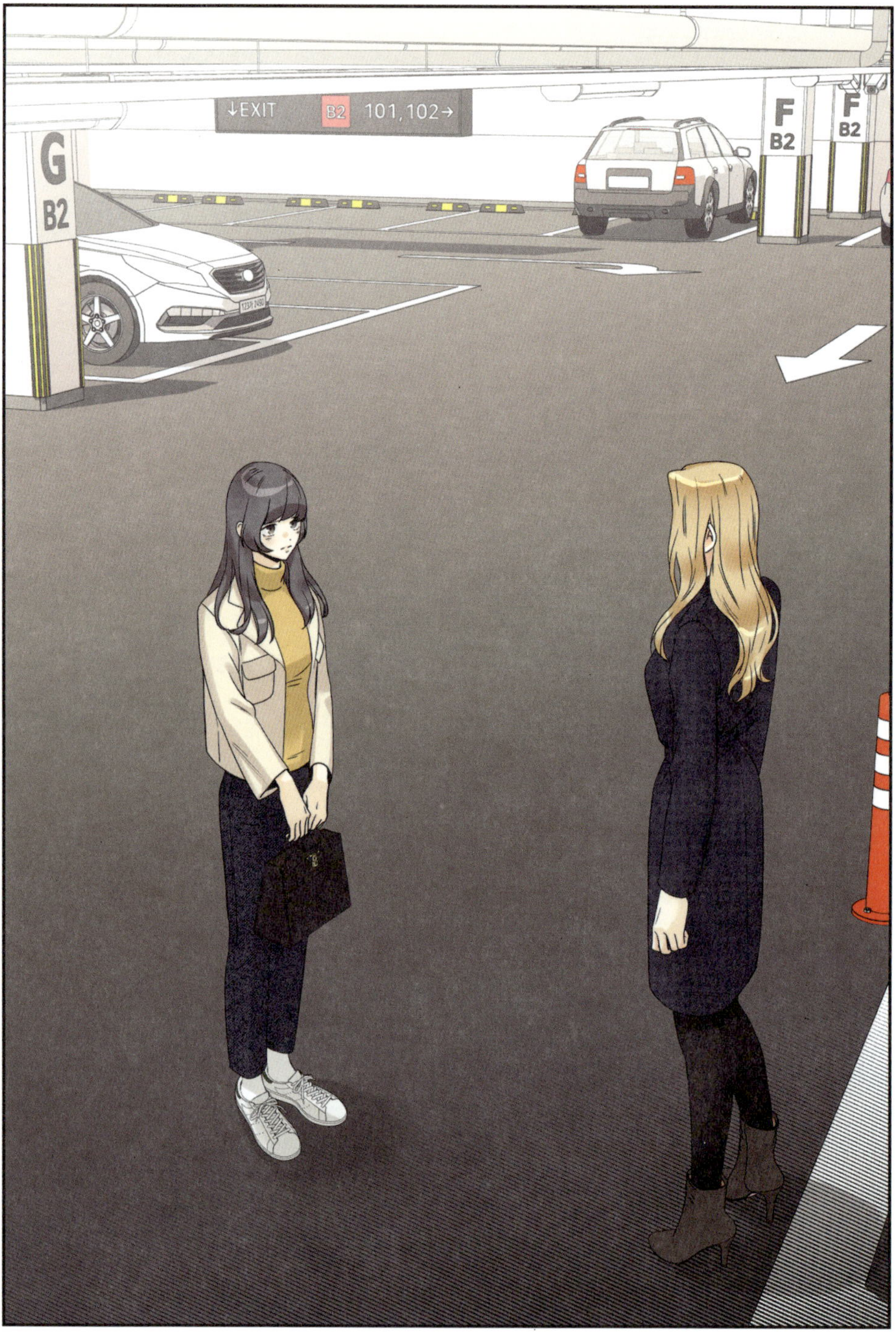
↓EXIT
B2 101,102→
G
B2
F
B2
F
B2

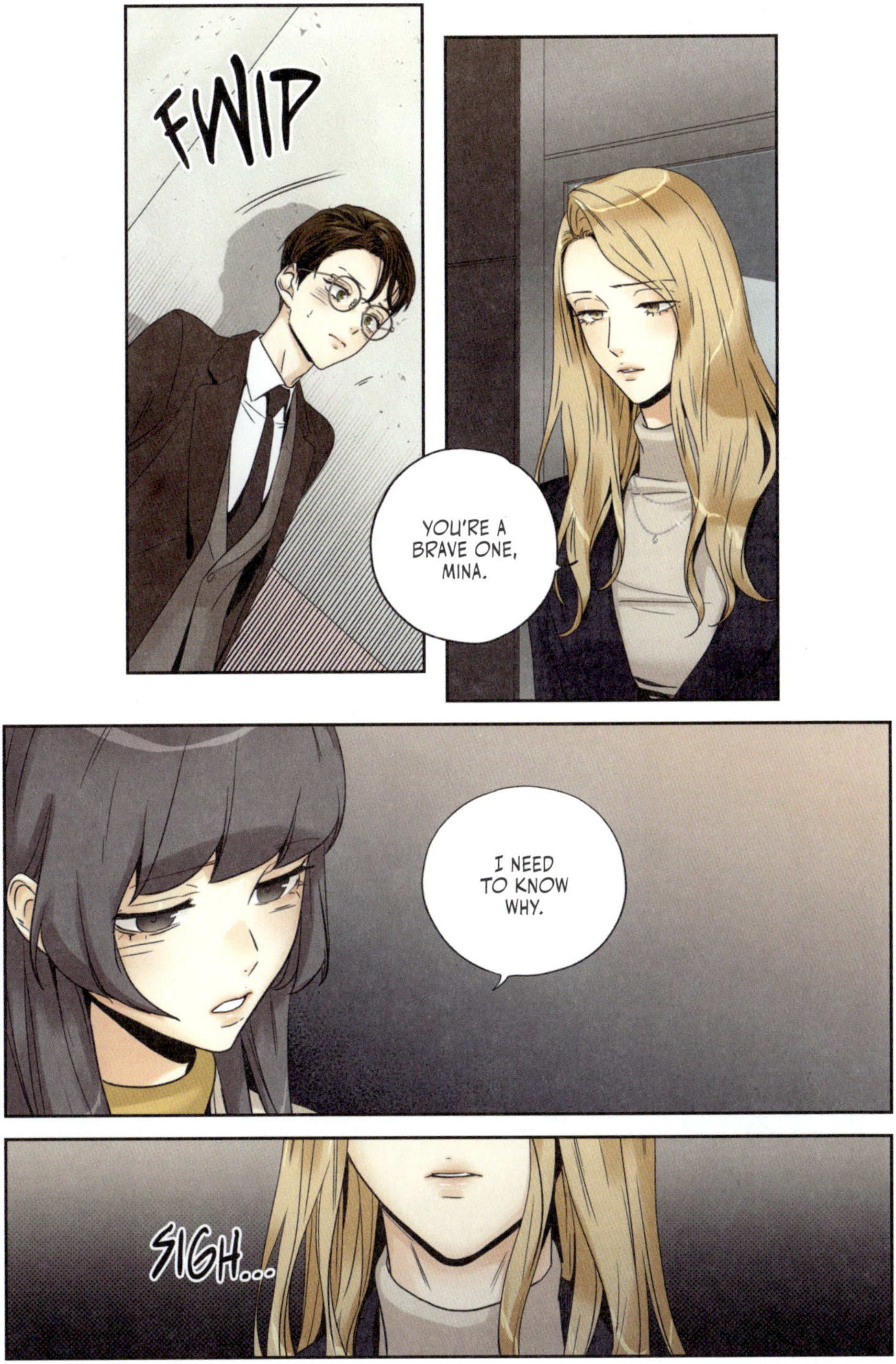
FWIP
YOU'RE A BRAVE ONE, MINA.
I NEED TO KNOW WHY.
SIGH...

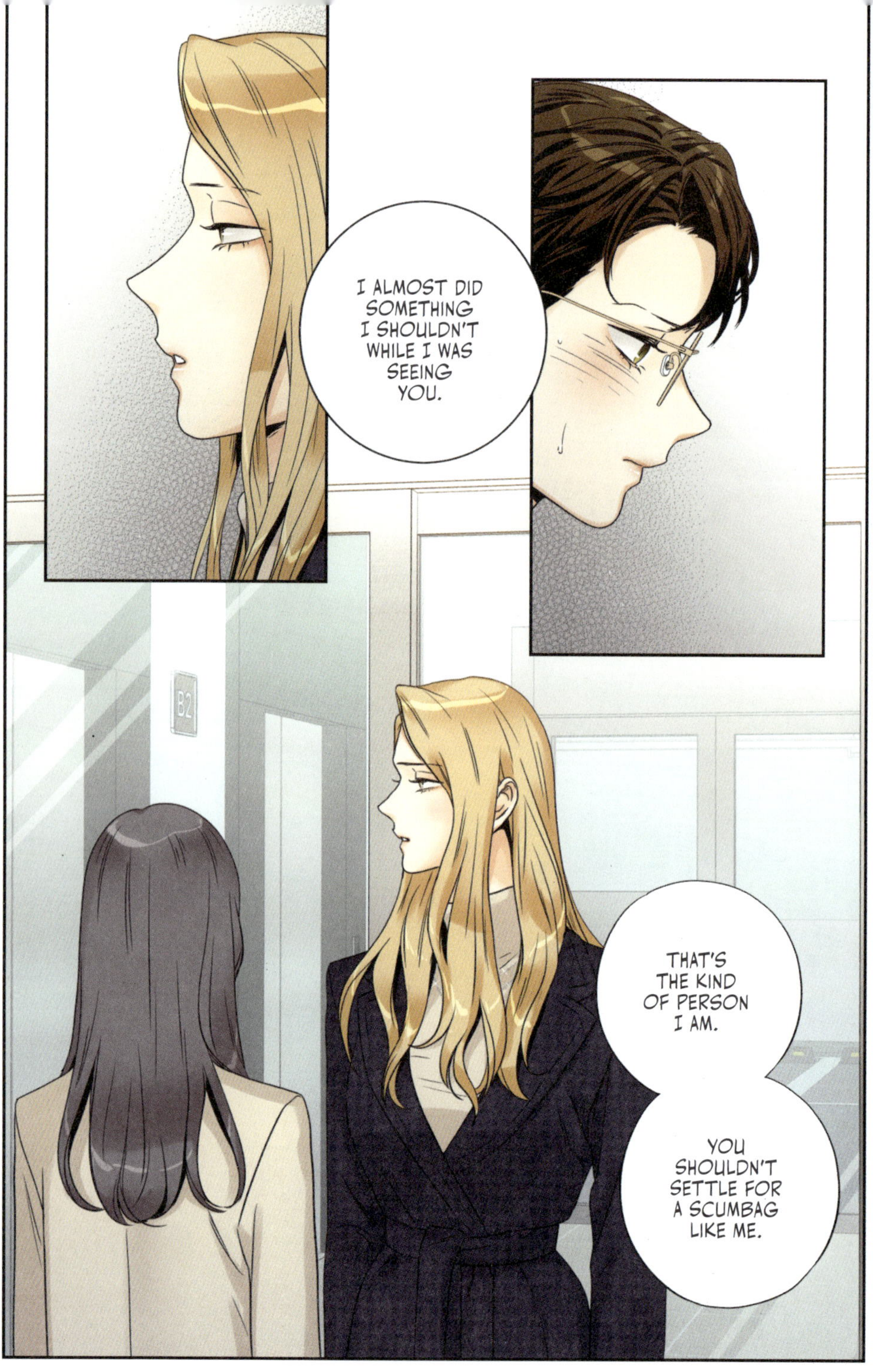
I ALMOST DID SOMETHING I SHOULDN'T WHILE I WAS SEEING YOU.
THAT'S THE KIND OF PERSON I AM.
YOU SHOULDN'T SETTLE FOR A SCUMBAG LIKE ME.

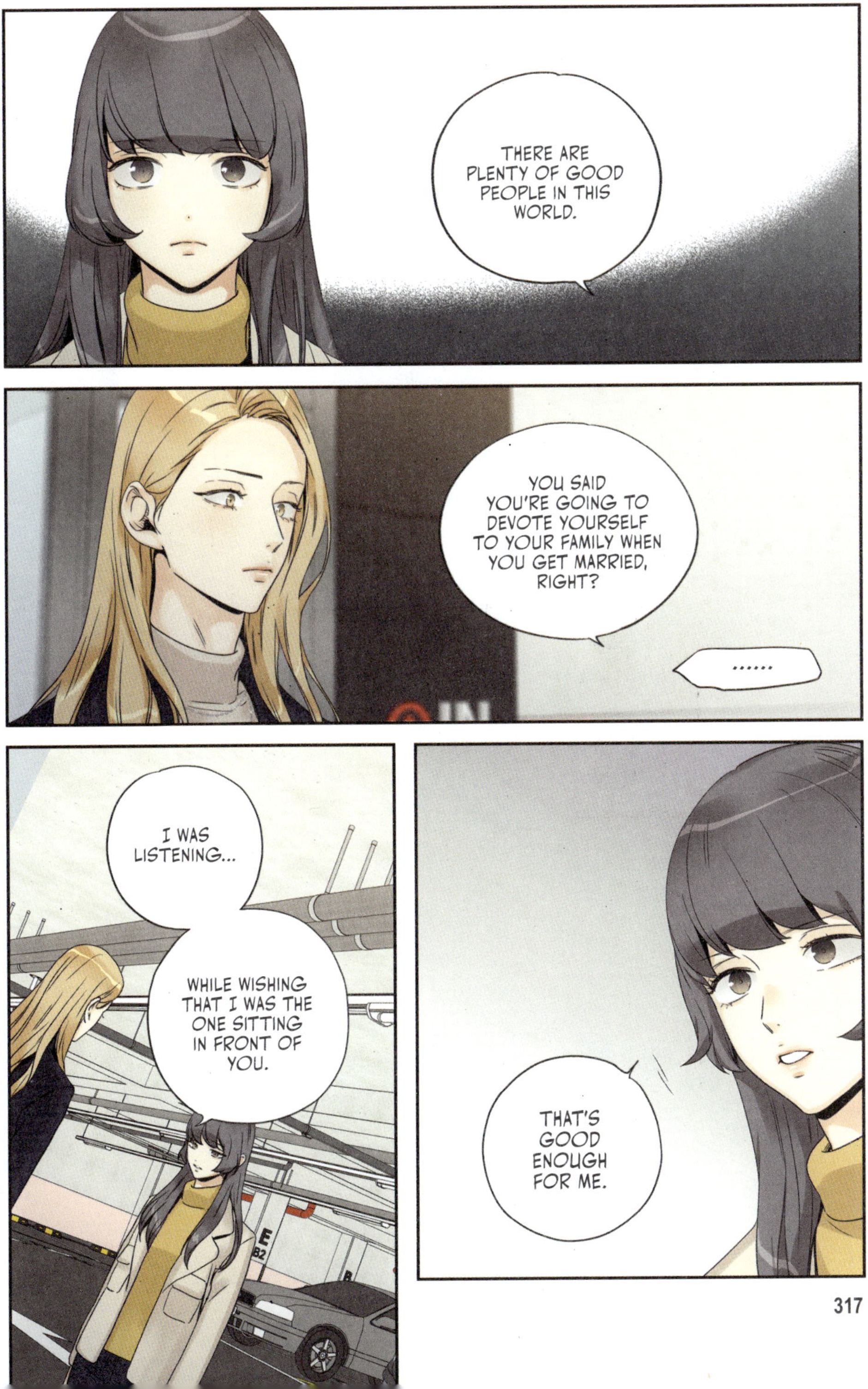
THERE ARE PLENTY OF GOOD PEOPLE IN THIS WORLD.
YOU SAID YOU'RE GOING TO DEVOTE YOURSELF TO YOUR FAMILY WHEN YOU GET MARRIED, RIGHT?
......
I WAS LISTENING...
WHILE WISHING THAT I WAS THE ONE SITTING IN FRONT OF YOU.
THAT'S GOOD ENOUGH FOR ME.

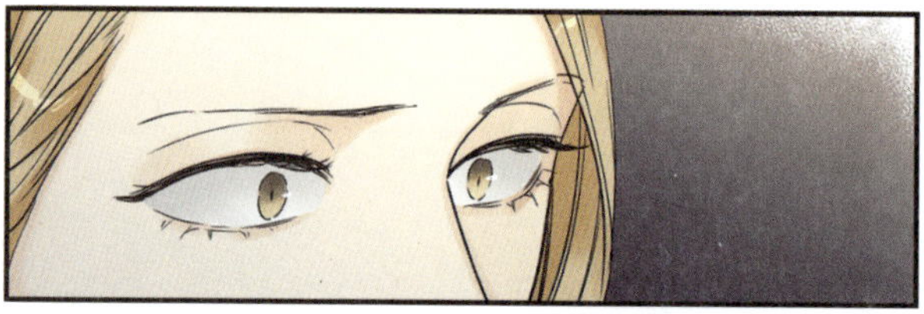

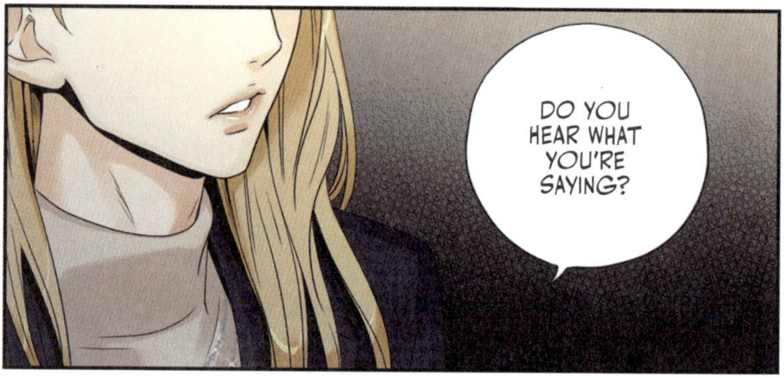
DO YOU HEAR WHAT YOU'RE SAYING?

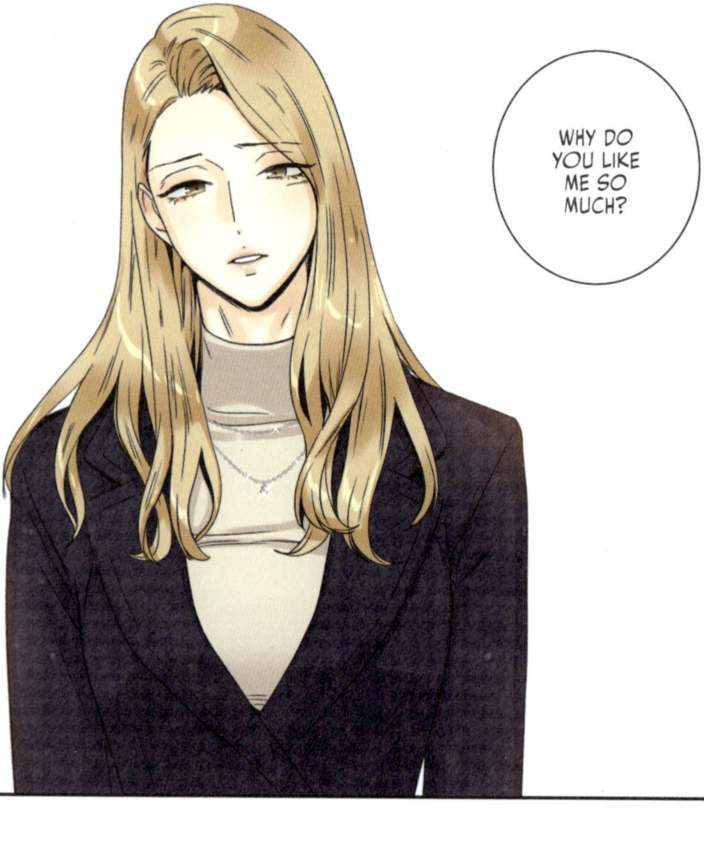
WHY DO YOU LIKE ME SO MUCH?

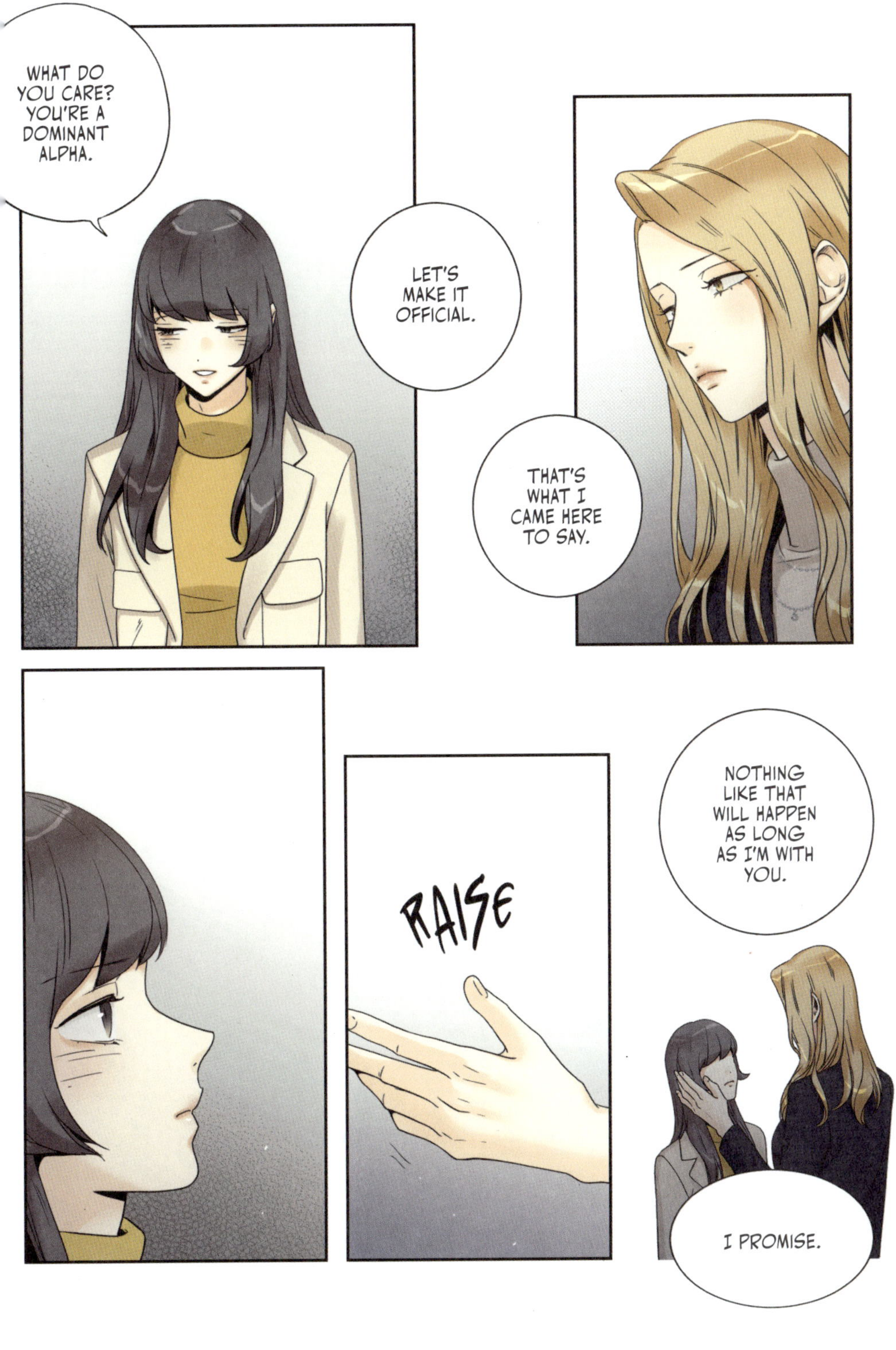
WHAT DO YOU CARE? YOU'RE A DOMINANT ALPHA.
LET'S MAKE IT OFFICIAL.
THAT'S WHAT I CAME HERE TO SAY.
RAISE
NOTHING LIKE THAT WILL HAPPEN AS LONG AS I'M WITH YOU.
I PROMISE.

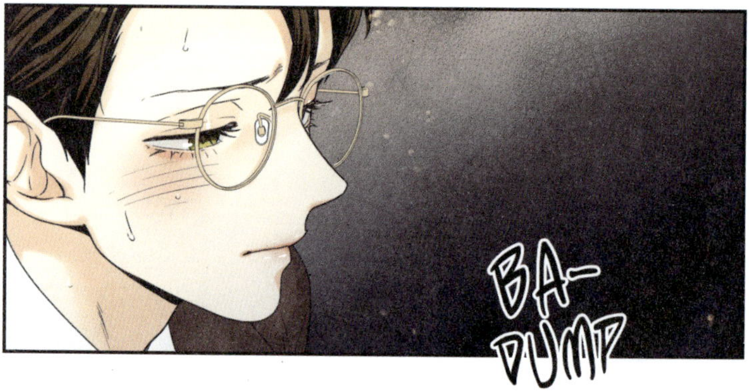
BA-
DUMP
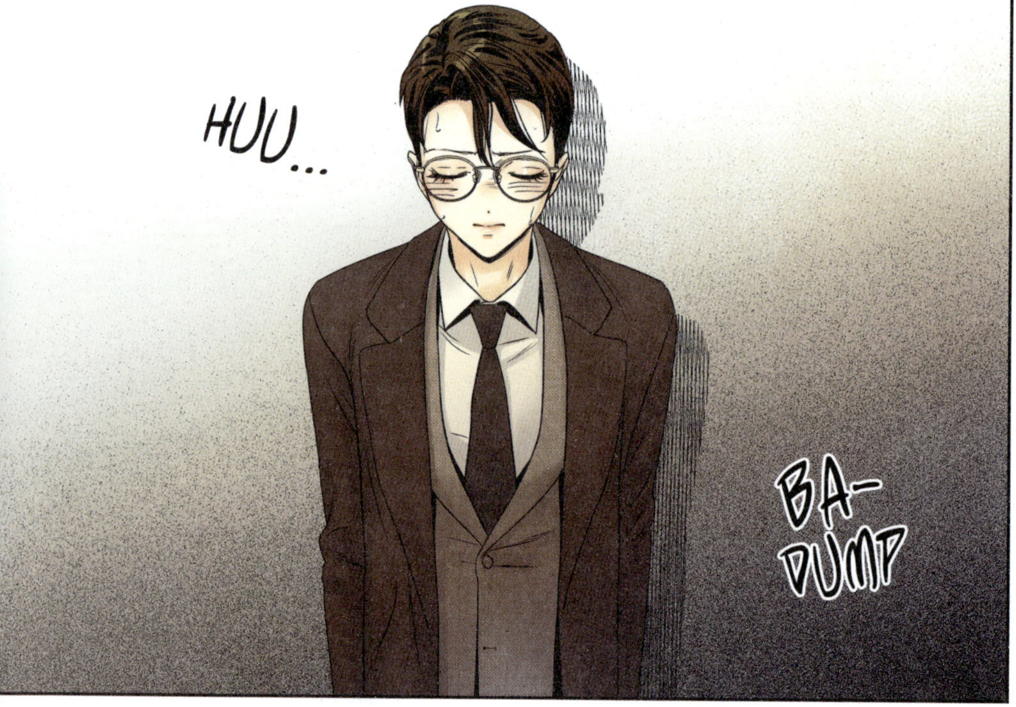
HUU...
BA-
DUMP

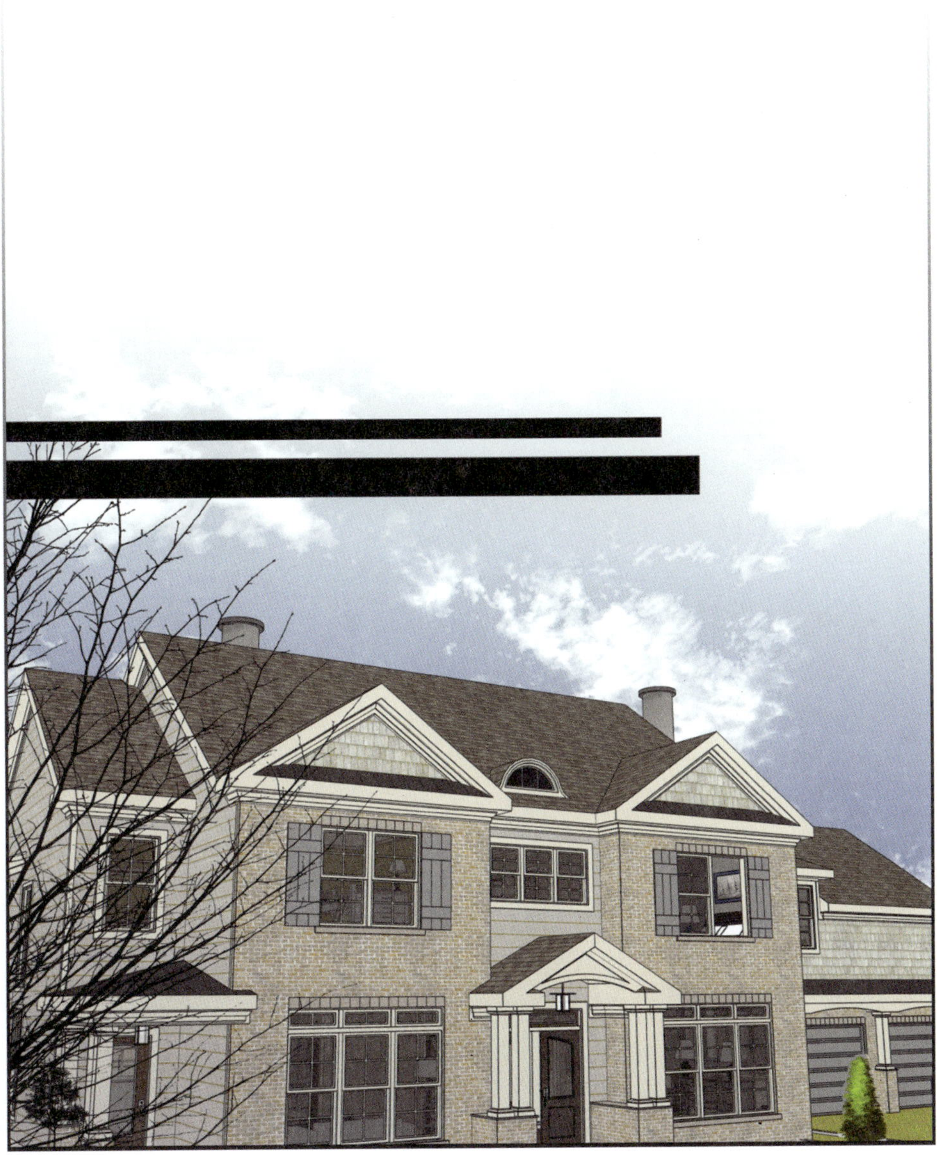

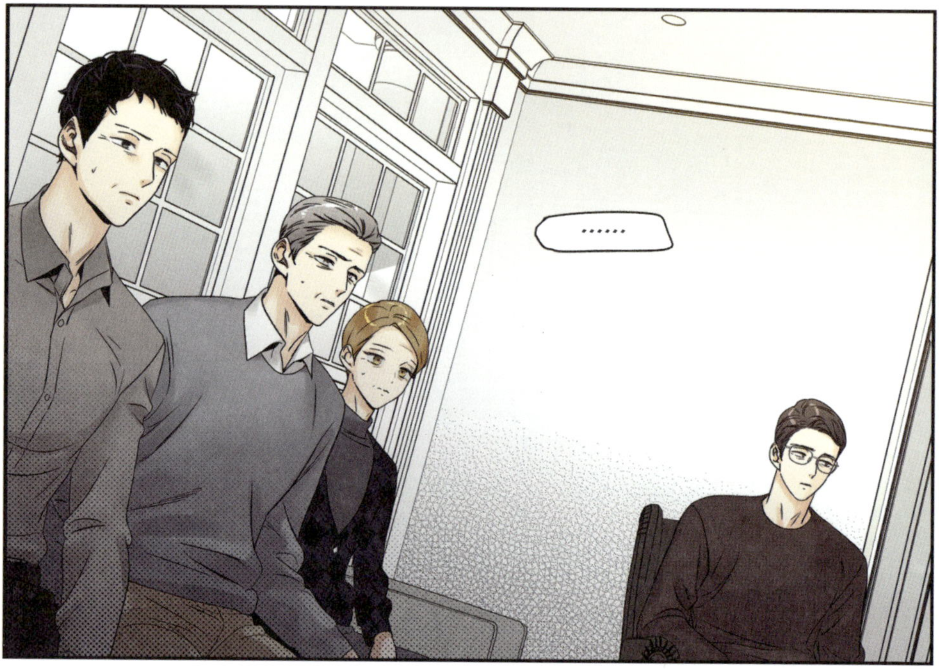
......
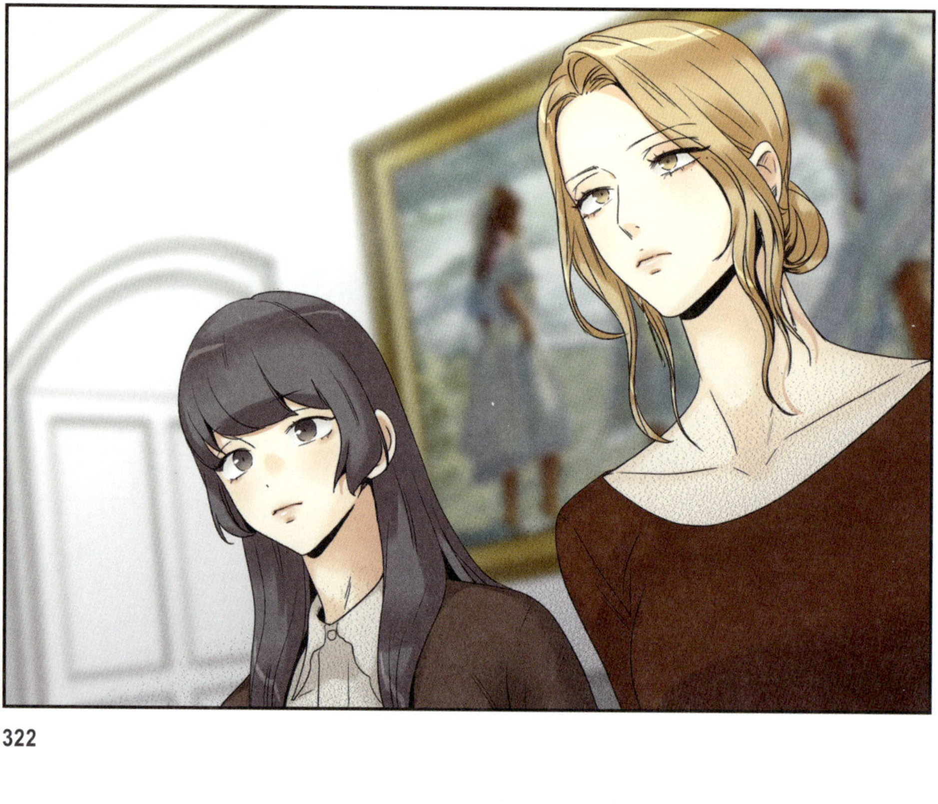

Love is an Illusion!
The Queen

Love is an Illusion! The Queen

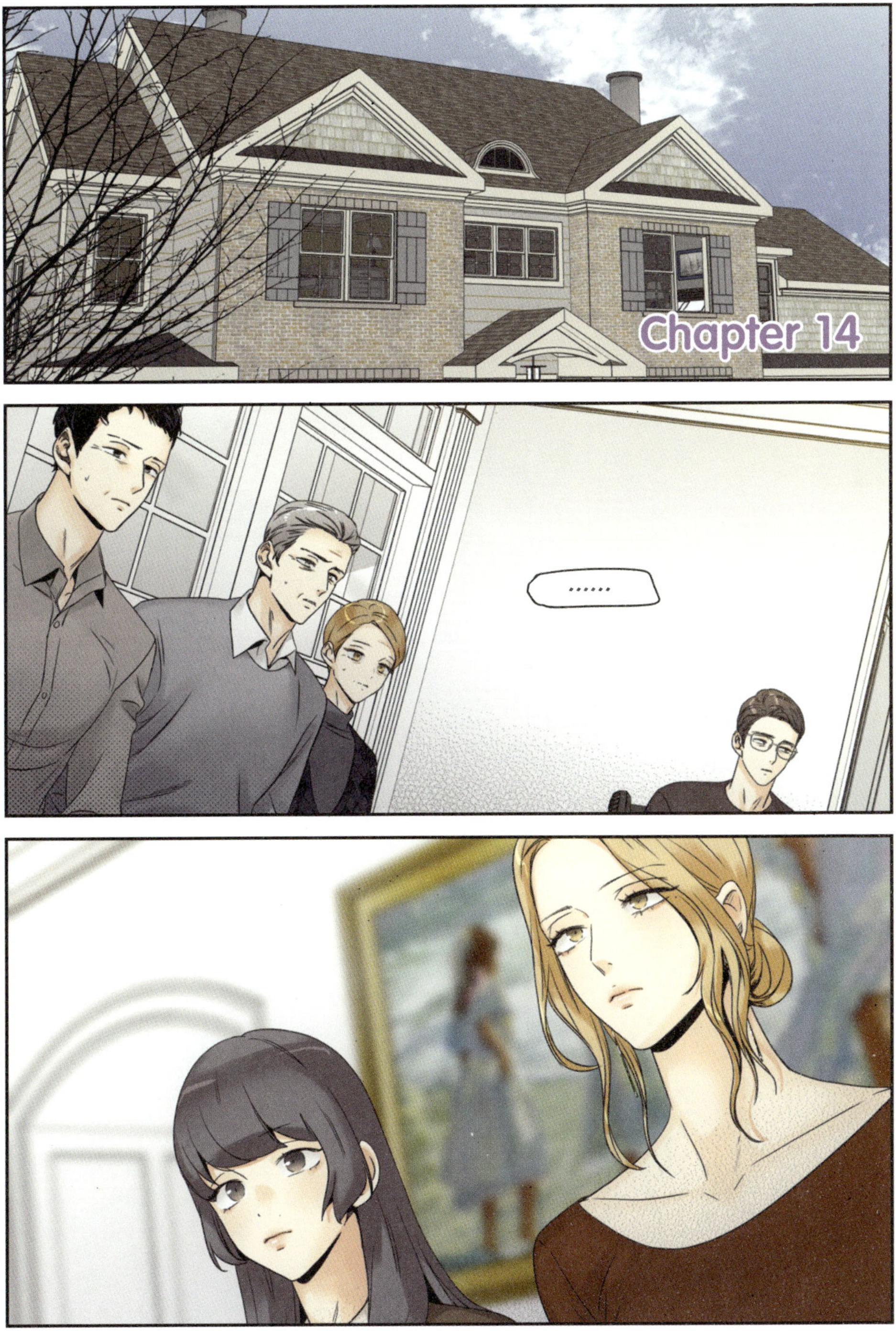
Chapter 14
......

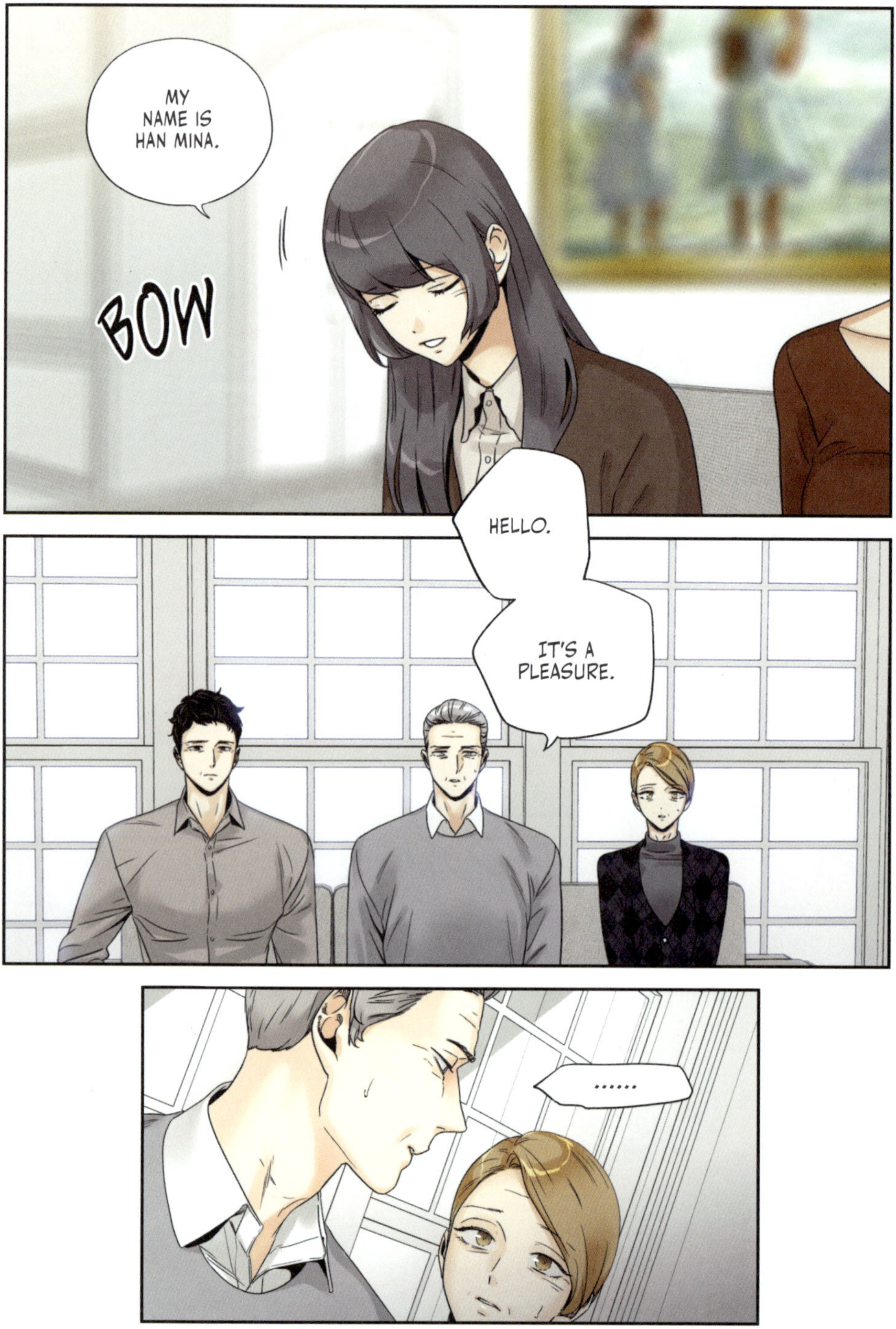
MY NAME IS HAN MINA.
BOW
HELLO.
IT'S A PLEASURE.
......

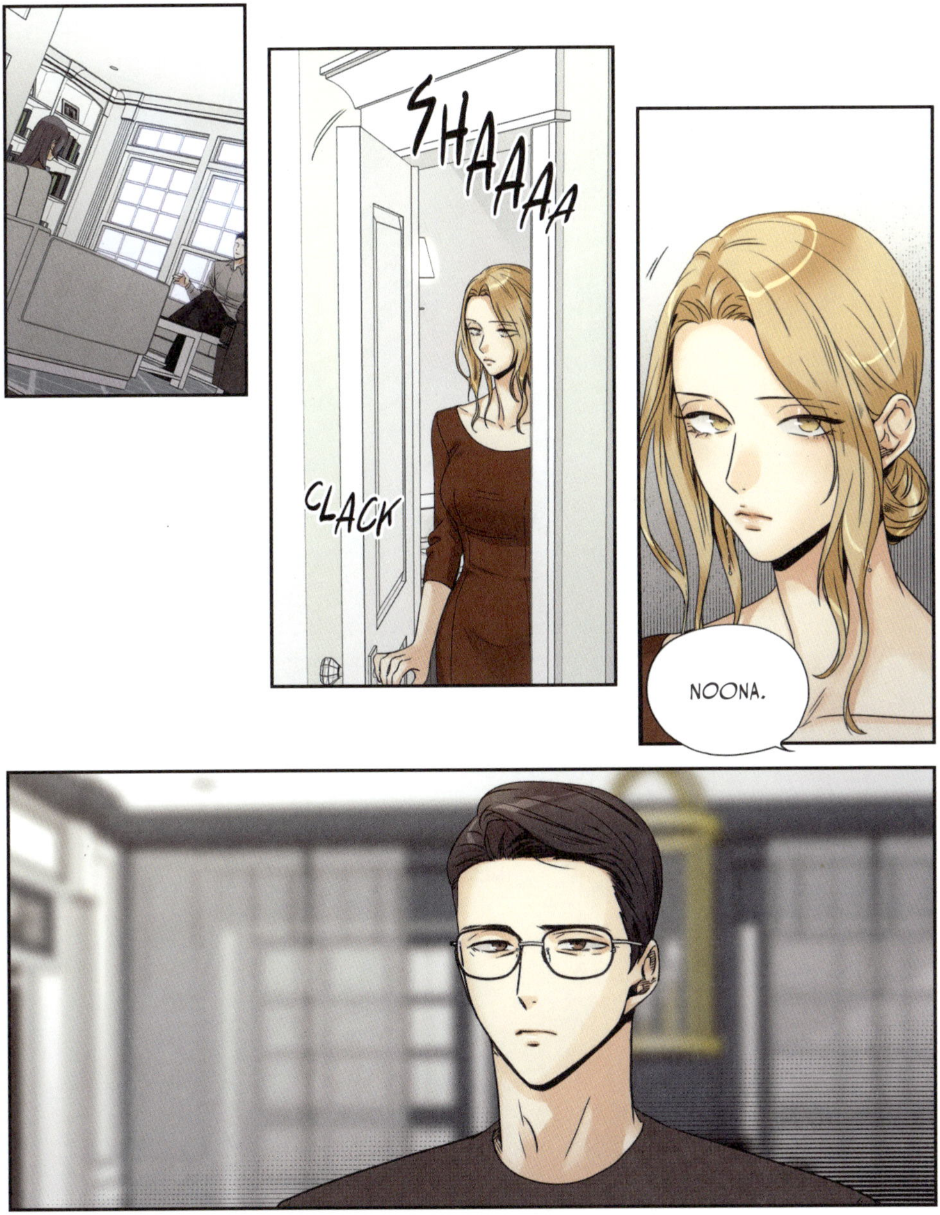
SHAAAAA
CLACK
NOONA.

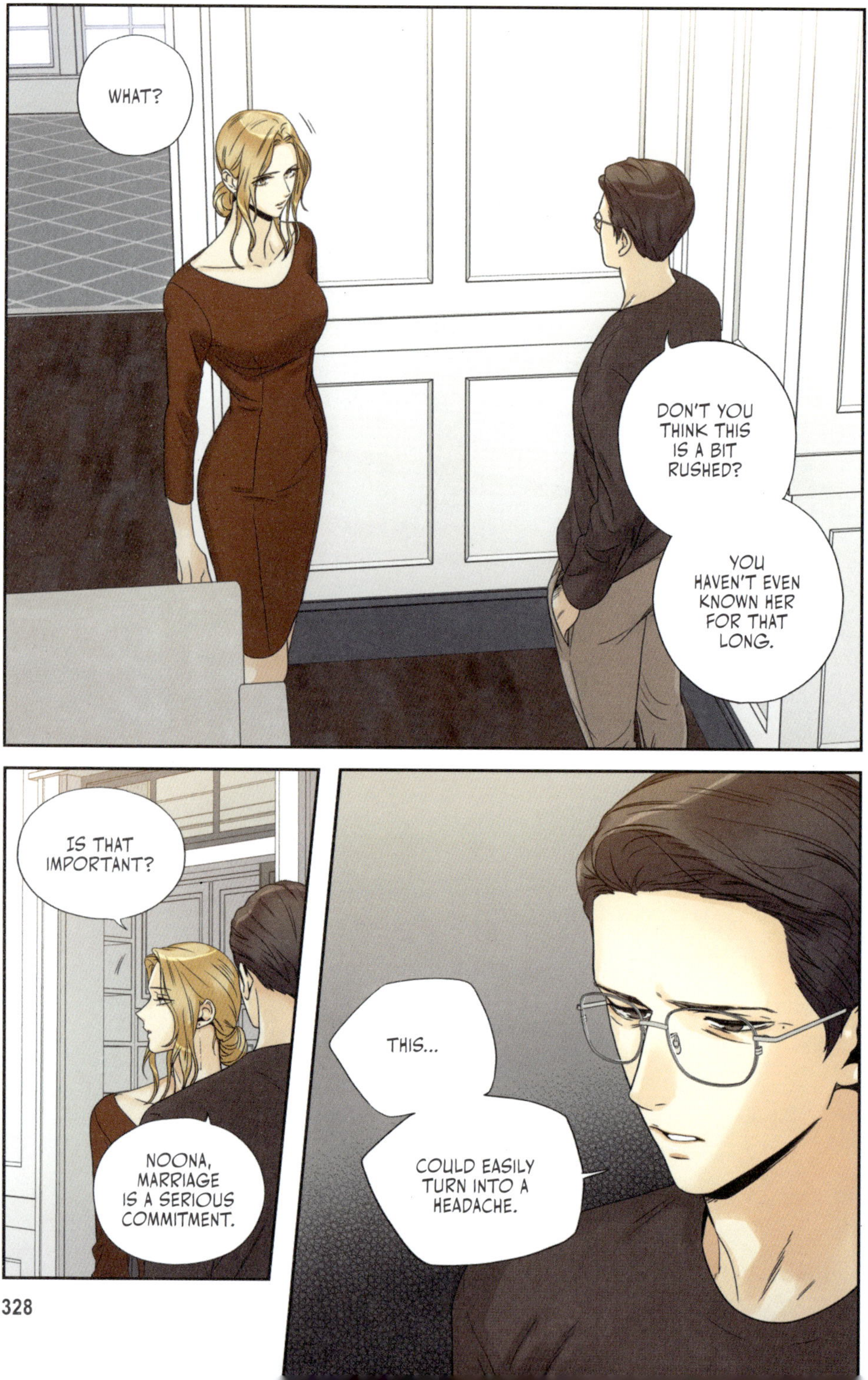
WHAT?
DON'T YOU THINK THIS IS A BIT RUSHED?
YOU HAVEN'T EVEN KNOWN HER FOR THAT LONG.
IS THAT IMPORTANT?
NOONA, MARRIAGE IS A SERIOUS COMMITMENT.
THIS...
COULD EASILY TURN INTO A HEADACHE.

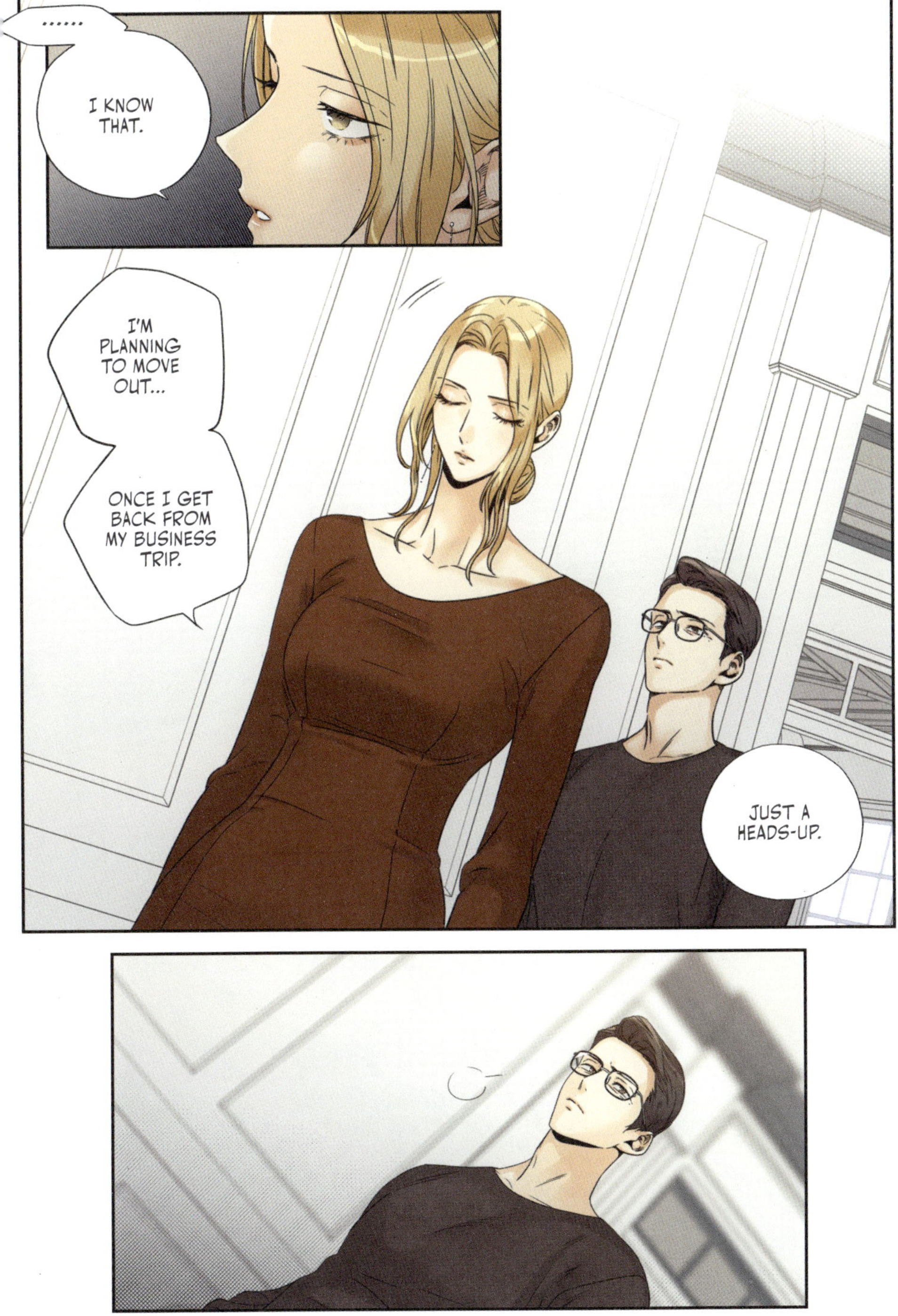
......
I KNOW THAT.
I'M PLANNING TO MOVE OUT...
ONCE I GET BACK FROM MY BUSINESS TRIP.
JUST A HEADS-UP.

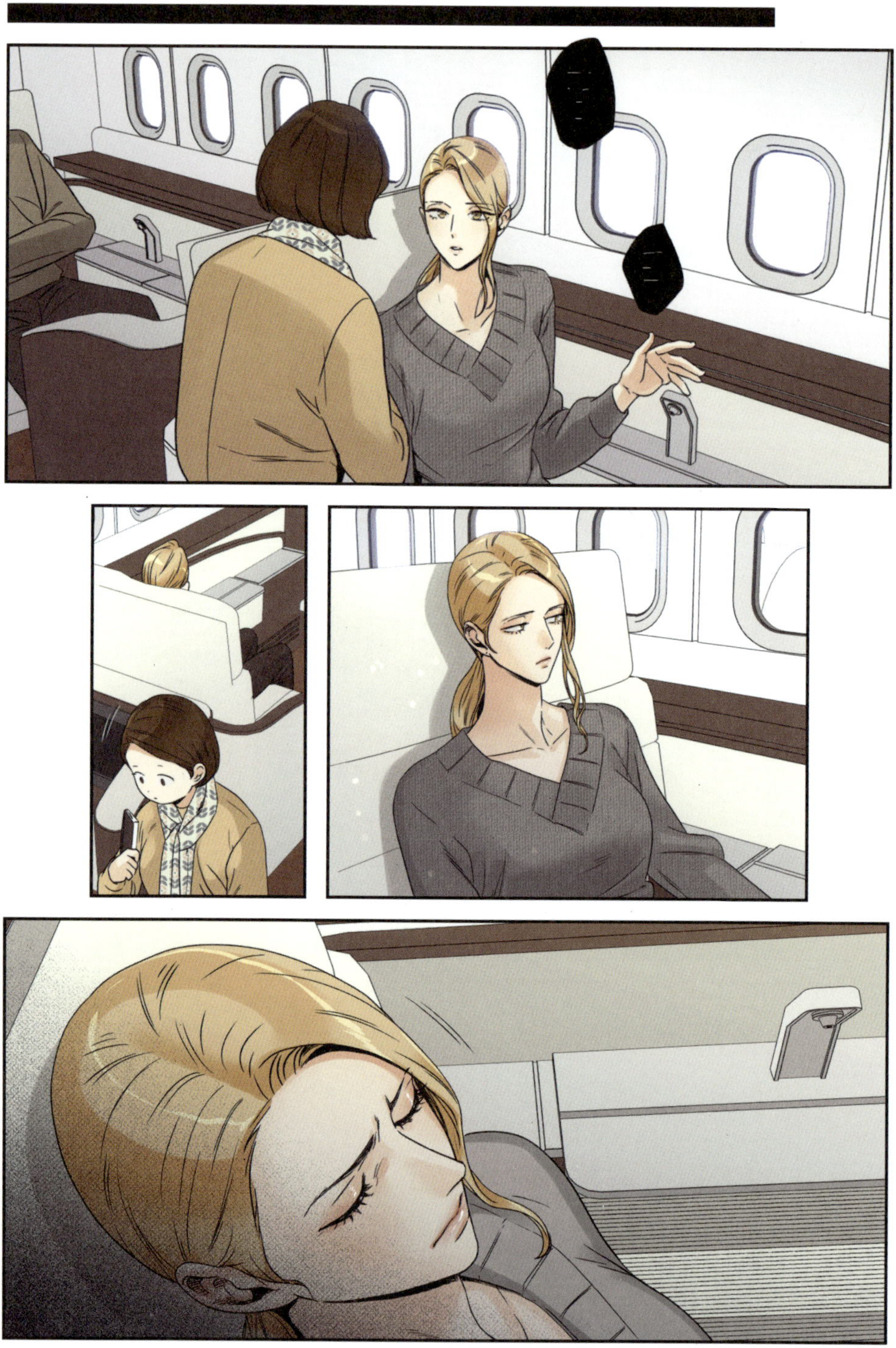

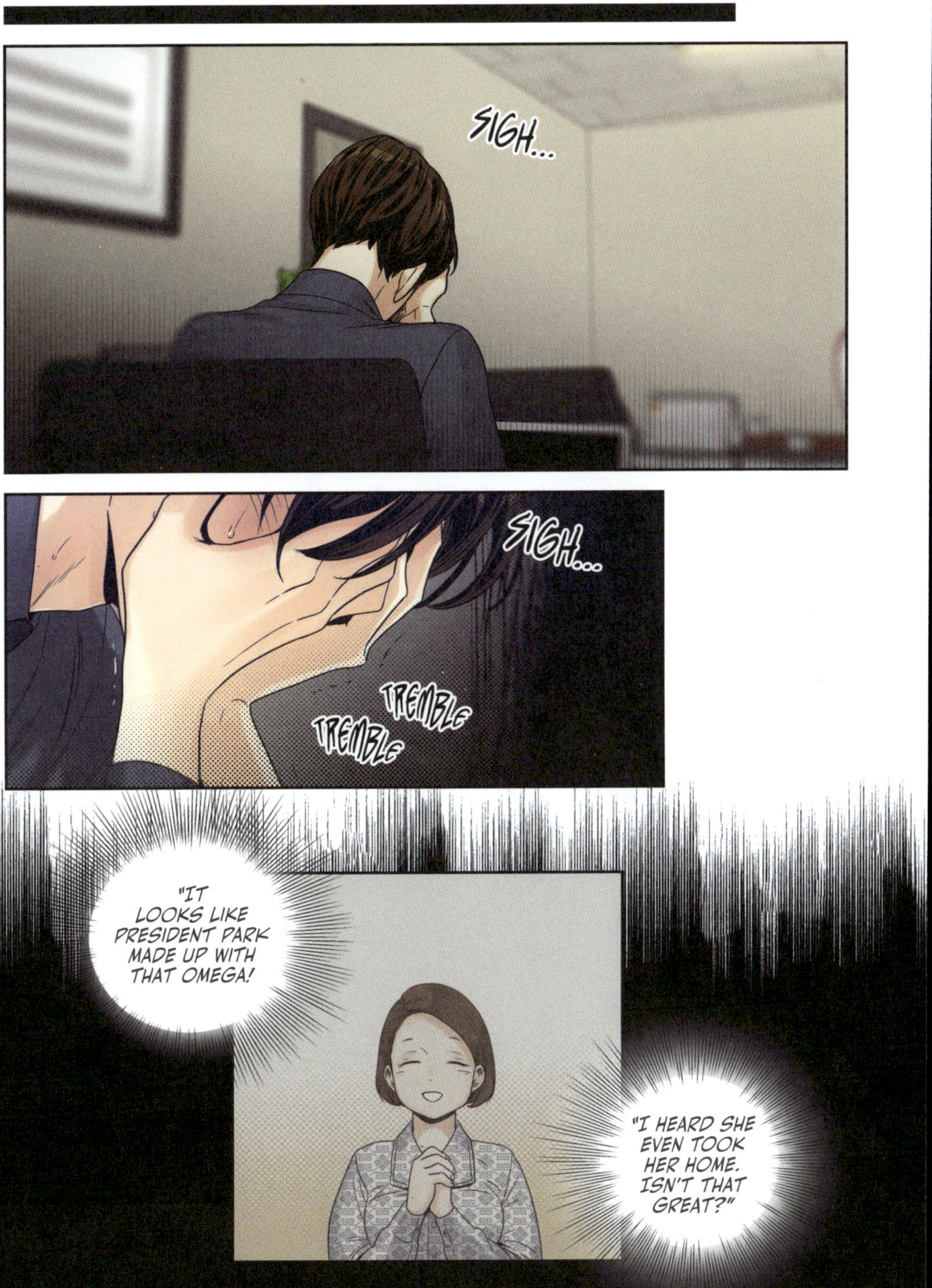
SIGH...
SIGH...
TREMBLE
TREMBLE
"IT LOOKS LIKE PRESIDENT PARK MADE UP WITH THAT OMEGA!
"I HEARD SHE EVEN TOOK HER HOME. ISN'T THAT GREAT?"

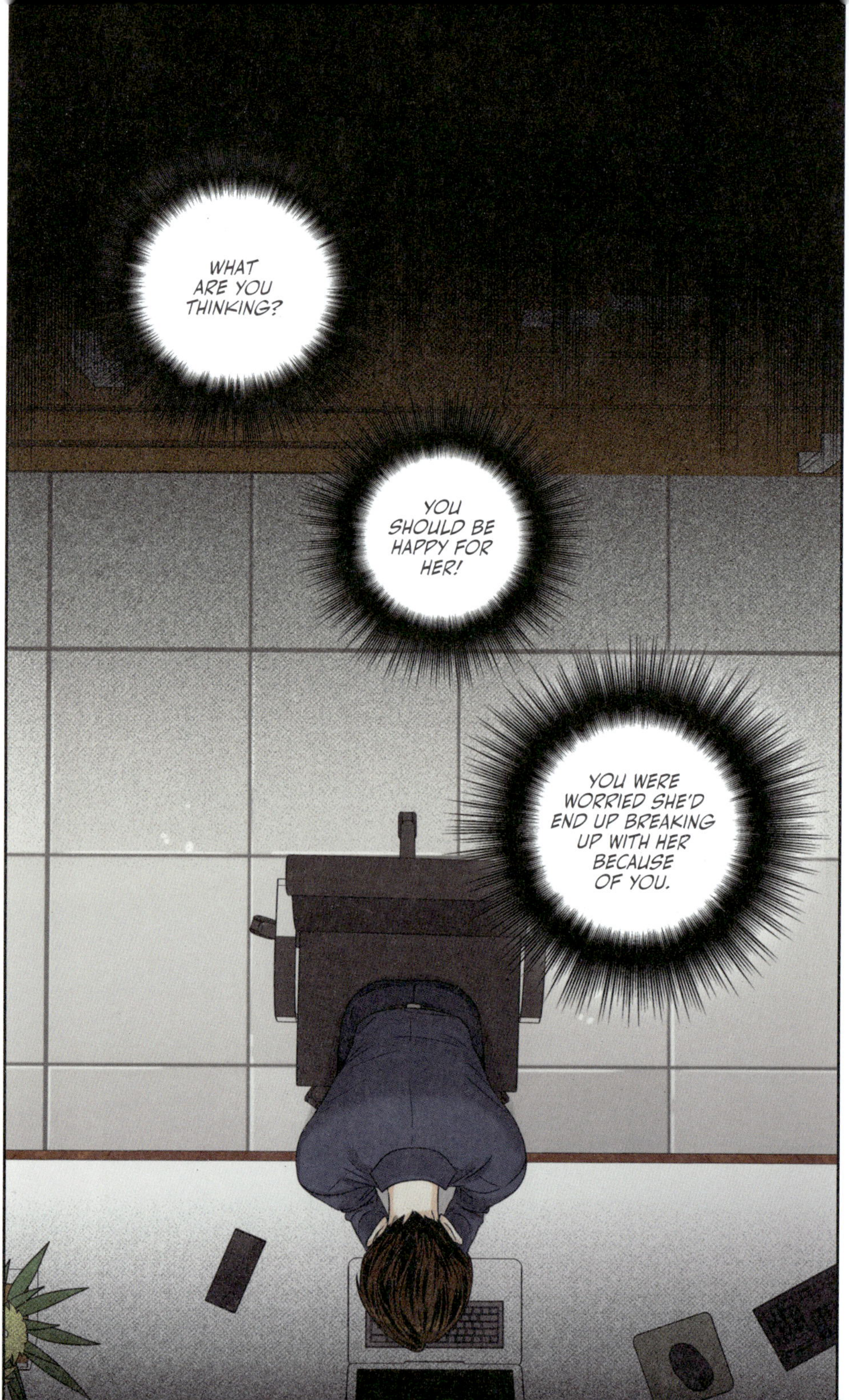
WHAT ARE YOU THINKING?
YOU SHOULD BE HAPPY FOR HER!
YOU WERE WORRIED SHE'D END UP BREAKING UP WITH HER BECAUSE OF YOU.

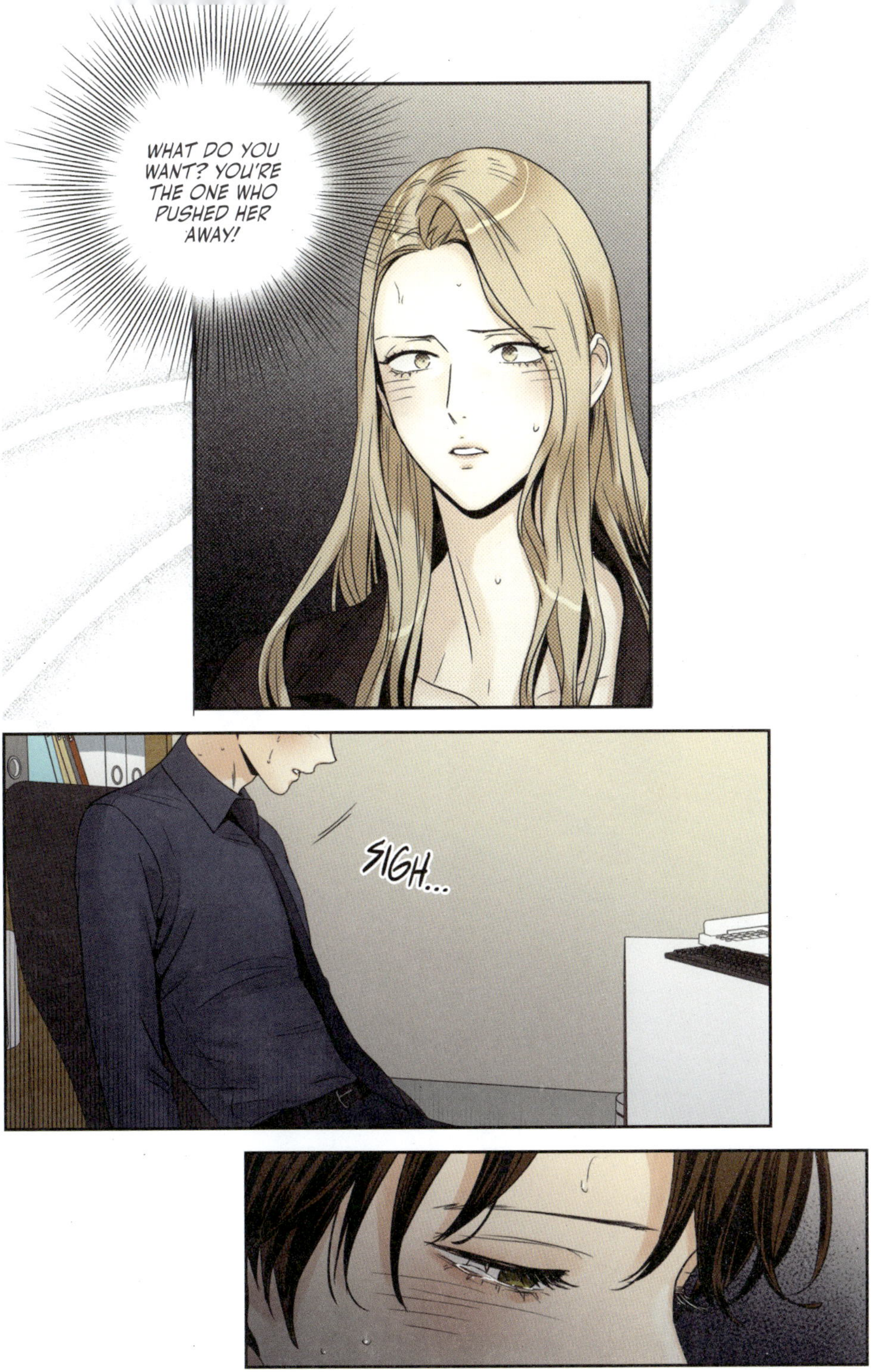
WHAT DO YOU WANT? YOU'RE THE ONE WHO PUSHED HER AWAY!
SIGH...

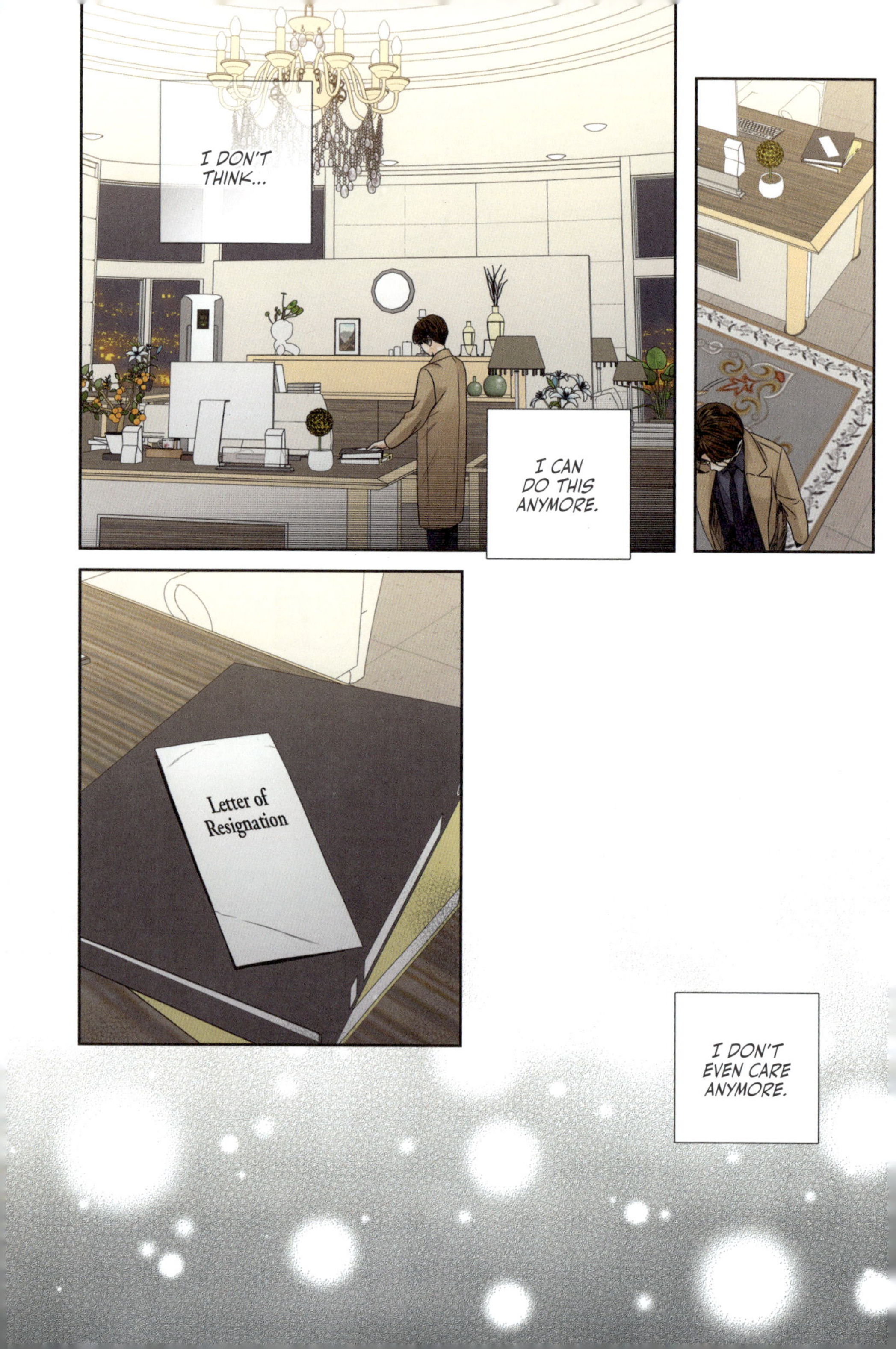
I DON'T THINK...
I CAN DO THIS ANYMORE.
Letter of Resignation
I DON'T EVEN CARE ANYMORE.

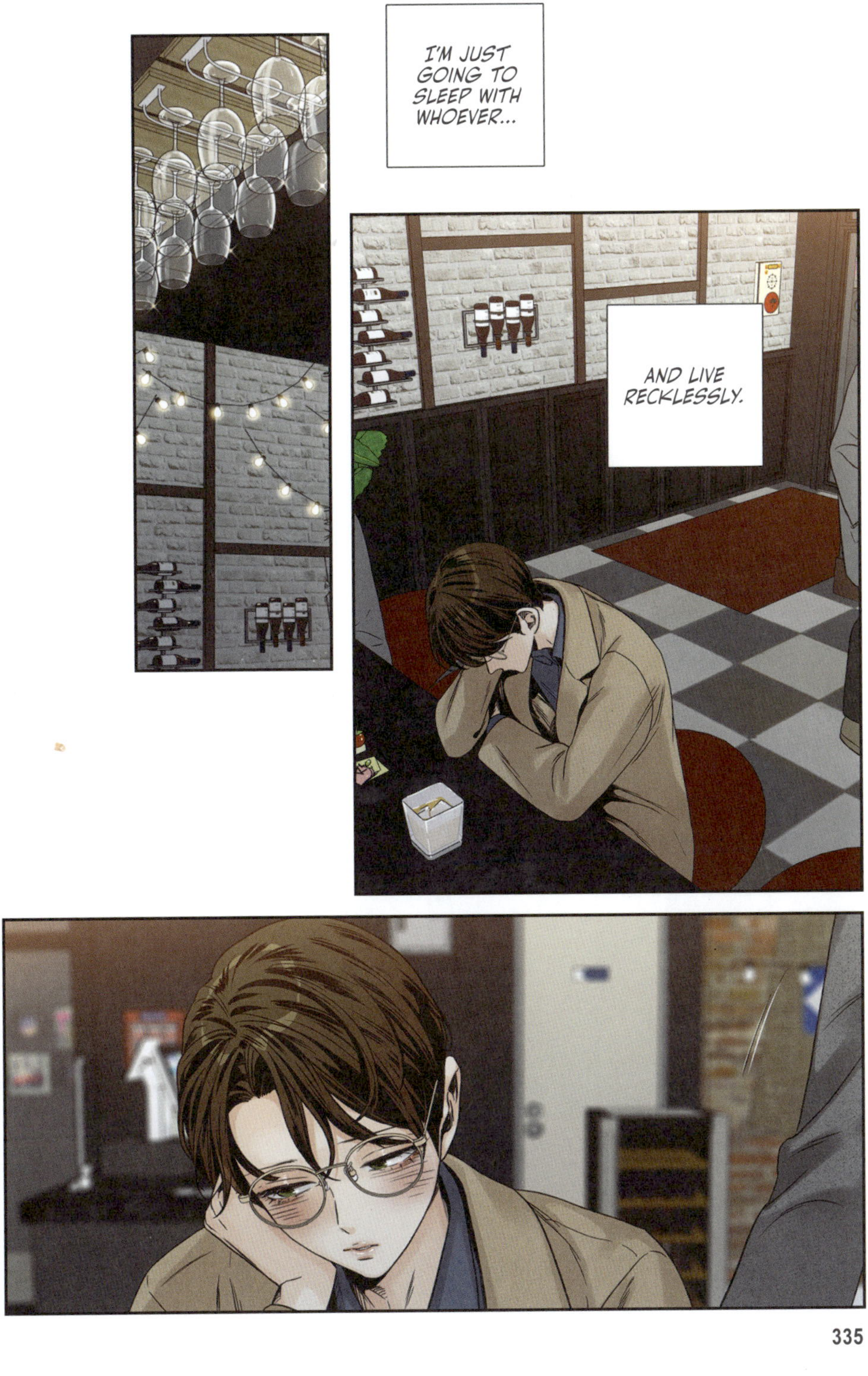
I'M JUST GOING TO SLEEP WITH WHOEVER...
AND LIVE RECKLESSLY.

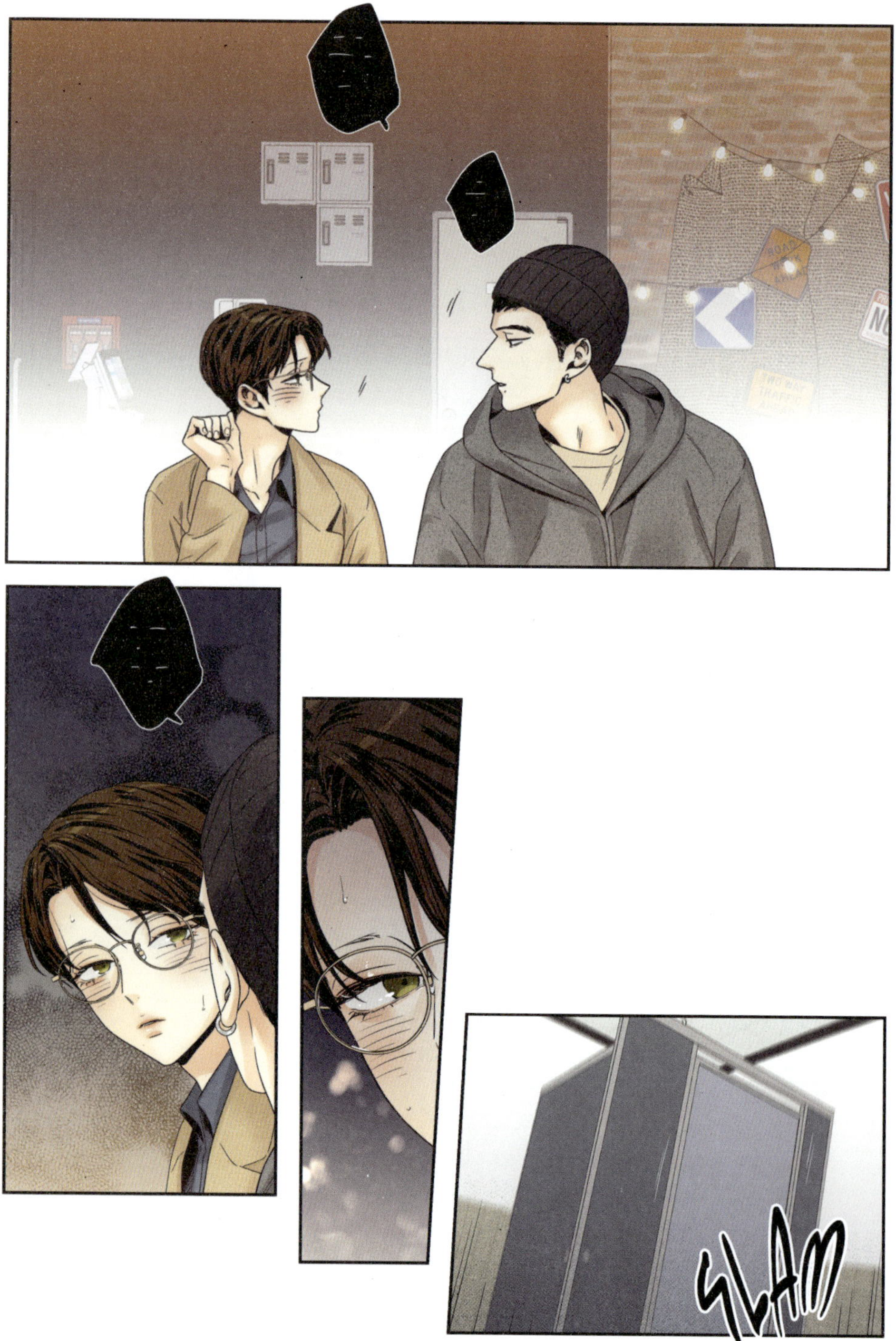
SLAM

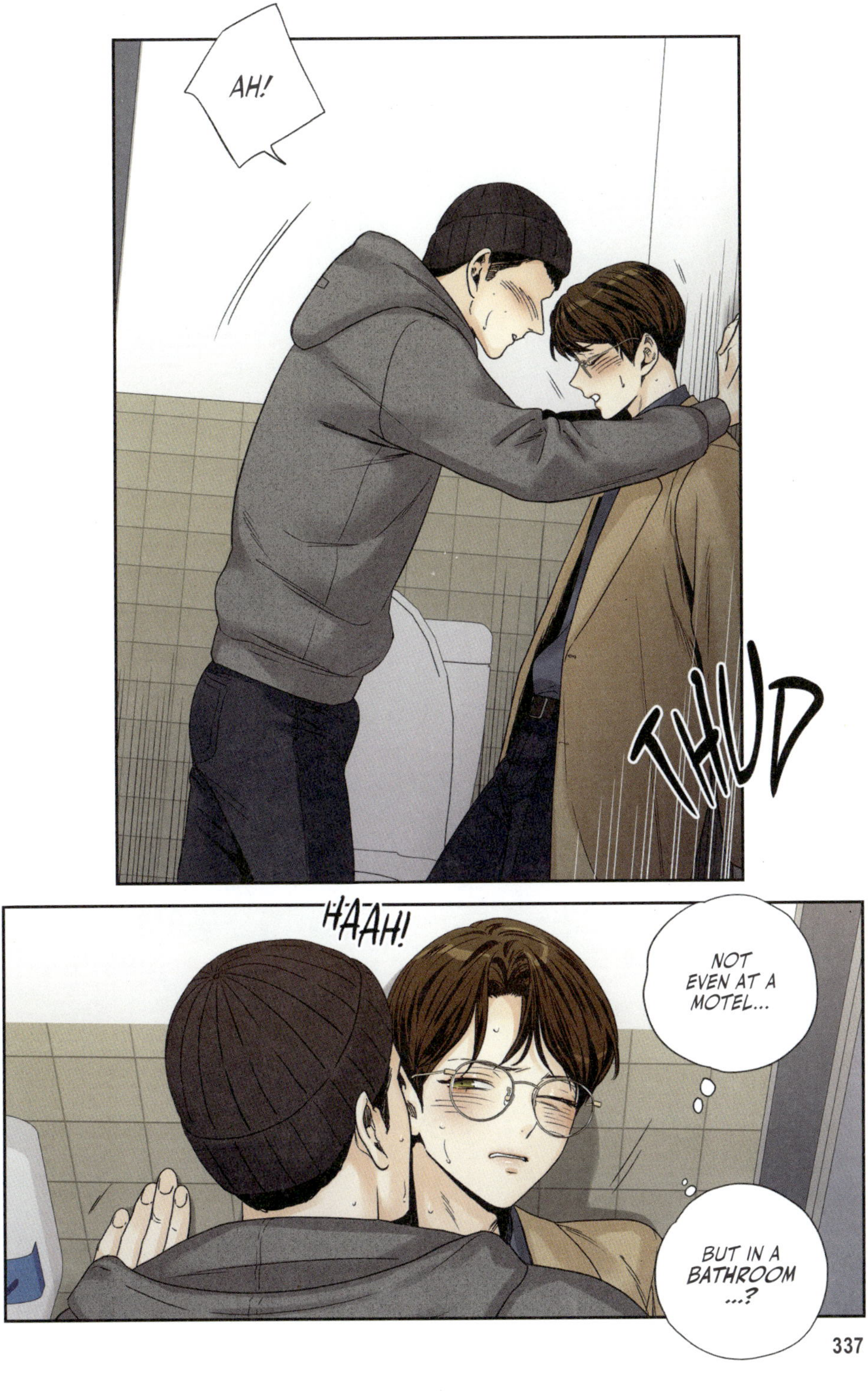
AH!
THUD
HAAAH!
NOT EVEN AT A MOTEL...
BUT IN A BATHROOM ...?

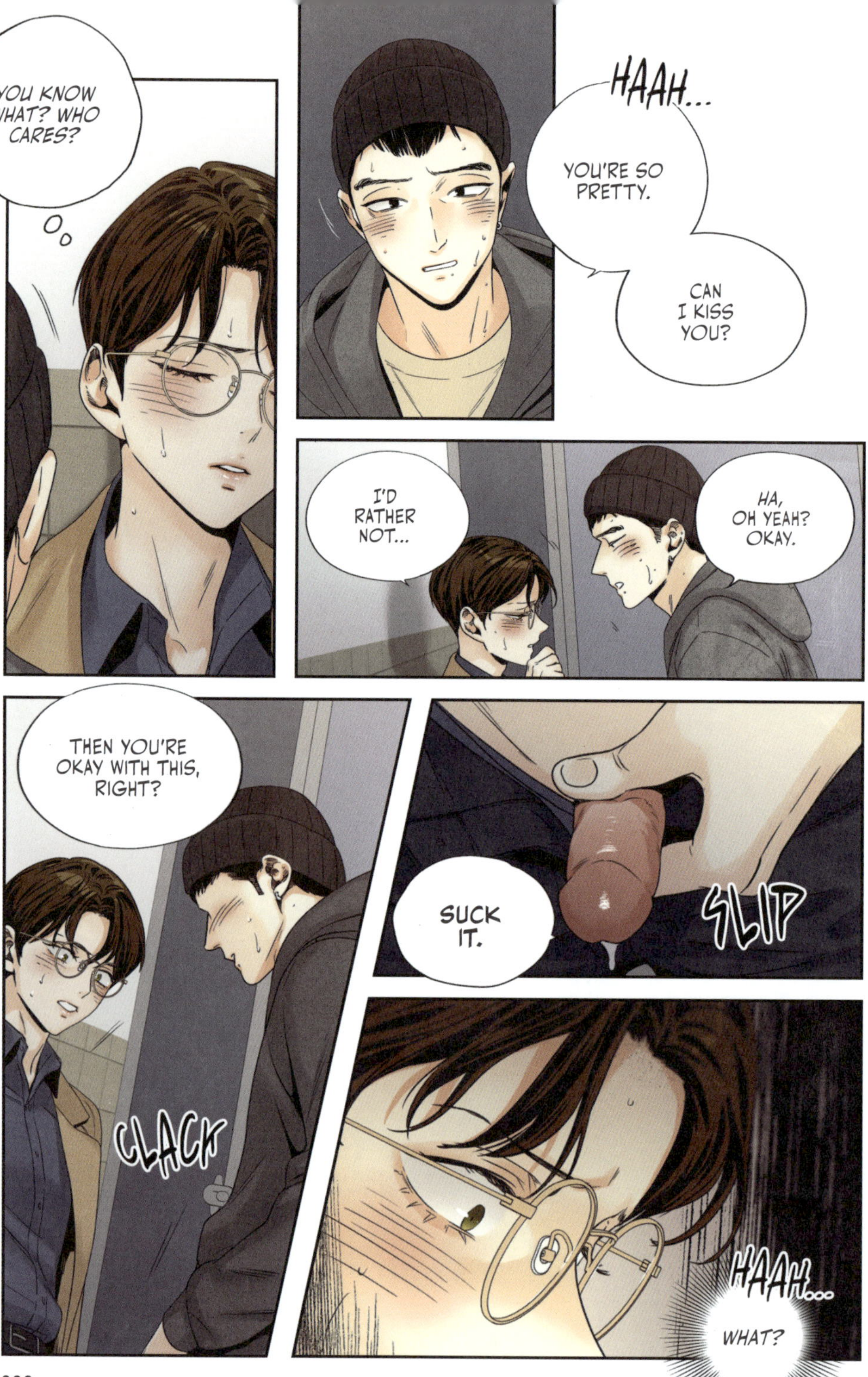
YOU KNOW WHAT? WHO CARES?
HAAH...
YOU'RE SO PRETTY.
CAN I KISS YOU?
I'D RATHER NOT...
HA, OH YEAH? OKAY.
THEN YOU'RE OKAY WITH THIS, RIGHT?
CLACK
SUCK IT.
SLIP
HAAH...
WHAT?

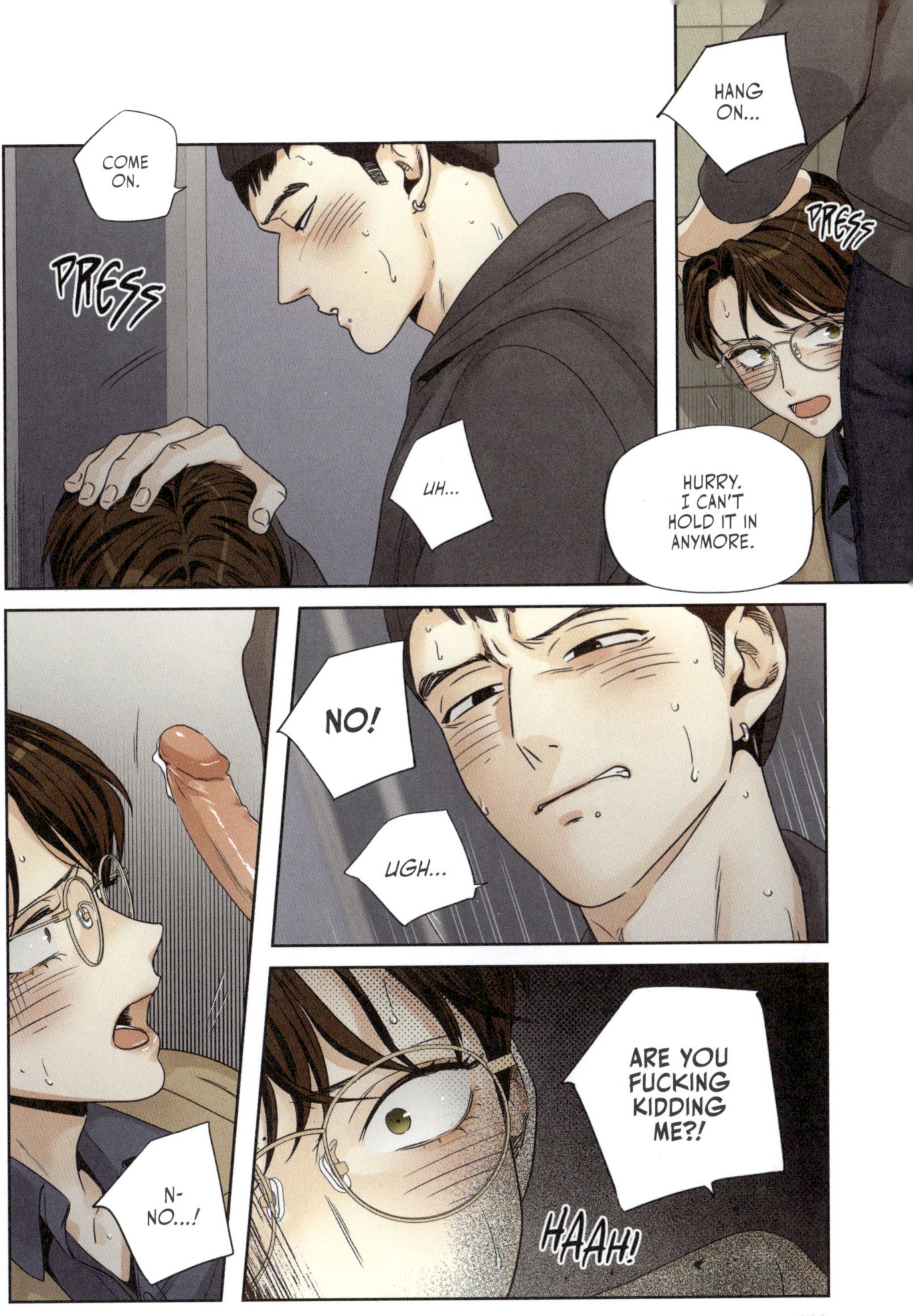
COME ON.
PRESS
UH...
HANG ON...
PRESS
HURRY. I CAN'T HOLD IT IN ANYMORE.
N- NO...!
NO!
UGH...
ARE YOU FUCKING KIDDING ME?!
HAAH!

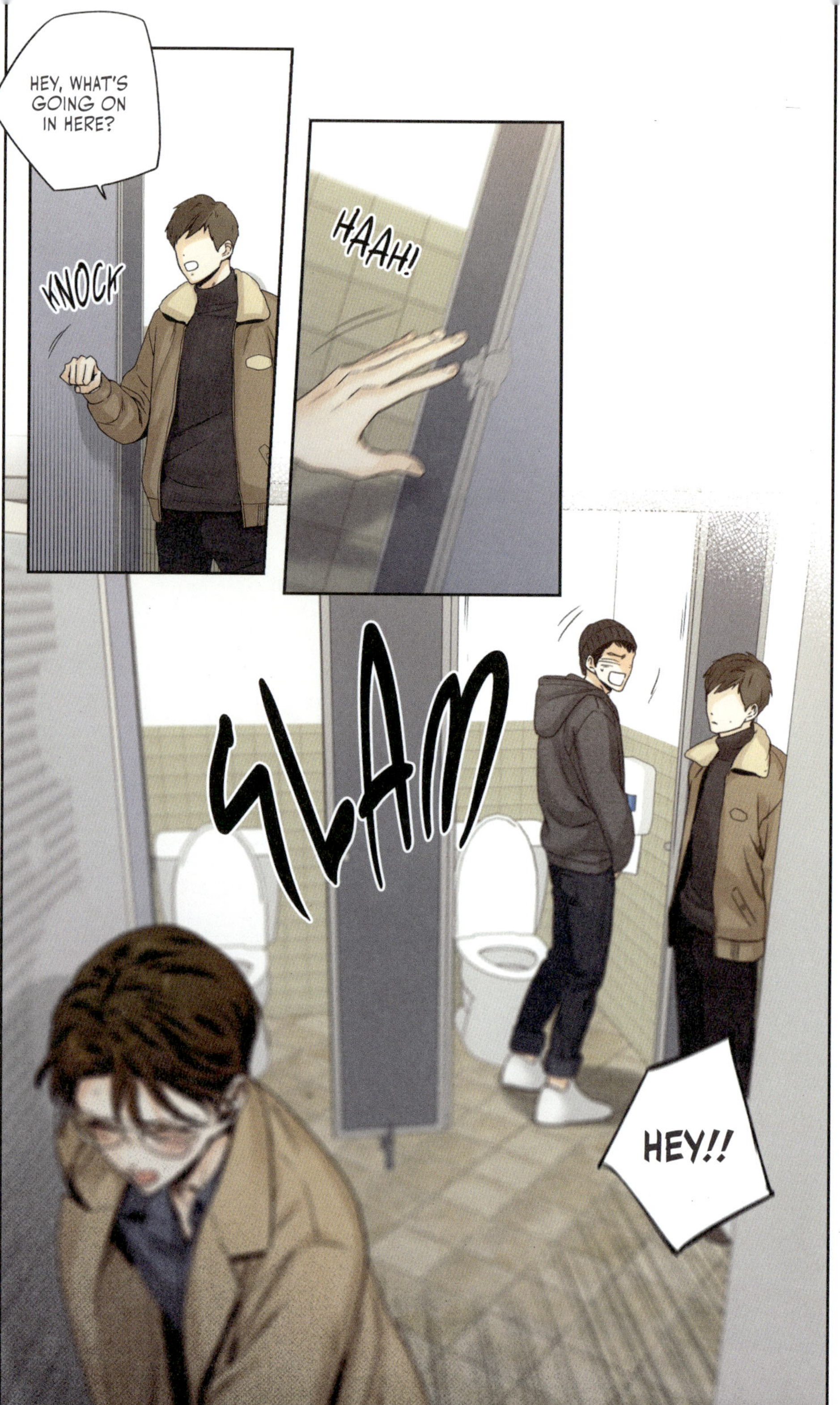
HEY, WHAT'S GOING ON IN HERE?
KNOCK
HAAAH!
SLAM
HEY!!

HAAH!

HAAH!

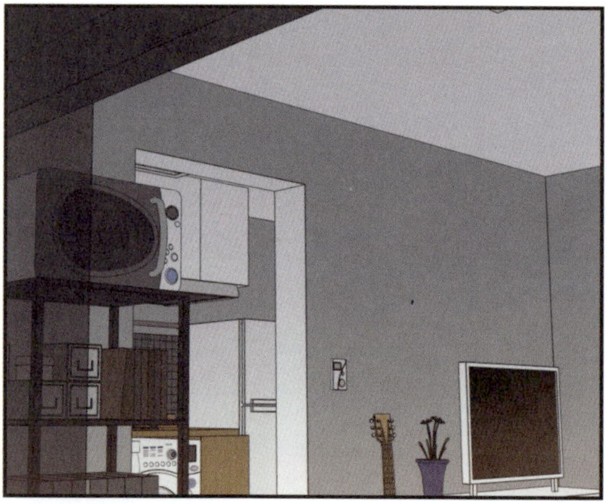

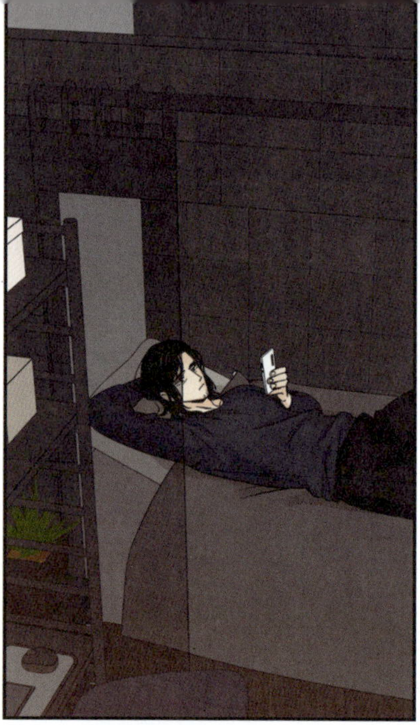

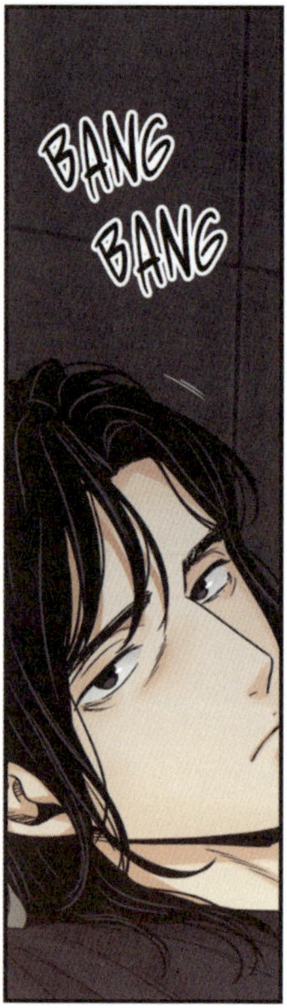
BANG
BANG

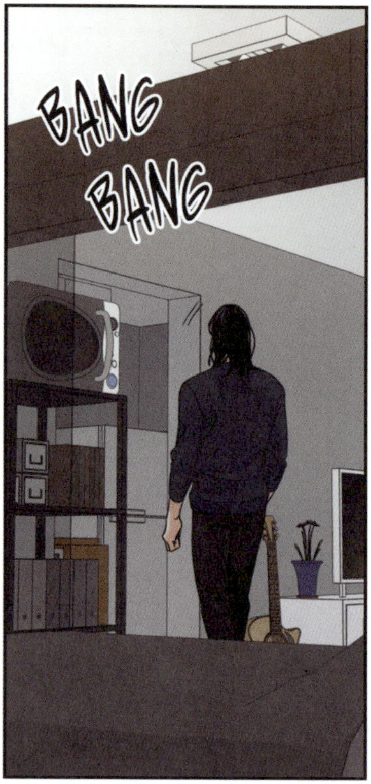
BANG
BANG

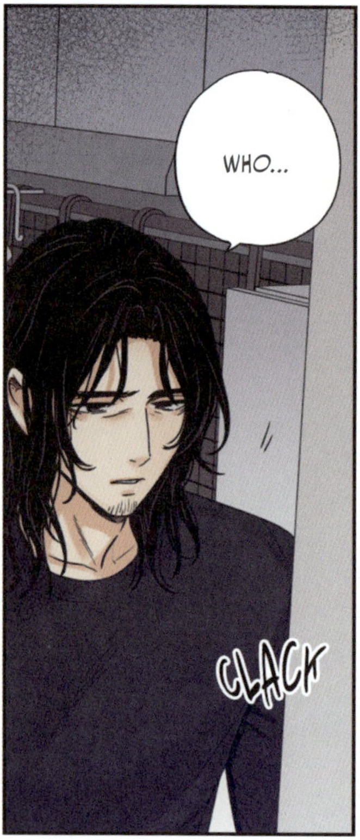
WHO...
CLACK

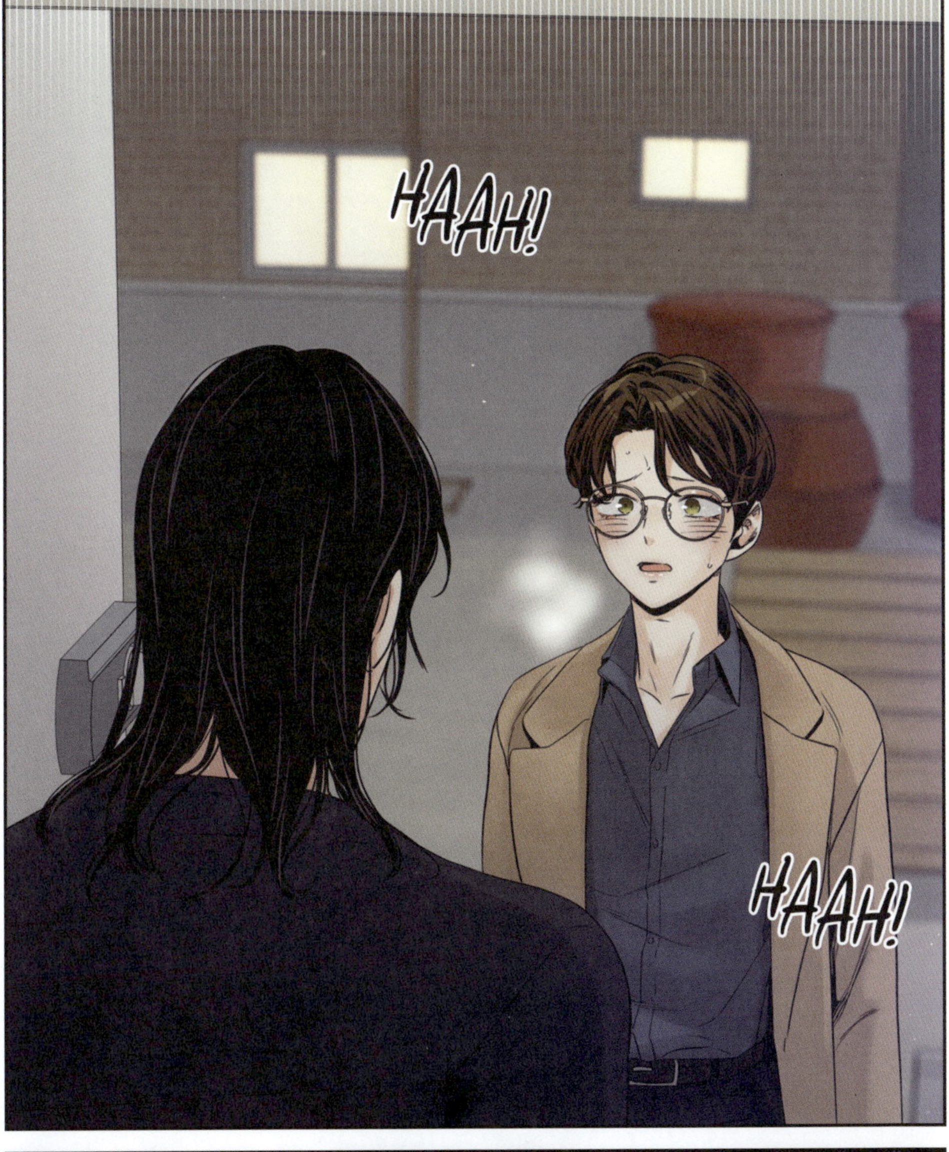
HAAAH!
HAAAH!
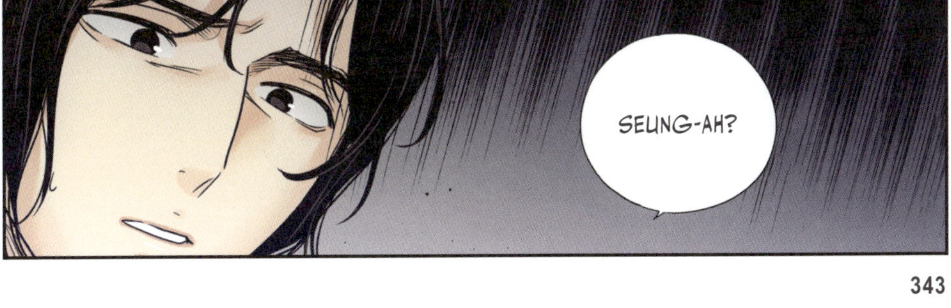
SEUNG-AH?

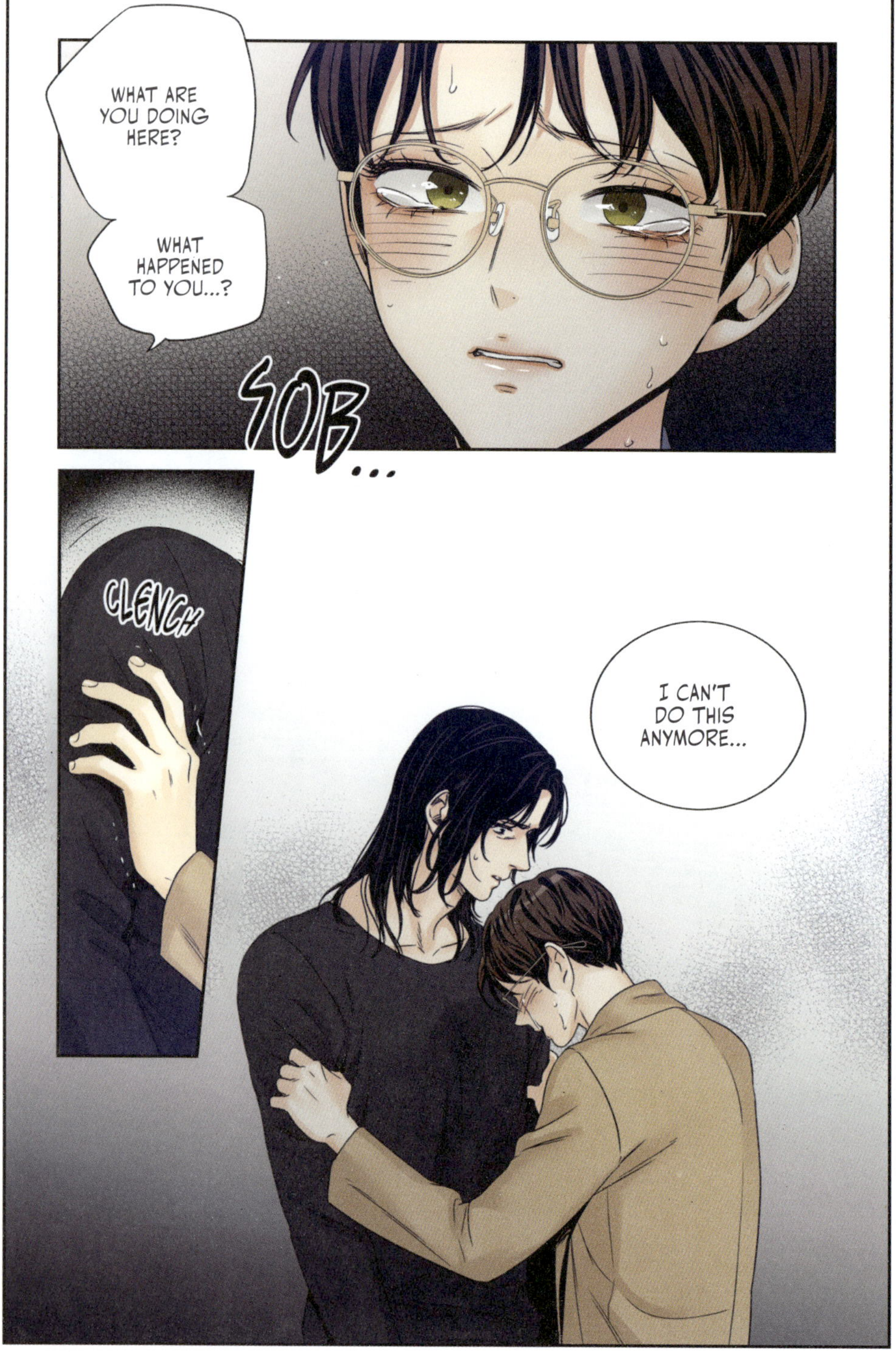
WHAT ARE YOU DOING HERE?
WHAT HAPPENED TO YOU...?
SOB...
CLENCH
I CAN'T DO THIS ANYMORE...

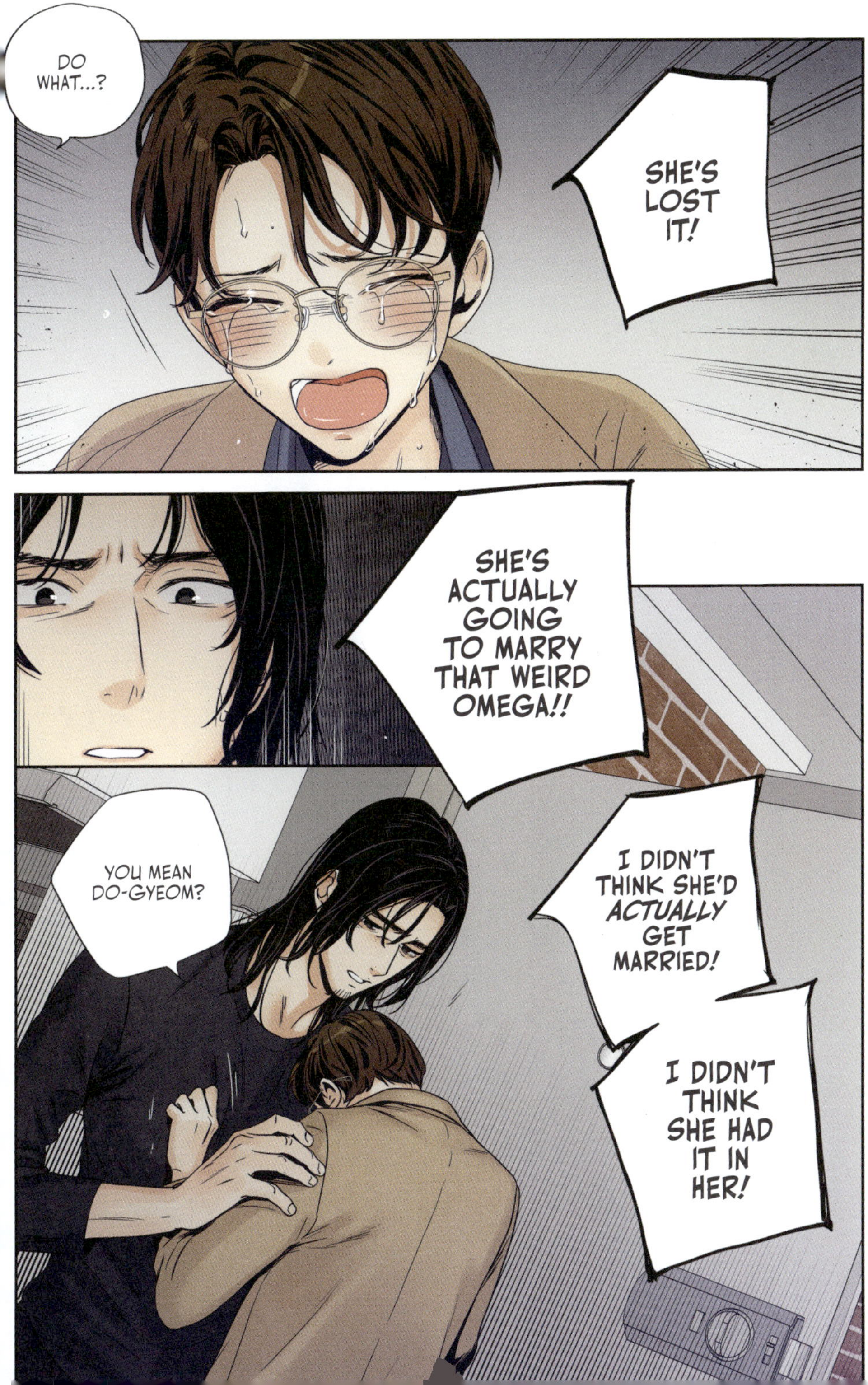
DO WHAT...?
SHE'S LOST IT!
SHE'S ACTUALLY GOING TO MARRY THAT WEIRD OMEGA!!
YOU MEAN DO-GYEOM?
I DIDN'T THINK SHE'D *ACTUALLY* GET MARRIED!
I DIDN'T THINK SHE HAD IT IN HER!

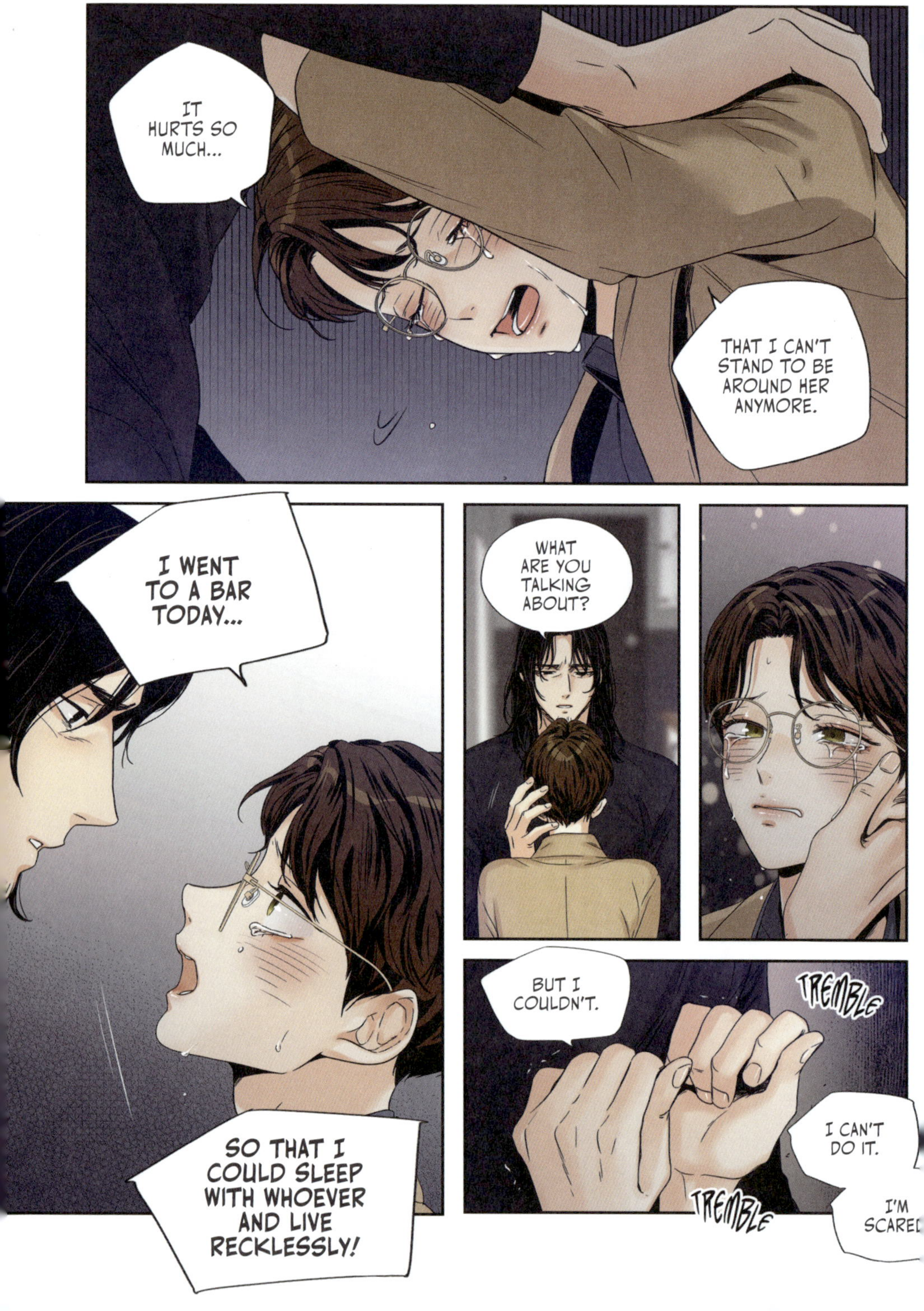
IT HURTS SO MUCH...
THAT I CAN'T STAND TO BE AROUND HER ANYMORE.
I WENT TO A BAR TODAY...
SO THAT I COULD SLEEP WITH WHOEVER AND LIVE RECKLESSLY!
WHAT ARE YOU TALKING ABOUT?
BUT I COULDN'T.
TREMBLE
TREMBLE
I CAN'T DO IT.
I'M SCARED

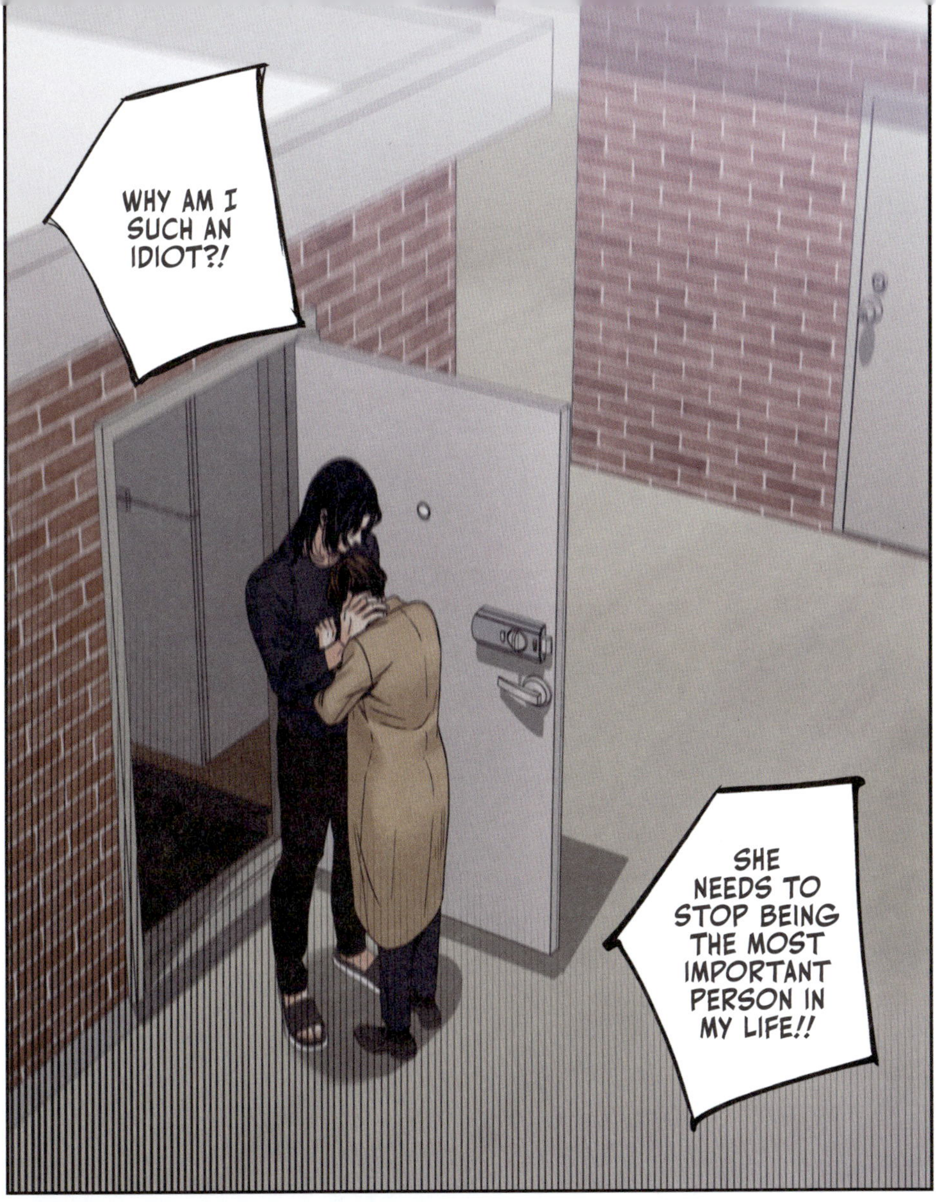
WHY AM I SUCH AN IDIOT?!
SHE NEEDS TO STOP BEING THE MOST IMPORTANT PERSON IN MY LIFE!!
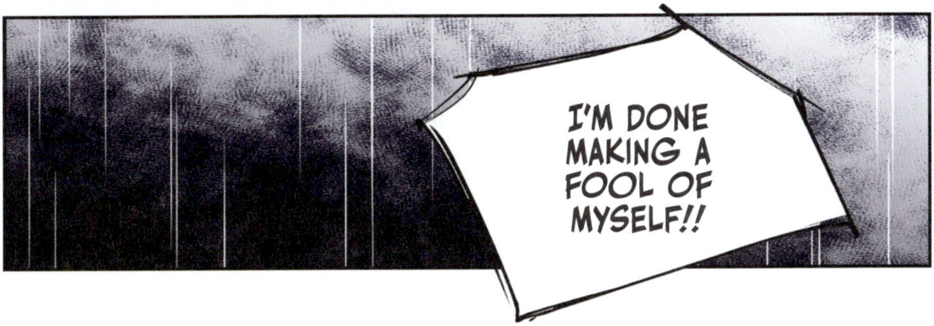
I'M DONE MAKING A FOOL OF MYSELF!!

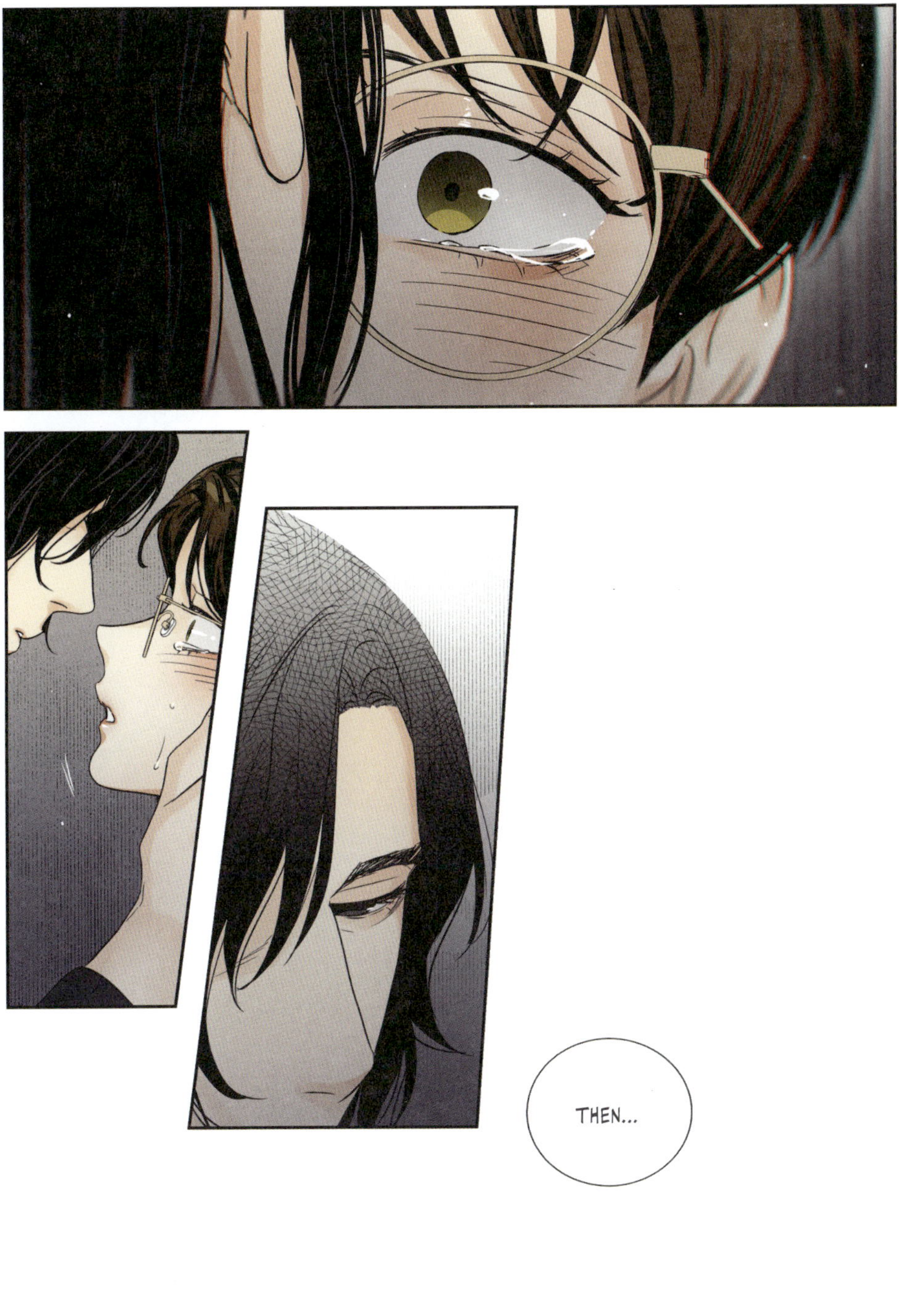
THEN...

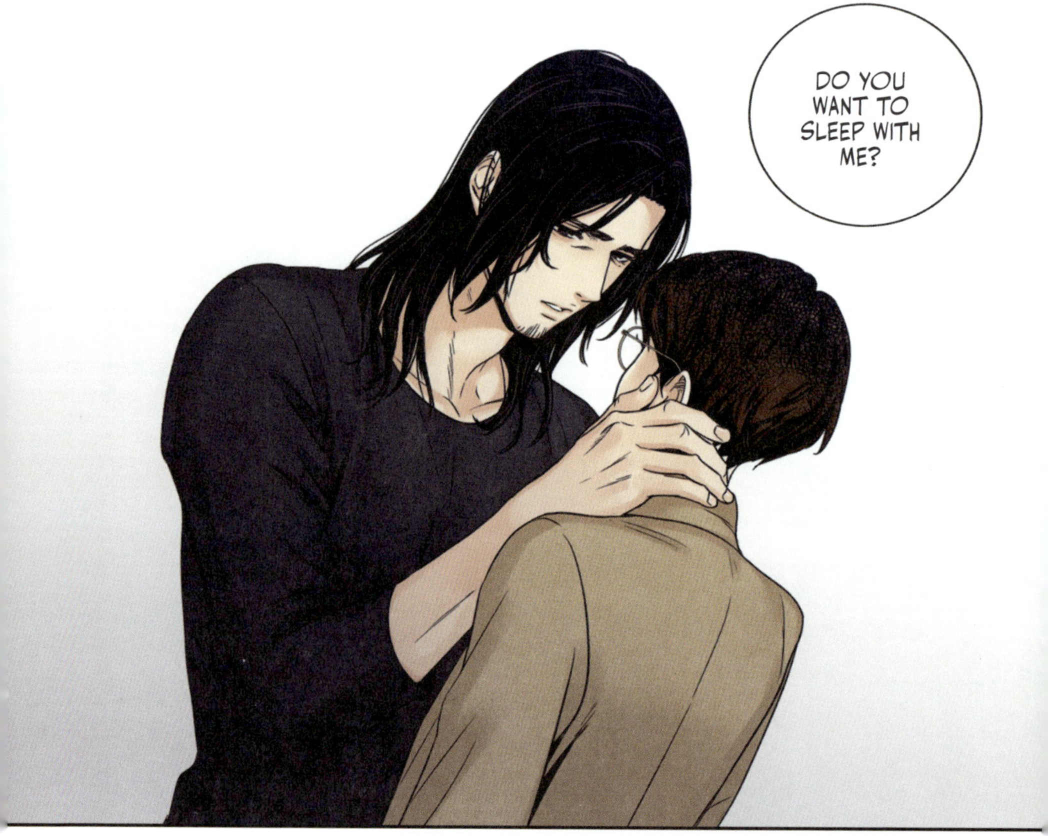
DO YOU WANT TO SLEEP WITH ME?
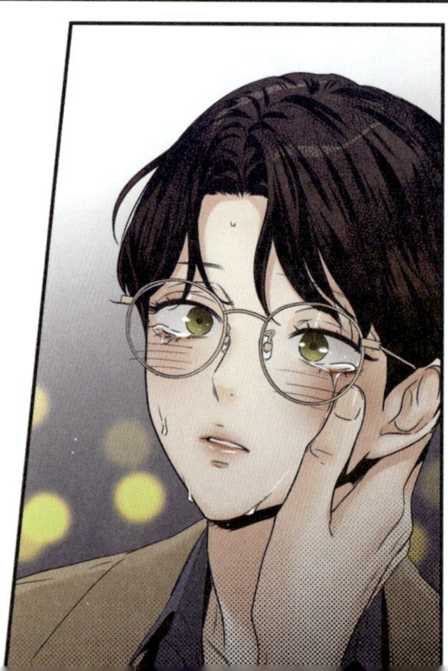

Love is an Illusion!
The Queen

Love is an Illusion!
The Queen

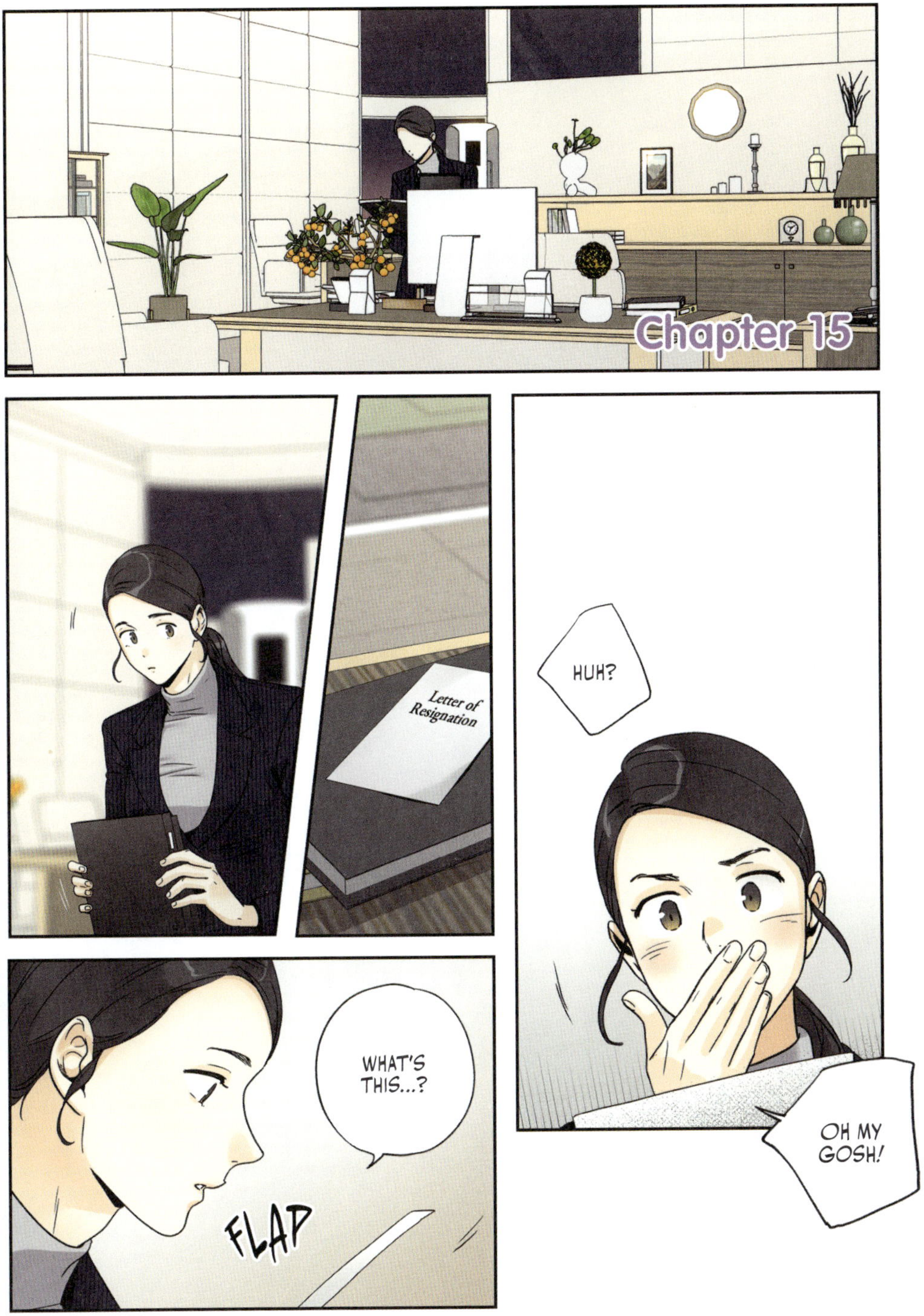
Chapter 15
Letter of Resignation
HUH?
WHAT'S THIS...?
FLAP
OH MY GOSH!

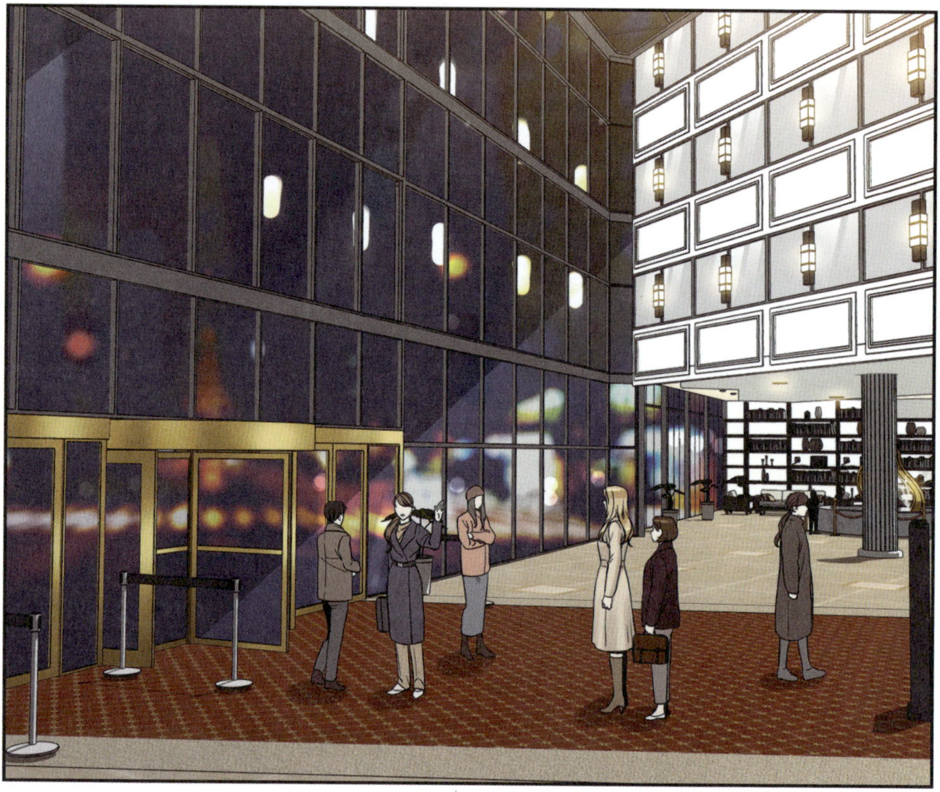

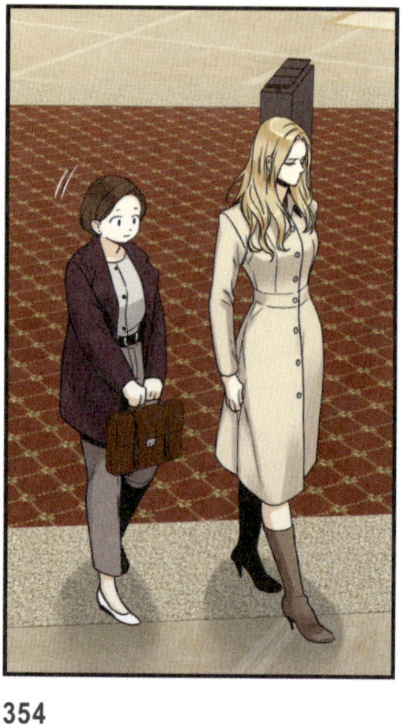

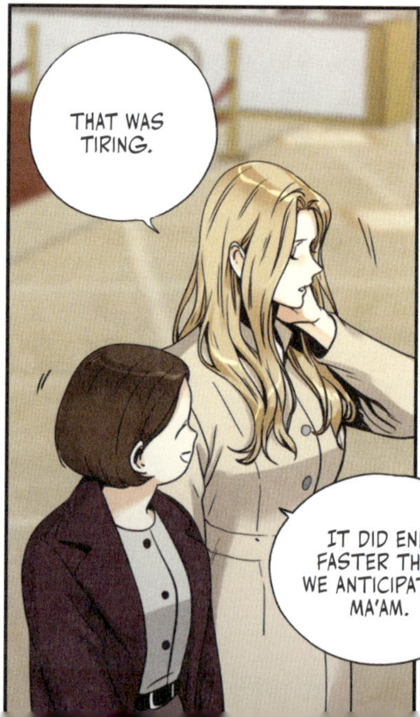
THAT WAS TIRING.
IT DID END FASTER THAN WE ANTICIPATED, MA'AM.

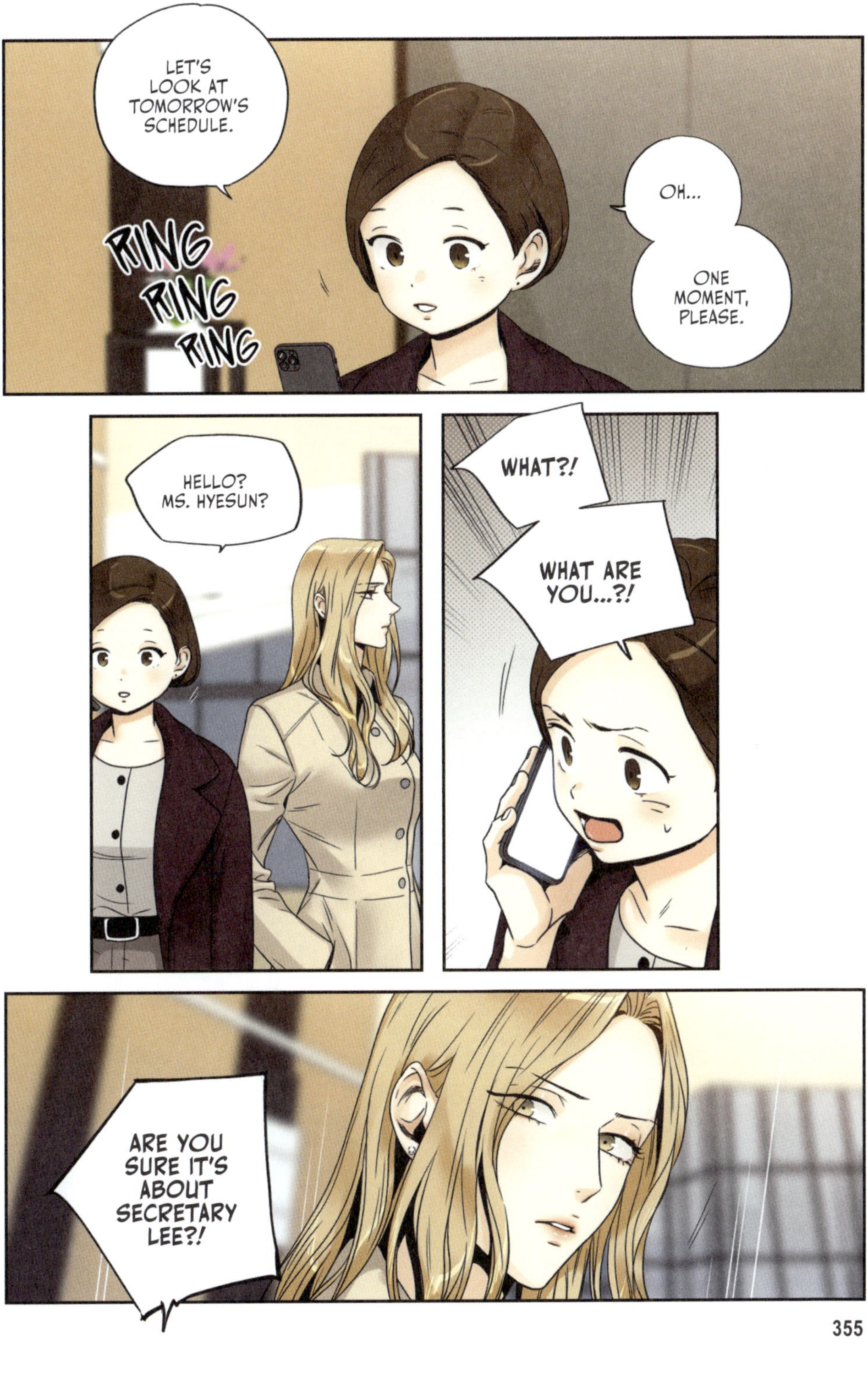
LET'S LOOK AT TOMORROW'S SCHEDULE.
RING RING RING
OH...
ONE MOMENT, PLEASE.
HELLO? MS. HYESUN?
WHAT?!
WHAT ARE YOU...?!
ARE YOU SURE IT'S ABOUT SECRETARY LEE?!

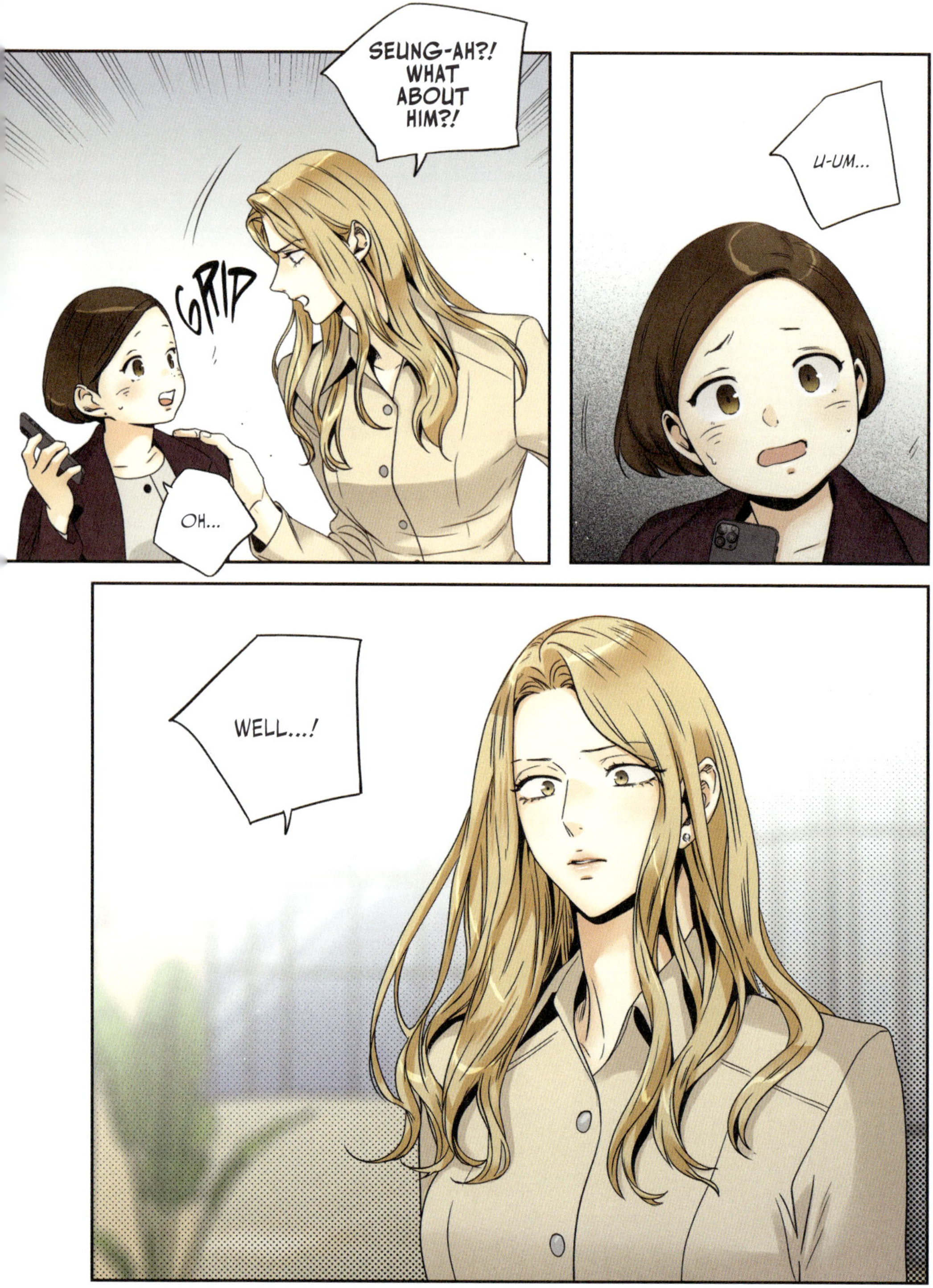
SEUNG-AH?! WHAT ABOUT HIM?!
GRIP
OH...
U-UM...
WELL...!

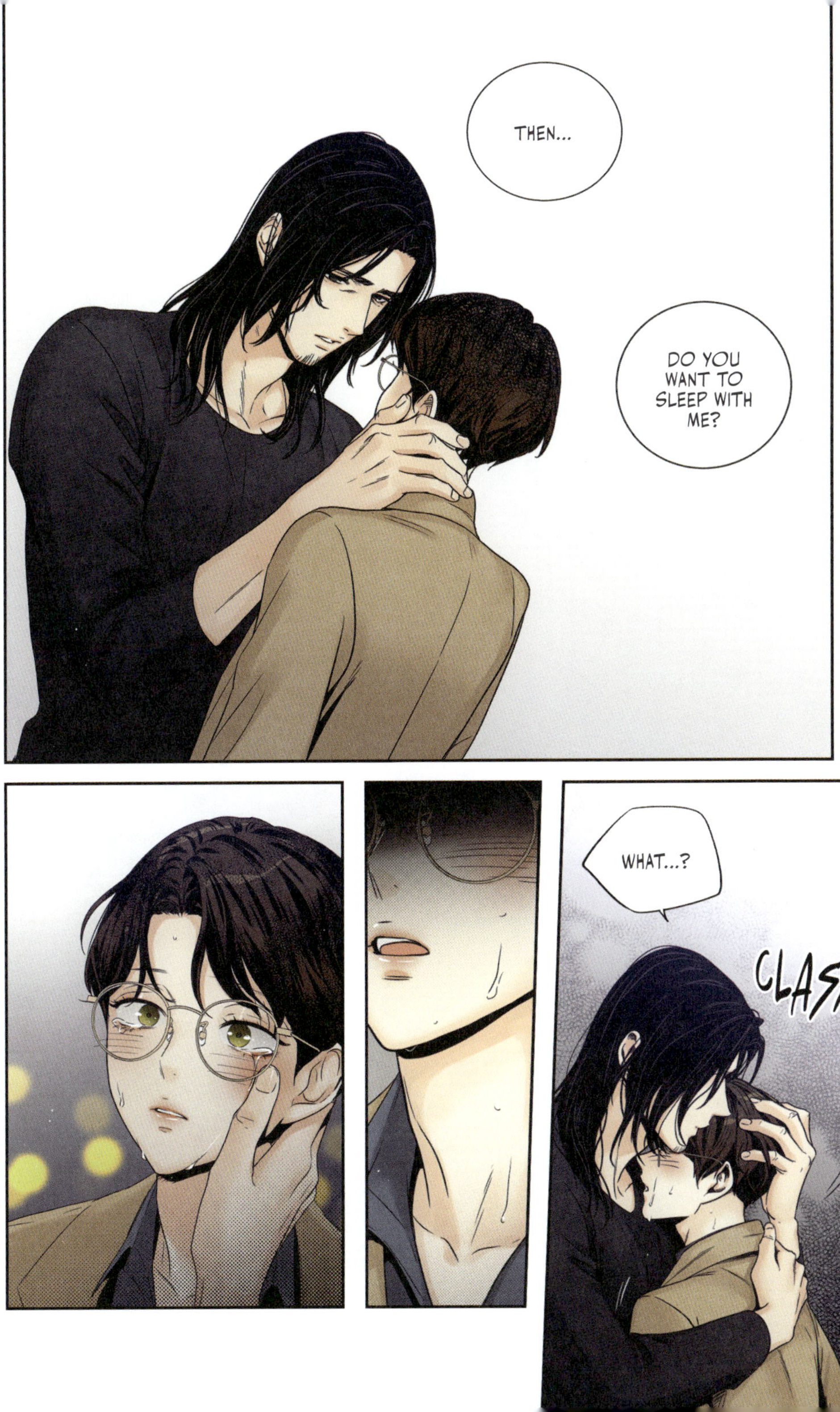
THEN...
DO YOU WANT TO SLEEP WITH ME?
WHAT...?
CLASP

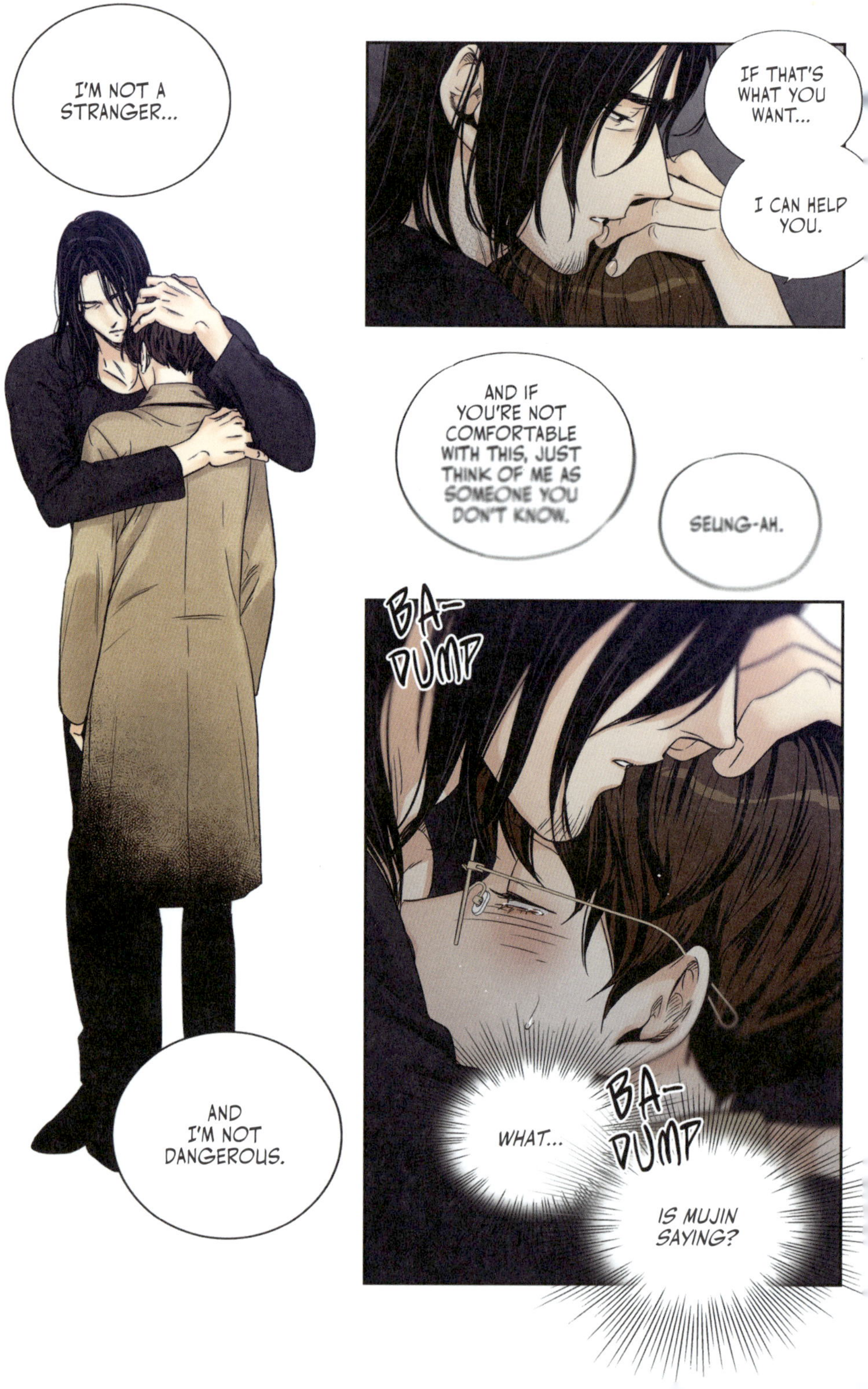
I'M NOT A STRANGER...
AND I'M NOT DANGEROUS.
IF THAT'S WHAT YOU WANT...
I CAN HELP YOU.
AND IF YOU'RE NOT COMFORTABLE WITH THIS, JUST THINK OF ME AS SOMEONE YOU DON'T KNOW.
SEUNG-AH.
BA-DUMP
WHAT...
BA-DUMP
IS MUJIN SAYING?

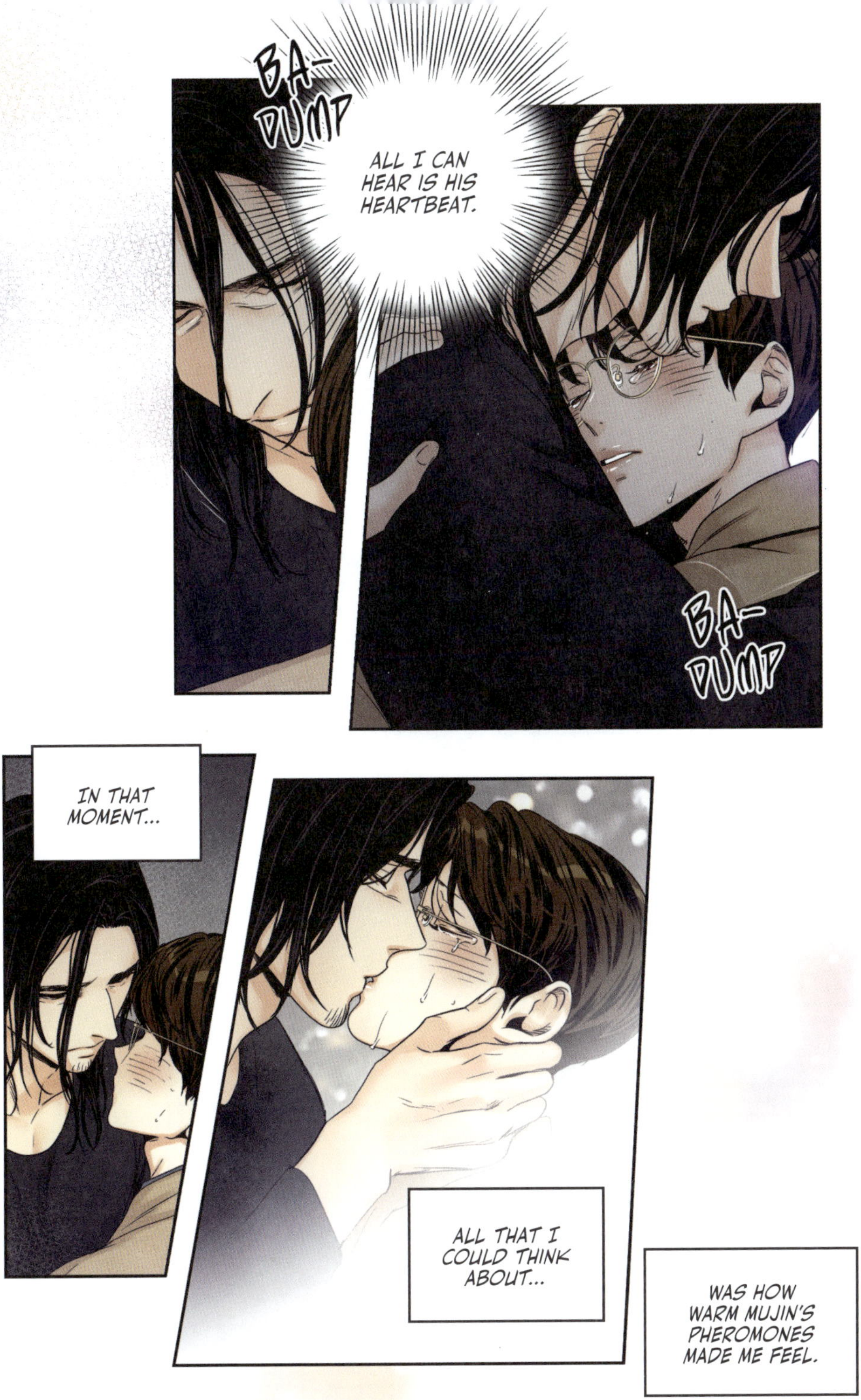
BA-DUMP
ALL I CAN HEAR IS HIS HEARTBEAT.
BA-DUMP
IN THAT MOMENT...
ALL THAT I COULD THINK ABOUT...
WAS HOW WARM MUJIN'S PHEROMONES MADE ME FEEL.

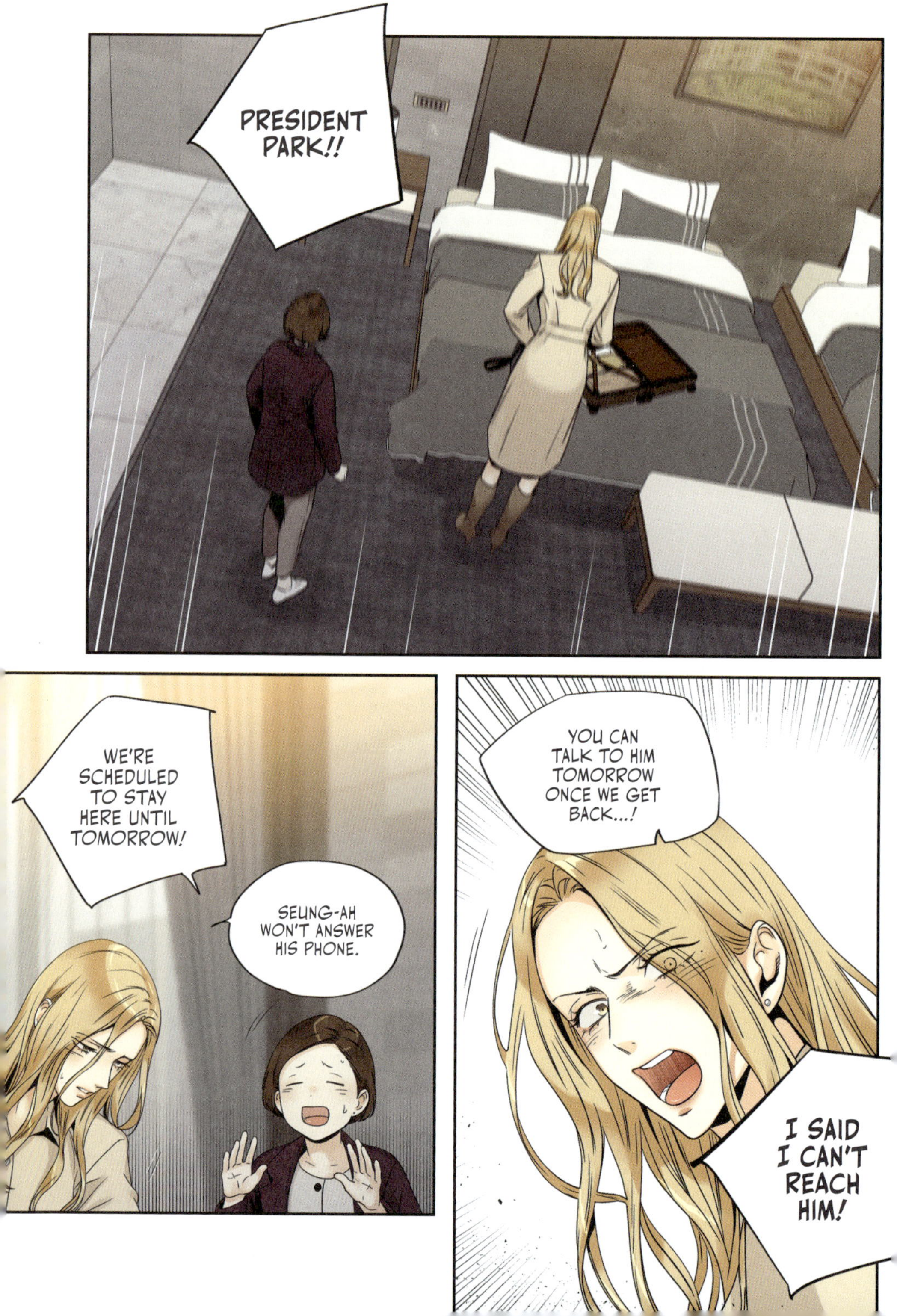
PRESIDENT PARK!!
WE'RE SCHEDULED TO STAY HERE UNTIL TOMORROW!
SEUNG-AH WON'T ANSWER HIS PHONE.
YOU CAN TALK TO HIM TOMORROW ONCE WE GET BACK...!
I SAID I CAN'T REACH HIM!

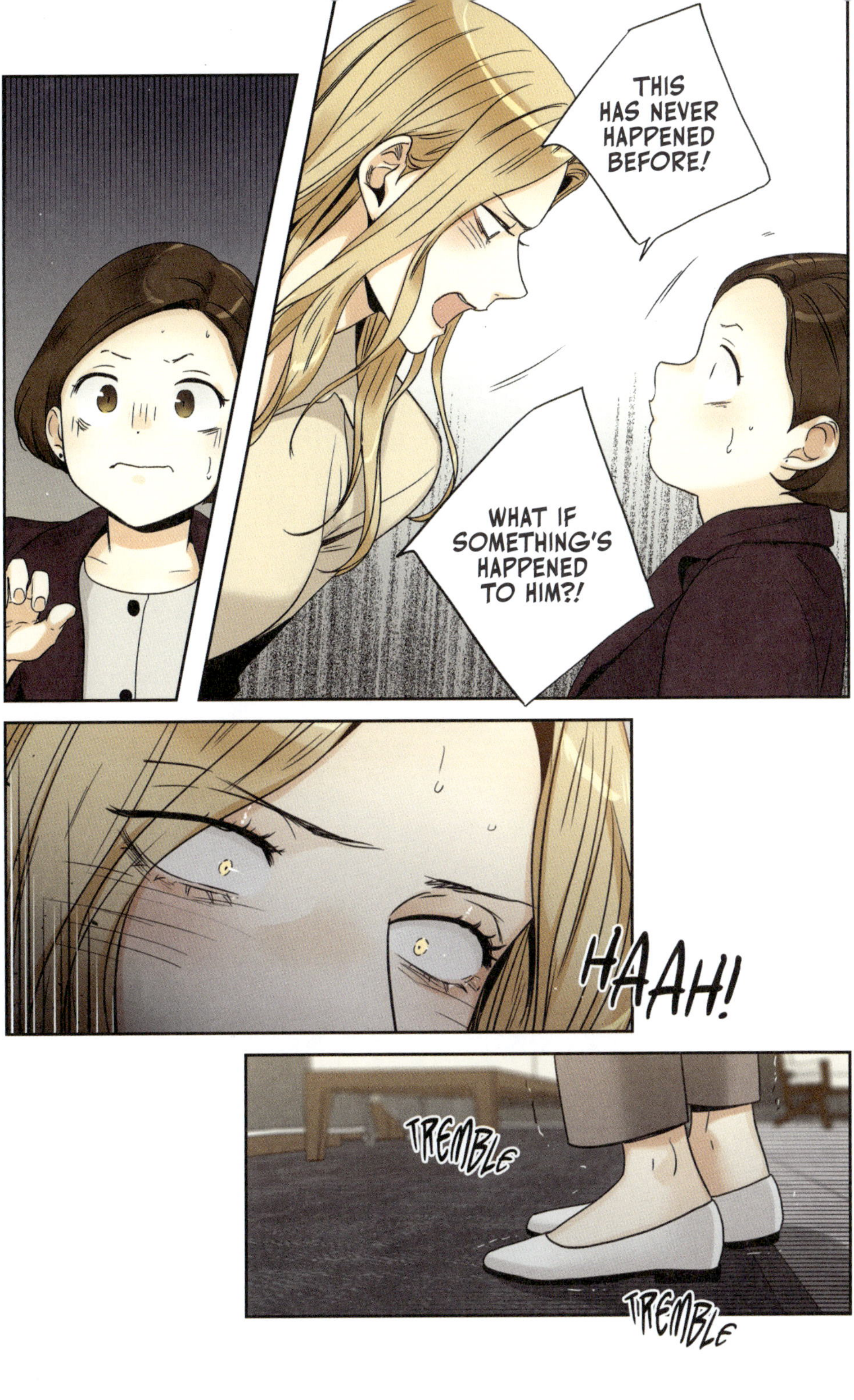
THIS HAS NEVER HAPPENED BEFORE!
WHAT IF SOMETHING'S HAPPENED TO HIM?!
HAAAH!
TREMBLE
TREMBLE

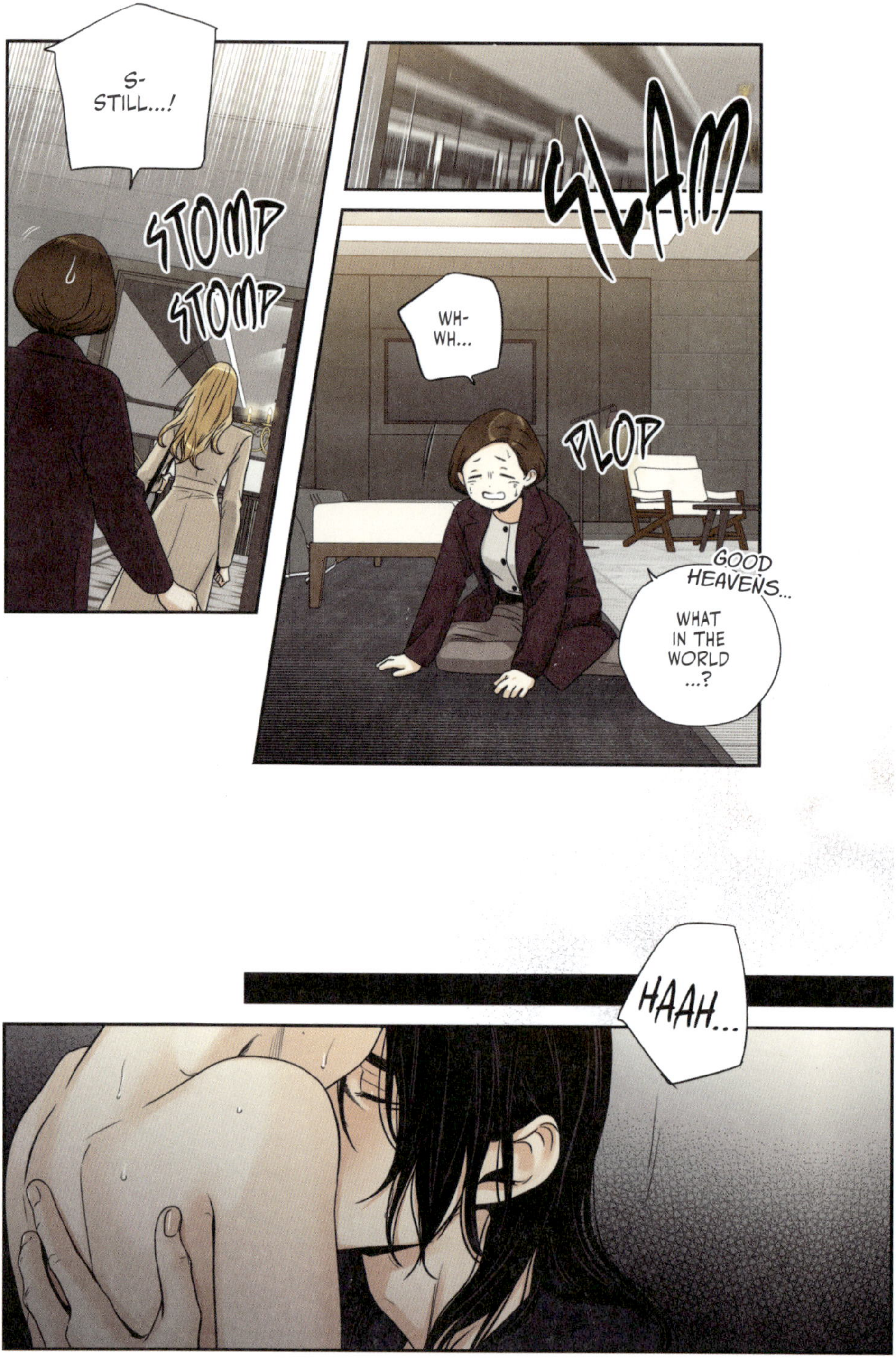
S-
STILL...!
STOMP
STOMP
SLAM
WH-
WH...
PLOP
GOOD HEAVENS...
WHAT IN THE WORLD ...?
HAAH...

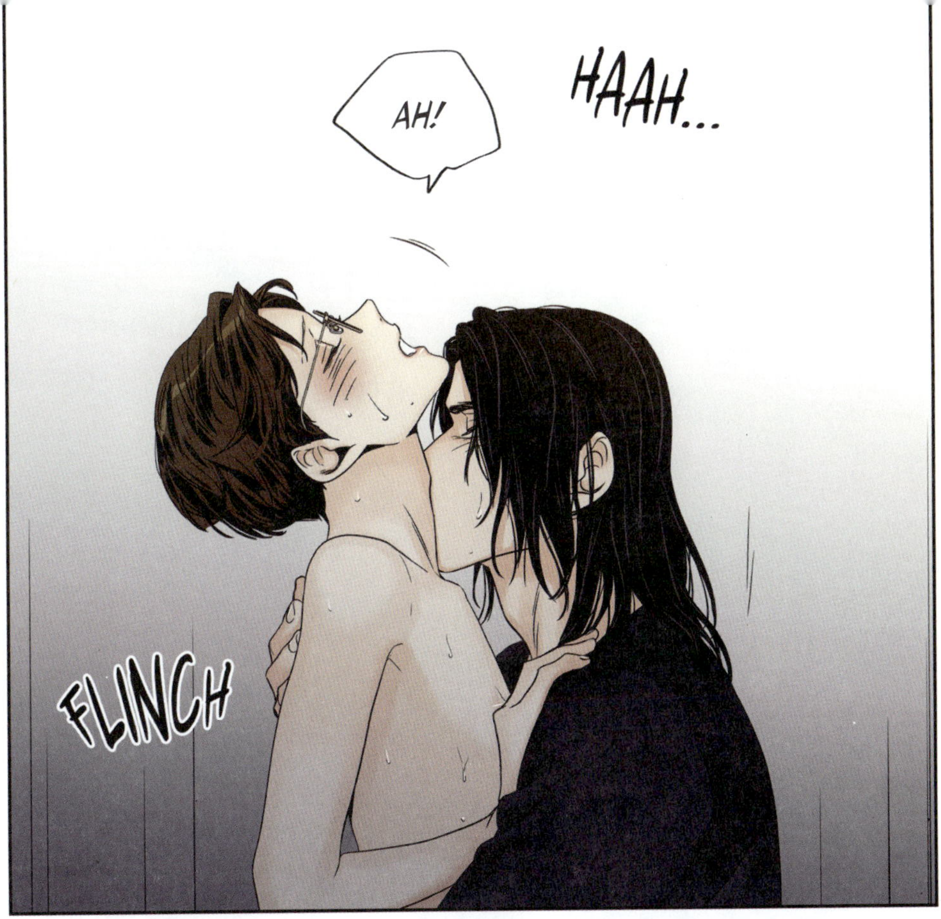
AH!
HAAH...
FLINCH

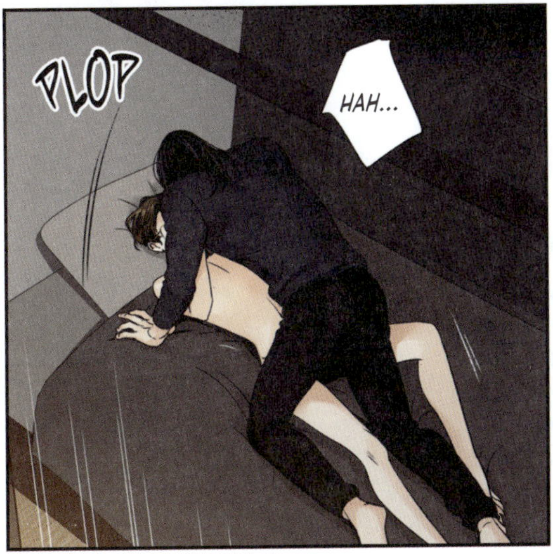
PLOP
HAH...

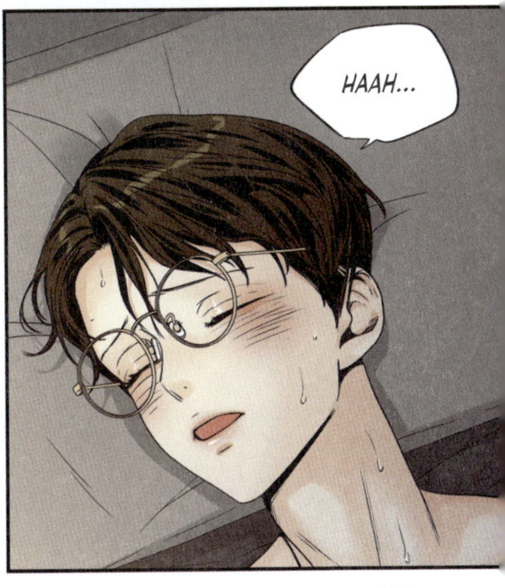
HAAH...

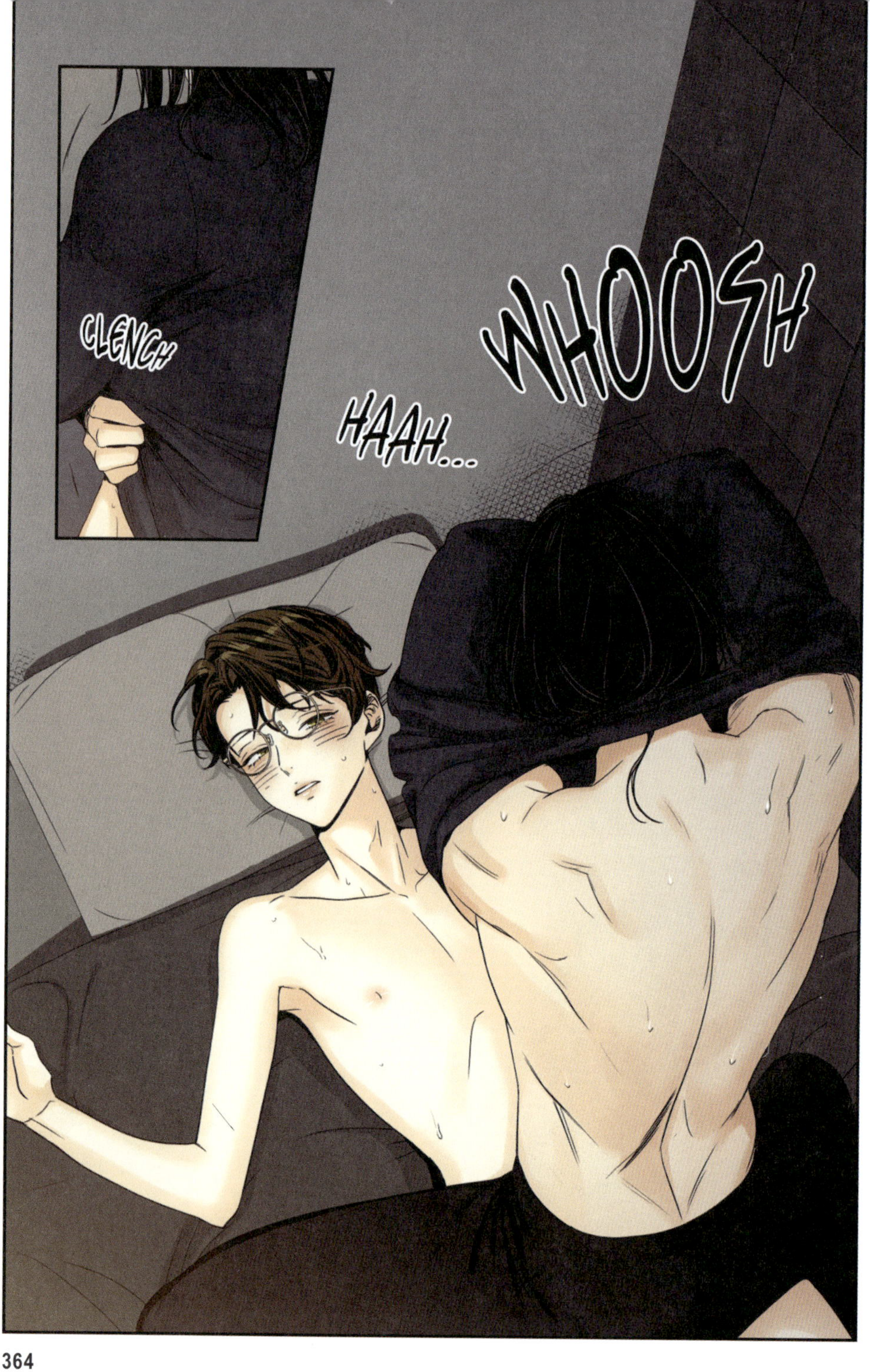
CLENCH
HAAH...
WHOOSH

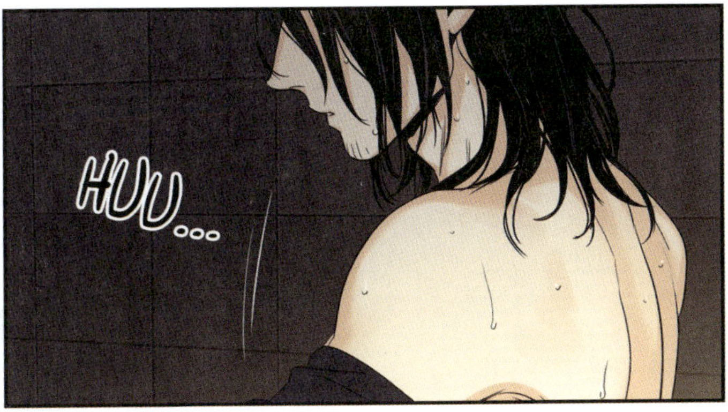
HUU...

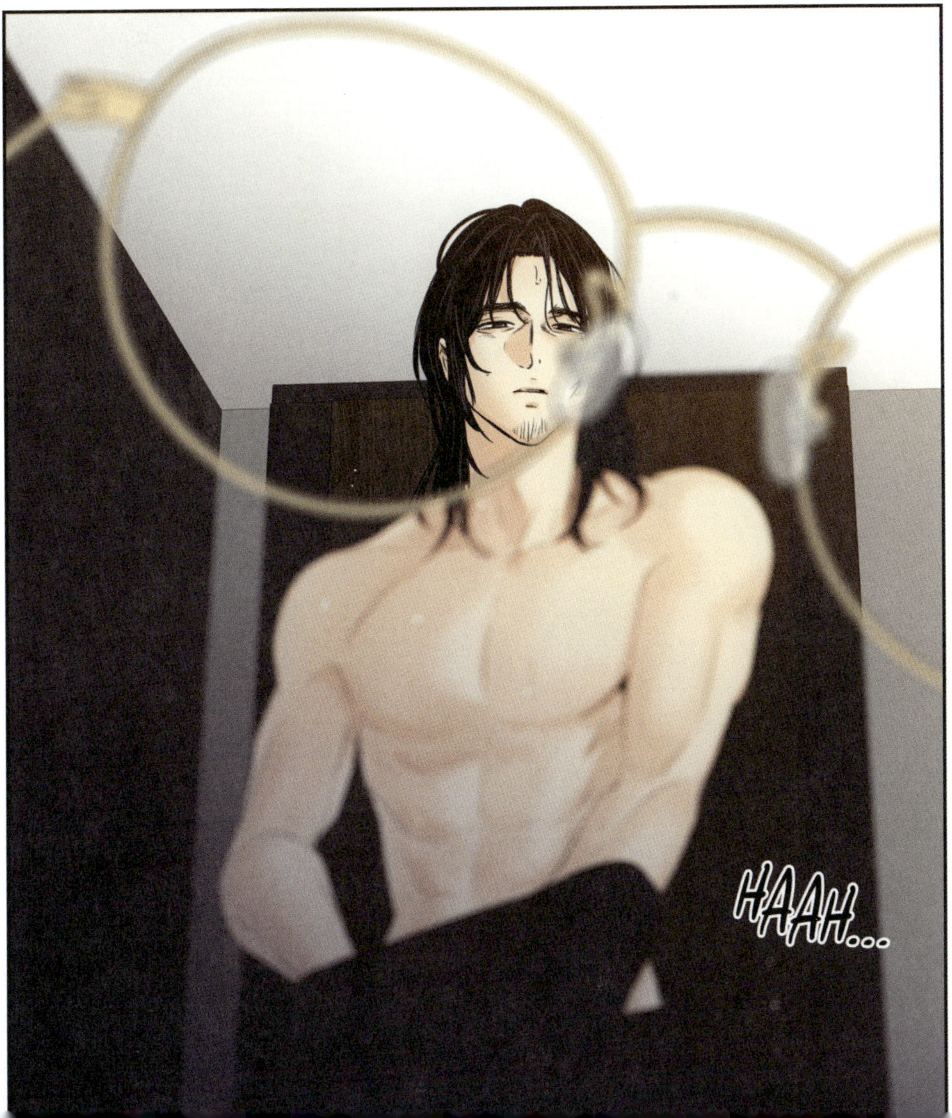
HAAH...

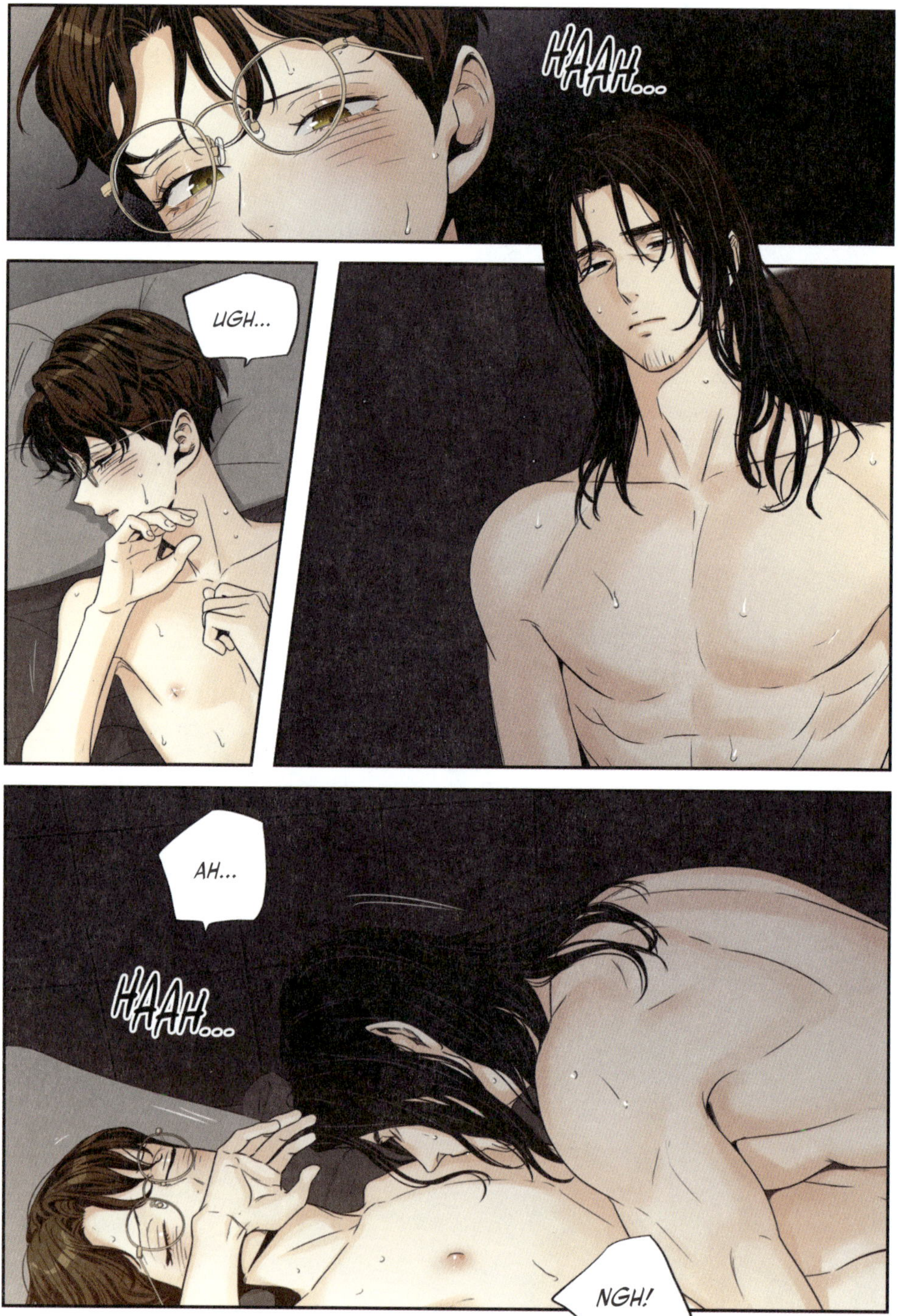
HAAH...
UGH...
AH...
HAAH...
NGH!

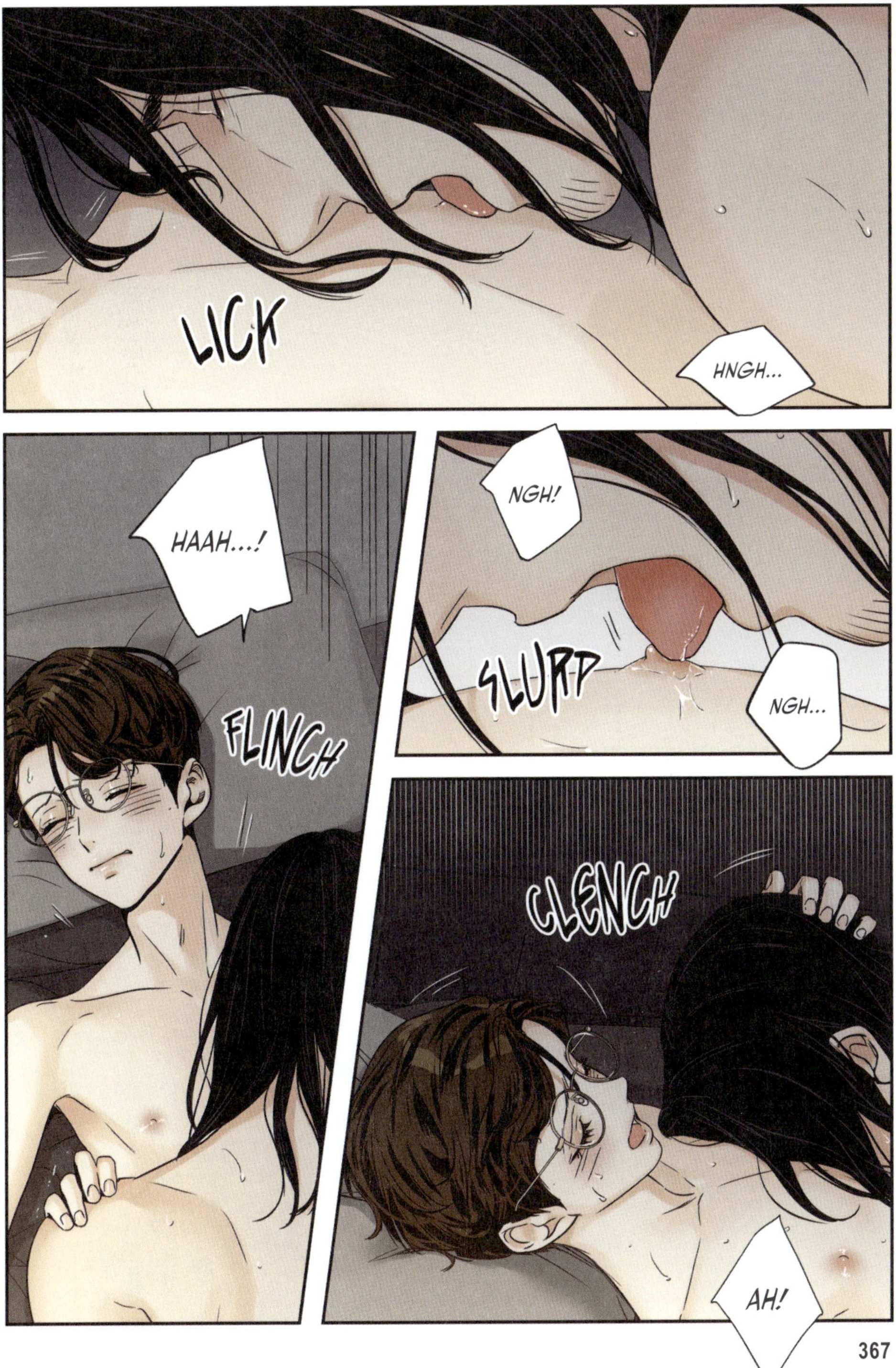
LICK
HNGH...
HAAH...!
FLINCH
NGH!
SLURP
NGH...
CLENCH
AH!

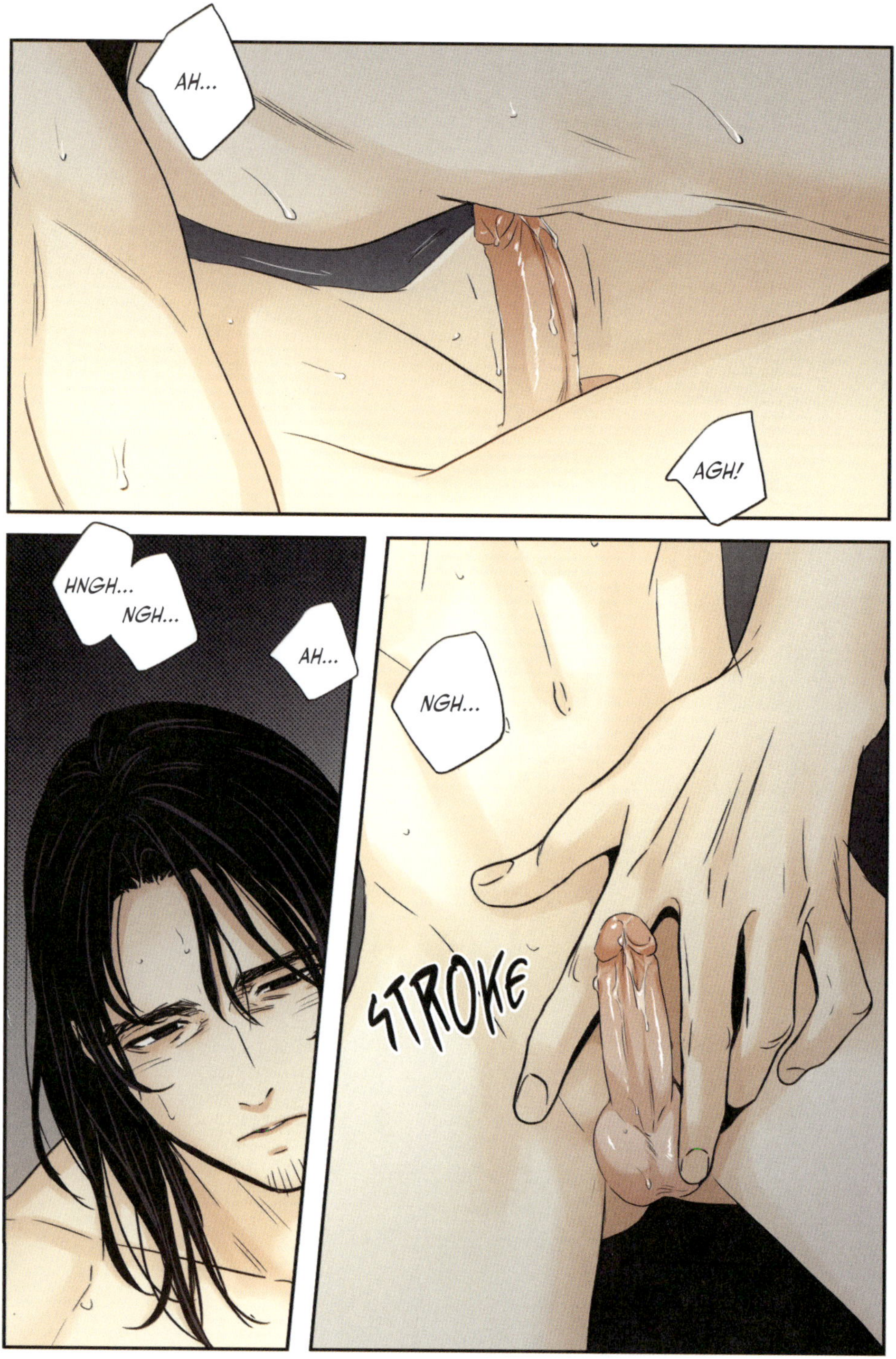
AH...
AGH!
HNGH...
NGH...
AH...
NGH...
STROKE

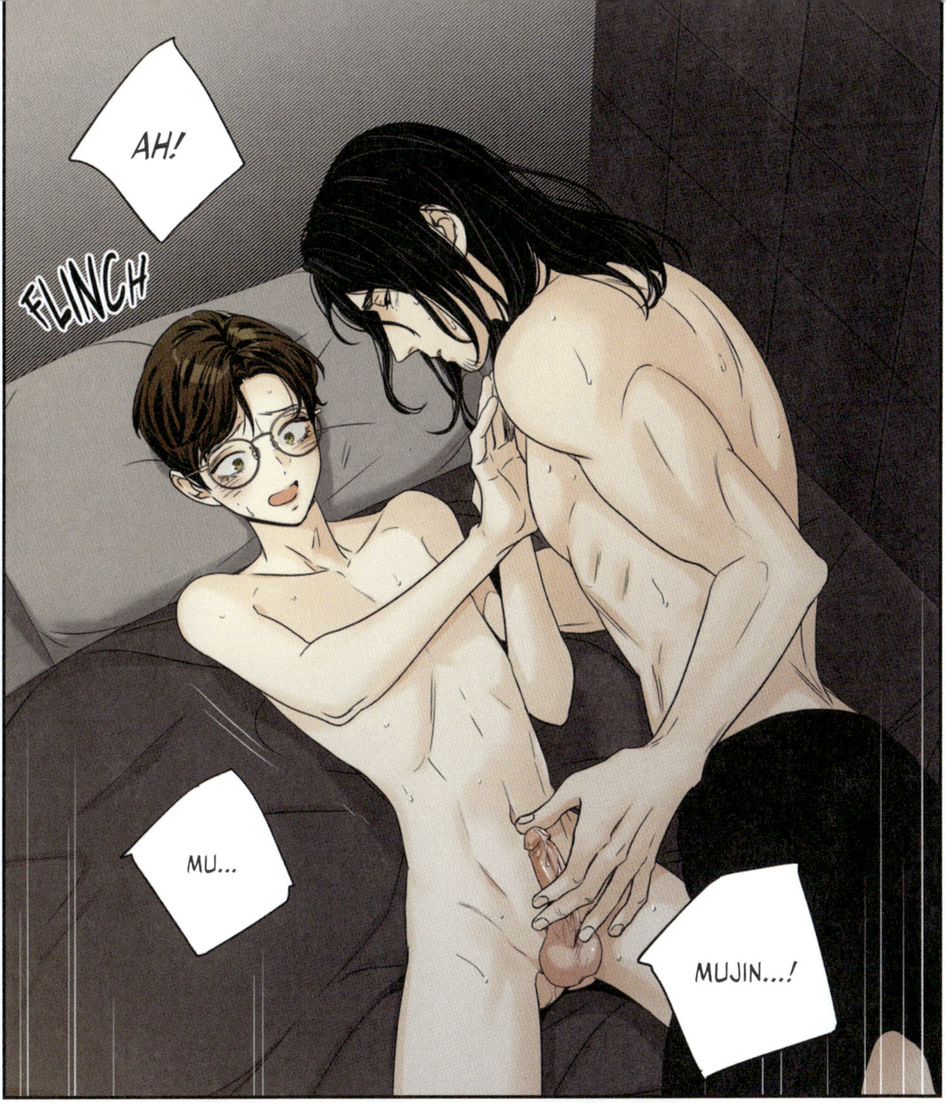
AH!
FLINCH
MU...
MUJIN...!

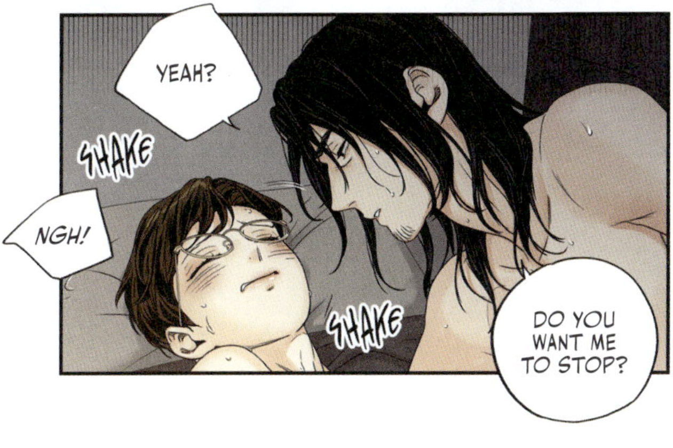
YEAH?
SHAKE
NGH!
SHAKE
DO YOU WANT ME TO STOP?

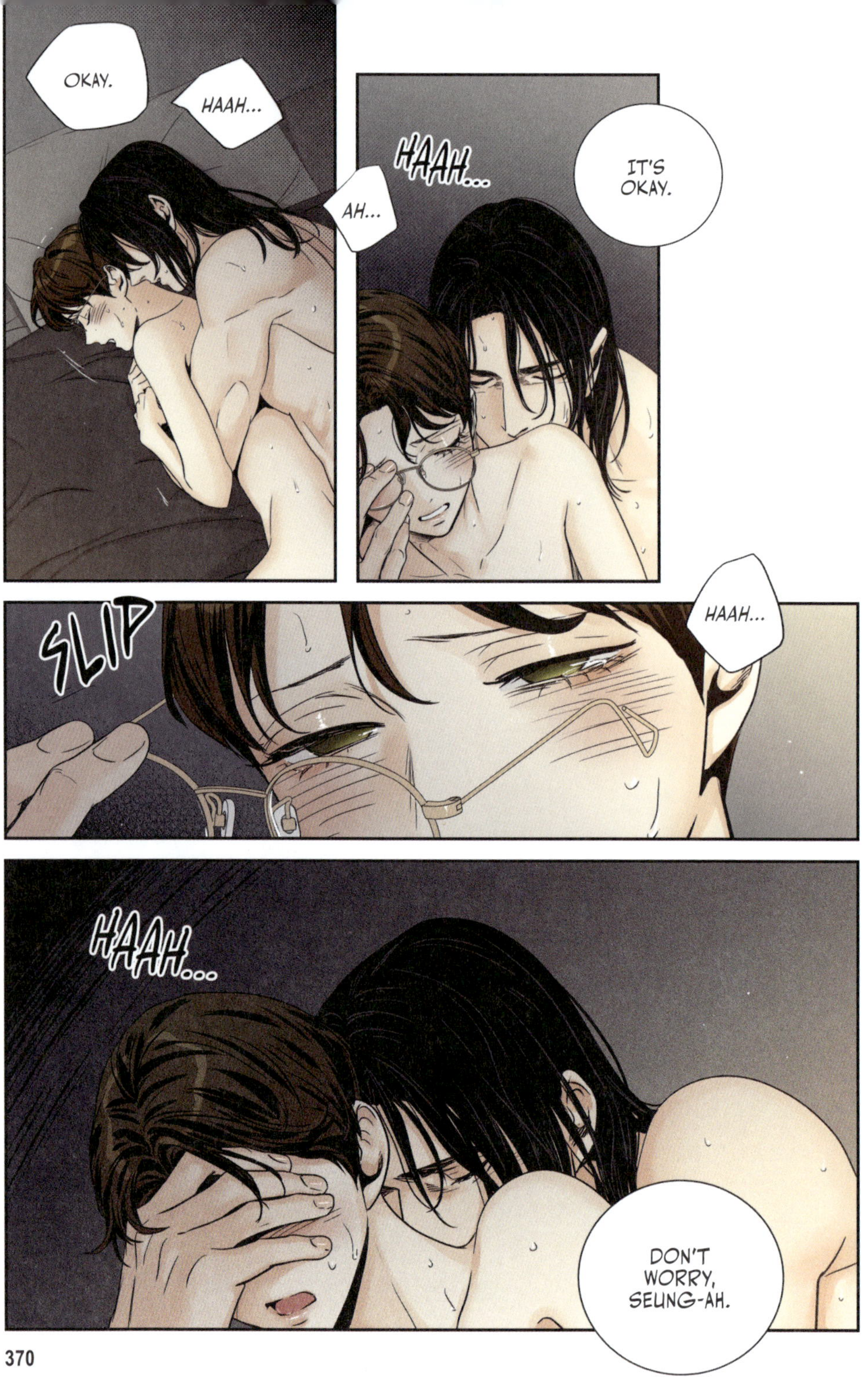
OKAY.
HAAH...
HAAH...
AH...
IT'S OKAY.
SLIP
HAAH...
HAAH...
DON'T WORRY, SEUNG-AH.

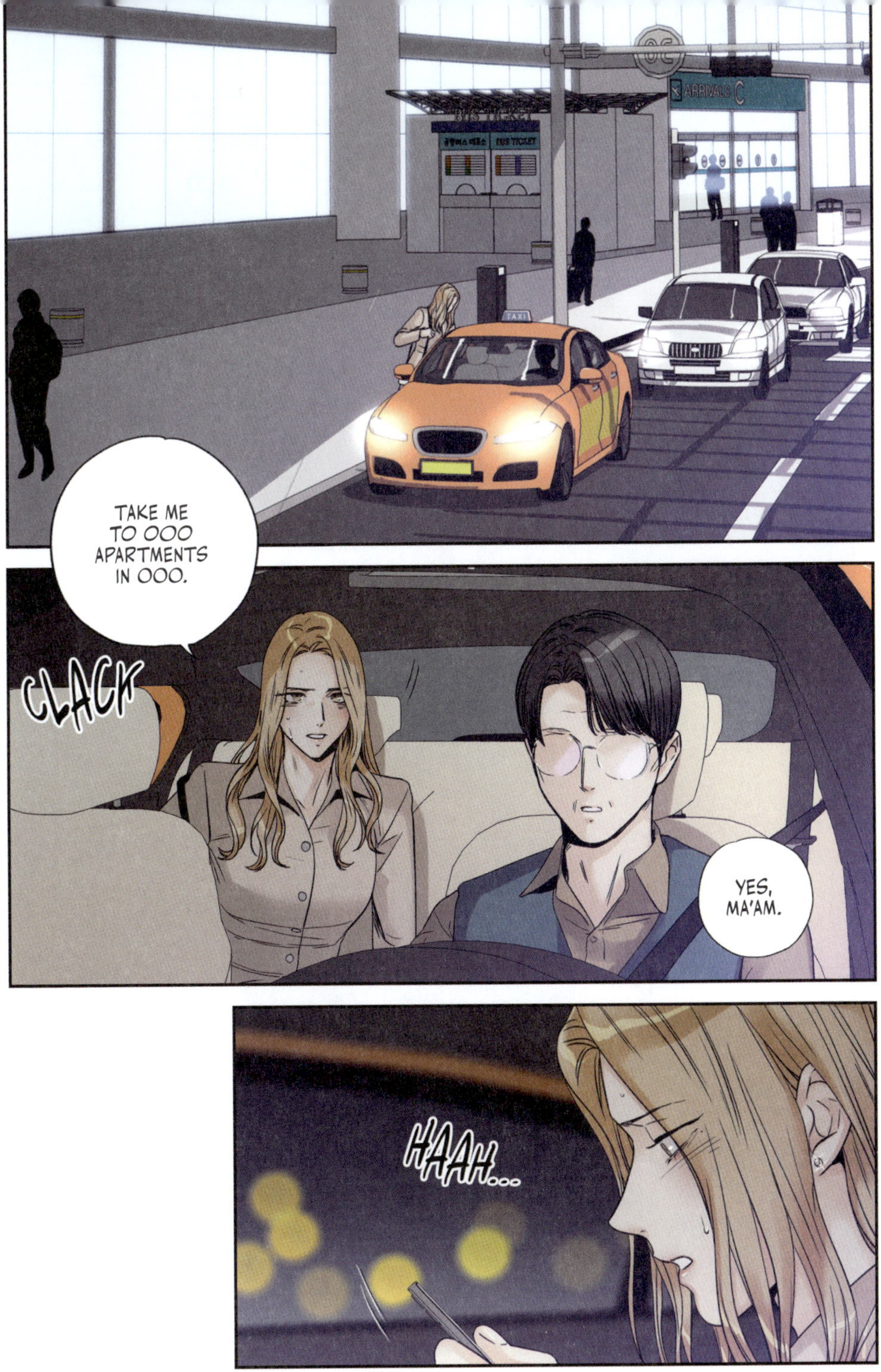
ARRIVALS C
BUS TICKET
TAXI
TAKE ME TO OOO APARTMENTS IN OOO.
CLACK
YES, MA'AM.
HAAH...

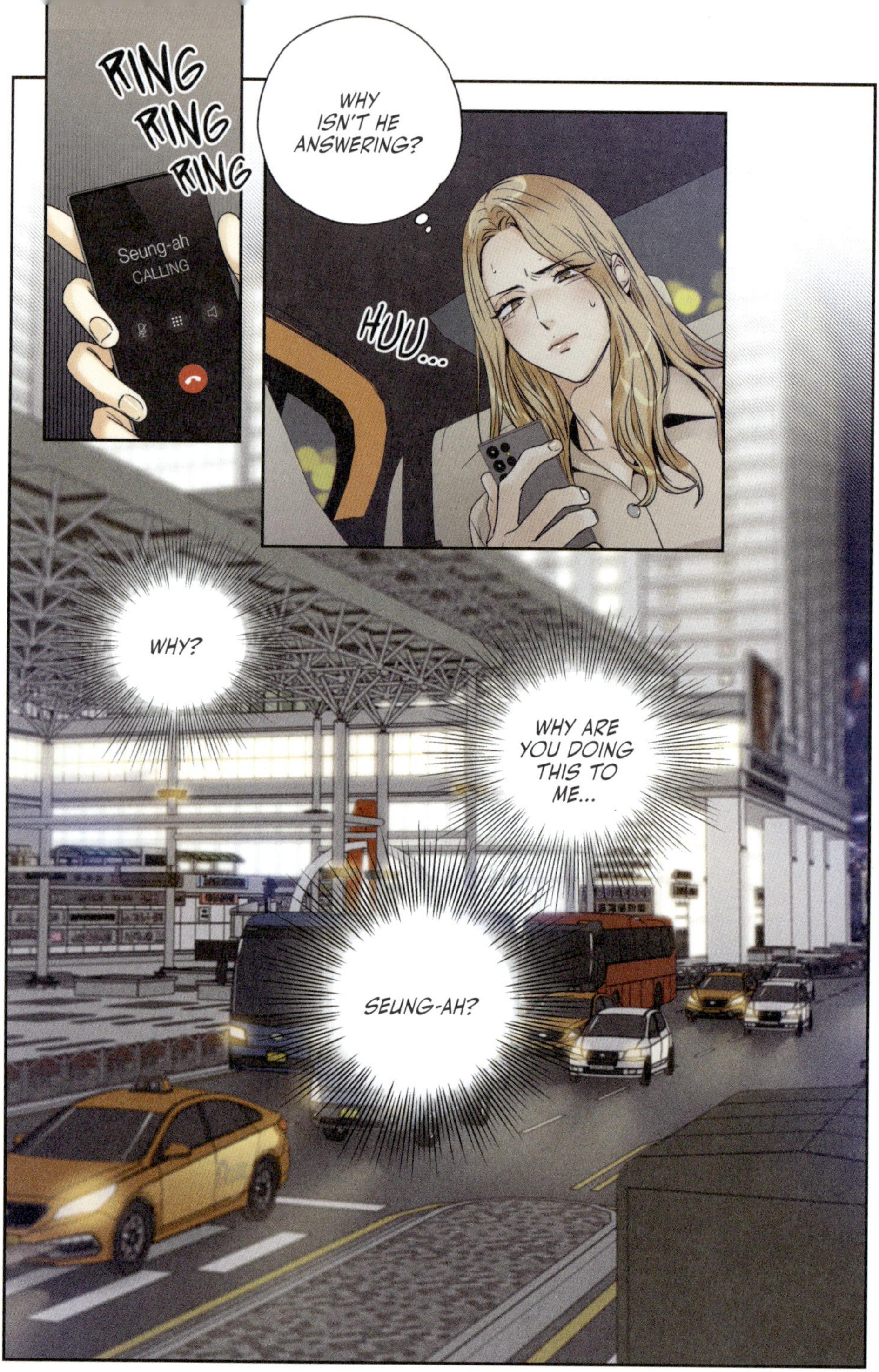
RING RING RING
Seung-ah
CALLING
WHY ISN'T HE ANSWERING?
HUU...
WHY?
WHY ARE YOU DOING THIS TO ME...
SEUNG-AH?

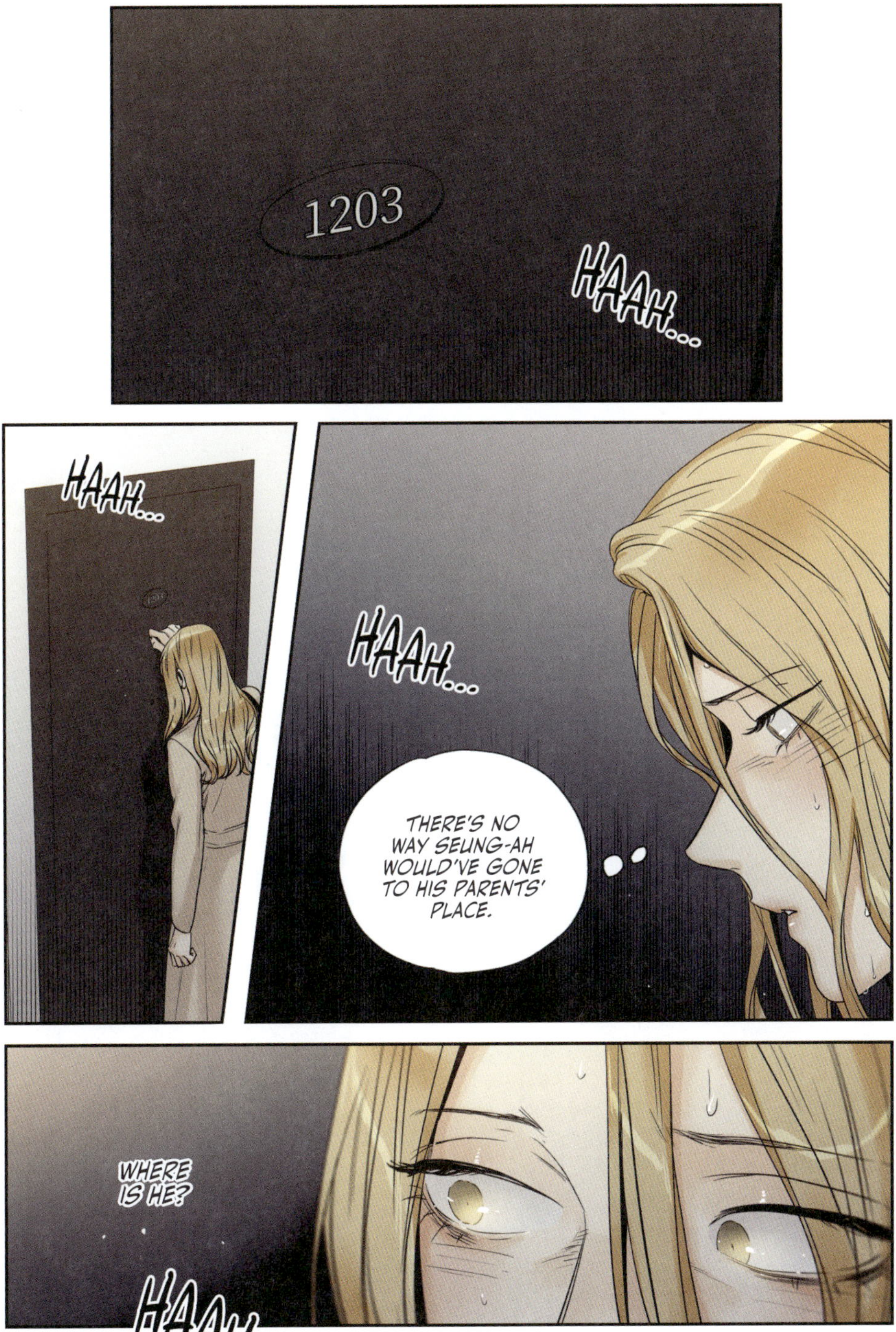
1203
HAAH...
HAAH...
HAAH...
THERE'S NO WAY SEUNG-AH WOULD'VE GONE TO HIS PARENTS' PLACE.
WHERE IS HE?
HAAH...

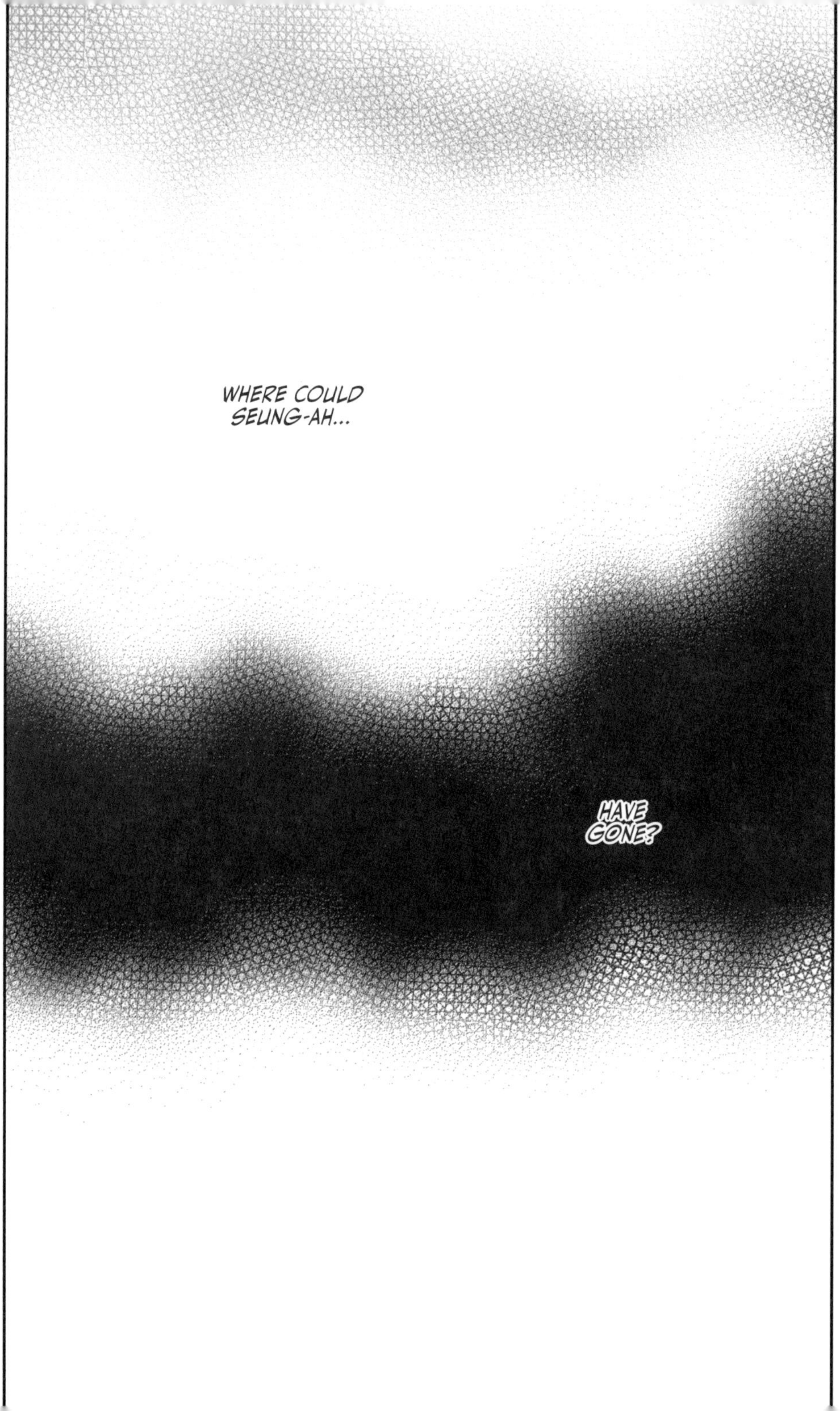
WHERE COULD SEUNG-AH...
HAVE GONE?

⸻•• To be Continued ••⸻

Love is an Illusion!

COMING SOON IN VOLUME TWO!

The Queen

HAAAH!
HAAAH!
IS...
SEUNG-AH HERE?

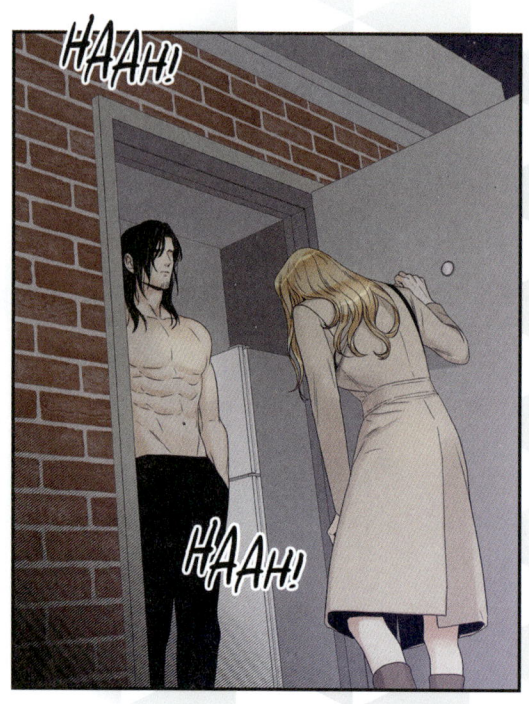

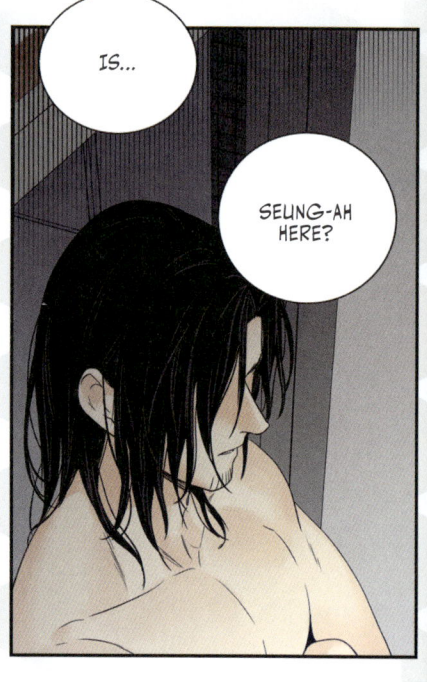

WHAT WILL HAPPEN TO SEUNG-AH, DO-GYEOM, AND MUJIN?

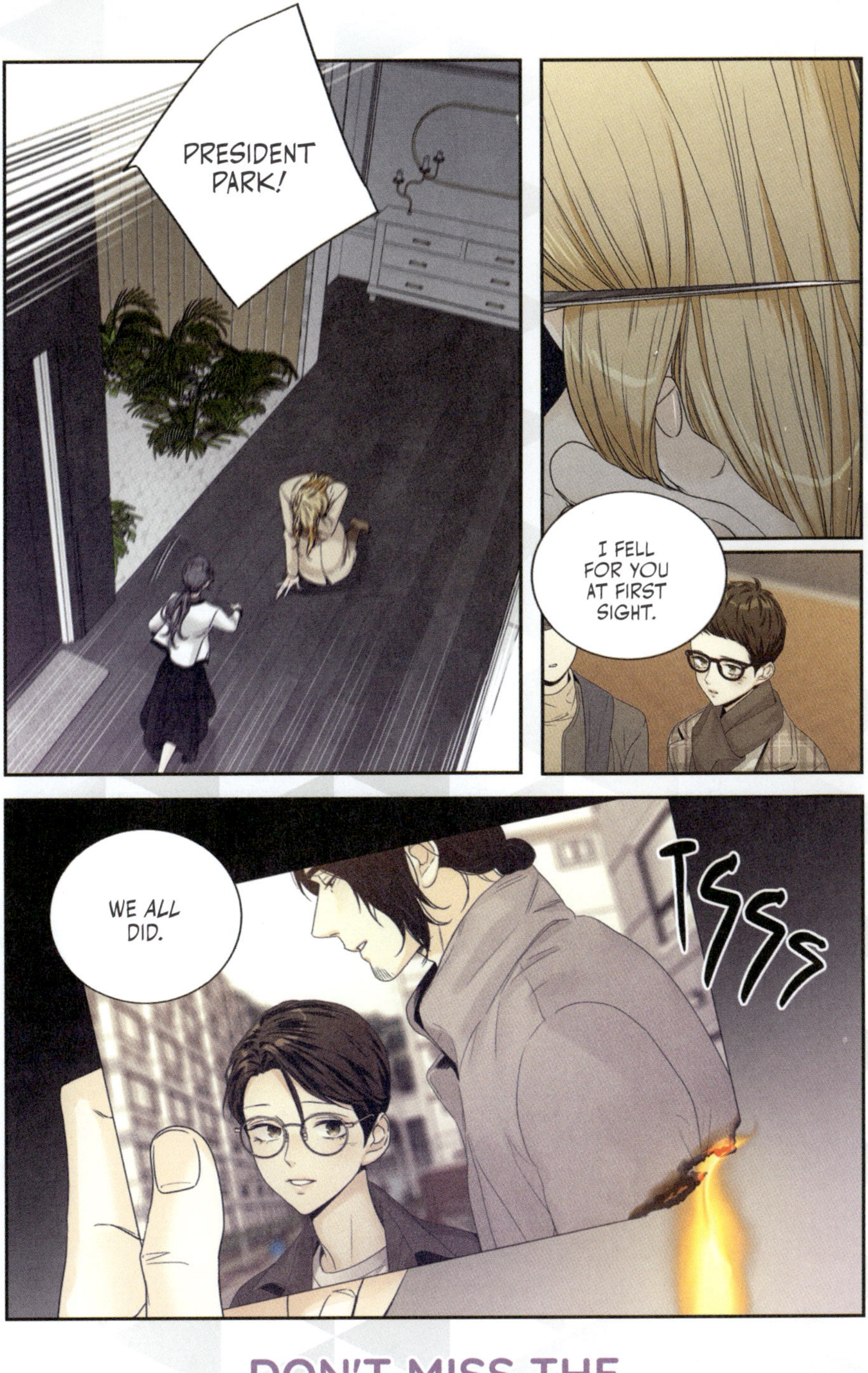
PRESIDENT PARK!
I FELL FOR YOU AT FIRST SIGHT.
WE ALL DID.
TSSS

DON'T MISS THE THRILLING CONCLUSION!

Fall in love all over again!
Romance, comedy, and heartache, from one-night stands to long-term plans!

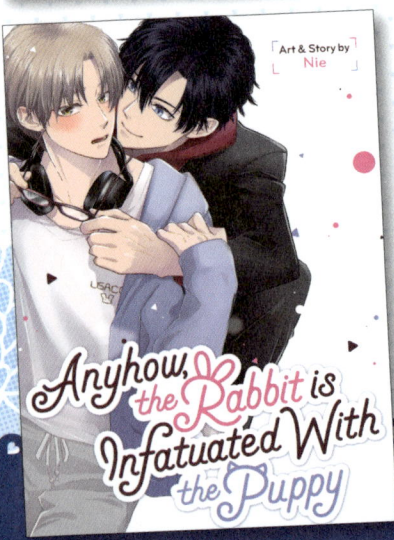

Discover your next great read at
www.sevenseasentertainment.com

Boys' Love

Seven Seas' label for BL manga and light novels.

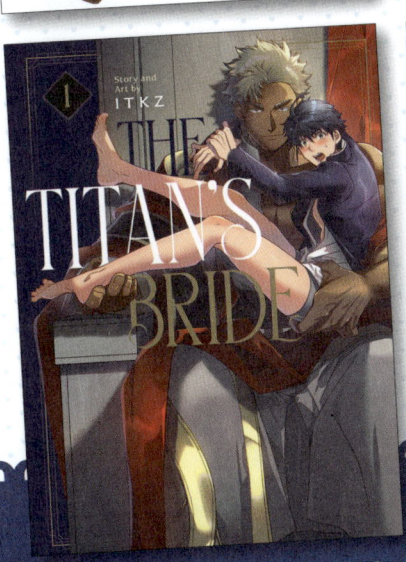
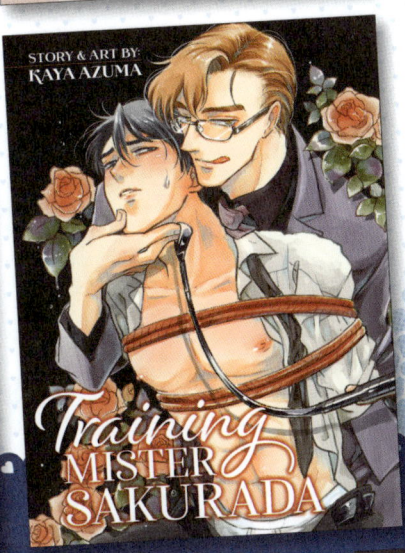

Print & digital editions available!
Visit and follow us on X (formerly Twitter) @gomanga and sign up for our newsletter for all Seven Seas has to offer.

Expand Your Horizons with Seven Seas!

Discover your next great read at
www.sevenseasentertainment.com

Experience a treasure trove
of manga, webtoons, and more!

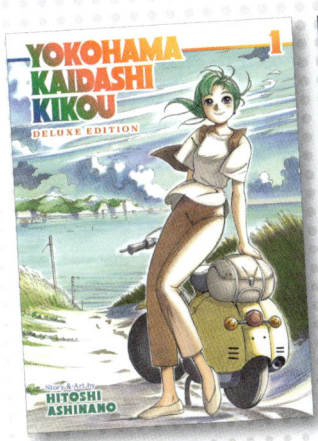

Print & digital editions available!
Visit and follow us on social media @gomanga and sign up for our newsletter for all Seven Seas has to offer.

Expand Your Horizons with Seven Seas!

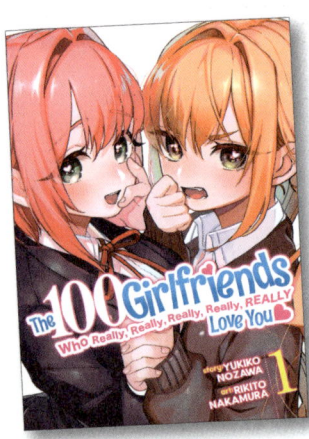

Discover your next great read at
www.sevenseasentertainment.com

Experience a treasure trove
of manga, webtoons, and more!

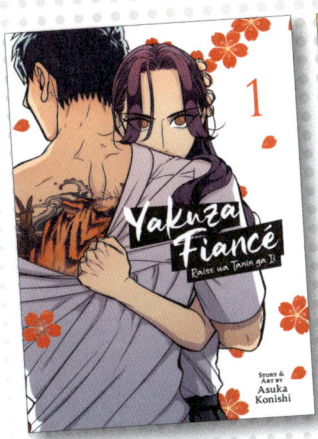
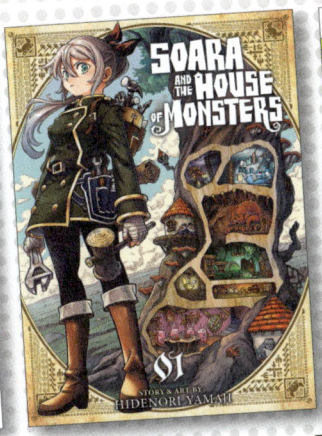

Print & digital editions available!
Visit and follow us on social media @gomanga and sign up for our newsletter for all Seven Seas has to offer.

Seven Seas

Love is an Illusion!
The Queen